Rick and

BOOK T

[adult swi

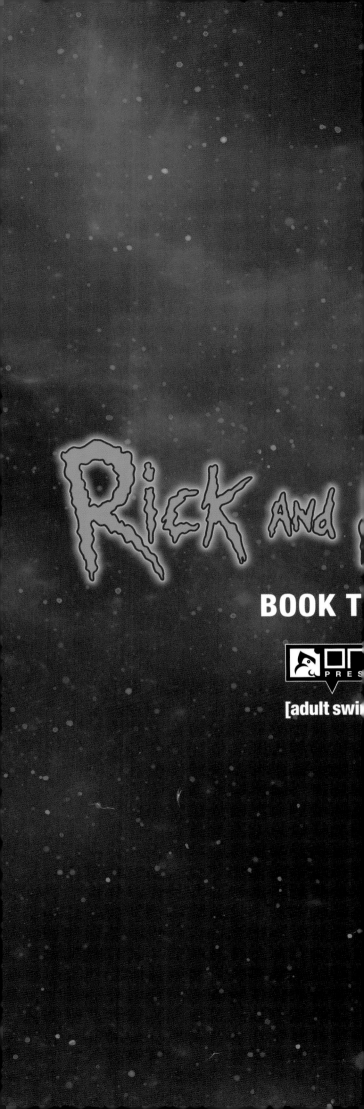

OK TWO

ORTY™ CREATED BY
ND JUSTIN ROILAND

CTION EDITED BY
YARWOOD

CTION DESIGNED BY
Y THOMPSON

NI PRESS PUBLICATION

[adult swim]™

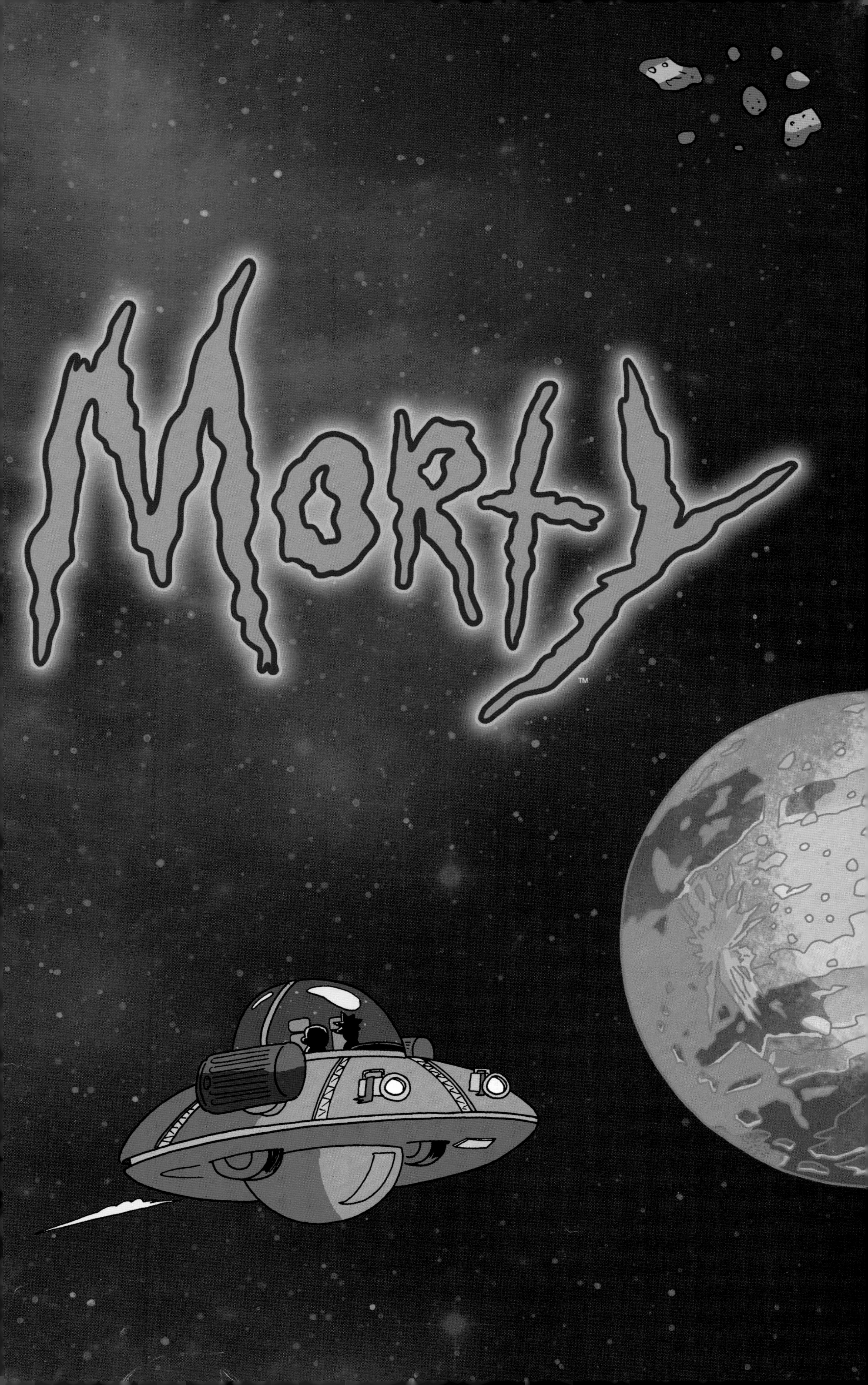
Morty™

PUBLISHED BY ONI PRESS, INC.

JOE NOZEMACK PUBLISHER

JAMES LUCAS JONES EDITOR IN CHIEF

BRAD ROOKS DIRECTOR OF OPERATIONS

DAVID DISSANAYAKE DIRECTOR OF SALES

RACHEL REED PUBLICITY MANAGER

MELISSA MESZAROS MACFADYEN MARKETING ASSISTANT

TROY LOOK DIRECTOR OF DESIGN & PRODUCTION

HILARY THOMPSON GRAPHIC DESIGNER

KATE Z. STONE JUNIOR GRAPHIC DESIGNER

ANGIE DOBSON DIGITAL PREPRESS TECHNICIAN

ARI YARWOOD MANAGING EDITOR

CHARLIE CHU SENIOR EDITOR

ROBIN HERRERA EDITOR

ALISSA SALLAH ADMINISTRATIVE ASSISTANT

JUNG LEE LOGISTICS ASSOCIATE

[adult swim]

ONIPRESS.COM
FACEBOOK.COM/ONIPRESS
TWITTER.COM/ONIPRESS
ONIPRESS.TUMBLR.COM
INSTAGRAM.COM/ONIPRESS

ADULTSWIM.COM
FACEBOOK.COM/RICKANDMORTY
TWITTER.COM/RICKANDMORTY

THIS VOLUME COLLECTS ISSUES #11-20 OF THE ONI PRESS SERIES *RICK AND MORTY*

FIRST EDITION: OCTOBER 2017

ISBN 978-1-62010-439-2

PRINTED IN CHINA.

LIBRARY OF CONGRESS CONTROL NUMBER: 2016940164

1 2 3 4 5 6 7 8 9 10

SPECIAL THANKS TO JUSTIN ROILAND, DAN HARMON, MARISA MARIONAKIS, AND MIKE MENDEL

INTRODUCTION

RUN, MORTY!

If you're hearing Rick's voice when you read that, then you've picked up the right hardcover collection of adult science fiction pseudo-nihilistic comedy comics.

Hi, I'm Mike. I'm not famous. (Usually introductions are written by someone cool like PATRICK STEWART, who wrote a pretty dope intro for *Transmetropolitan* back in the day.) I might not be a space captain, but in October of 2012 I got email from Justin Roiland:

"Hey, are you available at all for some writers assistant work? I'm not sure what the long term schedule is, but first day would be tomorrow."

He and Dan Harmon had already made the *Rick and Morty*™ pilot; now they needed to write a couple episode scripts to prove to Adult Swim™ that the show deserved a first season pickup. Dan, Justin, Ryan Ridley and I spent a couple weeks writing "Lawnmower Dog" and "Rick Potion #9"–which were enough to get the show on your TVs a year later.

I've been writing "RUN, MORTY!" ever since.

Seeing the show blow up has been surreal. I snatched up the first bootleg T-shirts that showed up online, because I couldn't believe they existed. Now, the audience and fandom of the show has blown up so quickly, and off of so few aired episodes, that it boggles the mind. Thankfully, part of that expansion was comics. I was so excited when Oni started publishing *Rick and Morty*™, and I'm not at all surprised that they've continued to sell out and get nominated for awards—because Oni brings it hard and never stops. (Some might say they can't stop, and won't stop— check out my faves: *Letter 44*, *The Bunker*, *Madman*, *Scott Pilgrim*, and *Whiteout*.)

The *Rick and Morty*™ comics are an interesting creature: they exist in a parallel universe, one that runs alongside the show, occasionally crossing paths. We keep our hands off of it, Dan and Justin approve the stories, but we aren't telling Oni where to take the characters, what jokes to tell, or what sci-fi rigmarole to encounter. It's amazing to see that Tom Fowler, Kyle Starks, Pamela Ribon, Marc Ellerby and CJ Cannon have had the same ideas that the writer's room has had— some plots and jokes that have been left on our whiteboard make it into the comics world (and more than a couple ideas that I wish we had done—Rick and Morty get mecha robots? G*****n it. I wanted to do that)—but their brains execute in ways we can't. They have longer, cross-issue stories, crazy fun bonus shorts, and I wish we could draw Rick's teeth the way they do. I mean, those teeth have some real character. Do I smell a spin-off comic? *Rick and Morty*™: *Rick's Teeth Go To College* (Oni: call me.) The *Rick and Morty*™ comics feel like a shadowy, alternate reality version of the show. (Obviously, no show is better served by this.) Just like the TV writers, the comics team knows that Summer's a badass who picks up a laser rifle at the first whiff of dystopia, Beth is a rock star who's trapped by her devotion to an absentee father, Rick doesn't try to control the chaos of the universe, Morty has crippling Earth-centric morality, and Jerry is such a Jerry.

The first collection of *Rick and Morty*™ comics (available now, SUCKA) definitely feels like it exists in a first season universe—they were basing stories and characters on what they saw at the time. This second collection is more like the second season of the show: bigger, darker, quicker to not give a f**k (LICK LICK LICK MY BALLS) and with a creeping sense that Bird Person won't be around much longer (viva Phoenix Person?). The Smith/Sanchez family has definitely gotten used to Rick being back in their lives. Morty and Summer aren't as thrown by sci-fi adventures anymore—they've developed a callous to mind-bending, earth-shattering danger—Beth is starting to question her life, and Jerry is cracking under the pressure of having Rick in his garage. If you liked season two of the show, then this collection is a great "RUN-MORTY" companion to your viewing experience.

Aw, jeeze, once these Oni folks see what we do in season three, s**t is going to go absolutely ham in the comics... BUT MIKE! SEASON THREE IS OUT! Look, I don't know when this is being published, but I know that Oni is still making new *Rick and Morty*™ comics, which means you can read them to help with the wait for season four. If you thought the wait for season three was hard...

Dooeeeee.

Hey, Adult Swim™: pick us up for Season Four. Nintendo: send us free stuff. McDonald's: you know what we want.)

MIKE MCMAHAN is a writer/producer on *Rick and Morty*™. You can tell him your dreams and exchange recipes at @mikemcmahanTM, and read his parody *Star Trek* guide *Star Trek: The Next Generation—Warped* either in book form, or in tweets at @tng_s8. His favorite *Star Wars* action figure is the AT-AT driver, his favorite fruit is pineapple, and he isn't good at writing his own bio.

HEAD SPACE

PART ONE

WRITTEN BY **TOM FOWLER**

DRAWN BY **CJ CANNON**

COLORED BY **RYAN HILL**

LETTERED BY **CRANK!**

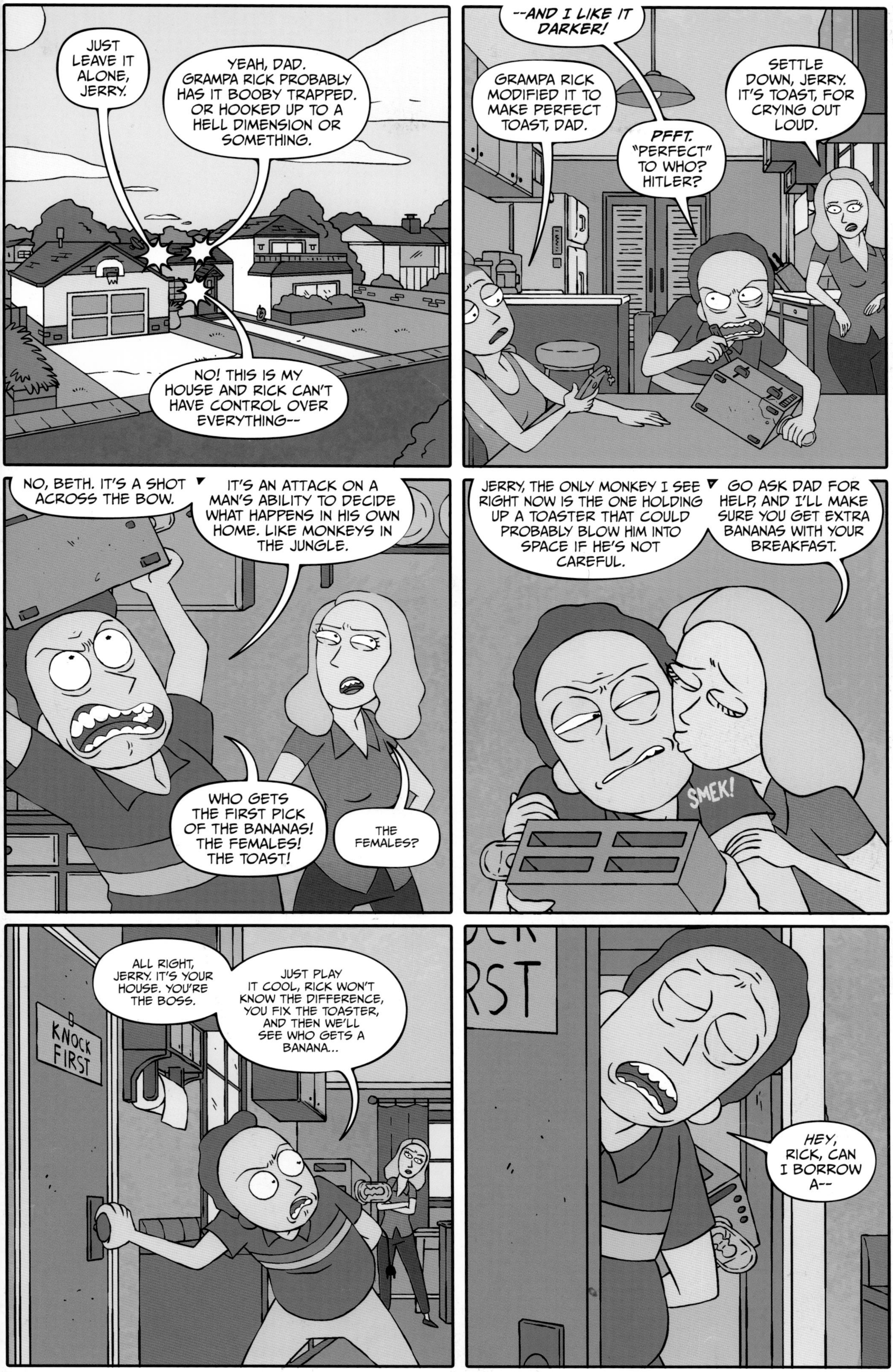
JUST LEAVE IT ALONE, JERRY.
YEAH, DAD. GRAMPA RICK PROBABLY HAS IT BOOBY TRAPPED. OR HOOKED UP TO A HELL DIMENSION OR SOMETHING.
NO! THIS IS MY HOUSE AND RICK CAN'T HAVE CONTROL OVER EVERYTHING--
--AND I LIKE IT DARKER!
GRAMPA RICK MODIFIED IT TO MAKE PERFECT TOAST, DAD.
PFFT. "PERFECT" TO WHO? HITLER?
SETTLE DOWN, JERRY. IT'S TOAST, FOR CRYING OUT LOUD.
NO, BETH. IT'S A SHOT ACROSS THE BOW.
IT'S AN ATTACK ON A MAN'S ABILITY TO DECIDE WHAT HAPPENS IN HIS OWN HOME. LIKE MONKEYS IN THE JUNGLE.
WHO GETS THE FIRST PICK OF THE BANANAS! THE FEMALES! THE TOAST!
THE FEMALES?
JERRY, THE ONLY MONKEY I SEE RIGHT NOW IS THE ONE HOLDING UP A TOASTER THAT COULD PROBABLY BLOW HIM INTO SPACE IF HE'S NOT CAREFUL.
GO ASK DAD FOR HELP, AND I'LL MAKE SURE YOU GET EXTRA BANANAS WITH YOUR BREAKFAST.
SMEK!
ALL RIGHT, JERRY. IT'S YOUR HOUSE. YOU'RE THE BOSS.
JUST PLAY IT COOL, RICK WON'T KNOW THE DIFFERENCE, YOU FIX THE TOASTER, AND THEN WE'LL SEE WHO GETS A BANANA...
KNOCK FIRST
HEY, RICK, CAN I BORROW A--

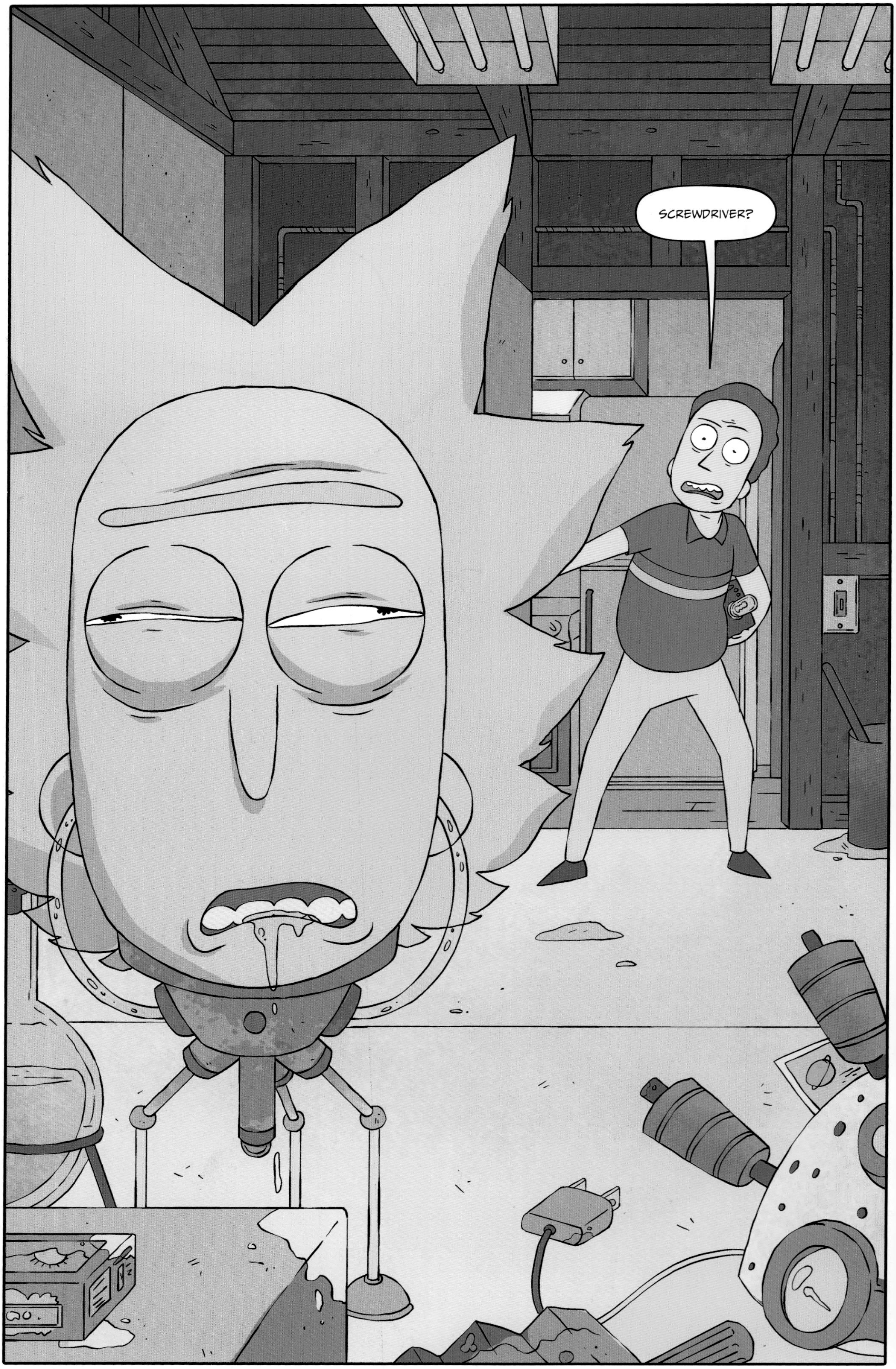
SCREWDRIVER?

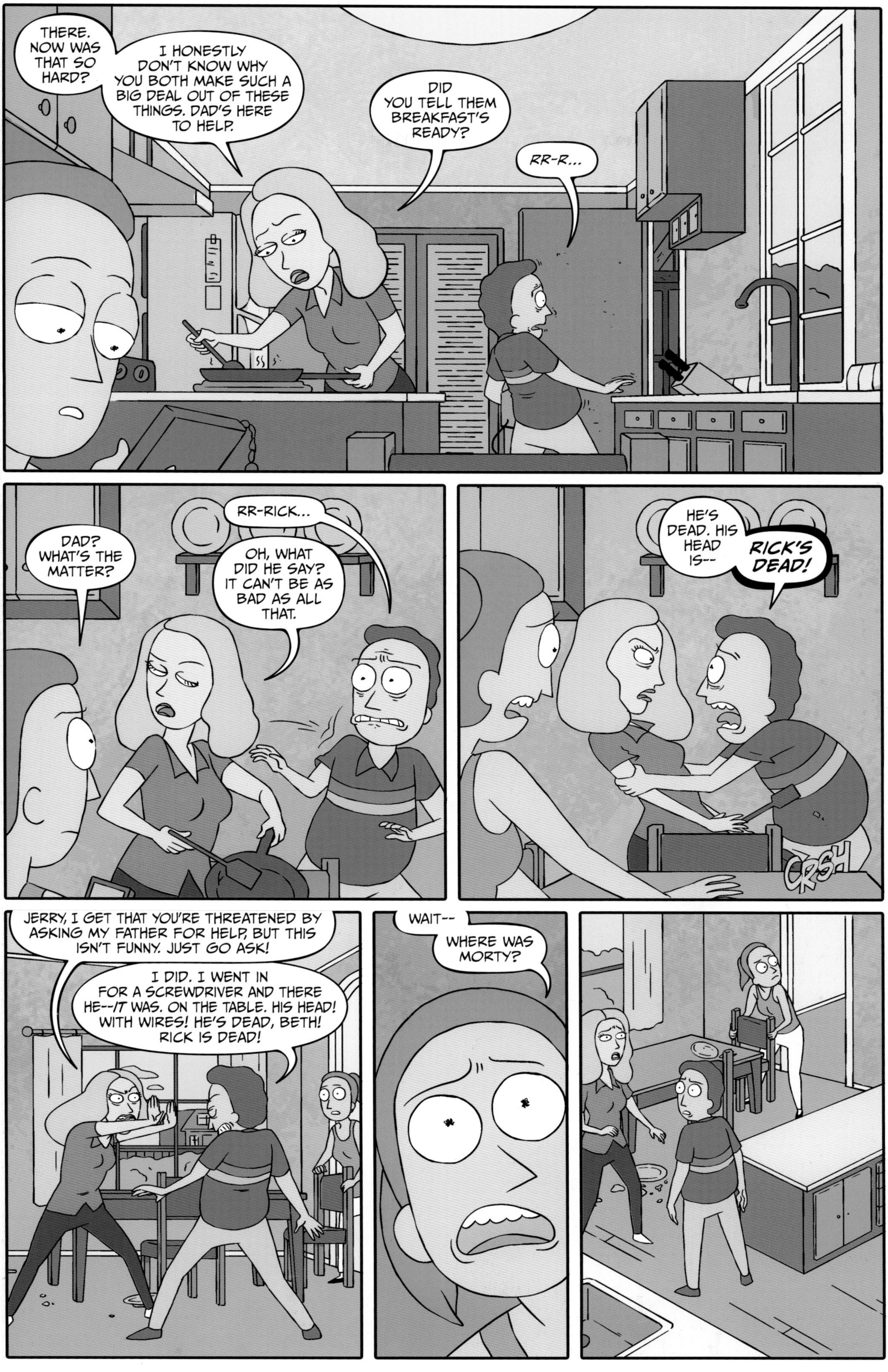
THERE. NOW WAS THAT SO HARD?
I HONESTLY DON'T KNOW WHY YOU BOTH MAKE SUCH A BIG DEAL OUT OF THESE THINGS. DAD'S HERE TO HELP.
DID YOU TELL THEM BREAKFAST'S READY?
RR-R...
DAD? WHAT'S THE MATTER?
RR-RICK...
OH, WHAT DID HE SAY? IT CAN'T BE AS BAD AS ALL THAT.
HE'S DEAD. HIS HEAD IS--
RICK'S DEAD!
CRSH
JERRY, I GET THAT YOU'RE THREATENED BY ASKING MY FATHER FOR HELP, BUT THIS ISN'T FUNNY. JUST GO ASK!
I DID. I WENT IN FOR A SCREWDRIVER AND THERE HE--*IT* WAS. ON THE TABLE. HIS HEAD! WITH WIRES! HE'S DEAD, BETH! RICK IS DEAD!
WAIT--
WHERE WAS MORTY?

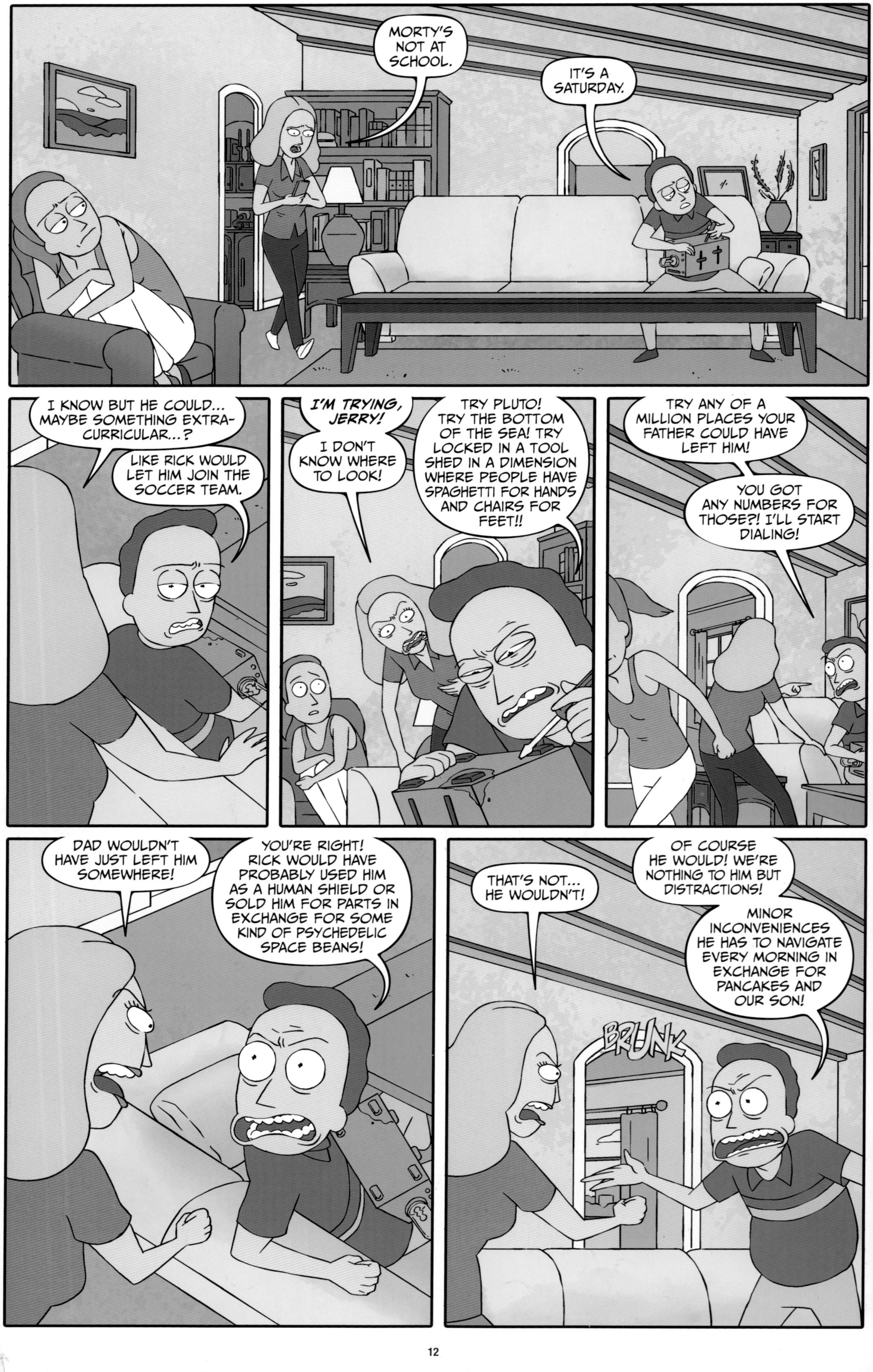
MORTY'S NOT AT SCHOOL.
IT'S A SATURDAY.
I KNOW BUT HE COULD... MAYBE SOMETHING EXTRA-CURRICULAR...?
LIKE RICK WOULD LET HIM JOIN THE SOCCER TEAM.
I'M TRYING, JERRY!
I DON'T KNOW WHERE TO LOOK!
TRY PLUTO! TRY THE BOTTOM OF THE SEA! TRY LOCKED IN A TOOL SHED IN A DIMENSION WHERE PEOPLE HAVE SPAGHETTI FOR HANDS AND CHAIRS FOR FEET!!
TRY ANY OF A MILLION PLACES YOUR FATHER COULD HAVE LEFT HIM!
YOU GOT ANY NUMBERS FOR THOSE?! I'LL START DIALING!
DAD WOULDN'T HAVE JUST LEFT HIM SOMEWHERE!
YOU'RE RIGHT! RICK WOULD HAVE PROBABLY USED HIM AS A HUMAN SHIELD OR SOLD HIM FOR PARTS IN EXCHANGE FOR SOME KIND OF PSYCHEDELIC SPACE BEANS!
THAT'S NOT... HE WOULDN'T!
OF COURSE HE WOULD! WE'RE NOTHING TO HIM BUT DISTRACTIONS!
MINOR INCONVENIENCES HE HAS TO NAVIGATE EVERY MORNING IN EXCHANGE FOR PANCAKES AND OUR SON!
BRUNK

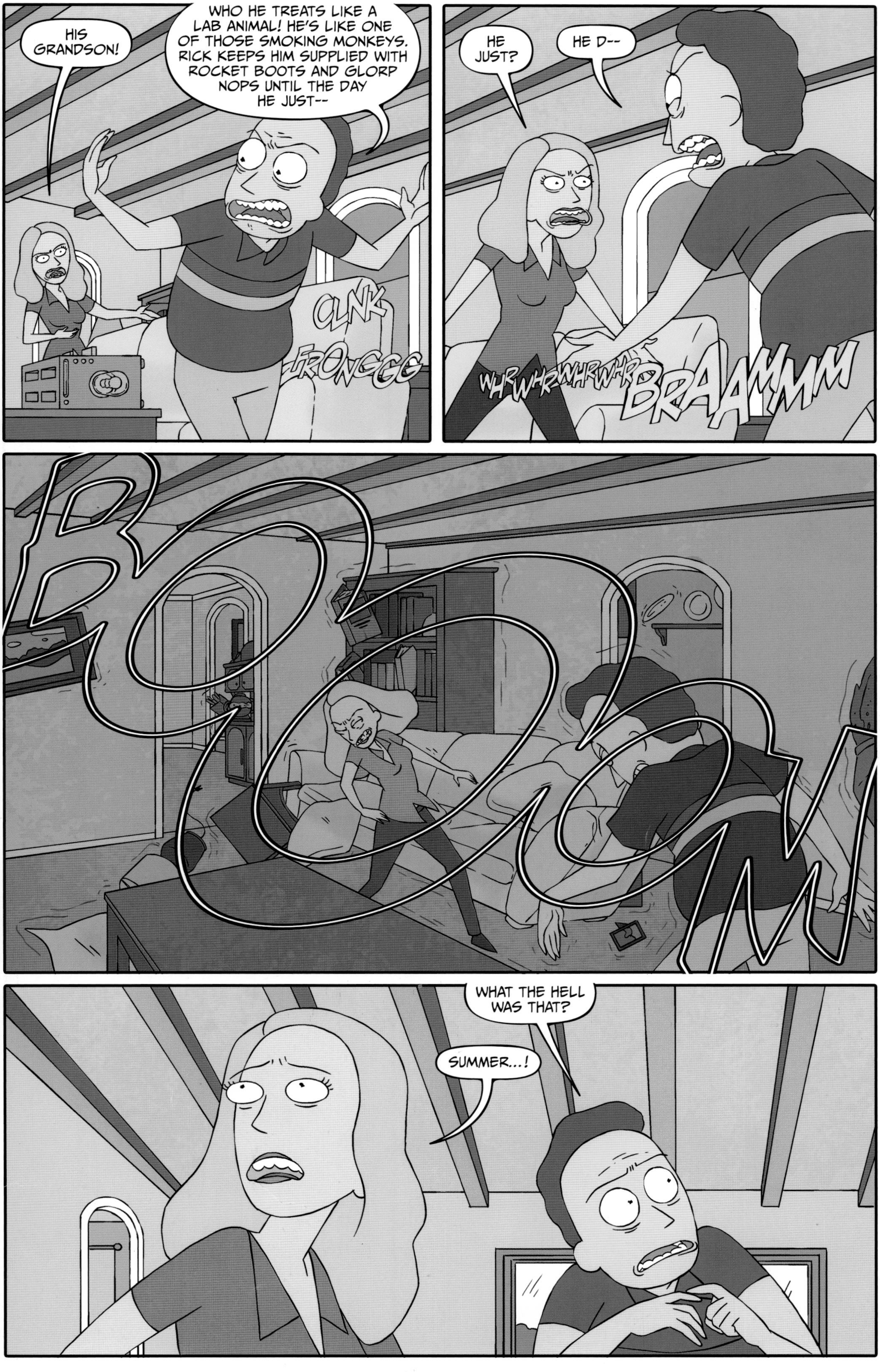
HIS GRANDSON!
WHO HE TREATS LIKE A LAB ANIMAL! HE'S LIKE ONE OF THOSE SMOKING MONKEYS. RICK KEEPS HIM SUPPLIED WITH ROCKET BOOTS AND GLORP NOPS UNTIL THE DAY HE JUST--
CLNK
FRONGGG
HE JUST?
HE D--
WHRWHRWHRWHR
BRAAMMM
BOOOOM
WHAT THE HELL WAS THAT?
SUMMER...!

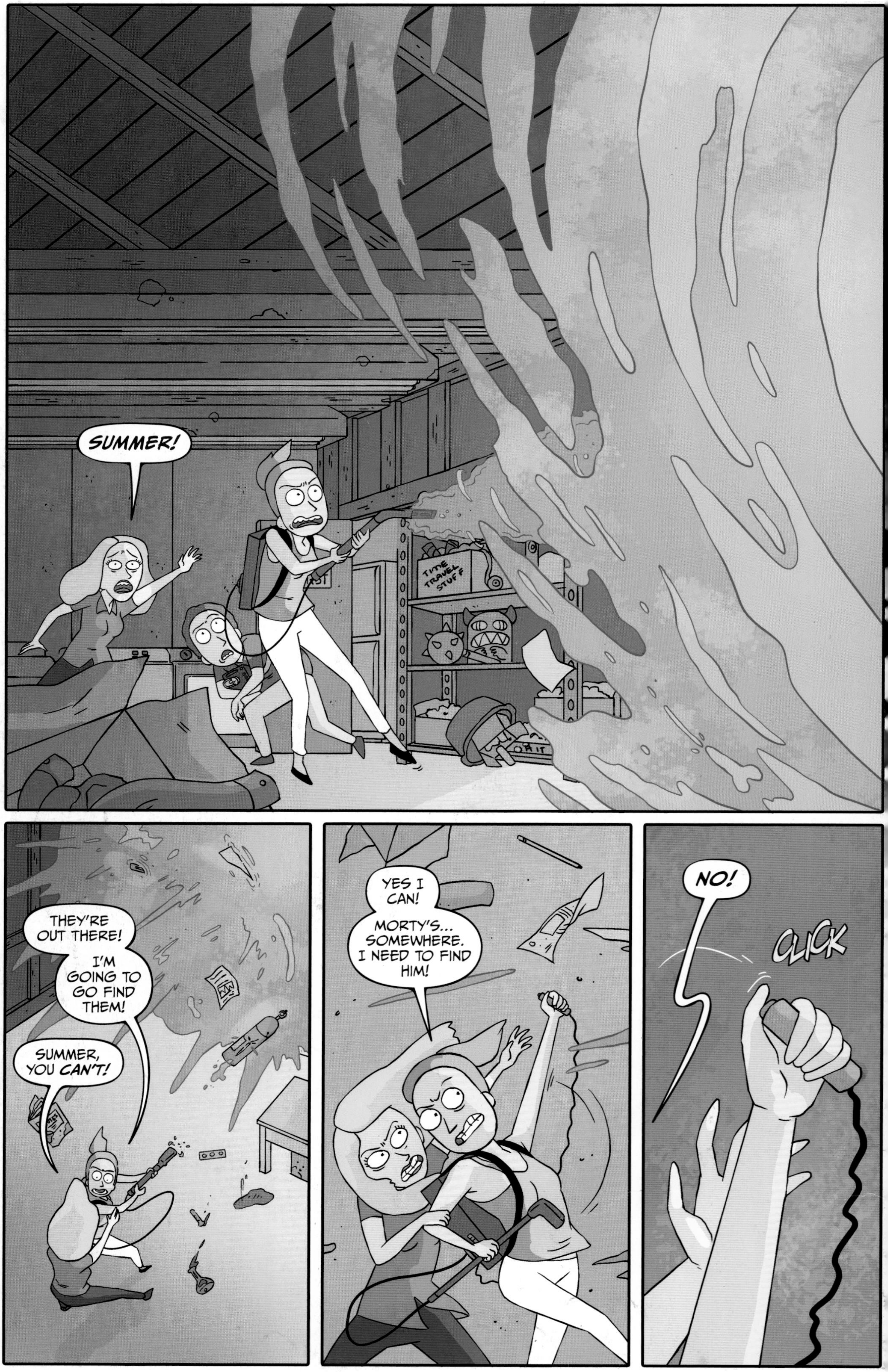
SUMMER!
TIME TRAVEL STUFF
THEY'RE OUT THERE!
I'M GOING TO GO FIND THEM!
SUMMER, YOU CAN'T!
YES I CAN!
MORTY'S... SOMEWHERE. I NEED TO FIND HIM!
NO!
CLICK

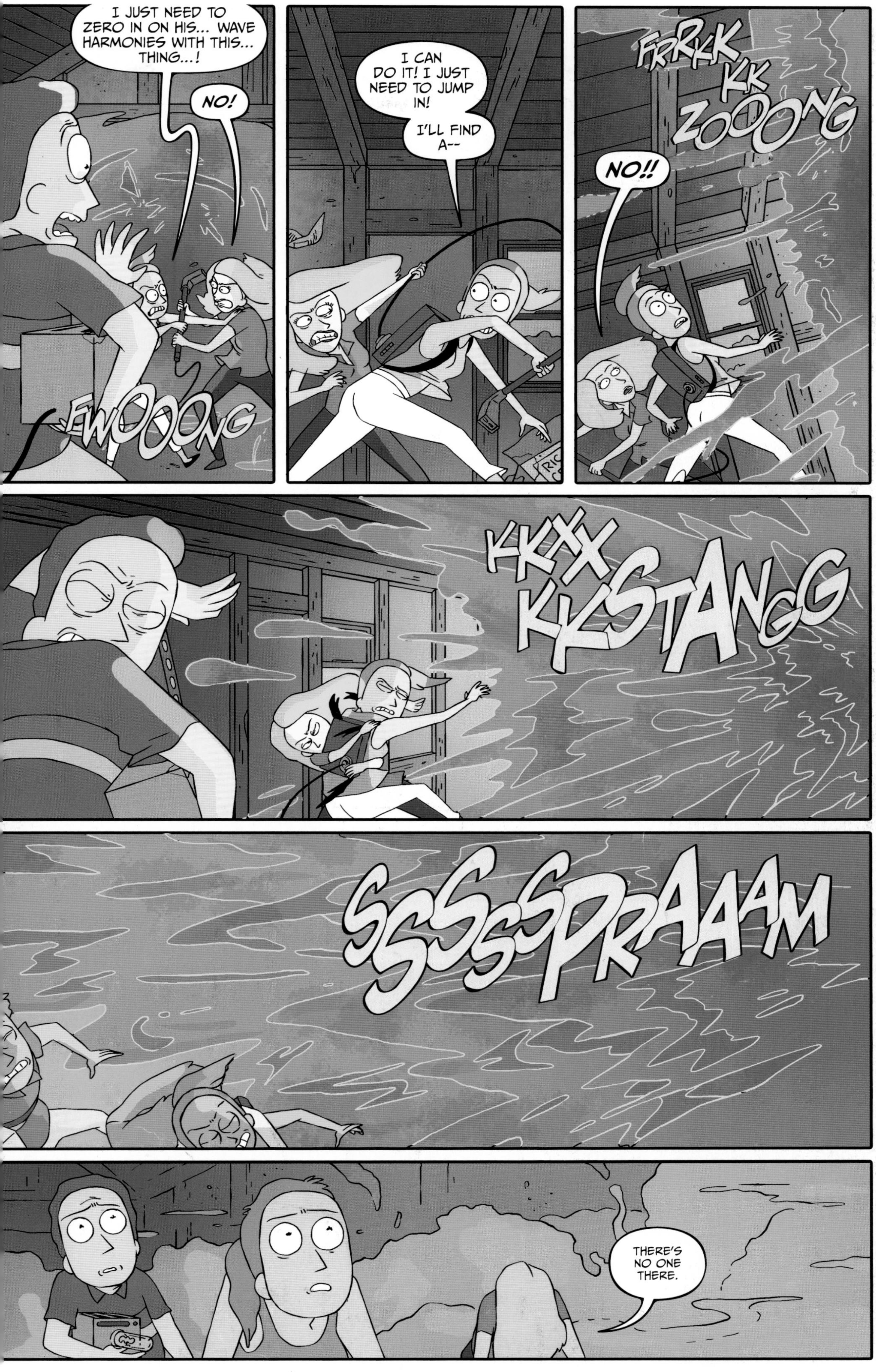
I JUST NEED TO ZERO IN ON HIS... WAVE HARMONIES WITH THIS... THING...!
NO!
EWOOOONG
I CAN DO IT! I JUST NEED TO JUMP IN!
I'LL FIND A--
FRRKK KK ZOOOONG
NO!!
KKXX KKSTANGG
SSSSSPRAAAM
THERE'S NO ONE THERE.

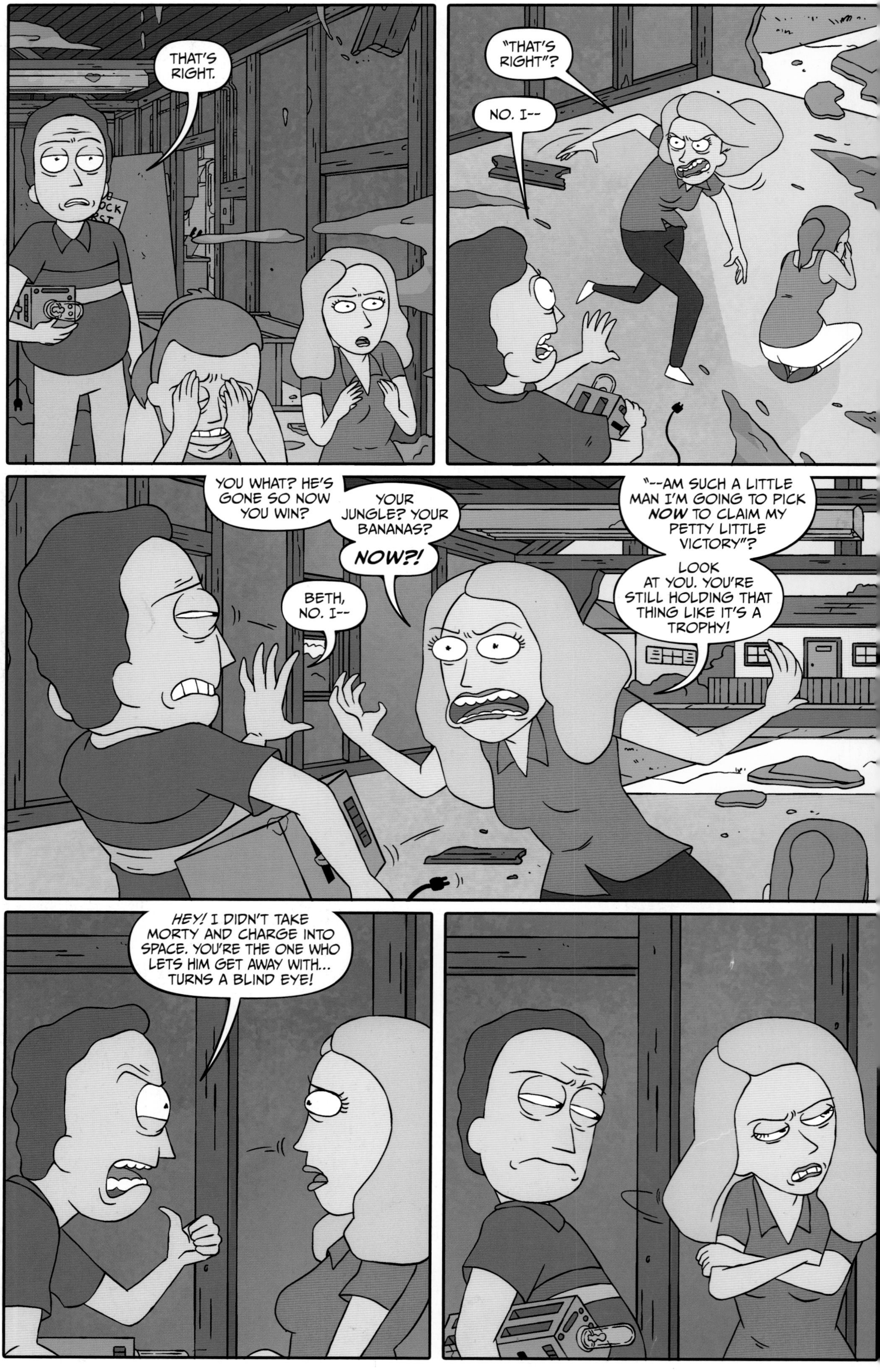
THAT'S RIGHT.
"THAT'S RIGHT"?
NO. I--
YOU WHAT? HE'S GONE SO NOW YOU WIN?
YOUR JUNGLE? YOUR BANANAS?
NOW?!
BETH, NO. I--
"--AM SUCH A LITTLE MAN I'M GOING TO PICK NOW TO CLAIM MY PETTY LITTLE VICTORY"?
LOOK AT YOU. YOU'RE STILL HOLDING THAT THING LIKE IT'S A TROPHY!
HEY! I DIDN'T TAKE MORTY AND CHARGE INTO SPACE. YOU'RE THE ONE WHO LETS HIM GET AWAY WITH... TURNS A BLIND EYE!

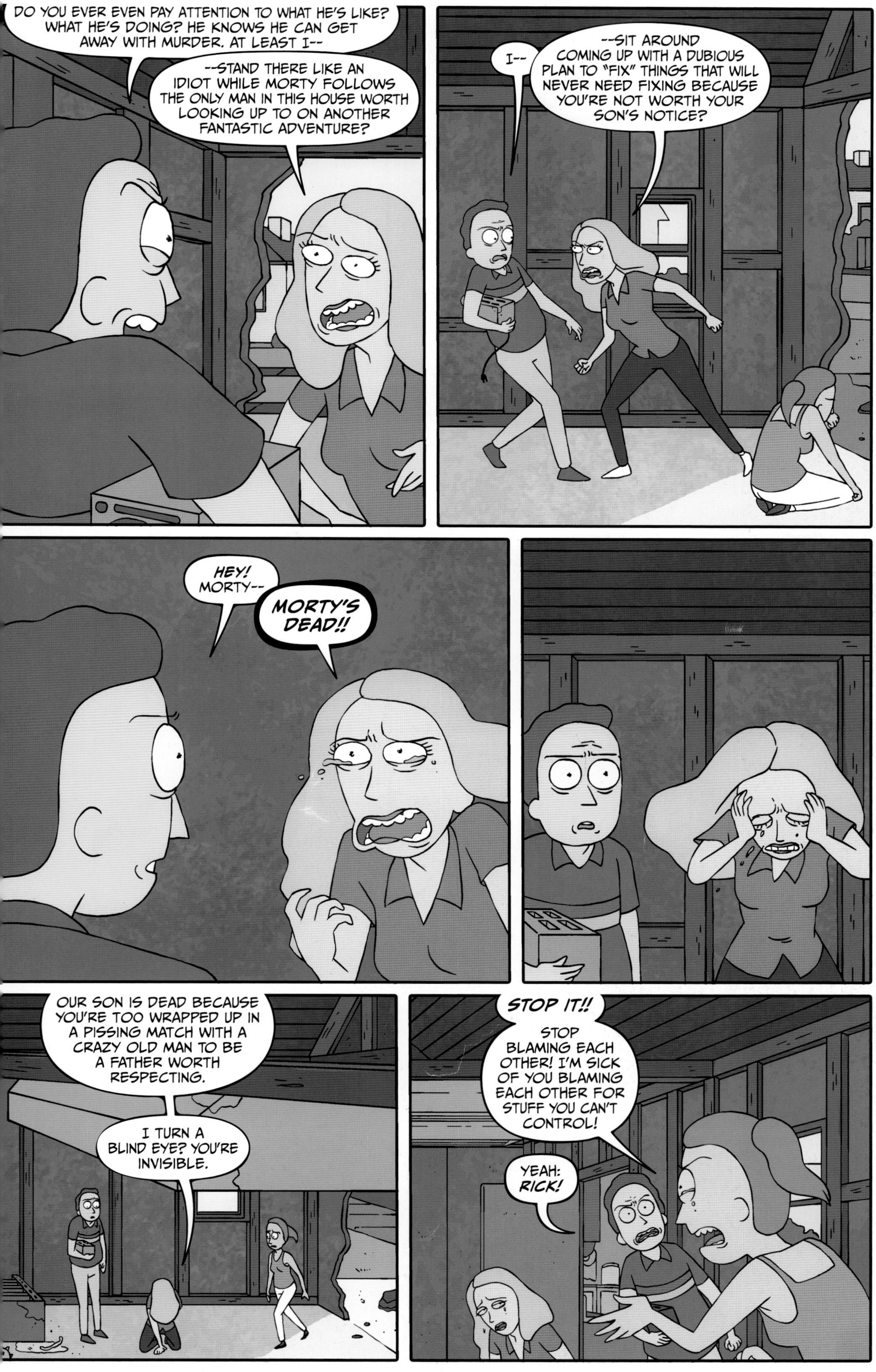
DO YOU EVER EVEN PAY ATTENTION TO WHAT HE'S LIKE? WHAT HE'S DOING? HE KNOWS HE CAN GET AWAY WITH MURDER. AT LEAST I--
--STAND THERE LIKE AN IDIOT WHILE MORTY FOLLOWS THE ONLY MAN IN THIS HOUSE WORTH LOOKING UP TO ON ANOTHER FANTASTIC ADVENTURE?
I--
--SIT AROUND COMING UP WITH A DUBIOUS PLAN TO "FIX" THINGS THAT WILL NEVER NEED FIXING BECAUSE YOU'RE NOT WORTH YOUR SON'S NOTICE?
HEY! MORTY--
MORTY'S DEAD!!
OUR SON IS DEAD BECAUSE YOU'RE TOO WRAPPED UP IN A PISSING MATCH WITH A CRAZY OLD MAN TO BE A FATHER WORTH RESPECTING.
I TURN A BLIND EYE? YOU'RE INVISIBLE.
STOP IT!!
STOP BLAMING EACH OTHER! I'M SICK OF YOU BLAMING EACH OTHER FOR STUFF YOU CAN'T CONTROL!
YEAH: RICK!

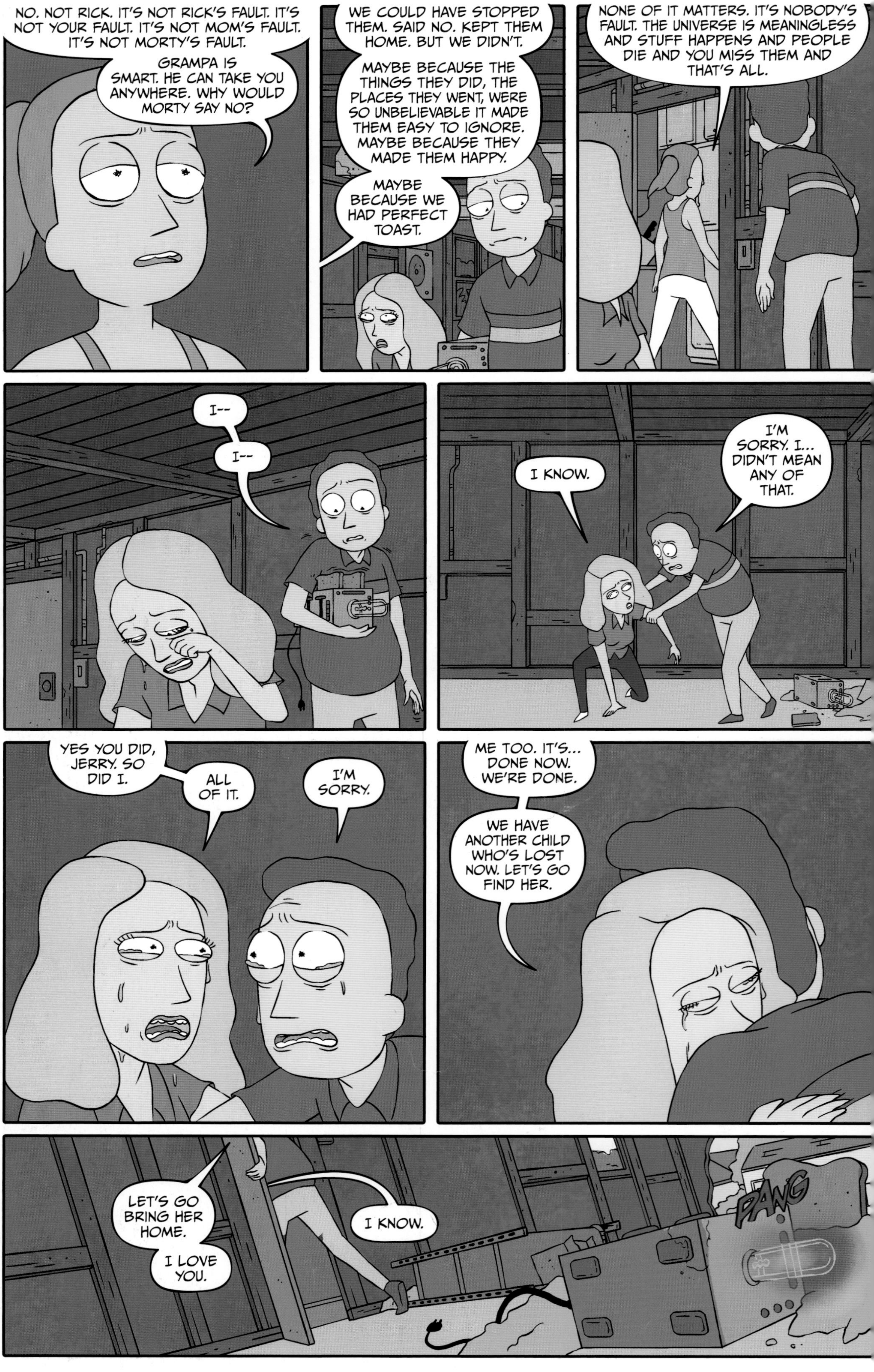
NO. NOT RICK. IT'S NOT RICK'S FAULT. IT'S NOT YOUR FAULT. IT'S NOT MOM'S FAULT. IT'S NOT MORTY'S FAULT.
GRAMPA IS SMART. HE CAN TAKE YOU ANYWHERE. WHY WOULD MORTY SAY NO?
WE COULD HAVE STOPPED THEM. SAID NO. KEPT THEM HOME. BUT WE DIDN'T.
MAYBE BECAUSE THE THINGS THEY DID, THE PLACES THEY WENT, WERE SO UNBELIEVABLE IT MADE THEM EASY TO IGNORE. MAYBE BECAUSE THEY MADE THEM HAPPY.
MAYBE BECAUSE WE HAD PERFECT TOAST.
NONE OF IT MATTERS. IT'S NOBODY'S FAULT. THE UNIVERSE IS MEANINGLESS AND STUFF HAPPENS AND PEOPLE DIE AND YOU MISS THEM AND THAT'S ALL.
I--
I--
I'M SORRY. I... DIDN'T MEAN ANY OF THAT.
I KNOW.
YES YOU DID, JERRY. SO DID I.
ALL OF IT.
I'M SORRY.
ME TOO. IT'S... DONE NOW. WE'RE DONE.
WE HAVE ANOTHER CHILD WHO'S LOST NOW. LET'S GO FIND HER.
LET'S GO BRING HER HOME.
I LOVE YOU.
I KNOW.
DANG

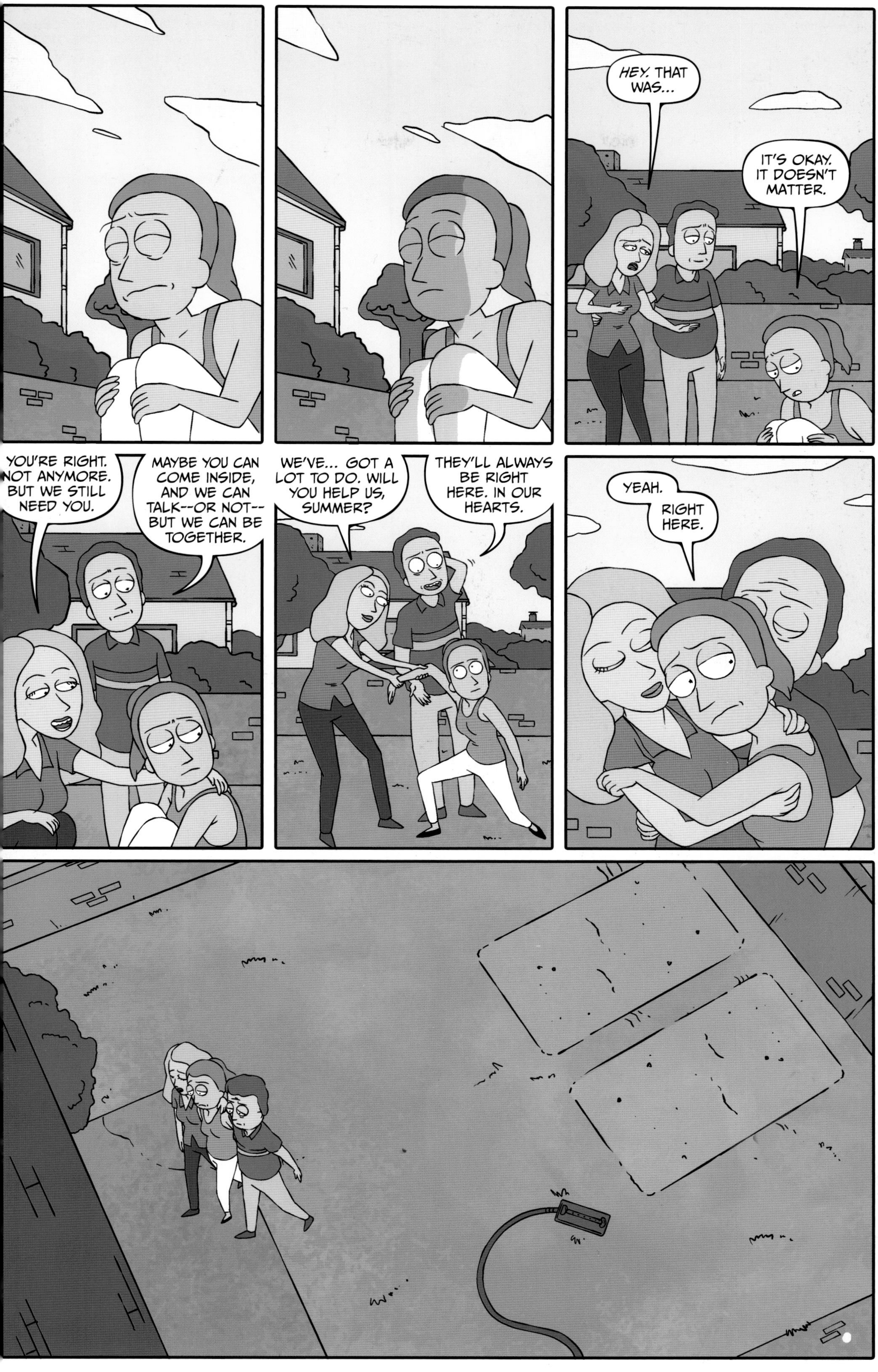
HEY. THAT WAS...
IT'S OKAY. IT DOESN'T MATTER.
YOU'RE RIGHT. NOT ANYMORE. BUT WE STILL NEED YOU.
MAYBE YOU CAN COME INSIDE, AND WE CAN TALK--OR NOT--BUT WE CAN BE TOGETHER.
WE'VE... GOT A LOT TO DO. WILL YOU HELP US, SUMMER?
THEY'LL ALWAYS BE RIGHT HERE. IN OUR HEARTS.
YEAH.
RIGHT HERE.

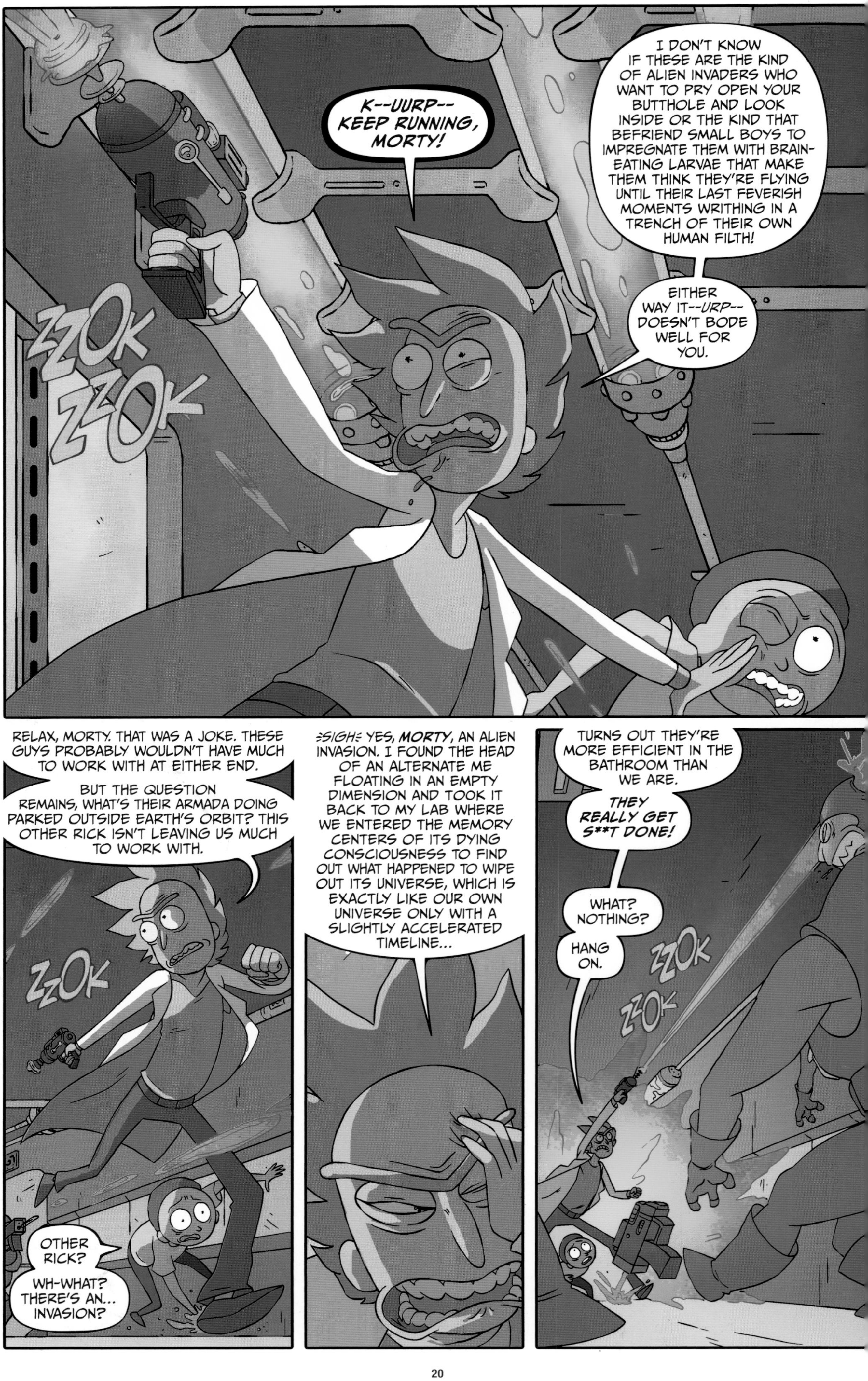
K--UURP--
KEEP RUNNING, MORTY!
I DON'T KNOW IF THESE ARE THE KIND OF ALIEN INVADERS WHO WANT TO PRY OPEN YOUR BUTTHOLE AND LOOK INSIDE OR THE KIND THAT BEFRIEND SMALL BOYS TO IMPREGNATE THEM WITH BRAIN-EATING LARVAE THAT MAKE THEM THINK THEY'RE FLYING UNTIL THEIR LAST FEVERISH MOMENTS WRITHING IN A TRENCH OF THEIR OWN HUMAN FILTH!
EITHER WAY IT--URP--DOESN'T BODE WELL FOR YOU.
ZZOK
ZZOK
RELAX, MORTY. THAT WAS A JOKE. THESE GUYS PROBABLY WOULDN'T HAVE MUCH TO WORK WITH AT EITHER END.
BUT THE QUESTION REMAINS, WHAT'S THEIR ARMADA DOING PARKED OUTSIDE EARTH'S ORBIT? THIS OTHER RICK ISN'T LEAVING US MUCH TO WORK WITH.
ZZOK
OTHER RICK?
WH-WHAT? THERE'S AN... INVASION?
=SIGH= YES, MORTY, AN ALIEN INVASION. I FOUND THE HEAD OF AN ALTERNATE ME FLOATING IN AN EMPTY DIMENSION AND TOOK IT BACK TO MY LAB WHERE WE ENTERED THE MEMORY CENTERS OF ITS DYING CONSCIOUSNESS TO FIND OUT WHAT HAPPENED TO WIPE OUT ITS UNIVERSE, WHICH IS EXACTLY LIKE OUR OWN UNIVERSE ONLY WITH A SLIGHTLY ACCELERATED TIMELINE...
TURNS OUT THEY'RE MORE EFFICIENT IN THE BATHROOM THAN WE ARE.
THEY REALLY GET S**T DONE!
WHAT? NOTHING?
HANG ON.
ZZOK
ZZOK

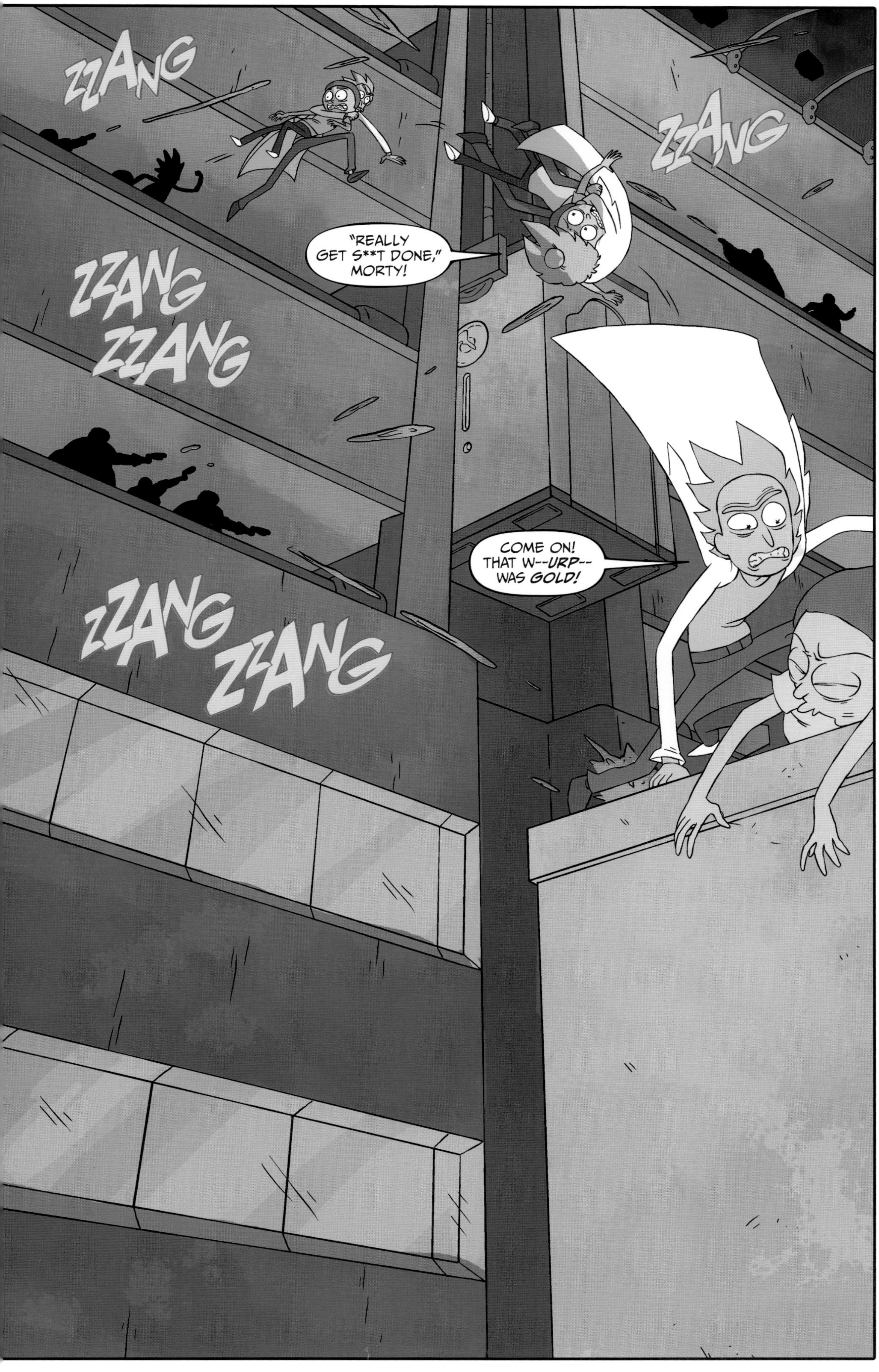
ZZANG
ZZANG
"REALLY GET S**T DONE," MORTY!
ZZANG
ZZANG
COME ON! THAT W--URP-- WAS GOLD!
ZZANG
ZZANG

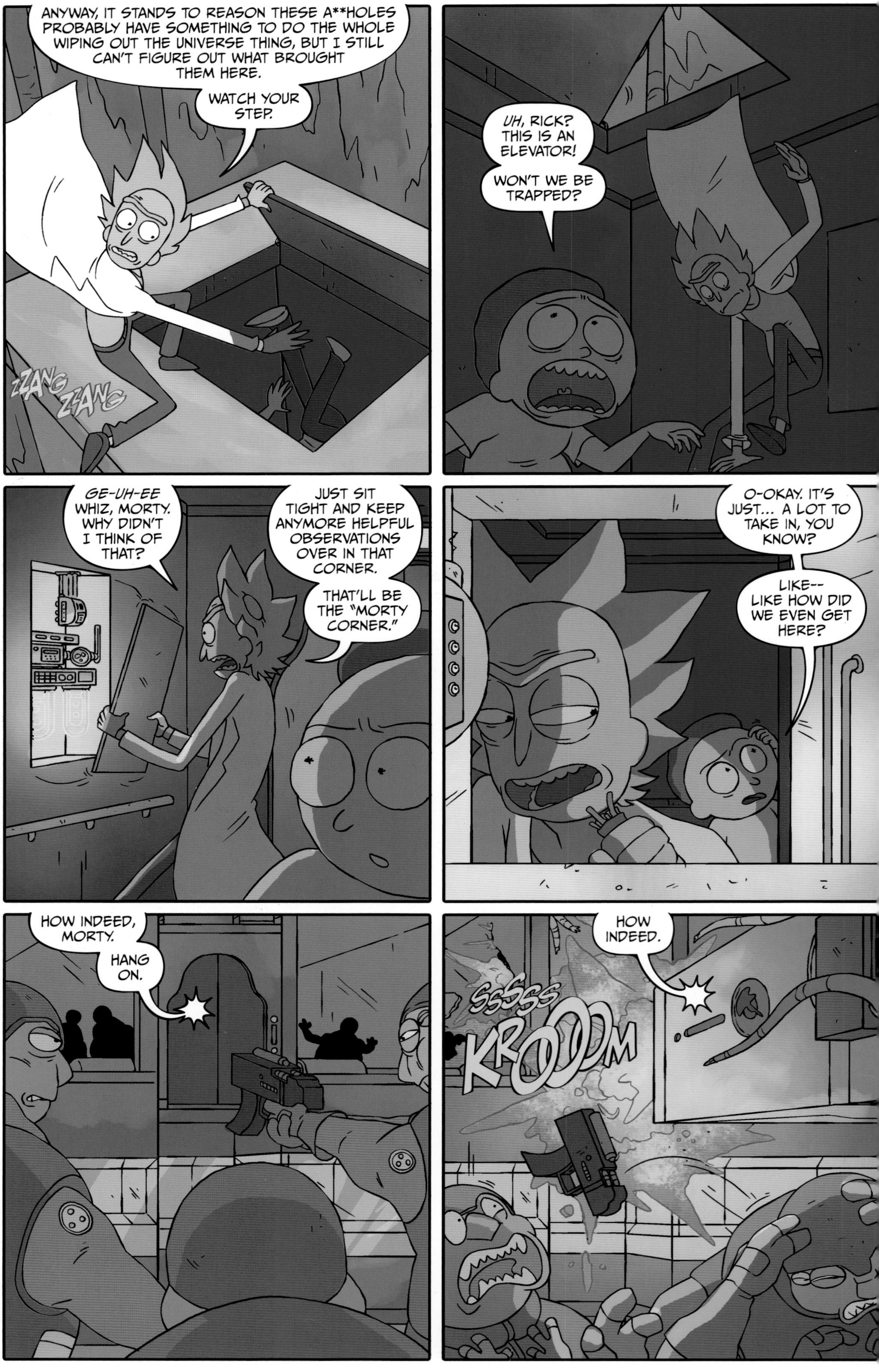

ANYWAY, IT STANDS TO REASON THESE A**HOLES PROBABLY HAVE SOMETHING TO DO THE WHOLE WIPING OUT THE UNIVERSE THING, BUT I STILL CAN'T FIGURE OUT WHAT BROUGHT THEM HERE.
WATCH YOUR STEP.
ZZANG ZZANG
UH, RICK? THIS IS AN ELEVATOR!
WON'T WE BE TRAPPED?
GE-UH-EE WHIZ, MORTY. WHY DIDN'T I THINK OF THAT?
JUST SIT TIGHT AND KEEP ANYMORE HELPFUL OBSERVATIONS OVER IN THAT CORNER.
THAT'LL BE THE "MORTY CORNER."
O-OKAY. IT'S JUST... A LOT TO TAKE IN, YOU KNOW?
LIKE-- LIKE HOW DID WE EVEN GET HERE?
HOW INDEED, MORTY.
HANG ON.
HOW INDEED.
SSSSS
KROOOM

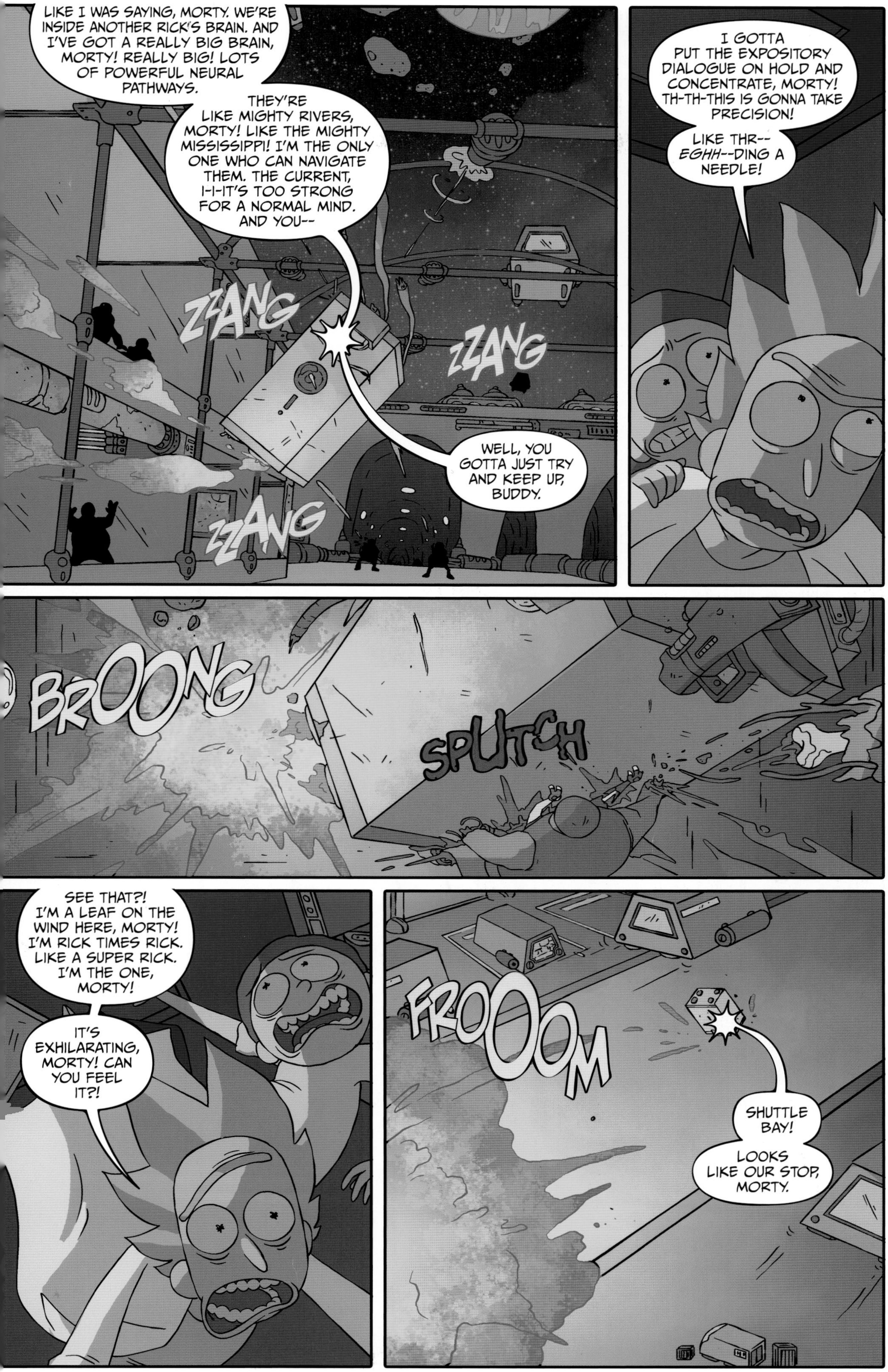
LIKE I WAS SAYING, MORTY. WE'RE INSIDE ANOTHER RICK'S BRAIN. AND I'VE GOT A REALLY BIG BRAIN, MORTY! REALLY BIG! LOTS OF POWERFUL NEURAL PATHWAYS.
THEY'RE LIKE MIGHTY RIVERS, MORTY! LIKE THE MIGHTY MISSISSIPPI! I'M THE ONLY ONE WHO CAN NAVIGATE THEM. THE CURRENT, I-I-IT'S TOO STRONG FOR A NORMAL MIND. AND YOU--
ZZANG
ZZANG
ZZANG
WELL, YOU GOTTA JUST TRY AND KEEP UP, BUDDY.
I GOTTA PUT THE EXPOSITORY DIALOGUE ON HOLD AND CONCENTRATE, MORTY! TH-TH-THIS IS GONNA TAKE PRECISION!
LIKE THR-- *EGHH*--DING A NEEDLE!
BROONG
SPLUTCH
SEE THAT?! I'M A LEAF ON THE WIND HERE, MORTY! I'M RICK TIMES RICK. LIKE A SUPER RICK. I'M THE ONE, MORTY!
IT'S EXHILARATING, MORTY! CAN YOU FEEL IT?!
FROOOOM
SHUTTLE BAY!
LOOKS LIKE OUR STOP, MORTY.

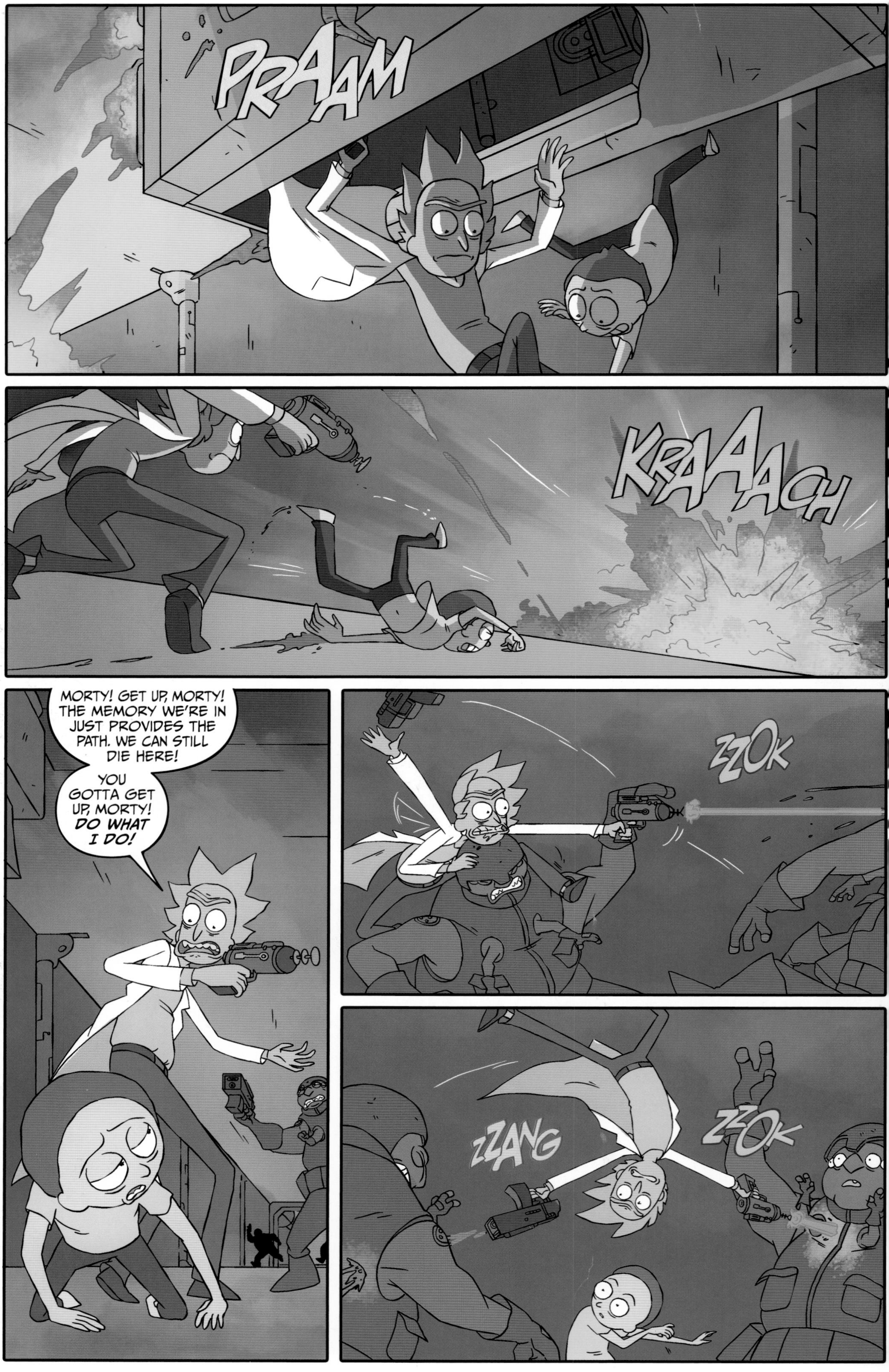
PRAAM
KRAAAACH
MORTY! GET UP, MORTY! THE MEMORY WE'RE IN JUST PROVIDES THE PATH. WE CAN STILL DIE HERE!
YOU GOTTA GET UP, MORTY! DO WHAT I DO!
ZZOK
ZZANG
ZZOK

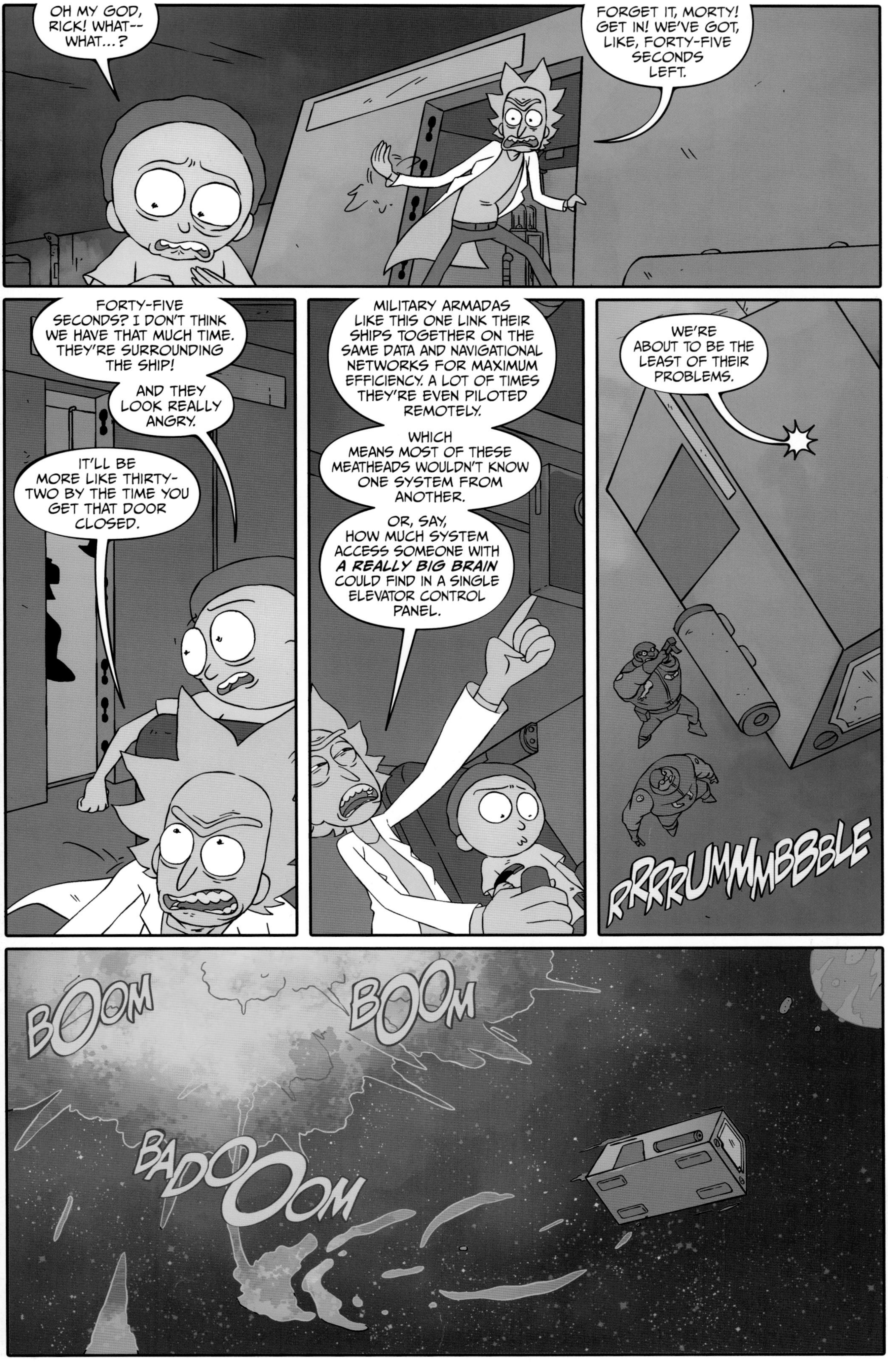

OH MY GOD, RICK! WHAT-- WHAT...?
FORGET IT, MORTY! GET IN! WE'VE GOT, LIKE, FORTY-FIVE SECONDS LEFT.
FORTY-FIVE SECONDS? I DON'T THINK WE HAVE THAT MUCH TIME. THEY'RE SURROUNDING THE SHIP!
AND THEY LOOK REALLY ANGRY.
IT'LL BE MORE LIKE THIRTY-TWO BY THE TIME YOU GET THAT DOOR CLOSED.
MILITARY ARMADAS LIKE THIS ONE LINK THEIR SHIPS TOGETHER ON THE SAME DATA AND NAVIGATIONAL NETWORKS FOR MAXIMUM EFFICIENCY. A LOT OF TIMES THEY'RE EVEN PILOTED REMOTELY.
WHICH MEANS MOST OF THESE MEATHEADS WOULDN'T KNOW ONE SYSTEM FROM ANOTHER.
OR, SAY, HOW MUCH SYSTEM ACCESS SOMEONE WITH ***A REALLY BIG BRAIN*** COULD FIND IN A SINGLE ELEVATOR CONTROL PANEL.
WE'RE ABOUT TO BE THE LEAST OF THEIR PROBLEMS.
RRRRUMMMBBBLE
BOOM
BOOM
BADOOOOM

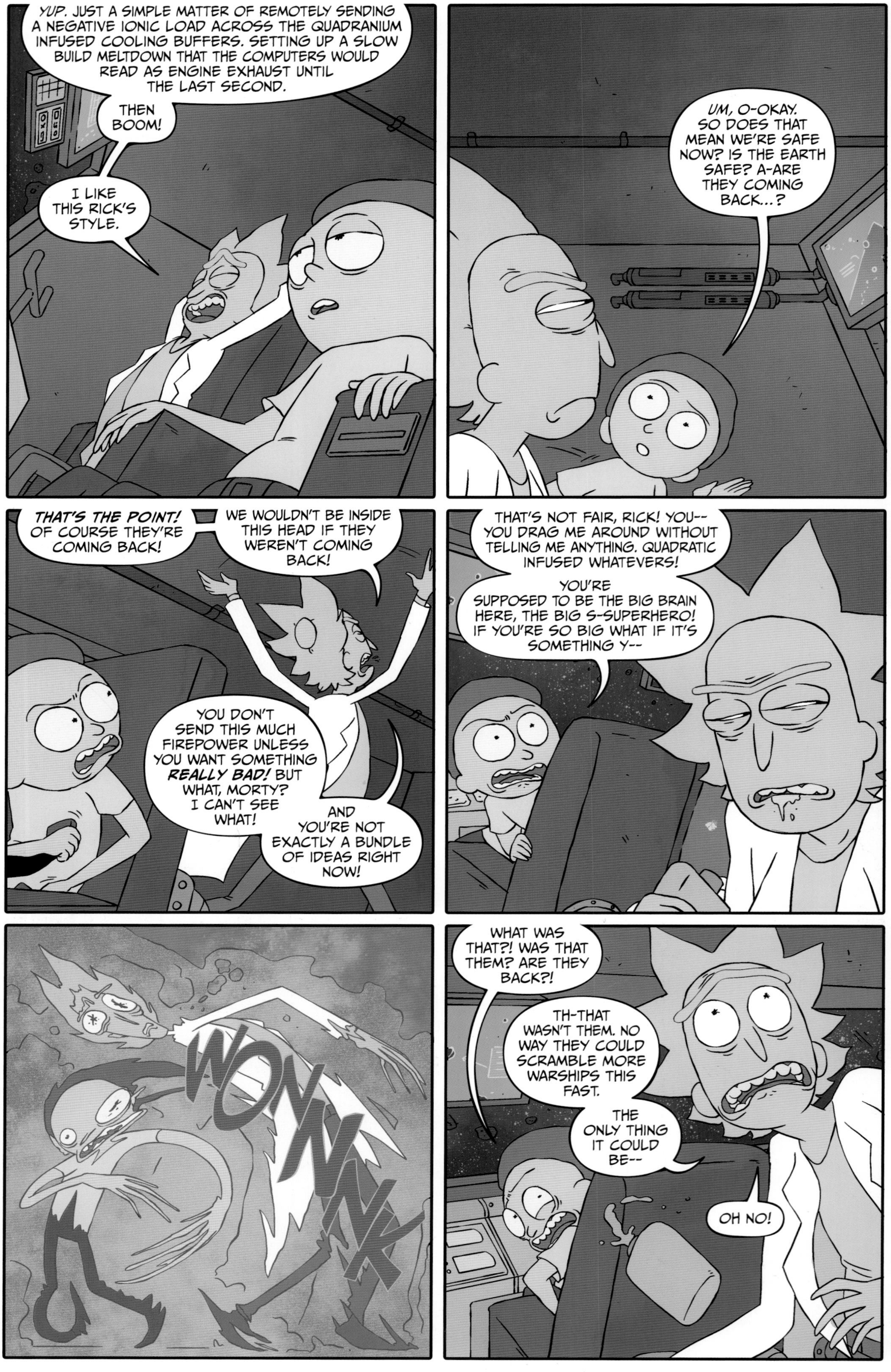
YUP. JUST A SIMPLE MATTER OF REMOTELY SENDING A NEGATIVE IONIC LOAD ACROSS THE QUADRANIUM INFUSED COOLING BUFFERS. SETTING UP A SLOW BUILD MELTDOWN THAT THE COMPUTERS WOULD READ AS ENGINE EXHAUST UNTIL THE LAST SECOND.
THEN BOOM!
I LIKE THIS RICK'S STYLE.
UM, O-OKAY. SO DOES THAT MEAN WE'RE SAFE NOW? IS THE EARTH SAFE? A-ARE THEY COMING BACK...?
THAT'S THE POINT! OF COURSE THEY'RE COMING BACK!
WE WOULDN'T BE INSIDE THIS HEAD IF THEY WEREN'T COMING BACK!
YOU DON'T SEND THIS MUCH FIREPOWER UNLESS YOU WANT SOMETHING REALLY BAD! BUT WHAT, MORTY? I CAN'T SEE WHAT!
AND YOU'RE NOT EXACTLY A BUNDLE OF IDEAS RIGHT NOW!
THAT'S NOT FAIR, RICK! YOU--YOU DRAG ME AROUND WITHOUT TELLING ME ANYTHING. QUADRATIC INFUSED WHATEVERS!
YOU'RE SUPPOSED TO BE THE BIG BRAIN HERE, THE BIG S-SUPERHERO! IF YOU'RE SO BIG WHAT IF IT'S SOMETHING Y--
WONNNK
WHAT WAS THAT?! WAS THAT THEM? ARE THEY BACK?!
TH-THAT WASN'T THEM. NO WAY THEY COULD SCRAMBLE MORE WARSHIPS THIS FAST.
THE ONLY THING IT COULD BE--
OH NO!

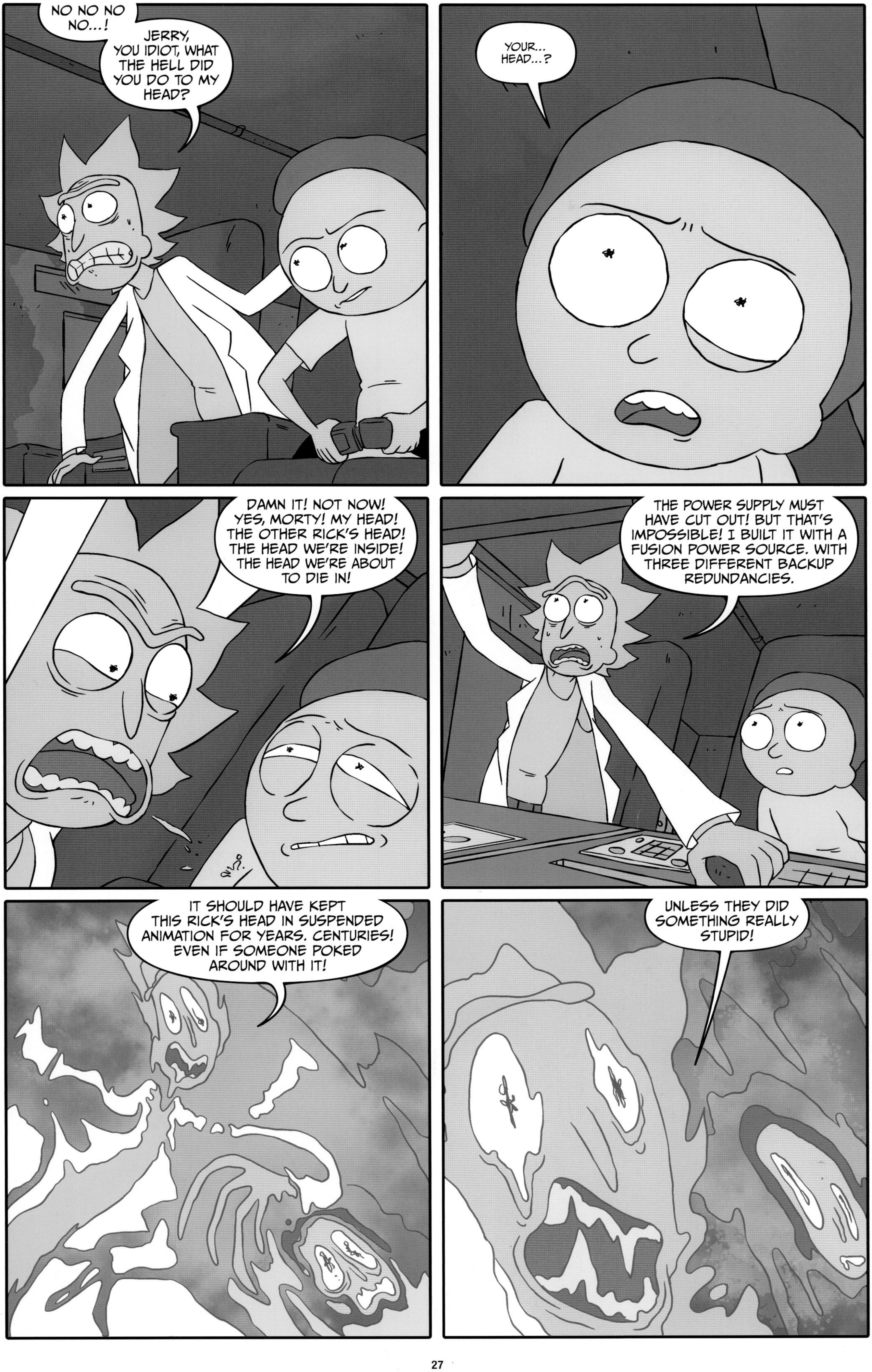
NO NO NO NO...!
JERRY, YOU IDIOT, WHAT THE HELL DID YOU DO TO MY HEAD?
YOUR... HEAD...?
DAMN IT! NOT NOW! YES, MORTY! MY HEAD! THE OTHER RICK'S HEAD! THE HEAD WE'RE INSIDE! THE HEAD WE'RE ABOUT TO DIE IN!
THE POWER SUPPLY MUST HAVE CUT OUT! BUT THAT'S IMPOSSIBLE! I BUILT IT WITH A FUSION POWER SOURCE. WITH THREE DIFFERENT BACKUP REDUNDANCIES.
IT SHOULD HAVE KEPT THIS RICK'S HEAD IN SUSPENDED ANIMATION FOR YEARS. CENTURIES! EVEN IF SOMEONE POKED AROUND WITH IT!
UNLESS THEY DID SOMETHING REALLY STUPID!

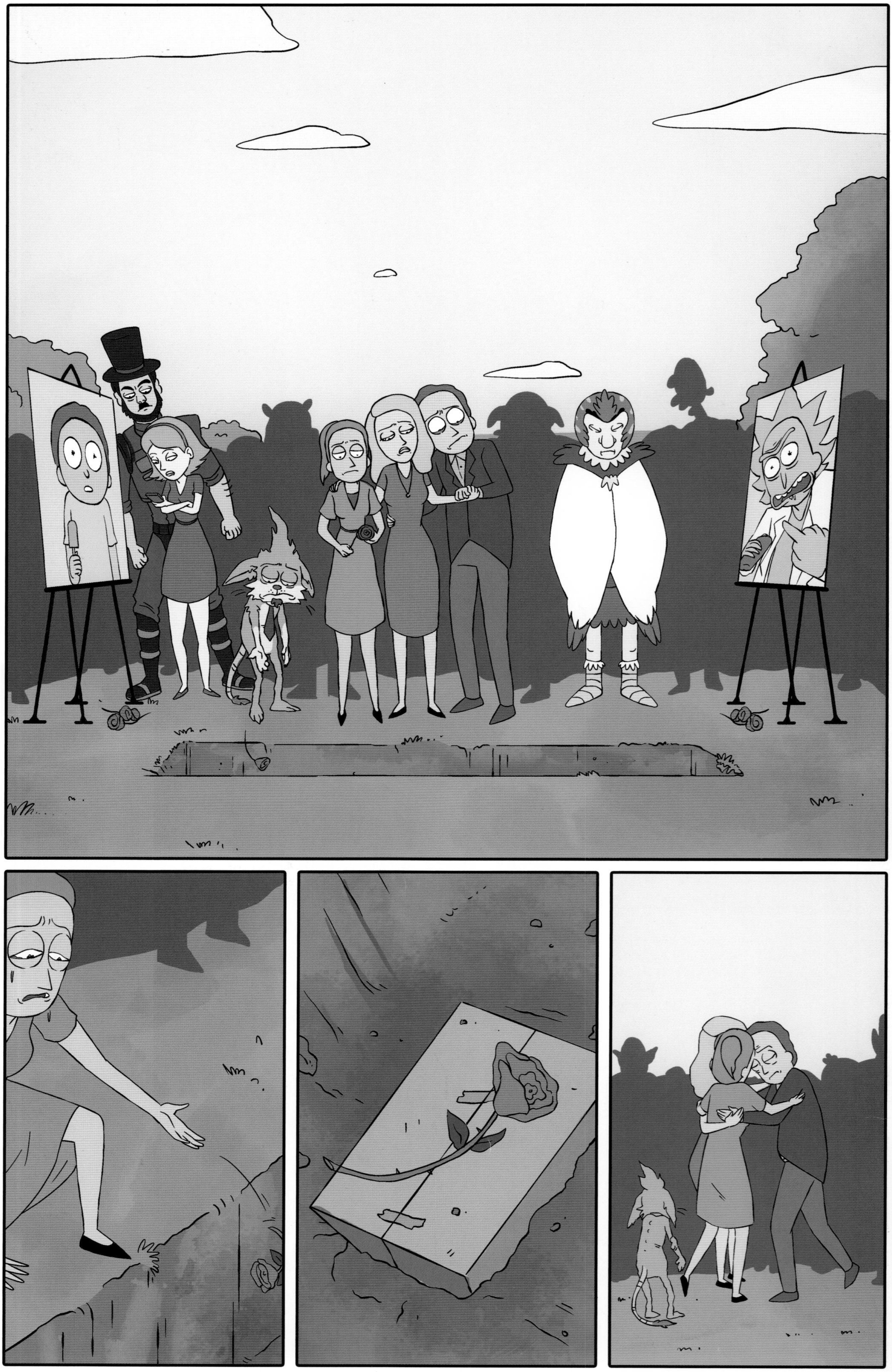

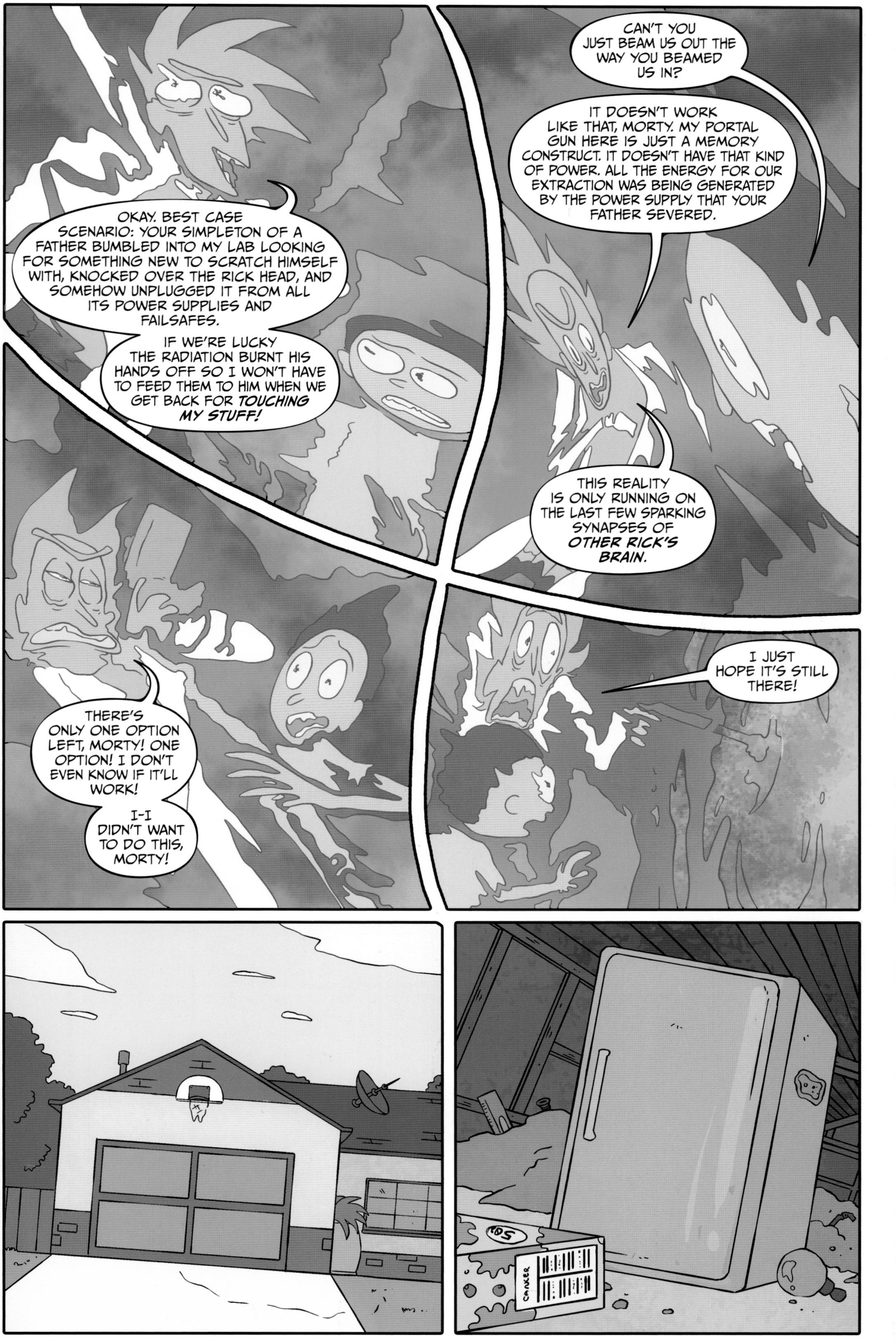
OKAY. BEST CASE SCENARIO: YOUR SIMPLETON OF A FATHER BUMBLED INTO MY LAB LOOKING FOR SOMETHING NEW TO SCRATCH HIMSELF WITH, KNOCKED OVER THE RICK HEAD, AND SOMEHOW UNPLUGGED IT FROM ALL ITS POWER SUPPLIES AND FAILSAFES.
IF WE'RE LUCKY THE RADIATION BURNT HIS HANDS OFF SO I WON'T HAVE TO FEED THEM TO HIM WHEN WE GET BACK FOR *TOUCHING MY STUFF!*
CAN'T YOU JUST BEAM US OUT THE WAY YOU BEAMED US IN?
IT DOESN'T WORK LIKE THAT, MORTY. MY PORTAL GUN HERE IS JUST A MEMORY CONSTRUCT. IT DOESN'T HAVE THAT KIND OF POWER. ALL THE ENERGY FOR OUR EXTRACTION WAS BEING GENERATED BY THE POWER SUPPLY THAT YOUR FATHER SEVERED.
THIS REALITY IS ONLY RUNNING ON THE LAST FEW SPARKING SYNAPSES OF *OTHER RICK'S BRAIN.*
THERE'S ONLY ONE OPTION LEFT, MORTY! ONE OPTION! I DON'T EVEN KNOW IF IT'LL WORK!
I-I DIDN'T WANT TO DO THIS, MORTY!
I JUST HOPE IT'S STILL THERE!

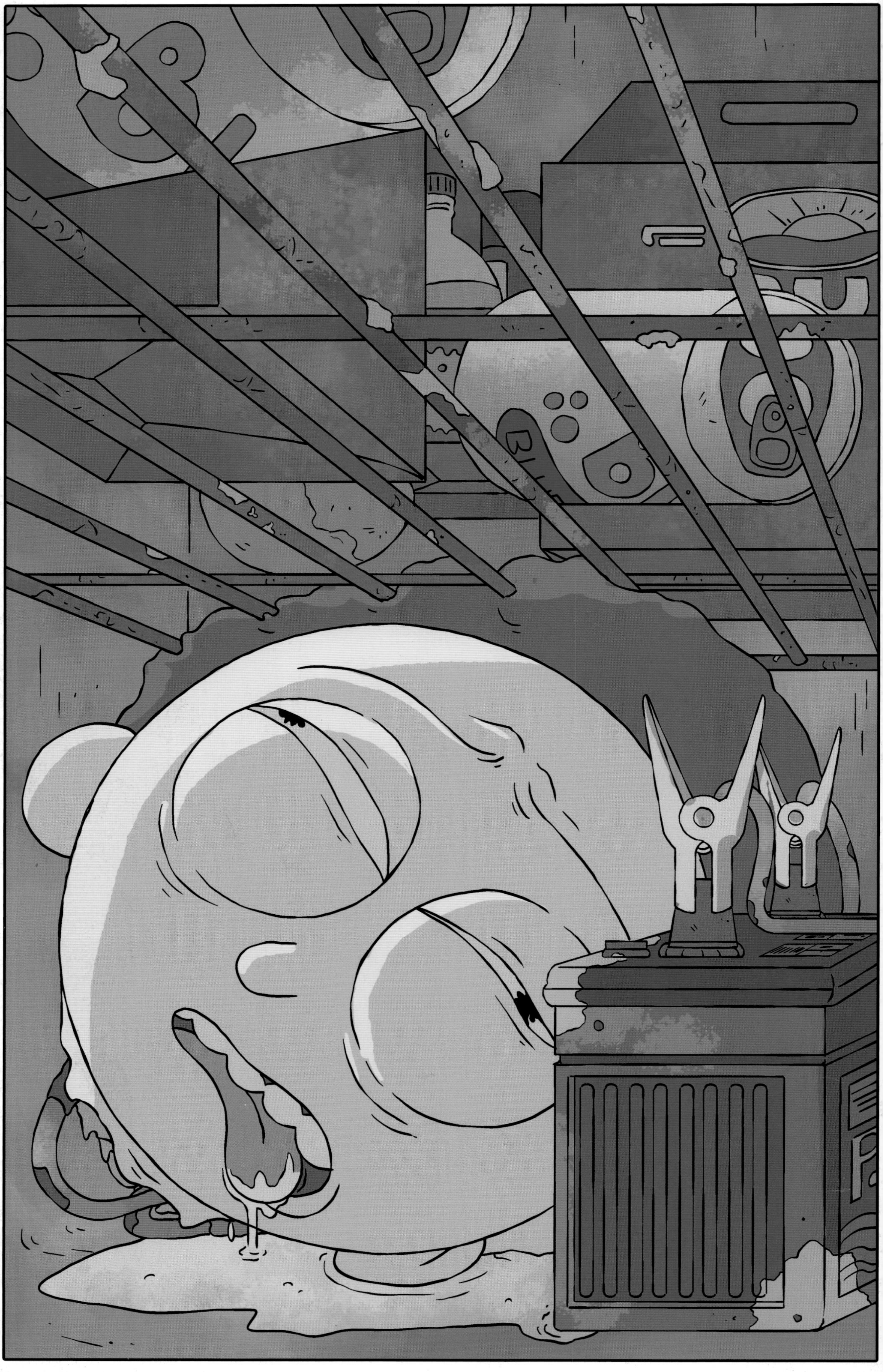

HEAD SPACE
PART TWO

WRITTEN BY **TOM FOWLER**
DRAWN BY **CJ CANNON**
COLORED BY **RYAN HILL**
LETTERED BY **CRANK!**

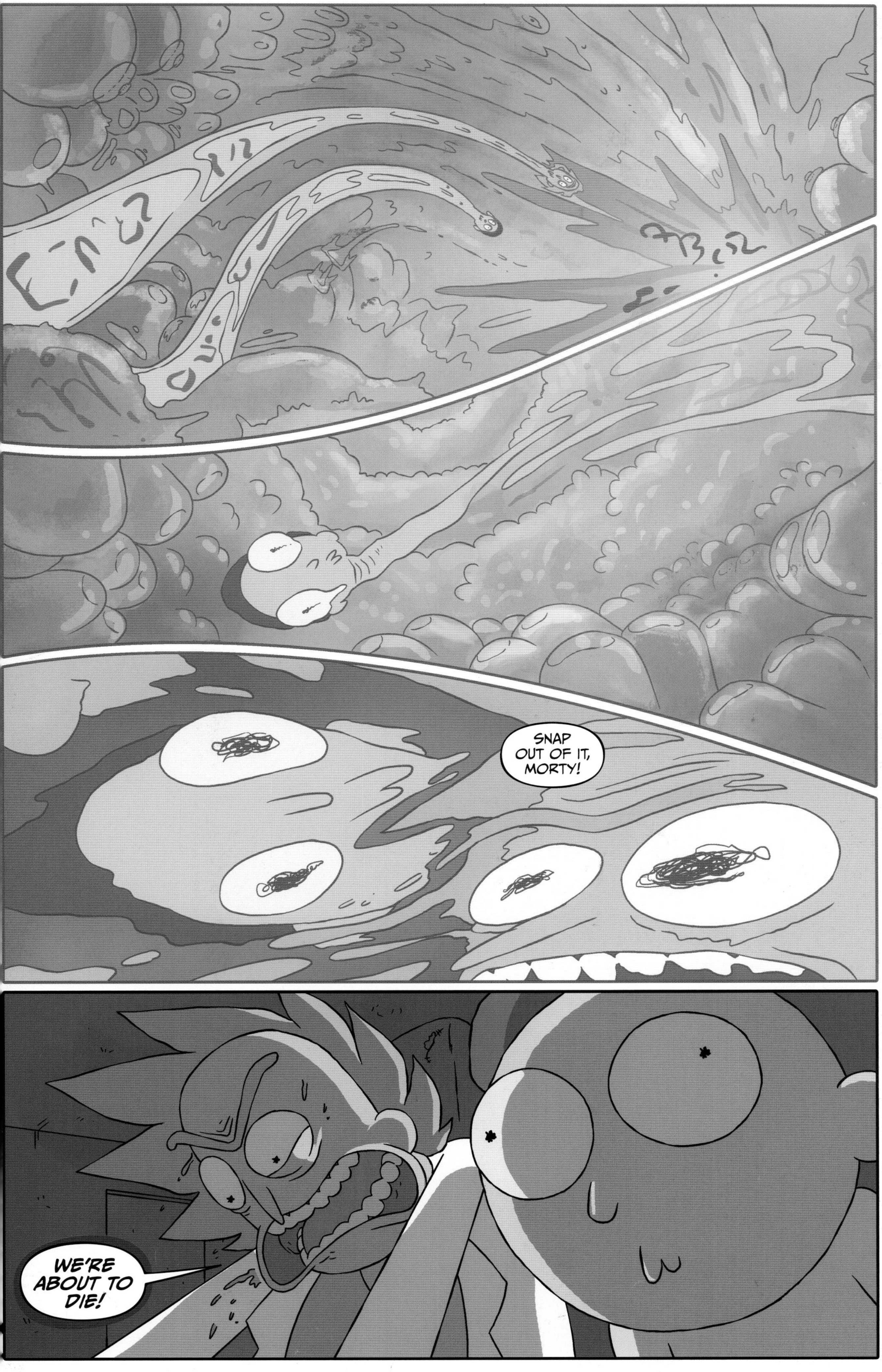
SNAP OUT OF IT, MORTY!
WE'RE ABOUT TO DIE!

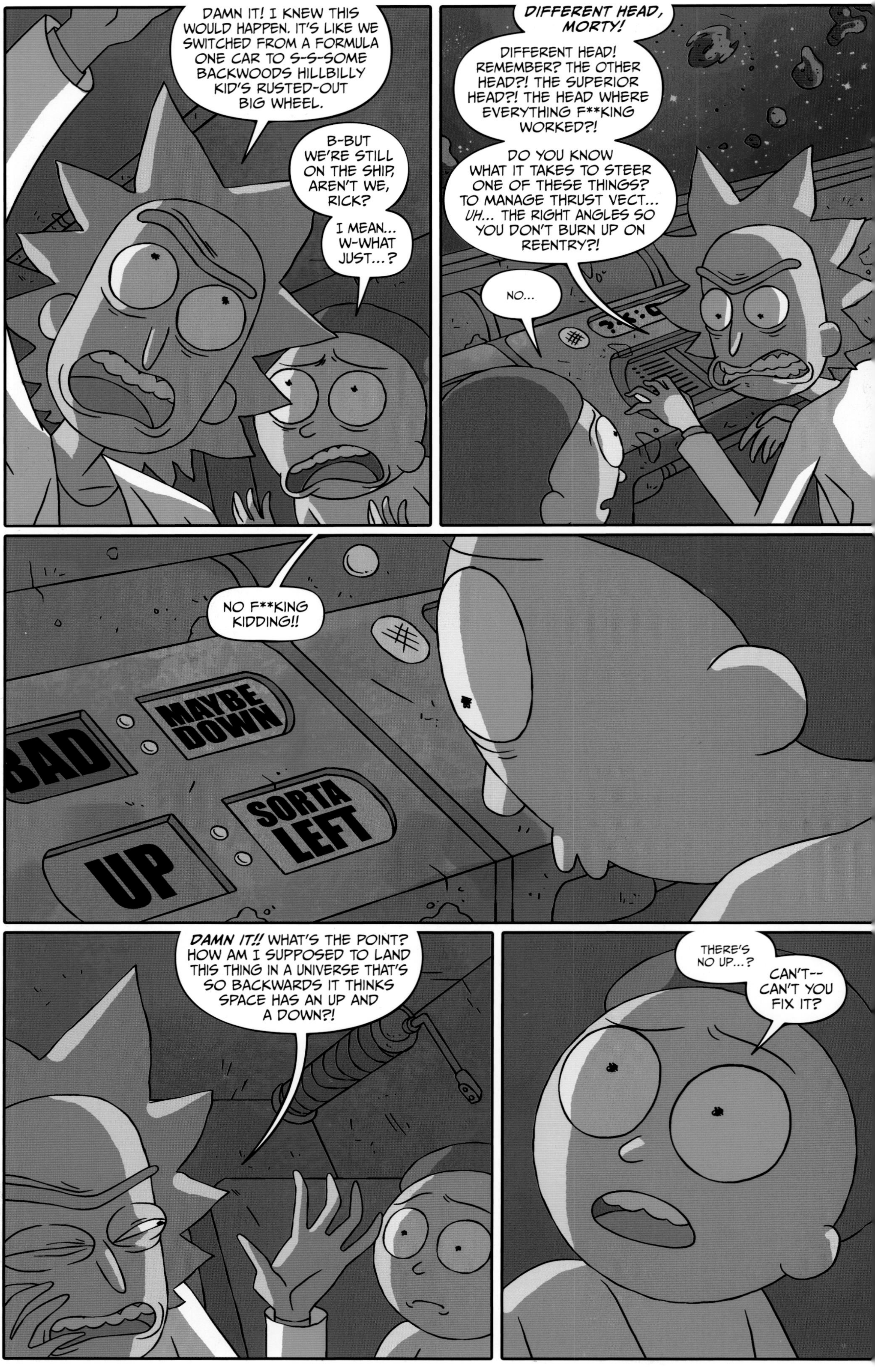
DAMN IT! I KNEW THIS WOULD HAPPEN. IT'S LIKE WE SWITCHED FROM A FORMULA ONE CAR TO S-S-SOME BACKWOODS HILLBILLY KID'S RUSTED-OUT BIG WHEEL.
B-BUT WE'RE STILL ON THE SHIP, AREN'T WE, RICK?
I MEAN... W-WHAT JUST...?
DIFFERENT HEAD, MORTY!
DIFFERENT HEAD! REMEMBER? THE OTHER HEAD?! THE SUPERIOR HEAD?! THE HEAD WHERE EVERYTHING F**KING WORKED?!
DO YOU KNOW WHAT IT TAKES TO STEER ONE OF THESE THINGS? TO MANAGE THRUST VECT... UH... THE RIGHT ANGLES SO YOU DON'T BURN UP ON REENTRY?!
NO...
NO F**KING KIDDING!!
BAD
MAYBE DOWN
UP
SORTA LEFT
DAMN IT!! WHAT'S THE POINT? HOW AM I SUPPOSED TO LAND THIS THING IN A UNIVERSE THAT'S SO BACKWARDS IT THINKS SPACE HAS AN UP AND A DOWN?!
THERE'S NO UP...?
CAN'T-- CAN'T YOU FIX IT?

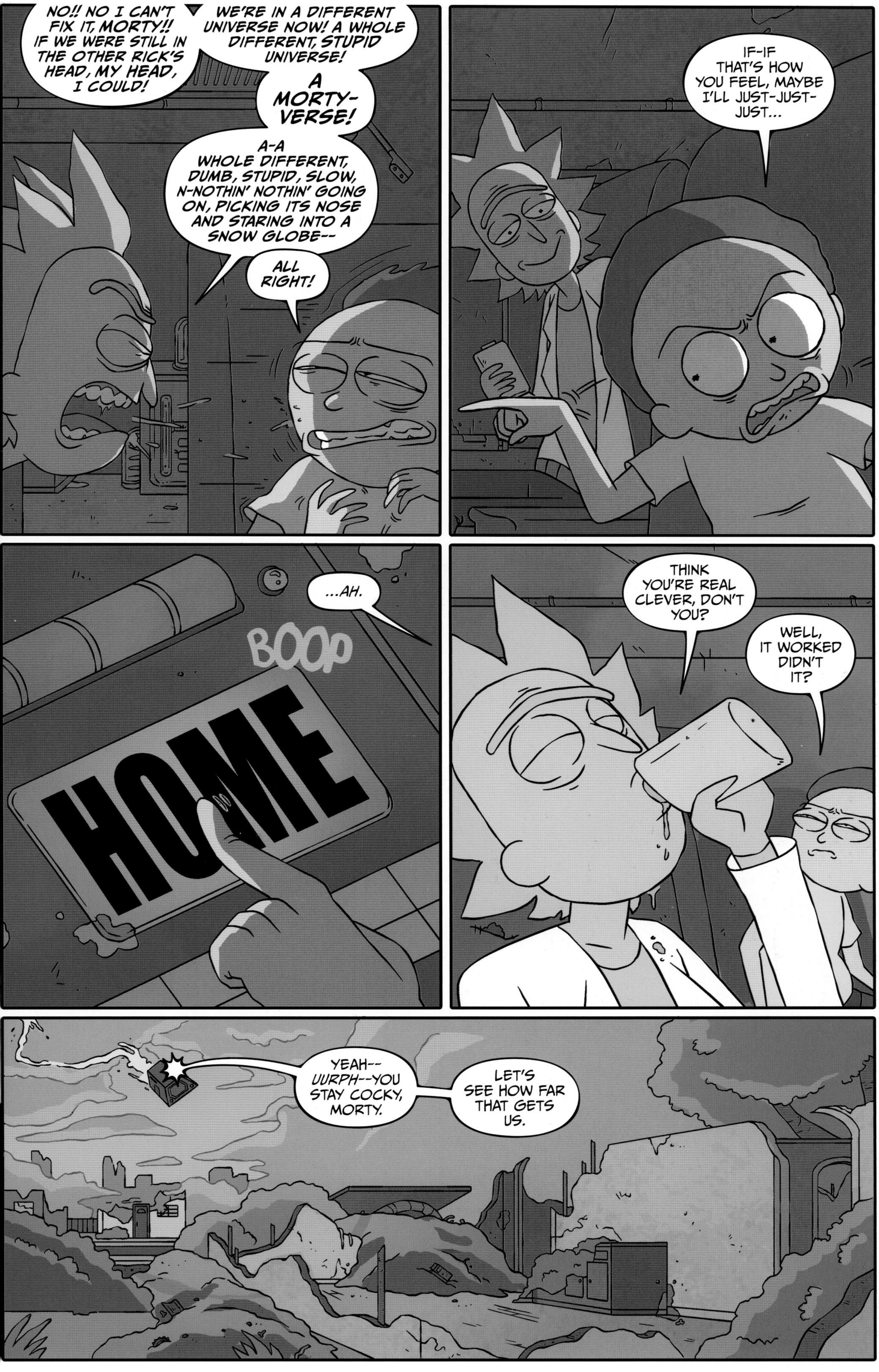
NO!! NO I CAN'T FIX IT, MORTY!! IF WE WERE STILL IN THE OTHER RICK'S HEAD, MY HEAD, I COULD!
WE'RE IN A DIFFERENT UNIVERSE NOW! A WHOLE DIFFERENT, STUPID UNIVERSE!
A MORTY-VERSE!
A-A WHOLE DIFFERENT, DUMB, STUPID, SLOW, N-NOTHIN' NOTHIN' GOING ON, PICKING ITS NOSE AND STARING INTO A SNOW GLOBE--
ALL RIGHT!
IF-IF THAT'S HOW YOU FEEL, MAYBE I'LL JUST-JUST-JUST...
...AH.
BOOP
HOME
THINK YOU'RE REAL CLEVER, DON'T YOU?
WELL, IT WORKED DIDN'T IT?
YEAH--UURPH--YOU STAY COCKY, MORTY.
LET'S SEE HOW FAR THAT GETS US.

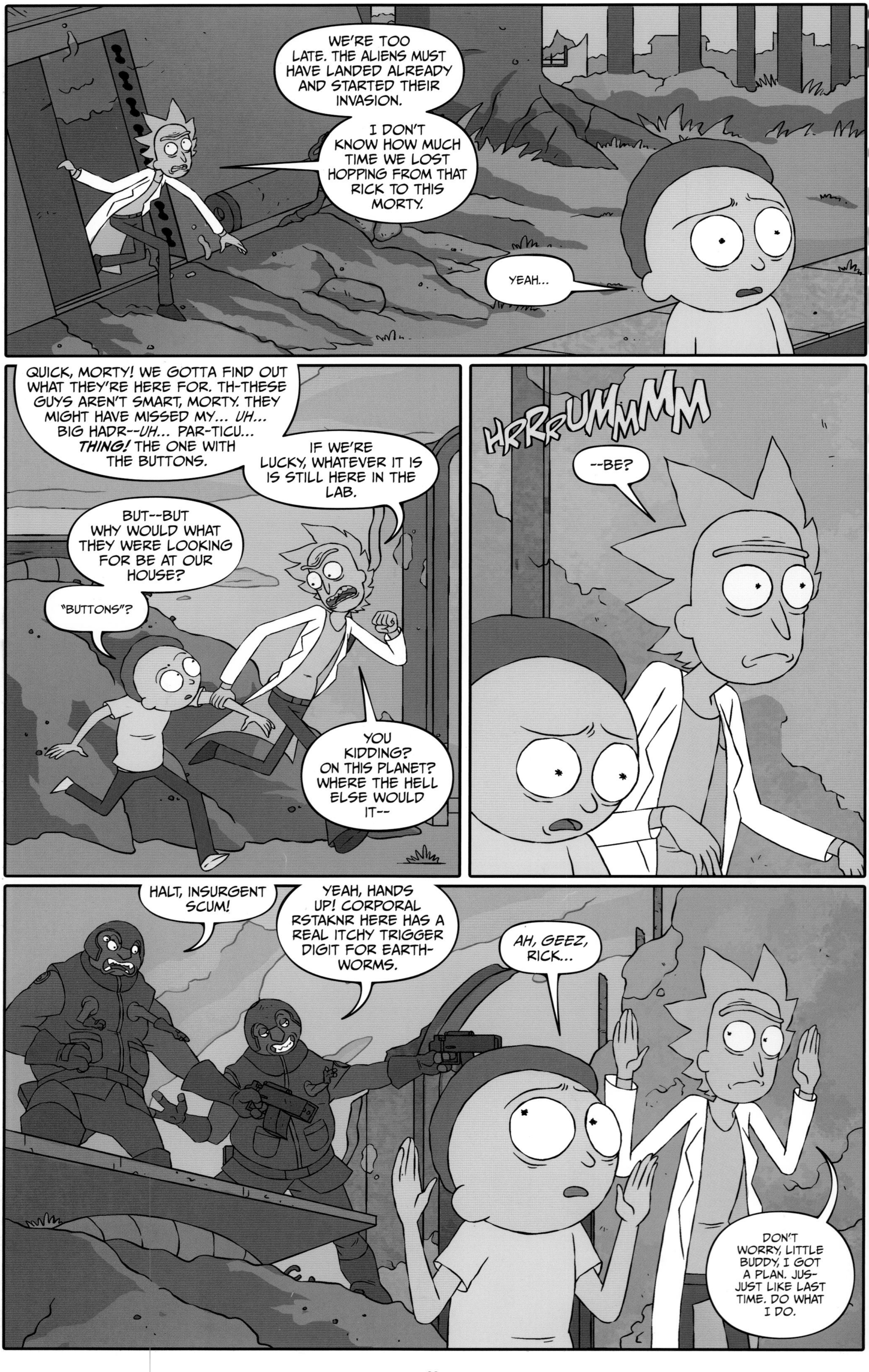
WE'RE TOO LATE. THE ALIENS MUST HAVE LANDED ALREADY AND STARTED THEIR INVASION.
I DON'T KNOW HOW MUCH TIME WE LOST HOPPING FROM THAT RICK TO THIS MORTY.
YEAH...
QUICK, MORTY! WE GOTTA FIND OUT WHAT THEY'RE HERE FOR. TH-THESE GUYS AREN'T SMART, MORTY. THEY MIGHT HAVE MISSED MY... *UH...* BIG HADR--*UH...* PAR-TICU... ***THING!*** THE ONE WITH THE BUTTONS.
IF WE'RE LUCKY, WHATEVER IT IS IS STILL HERE IN THE LAB.
BUT--BUT WHY WOULD WHAT THEY WERE LOOKING FOR BE AT OUR HOUSE?
"BUTTONS"?
YOU KIDDING? ON THIS PLANET? WHERE THE HELL ELSE WOULD IT--
HRRRUMMMM
--BE?
HALT, INSURGENT SCUM!
YEAH, HANDS UP! CORPORAL RSTAKNR HERE HAS A REAL ITCHY TRIGGER DIGIT FOR EARTH-WORMS.
AH, GEEZ, RICK...
DON'T WORRY, LITTLE BUDDY, I GOT A PLAN. JUS-JUST LIKE LAST TIME. DO WHAT I DO.

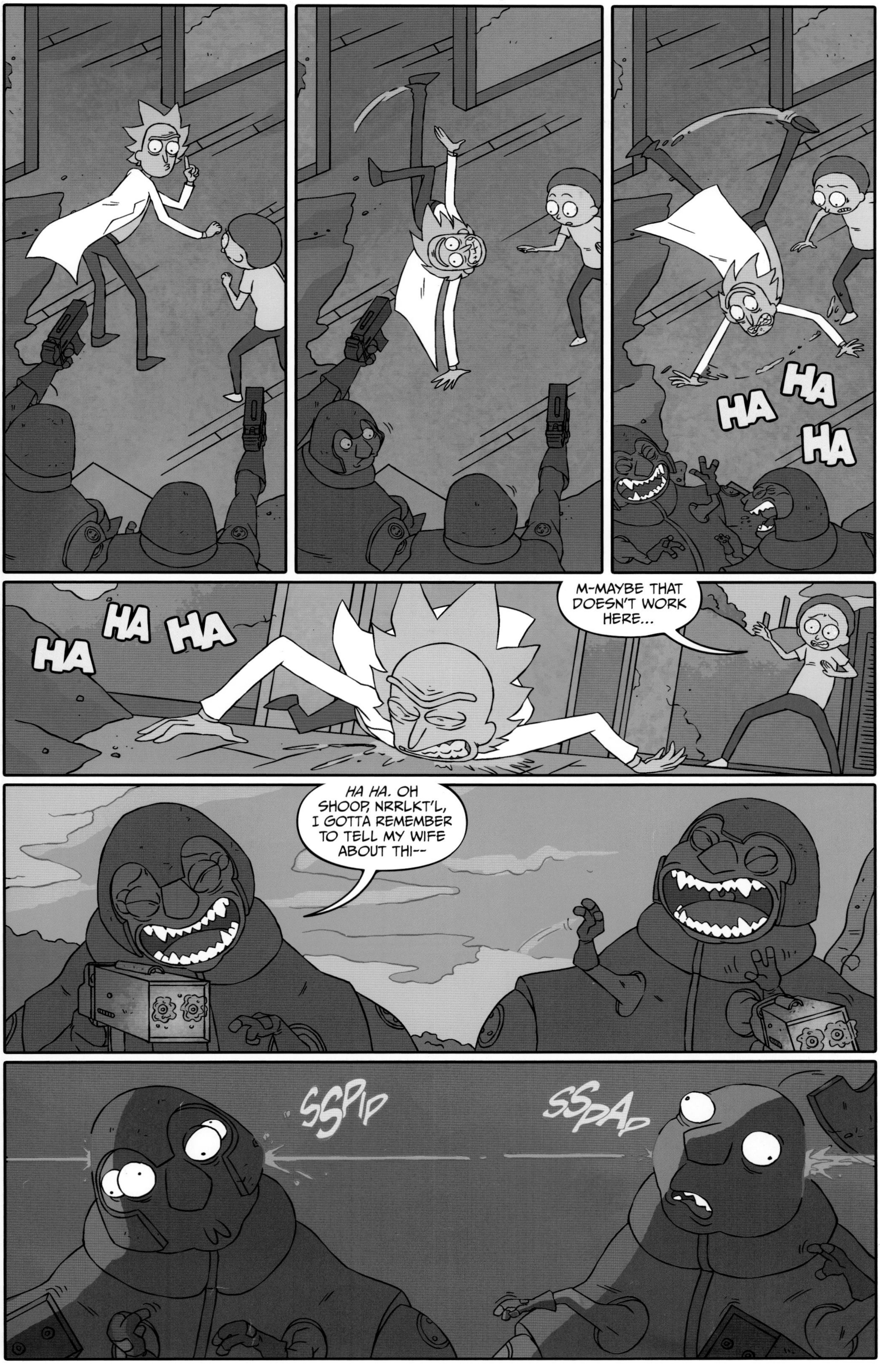
HA
HA
HA
HA HA HA
M-MAYBE THAT DOESN'T WORK HERE...
HA HA. OH SHOOP, NRRLKT'L, I GOTTA REMEMBER TO TELL MY WIFE ABOUT THI--
SSPIP
SSPAP

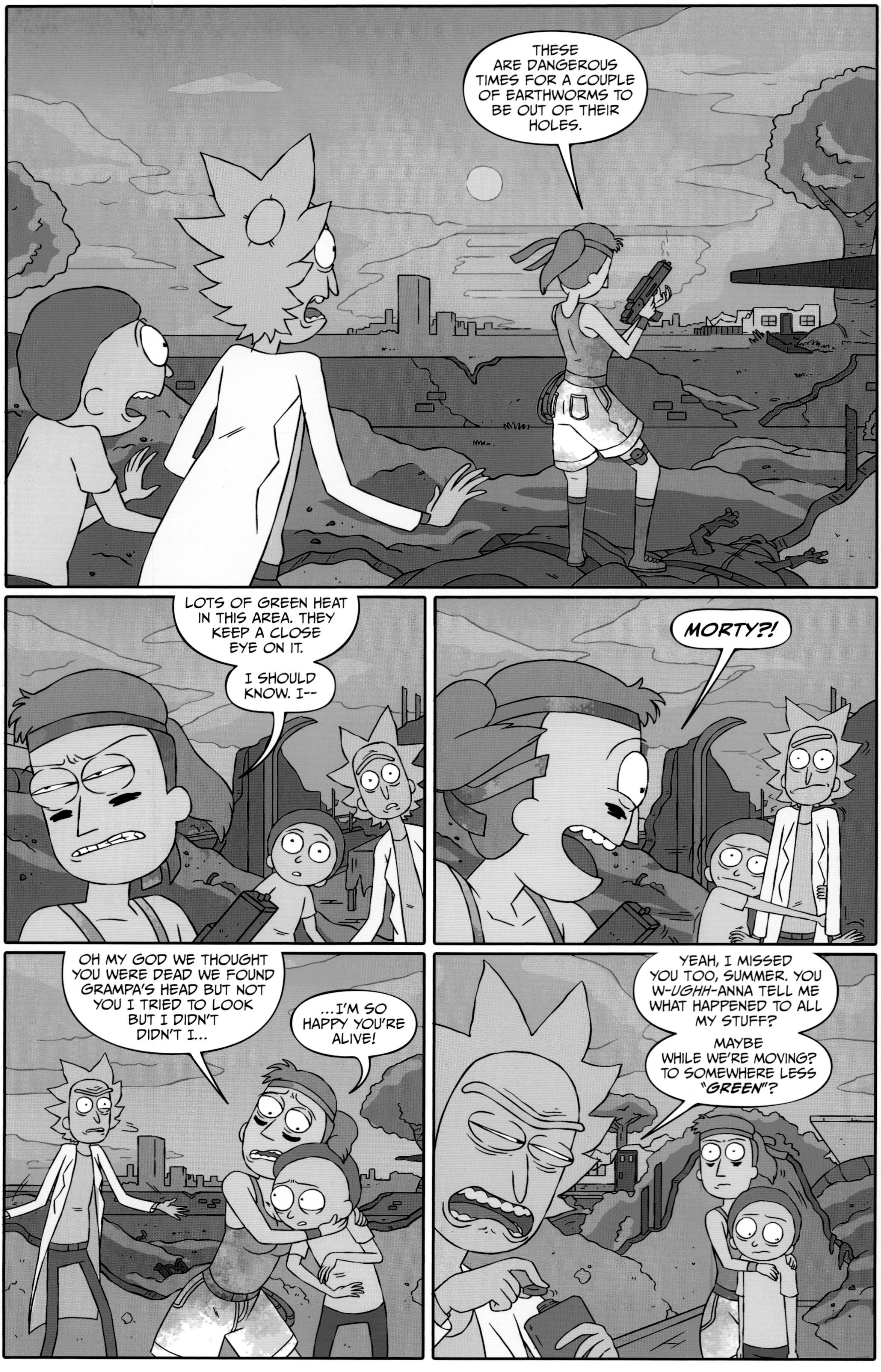
THESE ARE DANGEROUS TIMES FOR A COUPLE OF EARTHWORMS TO BE OUT OF THEIR HOLES.
LOTS OF GREEN HEAT IN THIS AREA. THEY KEEP A CLOSE EYE ON IT.
I SHOULD KNOW. I--
MORTY?!
OH MY GOD WE THOUGHT YOU WERE DEAD WE FOUND GRAMPA'S HEAD BUT NOT YOU I TRIED TO LOOK BUT I DIDN'T DIDN'T I...
...I'M SO HAPPY YOU'RE ALIVE!
YEAH, I MISSED YOU TOO, SUMMER. YOU W-UGHH-ANNA TELL ME WHAT HAPPENED TO ALL MY STUFF?
MAYBE WHILE WE'RE MOVING? TO SOMEWHERE LESS "GREEN"?

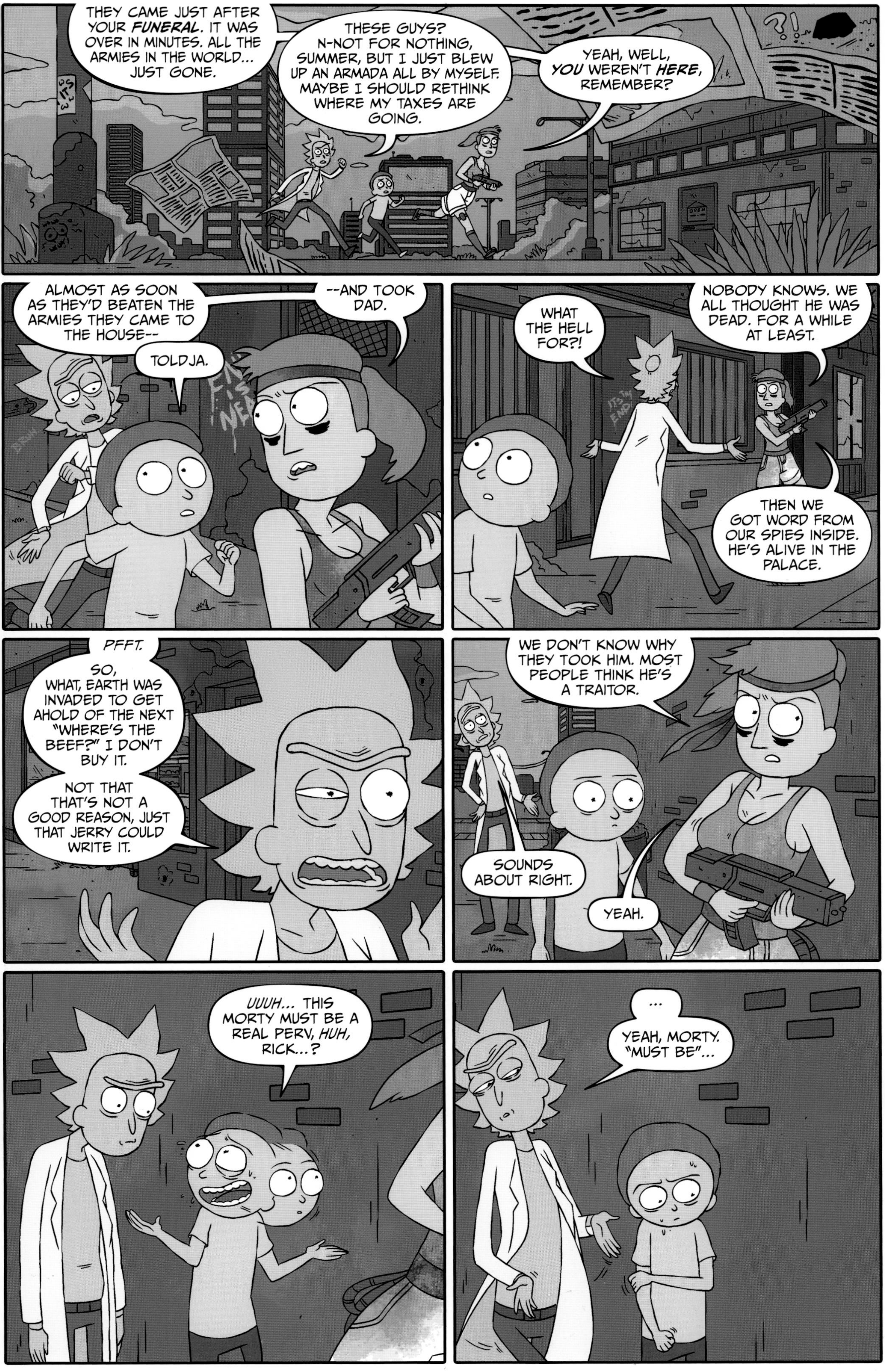
THEY CAME JUST AFTER YOUR FUNERAL. IT WAS OVER IN MINUTES. ALL THE ARMIES IN THE WORLD... JUST GONE.
THESE GUYS? N-NOT FOR NOTHING, SUMMER, BUT I JUST BLEW UP AN ARMADA ALL BY MYSELF. MAYBE I SHOULD RETHINK WHERE MY TAXES ARE GOING.
YEAH, WELL, YOU WEREN'T HERE, REMEMBER?
ALMOST AS SOON AS THEY'D BEATEN THE ARMIES THEY CAME TO THE HOUSE--
TOLDJA.
--AND TOOK DAD.
WHAT THE HELL FOR?!
NOBODY KNOWS. WE ALL THOUGHT HE WAS DEAD. FOR A WHILE AT LEAST.
THEN WE GOT WORD FROM OUR SPIES INSIDE. HE'S ALIVE IN THE PALACE.
PFFT.
SO, WHAT, EARTH WAS INVADED TO GET AHOLD OF THE NEXT "WHERE'S THE BEEF?" I DON'T BUY IT.
NOT THAT THAT'S NOT A GOOD REASON, JUST THAT JERRY COULD WRITE IT.
WE DON'T KNOW WHY THEY TOOK HIM. MOST PEOPLE THINK HE'S A TRAITOR.
SOUNDS ABOUT RIGHT.
YEAH.
UUUH... THIS MORTY MUST BE A REAL PERV, HUH, RICK...?
...
YEAH, MORTY. "MUST BE"...

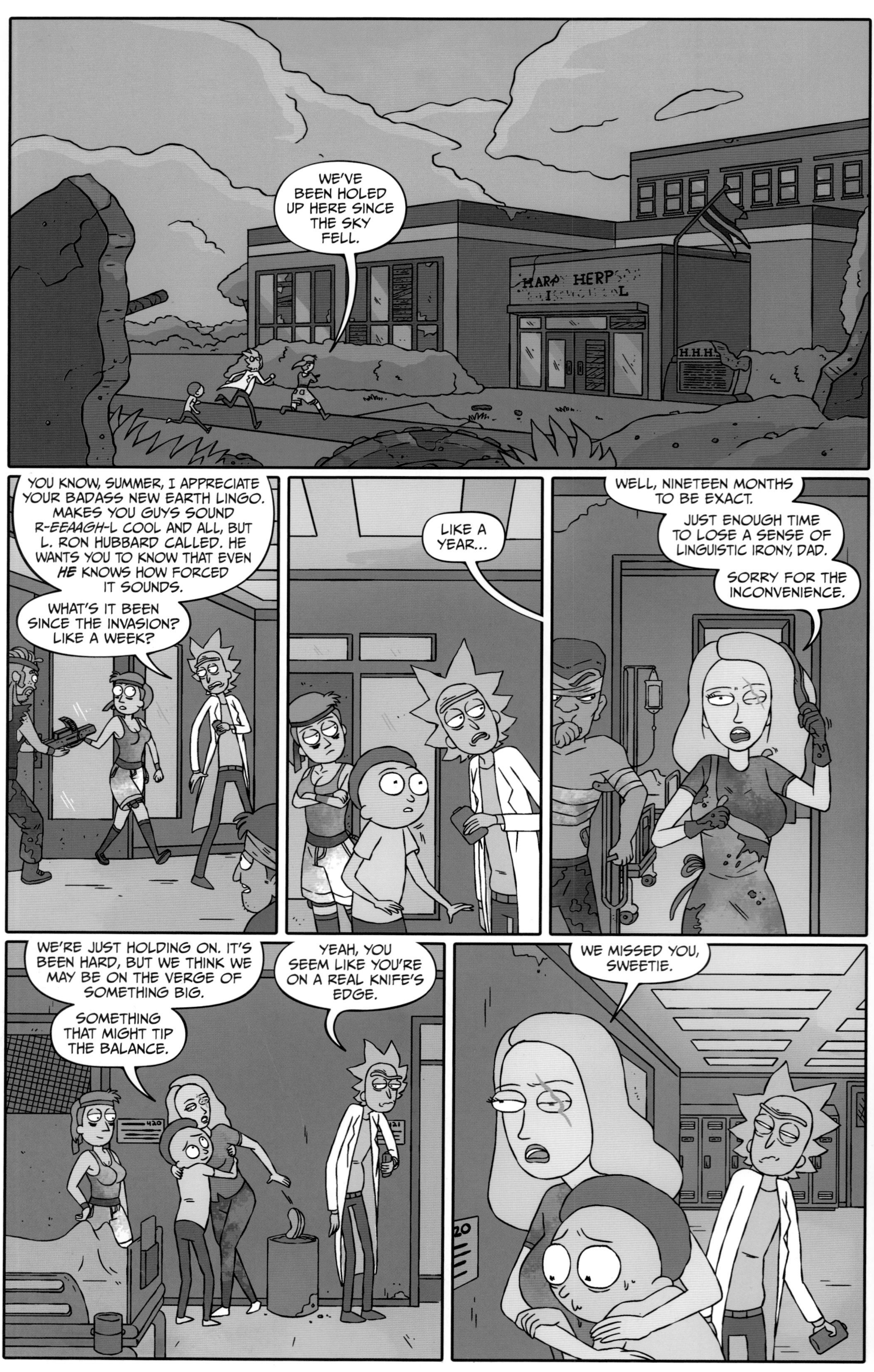
WE'VE BEEN HOLED UP HERE SINCE THE SKY FELL.
HARP HERP
H.H.H.
YOU KNOW, SUMMER, I APPRECIATE YOUR BADASS NEW EARTH LINGO. MAKES YOU GUYS SOUND R-EEAAGH-L COOL AND ALL, BUT L. RON HUBBARD CALLED. HE WANTS YOU TO KNOW THAT EVEN HE KNOWS HOW FORCED IT SOUNDS.
WHAT'S IT BEEN SINCE THE INVASION? LIKE A WEEK?
LIKE A YEAR...
WELL, NINETEEN MONTHS TO BE EXACT.
JUST ENOUGH TIME TO LOSE A SENSE OF LINGUISTIC IRONY, DAD.
SORRY FOR THE INCONVENIENCE.
WE'RE JUST HOLDING ON. IT'S BEEN HARD, BUT WE THINK WE MAY BE ON THE VERGE OF SOMETHING BIG.
SOMETHING THAT MIGHT TIP THE BALANCE.
YEAH, YOU SEEM LIKE YOU'RE ON A REAL KNIFE'S EDGE.
WE MISSED YOU, SWEETIE.

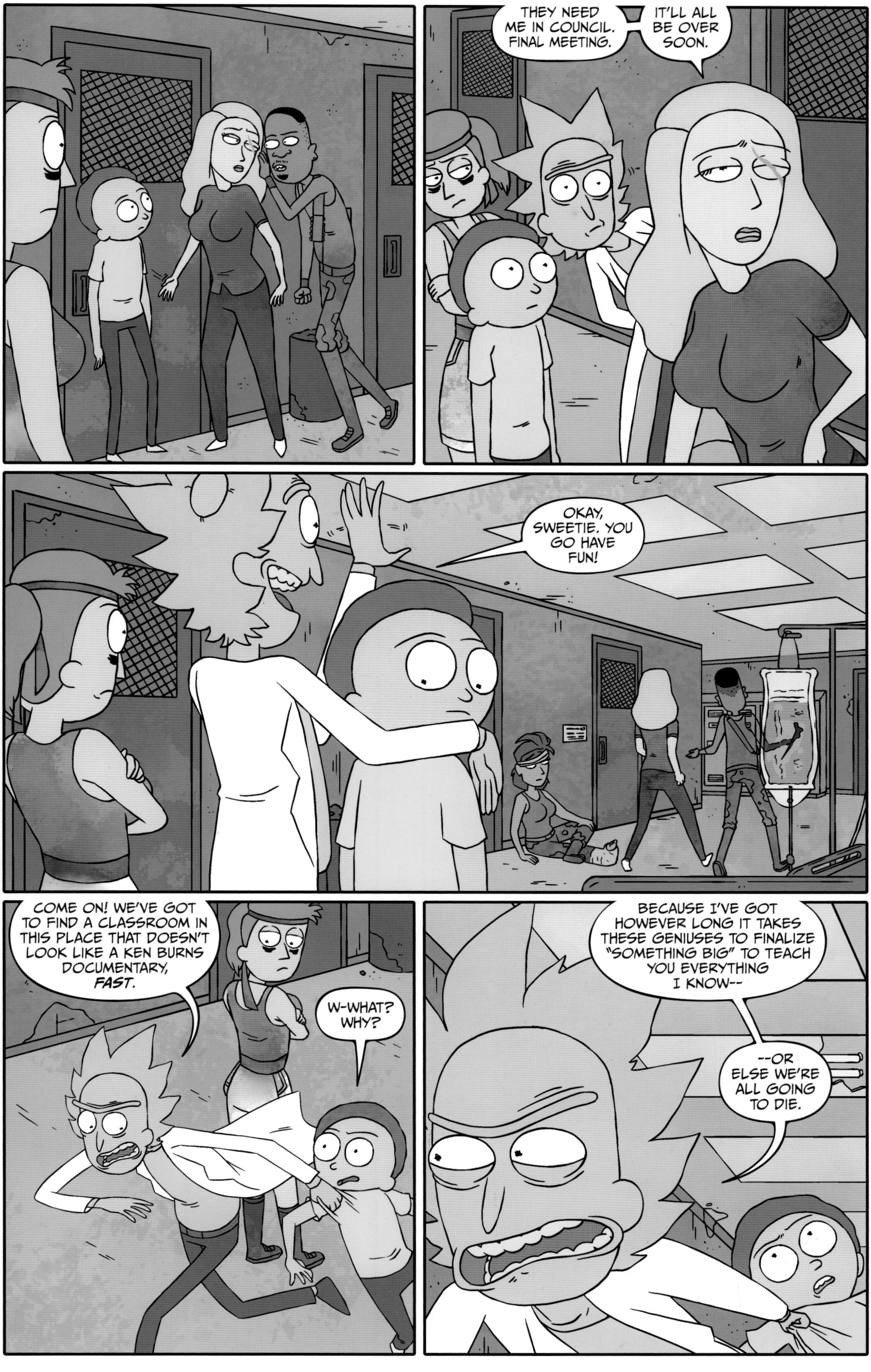
THEY NEED ME IN COUNCIL. FINAL MEETING.
IT'LL ALL BE OVER SOON.
OKAY, SWEETIE. YOU GO HAVE FUN!
COME ON! WE'VE GOT TO FIND A CLASSROOM IN THIS PLACE THAT DOESN'T LOOK LIKE A KEN BURNS DOCUMENTARY, *FAST*.
W-WHAT? WHY?
BECAUSE I'VE GOT HOWEVER LONG IT TAKES THESE GENIUSES TO FINALIZE "SOMETHING BIG" TO TEACH YOU EVERYTHING I KNOW--
--OR ELSE WE'RE ALL GOING TO DIE.

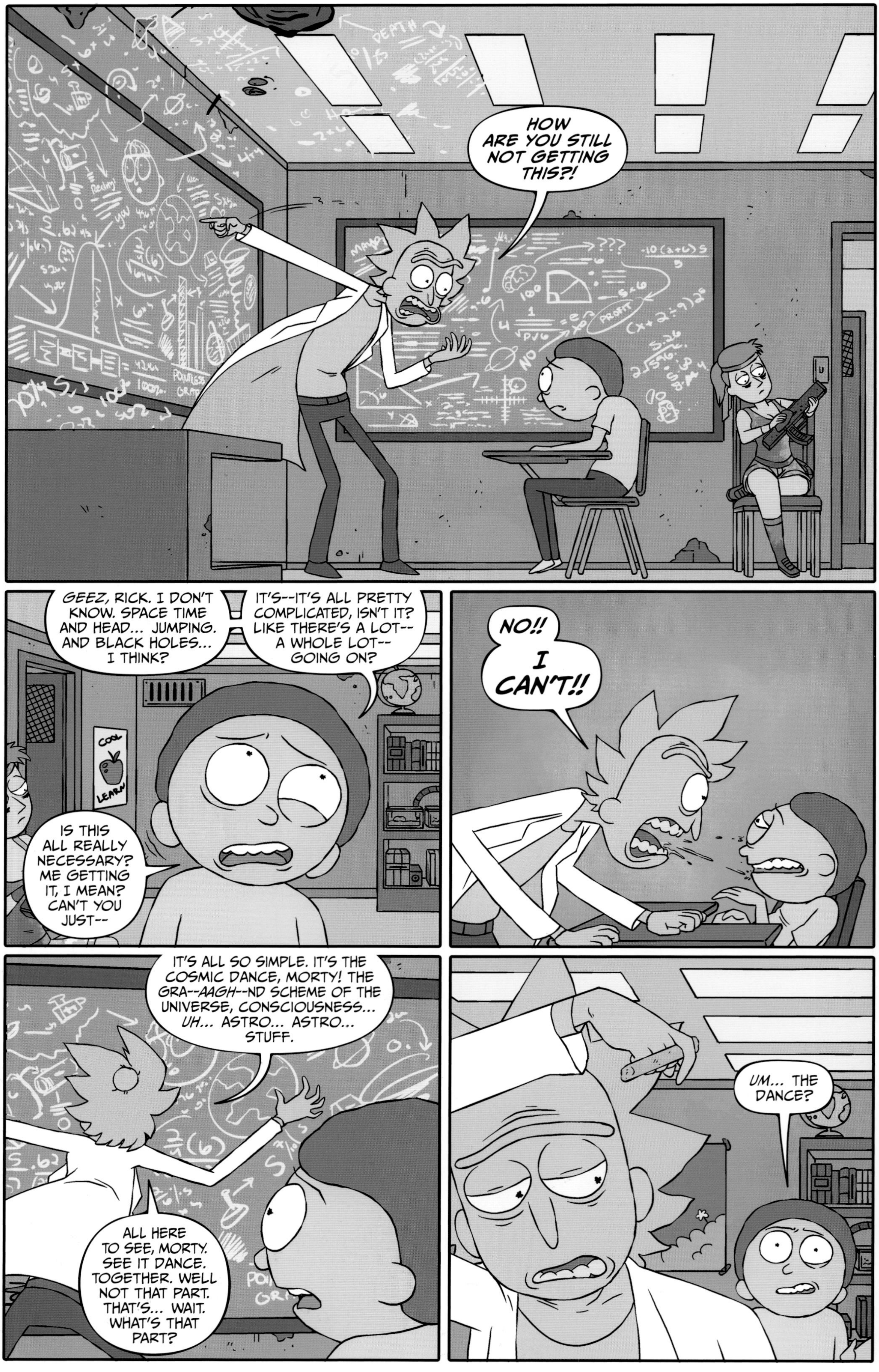
HOW ARE YOU STILL NOT GETTING THIS?!
GEEZ, RICK. I DON'T KNOW. SPACE TIME AND HEAD... JUMPING. AND BLACK HOLES... I THINK?
IT'S--IT'S ALL PRETTY COMPLICATED, ISN'T IT? LIKE THERE'S A LOT-- A WHOLE LOT-- GOING ON?
IS THIS ALL REALLY NECESSARY? ME GETTING IT, I MEAN? CAN'T YOU JUST--
NO!!
I CAN'T!!
IT'S ALL SO SIMPLE. IT'S THE COSMIC DANCE, MORTY! THE GRA--AAGH--ND SCHEME OF THE UNIVERSE, CONSCIOUSNESS... UH... ASTRO... ASTRO... STUFF.
ALL HERE TO SEE, MORTY. SEE IT DANCE. TOGETHER. WELL NOT THAT PART. THAT'S... WAIT. WHAT'S THAT PART?
UM... THE DANCE?

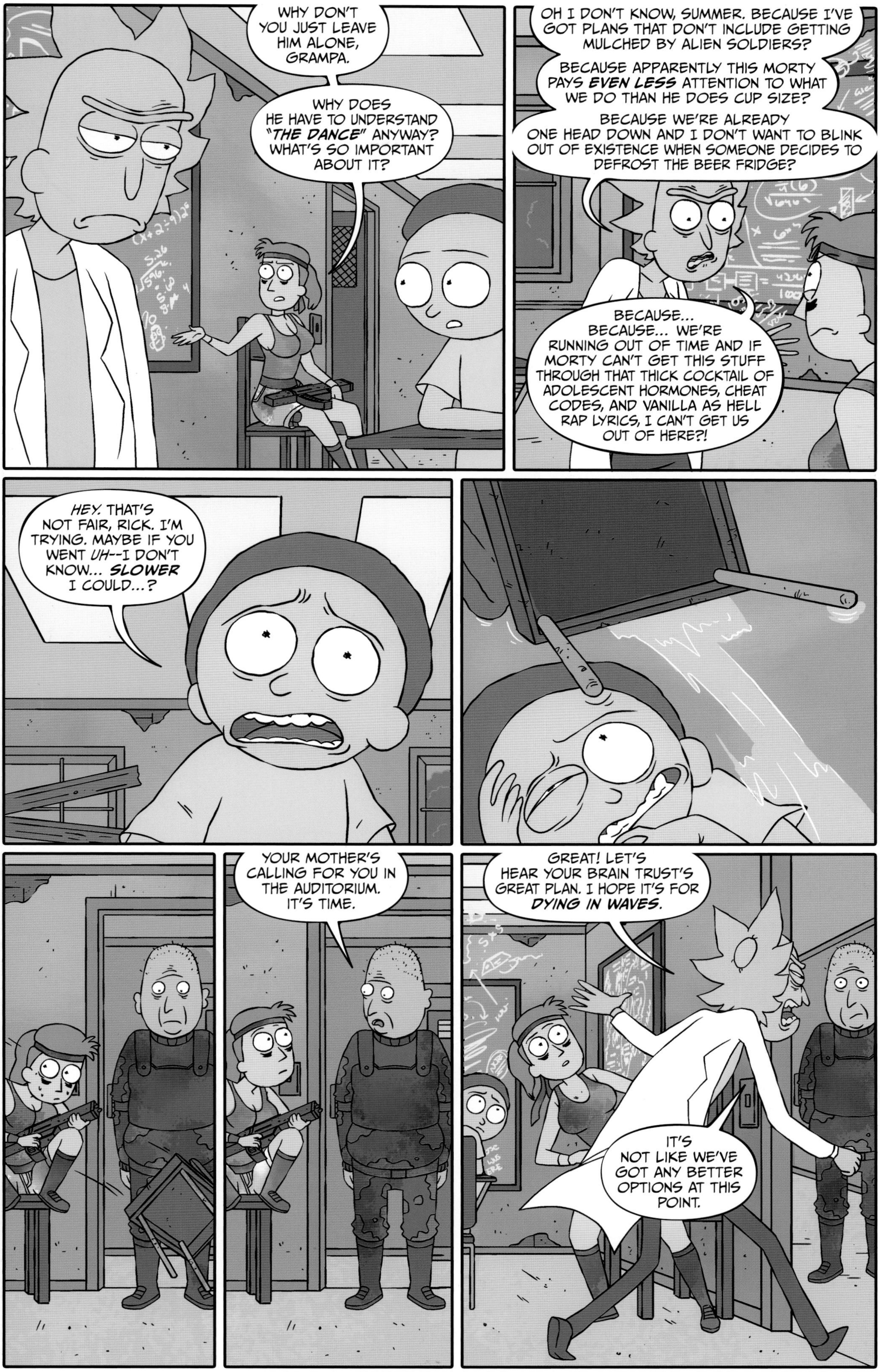
WHY DON'T YOU JUST LEAVE HIM ALONE, GRAMPA.
WHY DOES HE HAVE TO UNDERSTAND "THE DANCE" ANYWAY? WHAT'S SO IMPORTANT ABOUT IT?
OH I DON'T KNOW, SUMMER. BECAUSE I'VE GOT PLANS THAT DON'T INCLUDE GETTING MULCHED BY ALIEN SOLDIERS?
BECAUSE APPARENTLY THIS MORTY PAYS EVEN LESS ATTENTION TO WHAT WE DO THAN HE DOES CUP SIZE?
BECAUSE WE'RE ALREADY ONE HEAD DOWN AND I DON'T WANT TO BLINK OUT OF EXISTENCE WHEN SOMEONE DECIDES TO DEFROST THE BEER FRIDGE?
BECAUSE... BECAUSE... WE'RE RUNNING OUT OF TIME AND IF MORTY CAN'T GET THIS STUFF THROUGH THAT THICK COCKTAIL OF ADOLESCENT HORMONES, CHEAT CODES, AND VANILLA AS HELL RAP LYRICS, I CAN'T GET US OUT OF HERE?!
HEY. THAT'S NOT FAIR, RICK. I'M TRYING. MAYBE IF YOU WENT UH--I DON'T KNOW... SLOWER I COULD...?
YOUR MOTHER'S CALLING FOR YOU IN THE AUDITORIUM. IT'S TIME.
GREAT! LET'S HEAR YOUR BRAIN TRUST'S GREAT PLAN. I HOPE IT'S FOR DYING IN WAVES.
IT'S NOT LIKE WE'VE GOT ANY BETTER OPTIONS AT THIS POINT.

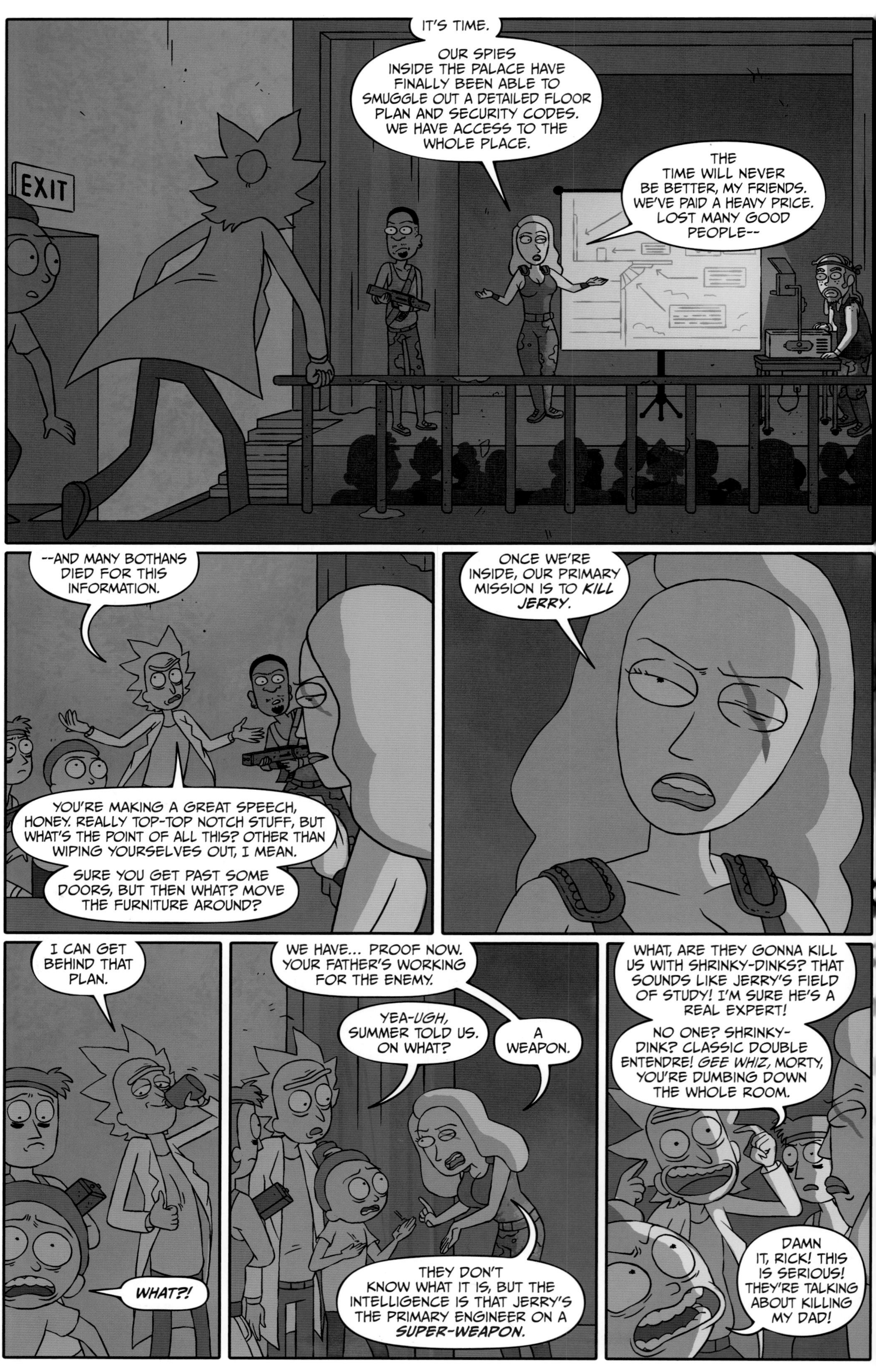
IT'S TIME.
OUR SPIES INSIDE THE PALACE HAVE FINALLY BEEN ABLE TO SMUGGLE OUT A DETAILED FLOOR PLAN AND SECURITY CODES. WE HAVE ACCESS TO THE WHOLE PLACE.
EXIT
THE TIME WILL NEVER BE BETTER, MY FRIENDS. WE'VE PAID A HEAVY PRICE. LOST MANY GOOD PEOPLE--
--AND MANY BOTHANS DIED FOR THIS INFORMATION.
YOU'RE MAKING A GREAT SPEECH, HONEY. REALLY TOP-TOP NOTCH STUFF, BUT WHAT'S THE POINT OF ALL THIS? OTHER THAN WIPING YOURSELVES OUT, I MEAN.
SURE YOU GET PAST SOME DOORS, BUT THEN WHAT? MOVE THE FURNITURE AROUND?
ONCE WE'RE INSIDE, OUR PRIMARY MISSION IS TO *KILL JERRY.*
I CAN GET BEHIND THAT PLAN.
WHAT?!
WE HAVE... PROOF NOW. YOUR FATHER'S WORKING FOR THE ENEMY.
YEA-*UGH,* SUMMER TOLD US. ON WHAT?
A WEAPON.
THEY DON'T KNOW WHAT IT IS, BUT THE INTELLIGENCE IS THAT JERRY'S THE PRIMARY ENGINEER ON A ***SUPER-WEAPON.***
WHAT, ARE THEY GONNA KILL US WITH SHRINKY-DINKS? THAT SOUNDS LIKE JERRY'S FIELD OF STUDY! I'M SURE HE'S A REAL EXPERT!
NO ONE? SHRINKY-DINK? CLASSIC DOUBLE ENTENDRE! *GEE WHIZ,* MORTY, YOU'RE DUMBING DOWN THE WHOLE ROOM.
DAMN IT, RICK! THIS IS SERIOUS! THEY'RE TALKING ABOUT KILLING MY DAD!

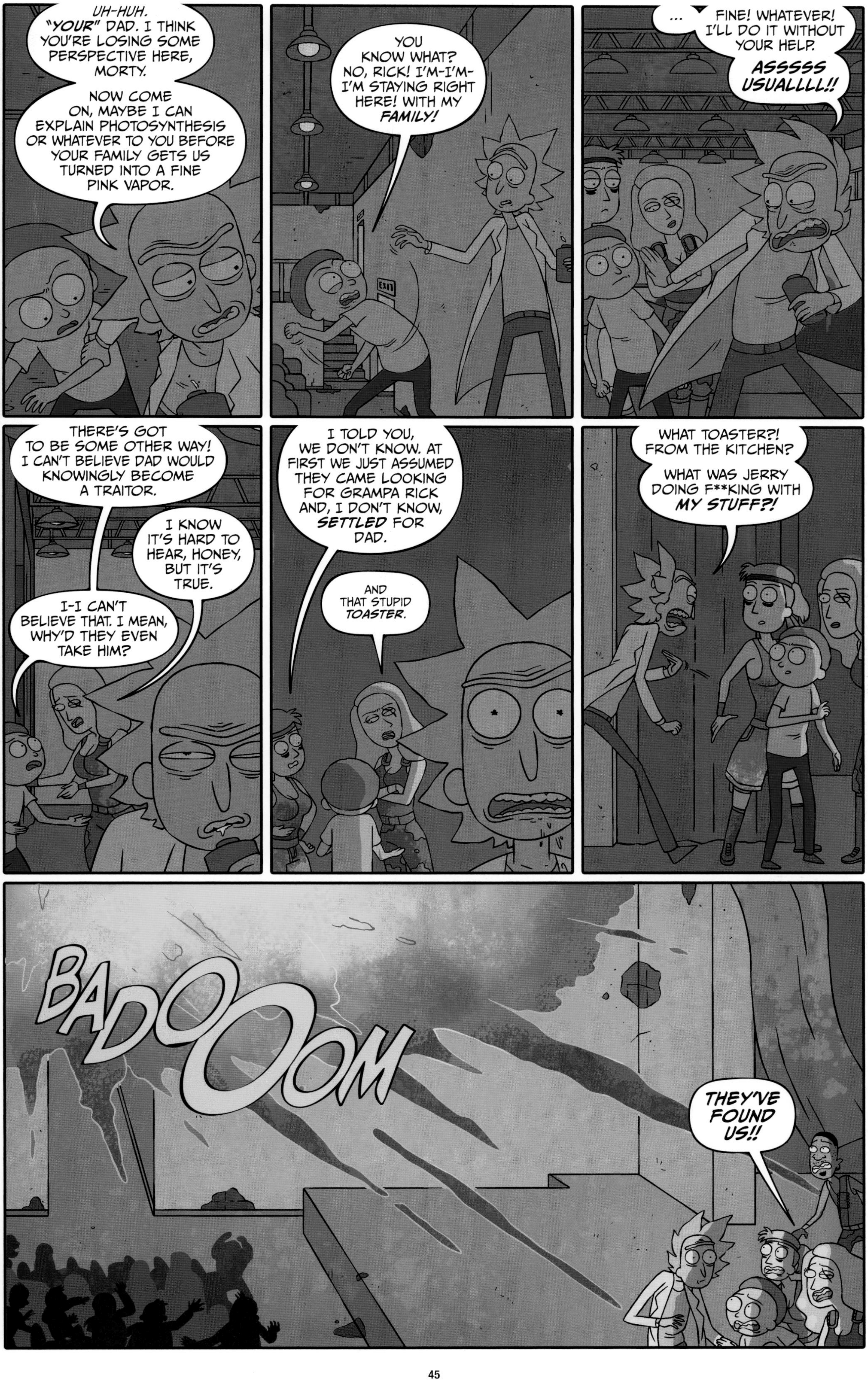
UH-HUH. "YOUR" DAD. I THINK YOU'RE LOSING SOME PERSPECTIVE HERE, MORTY.
NOW COME ON, MAYBE I CAN EXPLAIN PHOTOSYNTHESIS OR WHATEVER TO YOU BEFORE YOUR FAMILY GETS US TURNED INTO A FINE PINK VAPOR.
YOU KNOW WHAT? NO, RICK! I'M-I'M-I'M STAYING RIGHT HERE! WITH MY FAMILY!
EXIT
...
FINE! WHATEVER! I'LL DO IT WITHOUT YOUR HELP.
ASSSSS USUALLLL!!
THERE'S GOT TO BE SOME OTHER WAY! I CAN'T BELIEVE DAD WOULD KNOWINGLY BECOME A TRAITOR.
I KNOW IT'S HARD TO HEAR, HONEY, BUT IT'S TRUE.
I-I CAN'T BELIEVE THAT. I MEAN, WHY'D THEY EVEN TAKE HIM?
I TOLD YOU, WE DON'T KNOW. AT FIRST WE JUST ASSUMED THEY CAME LOOKING FOR GRAMPA RICK AND, I DON'T KNOW, SETTLED FOR DAD.
AND THAT STUPID TOASTER.
WHAT TOASTER?! FROM THE KITCHEN?
WHAT WAS JERRY DOING F**KING WITH MY STUFF?!
BADOOOM
THEY'VE FOUND US!!

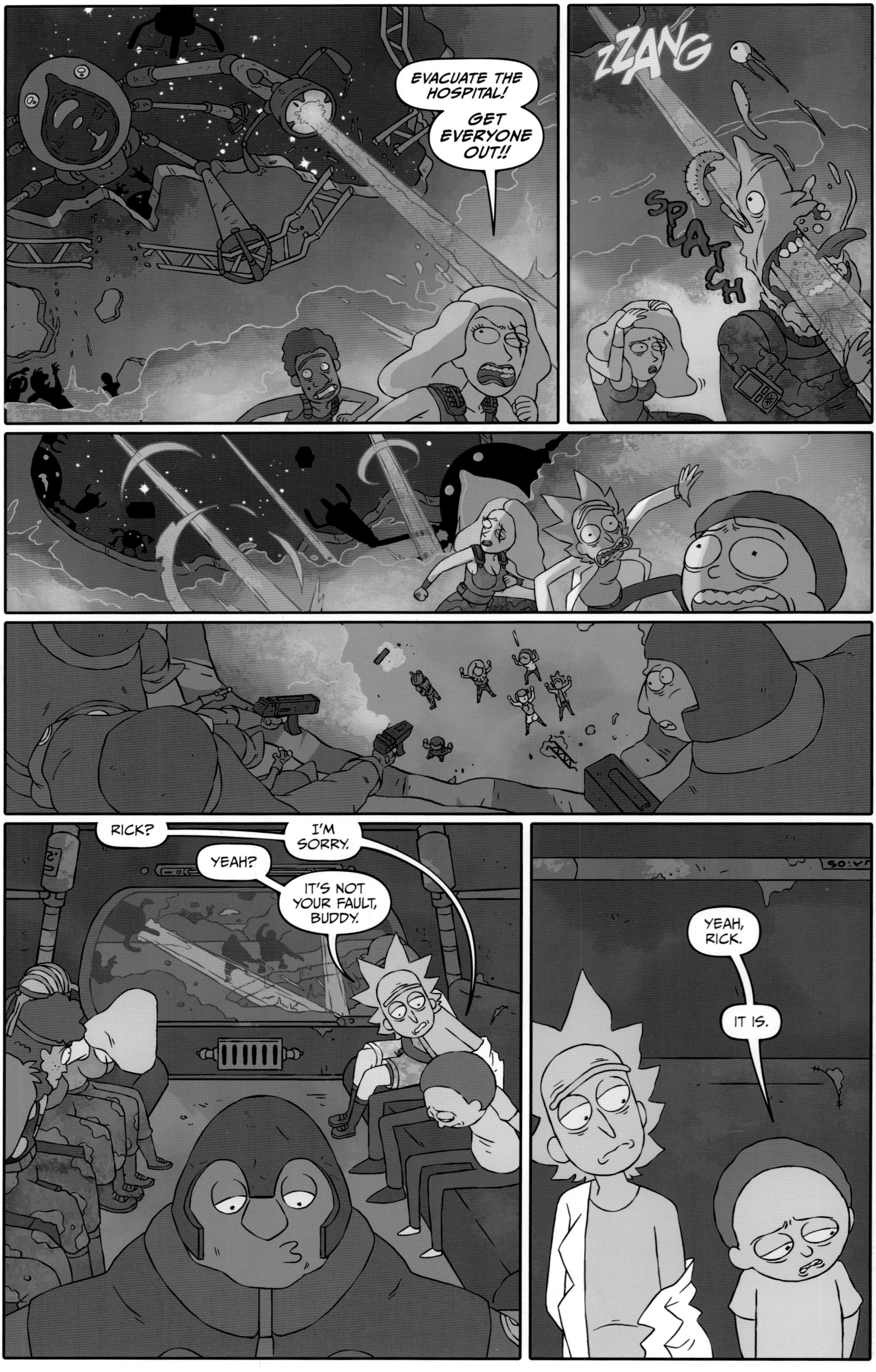
EVACUATE THE HOSPITAL!
GET EVERYONE OUT!!
ZZANG
SPLATCH
RICK?
YEAH?
I'M SORRY.
IT'S NOT YOUR FAULT, BUDDY.
YEAH, RICK.
IT IS.

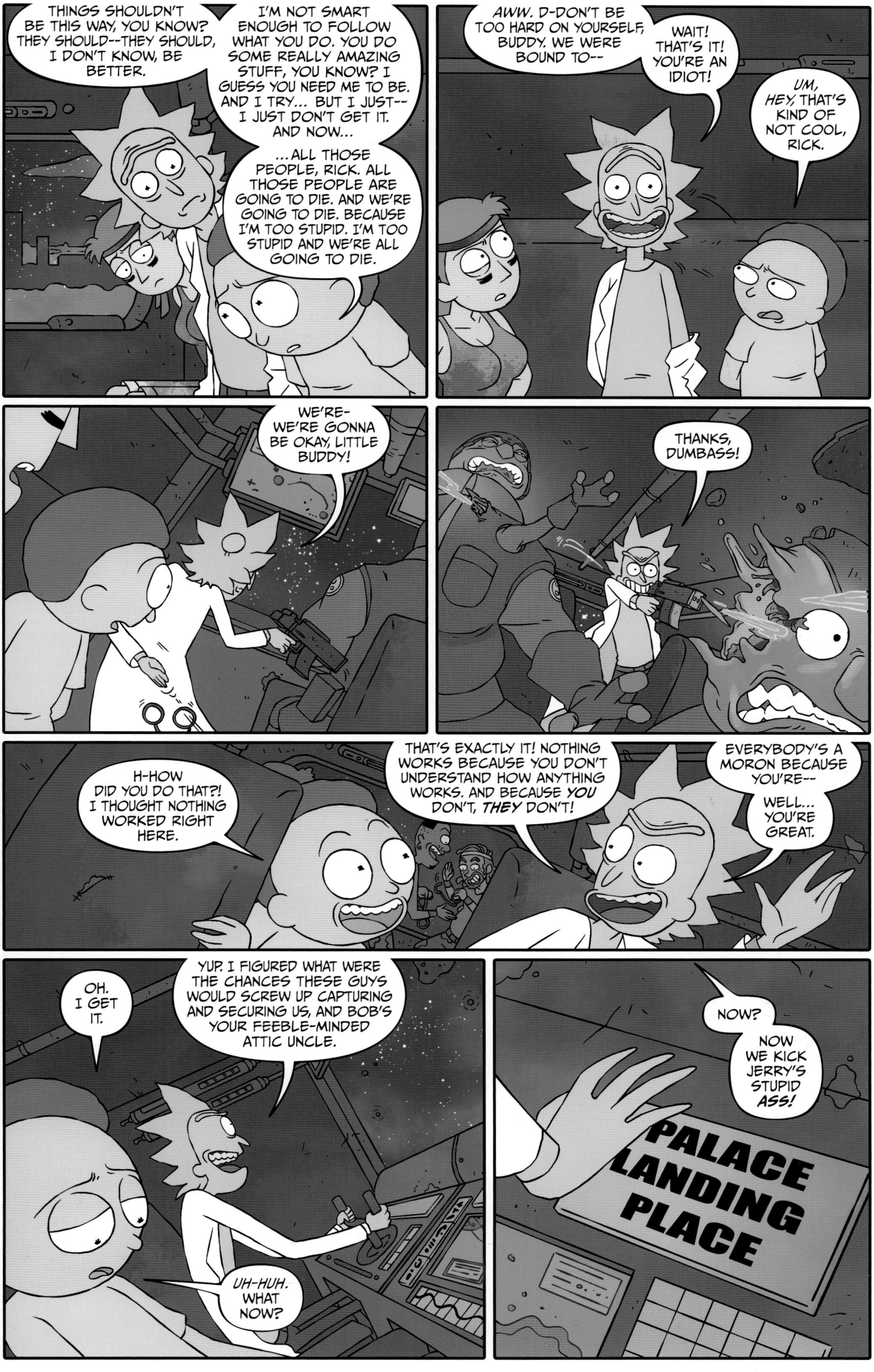
THINGS SHOULDN'T BE THIS WAY, YOU KNOW? THEY SHOULD--THEY SHOULD, I DON'T KNOW, BE BETTER.
I'M NOT SMART ENOUGH TO FOLLOW WHAT YOU DO. YOU DO SOME REALLY AMAZING STUFF, YOU KNOW? I GUESS YOU NEED ME TO BE. AND I TRY... BUT I JUST-- I JUST DON'T GET IT. AND NOW...
...ALL THOSE PEOPLE, RICK. ALL THOSE PEOPLE ARE GOING TO DIE. AND WE'RE GOING TO DIE. BECAUSE I'M TOO STUPID. I'M TOO STUPID AND WE'RE ALL GOING TO DIE.
AWW. D-DON'T BE TOO HARD ON YOURSELF, BUDDY. WE WERE BOUND TO--
WAIT! THAT'S IT! YOU'RE AN IDIOT!
UM, HEY, THAT'S KIND OF NOT COOL, RICK.
WE'RE- WE'RE GONNA BE OKAY, LITTLE BUDDY!
THANKS, DUMBASS!
H-HOW DID YOU DO THAT?! I THOUGHT NOTHING WORKED RIGHT HERE.
THAT'S EXACTLY IT! NOTHING WORKS BECAUSE YOU DON'T UNDERSTAND HOW ANYTHING WORKS. AND BECAUSE YOU DON'T, THEY DON'T!
EVERYBODY'S A MORON BECAUSE YOU'RE--
WELL... YOU'RE GREAT.
OH. I GET IT.
YUP. I FIGURED WHAT WERE THE CHANCES THESE GUYS WOULD SCREW UP CAPTURING AND SECURING US, AND BOB'S YOUR FEEBLE-MINDED ATTIC UNCLE.
UH-HUH. WHAT NOW?
NOW?
NOW WE KICK JERRY'S STUPID ASS!
PALACE LANDING PLACE

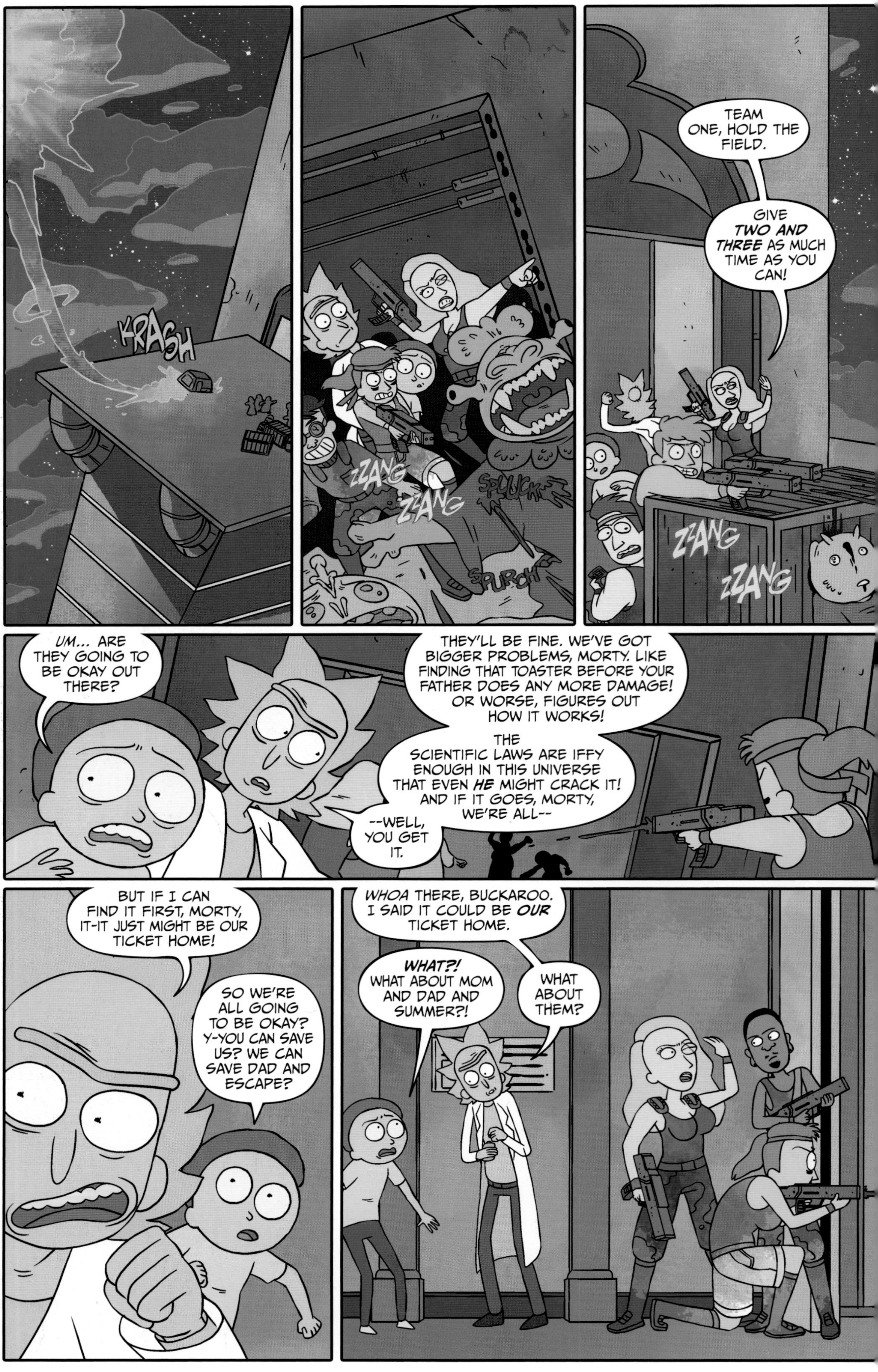
KRASH
ZZANG
ZZANG
SPLUCK
SPURCH
TEAM ONE, HOLD THE FIELD.
GIVE TWO AND THREE AS MUCH TIME AS YOU CAN!
ZZANG
ZZANG
UM... ARE THEY GOING TO BE OKAY OUT THERE?
THEY'LL BE FINE. WE'VE GOT BIGGER PROBLEMS, MORTY. LIKE FINDING THAT TOASTER BEFORE YOUR FATHER DOES ANY MORE DAMAGE! OR WORSE, FIGURES OUT HOW IT WORKS!
THE SCIENTIFIC LAWS ARE IFFY ENOUGH IN THIS UNIVERSE THAT EVEN HE MIGHT CRACK IT! AND IF IT GOES, MORTY, WE'RE ALL--
--WELL, YOU GET IT.
BUT IF I CAN FIND IT FIRST, MORTY, IT-IT JUST MIGHT BE OUR TICKET HOME!
SO WE'RE ALL GOING TO BE OKAY? Y-YOU CAN SAVE US? WE CAN SAVE DAD AND ESCAPE?
WHOA THERE, BUCKAROO. I SAID IT COULD BE OUR TICKET HOME.
WHAT?! WHAT ABOUT MOM AND DAD AND SUMMER?!
WHAT ABOUT THEM?

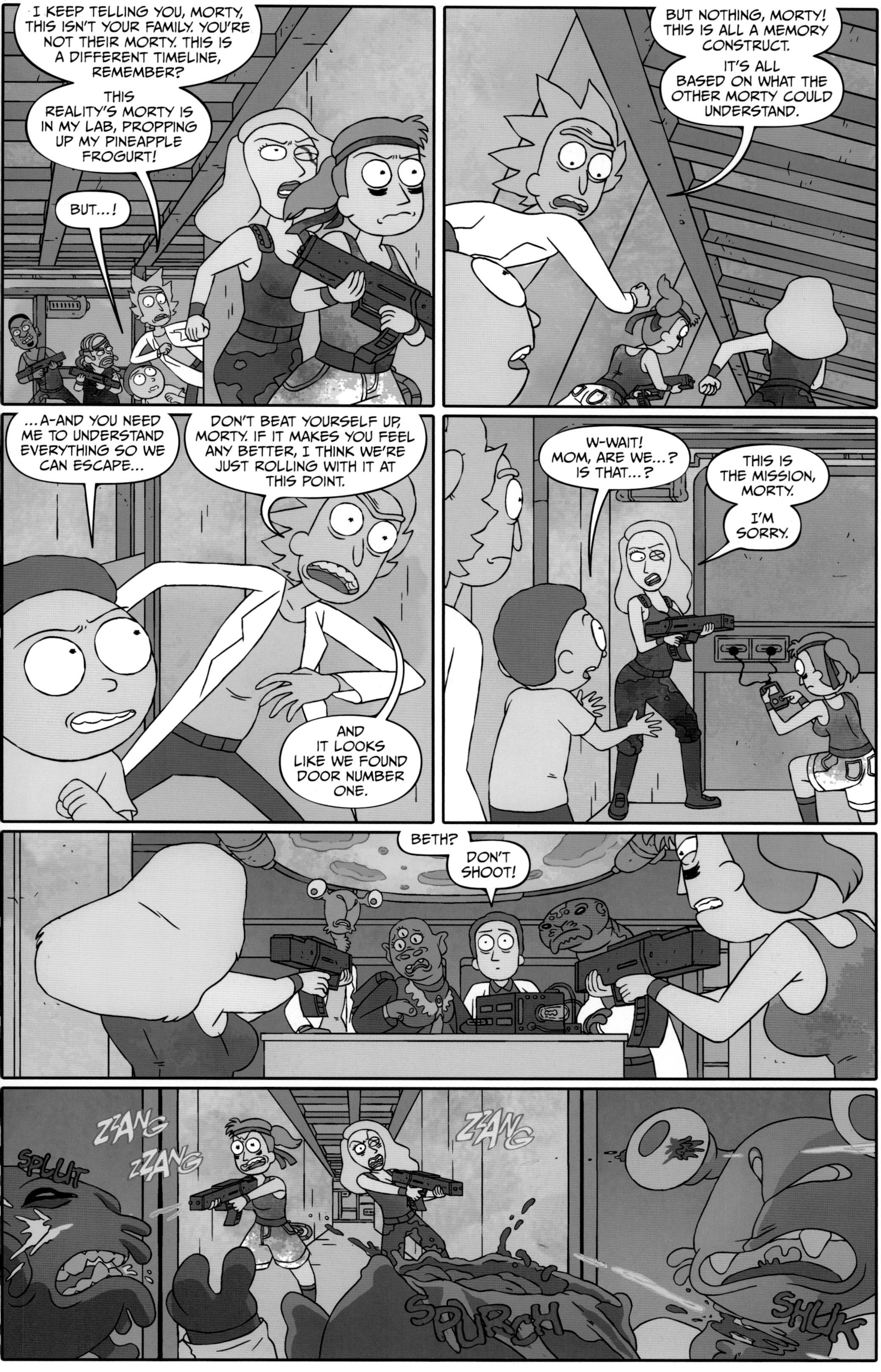
I KEEP TELLING YOU, MORTY, THIS ISN'T YOUR FAMILY. YOU'RE NOT THEIR MORTY. THIS IS A DIFFERENT TIMELINE, REMEMBER?
THIS REALITY'S MORTY IS IN MY LAB, PROPPING UP MY PINEAPPLE FROGURT!
BUT...!
BUT NOTHING, MORTY! THIS IS ALL A MEMORY CONSTRUCT.
IT'S ALL BASED ON WHAT THE OTHER MORTY COULD UNDERSTAND.
...A-AND YOU NEED ME TO UNDERSTAND EVERYTHING SO WE CAN ESCAPE...
DON'T BEAT YOURSELF UP, MORTY. IF IT MAKES YOU FEEL ANY BETTER, I THINK WE'RE JUST ROLLING WITH IT AT THIS POINT.
AND IT LOOKS LIKE WE FOUND DOOR NUMBER ONE.
W-WAIT! MOM, ARE WE...? IS THAT...?
THIS IS THE MISSION, MORTY.
I'M SORRY.
BETH?
DON'T SHOOT!
ZZANG
ZZANG
SPLUT
ZZANG
SPURCH
SHUK

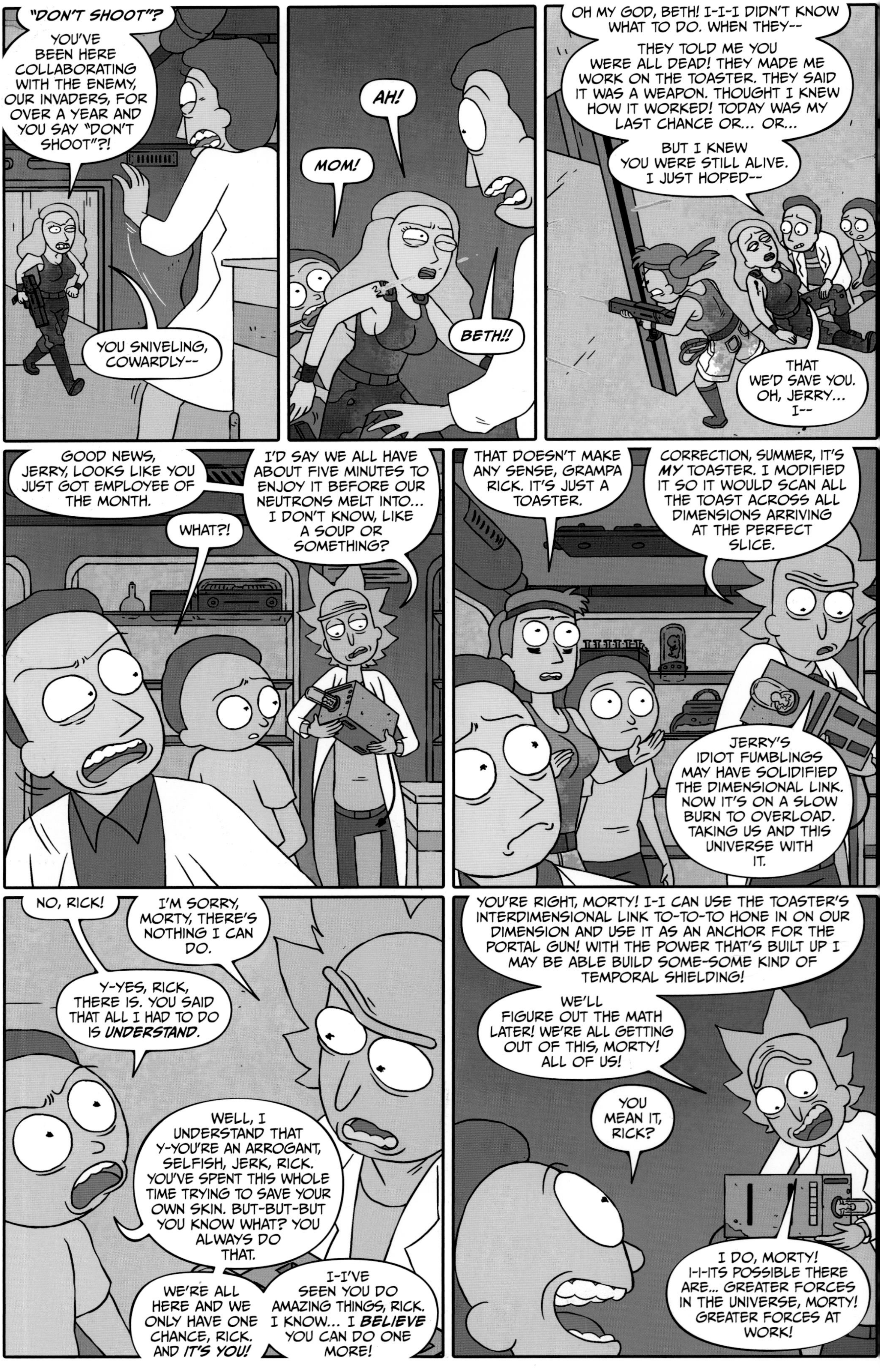
"DON'T SHOOT"?
YOU'VE BEEN HERE COLLABORATING WITH THE ENEMY, OUR INVADERS, FOR OVER A YEAR AND YOU SAY "DON'T SHOOT"?!
YOU SNIVELING, COWARDLY--
AH!
MOM!
BETH!!
OH MY GOD, BETH! I-I-I DIDN'T KNOW WHAT TO DO. WHEN THEY--
THEY TOLD ME YOU WERE ALL DEAD! THEY MADE ME WORK ON THE TOASTER. THEY SAID IT WAS A WEAPON. THOUGHT I KNEW HOW IT WORKED! TODAY WAS MY LAST CHANCE OR... OR...
BUT I KNEW YOU WERE STILL ALIVE. I JUST HOPED--
THAT WE'D SAVE YOU. OH, JERRY... I--
GOOD NEWS, JERRY, LOOKS LIKE YOU JUST GOT EMPLOYEE OF THE MONTH.
WHAT?!
I'D SAY WE ALL HAVE ABOUT FIVE MINUTES TO ENJOY IT BEFORE OUR NEUTRONS MELT INTO... I DON'T KNOW, LIKE A SOUP OR SOMETHING?
THAT DOESN'T MAKE ANY SENSE, GRAMPA RICK. IT'S JUST A TOASTER.
CORRECTION, SUMMER, IT'S MY TOASTER. I MODIFIED IT SO IT WOULD SCAN ALL THE TOAST ACROSS ALL DIMENSIONS ARRIVING AT THE PERFECT SLICE.
JERRY'S IDIOT FUMBLINGS MAY HAVE SOLIDIFIED THE DIMENSIONAL LINK. NOW IT'S ON A SLOW BURN TO OVERLOAD. TAKING US AND THIS UNIVERSE WITH IT.
NO, RICK!
I'M SORRY, MORTY, THERE'S NOTHING I CAN DO.
Y-YES, RICK, THERE IS. YOU SAID THAT ALL I HAD TO DO IS UNDERSTAND.
WELL, I UNDERSTAND THAT Y-YOU'RE AN ARROGANT, SELFISH, JERK, RICK. YOU'VE SPENT THIS WHOLE TIME TRYING TO SAVE YOUR OWN SKIN. BUT-BUT-BUT YOU KNOW WHAT? YOU ALWAYS DO THAT.
WE'RE ALL HERE AND WE ONLY HAVE ONE CHANCE, RICK. AND IT'S YOU!
I-I'VE SEEN YOU DO AMAZING THINGS, RICK. I KNOW... I BELIEVE YOU CAN DO ONE MORE!
YOU'RE RIGHT, MORTY! I-I CAN USE THE TOASTER'S INTERDIMENSIONAL LINK TO-TO-TO HONE IN ON OUR DIMENSION AND USE IT AS AN ANCHOR FOR THE PORTAL GUN! WITH THE POWER THAT'S BUILT UP I MAY BE ABLE BUILD SOME-SOME KIND OF TEMPORAL SHIELDING!
WE'LL FIGURE OUT THE MATH LATER! WE'RE ALL GETTING OUT OF THIS, MORTY! ALL OF US!
YOU MEAN IT, RICK?
I DO, MORTY! I-I-ITS POSSIBLE THERE ARE... GREATER FORCES IN THE UNIVERSE, MORTY! GREATER FORCES AT WORK!

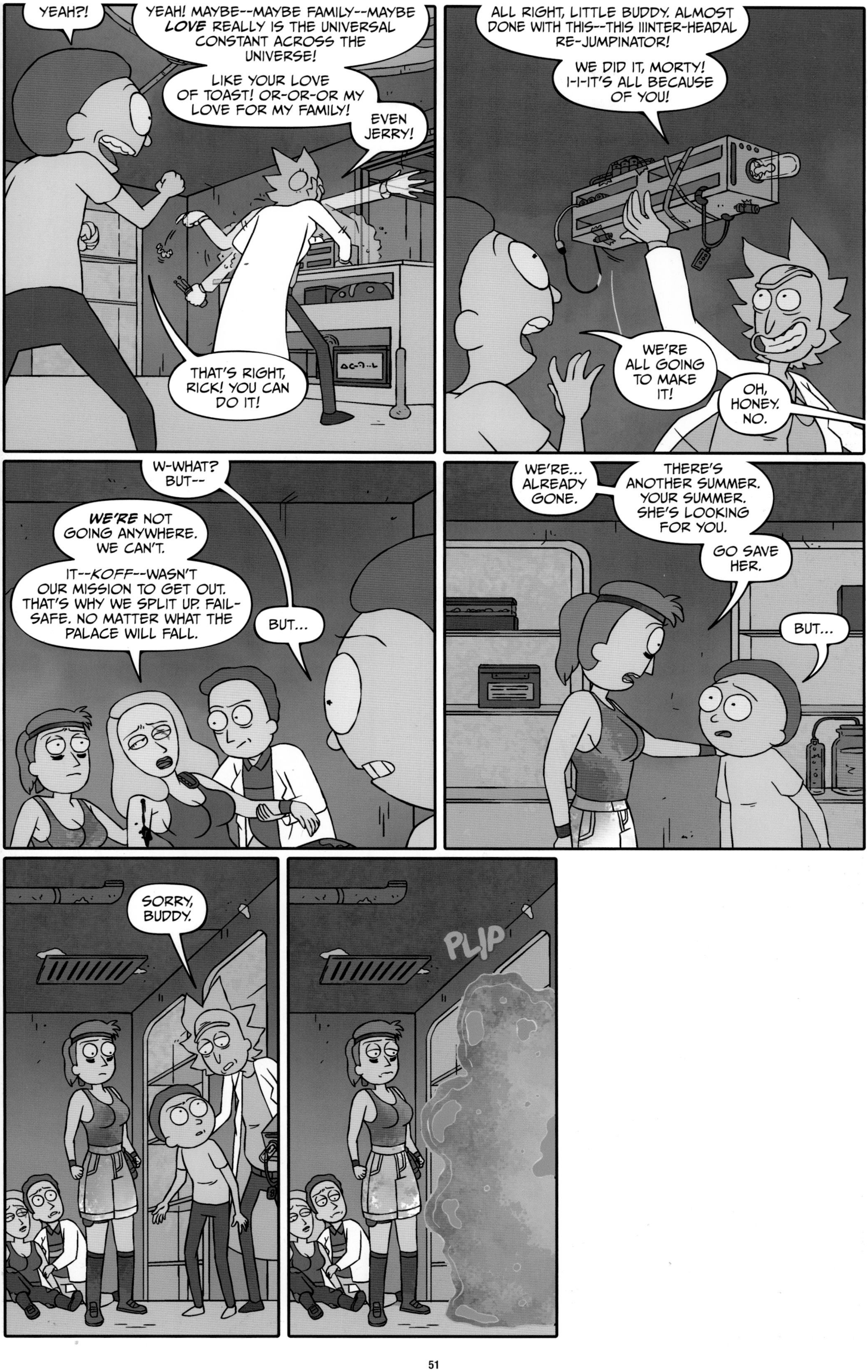
YEAH?!
YEAH! MAYBE--MAYBE FAMILY--MAYBE LOVE REALLY IS THE UNIVERSAL CONSTANT ACROSS THE UNIVERSE!
LIKE YOUR LOVE OF TOAST! OR-OR-OR MY LOVE FOR MY FAMILY!
EVEN JERRY!
THAT'S RIGHT, RICK! YOU CAN DO IT!
ALL RIGHT, LITTLE BUDDY. ALMOST DONE WITH THIS--THIS IIINTER-HEADAL RE-JUMPINATOR!
WE DID IT, MORTY! I-I-IT'S ALL BECAUSE OF YOU!
WE'RE ALL GOING TO MAKE IT!
OH, HONEY. NO.
W-WHAT? BUT--
WE'RE NOT GOING ANYWHERE. WE CAN'T.
IT--KOFF--WASN'T OUR MISSION TO GET OUT. THAT'S WHY WE SPLIT UP. FAIL-SAFE. NO MATTER WHAT THE PALACE WILL FALL.
BUT...
WE'RE... ALREADY GONE.
THERE'S ANOTHER SUMMER. YOUR SUMMER. SHE'S LOOKING FOR YOU.
GO SAVE HER.
BUT...
SORRY, BUDDY.
PLIP

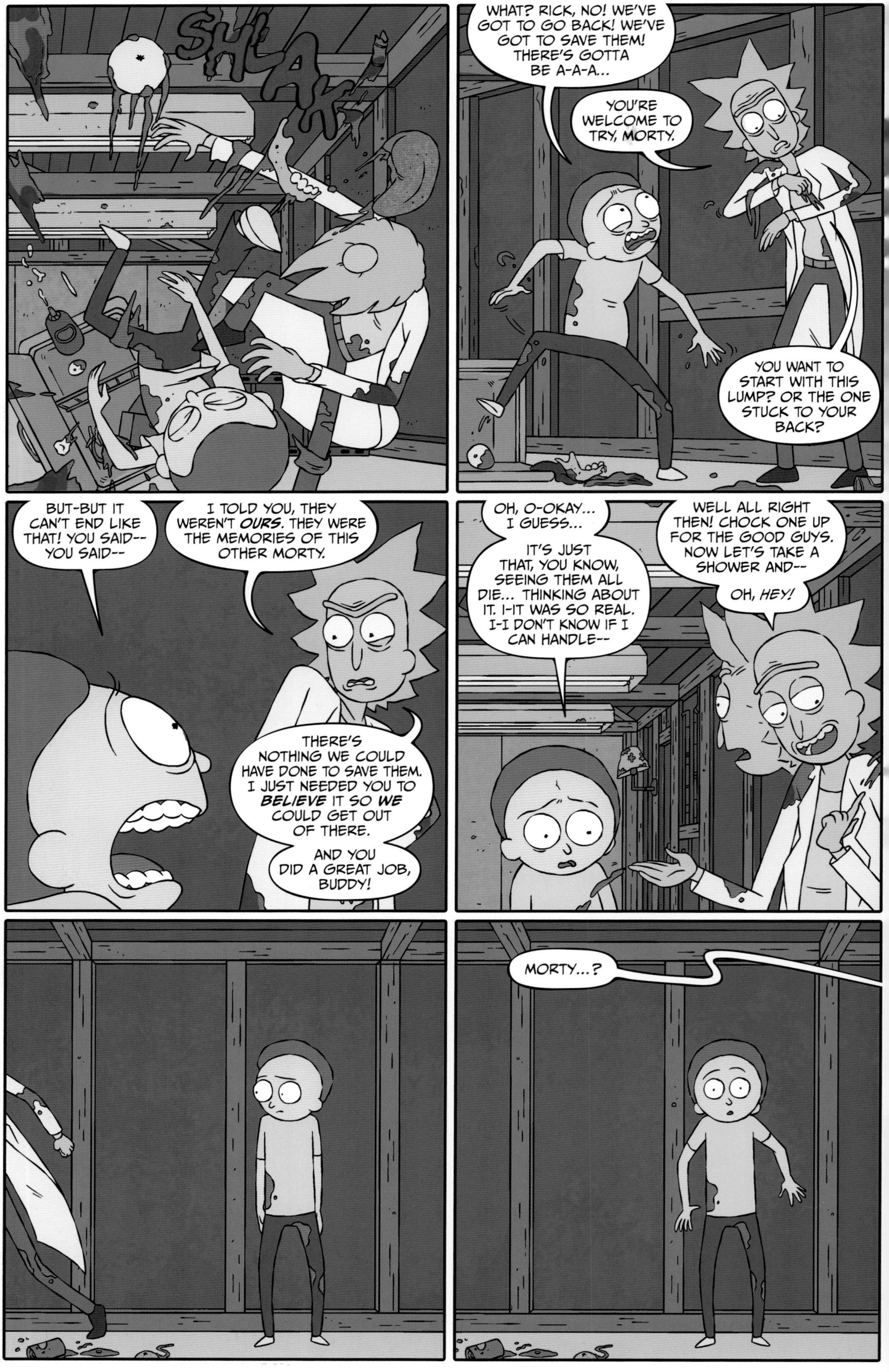
SHLAK
WHAT? RICK, NO! WE'VE GOT TO GO BACK! WE'VE GOT TO SAVE THEM! THERE'S GOTTA BE A-A-A...
YOU'RE WELCOME TO TRY, MORTY.
YOU WANT TO START WITH THIS LUMP? OR THE ONE STUCK TO YOUR BACK?
BUT-BUT IT CAN'T END LIKE THAT! YOU SAID-- YOU SAID--
I TOLD YOU, THEY WEREN'T OURS. THEY WERE THE MEMORIES OF THIS OTHER MORTY.
THERE'S NOTHING WE COULD HAVE DONE TO SAVE THEM. I JUST NEEDED YOU TO BELIEVE IT SO WE COULD GET OUT OF THERE.
AND YOU DID A GREAT JOB, BUDDY!
OH, O-OKAY... I GUESS...
IT'S JUST THAT, YOU KNOW, SEEING THEM ALL DIE... THINKING ABOUT IT. I-IT WAS SO REAL. I-I DON'T KNOW IF I CAN HANDLE--
WELL ALL RIGHT THEN! CHOCK ONE UP FOR THE GOOD GUYS. NOW LET'S TAKE A SHOWER AND--
OH, HEY!
MORTY...?

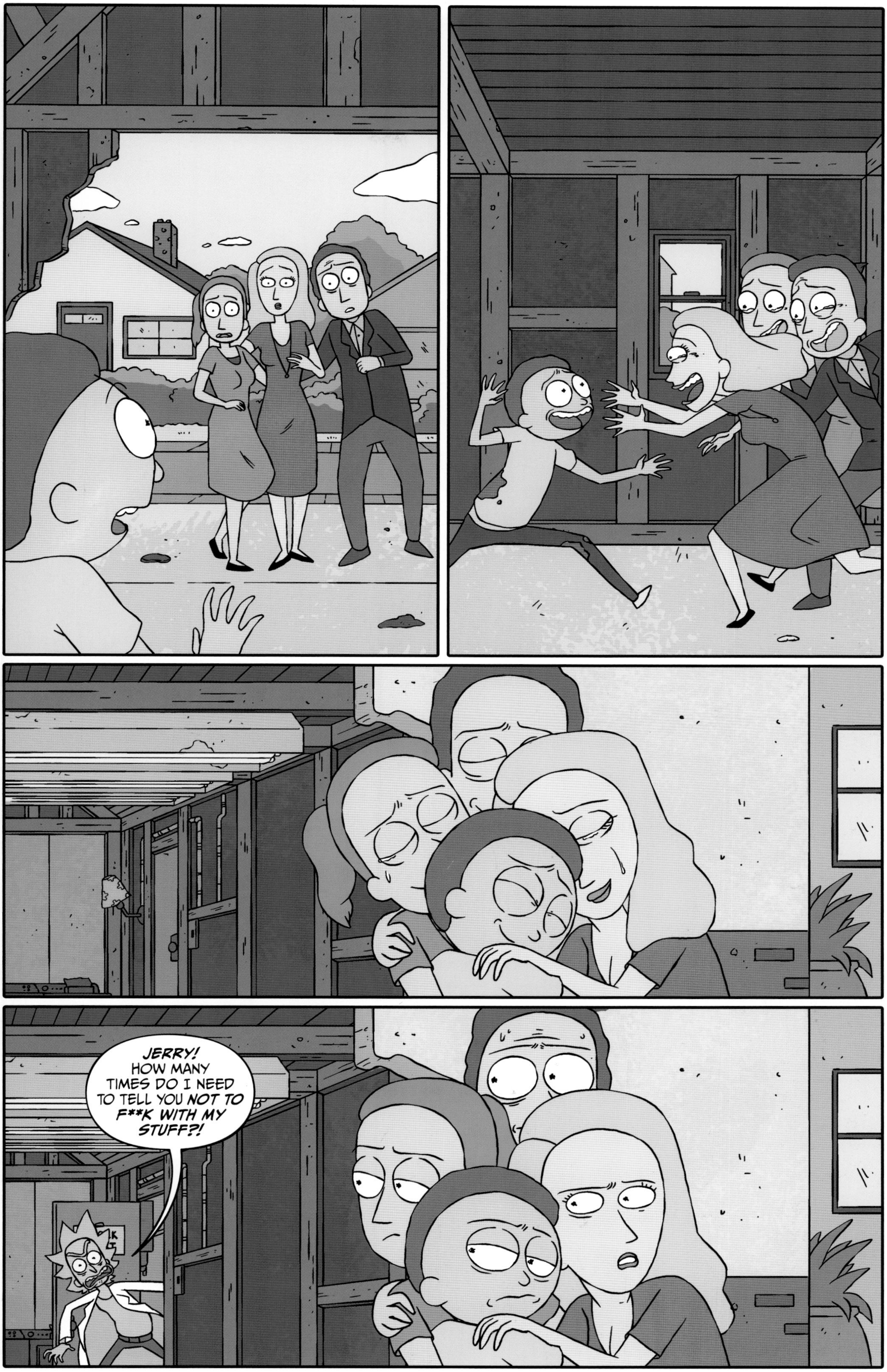
JERRY! HOW MANY TIMES DO I NEED TO TELL YOU NOT TO F**K WITH MY STUFF?!

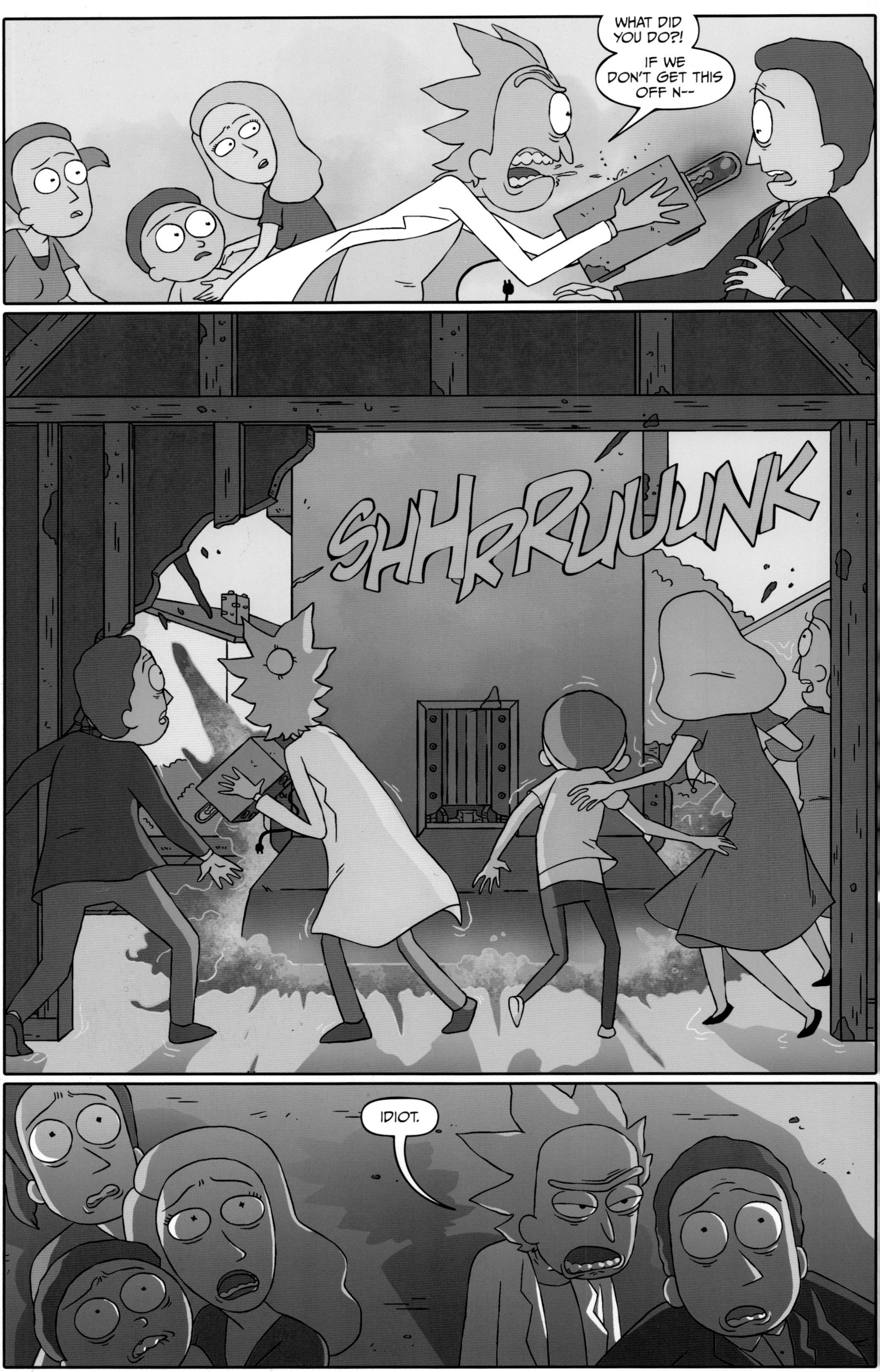
WHAT DID YOU DO?!
IF WE DON'T GET THIS OFF N--
SHHRRUUUNK
IDIOT.

HEAD SPACE
PART THREE

WRITTEN BY **TOM FOWLER**
DRAWN BY **CJ CANNON**
COLORED BY **RYAN HILL**
LETTERED BY **CRANK!**

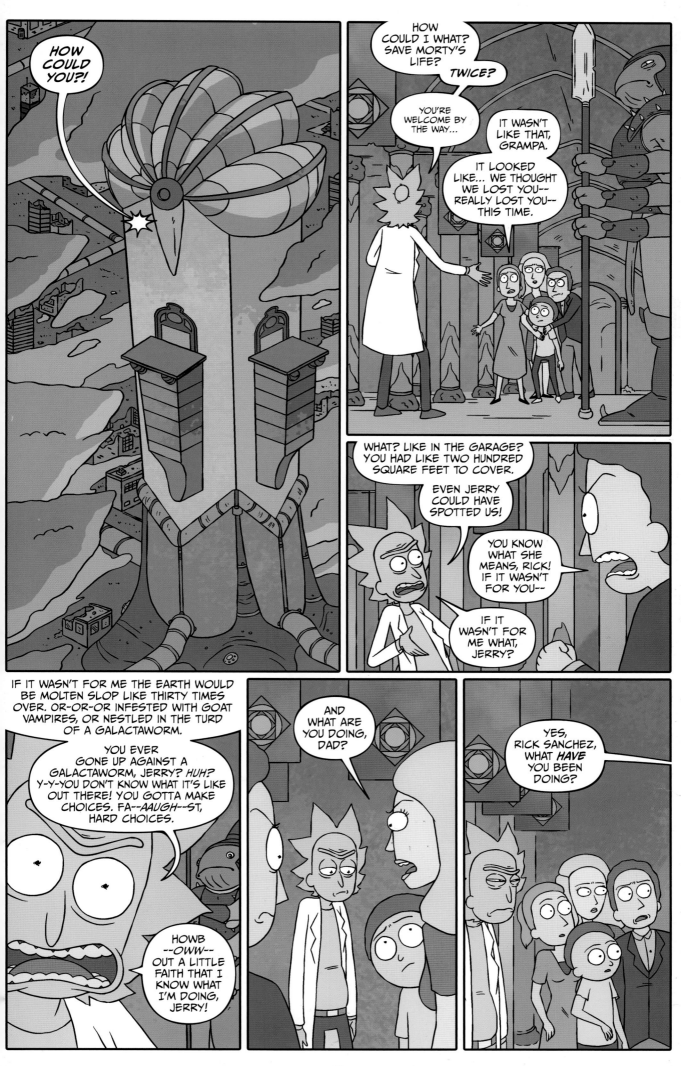

HOW COULD YOU?!

HOW COULD I WHAT? SAVE MORTY'S LIFE? *TWICE?*

YOU'RE WELCOME BY THE WAY...

IT WASN'T LIKE THAT, GRAMPA.

IT LOOKED LIKE... WE THOUGHT WE LOST YOU-- REALLY LOST YOU-- THIS TIME.

WHAT? LIKE IN THE GARAGE? YOU HAD LIKE TWO HUNDRED SQUARE FEET TO COVER.

EVEN JERRY COULD HAVE SPOTTED US!

YOU KNOW WHAT SHE MEANS, RICK! IF IT WASN'T FOR YOU--

IF IT WASN'T FOR ME WHAT, JERRY?

IF IT WASN'T FOR ME THE EARTH WOULD BE MOLTEN SLOP LIKE THIRTY TIMES OVER. OR-OR-OR INFESTED WITH GOAT VAMPIRES, OR NESTLED IN THE TURD OF A GALACTAWORM.

YOU EVER GONE UP AGAINST A GALACTAWORM, JERRY? *HUH?* Y-Y-YOU DON'T KNOW WHAT IT'S LIKE OUT THERE! YOU GOTTA MAKE CHOICES. FA--AAUGH--ST, HARD CHOICES.

HOWB --OWW-- OUT A LITTLE FAITH THAT I KNOW WHAT I'M DOING, JERRY!

AND WHAT ARE YOU DOING, DAD?

YES, RICK SANCHEZ, WHAT *HAVE* YOU BEEN DOING?

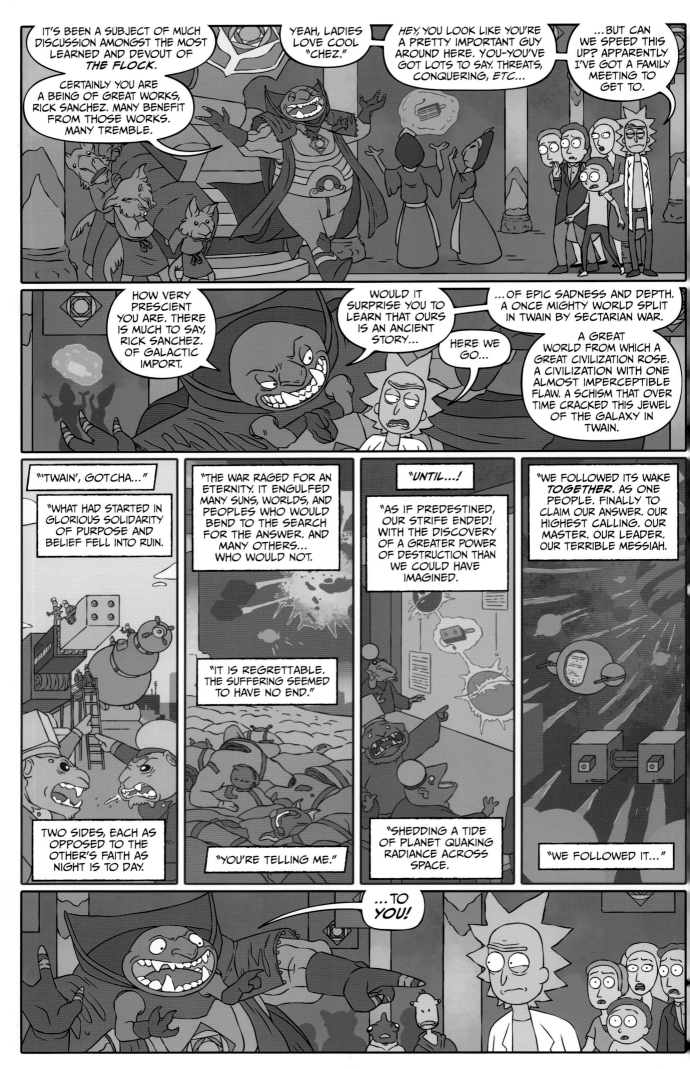

IT'S BEEN A SUBJECT OF MUCH DISCUSSION AMONGST THE MOST LEARNED AND DEVOUT OF *THE FLOCK.*

CERTAINLY YOU ARE A BEING OF GREAT WORKS, RICK SANCHEZ. MANY BENEFIT FROM THOSE WORKS. MANY TREMBLE.

YEAH, LADIES LOVE COOL "CHEZ."

HEY, YOU LOOK LIKE YOU'RE A PRETTY IMPORTANT GUY AROUND HERE. YOU-YOU'VE GOT LOTS TO SAY. THREATS, CONQUERING, *ETC...*

...BUT CAN WE SPEED THIS UP? APPARENTLY I'VE GOT A FAMILY MEETING TO GET TO.

HOW VERY PRESCIENT YOU ARE. THERE IS MUCH TO SAY, RICK SANCHEZ. OF GALACTIC IMPORT.

WOULD IT SURPRISE YOU TO LEARN THAT OURS IS AN ANCIENT STORY...

HERE WE GO...

...OF EPIC SADNESS AND DEPTH. A ONCE MIGHTY WORLD SPLIT IN TWAIN BY SECTARIAN WAR.

A GREAT WORLD FROM WHICH A GREAT CIVILIZATION ROSE. A CIVILIZATION WITH ONE ALMOST IMPERCEPTIBLE FLAW. A SCHISM THAT OVER TIME CRACKED THIS JEWEL OF THE GALAXY IN TWAIN.

"'TWAIN', GOTCHA..."

"WHAT HAD STARTED IN GLORIOUS SOLIDARITY OF PURPOSE AND BELIEF FELL INTO RUIN.

TWO SIDES, EACH AS OPPOSED TO THE OTHER'S FAITH AS NIGHT IS TO DAY.

"THE WAR RAGED FOR AN ETERNITY. IT ENGULFED MANY SUNS, WORLDS, AND PEOPLES WHO WOULD BEND TO THE SEARCH FOR THE ANSWER. AND MANY OTHERS... WHO WOULD NOT.

"IT IS REGRETTABLE. THE SUFFERING SEEMED TO HAVE NO END."

"YOU'RE TELLING ME."

"UNTIL...!

"AS IF PREDESTINED, OUR STRIFE ENDED! WITH THE DISCOVERY OF A GREATER POWER OF DESTRUCTION THAN WE COULD HAVE IMAGINED.

"SHEDDING A TIDE OF PLANET QUAKING RADIANCE ACROSS SPACE.

"WE FOLLOWED ITS WAKE *TOGETHER.* AS ONE PEOPLE. FINALLY TO CLAIM OUR ANSWER. OUR HIGHEST CALLING. OUR MASTER. OUR LEADER. OUR TERRIBLE MESSIAH.

"WE FOLLOWED IT..."

...TO *YOU!*

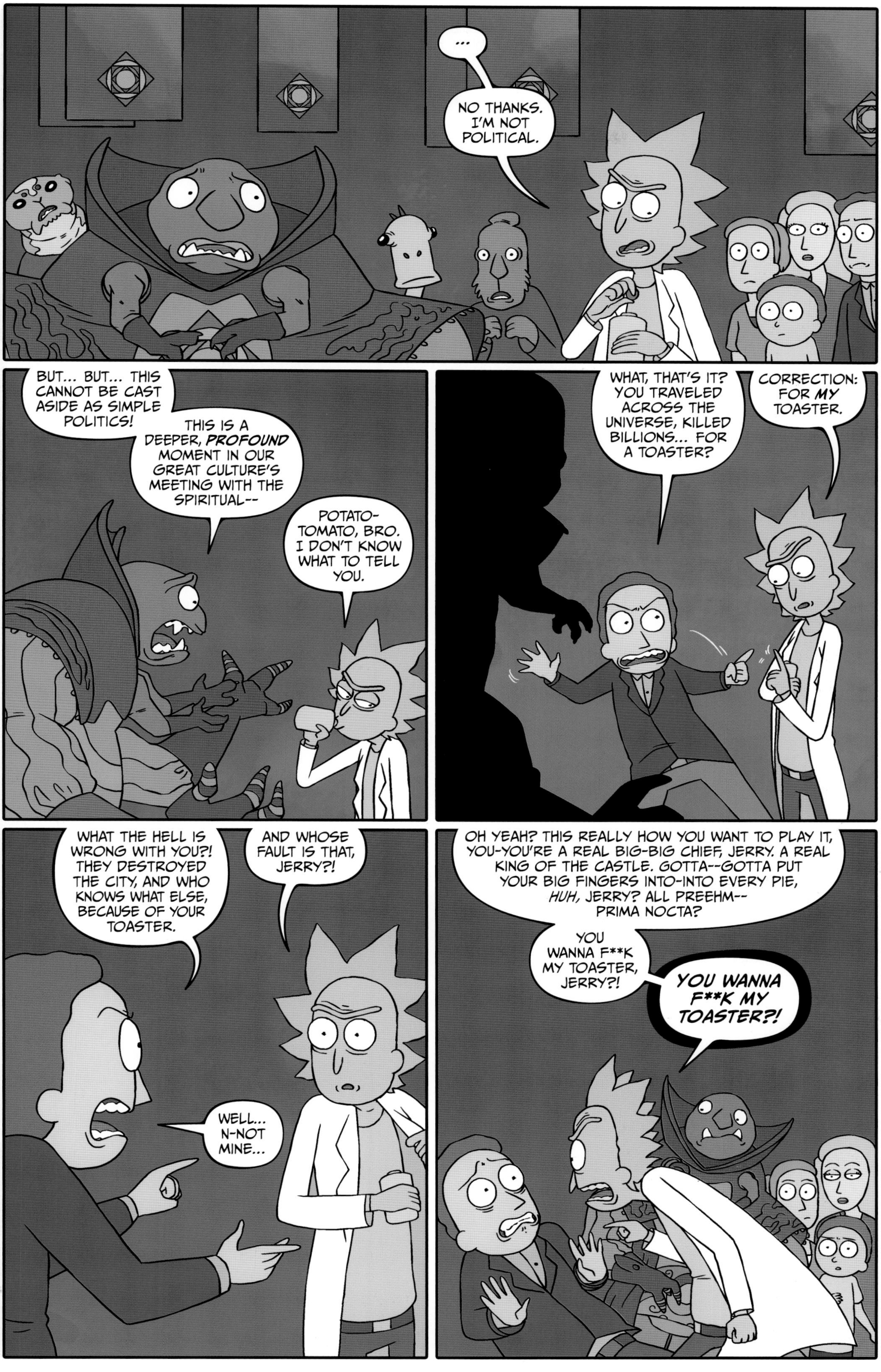
...
NO THANKS. I'M NOT POLITICAL.
BUT... BUT... THIS CANNOT BE CAST ASIDE AS SIMPLE POLITICS!
THIS IS A DEEPER, PROFOUND MOMENT IN OUR GREAT CULTURE'S MEETING WITH THE SPIRITUAL--
POTATO-TOMATO, BRO. I DON'T KNOW WHAT TO TELL YOU.
WHAT, THAT'S IT? YOU TRAVELED ACROSS THE UNIVERSE, KILLED BILLIONS... FOR A TOASTER?
CORRECTION: FOR MY TOASTER.
WHAT THE HELL IS WRONG WITH YOU?! THEY DESTROYED THE CITY, AND WHO KNOWS WHAT ELSE, BECAUSE OF YOUR TOASTER.
AND WHOSE FAULT IS THAT, JERRY?!
WELL... N-NOT MINE...
OH YEAH? THIS REALLY HOW YOU WANT TO PLAY IT, YOU-YOU'RE A REAL BIG-BIG CHIEF, JERRY. A REAL KING OF THE CASTLE. GOTTA--GOTTA PUT YOUR BIG FINGERS INTO-INTO EVERY PIE, HUH, JERRY? ALL PREEHM-- PRIMA NOCTA?
YOU WANNA F**K MY TOASTER, JERRY?!
YOU WANNA F**K MY TOASTER?!

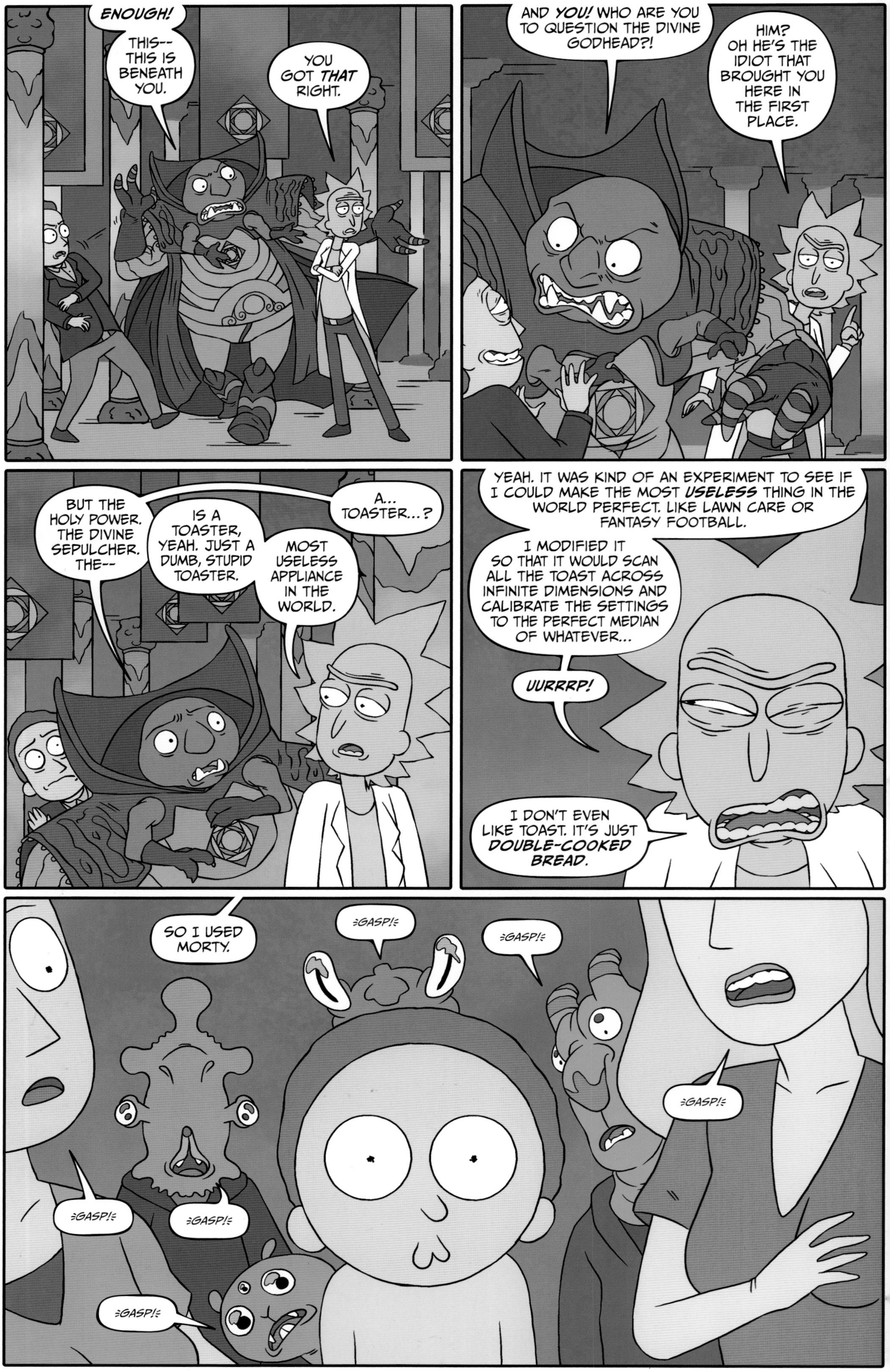
ENOUGH!
THIS-- THIS IS BENEATH YOU.
YOU GOT THAT RIGHT.
AND YOU! WHO ARE YOU TO QUESTION THE DIVINE GODHEAD?!
HIM? OH HE'S THE IDIOT THAT BROUGHT YOU HERE IN THE FIRST PLACE.
A... TOASTER...?
BUT THE HOLY POWER. THE DIVINE SEPULCHER. THE--
IS A TOASTER, YEAH. JUST A DUMB, STUPID TOASTER.
MOST USELESS APPLIANCE IN THE WORLD.
YEAH. IT WAS KIND OF AN EXPERIMENT TO SEE IF I COULD MAKE THE MOST USELESS THING IN THE WORLD PERFECT. LIKE LAWN CARE OR FANTASY FOOTBALL.
I MODIFIED IT SO THAT IT WOULD SCAN ALL THE TOAST ACROSS INFINITE DIMENSIONS AND CALIBRATE THE SETTINGS TO THE PERFECT MEDIAN OF WHATEVER...
UURRRP!
I DON'T EVEN LIKE TOAST. IT'S JUST DOUBLE-COOKED BREAD.
SO I USED MORTY.
GASP!
GASP!
GASP!
GASP!
GASP!
GASP!

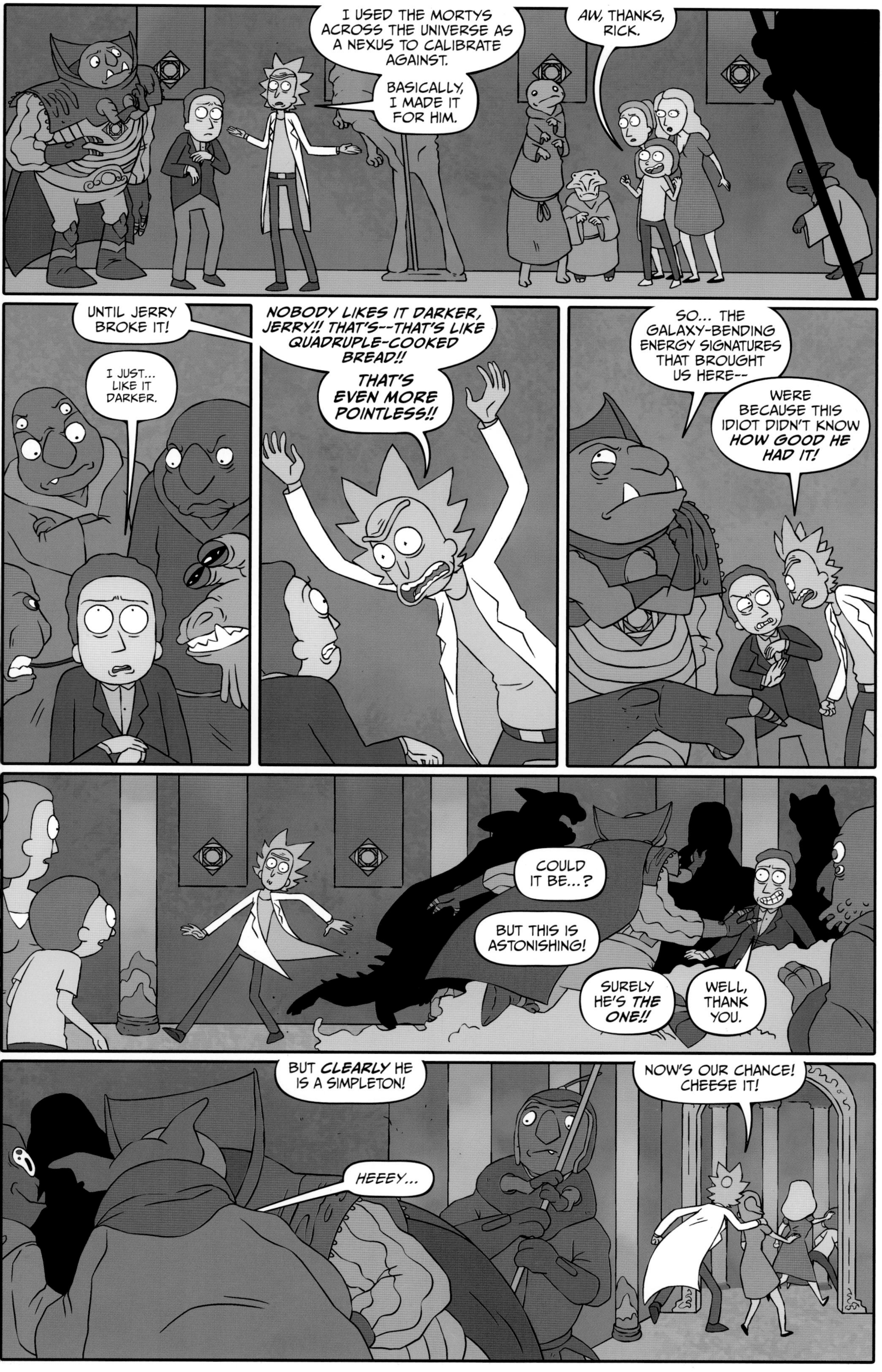
I USED THE MORTYS ACROSS THE UNIVERSE AS A NEXUS TO CALIBRATE AGAINST.
BASICALLY, I MADE IT FOR HIM.
AW, THANKS, RICK.
UNTIL JERRY BROKE IT!
I JUST... LIKE IT DARKER.
NOBODY LIKES IT DARKER, JERRY!! THAT'S--THAT'S LIKE QUADRUPLE-COOKED BREAD!!
THAT'S EVEN MORE POINTLESS!!
SO... THE GALAXY-BENDING ENERGY SIGNATURES THAT BROUGHT US HERE--
WERE BECAUSE THIS IDIOT DIDN'T KNOW HOW GOOD HE HAD IT!
COULD IT BE...?
BUT THIS IS ASTONISHING!
SURELY HE'S THE ONE!!
WELL, THANK YOU.
BUT CLEARLY HE IS A SIMPLETON!
HEEEY...
NOW'S OUR CHANCE! CHEESE IT!

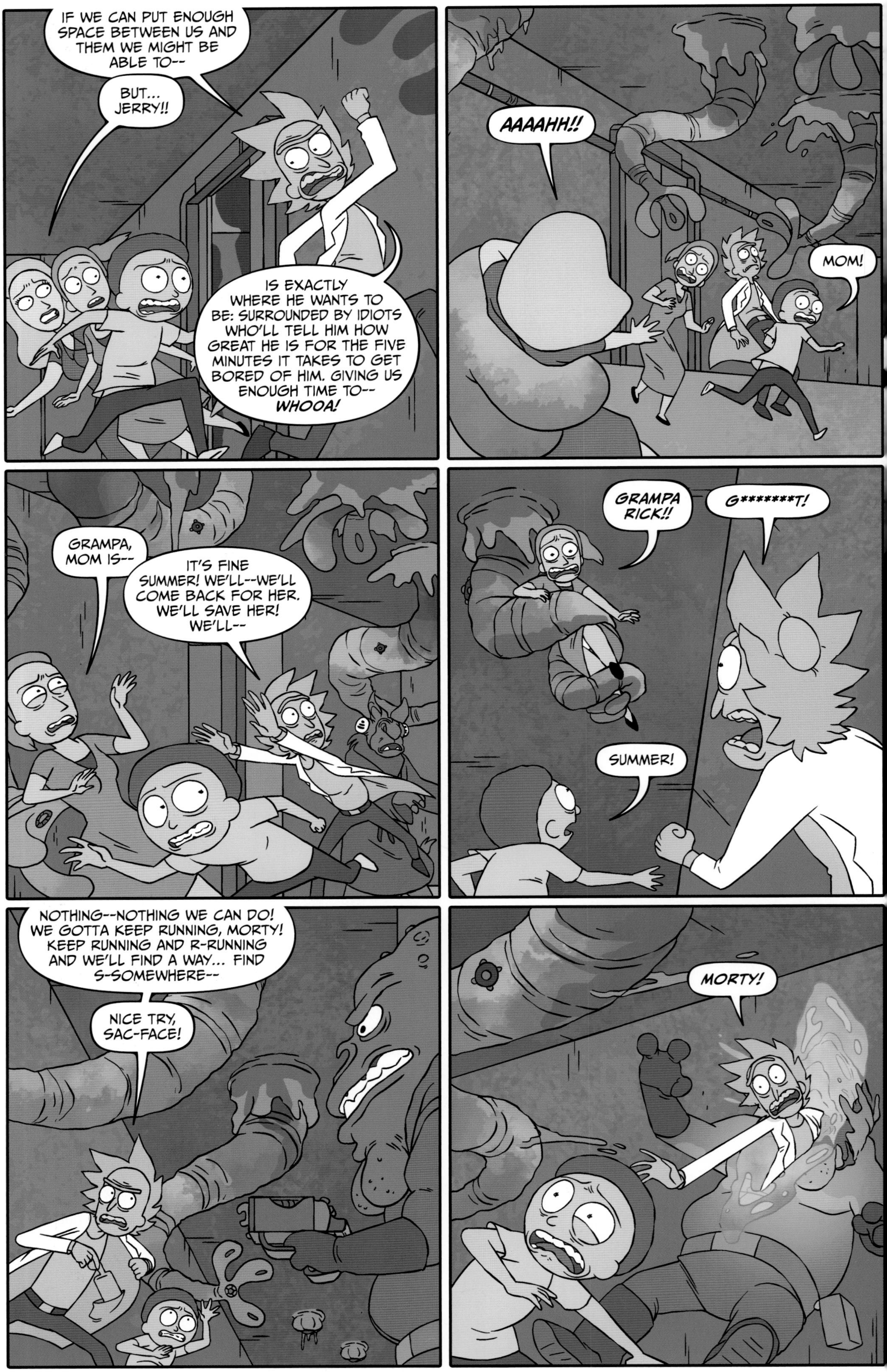
IF WE CAN PUT ENOUGH SPACE BETWEEN US AND THEM WE MIGHT BE ABLE TO--
BUT... JERRY!!
IS EXACTLY WHERE HE WANTS TO BE: SURROUNDED BY IDIOTS WHO'LL TELL HIM HOW GREAT HE IS FOR THE FIVE MINUTES IT TAKES TO GET BORED OF HIM. GIVING US ENOUGH TIME TO-- WHOOA!
AAAAHH!!
MOM!
GRAMPA, MOM IS--
IT'S FINE SUMMER! WE'LL--WE'LL COME BACK FOR HER. WE'LL SAVE HER! WE'LL--
GRAMPA RICK!!
G*******T!
SUMMER!
NOTHING--NOTHING WE CAN DO! WE GOTTA KEEP RUNNING, MORTY! KEEP RUNNING AND R-RUNNING AND WE'LL FIND A WAY... FIND S-SOMEWHERE--
NICE TRY, SAC-FACE!
MORTY!

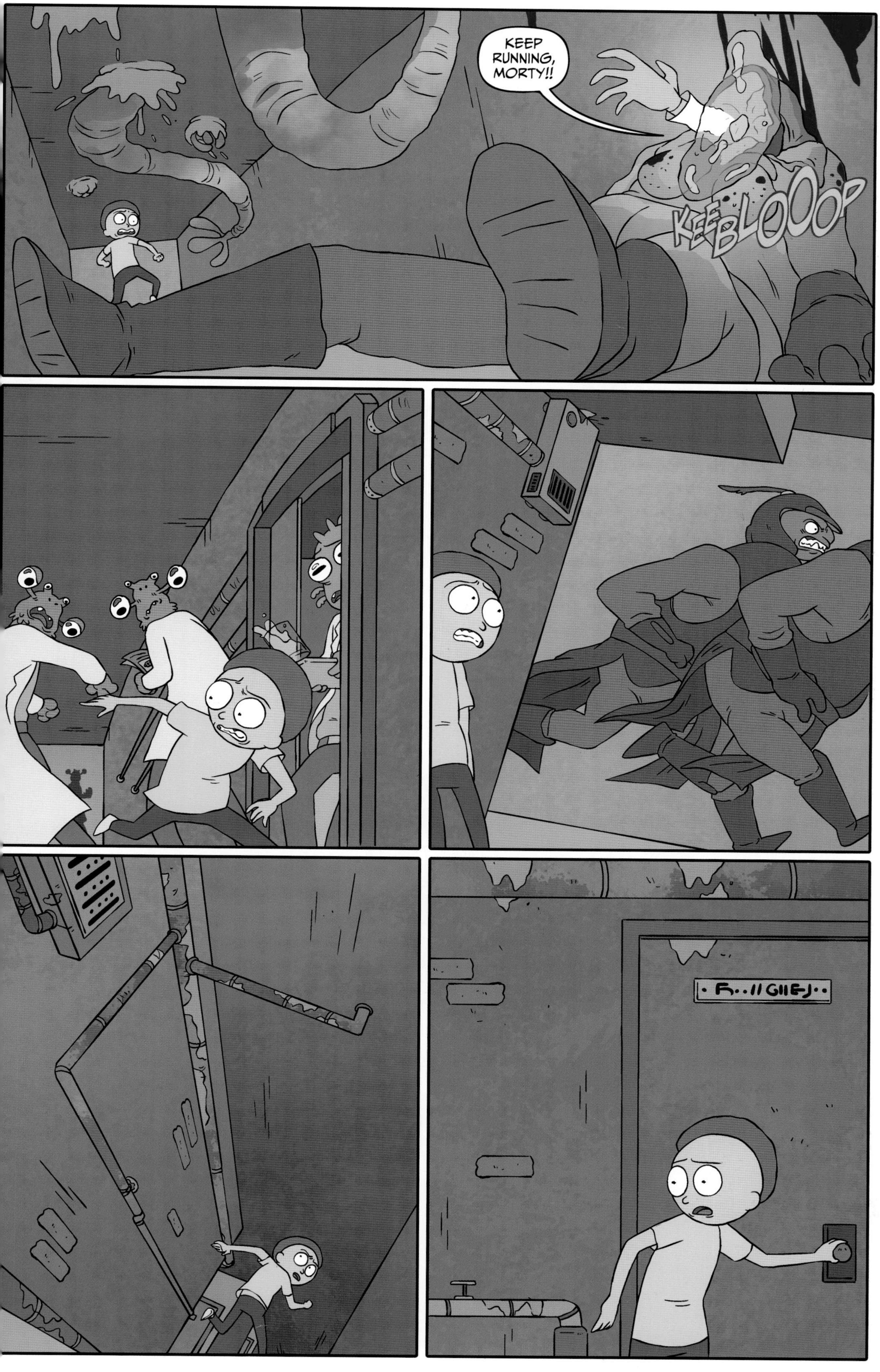
KEEP RUNNING, MORTY!!
KEEBLOOOOP

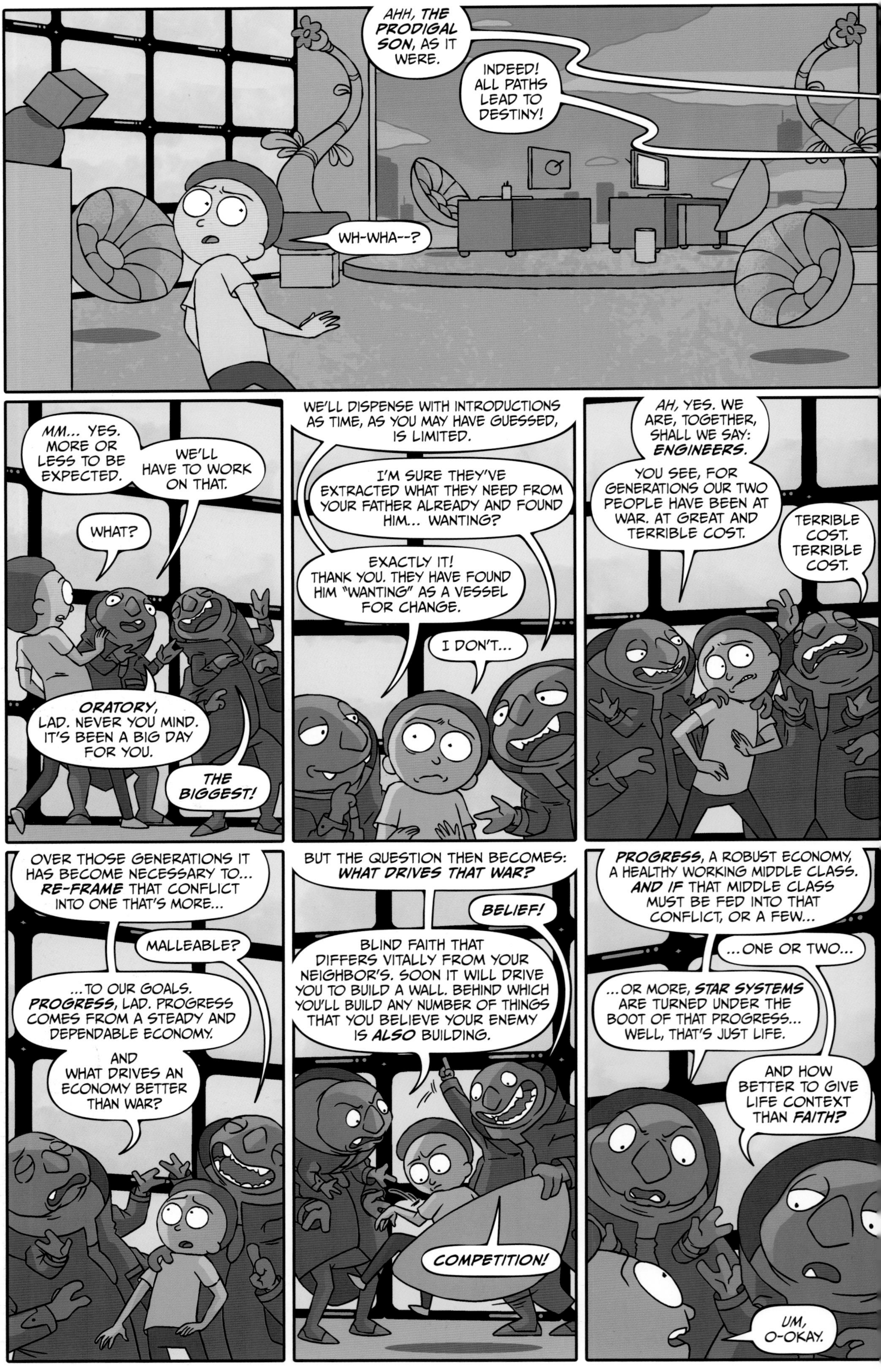
AHH, THE PRODIGAL SON, AS IT WERE.
INDEED! ALL PATHS LEAD TO DESTINY!
WH-WHA--?
MM... YES. MORE OR LESS TO BE EXPECTED.
WE'LL HAVE TO WORK ON THAT.
WHAT?
ORATORY, LAD. NEVER YOU MIND. IT'S BEEN A BIG DAY FOR YOU.
THE BIGGEST!
WE'LL DISPENSE WITH INTRODUCTIONS AS TIME, AS YOU MAY HAVE GUESSED, IS LIMITED.
I'M SURE THEY'VE EXTRACTED WHAT THEY NEED FROM YOUR FATHER ALREADY AND FOUND HIM... WANTING?
EXACTLY IT! THANK YOU. THEY HAVE FOUND HIM "WANTING" AS A VESSEL FOR CHANGE.
I DON'T...
AH, YES. WE ARE, TOGETHER, SHALL WE SAY: ENGINEERS.
YOU SEE, FOR GENERATIONS OUR TWO PEOPLE HAVE BEEN AT WAR. AT GREAT AND TERRIBLE COST.
TERRIBLE COST. TERRIBLE COST.
OVER THOSE GENERATIONS IT HAS BECOME NECESSARY TO... RE-FRAME THAT CONFLICT INTO ONE THAT'S MORE...
MALLEABLE?
...TO OUR GOALS. PROGRESS, LAD. PROGRESS COMES FROM A STEADY AND DEPENDABLE ECONOMY.
AND WHAT DRIVES AN ECONOMY BETTER THAN WAR?
BUT THE QUESTION THEN BECOMES: WHAT DRIVES THAT WAR?
BELIEF!
BLIND FAITH THAT DIFFERS VITALLY FROM YOUR NEIGHBOR'S. SOON IT WILL DRIVE YOU TO BUILD A WALL. BEHIND WHICH YOU'LL BUILD ANY NUMBER OF THINGS THAT YOU BELIEVE YOUR ENEMY IS ALSO BUILDING.
COMPETITION!
PROGRESS, A ROBUST ECONOMY, A HEALTHY WORKING MIDDLE CLASS. AND IF THAT MIDDLE CLASS MUST BE FED INTO THAT CONFLICT, OR A FEW...
...ONE OR TWO...
...OR MORE, STAR SYSTEMS ARE TURNED UNDER THE BOOT OF THAT PROGRESS... WELL, THAT'S JUST LIFE.
AND HOW BETTER TO GIVE LIFE CONTEXT THAN FAITH?
UM, O-OKAY.

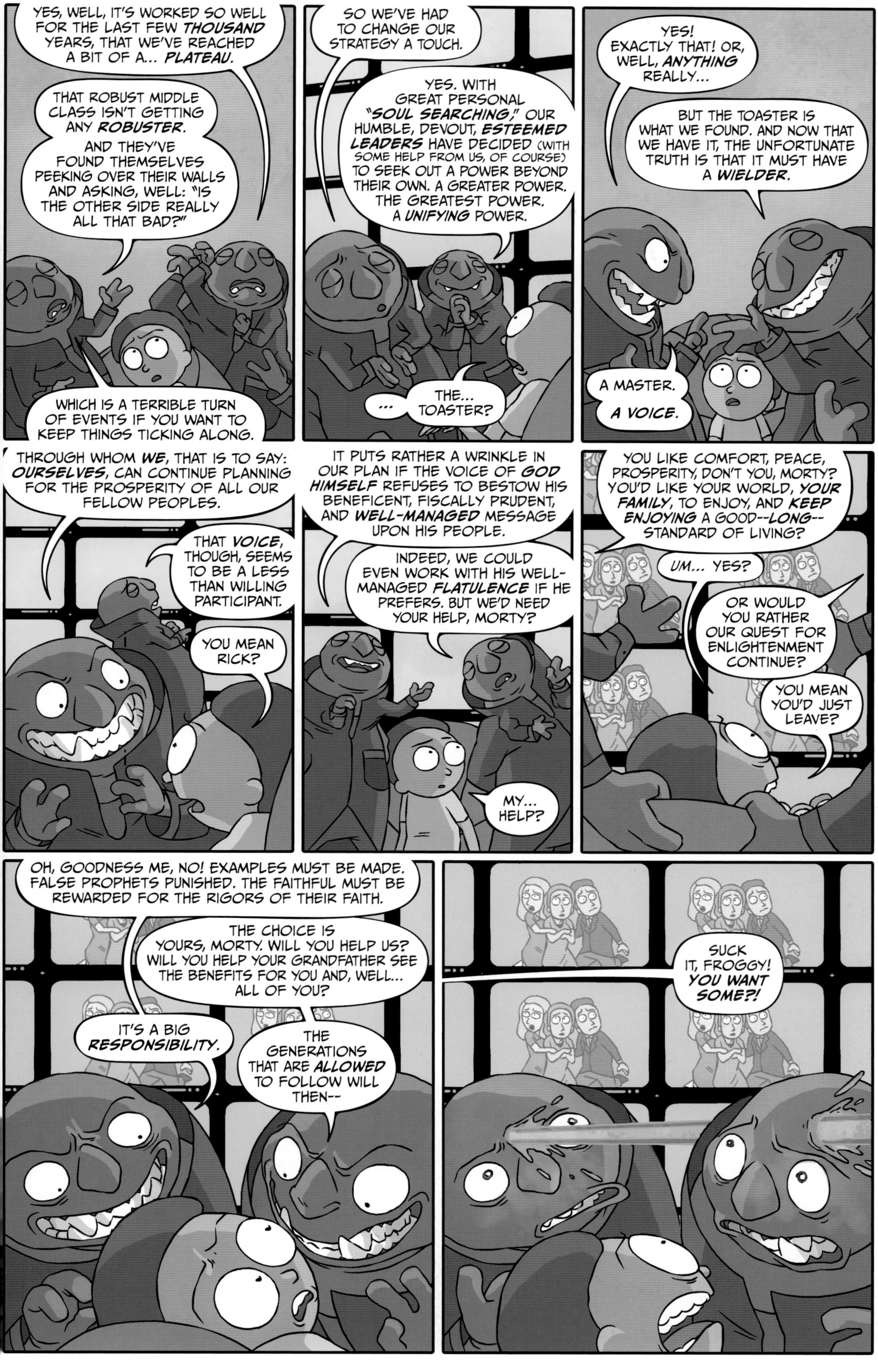
YES, WELL, IT'S WORKED SO WELL FOR THE LAST FEW THOUSAND YEARS, THAT WE'VE REACHED A BIT OF A... PLATEAU.
THAT ROBUST MIDDLE CLASS ISN'T GETTING ANY ROBUSTER.
AND THEY'VE FOUND THEMSELVES PEEKING OVER THEIR WALLS AND ASKING, WELL: "IS THE OTHER SIDE REALLY ALL THAT BAD?"
WHICH IS A TERRIBLE TURN OF EVENTS IF YOU WANT TO KEEP THINGS TICKING ALONG.
SO WE'VE HAD TO CHANGE OUR STRATEGY A TOUCH.
YES. WITH GREAT PERSONAL "SOUL SEARCHING," OUR HUMBLE, DEVOUT, ESTEEMED LEADERS HAVE DECIDED (WITH SOME HELP FROM US, OF COURSE) TO SEEK OUT A POWER BEYOND THEIR OWN. A GREATER POWER. THE GREATEST POWER. A UNIFYING POWER.
...
THE... TOASTER?
YES! EXACTLY THAT! OR, WELL, ANYTHING REALLY...
BUT THE TOASTER IS WHAT WE FOUND. AND NOW THAT WE HAVE IT, THE UNFORTUNATE TRUTH IS THAT IT MUST HAVE A WIELDER.
A MASTER.
A VOICE.
THROUGH WHOM WE, THAT IS TO SAY: OURSELVES, CAN CONTINUE PLANNING FOR THE PROSPERITY OF ALL OUR FELLOW PEOPLES.
THAT VOICE, THOUGH, SEEMS TO BE A LESS THAN WILLING PARTICIPANT.
YOU MEAN RICK?
IT PUTS RATHER A WRINKLE IN OUR PLAN IF THE VOICE OF GOD HIMSELF REFUSES TO BESTOW HIS BENEFICENT, FISCALLY PRUDENT, AND WELL-MANAGED MESSAGE UPON HIS PEOPLE.
INDEED, WE COULD EVEN WORK WITH HIS WELL-MANAGED FLATULENCE IF HE PREFERS. BUT WE'D NEED YOUR HELP, MORTY?
MY... HELP?
YOU LIKE COMFORT, PEACE, PROSPERITY, DON'T YOU, MORTY? YOU'D LIKE YOUR WORLD, YOUR FAMILY, TO ENJOY, AND KEEP ENJOYING A GOOD--LONG--STANDARD OF LIVING?
UM... YES?
OR WOULD YOU RATHER OUR QUEST FOR ENLIGHTENMENT CONTINUE?
YOU MEAN YOU'D JUST LEAVE?
OH, GOODNESS ME, NO! EXAMPLES MUST BE MADE. FALSE PROPHETS PUNISHED. THE FAITHFUL MUST BE REWARDED FOR THE RIGORS OF THEIR FAITH.
THE CHOICE IS YOURS, MORTY. WILL YOU HELP US? WILL YOU HELP YOUR GRANDFATHER SEE THE BENEFITS FOR YOU AND, WELL... ALL OF YOU?
IT'S A BIG RESPONSIBILITY.
THE GENERATIONS THAT ARE ALLOWED TO FOLLOW WILL THEN--
SUCK IT, FROGGY! YOU WANT SOME?!

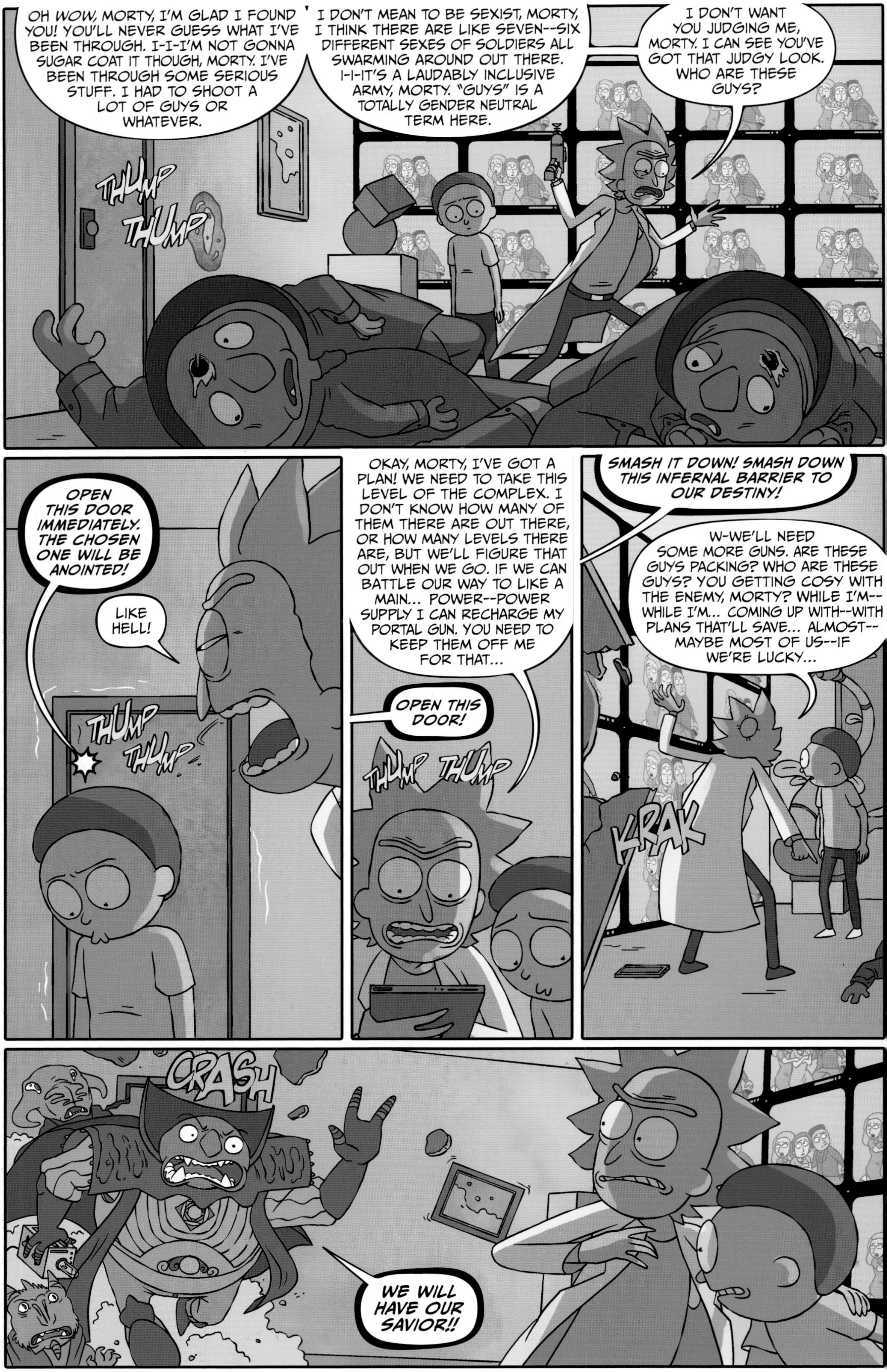
OH WOW, MORTY, I'M GLAD I FOUND YOU! YOU'LL NEVER GUESS WHAT I'VE BEEN THROUGH. I-I-I'M NOT GONNA SUGAR COAT IT THOUGH, MORTY. I'VE BEEN THROUGH SOME SERIOUS STUFF. I HAD TO SHOOT A LOT OF GUYS OR WHATEVER.
I DON'T MEAN TO BE SEXIST, MORTY, I THINK THERE ARE LIKE SEVEN--SIX DIFFERENT SEXES OF SOLDIERS ALL SWARMING AROUND OUT THERE. I-I-IT'S A LAUDABLY INCLUSIVE ARMY, MORTY. "GUYS" IS A TOTALLY GENDER NEUTRAL TERM HERE.
I DON'T WANT YOU JUDGING ME, MORTY. I CAN SEE YOU'VE GOT THAT JUDGY LOOK. WHO ARE THESE GUYS?
THUMP
THUMP
OPEN THIS DOOR IMMEDIATELY. THE CHOSEN ONE WILL BE ANOINTED!
LIKE HELL!
THUMP
THUMP
OKAY, MORTY, I'VE GOT A PLAN! WE NEED TO TAKE THIS LEVEL OF THE COMPLEX. I DON'T KNOW HOW MANY OF THEM THERE ARE OUT THERE, OR HOW MANY LEVELS THERE ARE, BUT WE'LL FIGURE THAT OUT WHEN WE GO. IF WE CAN BATTLE OUR WAY TO LIKE A MAIN... POWER--POWER SUPPLY I CAN RECHARGE MY PORTAL GUN. YOU NEED TO KEEP THEM OFF ME FOR THAT...
OPEN THIS DOOR!
THUMP THUMP
SMASH IT DOWN! SMASH DOWN THIS INFERNAL BARRIER TO OUR DESTINY!
W-WE'LL NEED SOME MORE GUNS. ARE THESE GUYS PACKING? WHO ARE THESE GUYS? YOU GETTING COSY WITH THE ENEMY, MORTY? WHILE I'M-- WHILE I'M... COMING UP WITH--WITH PLANS THAT'LL SAVE... ALMOST-- MAYBE MOST OF US--IF WE'RE LUCKY...
KRAK
CRASH
WE WILL HAVE OUR SAVIOR!!

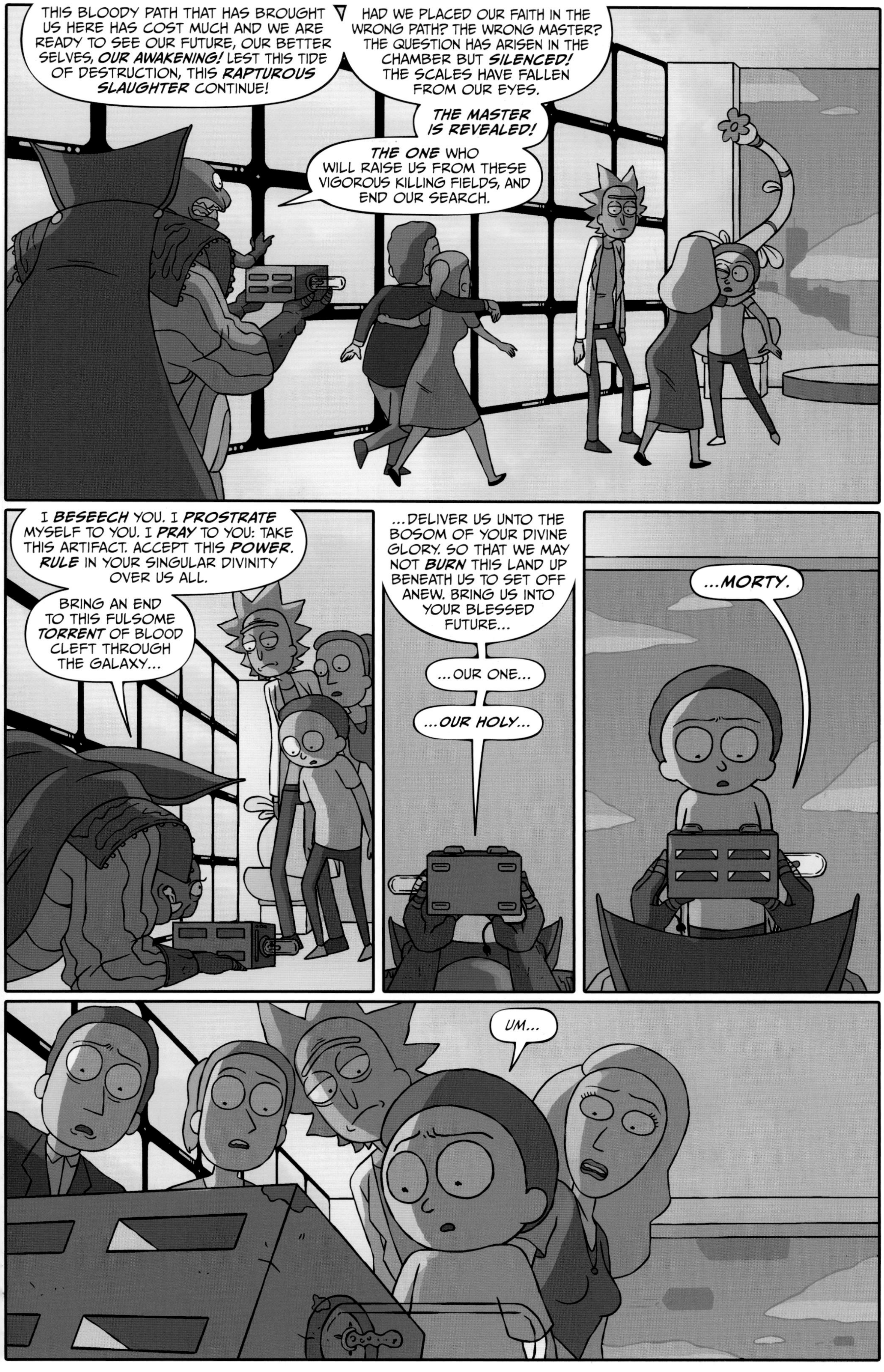
THIS BLOODY PATH THAT HAS BROUGHT US HERE HAS COST MUCH AND WE ARE READY TO SEE OUR FUTURE, OUR BETTER SELVES, OUR AWAKENING! LEST THIS TIDE OF DESTRUCTION, THIS RAPTUROUS SLAUGHTER CONTINUE!
HAD WE PLACED OUR FAITH IN THE WRONG PATH? THE WRONG MASTER? THE QUESTION HAS ARISEN IN THE CHAMBER BUT SILENCED! THE SCALES HAVE FALLEN FROM OUR EYES.
THE MASTER IS REVEALED!
THE ONE WHO WILL RAISE US FROM THESE VIGOROUS KILLING FIELDS, AND END OUR SEARCH.
I BESEECH YOU. I PROSTRATE MYSELF TO YOU. I PRAY TO YOU: TAKE THIS ARTIFACT. ACCEPT THIS POWER. RULE IN YOUR SINGULAR DIVINITY OVER US ALL.
BRING AN END TO THIS FULSOME TORRENT OF BLOOD CLEFT THROUGH THE GALAXY...
...DELIVER US UNTO THE BOSOM OF YOUR DIVINE GLORY. SO THAT WE MAY NOT BURN THIS LAND UP BENEATH US TO SET OFF ANEW. BRING US INTO YOUR BLESSED FUTURE...
...OUR ONE...
...OUR HOLY...
...MORTY.
UM...

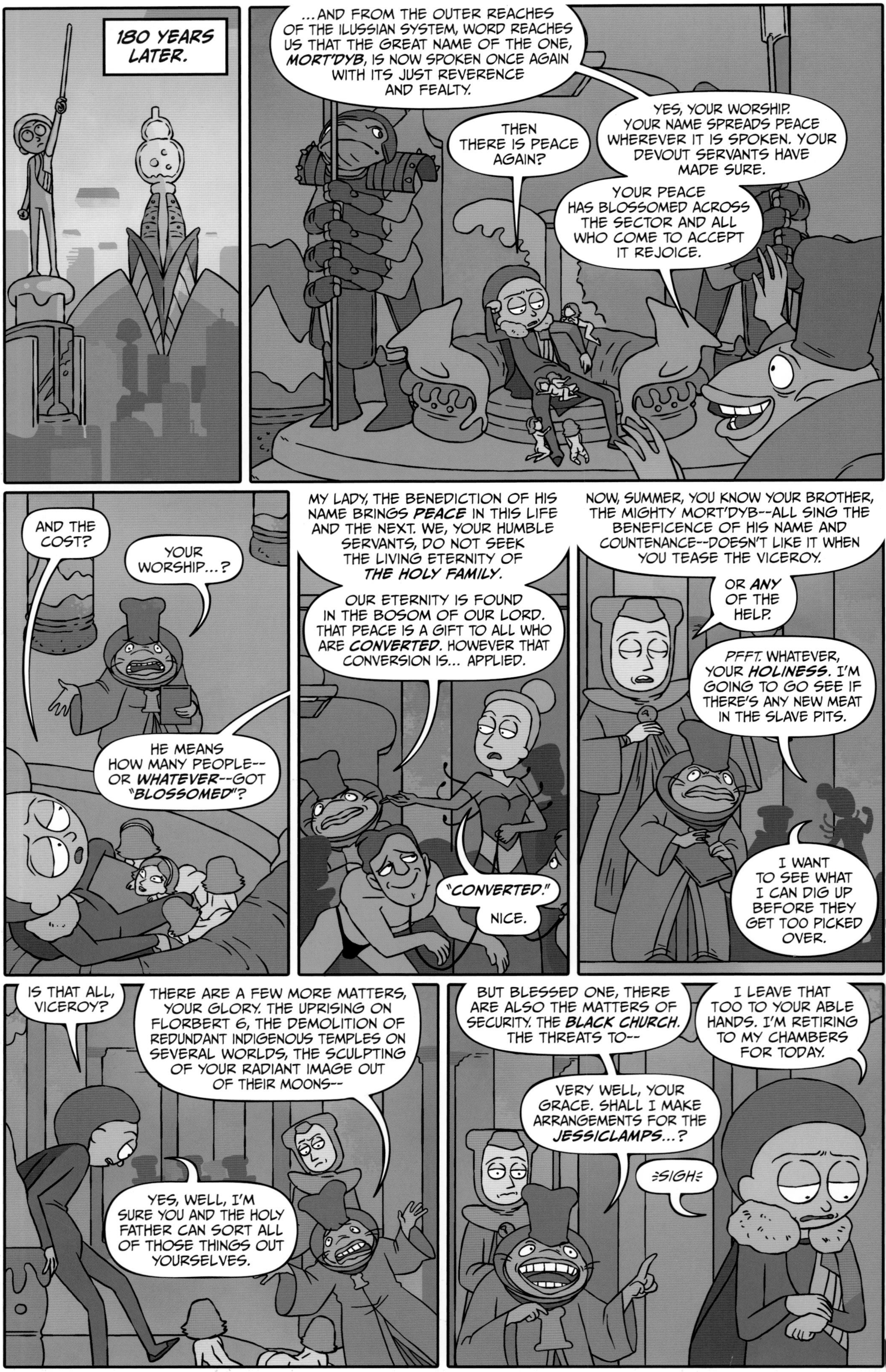
180 YEARS LATER.
...AND FROM THE OUTER REACHES OF THE ILUSSIAN SYSTEM, WORD REACHES US THAT THE GREAT NAME OF THE ONE, MORT'DYB, IS NOW SPOKEN ONCE AGAIN WITH ITS JUST REVERENCE AND FEALTY.
THEN THERE IS PEACE AGAIN?
YES, YOUR WORSHIP. YOUR NAME SPREADS PEACE WHEREVER IT IS SPOKEN. YOUR DEVOUT SERVANTS HAVE MADE SURE.
YOUR PEACE HAS BLOSSOMED ACROSS THE SECTOR AND ALL WHO COME TO ACCEPT IT REJOICE.
AND THE COST?
YOUR WORSHIP...?
HE MEANS HOW MANY PEOPLE--OR WHATEVER--GOT "BLOSSOMED"?
MY LADY, THE BENEDICTION OF HIS NAME BRINGS PEACE IN THIS LIFE AND THE NEXT. WE, YOUR HUMBLE SERVANTS, DO NOT SEEK THE LIVING ETERNITY OF THE HOLY FAMILY.
OUR ETERNITY IS FOUND IN THE BOSOM OF OUR LORD. THAT PEACE IS A GIFT TO ALL WHO ARE CONVERTED. HOWEVER THAT CONVERSION IS... APPLIED.
"CONVERTED."
NICE.
NOW, SUMMER, YOU KNOW YOUR BROTHER, THE MIGHTY MORT'DYB--ALL SING THE BENEFICENCE OF HIS NAME AND COUNTENANCE--DOESN'T LIKE IT WHEN YOU TEASE THE VICEROY.
OR ANY OF THE HELP.
PFFT. WHATEVER, YOUR HOLINESS. I'M GOING TO GO SEE IF THERE'S ANY NEW MEAT IN THE SLAVE PITS.
I WANT TO SEE WHAT I CAN DIG UP BEFORE THEY GET TOO PICKED OVER.
IS THAT ALL, VICEROY?
THERE ARE A FEW MORE MATTERS, YOUR GLORY. THE UPRISING ON FLORBERT 6, THE DEMOLITION OF REDUNDANT INDIGENOUS TEMPLES ON SEVERAL WORLDS, THE SCULPTING OF YOUR RADIANT IMAGE OUT OF THEIR MOONS--
YES, WELL, I'M SURE YOU AND THE HOLY FATHER CAN SORT ALL OF THOSE THINGS OUT YOURSELVES.
BUT BLESSED ONE, THERE ARE ALSO THE MATTERS OF SECURITY. THE BLACK CHURCH. THE THREATS TO--
I LEAVE THAT TOO TO YOUR ABLE HANDS. I'M RETIRING TO MY CHAMBERS FOR TODAY.
VERY WELL, YOUR GRACE. SHALL I MAKE ARRANGEMENTS FOR THE JESSICLAMPS...?
SIGH

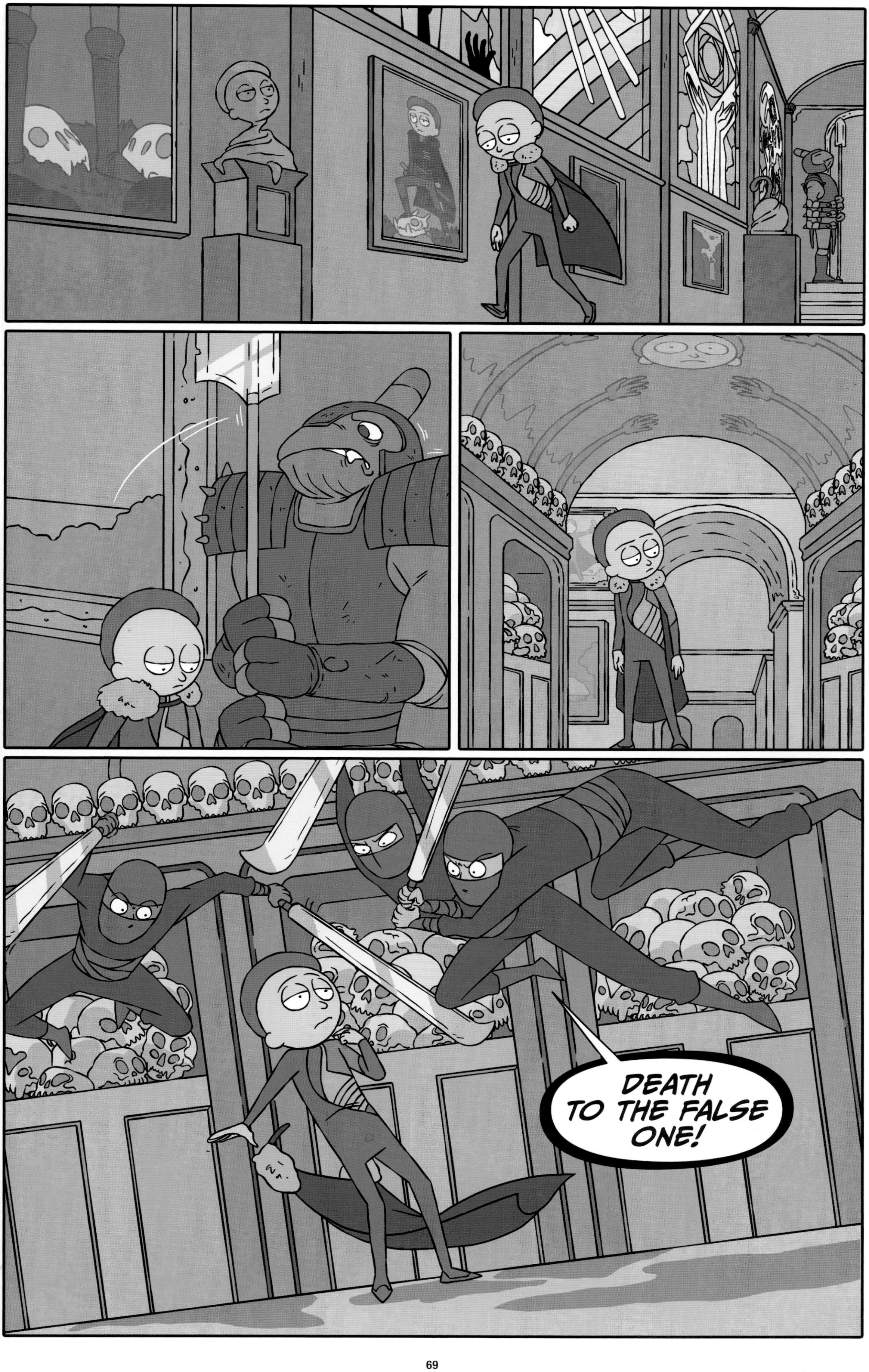
DEATH TO THE FALSE ONE!

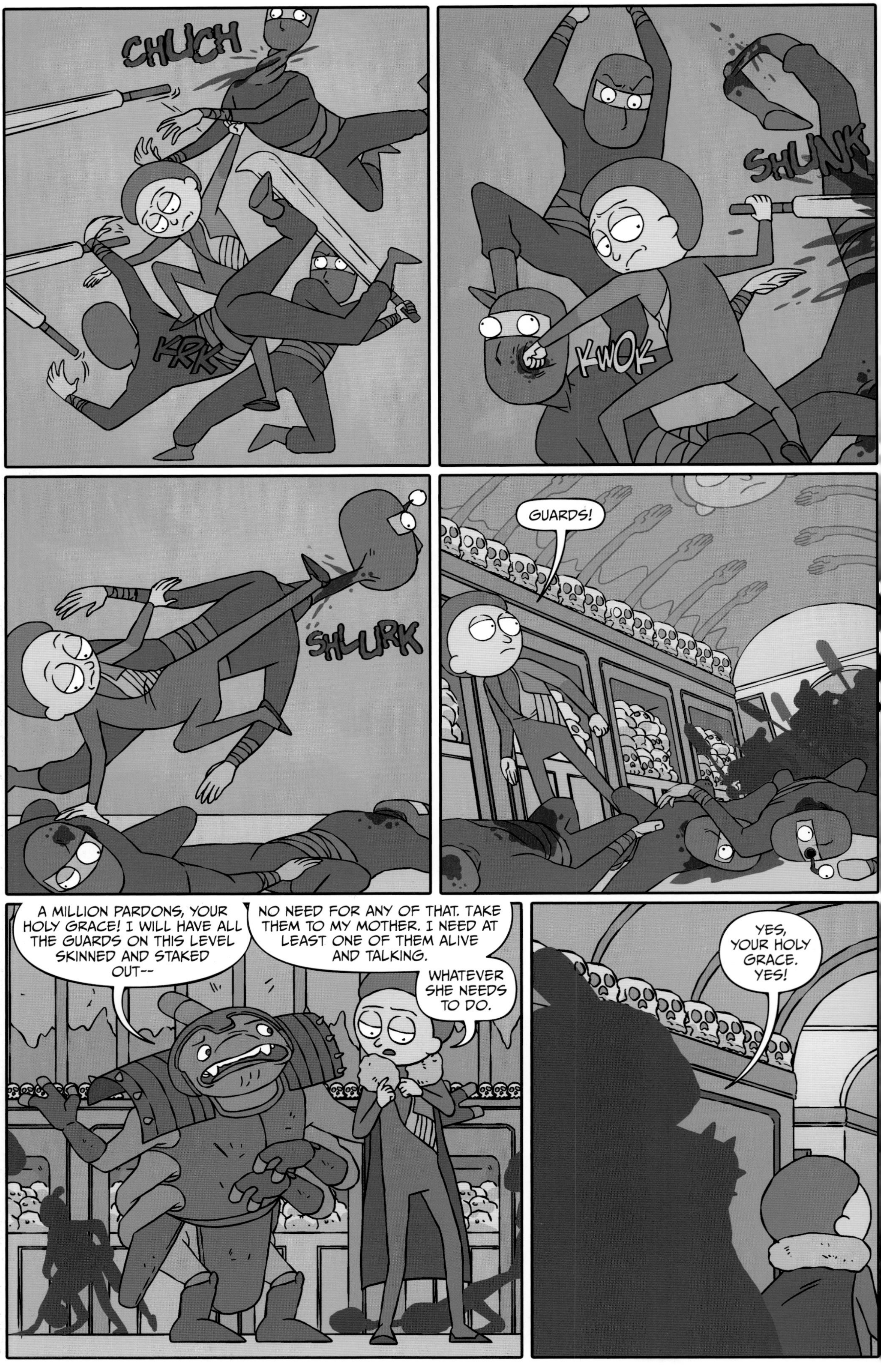
CHUCH
SHUNK
KRK
KWOK
SHLURK
GUARDS!
A MILLION PARDONS, YOUR HOLY GRACE! I WILL HAVE ALL THE GUARDS ON THIS LEVEL SKINNED AND STAKED OUT--
NO NEED FOR ANY OF THAT. TAKE THEM TO MY MOTHER. I NEED AT LEAST ONE OF THEM ALIVE AND TALKING.
WHATEVER SHE NEEDS TO DO.
YES, YOUR HOLY GRACE. YES!

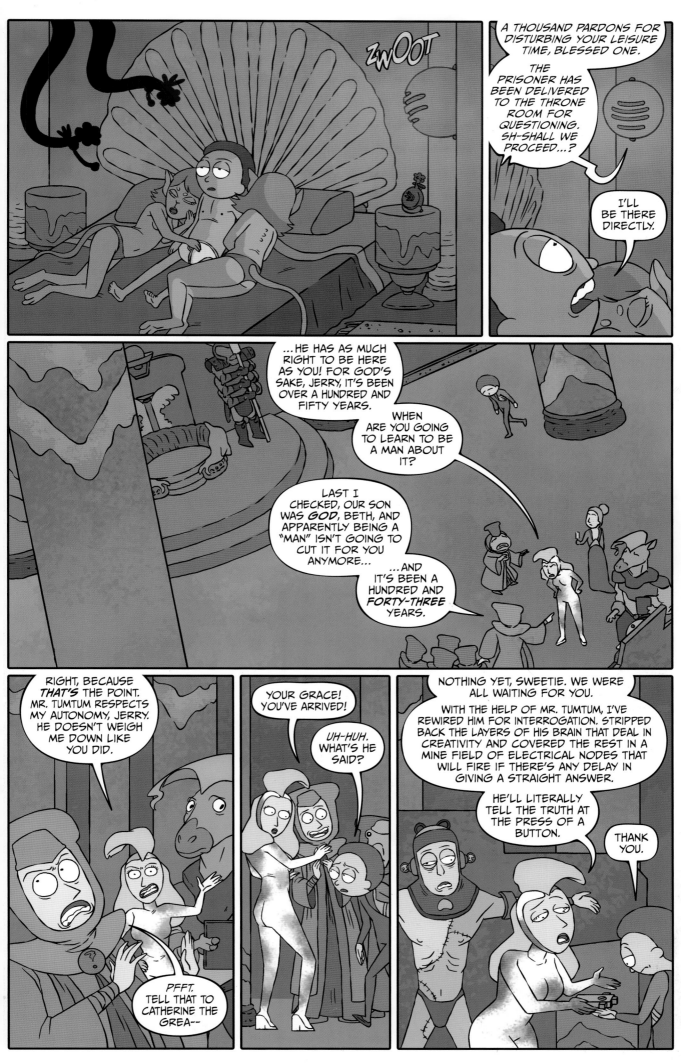

ZWOOT

A THOUSAND PARDONS FOR DISTURBING YOUR LEISURE TIME, BLESSED ONE.

THE PRISONER HAS BEEN DELIVERED TO THE THRONE ROOM FOR QUESTIONING. SH-SHALL WE PROCEED...?

I'LL BE THERE DIRECTLY.

...HE HAS AS MUCH RIGHT TO BE HERE AS YOU! FOR GOD'S SAKE, JERRY, IT'S BEEN OVER A HUNDRED AND FIFTY YEARS.

WHEN ARE YOU GOING TO LEARN TO BE A MAN ABOUT IT?

LAST I CHECKED, OUR SON WAS *GOD*, BETH, AND APPARENTLY BEING A "MAN" ISN'T GOING TO CUT IT FOR YOU ANYMORE...

...AND IT'S BEEN A HUNDRED AND *FORTY-THREE* YEARS.

RIGHT, BECAUSE *THAT'S* THE POINT. MR. TUMTUM RESPECTS MY AUTONOMY, JERRY. HE DOESN'T WEIGH ME DOWN LIKE YOU DID.

PFFT. TELL THAT TO CATHERINE THE GREA--

YOUR GRACE! YOU'VE ARRIVED!

UH-HUH. WHAT'S HE SAID?

NOTHING YET, SWEETIE. WE WERE ALL WAITING FOR YOU.

WITH THE HELP OF MR. TUMTUM, I'VE REWIRED HIM FOR INTERROGATION. STRIPPED BACK THE LAYERS OF HIS BRAIN THAT DEAL IN CREATIVITY AND COVERED THE REST IN A MINE FIELD OF ELECTRICAL NODES THAT WILL FIRE IF THERE'S ANY DELAY IN GIVING A STRAIGHT ANSWER.

HE'LL LITERALLY TELL THE TRUTH AT THE PRESS OF A BUTTON.

THANK YOU.

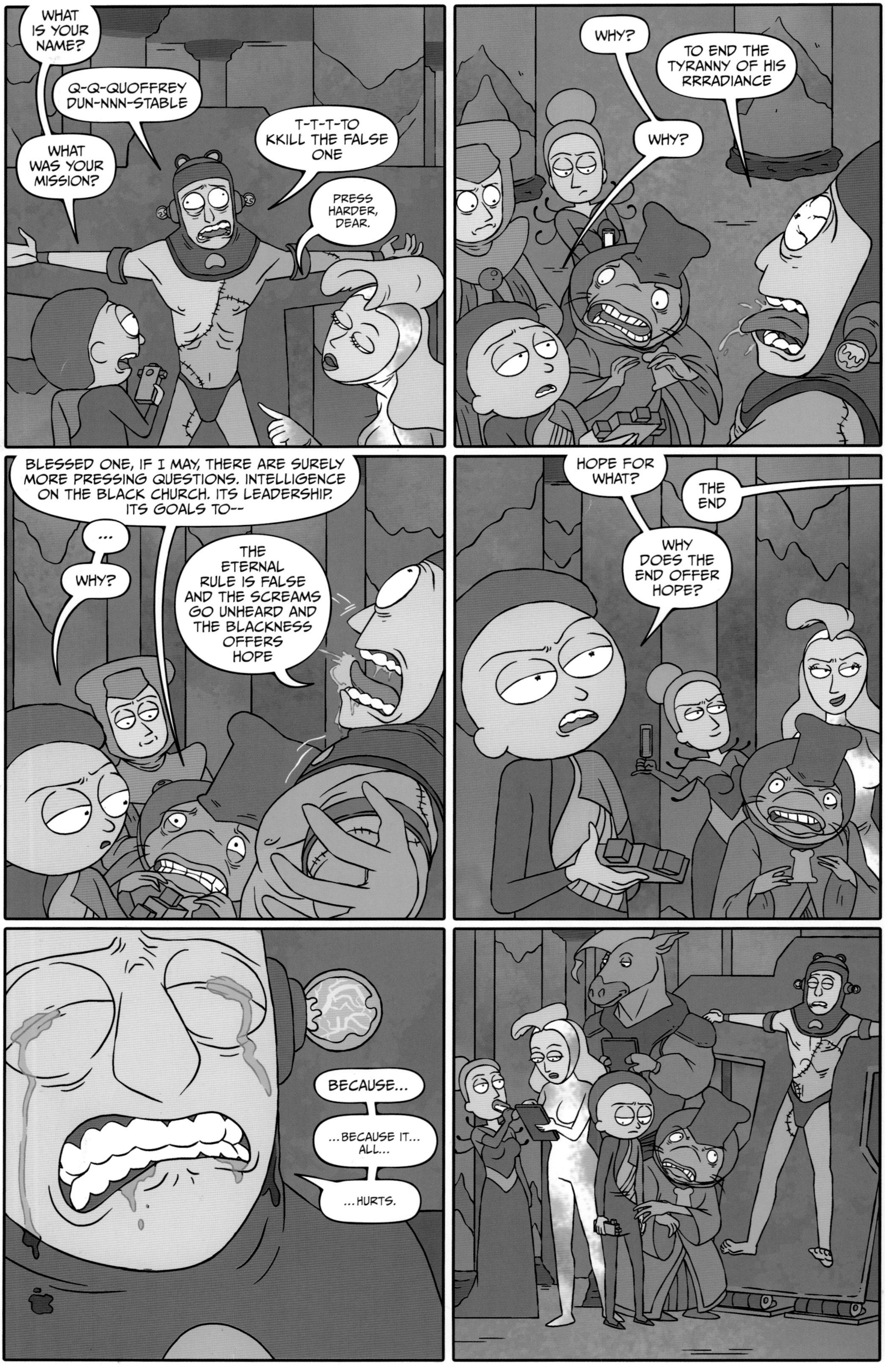
WHAT IS YOUR NAME?
Q-Q-QUOFFREY DUN-NNN-STABLE
WHAT WAS YOUR MISSION?
T-T-T-TO KKILL THE FALSE ONE
PRESS HARDER, DEAR.
WHY?
TO END THE TYRANNY OF HIS RRRADIANCE
WHY?
BLESSED ONE, IF I MAY, THERE ARE SURELY MORE PRESSING QUESTIONS. INTELLIGENCE ON THE BLACK CHURCH. ITS LEADERSHIP. ITS GOALS TO--
...
WHY?
THE ETERNAL RULE IS FALSE AND THE SCREAMS GO UNHEARD AND THE BLACKNESS OFFERS HOPE
HOPE FOR WHAT?
THE END
WHY DOES THE END OFFER HOPE?
BECAUSE...
...BECAUSE IT... ALL...
...HURTS.

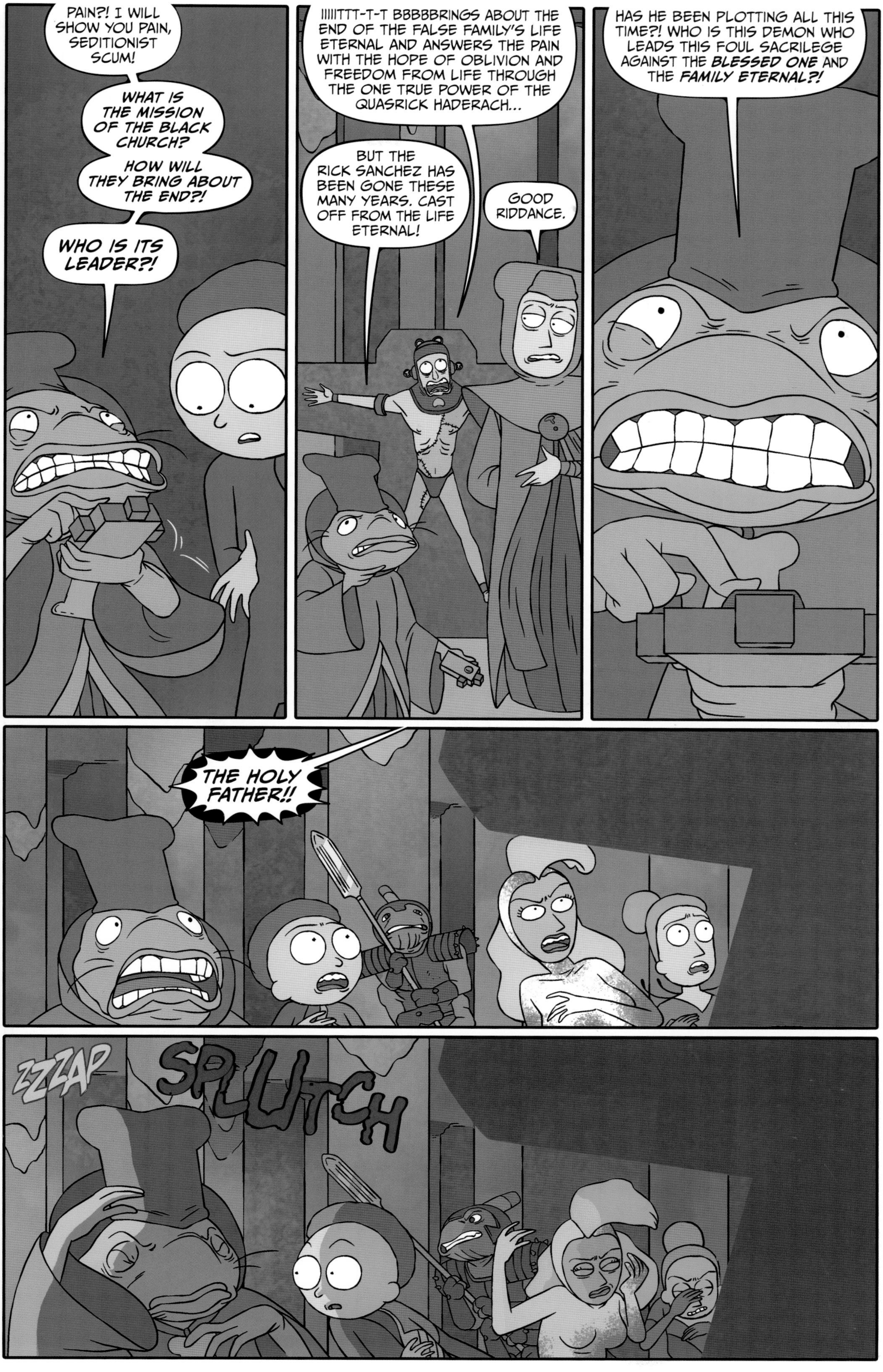

PAIN?! I WILL SHOW YOU PAIN, SEDITIONIST SCUM!
WHAT IS THE MISSION OF THE BLACK CHURCH?
HOW WILL THEY BRING ABOUT THE END?!
WHO IS ITS LEADER?!
IIIIITTT-T-T BBBBBRINGS ABOUT THE END OF THE FALSE FAMILY'S LIFE ETERNAL AND ANSWERS THE PAIN WITH THE HOPE OF OBLIVION AND FREEDOM FROM LIFE THROUGH THE ONE TRUE POWER OF THE QUASRICK HADERACH...
BUT THE RICK SANCHEZ HAS BEEN GONE THESE MANY YEARS. CAST OFF FROM THE LIFE ETERNAL!
GOOD RIDDANCE.
HAS HE BEEN PLOTTING ALL THIS TIME?! WHO IS THIS DEMON WHO LEADS THIS FOUL SACRILEGE AGAINST THE BLESSED ONE AND THE FAMILY ETERNAL?!
THE HOLY FATHER!!
ZZZAP
SPLUTCH

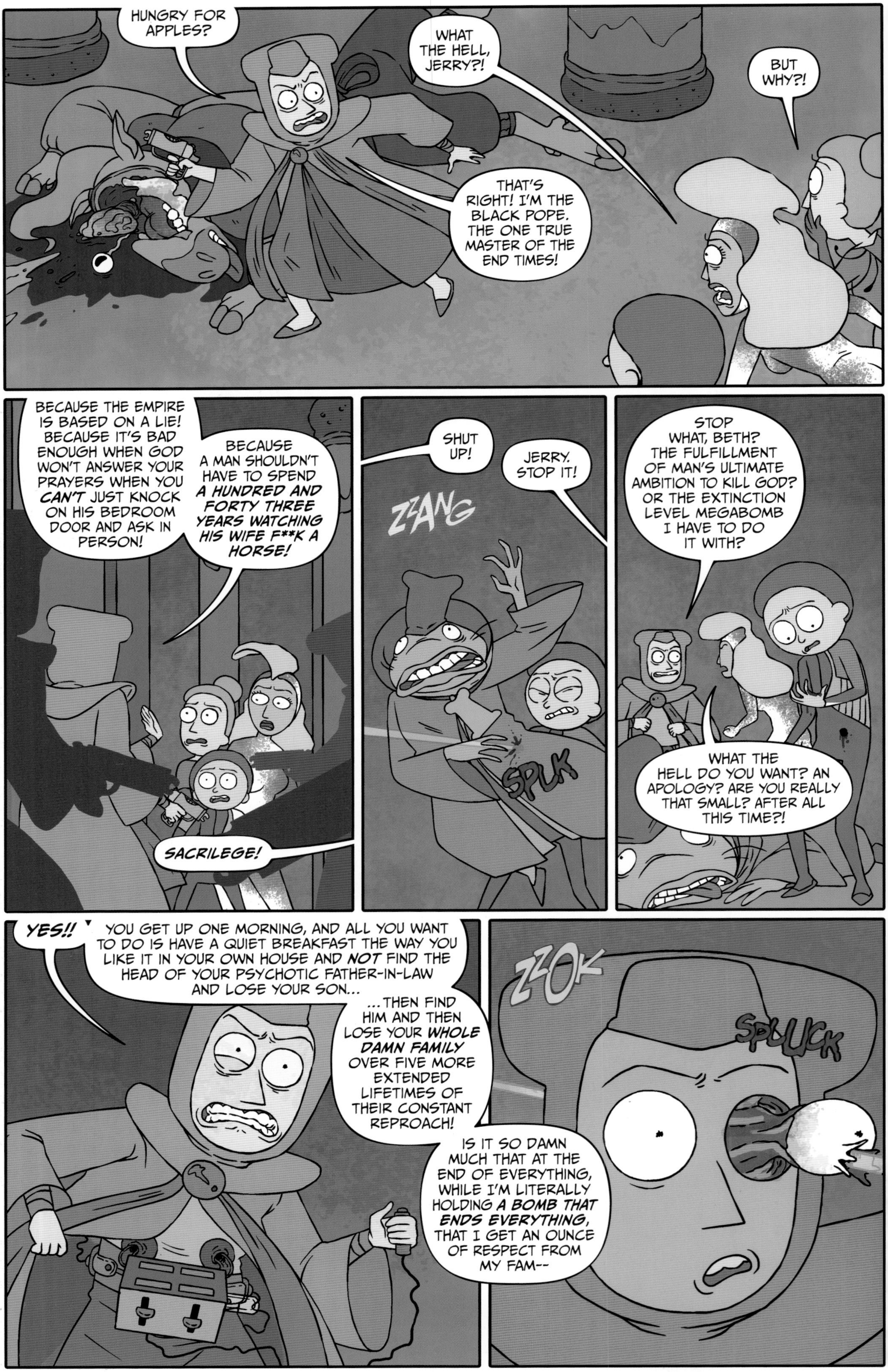
HUNGRY FOR APPLES?
WHAT THE HELL, JERRY?!
BUT WHY?!
THAT'S RIGHT! I'M THE BLACK POPE. THE ONE TRUE MASTER OF THE END TIMES!
BECAUSE THE EMPIRE IS BASED ON A LIE! BECAUSE IT'S BAD ENOUGH WHEN GOD WON'T ANSWER YOUR PRAYERS WHEN YOU CAN'T JUST KNOCK ON HIS BEDROOM DOOR AND ASK IN PERSON!
BECAUSE A MAN SHOULDN'T HAVE TO SPEND A HUNDRED AND FORTY THREE YEARS WATCHING HIS WIFE F**K A HORSE!
SACRILEGE!
SHUT UP!
JERRY. STOP IT!
ZZANG
SPLK
STOP WHAT, BETH? THE FULFILLMENT OF MAN'S ULTIMATE AMBITION TO KILL GOD? OR THE EXTINCTION LEVEL MEGABOMB I HAVE TO DO IT WITH?
WHAT THE HELL DO YOU WANT? AN APOLOGY? ARE YOU REALLY THAT SMALL? AFTER ALL THIS TIME?!
YES!!
YOU GET UP ONE MORNING, AND ALL YOU WANT TO DO IS HAVE A QUIET BREAKFAST THE WAY YOU LIKE IT IN YOUR OWN HOUSE AND NOT FIND THE HEAD OF YOUR PSYCHOTIC FATHER-IN-LAW AND LOSE YOUR SON...
...THEN FIND HIM AND THEN LOSE YOUR WHOLE DAMN FAMILY OVER FIVE MORE EXTENDED LIFETIMES OF THEIR CONSTANT REPROACH!
IS IT SO DAMN MUCH THAT AT THE END OF EVERYTHING, WHILE I'M LITERALLY HOLDING A BOMB THAT ENDS EVERYTHING, THAT I GET AN OUNCE OF RESPECT FROM MY FAM--
ZZOK
SPLUCK

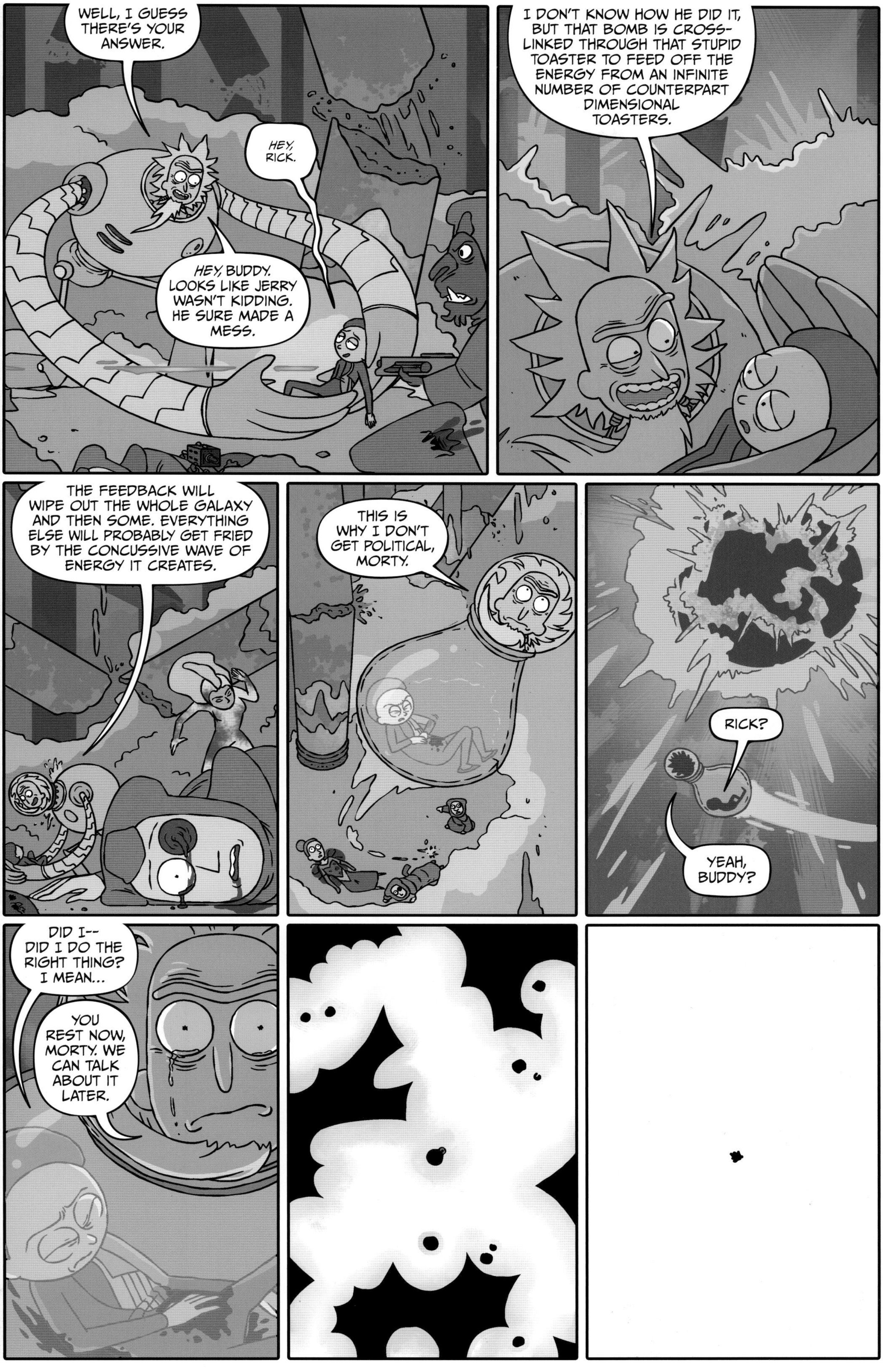
WELL, I GUESS THERE'S YOUR ANSWER.
HEY, RICK.
HEY, BUDDY. LOOKS LIKE JERRY WASN'T KIDDING. HE SURE MADE A MESS.
I DON'T KNOW HOW HE DID IT, BUT THAT BOMB IS CROSS-LINKED THROUGH THAT STUPID TOASTER TO FEED OFF THE ENERGY FROM AN INFINITE NUMBER OF COUNTERPART DIMENSIONAL TOASTERS.
THE FEEDBACK WILL WIPE OUT THE WHOLE GALAXY AND THEN SOME. EVERYTHING ELSE WILL PROBABLY GET FRIED BY THE CONCUSSIVE WAVE OF ENERGY IT CREATES.
THIS IS WHY I DON'T GET POLITICAL, MORTY.
RICK?
YEAH, BUDDY?
DID I-- DID I DO THE RIGHT THING? I MEAN...
YOU REST NOW, MORTY. WE CAN TALK ABOUT IT LATER.

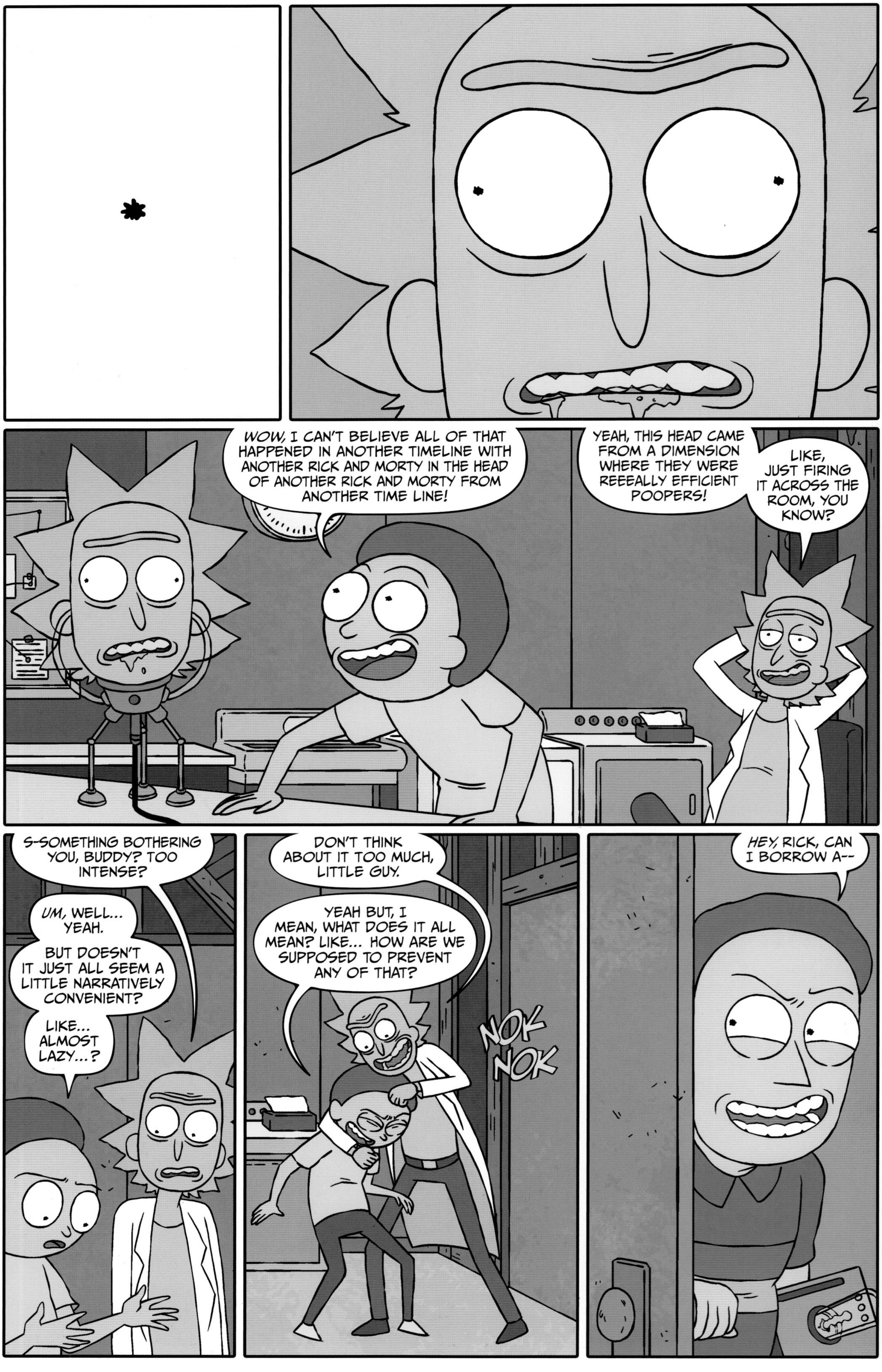
WOW, I CAN'T BELIEVE ALL OF THAT HAPPENED IN ANOTHER TIMELINE WITH ANOTHER RICK AND MORTY IN THE HEAD OF ANOTHER RICK AND MORTY FROM ANOTHER TIME LINE!
YEAH, THIS HEAD CAME FROM A DIMENSION WHERE THEY WERE REEEALLY EFFICIENT POOPERS!
LIKE, JUST FIRING IT ACROSS THE ROOM, YOU KNOW?
S-SOMETHING BOTHERING YOU, BUDDY? TOO INTENSE?
UM, WELL... YEAH.
BUT DOESN'T IT JUST ALL SEEM A LITTLE NARRATIVELY CONVENIENT?
LIKE... ALMOST LAZY...?
DON'T THINK ABOUT IT TOO MUCH, LITTLE GUY.
YEAH BUT, I MEAN, WHAT DOES IT ALL MEAN? LIKE... HOW ARE WE SUPPOSED TO PREVENT ANY OF THAT?
NOK NOK
HEY, RICK, CAN I BORROW A--

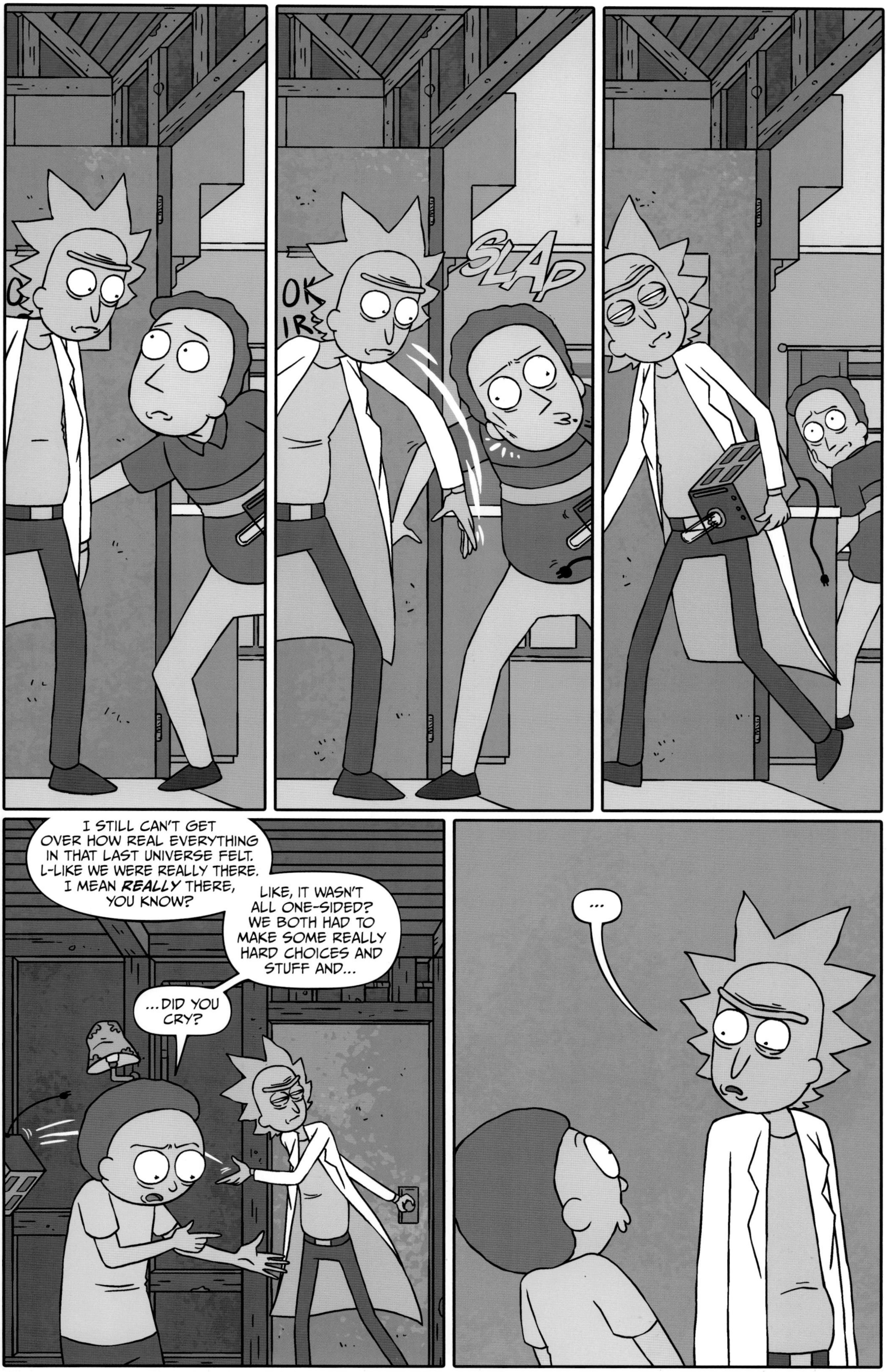
SLAP
I STILL CAN'T GET OVER HOW REAL EVERYTHING IN THAT LAST UNIVERSE FELT. L-LIKE WE WERE REALLY THERE. I MEAN **REALLY** THERE, YOU KNOW?
LIKE, IT WASN'T ALL ONE-SIDED? WE BOTH HAD TO MAKE SOME REALLY HARD CHOICES AND STUFF AND...
...DID YOU CRY?
...

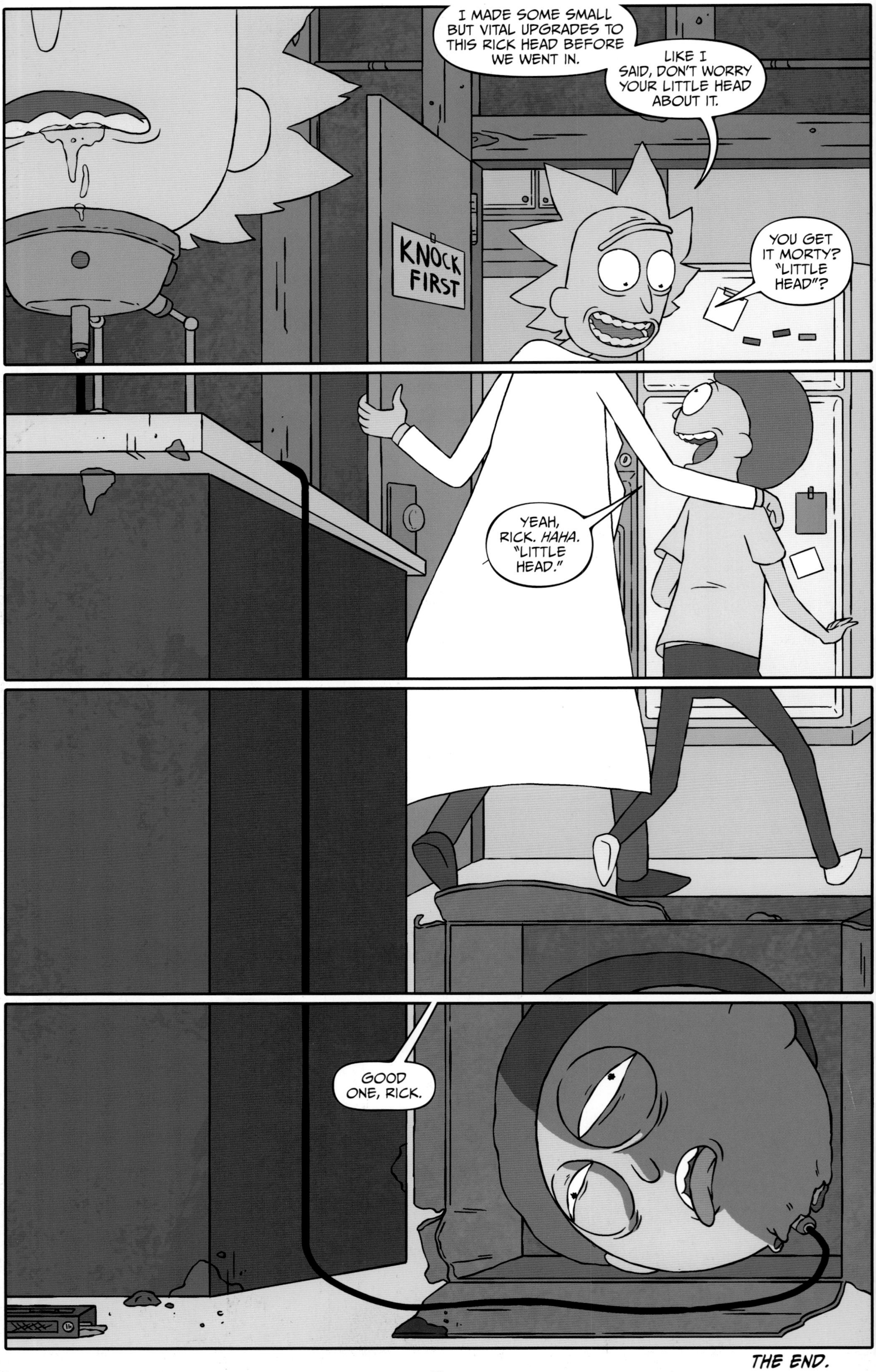
I MADE SOME SMALL BUT VITAL UPGRADES TO THIS RICK HEAD BEFORE WE WENT IN.
LIKE I SAID, DON'T WORRY YOUR LITTLE HEAD ABOUT IT.
KNOCK FIRST
YOU GET IT MORTY? "LITTLE HEAD"?
YEAH, RICK. *HAHA.* "LITTLE HEAD."
GOOD ONE, RICK.

THE END.

BIG GAME

WRITTEN AND DRAWN BY **TOM FOWLER**
COLORED BY **RYAN HILL**
LETTERED BY **CRANK!**

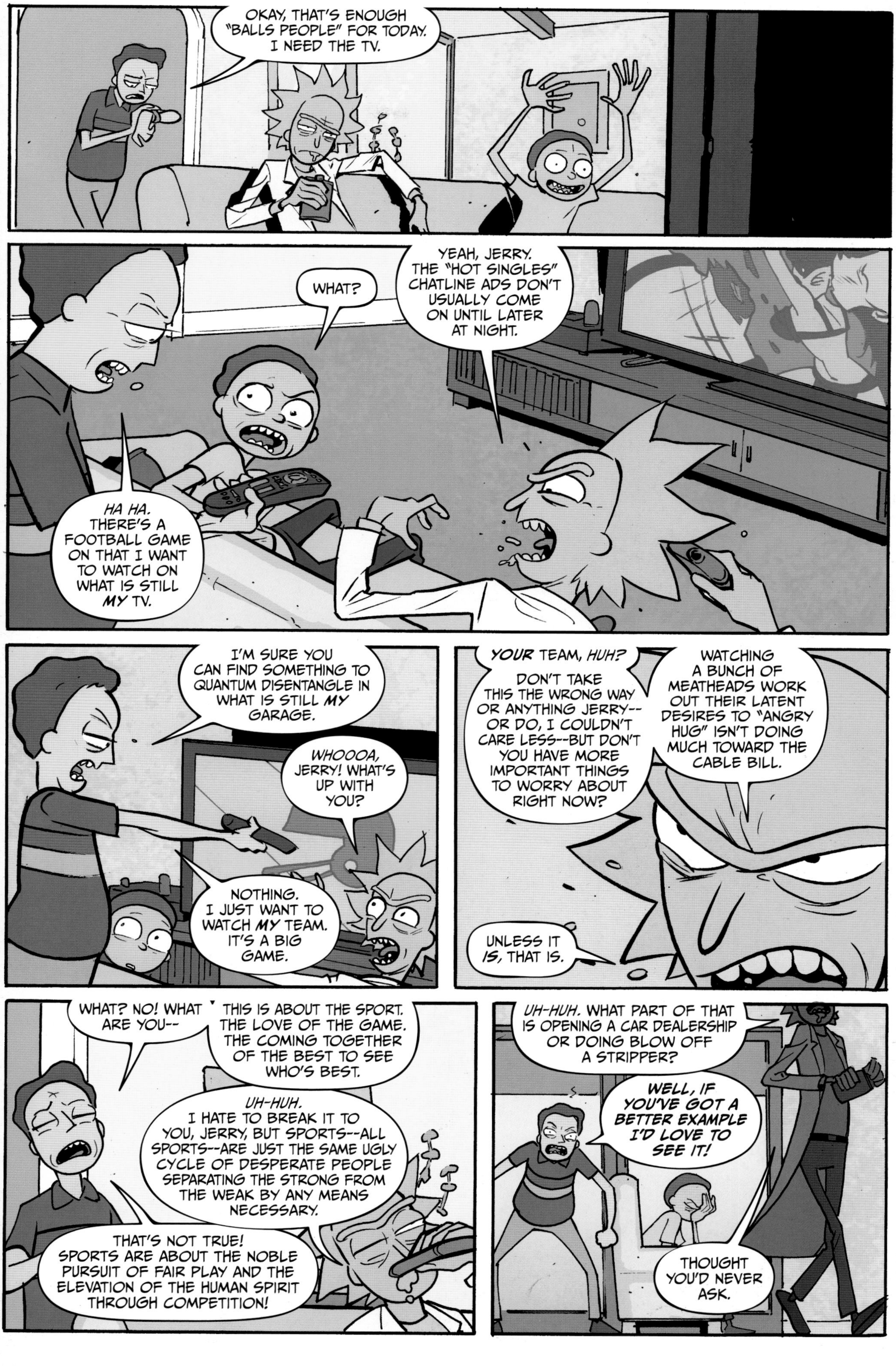
OKAY, THAT'S ENOUGH "BALLS PEOPLE" FOR TODAY. I NEED THE TV.
WHAT?
YEAH, JERRY. THE "HOT SINGLES" CHATLINE ADS DON'T USUALLY COME ON UNTIL LATER AT NIGHT.
HA HA. THERE'S A FOOTBALL GAME ON THAT I WANT TO WATCH ON WHAT IS STILL *MY* TV.
I'M SURE YOU CAN FIND SOMETHING TO QUANTUM DISENTANGLE IN WHAT IS STILL *MY* GARAGE.
WHOOOA, JERRY! WHAT'S UP WITH YOU?
NOTHING. I JUST WANT TO WATCH *MY* TEAM. IT'S A BIG GAME.
YOUR TEAM, *HUH?*
DON'T TAKE THIS THE WRONG WAY OR ANYTHING JERRY-- OR DO, I COULDN'T CARE LESS--BUT DON'T YOU HAVE MORE IMPORTANT THINGS TO WORRY ABOUT RIGHT NOW?
WATCHING A BUNCH OF MEATHEADS WORK OUT THEIR LATENT DESIRES TO "ANGRY HUG" ISN'T DOING MUCH TOWARD THE CABLE BILL.
UNLESS IT *IS,* THAT IS.
WHAT? NO! WHAT ARE YOU--
THIS IS ABOUT THE SPORT. THE LOVE OF THE GAME. THE COMING TOGETHER OF THE BEST TO SEE WHO'S BEST.
UH-HUH. I HATE TO BREAK IT TO YOU, JERRY, BUT SPORTS--ALL SPORTS--ARE JUST THE SAME UGLY CYCLE OF DESPERATE PEOPLE SEPARATING THE STRONG FROM THE WEAK BY ANY MEANS NECESSARY.
THAT'S NOT TRUE! SPORTS ARE ABOUT THE NOBLE PURSUIT OF FAIR PLAY AND THE ELEVATION OF THE HUMAN SPIRIT THROUGH COMPETITION!
UH-HUH. WHAT PART OF THAT IS OPENING A CAR DEALERSHIP OR DOING BLOW OFF A STRIPPER?
WELL, IF YOU'VE GOT A BETTER EXAMPLE I'D LOVE TO SEE IT!
THOUGHT YOU'D NEVER ASK.

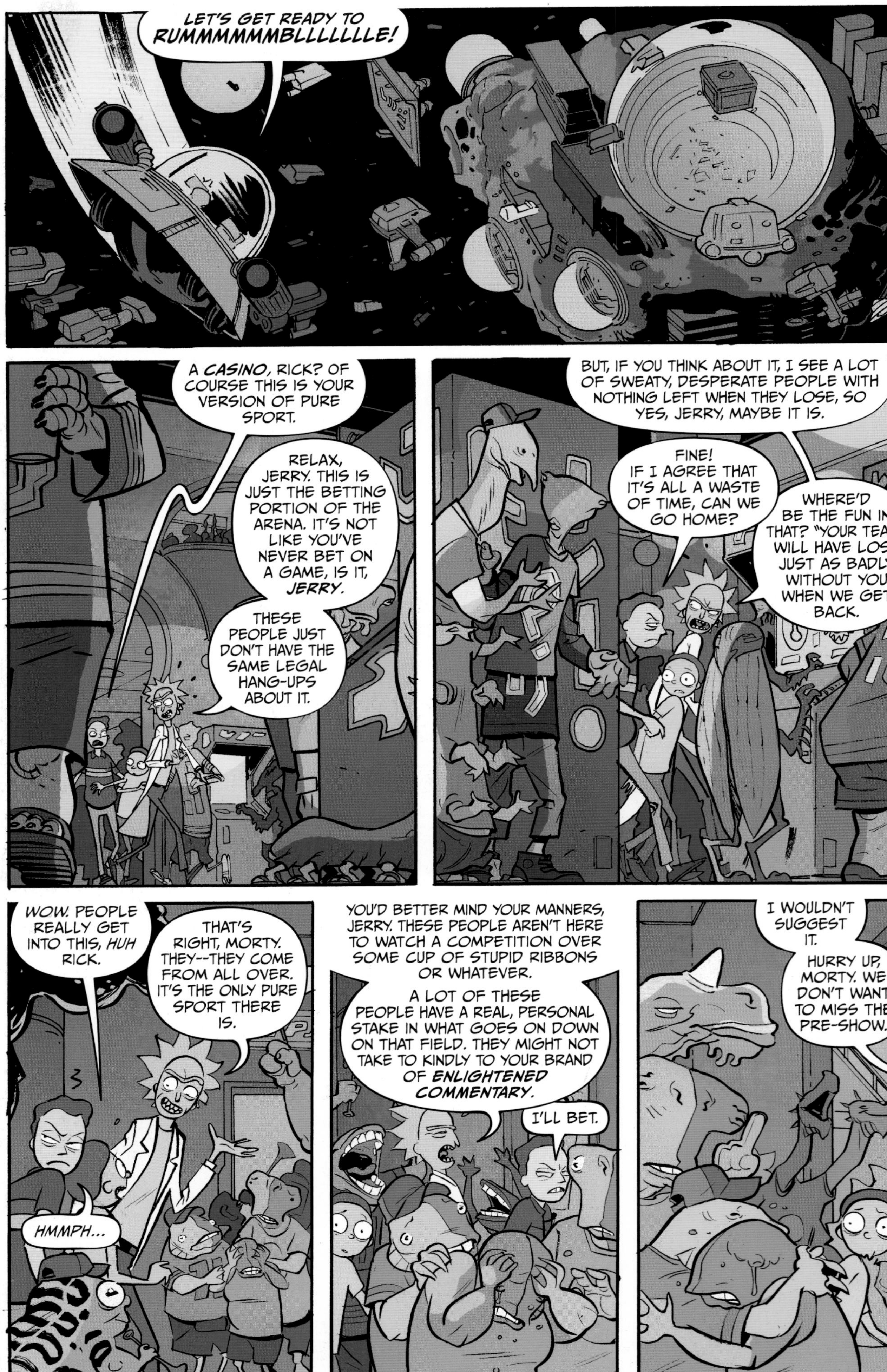
LET'S GET READY TO RUMMMMMMBLLLLLLLE!
A CASINO, RICK? OF COURSE THIS IS YOUR VERSION OF PURE SPORT.
RELAX, JERRY. THIS IS JUST THE BETTING PORTION OF THE ARENA. IT'S NOT LIKE YOU'VE NEVER BET ON A GAME, IS IT, JERRY.
THESE PEOPLE JUST DON'T HAVE THE SAME LEGAL HANG-UPS ABOUT IT.
BUT, IF YOU THINK ABOUT IT, I SEE A LOT OF SWEATY, DESPERATE PEOPLE WITH NOTHING LEFT WHEN THEY LOSE, SO YES, JERRY, MAYBE IT IS.
FINE! IF I AGREE THAT IT'S ALL A WASTE OF TIME, CAN WE GO HOME?
WHERE'D BE THE FUN IN THAT? "YOUR TEAM" WILL HAVE LOST JUST AS BADLY WITHOUT YOU WHEN WE GET BACK.
WOW. PEOPLE REALLY GET INTO THIS, HUH RICK.
THAT'S RIGHT, MORTY. THEY--THEY COME FROM ALL OVER. IT'S THE ONLY PURE SPORT THERE IS.
HMMPH...
YOU'D BETTER MIND YOUR MANNERS, JERRY. THESE PEOPLE AREN'T HERE TO WATCH A COMPETITION OVER SOME CUP OF STUPID RIBBONS OR WHATEVER.
A LOT OF THESE PEOPLE HAVE A REAL, PERSONAL STAKE IN WHAT GOES ON DOWN ON THAT FIELD. THEY MIGHT NOT TAKE TO KINDLY TO YOUR BRAND OF ENLIGHTENED COMMENTARY.
I'LL BET.
I WOULDN'T SUGGEST IT.
HURRY UP, MORTY. WE DON'T WANT TO MISS THE PRE-SHOW.

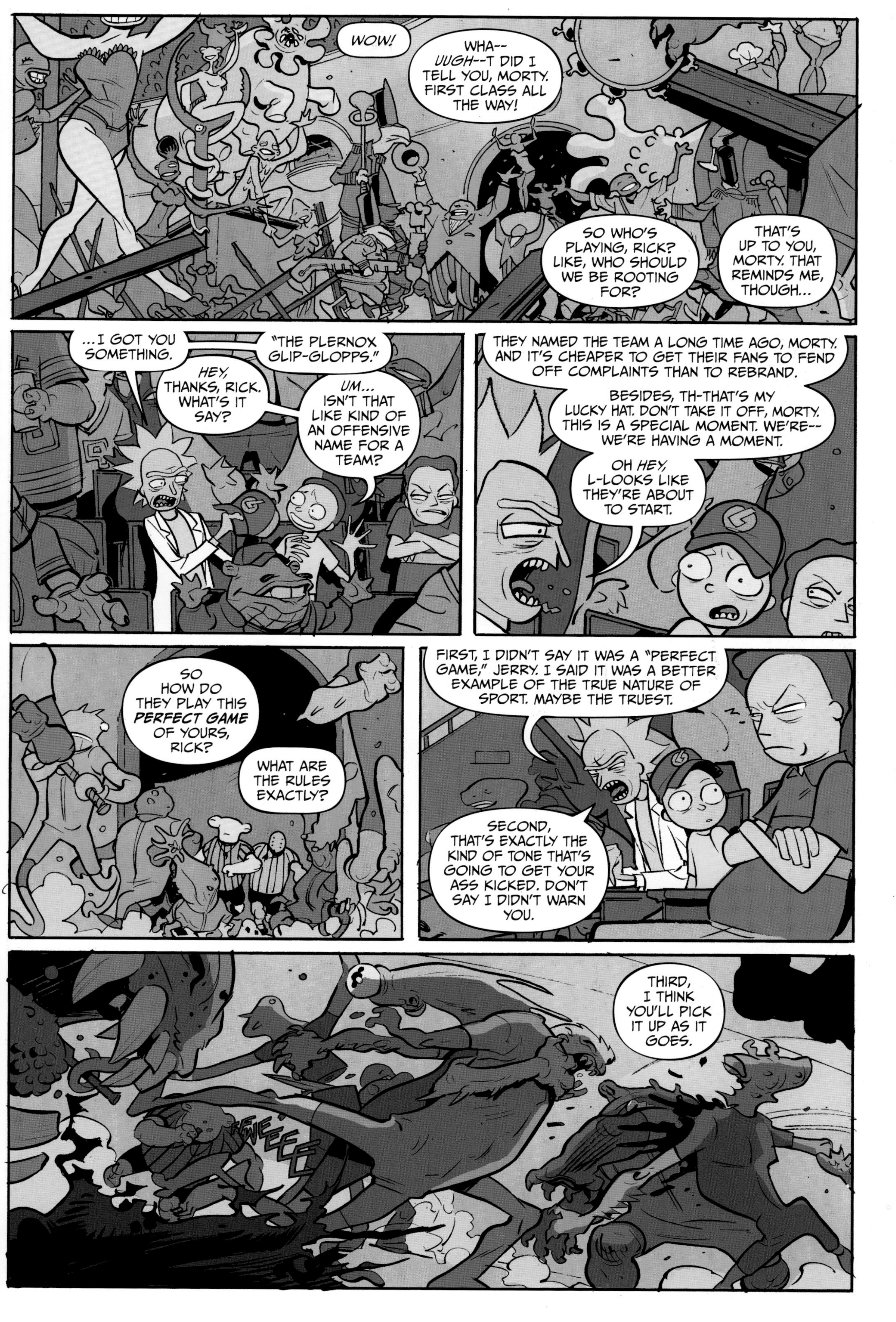
WOW!
WHA-- UUGH--T DID I TELL YOU, MORTY. FIRST CLASS ALL THE WAY!
SO WHO'S PLAYING, RICK? LIKE, WHO SHOULD WE BE ROOTING FOR?
THAT'S UP TO YOU, MORTY. THAT REMINDS ME, THOUGH...
...I GOT YOU SOMETHING.
HEY, THANKS, RICK. WHAT'S IT SAY?
"THE PLERNOX GLIP-GLOPPS."
UM... ISN'T THAT LIKE KIND OF AN OFFENSIVE NAME FOR A TEAM?
THEY NAMED THE TEAM A LONG TIME AGO, MORTY. AND IT'S CHEAPER TO GET THEIR FANS TO FEND OFF COMPLAINTS THAN TO REBRAND.
BESIDES, TH-THAT'S MY LUCKY HAT. DON'T TAKE IT OFF, MORTY. THIS IS A SPECIAL MOMENT. WE'RE-- WE'RE HAVING A MOMENT.
OH HEY, L-LOOKS LIKE THEY'RE ABOUT TO START.
SO HOW DO THEY PLAY THIS PERFECT GAME OF YOURS, RICK?
WHAT ARE THE RULES EXACTLY?
FIRST, I DIDN'T SAY IT WAS A "PERFECT GAME," JERRY. I SAID IT WAS A BETTER EXAMPLE OF THE TRUE NATURE OF SPORT. MAYBE THE TRUEST.
SECOND, THAT'S EXACTLY THE KIND OF TONE THAT'S GOING TO GET YOUR ASS KICKED. DON'T SAY I DIDN'T WARN YOU.
THIRD, I THINK YOU'LL PICK IT UP AS IT GOES.
FWEEEE

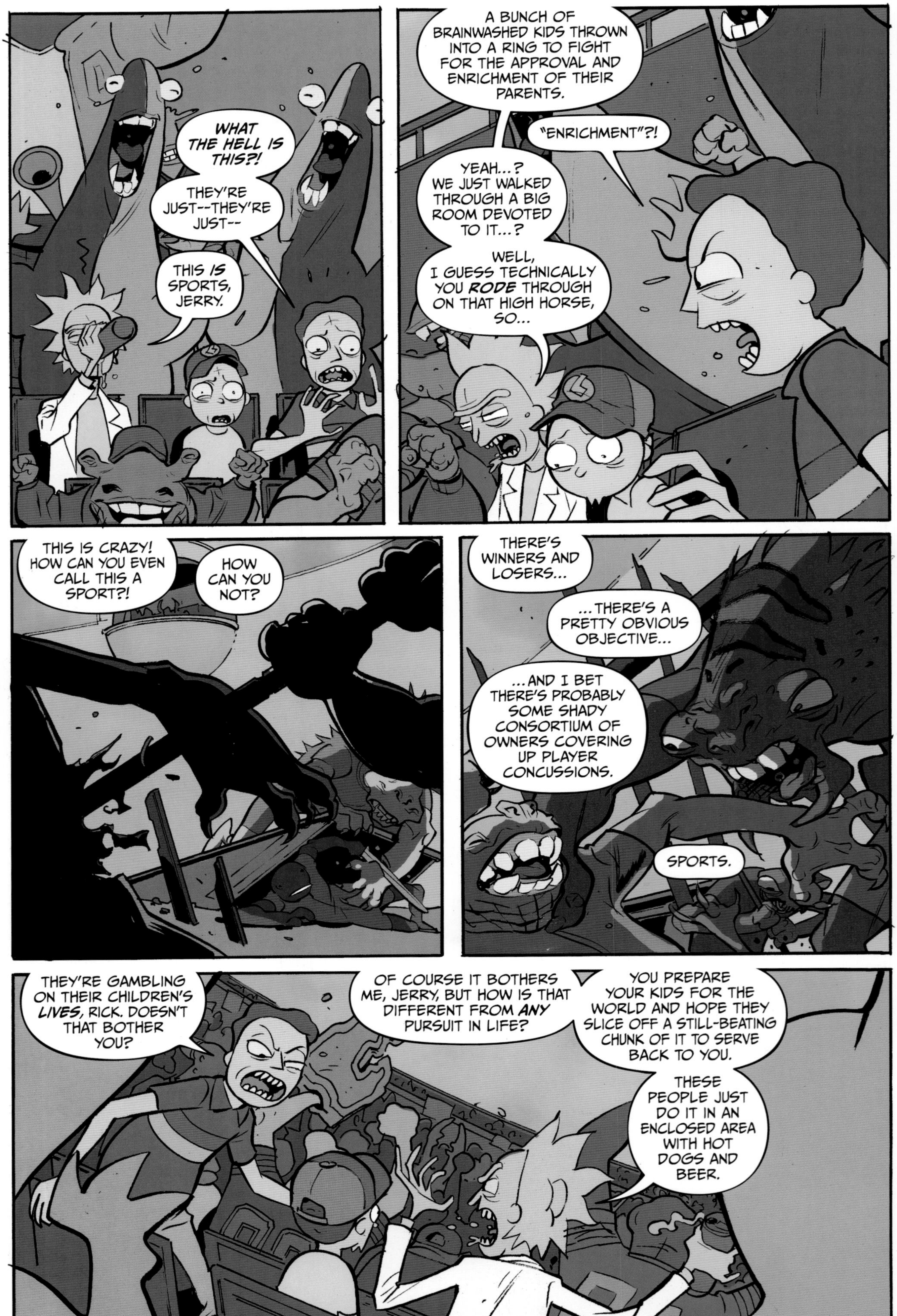
WHAT THE HELL IS THIS?!
THEY'RE JUST--THEY'RE JUST--
THIS IS SPORTS, JERRY.
A BUNCH OF BRAINWASHED KIDS THROWN INTO A RING TO FIGHT FOR THE APPROVAL AND ENRICHMENT OF THEIR PARENTS.
"ENRICHMENT"?!
YEAH...? WE JUST WALKED THROUGH A BIG ROOM DEVOTED TO IT...?
WELL, I GUESS TECHNICALLY YOU RODE THROUGH ON THAT HIGH HORSE, SO...
THIS IS CRAZY! HOW CAN YOU EVEN CALL THIS A SPORT?!
HOW CAN YOU NOT?
THERE'S WINNERS AND LOSERS...
...THERE'S A PRETTY OBVIOUS OBJECTIVE...
...AND I BET THERE'S PROBABLY SOME SHADY CONSORTIUM OF OWNERS COVERING UP PLAYER CONCUSSIONS.
SPORTS.
THEY'RE GAMBLING ON THEIR CHILDREN'S LIVES, RICK. DOESN'T THAT BOTHER YOU?
OF COURSE IT BOTHERS ME, JERRY, BUT HOW IS THAT DIFFERENT FROM ANY PURSUIT IN LIFE?
YOU PREPARE YOUR KIDS FOR THE WORLD AND HOPE THEY SLICE OFF A STILL-BEATING CHUNK OF IT TO SERVE BACK TO YOU.
THESE PEOPLE JUST DO IT IN AN ENCLOSED AREA WITH HOT DOGS AND BEER.

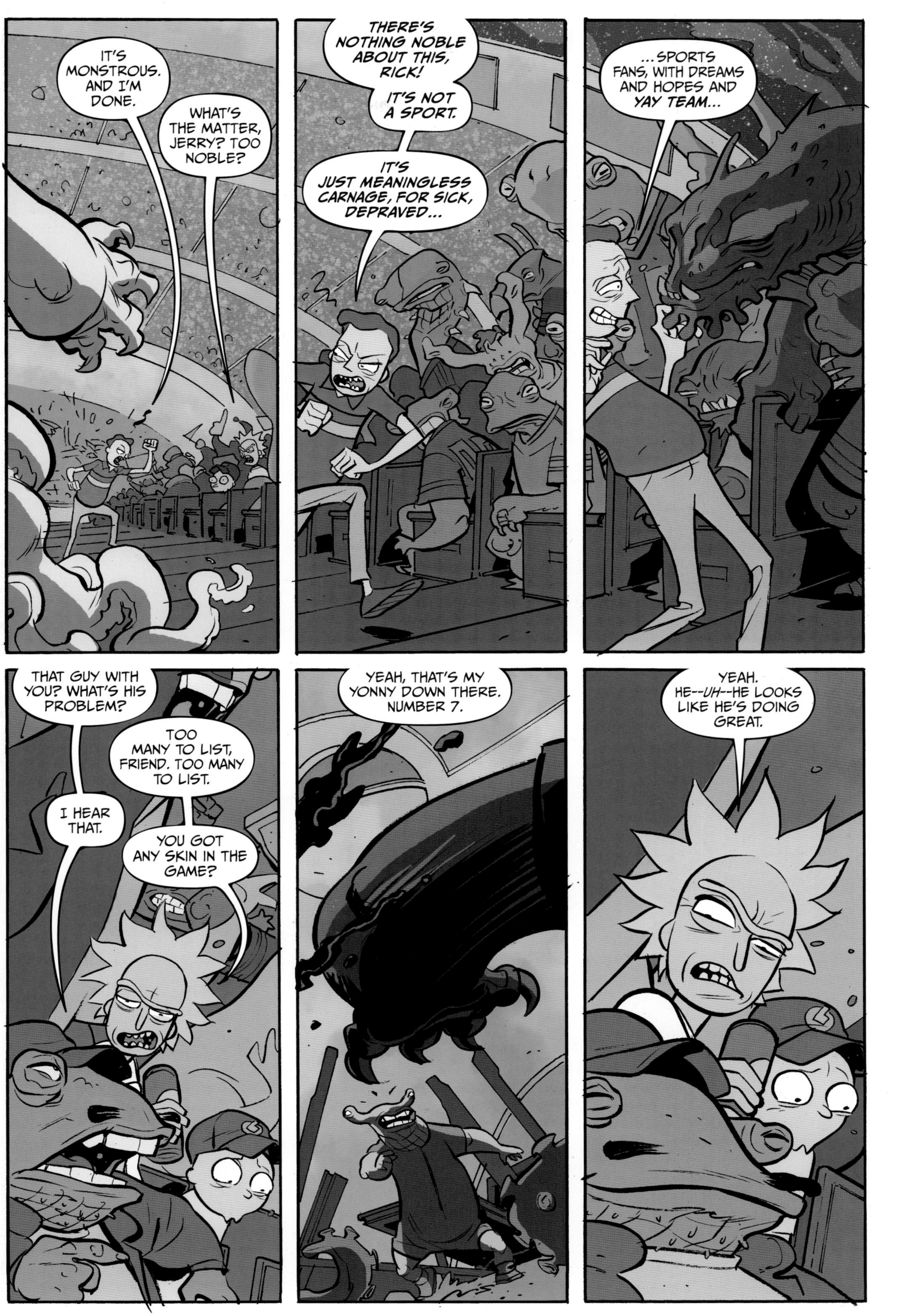
IT'S MONSTROUS. AND I'M DONE.
WHAT'S THE MATTER, JERRY? TOO NOBLE?
THERE'S NOTHING NOBLE ABOUT THIS, RICK!
IT'S NOT A SPORT.
IT'S JUST MEANINGLESS CARNAGE, FOR SICK, DEPRAVED...
...SPORTS FANS, WITH DREAMS AND HOPES AND YAY TEAM...
THAT GUY WITH YOU? WHAT'S HIS PROBLEM?
TOO MANY TO LIST, FRIEND. TOO MANY TO LIST.
I HEAR THAT.
YOU GOT ANY SKIN IN THE GAME?
YEAH, THAT'S MY YONNY DOWN THERE. NUMBER 7.
YEAH. HE--UH--HE LOOKS LIKE HE'S DOING GREAT.

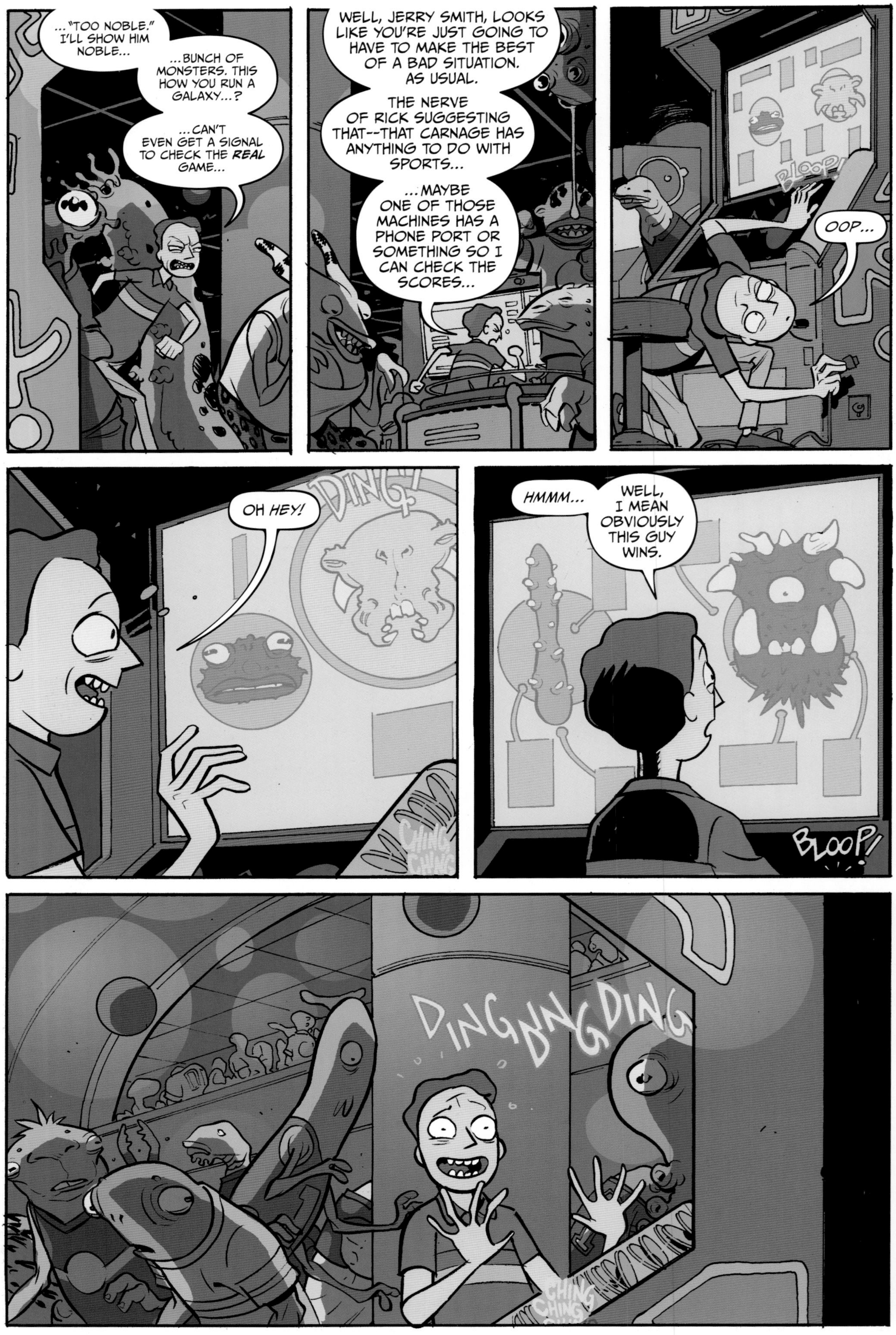

..."TOO NOBLE." I'LL SHOW HIM NOBLE...
...BUNCH OF MONSTERS. THIS HOW YOU RUN A GALAXY...?
...CAN'T EVEN GET A SIGNAL TO CHECK THE REAL GAME...
WELL, JERRY SMITH, LOOKS LIKE YOU'RE JUST GOING TO HAVE TO MAKE THE BEST OF A BAD SITUATION. AS USUAL.
THE NERVE OF RICK SUGGESTING THAT--THAT CARNAGE HAS ANYTHING TO DO WITH SPORTS...
...MAYBE ONE OF THOSE MACHINES HAS A PHONE PORT OR SOMETHING SO I CAN CHECK THE SCORES...
BLOOP!
OOP...
DING!
OH HEY!
CHING CHING
HMMM...
WELL, I MEAN OBVIOUSLY THIS GUY WINS.
BLOOP!
DING DING DING
CHING CHING

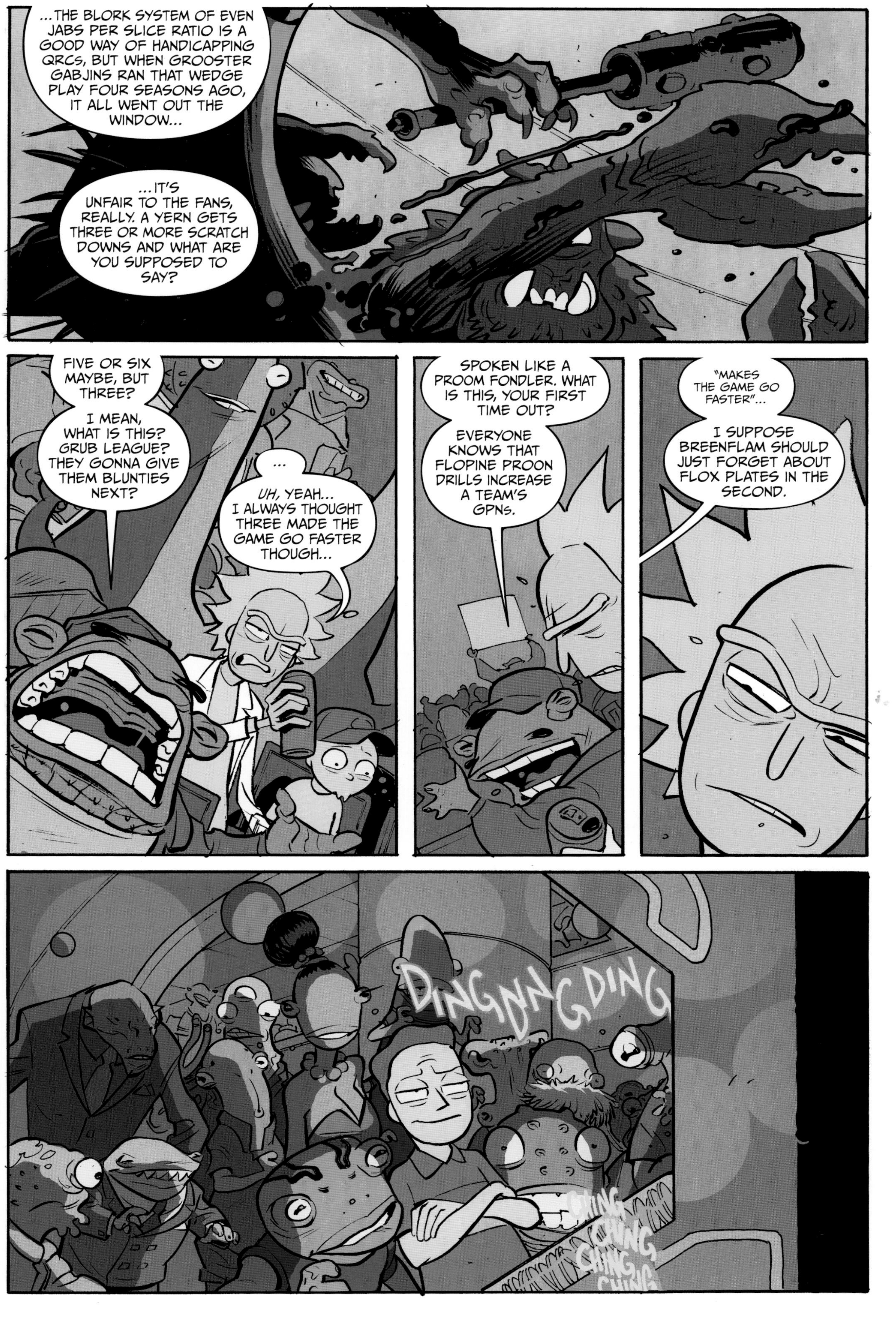
...THE BLORK SYSTEM OF EVEN JABS PER SLICE RATIO IS A GOOD WAY OF HANDICAPPING QRCS, BUT WHEN GROOSTER GABJINS RAN THAT WEDGE PLAY FOUR SEASONS AGO, IT ALL WENT OUT THE WINDOW...
...IT'S UNFAIR TO THE FANS, REALLY. A YERN GETS THREE OR MORE SCRATCH DOWNS AND WHAT ARE YOU SUPPOSED TO SAY?
FIVE OR SIX MAYBE, BUT THREE?
I MEAN, WHAT IS THIS? GRUB LEAGUE? THEY GONNA GIVE THEM BLUNTIES NEXT?
...
UH, YEAH... I ALWAYS THOUGHT THREE MADE THE GAME GO FASTER THOUGH...
SPOKEN LIKE A PROOM FONDLER. WHAT IS THIS, YOUR FIRST TIME OUT?
EVERYONE KNOWS THAT FLOPINE PROON DRILLS INCREASE A TEAM'S GPNS.
"MAKES THE GAME GO FASTER"...
I SUPPOSE BREENFLAM SHOULD JUST FORGET ABOUT FLOX PLATES IN THE SECOND.
DINGDINGDING
CHING CHING CHING CHING

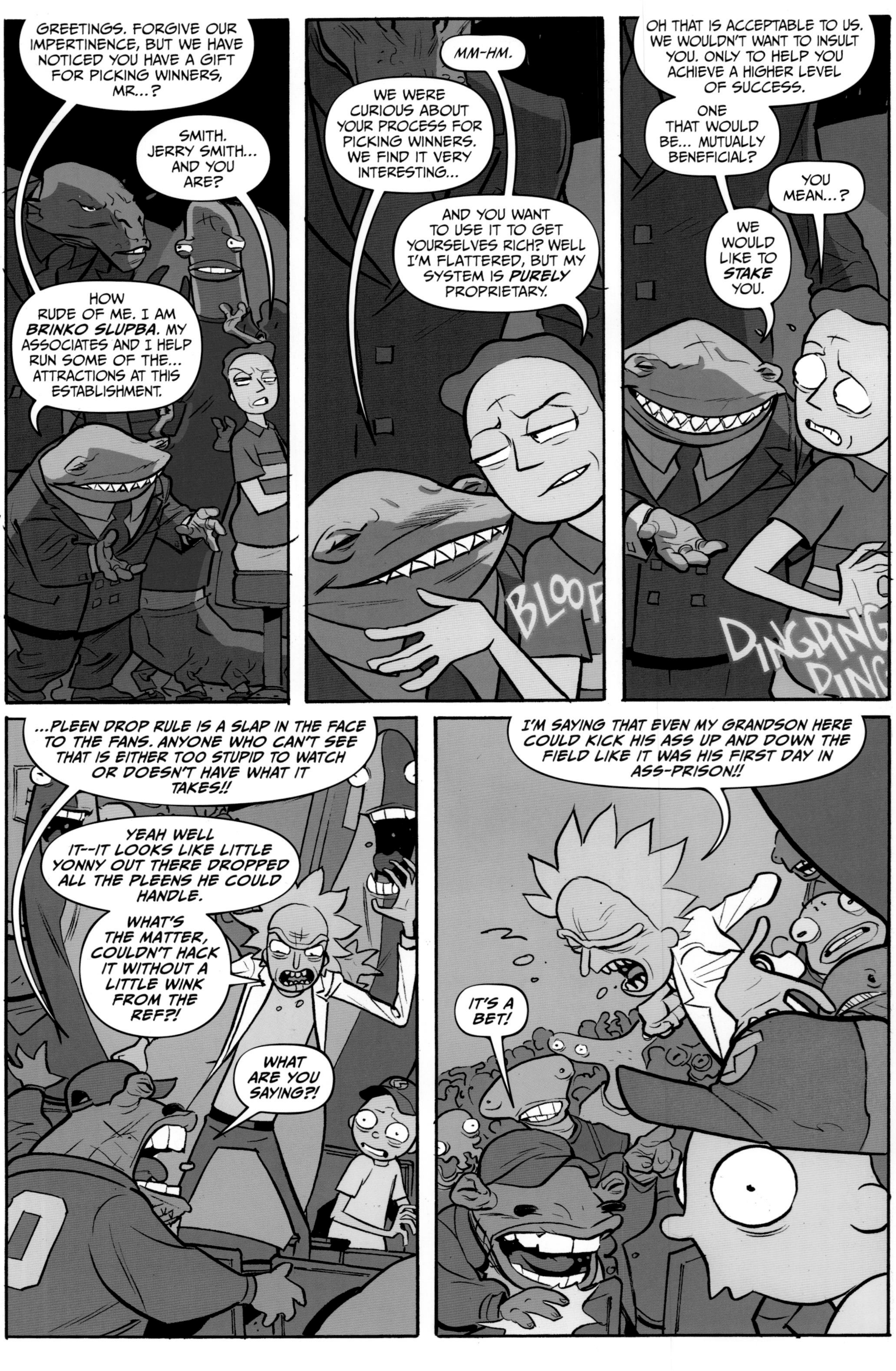
GREETINGS. FORGIVE OUR IMPERTINENCE, BUT WE HAVE NOTICED YOU HAVE A GIFT FOR PICKING WINNERS, MR...?
SMITH. JERRY SMITH... AND YOU ARE?
HOW RUDE OF ME. I AM BRINKO SLUPBA. MY ASSOCIATES AND I HELP RUN SOME OF THE... ATTRACTIONS AT THIS ESTABLISHMENT.
MM-HM.
WE WERE CURIOUS ABOUT YOUR PROCESS FOR PICKING WINNERS. WE FIND IT VERY INTERESTING...
AND YOU WANT TO USE IT TO GET YOURSELVES RICH? WELL I'M FLATTERED, BUT MY SYSTEM IS PURELY PROPRIETARY.
BLOOP
OH THAT IS ACCEPTABLE TO US. WE WOULDN'T WANT TO INSULT YOU. ONLY TO HELP YOU ACHIEVE A HIGHER LEVEL OF SUCCESS.
ONE THAT WOULD BE... MUTUALLY BENEFICIAL?
YOU MEAN...?
WE WOULD LIKE TO STAKE YOU.
DINGRNG DING
...PLEEN DROP RULE IS A SLAP IN THE FACE TO THE FANS. ANYONE WHO CAN'T SEE THAT IS EITHER TOO STUPID TO WATCH OR DOESN'T HAVE WHAT IT TAKES!!
YEAH WELL IT--IT LOOKS LIKE LITTLE YONNY OUT THERE DROPPED ALL THE PLEENS HE COULD HANDLE.
WHAT'S THE MATTER, COULDN'T HACK IT WITHOUT A LITTLE WINK FROM THE REF?!
WHAT ARE YOU SAYING?!
I'M SAYING THAT EVEN MY GRANDSON HERE COULD KICK HIS ASS UP AND DOWN THE FIELD LIKE IT WAS HIS FIRST DAY IN ASS-PRISON!!
IT'S A BET!

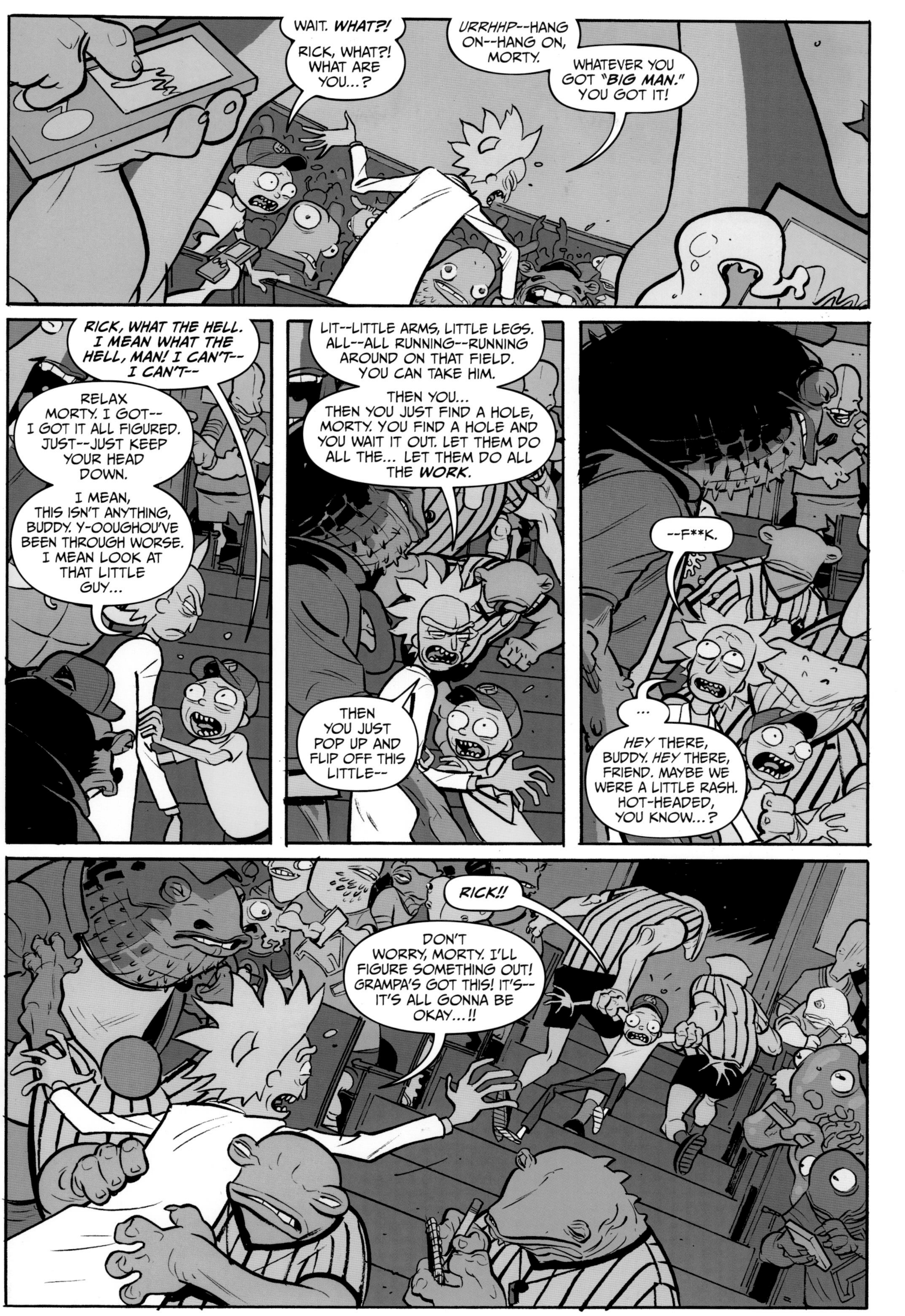
WAIT. WHAT?!
RICK, WHAT?! WHAT ARE YOU...?
URRHHP--HANG ON--HANG ON, MORTY.
WHATEVER YOU GOT "BIG MAN." YOU GOT IT!
RICK, WHAT THE HELL. I MEAN WHAT THE HELL, MAN! I CAN'T-- I CAN'T--
RELAX MORTY. I GOT-- I GOT IT ALL FIGURED. JUST--JUST KEEP YOUR HEAD DOWN.
I MEAN, THIS ISN'T ANYTHING, BUDDY. Y-OOUGHOU'VE BEEN THROUGH WORSE. I MEAN LOOK AT THAT LITTLE GUY...
LIT--LITTLE ARMS, LITTLE LEGS. ALL--ALL RUNNING--RUNNING AROUND ON THAT FIELD. YOU CAN TAKE HIM.
THEN YOU... THEN YOU JUST FIND A HOLE, MORTY. YOU FIND A HOLE AND YOU WAIT IT OUT. LET THEM DO ALL THE... LET THEM DO ALL THE WORK.
THEN YOU JUST POP UP AND FLIP OFF THIS LITTLE--
--F**K.
...
HEY THERE, BUDDY. HEY THERE, FRIEND. MAYBE WE WERE A LITTLE RASH. HOT-HEADED, YOU KNOW...?
RICK!!
DON'T WORRY, MORTY. I'LL FIGURE SOMETHING OUT! GRAMPA'S GOT THIS! IT'S-- IT'S ALL GONNA BE OKAY...!!

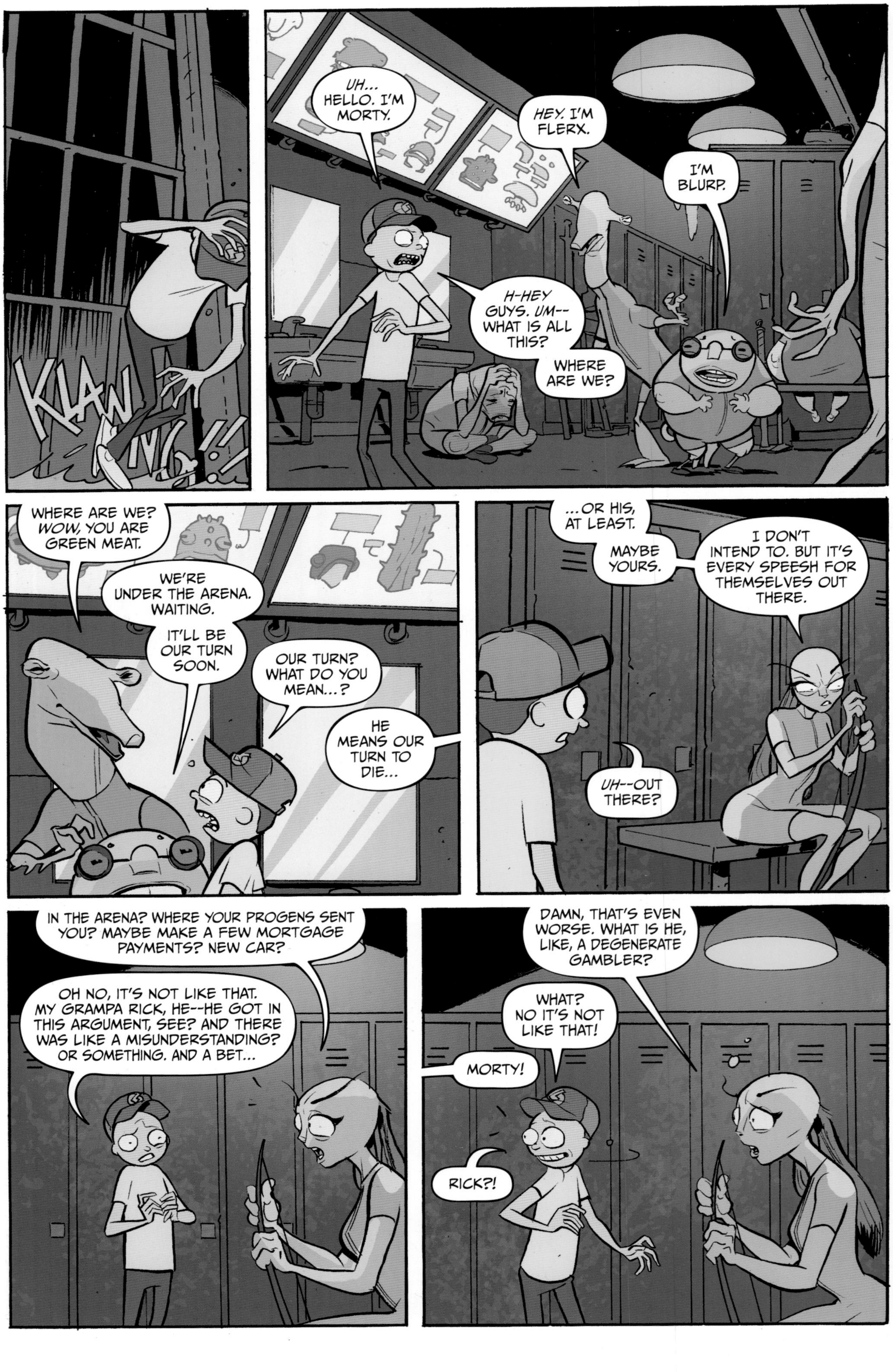
KLANNNG!!
UH... HELLO. I'M MORTY.
HEY. I'M FLERX.
I'M BLURP.
H-HEY GUYS. UM-- WHAT IS ALL THIS?
WHERE ARE WE?
WHERE ARE WE? WOW, YOU ARE GREEN MEAT.
WE'RE UNDER THE ARENA. WAITING.
IT'LL BE OUR TURN SOON.
OUR TURN? WHAT DO YOU MEAN...?
HE MEANS OUR TURN TO DIE...
...OR HIS, AT LEAST.
MAYBE YOURS.
I DON'T INTEND TO. BUT IT'S EVERY SPEESH FOR THEMSELVES OUT THERE.
UH--OUT THERE?
IN THE ARENA? WHERE YOUR PROGENS SENT YOU? MAYBE MAKE A FEW MORTGAGE PAYMENTS? NEW CAR?
OH NO, IT'S NOT LIKE THAT. MY GRAMPA RICK, HE--HE GOT IN THIS ARGUMENT, SEE? AND THERE WAS LIKE A MISUNDERSTANDING? OR SOMETHING. AND A BET...
DAMN, THAT'S EVEN WORSE. WHAT IS HE, LIKE, A DEGENERATE GAMBLER?
WHAT? NO IT'S NOT LIKE THAT!
MORTY!
RICK?!

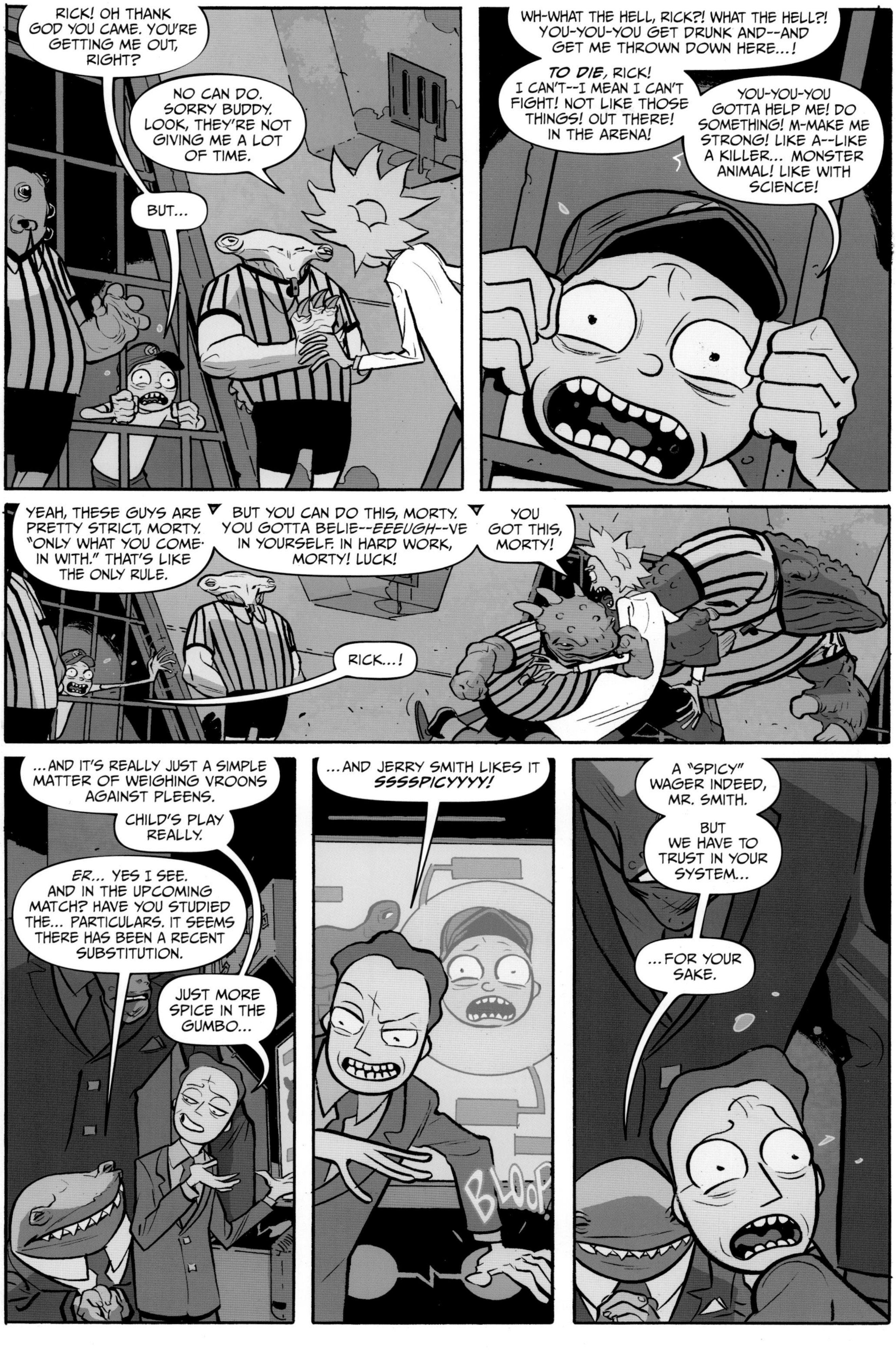
RICK! OH THANK GOD YOU CAME. YOU'RE GETTING ME OUT, RIGHT?
NO CAN DO. SORRY BUDDY. LOOK, THEY'RE NOT GIVING ME A LOT OF TIME.
BUT...
WH-WHAT THE HELL, RICK?! WHAT THE HELL?! YOU-YOU-YOU GET DRUNK AND--AND GET ME THROWN DOWN HERE...!
TO DIE, RICK! I CAN'T--I MEAN I CAN'T FIGHT! NOT LIKE THOSE THINGS! OUT THERE! IN THE ARENA!
YOU-YOU-YOU GOTTA HELP ME! DO SOMETHING! M-MAKE ME STRONG! LIKE A--LIKE A KILLER... MONSTER ANIMAL! LIKE WITH SCIENCE!
YEAH, THESE GUYS ARE PRETTY STRICT, MORTY. "ONLY WHAT YOU COME-IN WITH." THAT'S LIKE THE ONLY RULE.
BUT YOU CAN DO THIS, MORTY. YOU GOTTA BELIE--EEEUGH--VE IN YOURSELF. IN HARD WORK, MORTY! LUCK!
YOU GOT THIS, MORTY!
RICK...!
...AND IT'S REALLY JUST A SIMPLE MATTER OF WEIGHING VROONS AGAINST PLEENS.
CHILD'S PLAY REALLY.
ER... YES I SEE. AND IN THE UPCOMING MATCH? HAVE YOU STUDIED THE... PARTICULARS. IT SEEMS THERE HAS BEEN A RECENT SUBSTITUTION.
JUST MORE SPICE IN THE GUMBO...
...AND JERRY SMITH LIKES IT SSSSPICYYYY!
BLOOP
A "SPICY" WAGER INDEED, MR. SMITH.
BUT WE HAVE TO TRUST IN YOUR SYSTEM...
...FOR YOUR SAKE.

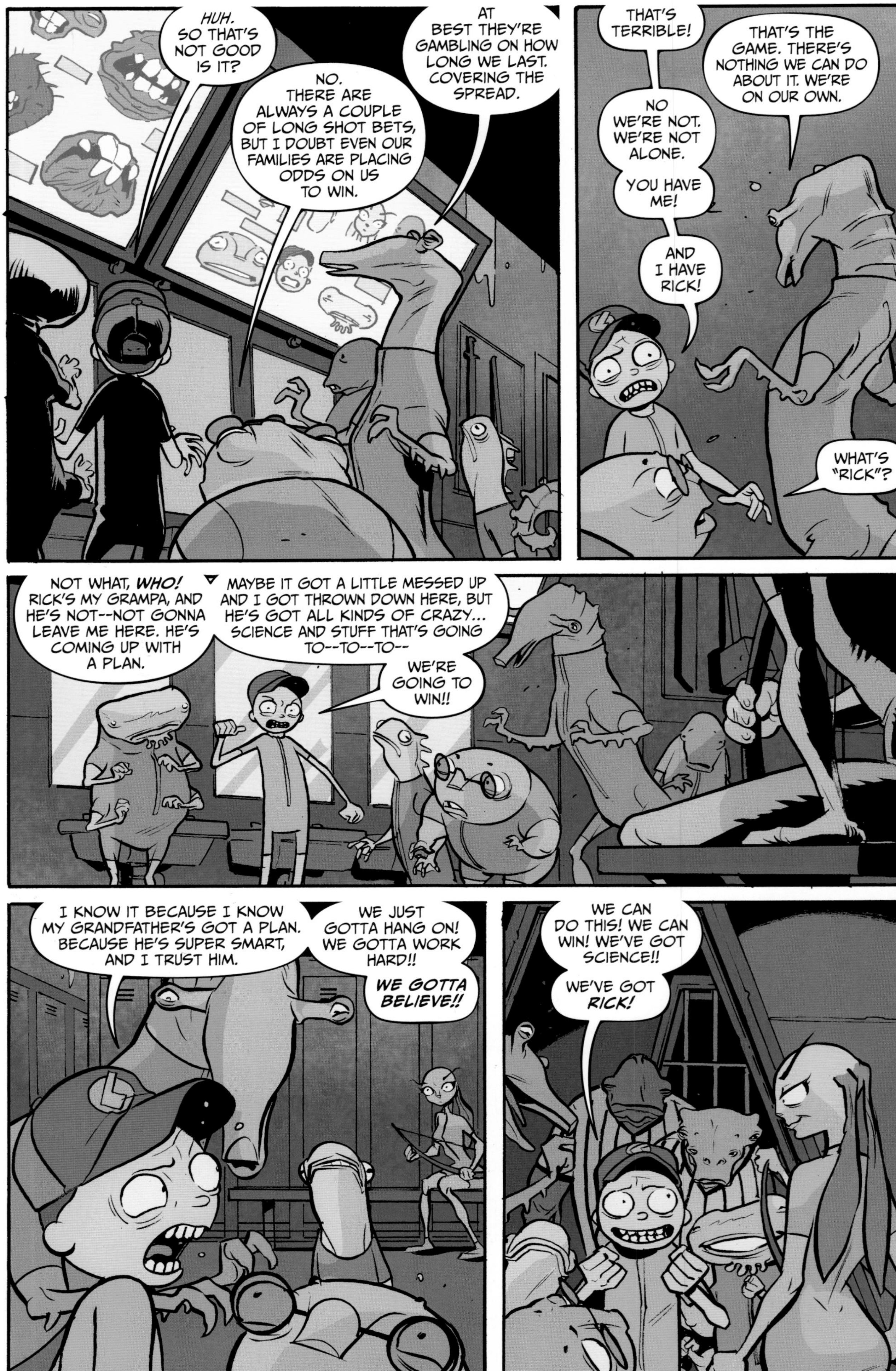
HUH. SO THAT'S NOT GOOD IS IT?
NO. THERE ARE ALWAYS A COUPLE OF LONG SHOT BETS, BUT I DOUBT EVEN OUR FAMILIES ARE PLACING ODDS ON US TO WIN.
AT BEST THEY'RE GAMBLING ON HOW LONG WE LAST. COVERING THE SPREAD.
THAT'S TERRIBLE!
THAT'S THE GAME. THERE'S NOTHING WE CAN DO ABOUT IT. WE'RE ON OUR OWN.
NO WE'RE NOT. WE'RE NOT ALONE.
YOU HAVE ME!
AND I HAVE RICK!
WHAT'S "RICK"?
NOT WHAT, WHO! RICK'S MY GRAMPA, AND HE'S NOT--NOT GONNA LEAVE ME HERE. HE'S COMING UP WITH A PLAN.
MAYBE IT GOT A LITTLE MESSED UP AND I GOT THROWN DOWN HERE, BUT HE'S GOT ALL KINDS OF CRAZY... SCIENCE AND STUFF THAT'S GOING TO--TO--TO--
WE'RE GOING TO WIN!!
I KNOW IT BECAUSE I KNOW MY GRANDFATHER'S GOT A PLAN. BECAUSE HE'S SUPER SMART, AND I TRUST HIM.
WE JUST GOTTA HANG ON! WE GOTTA WORK HARD!!
WE GOTTA BELIEVE!!
WE CAN DO THIS! WE CAN WIN! WE'VE GOT SCIENCE!!
WE'VE GOT RICK!

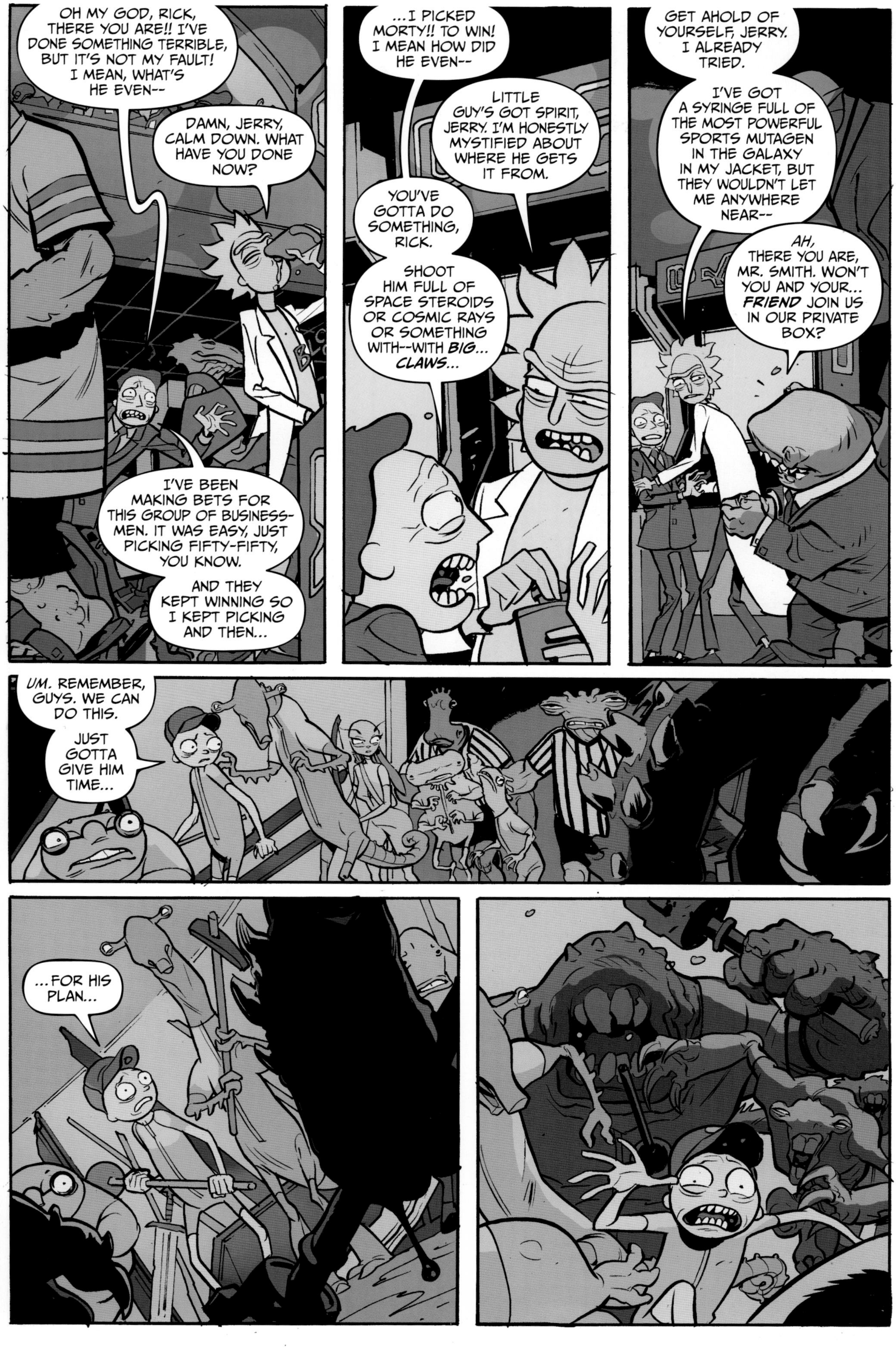
OH MY GOD, RICK, THERE YOU ARE!! I'VE DONE SOMETHING TERRIBLE, BUT IT'S NOT MY FAULT! I MEAN, WHAT'S HE EVEN--
DAMN, JERRY, CALM DOWN. WHAT HAVE YOU DONE NOW?
I'VE BEEN MAKING BETS FOR THIS GROUP OF BUSINESS-MEN. IT WAS EASY, JUST PICKING FIFTY-FIFTY, YOU KNOW.
AND THEY KEPT WINNING SO I KEPT PICKING AND THEN...
...I PICKED MORTY!! TO WIN! I MEAN HOW DID HE EVEN--
LITTLE GUY'S GOT SPIRIT, JERRY. I'M HONESTLY MYSTIFIED ABOUT WHERE HE GETS IT FROM.
YOU'VE GOTTA DO SOMETHING, RICK.
SHOOT HIM FULL OF SPACE STEROIDS OR COSMIC RAYS OR SOMETHING WITH--WITH *BIG... CLAWS...*
GET AHOLD OF YOURSELF, JERRY. I ALREADY TRIED.
I'VE GOT A SYRINGE FULL OF THE MOST POWERFUL SPORTS MUTAGEN IN THE GALAXY IN MY JACKET, BUT THEY WOULDN'T LET ME ANYWHERE NEAR--
AH, THERE YOU ARE, MR. SMITH. WON'T YOU AND YOUR... ***FRIEND*** JOIN US IN OUR PRIVATE BOX?
UM. REMEMBER, GUYS. WE CAN DO THIS.
JUST GOTTA GIVE HIM TIME...
...FOR HIS PLAN...

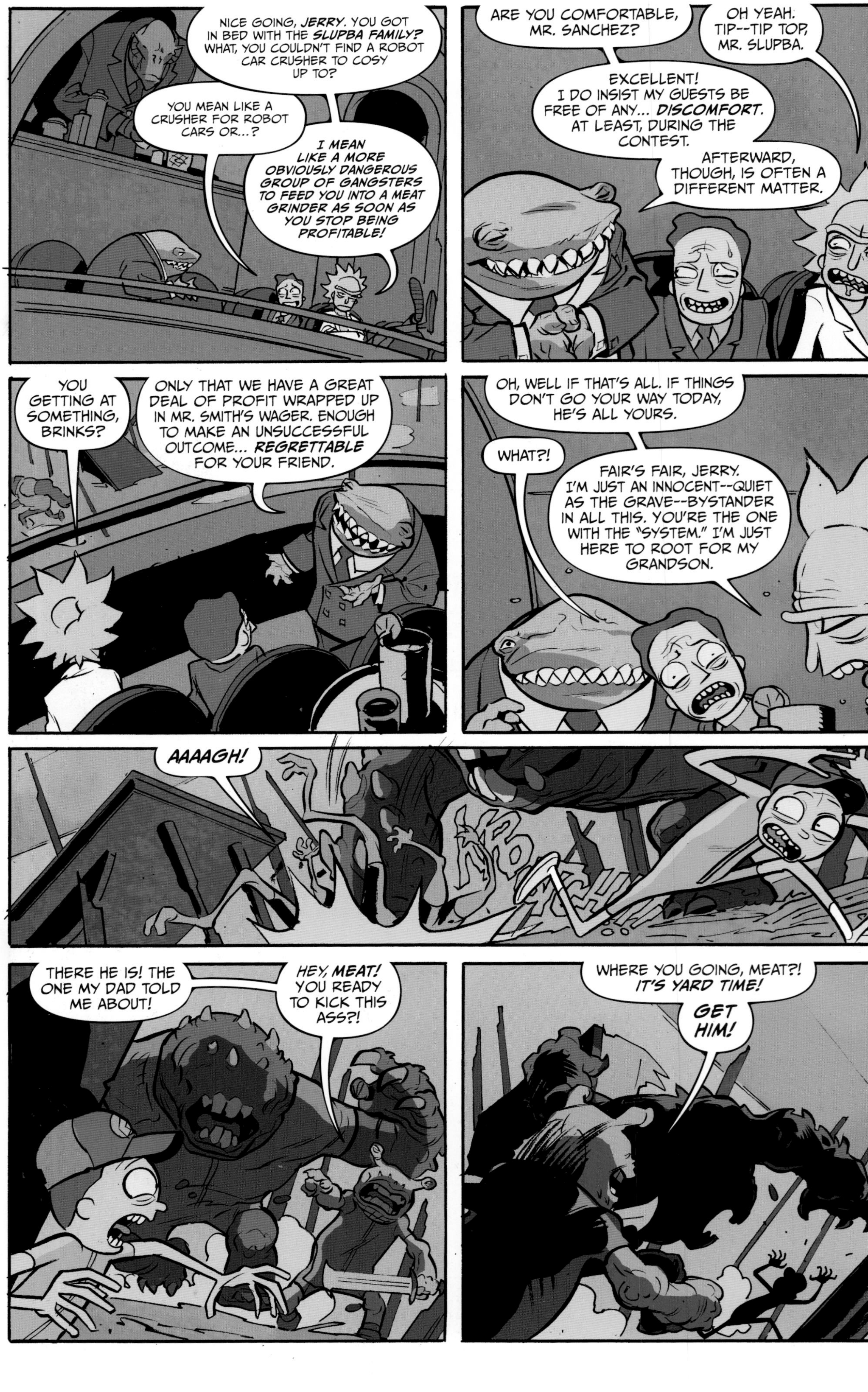
NICE GOING, JERRY. YOU GOT IN BED WITH THE SLUPBA FAMILY? WHAT, YOU COULDN'T FIND A ROBOT CAR CRUSHER TO COSY UP TO?
YOU MEAN LIKE A CRUSHER FOR ROBOT CARS OR...?
I MEAN LIKE A MORE OBVIOUSLY DANGEROUS GROUP OF GANGSTERS TO FEED YOU INTO A MEAT GRINDER AS SOON AS YOU STOP BEING PROFITABLE!
ARE YOU COMFORTABLE, MR. SANCHEZ?
OH YEAH. TIP--TIP TOP, MR. SLUPBA.
EXCELLENT! I DO INSIST MY GUESTS BE FREE OF ANY... DISCOMFORT. AT LEAST, DURING THE CONTEST.
AFTERWARD, THOUGH, IS OFTEN A DIFFERENT MATTER.
YOU GETTING AT SOMETHING, BRINKS?
ONLY THAT WE HAVE A GREAT DEAL OF PROFIT WRAPPED UP IN MR. SMITH'S WAGER. ENOUGH TO MAKE AN UNSUCCESSFUL OUTCOME... REGRETTABLE FOR YOUR FRIEND.
OH, WELL IF THAT'S ALL. IF THINGS DON'T GO YOUR WAY TODAY, HE'S ALL YOURS.
WHAT?!
FAIR'S FAIR, JERRY. I'M JUST AN INNOCENT--QUIET AS THE GRAVE--BYSTANDER IN ALL THIS. YOU'RE THE ONE WITH THE "SYSTEM." I'M JUST HERE TO ROOT FOR MY GRANDSON.
AAAAGH!
THERE HE IS! THE ONE MY DAD TOLD ME ABOUT!
HEY, MEAT! YOU READY TO KICK THIS ASS?!
WHERE YOU GOING, MEAT?! IT'S YARD TIME!
GET HIM!

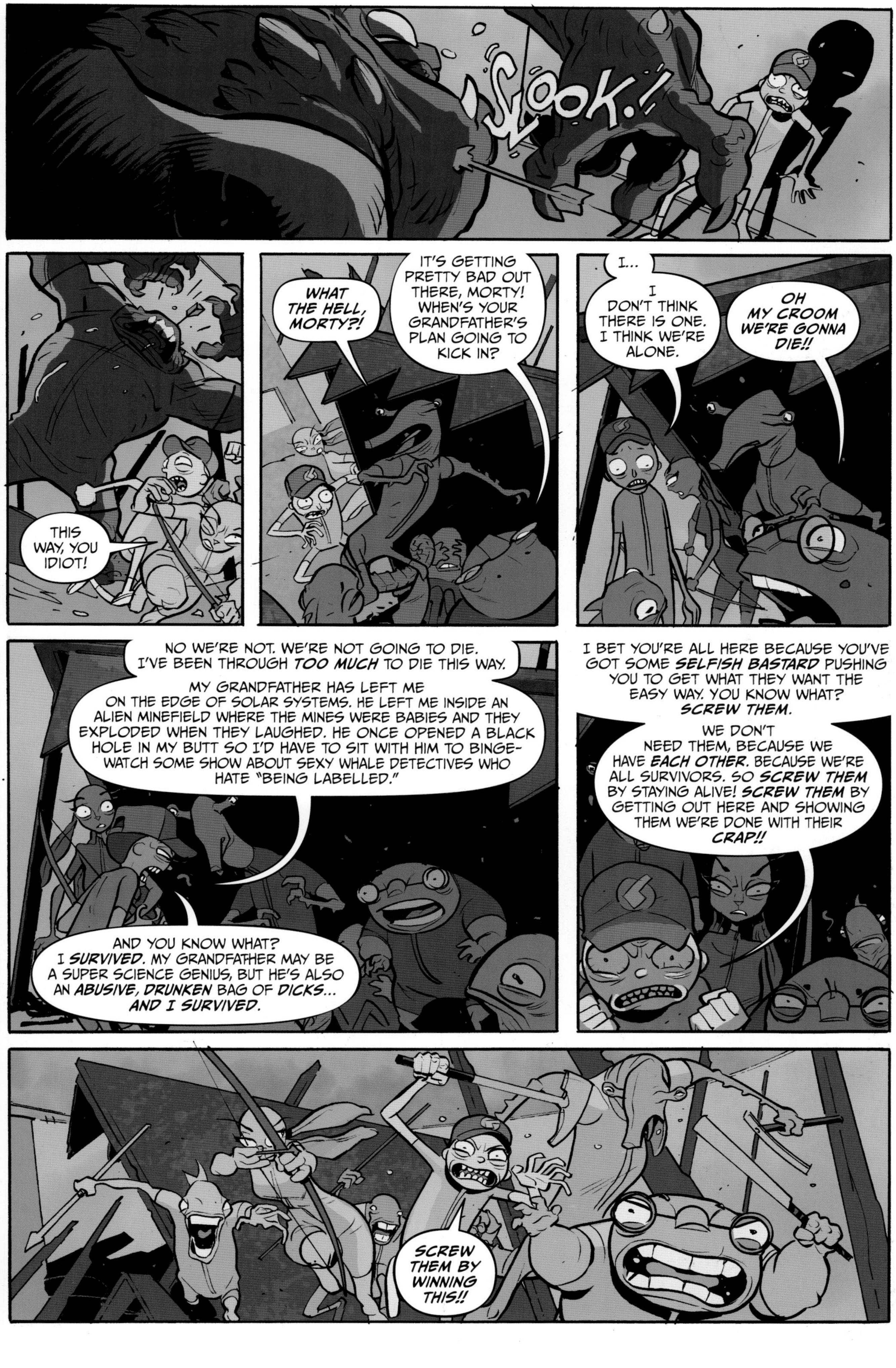
SLOOK!!
THIS WAY, YOU IDIOT!
WHAT THE HELL, MORTY?!
IT'S GETTING PRETTY BAD OUT THERE, MORTY! WHEN'S YOUR GRANDFATHER'S PLAN GOING TO KICK IN?
I...
I DON'T THINK THERE IS ONE. I THINK WE'RE ALONE.
OH MY CROOM WE'RE GONNA DIE!!
NO WE'RE NOT. WE'RE NOT GOING TO DIE. I'VE BEEN THROUGH TOO MUCH TO DIE THIS WAY.
MY GRANDFATHER HAS LEFT ME ON THE EDGE OF SOLAR SYSTEMS. HE LEFT ME INSIDE AN ALIEN MINEFIELD WHERE THE MINES WERE BABIES AND THEY EXPLODED WHEN THEY LAUGHED. HE ONCE OPENED A BLACK HOLE IN MY BUTT SO I'D HAVE TO SIT WITH HIM TO BINGE-WATCH SOME SHOW ABOUT SEXY WHALE DETECTIVES WHO HATE "BEING LABELLED."
AND YOU KNOW WHAT? I SURVIVED. MY GRANDFATHER MAY BE A SUPER SCIENCE GENIUS, BUT HE'S ALSO AN ABUSIVE, DRUNKEN BAG OF DICKS... AND I SURVIVED.
I BET YOU'RE ALL HERE BECAUSE YOU'VE GOT SOME SELFISH BASTARD PUSHING YOU TO GET WHAT THEY WANT THE EASY WAY. YOU KNOW WHAT? SCREW THEM.
WE DON'T NEED THEM, BECAUSE WE HAVE EACH OTHER. BECAUSE WE'RE ALL SURVIVORS. SO SCREW THEM BY STAYING ALIVE! SCREW THEM BY GETTING OUT HERE AND SHOWING THEM WE'RE DONE WITH THEIR CRAP!!
SCREW THEM BY WINNING THIS!!

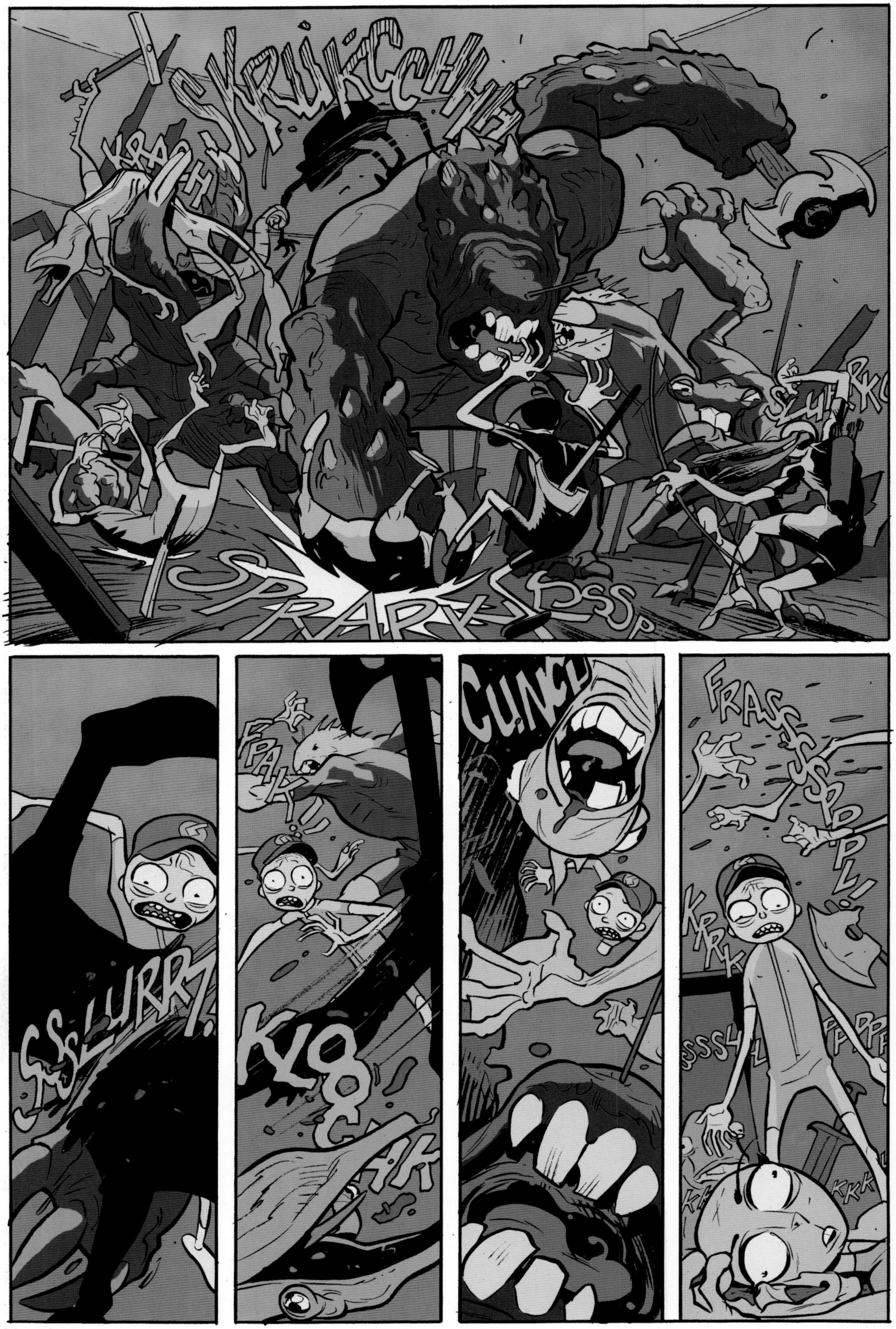
SKRUKCCHHH
SPRAK
SSSP
SSSLURRT...
FRAK!!
KLOCK
FRASSSSPPL!
KRRK

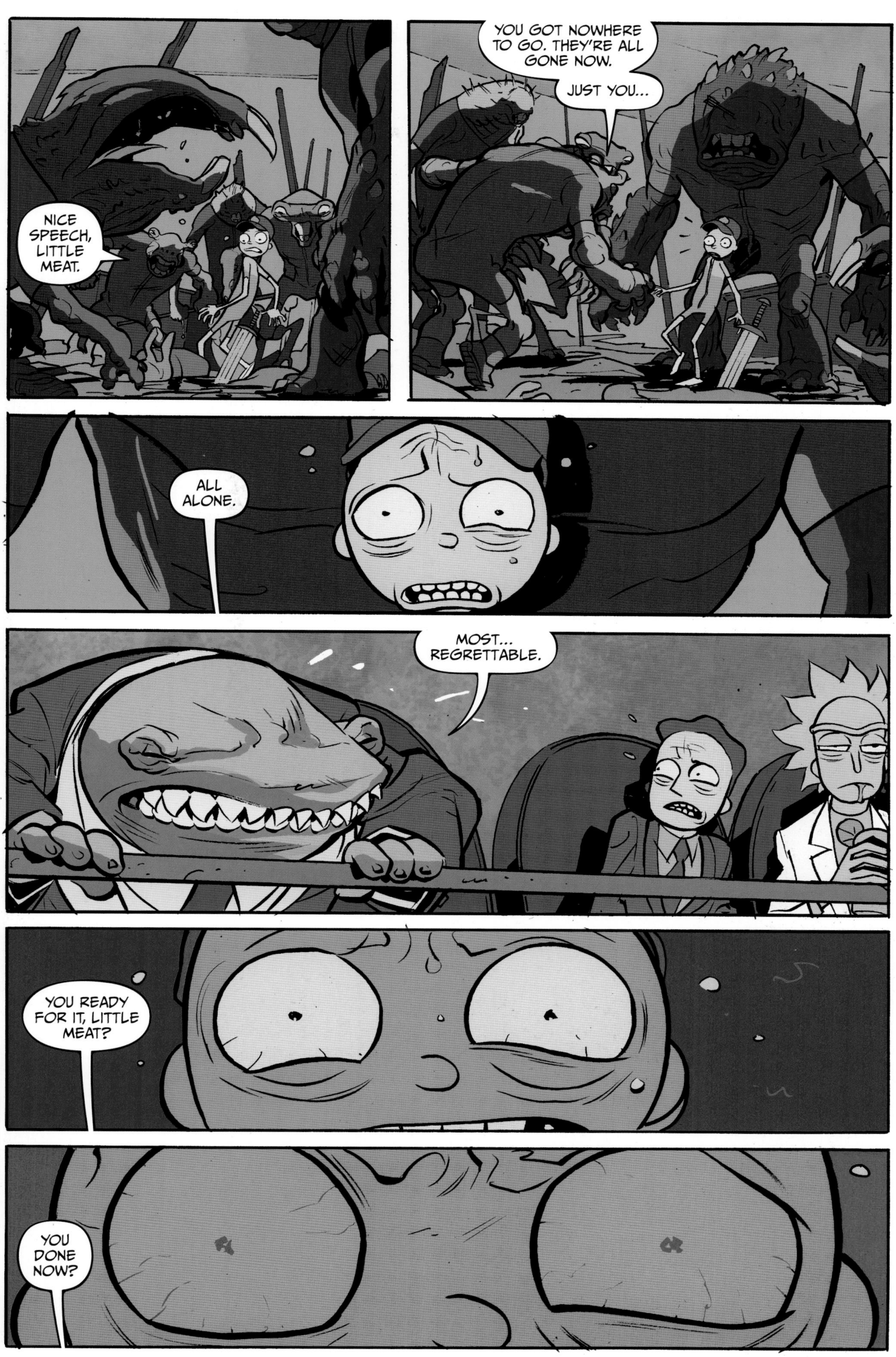
NICE SPEECH, LITTLE MEAT.
YOU GOT NOWHERE TO GO. THEY'RE ALL GONE NOW.
JUST YOU...
ALL ALONE.
MOST... REGRETTABLE.
YOU READY FOR IT, LITTLE MEAT?
YOU DONE NOW?

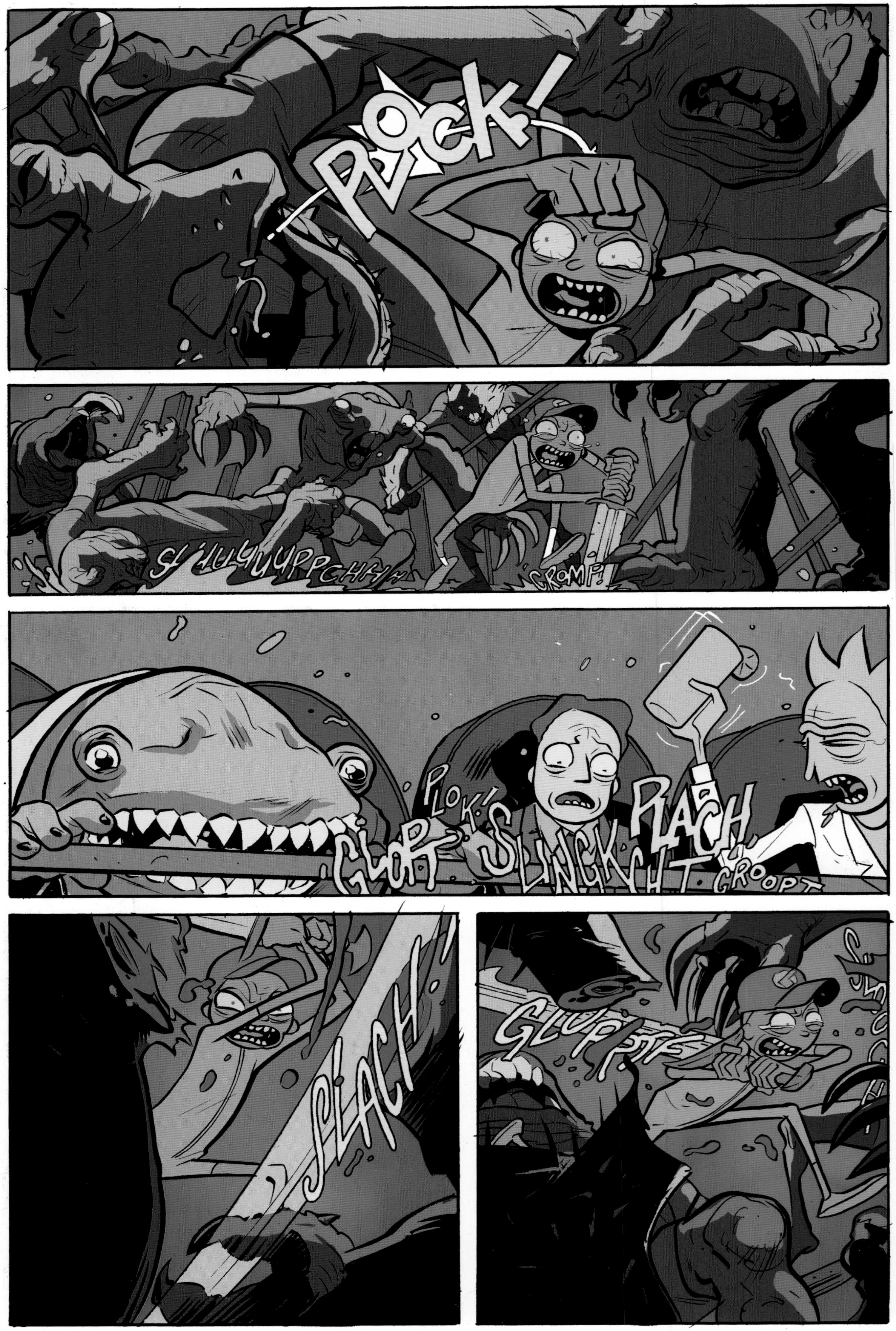
PLOCK!
CROMP!
PLOK!
GLOPT
SLUNCK
PLACH
CHT
GROOPT
SPLACH!
GLUPPPTF

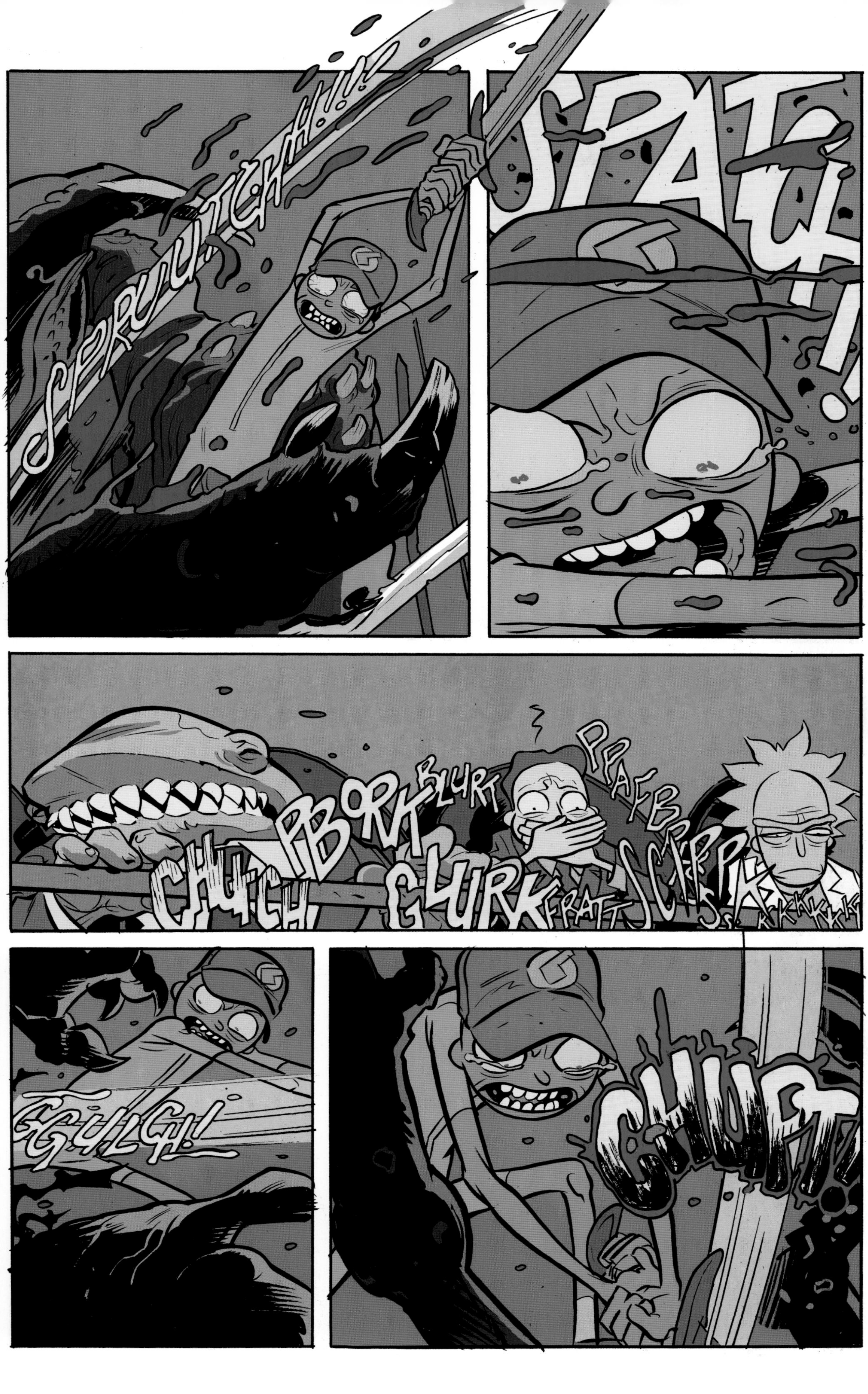
SPRUUTCHH!!?
SPATCH!!
CHUCH
PBORK
BLURT
PPAFB
GLURK
FRATT
GGULCH!
CHUPT!

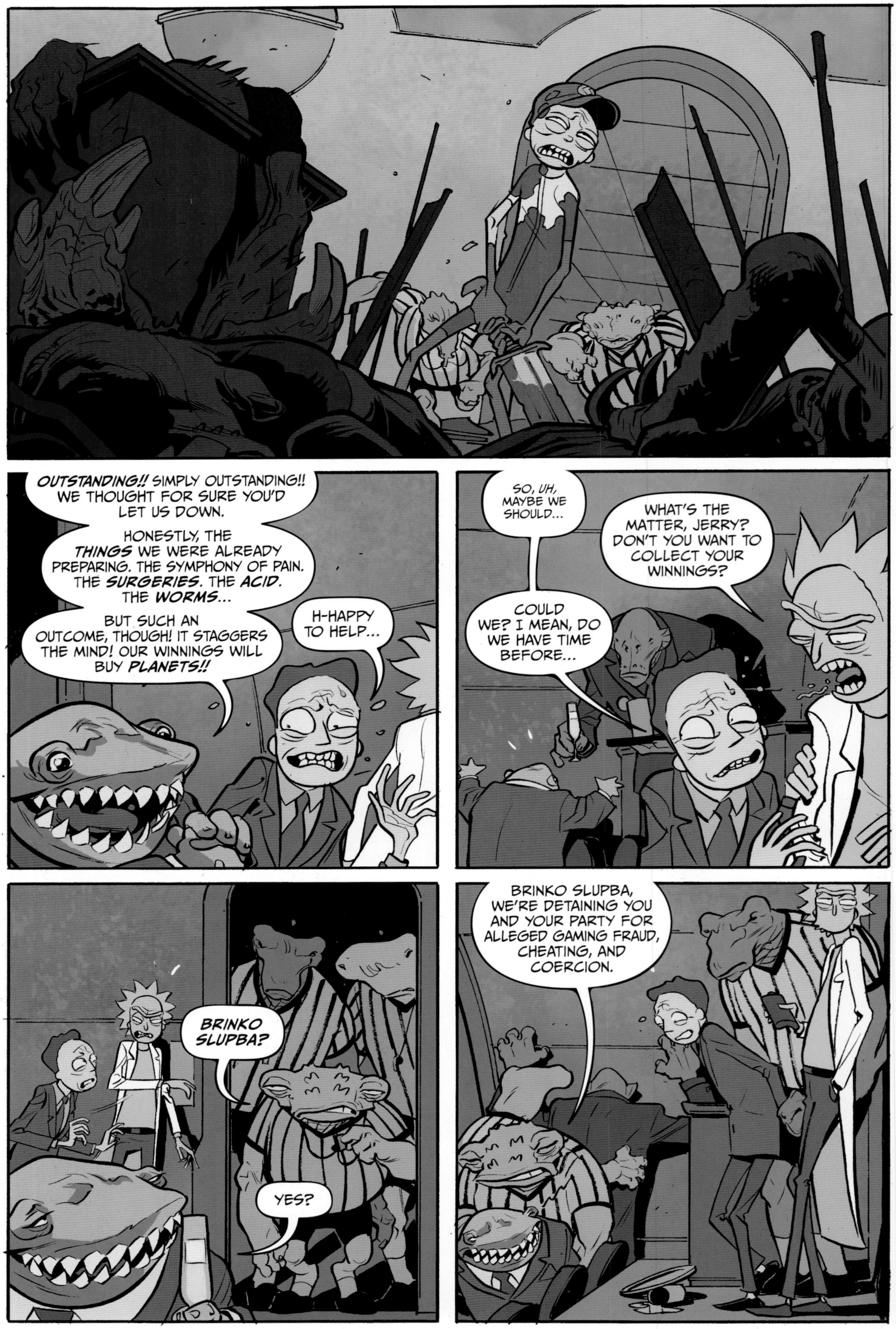
OUTSTANDING!! SIMPLY OUTSTANDING!! WE THOUGHT FOR SURE YOU'D LET US DOWN.
HONESTLY, THE THINGS WE WERE ALREADY PREPARING. THE SYMPHONY OF PAIN. THE SURGERIES. THE ACID. THE WORMS...
BUT SUCH AN OUTCOME, THOUGH! IT STAGGERS THE MIND! OUR WINNINGS WILL BUY PLANETS!!
H-HAPPY TO HELP...
SO, UH, MAYBE WE SHOULD...
COULD WE? I MEAN, DO WE HAVE TIME BEFORE...
WHAT'S THE MATTER, JERRY? DON'T YOU WANT TO COLLECT YOUR WINNINGS?
BRINKO SLUPBA?
YES?
BRINKO SLUPBA, WE'RE DETAINING YOU AND YOUR PARTY FOR ALLEGED GAMING FRAUD, CHEATING, AND COERCION.

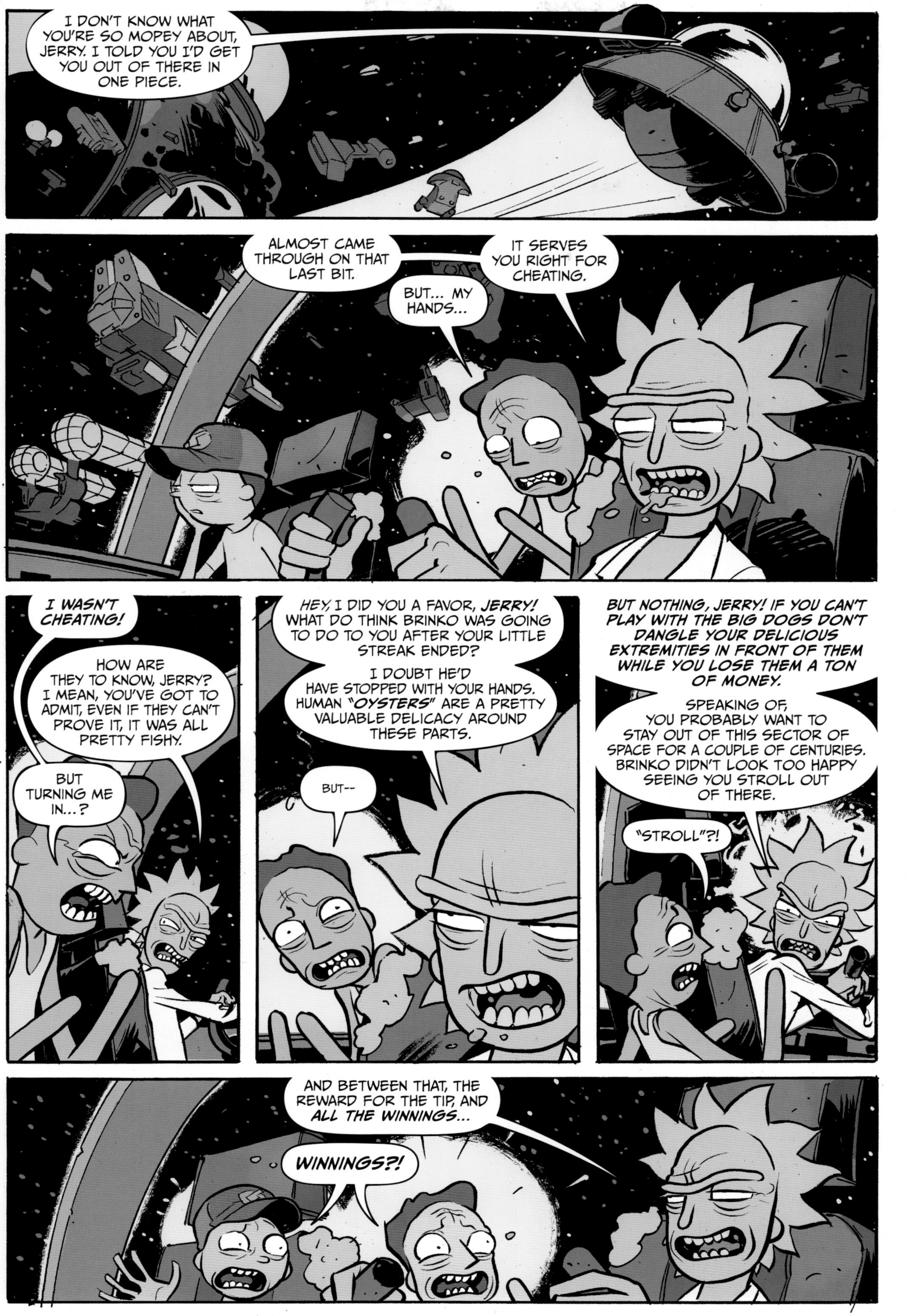
I DON'T KNOW WHAT YOU'RE SO MOPEY ABOUT, JERRY. I TOLD YOU I'D GET YOU OUT OF THERE IN ONE PIECE.
ALMOST CAME THROUGH ON THAT LAST BIT.
BUT... MY HANDS...
IT SERVES YOU RIGHT FOR CHEATING.
I WASN'T CHEATING!
HOW ARE THEY TO KNOW, JERRY? I MEAN, YOU'VE GOT TO ADMIT, EVEN IF THEY CAN'T PROVE IT, IT WAS ALL PRETTY FISHY.
BUT TURNING ME IN...?
HEY, I DID YOU A FAVOR, JERRY! WHAT DO THINK BRINKO WAS GOING TO DO TO YOU AFTER YOUR LITTLE STREAK ENDED?
I DOUBT HE'D HAVE STOPPED WITH YOUR HANDS. HUMAN "OYSTERS" ARE A PRETTY VALUABLE DELICACY AROUND THESE PARTS.
BUT--
BUT NOTHING, JERRY! IF YOU CAN'T PLAY WITH THE BIG DOGS DON'T DANGLE YOUR DELICIOUS EXTREMITIES IN FRONT OF THEM WHILE YOU LOSE THEM A TON OF MONEY.
SPEAKING OF, YOU PROBABLY WANT TO STAY OUT OF THIS SECTOR OF SPACE FOR A COUPLE OF CENTURIES. BRINKO DIDN'T LOOK TOO HAPPY SEEING YOU STROLL OUT OF THERE.
"STROLL"?!
AND BETWEEN THAT, THE REWARD FOR THE TIP, AND ALL THE WINNINGS...
WINNINGS?!

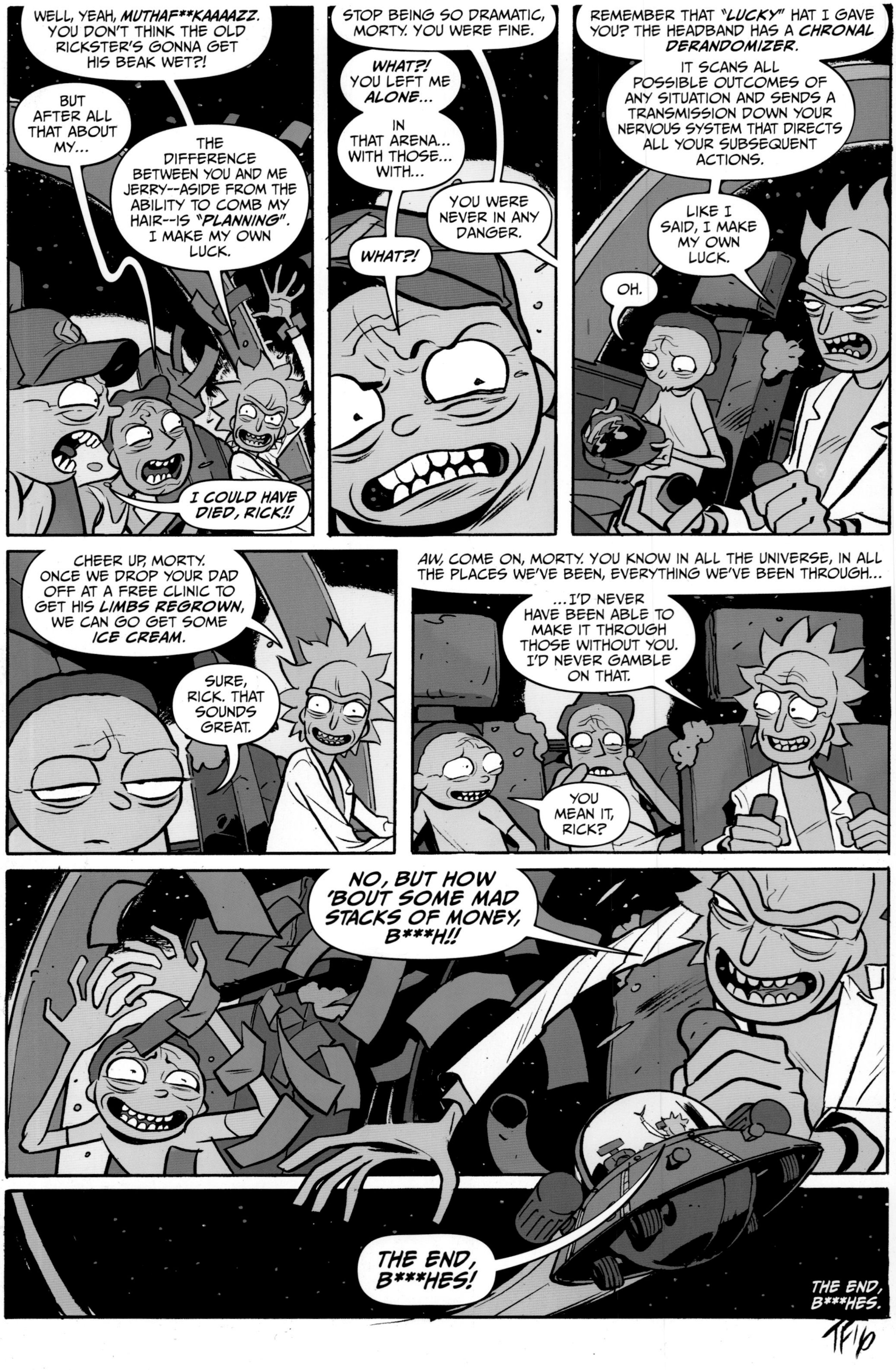
WELL, YEAH, MUTHAF**KAAAAZZ. YOU DON'T THINK THE OLD RICKSTER'S GONNA GET HIS BEAK WET?!
BUT AFTER ALL THAT ABOUT MY...
THE DIFFERENCE BETWEEN YOU AND ME JERRY--ASIDE FROM THE ABILITY TO COMB MY HAIR--IS "PLANNING". I MAKE MY OWN LUCK.
I COULD HAVE DIED, RICK!!
STOP BEING SO DRAMATIC, MORTY. YOU WERE FINE.
WHAT?! YOU LEFT ME ALONE...
IN THAT ARENA... WITH THOSE... WITH...
YOU WERE NEVER IN ANY DANGER.
WHAT?!
REMEMBER THAT "LUCKY" HAT I GAVE YOU? THE HEADBAND HAS A CHRONAL DERANDOMIZER.
IT SCANS ALL POSSIBLE OUTCOMES OF ANY SITUATION AND SENDS A TRANSMISSION DOWN YOUR NERVOUS SYSTEM THAT DIRECTS ALL YOUR SUBSEQUENT ACTIONS.
LIKE I SAID, I MAKE MY OWN LUCK.
OH.
CHEER UP, MORTY. ONCE WE DROP YOUR DAD OFF AT A FREE CLINIC TO GET HIS LIMBS REGROWN, WE CAN GO GET SOME ICE CREAM.
SURE, RICK. THAT SOUNDS GREAT.
AW, COME ON, MORTY. YOU KNOW IN ALL THE UNIVERSE, IN ALL THE PLACES WE'VE BEEN, EVERYTHING WE'VE BEEN THROUGH...
...I'D NEVER HAVE BEEN ABLE TO MAKE IT THROUGH THOSE WITHOUT YOU. I'D NEVER GAMBLE ON THAT.
YOU MEAN IT, RICK?
NO, BUT HOW 'BOUT SOME MAD STACKS OF MONEY, B***H!!
THE END, B***HES!
THE END, B***HES.
TF'16

READY PLAYER MORTY

WRITTEN BY **PAMELA RIBON**
DRAWN BY **MARC ELLERBY**
COLORED BY **RYAN HILL**
LETTERED BY **CRANK!**

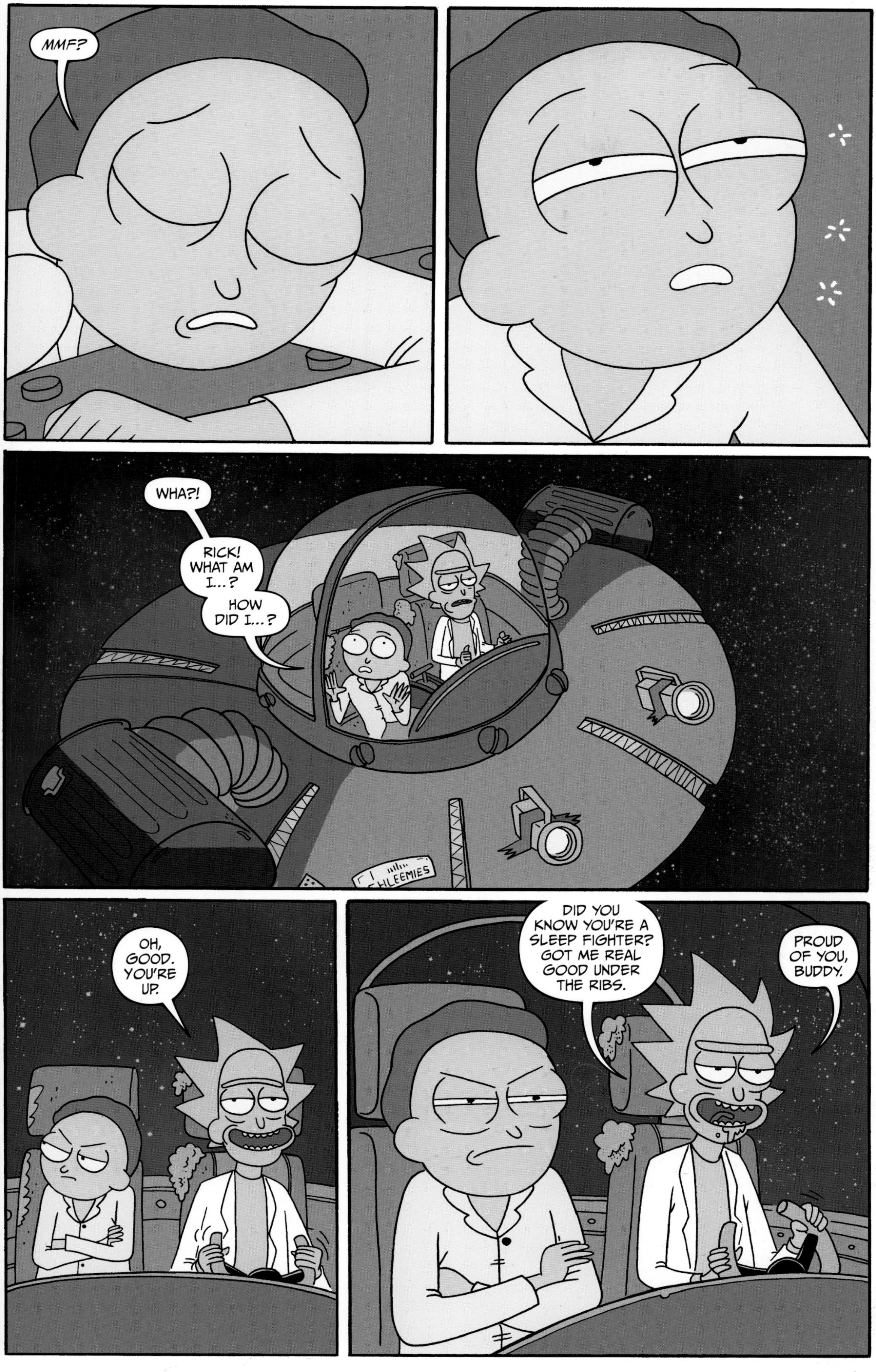
MMF?
WHA?!
RICK! WHAT AM I...?
HOW DID I...?
OH, GOOD. YOU'RE UP.
DID YOU KNOW YOU'RE A SLEEP FIGHTER? GOT ME REAL GOOD UNDER THE RIBS.
PROUD OF YOU, BUDDY.

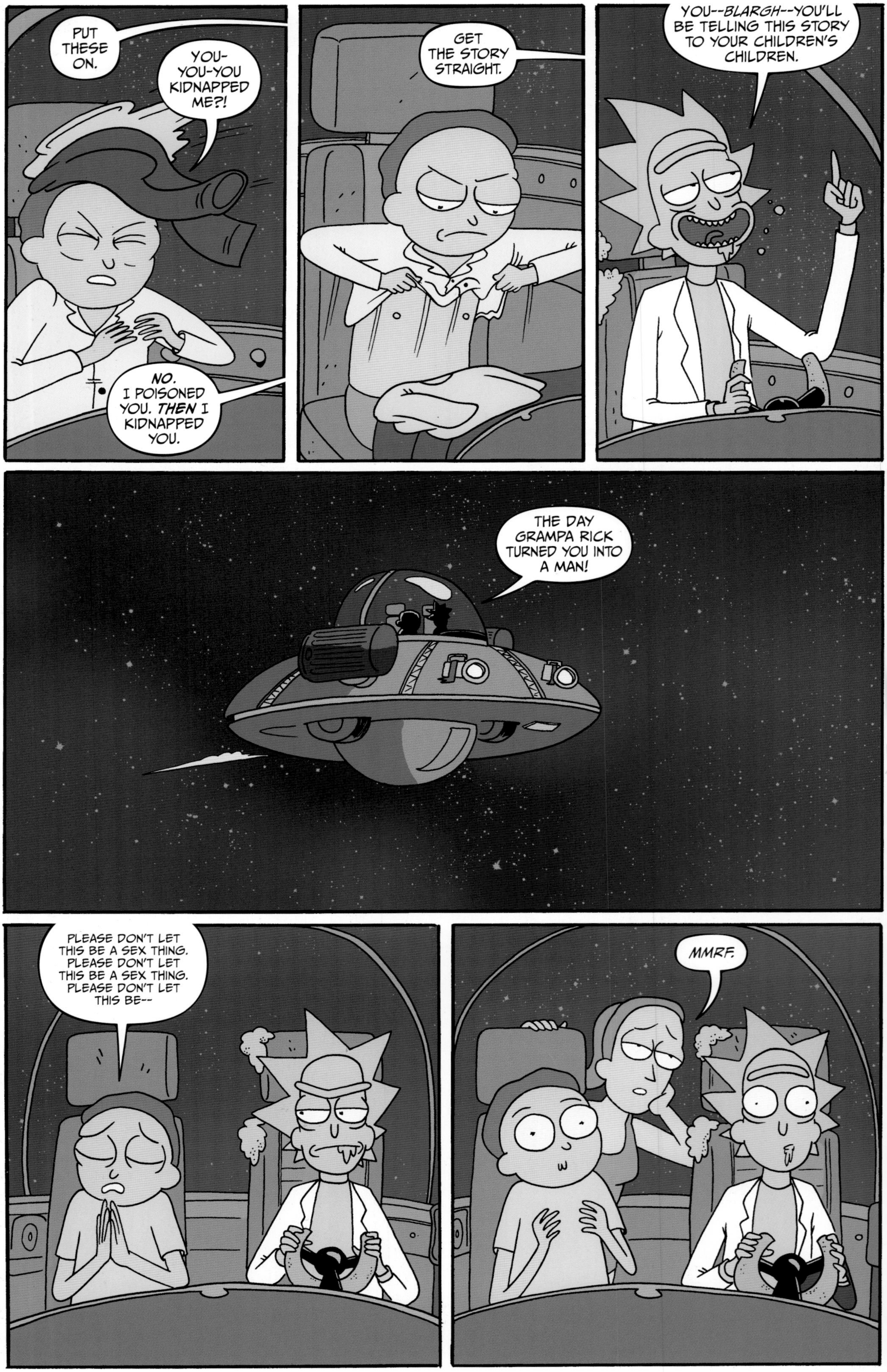
PUT THESE ON.
YOU-YOU-YOU KIDNAPPED ME?!
NO. I POISONED YOU. THEN I KIDNAPPED YOU.
GET THE STORY STRAIGHT.
YOU--BLARGH--YOU'LL BE TELLING THIS STORY TO YOUR CHILDREN'S CHILDREN.
THE DAY GRAMPA RICK TURNED YOU INTO A MAN!
PLEASE DON'T LET THIS BE A SEX THING. PLEASE DON'T LET THIS BE A SEX THING. PLEASE DON'T LET THIS BE--
MMRF.

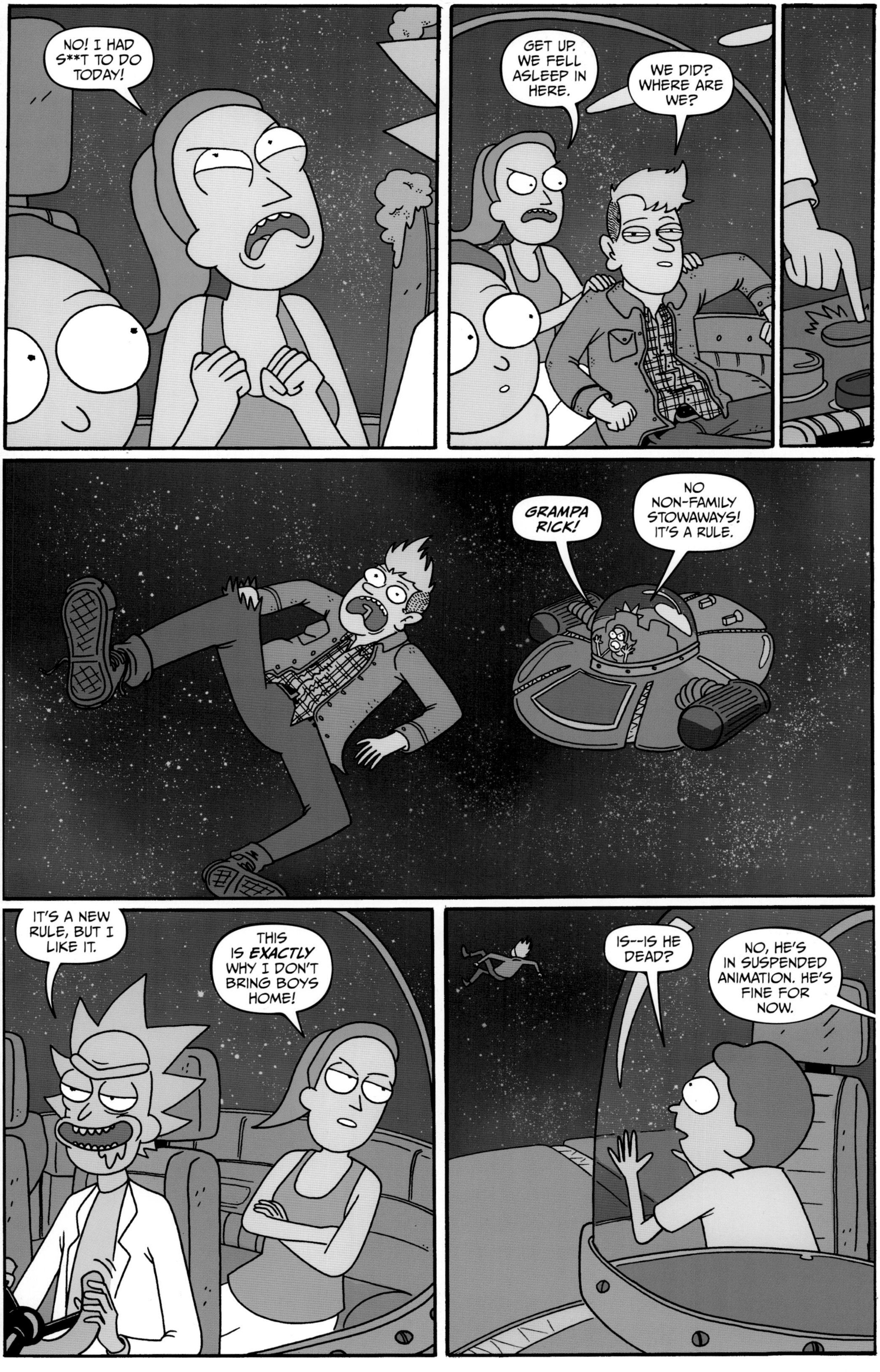

NO! I HAD S**T TO DO TODAY!
GET UP. WE FELL ASLEEP IN HERE.
WE DID? WHERE ARE WE?
GRAMPA RICK!
NO NON-FAMILY STOWAWAYS! IT'S A RULE.
IT'S A NEW RULE, BUT I LIKE IT.
THIS IS EXACTLY WHY I DON'T BRING BOYS HOME!
IS--IS HE DEAD?
NO, HE'S IN SUSPENDED ANIMATION. HE'S FINE FOR NOW.

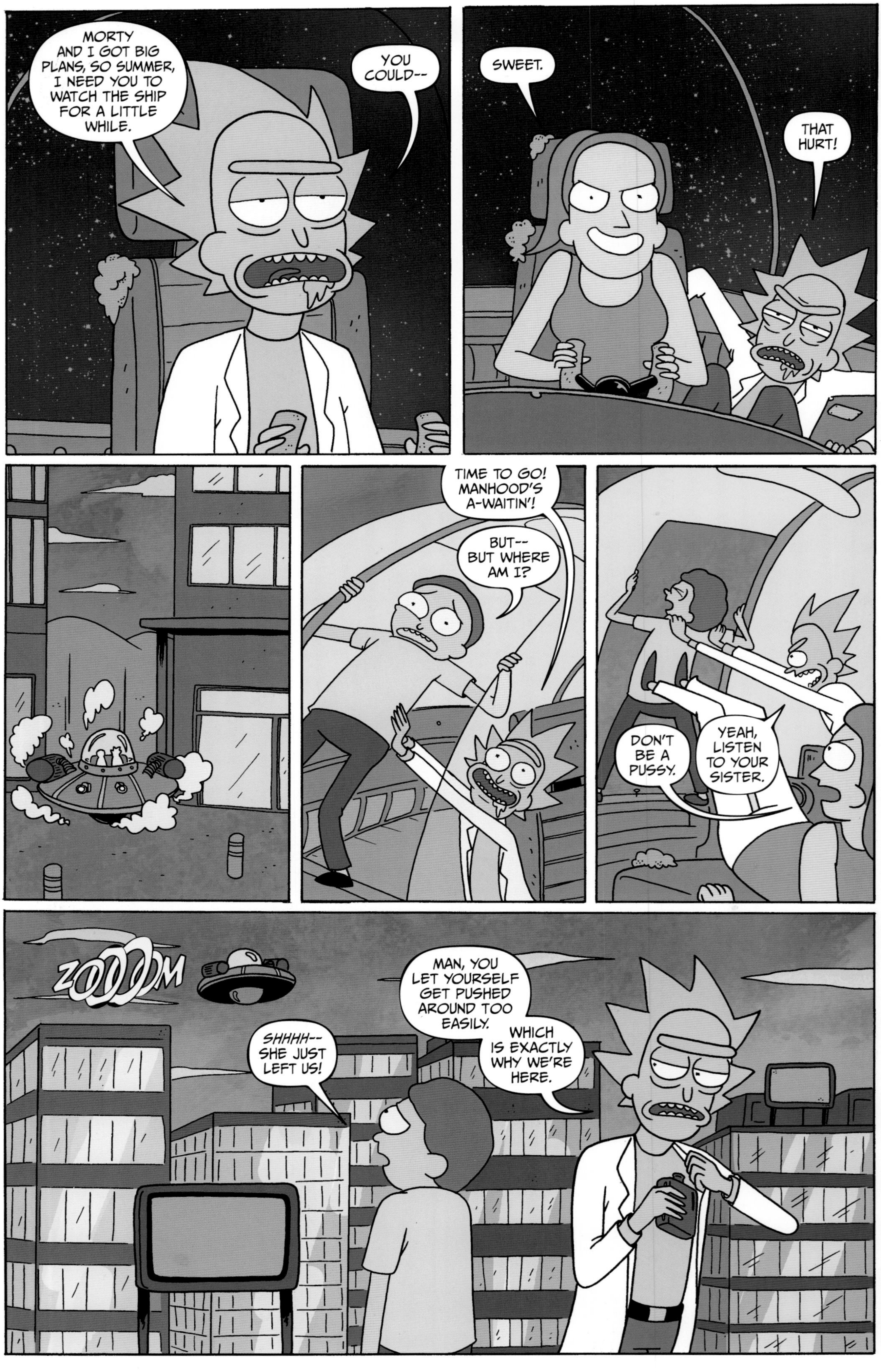
MORTY AND I GOT BIG PLANS, SO SUMMER, I NEED YOU TO WATCH THE SHIP FOR A LITTLE WHILE.
YOU COULD--
SWEET.
THAT HURT!
TIME TO GO! MANHOOD'S A-WAITIN'!
BUT-- BUT WHERE AM I?
DON'T BE A PUSSY.
YEAH, LISTEN TO YOUR SISTER.
ZOOOOM
MAN, YOU LET YOURSELF GET PUSHED AROUND TOO EASILY.
SHHHH-- SHE JUST LEFT US!
WHICH IS EXACTLY WHY WE'RE HERE.

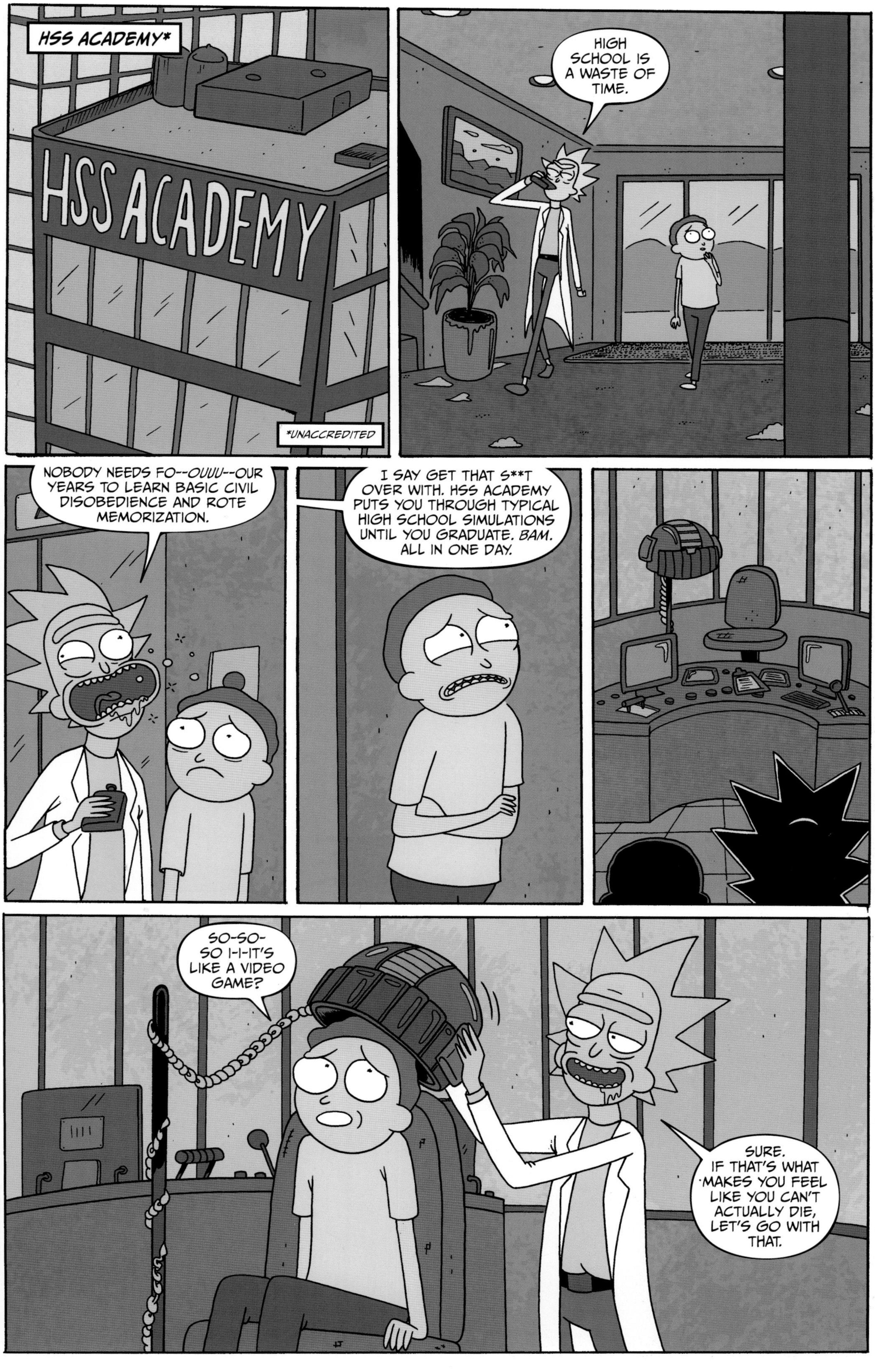
HSS ACADEMY*
HSS ACADEMY
*UNACCREDITED
HIGH SCHOOL IS A WASTE OF TIME.
NOBODY NEEDS FO--OUUU--OUR YEARS TO LEARN BASIC CIVIL DISOBEDIENCE AND ROTE MEMORIZATION.
I SAY GET THAT S**T OVER WITH. HSS ACADEMY PUTS YOU THROUGH TYPICAL HIGH SCHOOL SIMULATIONS UNTIL YOU GRADUATE. BAM. ALL IN ONE DAY.
SO-SO-SO I-I-IT'S LIKE A VIDEO GAME?
SURE. IF THAT'S WHAT MAKES YOU FEEL LIKE YOU CAN'T ACTUALLY DIE, LET'S GO WITH THAT.

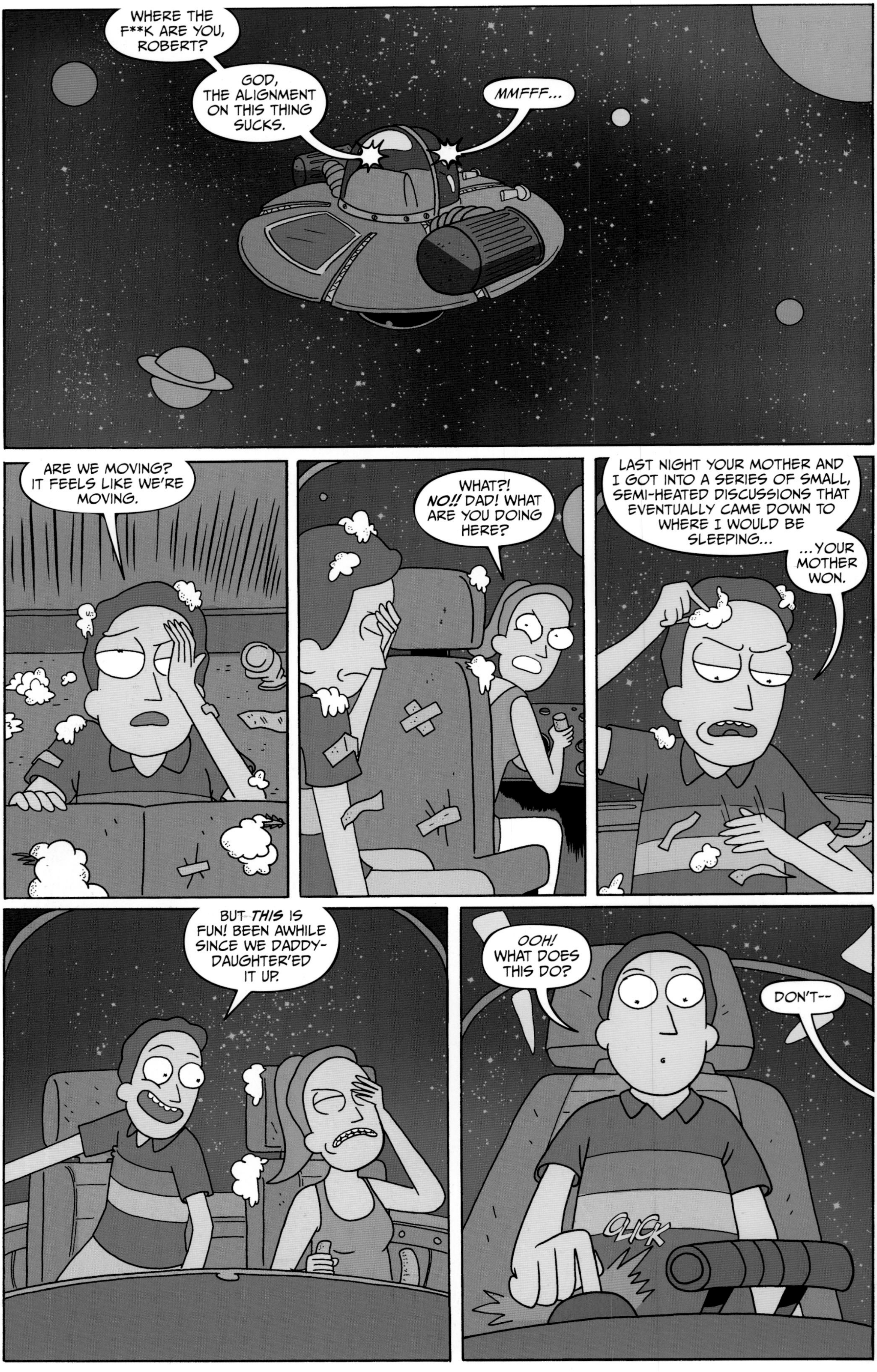
WHERE THE F**K ARE YOU, ROBERT?
GOD, THE ALIGNMENT ON THIS THING SUCKS.
MMFFF...
ARE WE MOVING? IT FEELS LIKE WE'RE MOVING.
WHAT?! NO!! DAD! WHAT ARE YOU DOING HERE?
LAST NIGHT YOUR MOTHER AND I GOT INTO A SERIES OF SMALL, SEMI-HEATED DISCUSSIONS THAT EVENTUALLY CAME DOWN TO WHERE I WOULD BE SLEEPING...
...YOUR MOTHER WON.
BUT THIS IS FUN! BEEN AWHILE SINCE WE DADDY-DAUGHTER'ED IT UP.
OOH! WHAT DOES THIS DO?
DON'T--
CLICK

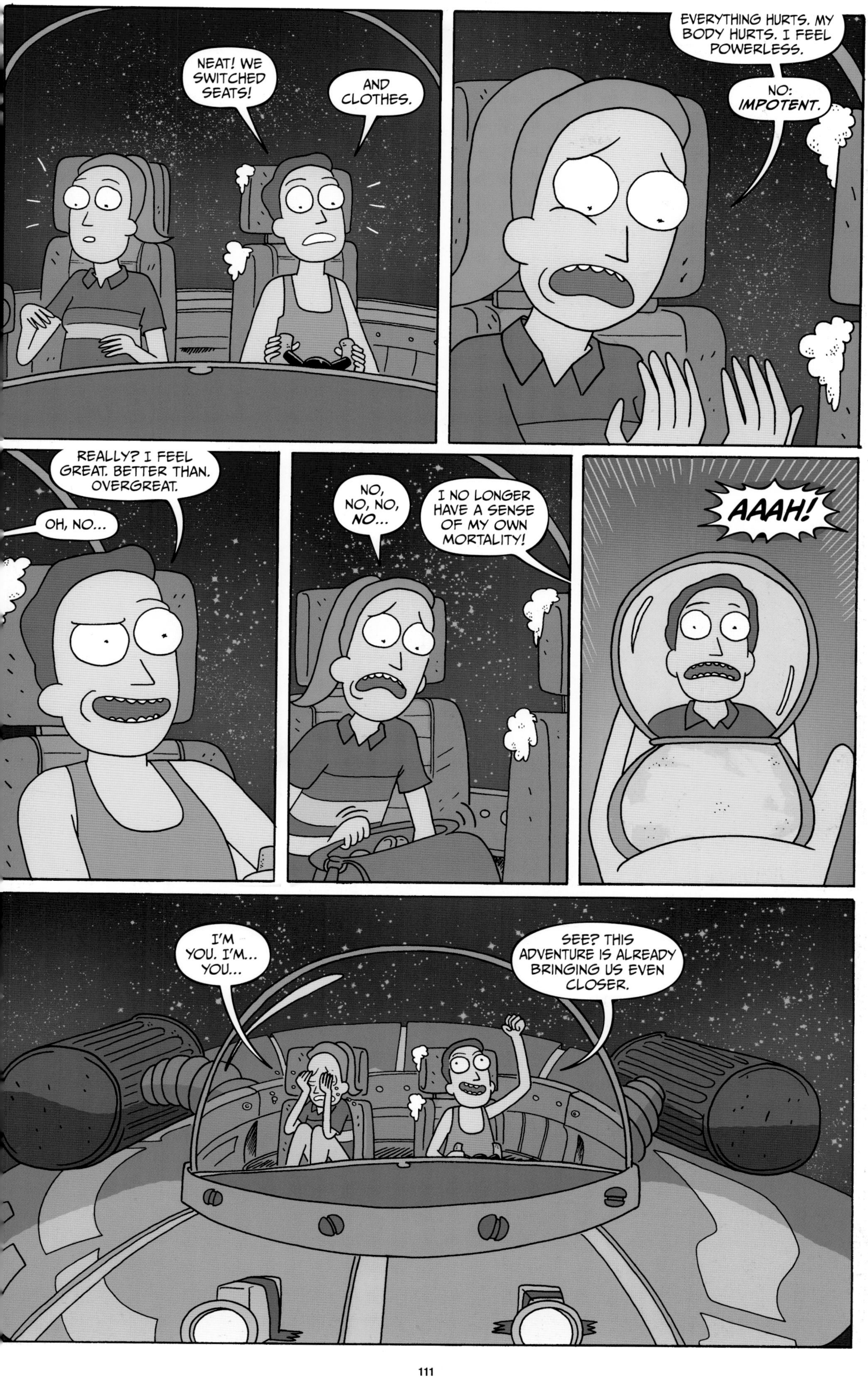
NEAT! WE SWITCHED SEATS!
AND CLOTHES.
EVERYTHING HURTS. MY BODY HURTS. I FEEL POWERLESS.
NO: *IMPOTENT.*
REALLY? I FEEL GREAT. BETTER THAN. OVERGREAT.
OH, NO...
NO, NO, NO, *NO*...
I NO LONGER HAVE A SENSE OF MY OWN MORTALITY!
AAAH!
I'M YOU. I'M... YOU...
SEE? THIS ADVENTURE IS ALREADY BRINGING US EVEN CLOSER.

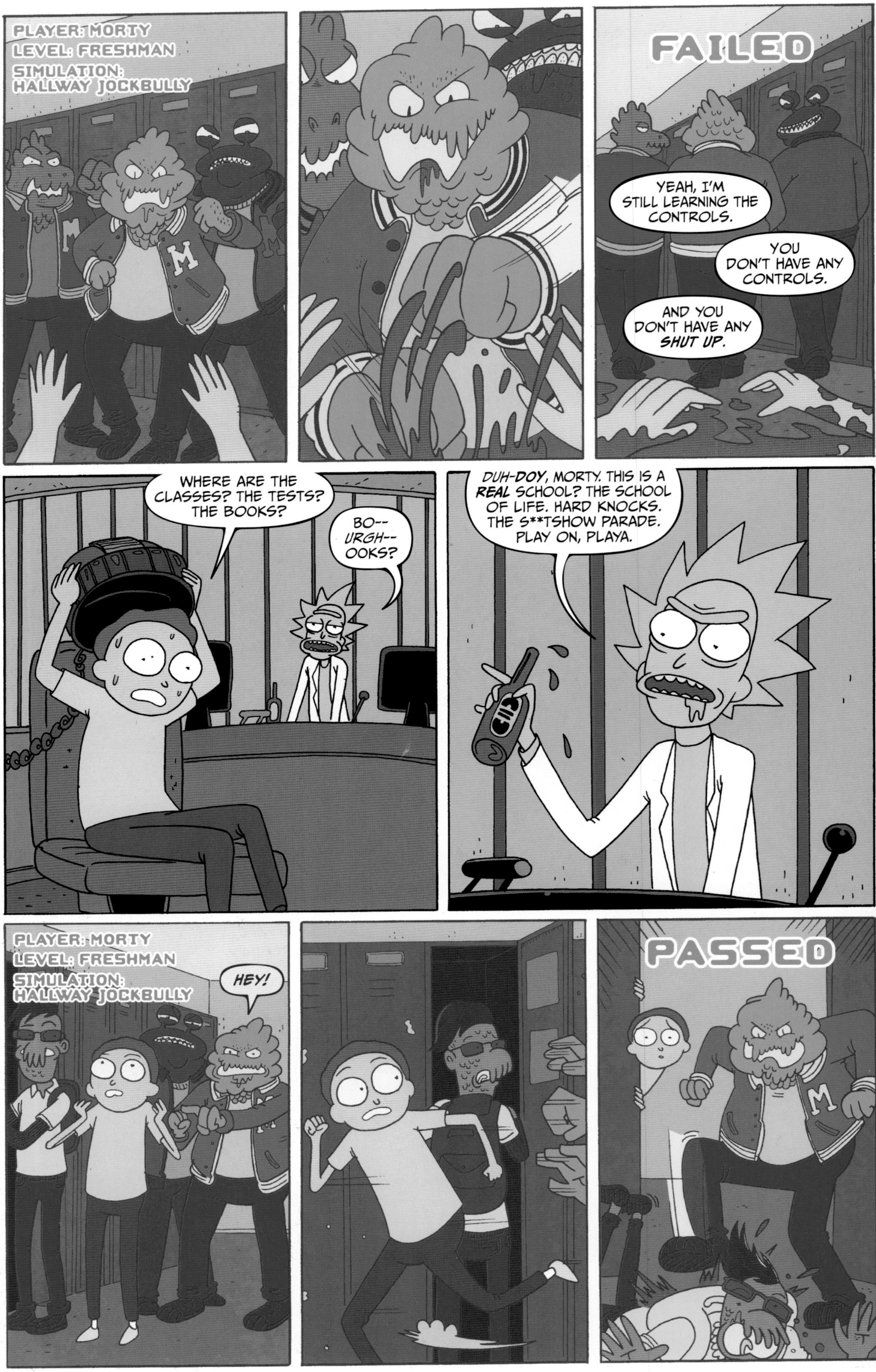
PLAYER: MORTY
LEVEL: FRESHMAN
SIMULATION: HALLWAY JOCKBULLY
FAILED
YEAH, I'M STILL LEARNING THE CONTROLS.
YOU DON'T HAVE ANY CONTROLS.
AND YOU DON'T HAVE ANY *SHUT UP*.
WHERE ARE THE CLASSES? THE TESTS? THE BOOKS?
BO-- *URGH*-- OOKS?
DUH-DOY, MORTY. THIS IS A ***REAL*** SCHOOL? THE SCHOOL OF LIFE. HARD KNOCKS. THE S**TSHOW PARADE. PLAY ON, PLAYA.
PLAYER: MORTY
LEVEL: FRESHMAN
SIMULATION: HALLWAY JOCKBULLY
HEY!
PASSED

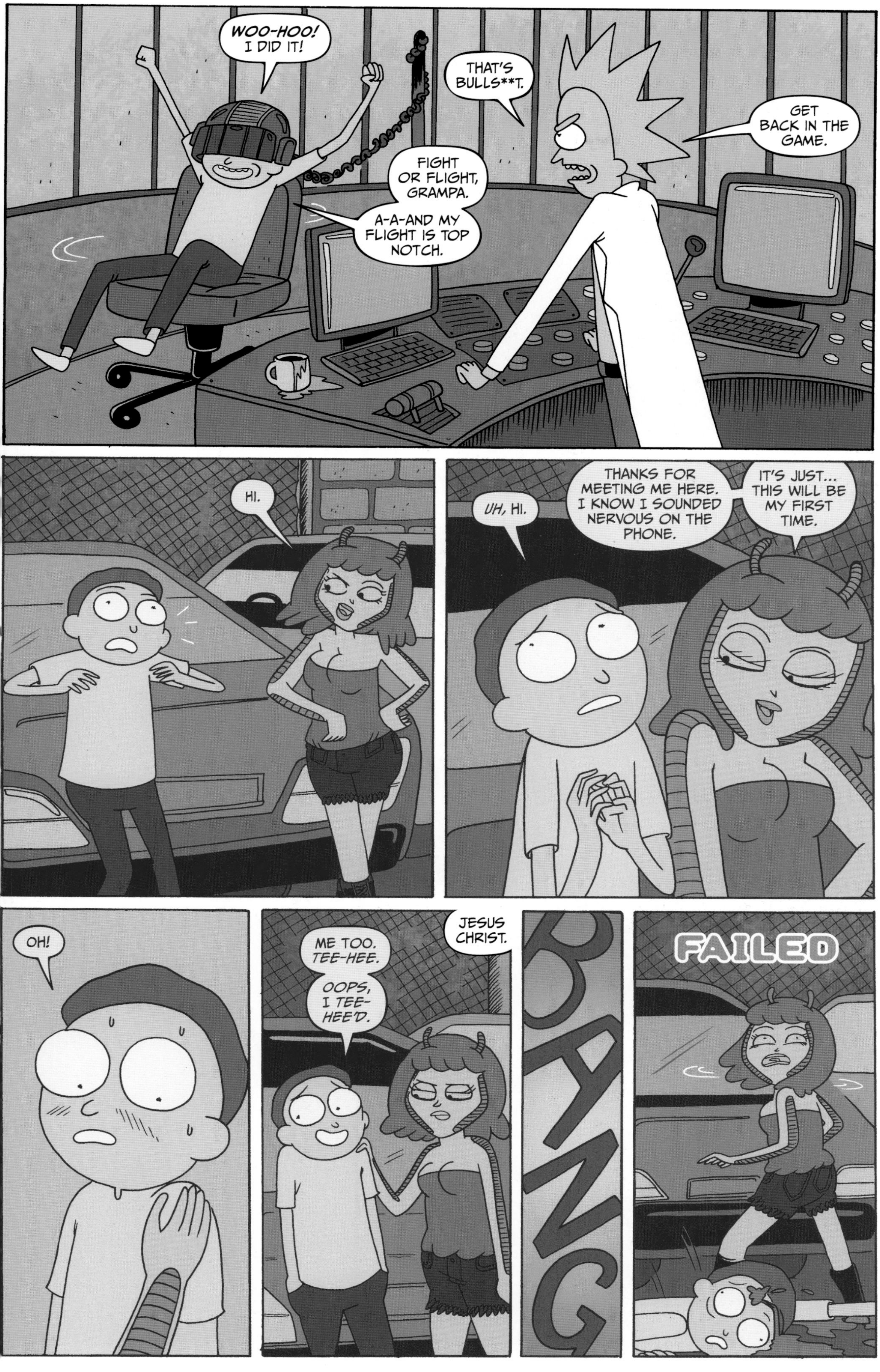

WOO-HOO! I DID IT!
THAT'S BULLS**T.
GET BACK IN THE GAME.
FIGHT OR FLIGHT, GRAMPA.
A-A-AND MY FLIGHT IS TOP NOTCH.
HI.
UH, HI.
THANKS FOR MEETING ME HERE. I KNOW I SOUNDED NERVOUS ON THE PHONE.
IT'S JUST... THIS WILL BE MY FIRST TIME.
OH!
ME TOO. TEE-HEE.
OOPS, I TEE-HEE'D.
JESUS CHRIST.
BANG
FAILED

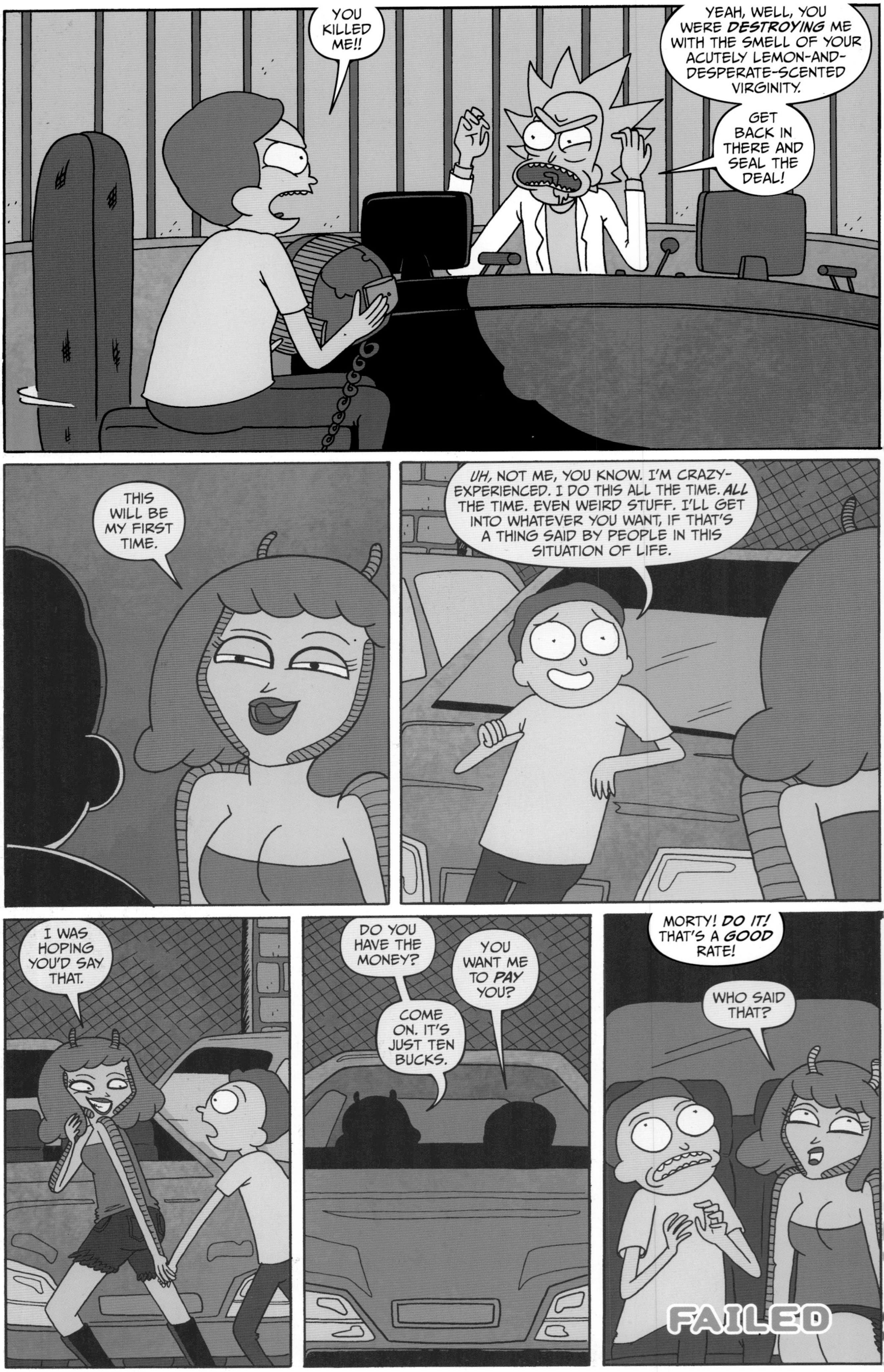
YOU KILLED ME!!
YEAH, WELL, YOU WERE DESTROYING ME WITH THE SMELL OF YOUR ACUTELY LEMON-AND-DESPERATE-SCENTED VIRGINITY.
GET BACK IN THERE AND SEAL THE DEAL!
THIS WILL BE MY FIRST TIME.
UH, NOT ME, YOU KNOW. I'M CRAZY-EXPERIENCED. I DO THIS ALL THE TIME. ALL THE TIME. EVEN WEIRD STUFF. I'LL GET INTO WHATEVER YOU WANT, IF THAT'S A THING SAID BY PEOPLE IN THIS SITUATION OF LIFE.
I WAS HOPING YOU'D SAY THAT.
DO YOU HAVE THE MONEY?
YOU WANT ME TO PAY YOU?
COME ON. IT'S JUST TEN BUCKS.
MORTY! DO IT! THAT'S A GOOD RATE!
WHO SAID THAT?
FAILED

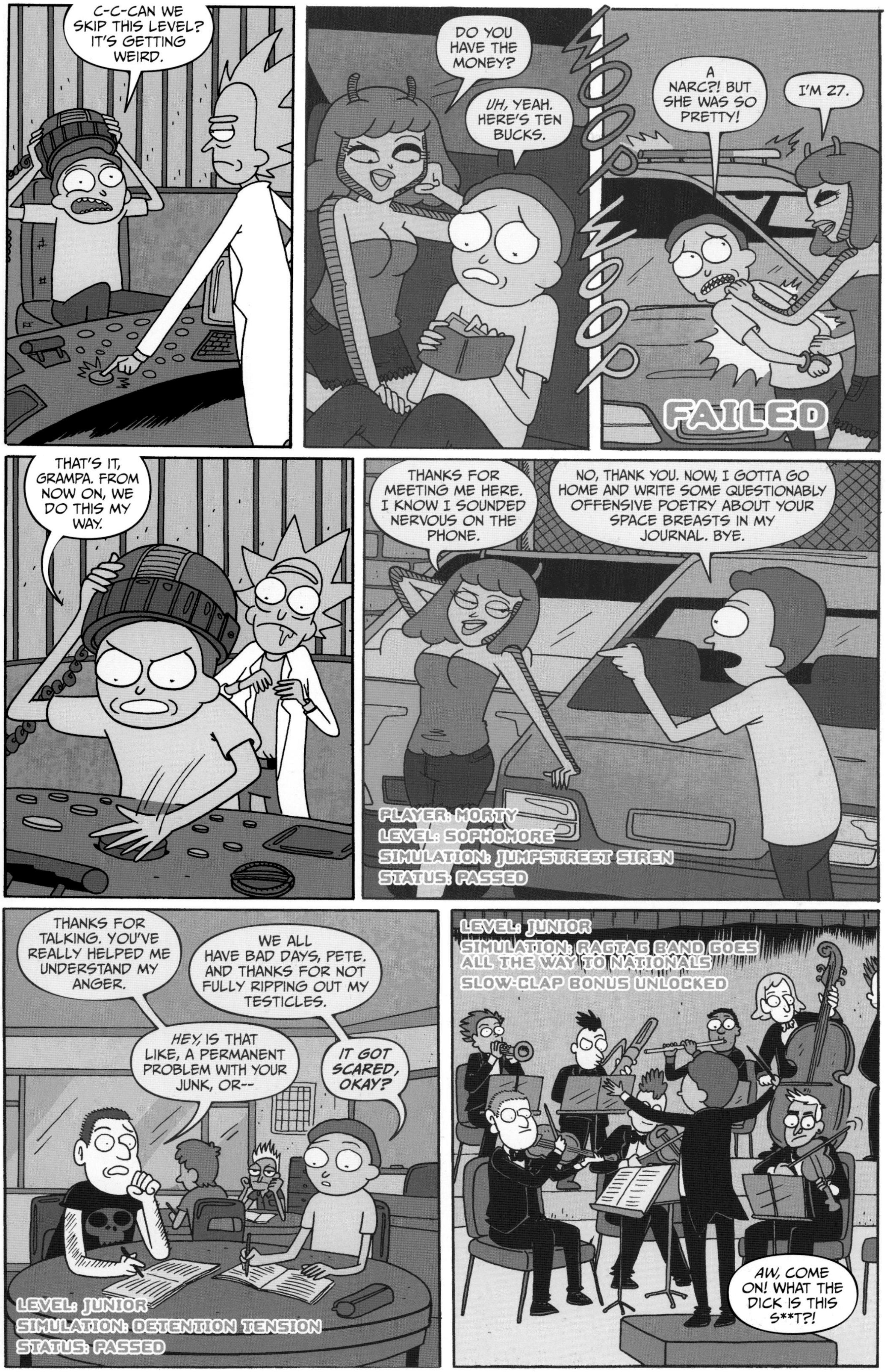
C-C-CAN WE SKIP THIS LEVEL? IT'S GETTING WEIRD.
DO YOU HAVE THE MONEY?
UH, YEAH. HERE'S TEN BUCKS.
WOOP WOOP
A NARC?! BUT SHE WAS SO PRETTY!
I'M 27.
FAILED
THAT'S IT, GRAMPA. FROM NOW ON, WE DO THIS MY WAY.
THANKS FOR MEETING ME HERE. I KNOW I SOUNDED NERVOUS ON THE PHONE.
NO, THANK YOU. NOW, I GOTTA GO HOME AND WRITE SOME QUESTIONABLY OFFENSIVE POETRY ABOUT YOUR SPACE BREASTS IN MY JOURNAL. BYE.
PLAYER: MORTY
LEVEL: SOPHOMORE
SIMULATION: JUMPSTREET SIREN
STATUS: PASSED
THANKS FOR TALKING. YOU'VE REALLY HELPED ME UNDERSTAND MY ANGER.
WE ALL HAVE BAD DAYS, PETE. AND THANKS FOR NOT FULLY RIPPING OUT MY TESTICLES.
HEY, IS THAT LIKE, A PERMANENT PROBLEM WITH YOUR JUNK, OR--
IT GOT SCARED, OKAY?
LEVEL: JUNIOR
SIMULATION: DETENTION TENSION
STATUS: PASSED
LEVEL: JUNIOR
SIMULATION: RAGTAG BAND GOES ALL THE WAY TO NATIONALS
SLOW-CLAP BONUS UNLOCKED
AW, COME ON! WHAT THE DICK IS THIS S**T?!

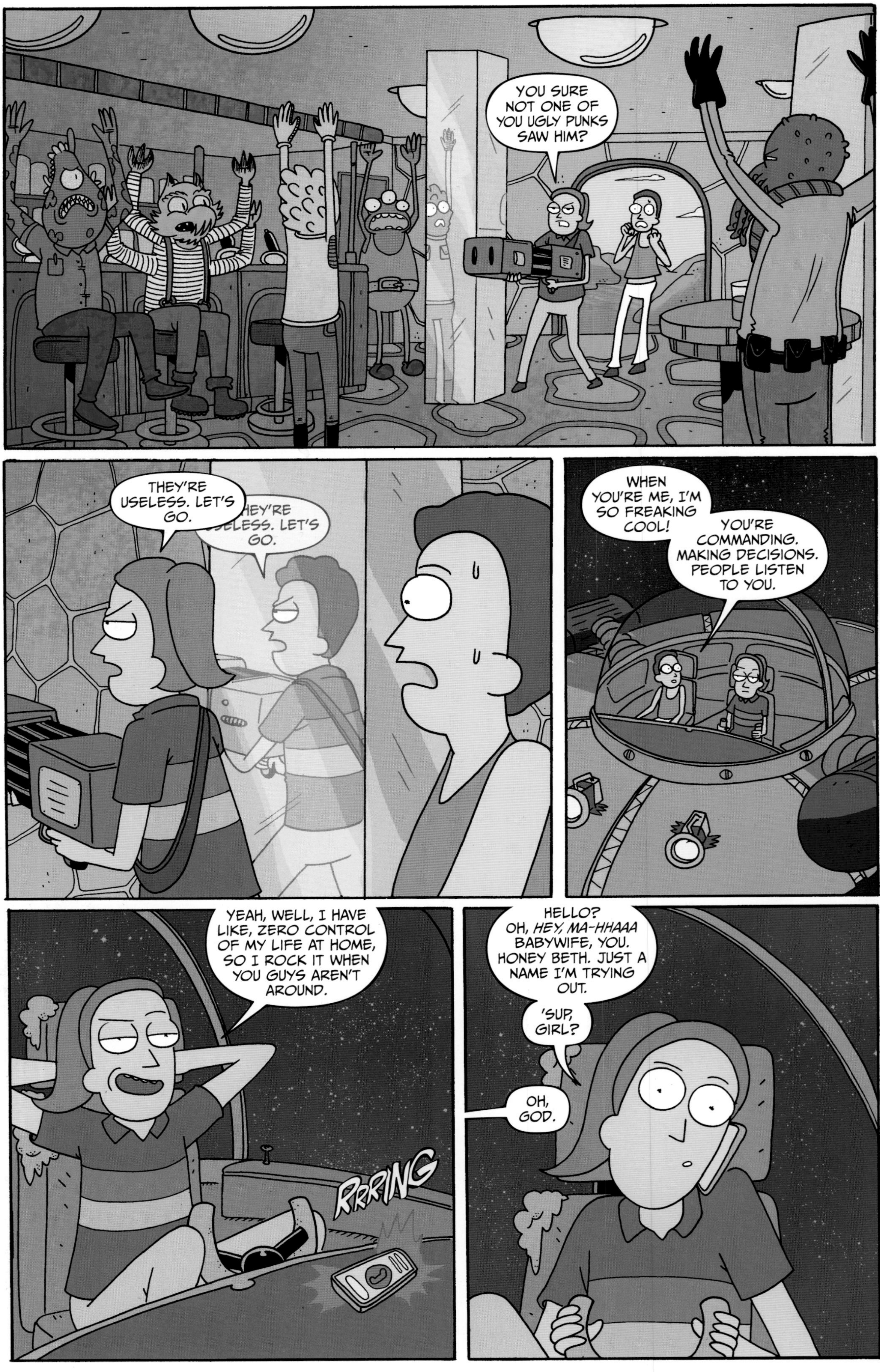
YOU SURE NOT ONE OF YOU UGLY PUNKS SAW HIM?
THEY'RE USELESS. LET'S GO.
THEY'RE USELESS. LET'S GO.
WHEN YOU'RE ME, I'M SO FREAKING COOL!
YOU'RE COMMANDING. MAKING DECISIONS. PEOPLE LISTEN TO YOU.
YEAH, WELL, I HAVE LIKE, ZERO CONTROL OF MY LIFE AT HOME, SO I ROCK IT WHEN YOU GUYS AREN'T AROUND.
RRRING
HELLO? OH, *HEY, MA-HHAAA* BABYWIFE, YOU. HONEY BETH. JUST A NAME I'M TRYING OUT.
'SUP, GIRL?
OH, GOD.

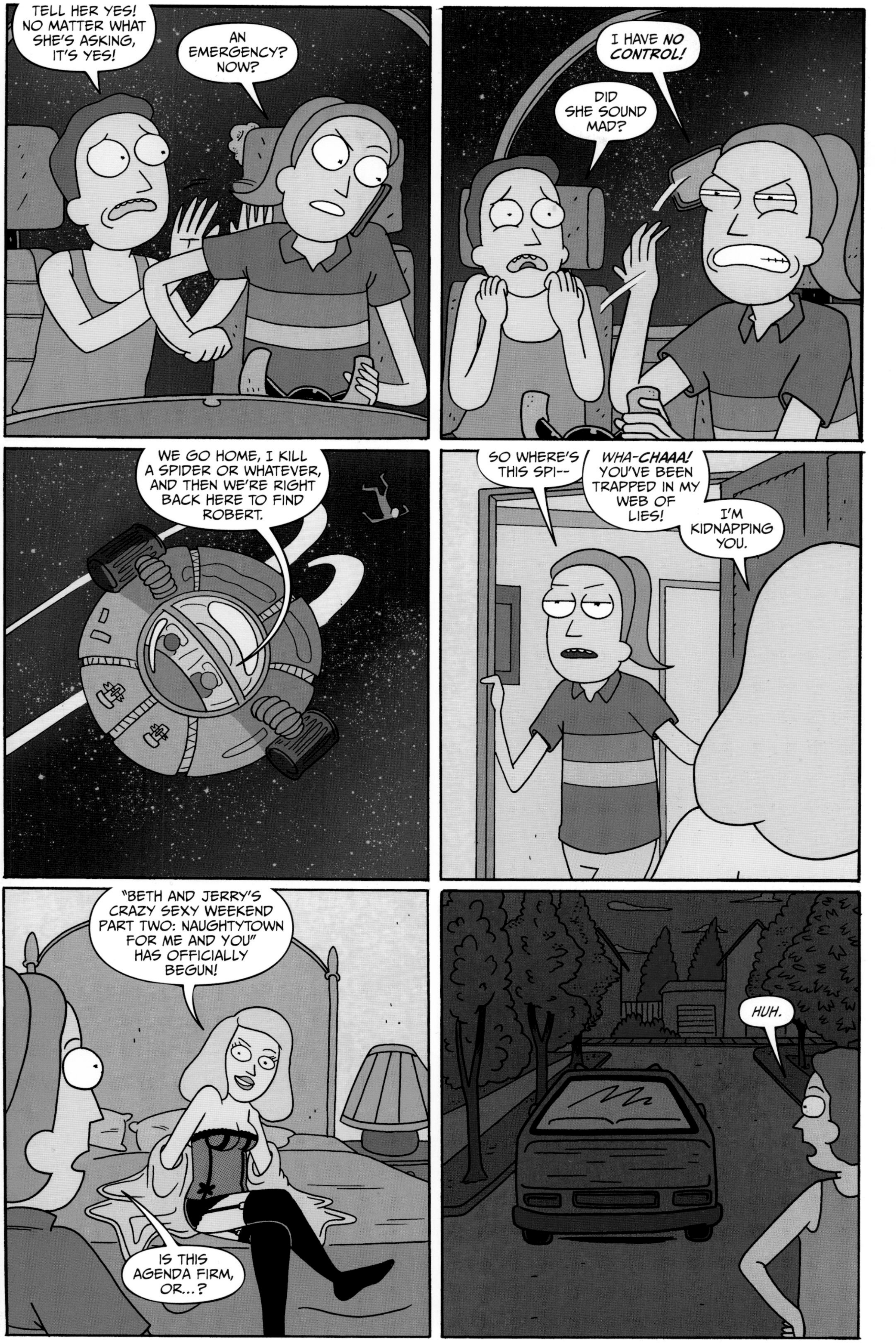
TELL HER YES! NO MATTER WHAT SHE'S ASKING, IT'S YES!
AN EMERGENCY? NOW?
I HAVE NO CONTROL!
DID SHE SOUND MAD?
WE GO HOME, I KILL A SPIDER OR WHATEVER, AND THEN WE'RE RIGHT BACK HERE TO FIND ROBERT.
SO WHERE'S THIS SPI--
WHA-CHAAA! YOU'VE BEEN TRAPPED IN MY WEB OF LIES!
I'M KIDNAPPING YOU.
"BETH AND JERRY'S CRAZY SEXY WEEKEND PART TWO: NAUGHTYTOWN FOR ME AND YOU" HAS OFFICIALLY BEGUN!
IS THIS AGENDA FIRM, OR...?
HUH.

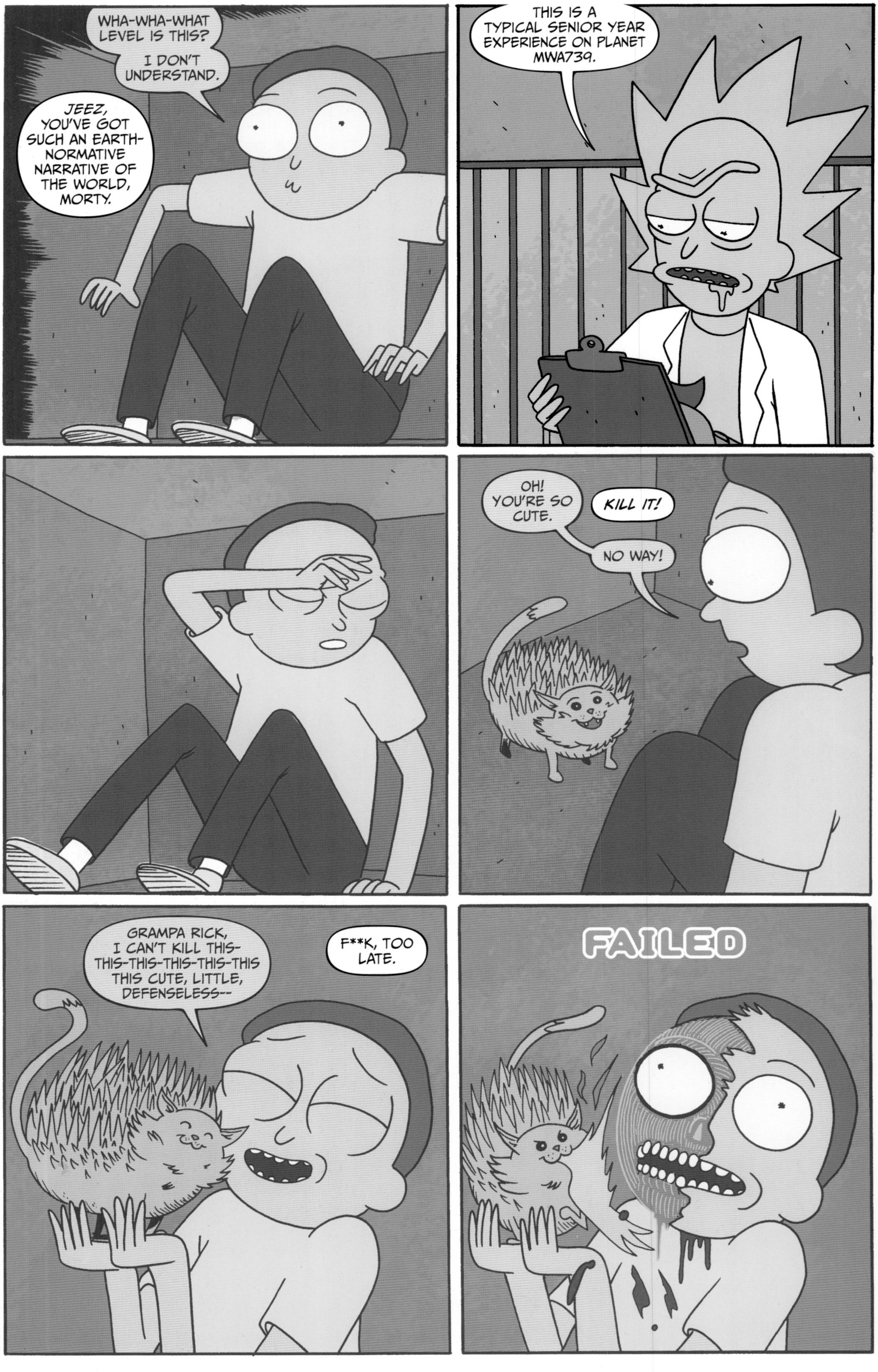
WHA-WHA-WHAT LEVEL IS THIS?
I DON'T UNDERSTAND.
JEEZ, YOU'VE GOT SUCH AN EARTH-NORMATIVE NARRATIVE OF THE WORLD, MORTY.
THIS IS A TYPICAL SENIOR YEAR EXPERIENCE ON PLANET MWA739.
OH! YOU'RE SO CUTE.
KILL IT!
NO WAY!
GRAMPA RICK, I CAN'T KILL THIS-THIS-THIS-THIS-THIS-THIS THIS CUTE, LITTLE, DEFENSELESS--
F**K, TOO LATE.
FAILED

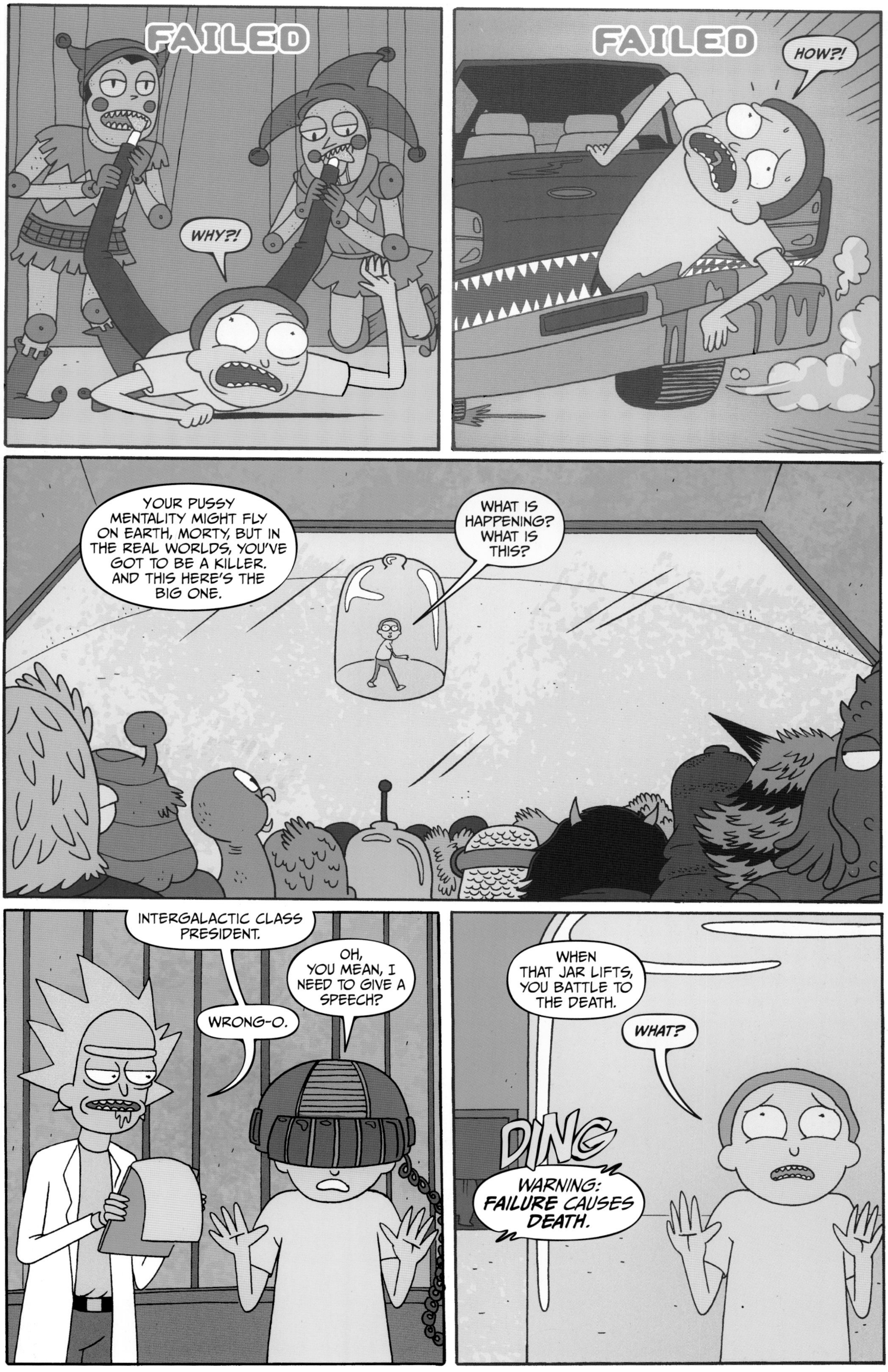
FAILED
WHY?!
FAILED
HOW?!
YOUR PUSSY MENTALITY MIGHT FLY ON EARTH, MORTY, BUT IN THE REAL WORLDS, YOU'VE GOT TO BE A KILLER. AND THIS HERE'S THE BIG ONE.
WHAT IS HAPPENING? WHAT IS THIS?
INTERGALACTIC CLASS PRESIDENT.
OH, YOU MEAN, I NEED TO GIVE A SPEECH?
WRONG-O.
WHEN THAT JAR LIFTS, YOU BATTLE TO THE DEATH.
WHAT?
DING
WARNING: FAILURE CAUSES DEATH.

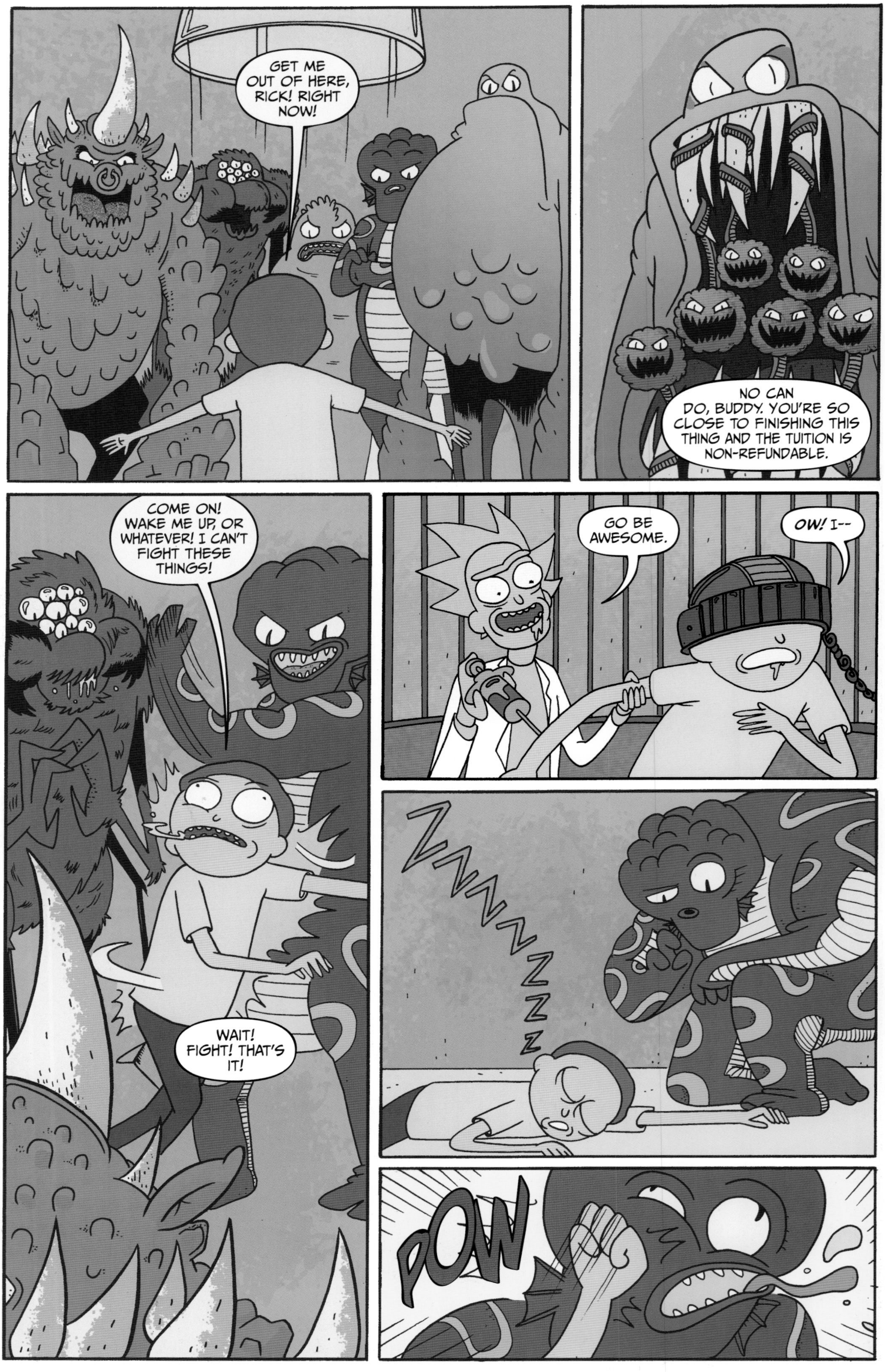
GET ME OUT OF HERE, RICK! RIGHT NOW!
NO CAN DO, BUDDY. YOU'RE SO CLOSE TO FINISHING THIS THING AND THE TUITION IS NON-REFUNDABLE.
COME ON! WAKE ME UP, OR WHATEVER! I CAN'T FIGHT THESE THINGS!
WAIT! FIGHT! THAT'S IT!
GO BE AWESOME.
OW! I--
ZZZZZZZZZ
POW

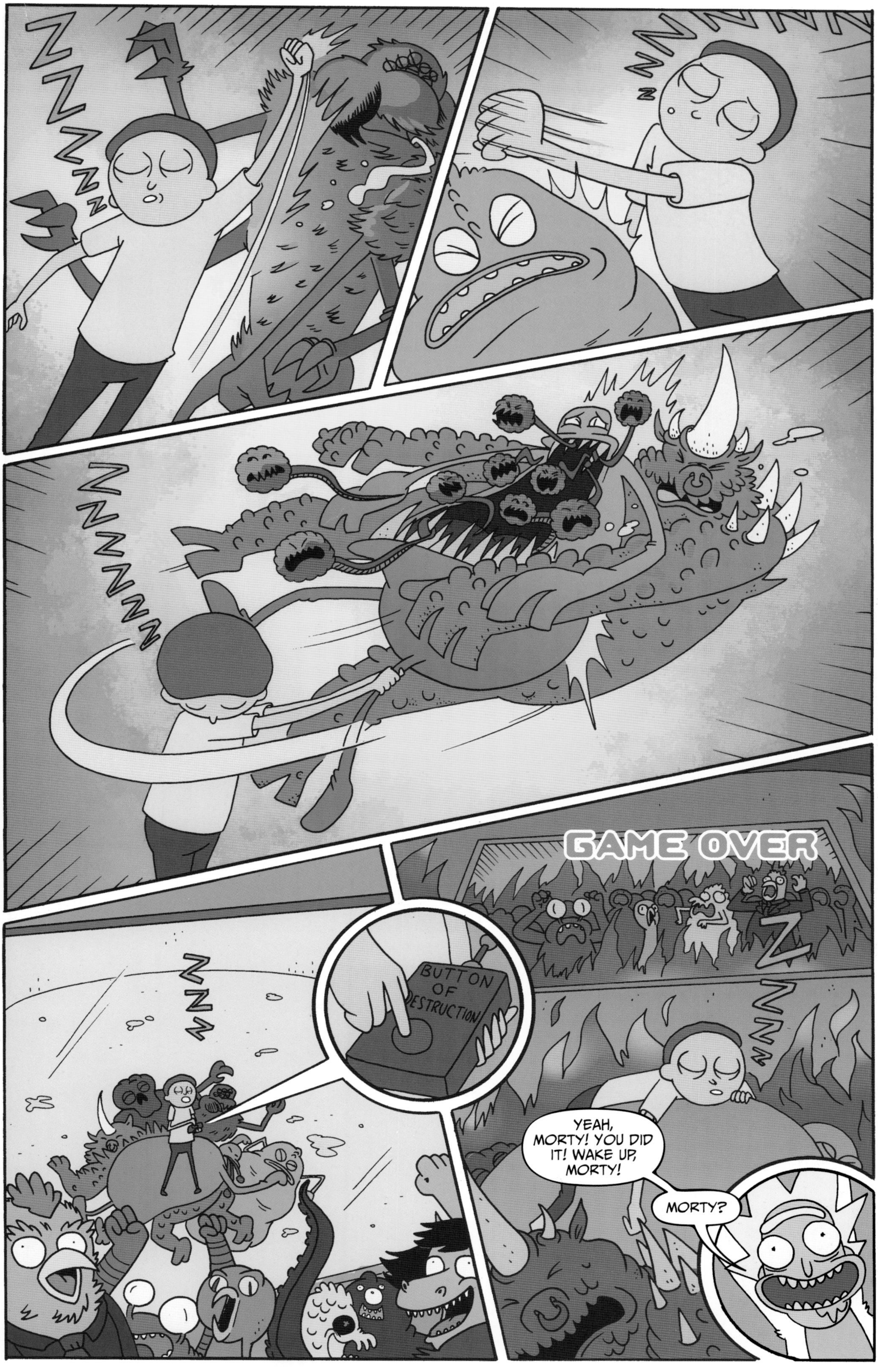
ZZZZZZ
ZZZZ
ZZZZZZZ
GAME OVER
BUTTON OF DESTRUCTION
ZZZ
ZZZ
YEAH, MORTY! YOU DID IT! WAKE UP, MORTY!
MORTY?

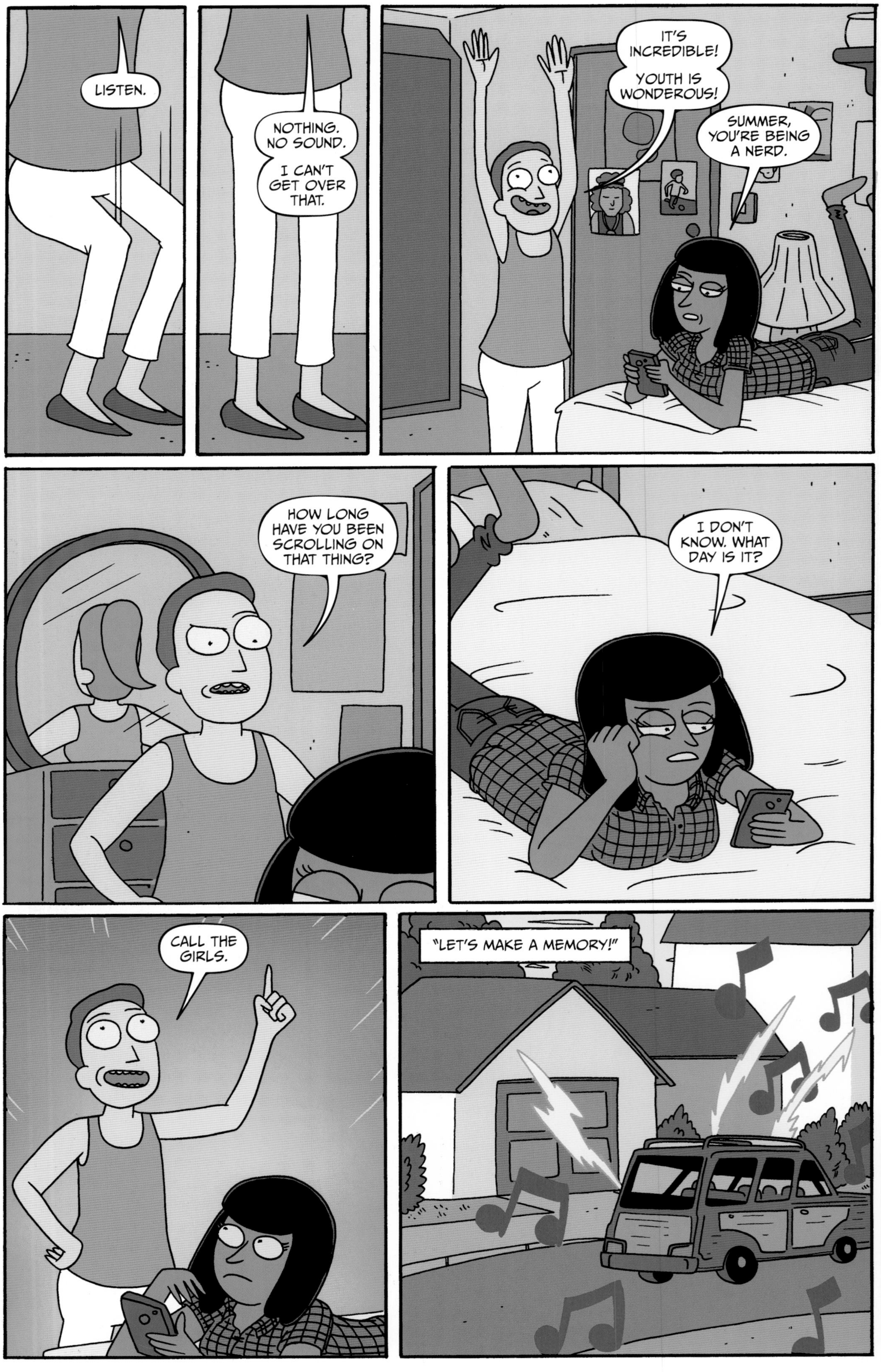
LISTEN.
NOTHING. NO SOUND.
I CAN'T GET OVER THAT.
IT'S INCREDIBLE!
YOUTH IS WONDEROUS!
SUMMER, YOU'RE BEING A NERD.
HOW LONG HAVE YOU BEEN SCROLLING ON THAT THING?
I DON'T KNOW. WHAT DAY IS IT?
CALL THE GIRLS.
"LET'S MAKE A MEMORY!"

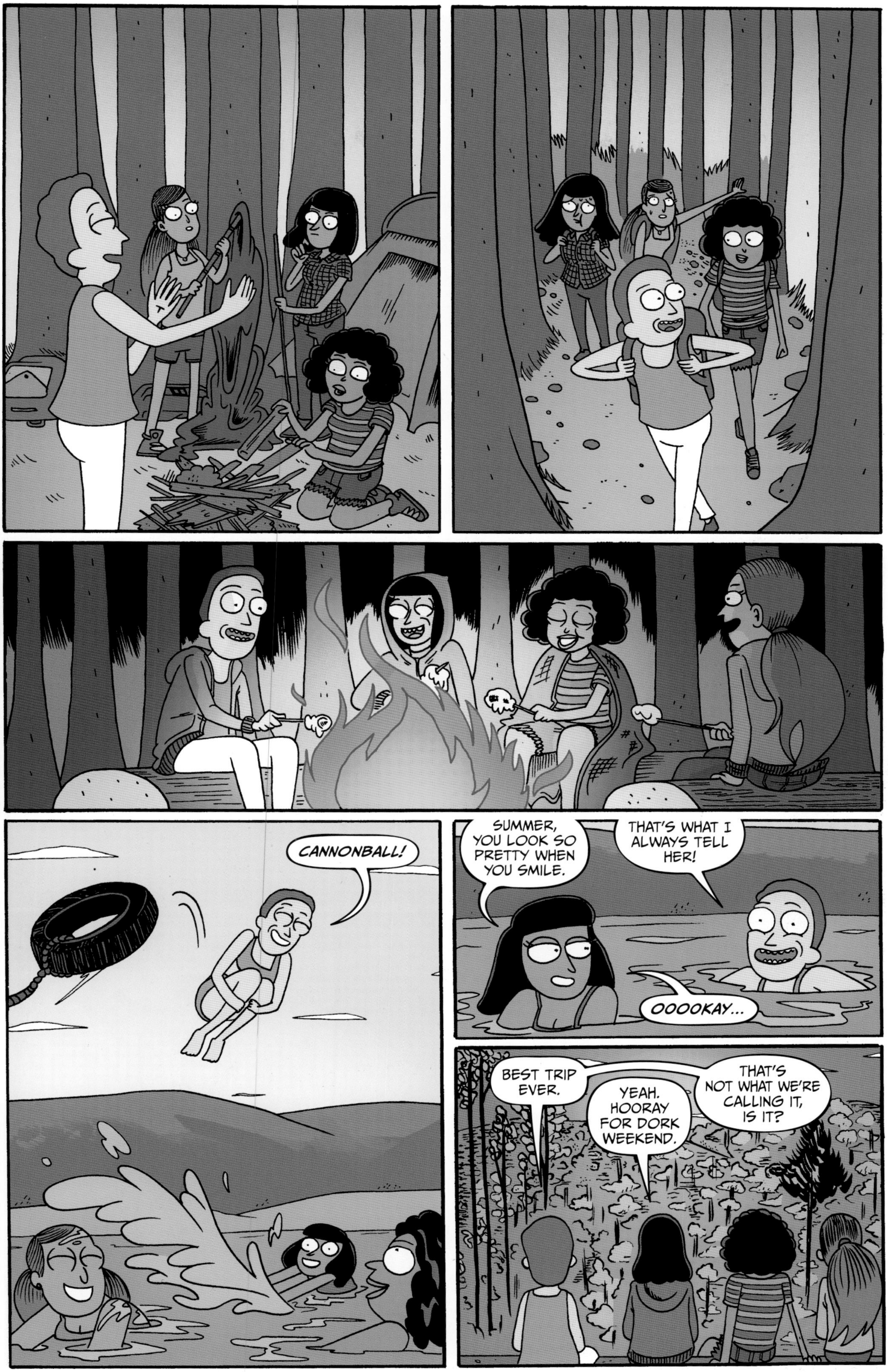
CANNONBALL!
SUMMER, YOU LOOK SO PRETTY WHEN YOU SMILE.
THAT'S WHAT I ALWAYS TELL HER!
OOOOKAY...
BEST TRIP EVER.
THAT'S NOT WHAT WE'RE CALLING IT, IS IT?
YEAH. HOORAY FOR DORK WEEKEND.

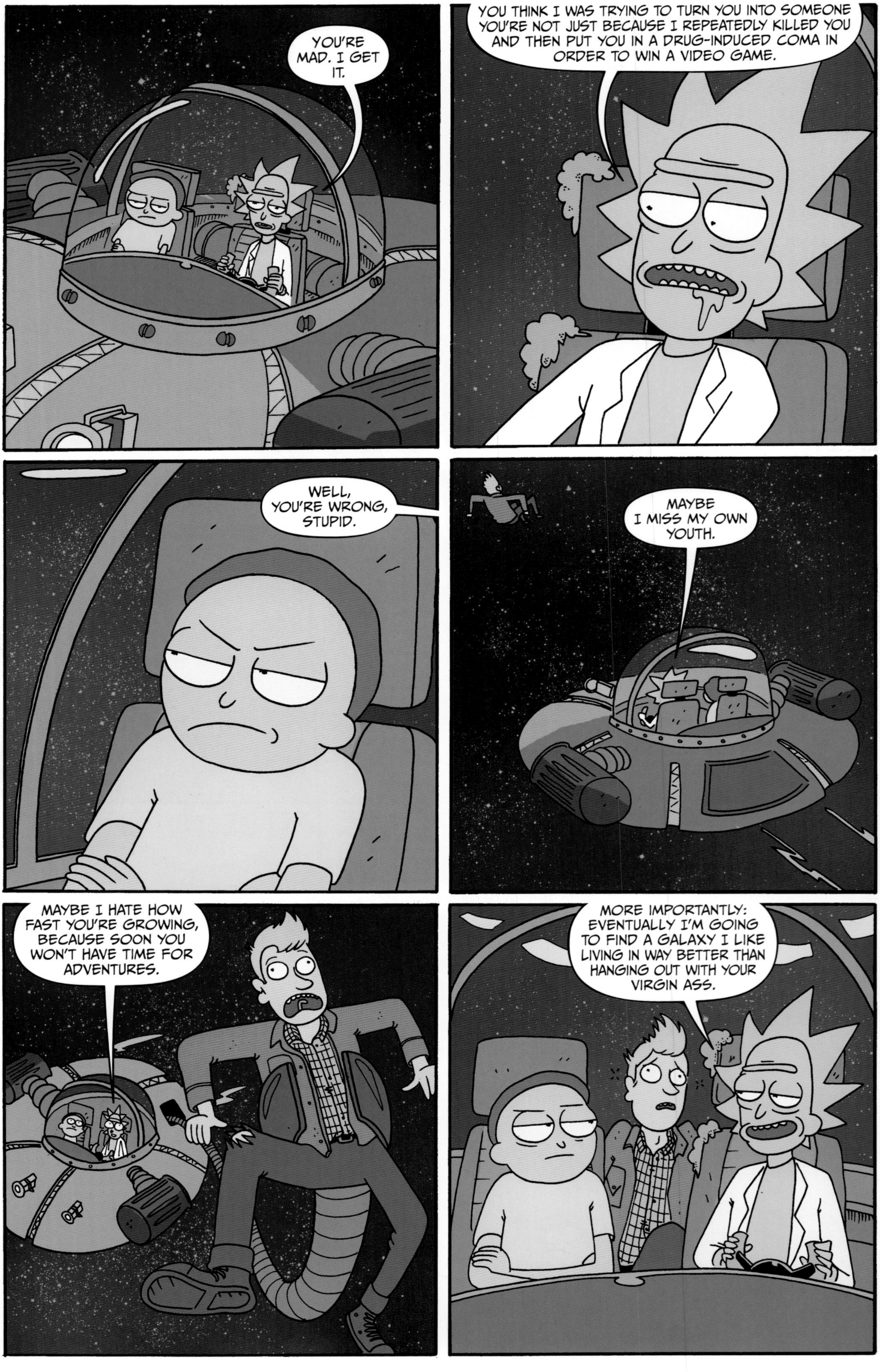
YOU'RE MAD. I GET IT.
YOU THINK I WAS TRYING TO TURN YOU INTO SOMEONE YOU'RE NOT JUST BECAUSE I REPEATEDLY KILLED YOU AND THEN PUT YOU IN A DRUG-INDUCED COMA IN ORDER TO WIN A VIDEO GAME.
WELL, YOU'RE WRONG, STUPID.
MAYBE I MISS MY OWN YOUTH.
MAYBE I HATE HOW FAST YOU'RE GROWING, BECAUSE SOON YOU WON'T HAVE TIME FOR ADVENTURES.
MORE IMPORTANTLY: EVENTUALLY I'M GOING TO FIND A GALAXY I LIKE LIVING IN WAY BETTER THAN HANGING OUT WITH YOUR VIRGIN ASS.

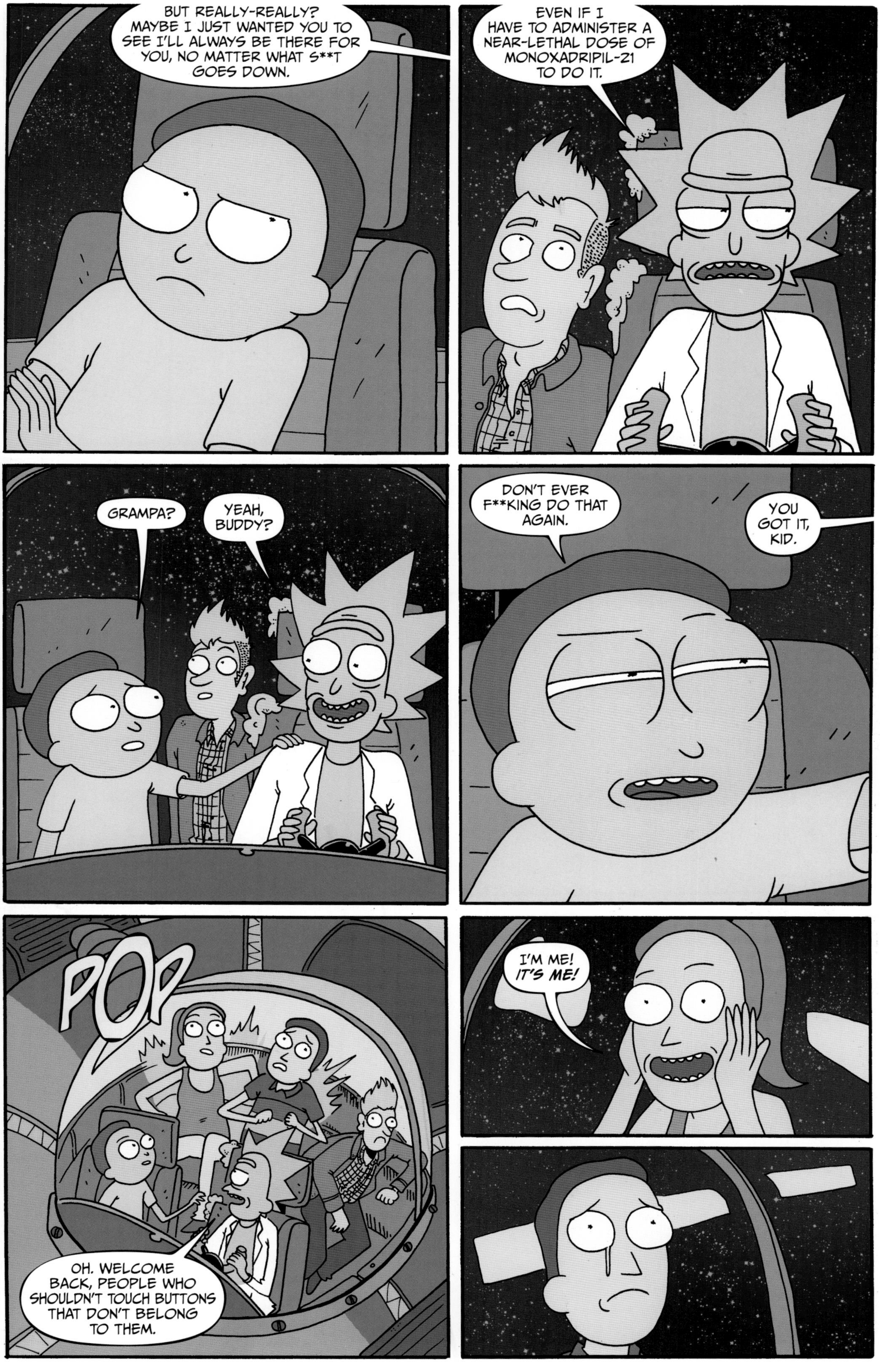
BUT REALLY-REALLY? MAYBE I JUST WANTED YOU TO SEE I'LL ALWAYS BE THERE FOR YOU, NO MATTER WHAT S**T GOES DOWN.
EVEN IF I HAVE TO ADMINISTER A NEAR-LETHAL DOSE OF MONOXADRIPIL-21 TO DO IT.
GRAMPA?
YEAH, BUDDY?
DON'T EVER F**KING DO THAT AGAIN.
YOU GOT IT, KID.
POP
OH. WELCOME BACK, PEOPLE WHO SHOULDN'T TOUCH BUTTONS THAT DON'T BELONG TO THEM.
I'M ME! *IT'S ME!*

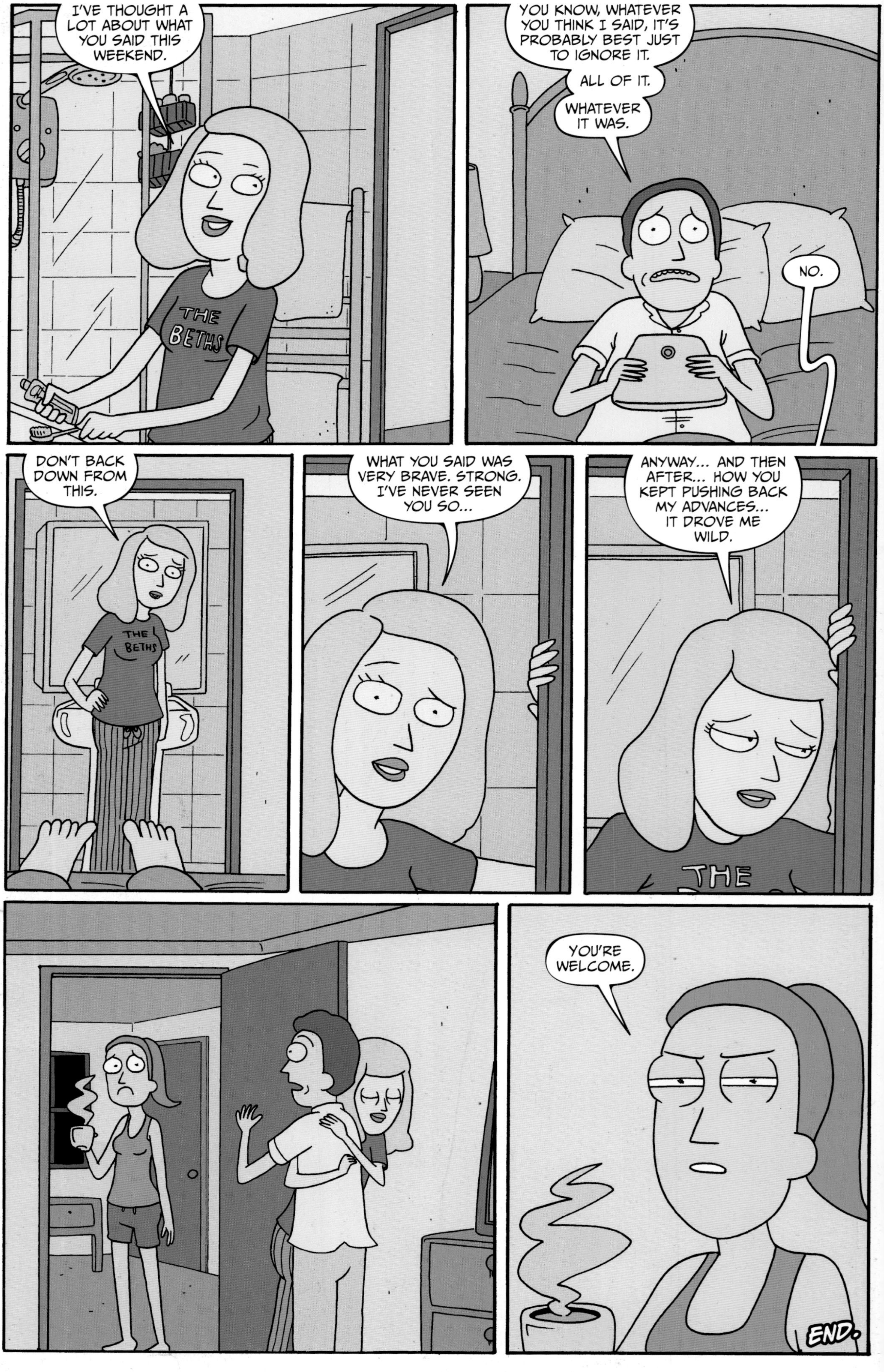
I'VE THOUGHT A LOT ABOUT WHAT YOU SAID THIS WEEKEND.
THE BETHS
YOU KNOW, WHATEVER YOU THINK I SAID, IT'S PROBABLY BEST JUST TO IGNORE IT.
ALL OF IT.
WHATEVER IT WAS.
NO.
DON'T BACK DOWN FROM THIS.
THE BETHS
WHAT YOU SAID WAS VERY BRAVE. STRONG. I'VE NEVER SEEN YOU SO...
ANYWAY... AND THEN AFTER... HOW YOU KEPT PUSHING BACK MY ADVANCES... IT DROVE ME WILD.
THE
YOU'RE WELCOME.
END.

BR-RICKING BAD, PART ONE:
THE RICKY HORROR PEACOCK SHOW

WRITTEN BY **KYLE STARKS**
DRAWN BY **CJ CANNON**
COLORED BY **RYAN HILL**
LETTERED BY **CRANK!**

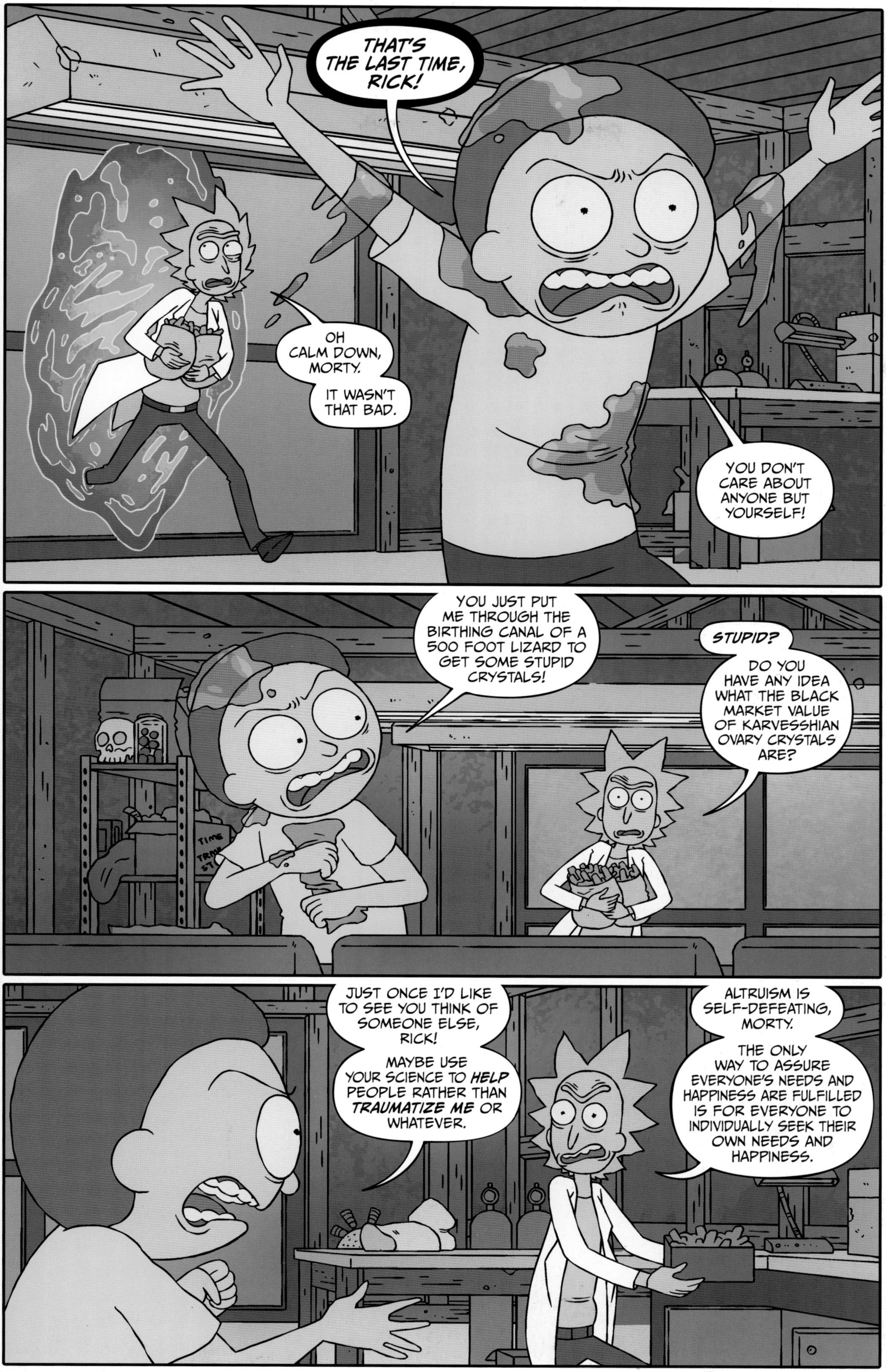
THAT'S THE LAST TIME, RICK!
OH CALM DOWN, MORTY.
IT WASN'T THAT BAD.
YOU DON'T CARE ABOUT ANYONE BUT YOURSELF!
YOU JUST PUT ME THROUGH THE BIRTHING CANAL OF A 500 FOOT LIZARD TO GET SOME STUPID CRYSTALS!
STUPID?
DO YOU HAVE ANY IDEA WHAT THE BLACK MARKET VALUE OF KARVESSHIAN OVARY CRYSTALS ARE?
JUST ONCE I'D LIKE TO SEE YOU THINK OF SOMEONE ELSE, RICK!
MAYBE USE YOUR SCIENCE TO HELP PEOPLE RATHER THAN TRAUMATIZE ME OR WHATEVER.
ALTRUISM IS SELF-DEFEATING, MORTY.
THE ONLY WAY TO ASSURE EVERYONE'S NEEDS AND HAPPINESS ARE FULFILLED IS FOR EVERYONE TO INDIVIDUALLY SEEK THEIR OWN NEEDS AND HAPPINESS.

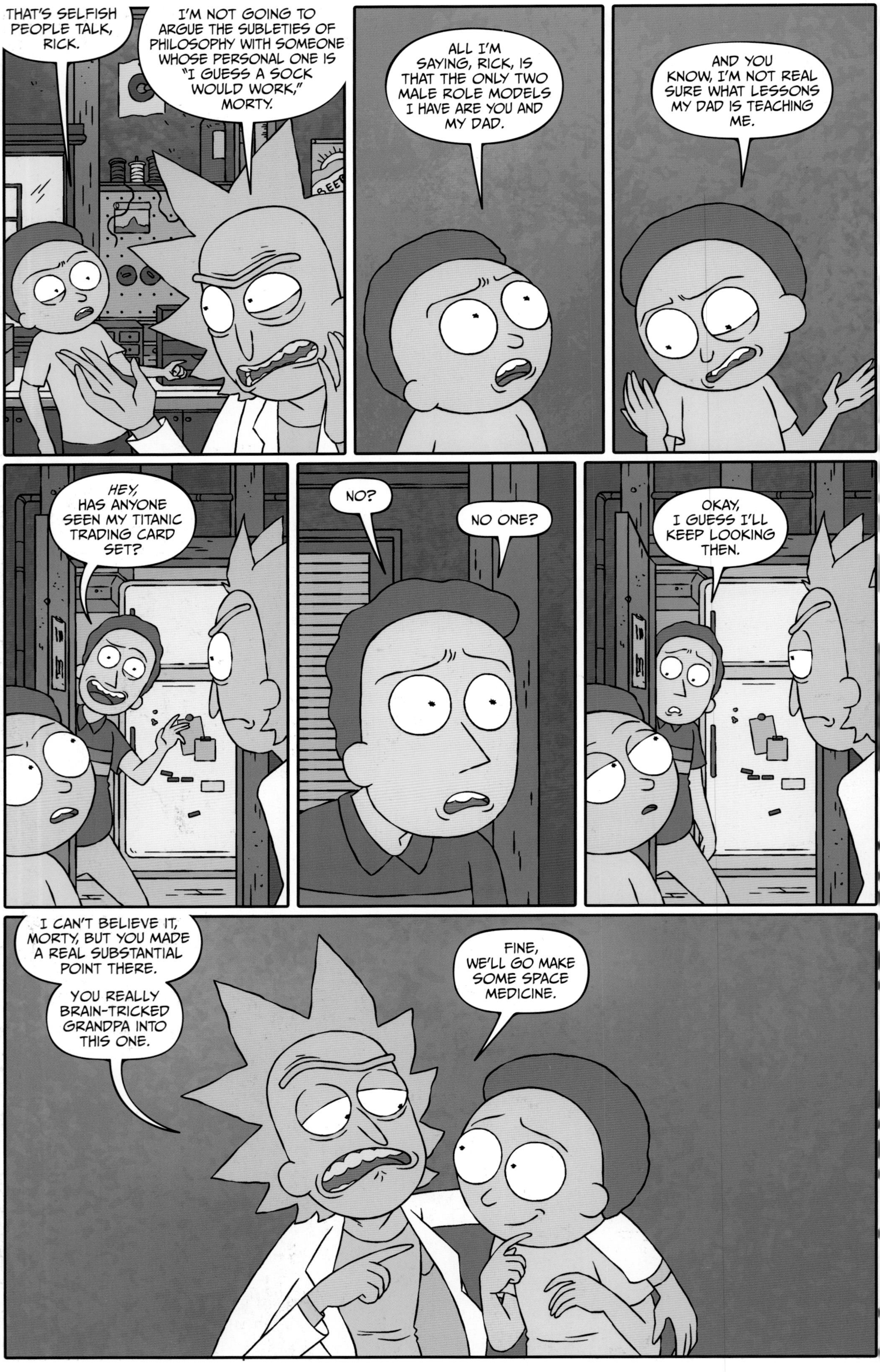
THAT'S SELFISH PEOPLE TALK, RICK.
I'M NOT GOING TO ARGUE THE SUBLETIES OF PHILOSOPHY WITH SOMEONE WHOSE PERSONAL ONE IS "I GUESS A SOCK WOULD WORK," MORTY.
BEER
ALL I'M SAYING, RICK, IS THAT THE ONLY TWO MALE ROLE MODELS I HAVE ARE YOU AND MY DAD.
AND YOU KNOW, I'M NOT REAL SURE WHAT LESSONS MY DAD IS TEACHING ME.
HEY, HAS ANYONE SEEN MY TITANIC TRADING CARD SET?
NO?
NO ONE?
OKAY, I GUESS I'LL KEEP LOOKING THEN.
I CAN'T BELIEVE IT, MORTY, BUT YOU MADE A REAL SUBSTANTIAL POINT THERE.
YOU REALLY BRAIN-TRICKED GRANDPA INTO THIS ONE.
FINE, WE'LL GO MAKE SOME SPACE MEDICINE.

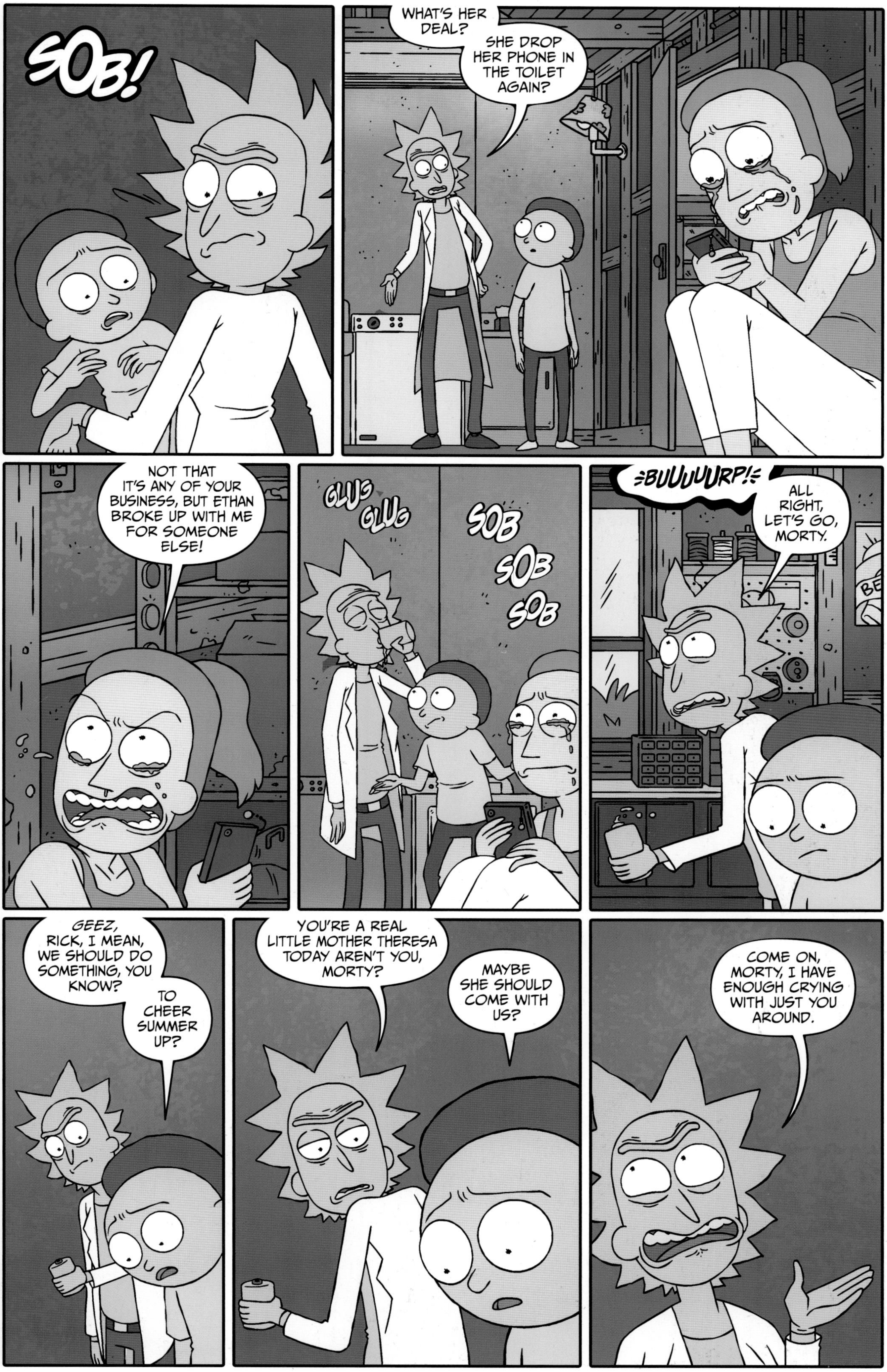
SOB!
WHAT'S HER DEAL?
SHE DROP HER PHONE IN THE TOILET AGAIN?
NOT THAT IT'S ANY OF YOUR BUSINESS, BUT ETHAN BROKE UP WITH ME FOR SOMEONE ELSE!
GLUG GLUG
SOB SOB SOB
BUUUUURP!
ALL RIGHT, LET'S GO, MORTY.
GEEZ, RICK, I MEAN, WE SHOULD DO SOMETHING, YOU KNOW?
TO CHEER SUMMER UP?
YOU'RE A REAL LITTLE MOTHER THERESA TODAY AREN'T YOU, MORTY?
MAYBE SHE SHOULD COME WITH US?
COME ON, MORTY, I HAVE ENOUGH CRYING WITH JUST YOU AROUND.

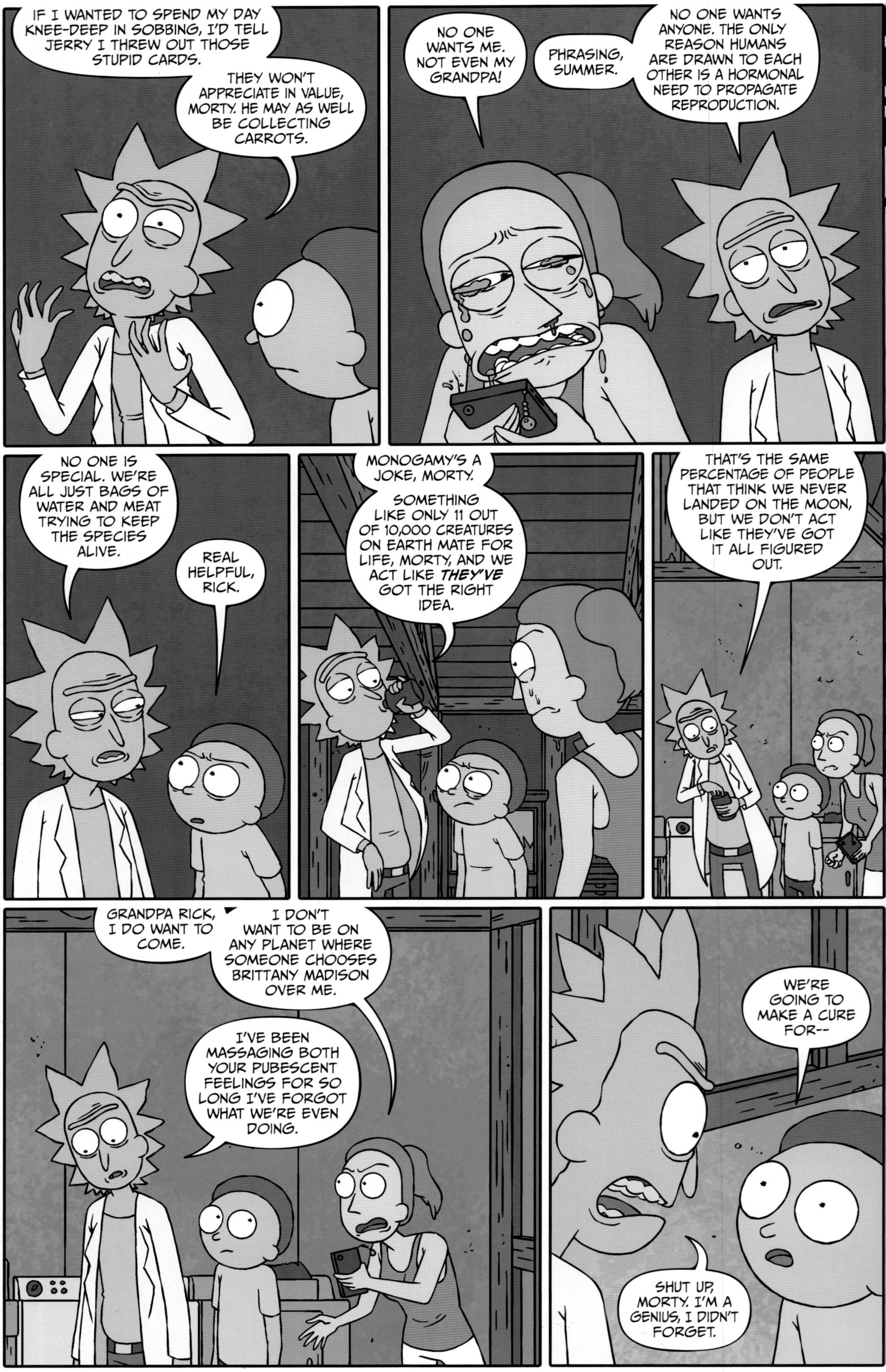
IF I WANTED TO SPEND MY DAY KNEE-DEEP IN SOBBING, I'D TELL JERRY I THREW OUT THOSE STUPID CARDS.
THEY WON'T APPRECIATE IN VALUE, MORTY. HE MAY AS WELL BE COLLECTING CARROTS.
NO ONE WANTS ME. NOT EVEN MY GRANDPA!
PHRASING, SUMMER.
NO ONE WANTS ANYONE. THE ONLY REASON HUMANS ARE DRAWN TO EACH OTHER IS A HORMONAL NEED TO PROPAGATE REPRODUCTION.
NO ONE IS SPECIAL. WE'RE ALL JUST BAGS OF WATER AND MEAT TRYING TO KEEP THE SPECIES ALIVE.
REAL HELPFUL, RICK.
MONOGAMY'S A JOKE, MORTY.
SOMETHING LIKE ONLY 11 OUT OF 10,000 CREATURES ON EARTH MATE FOR LIFE, MORTY, AND WE ACT LIKE ***THEY'VE*** GOT THE RIGHT IDEA.
THAT'S THE SAME PERCENTAGE OF PEOPLE THAT THINK WE NEVER LANDED ON THE MOON, BUT WE DON'T ACT LIKE THEY'VE GOT IT ALL FIGURED OUT.
GRANDPA RICK, I DO WANT TO COME.
I DON'T WANT TO BE ON ANY PLANET WHERE SOMEONE CHOOSES BRITTANY MADISON OVER ME.
I'VE BEEN MASSAGING BOTH YOUR PUBESCENT FEELINGS FOR SO LONG I'VE FORGOT WHAT WE'RE EVEN DOING.
WE'RE GOING TO MAKE A CURE FOR--
SHUT UP, MORTY. I'M A GENIUS, I DIDN'T FORGET.

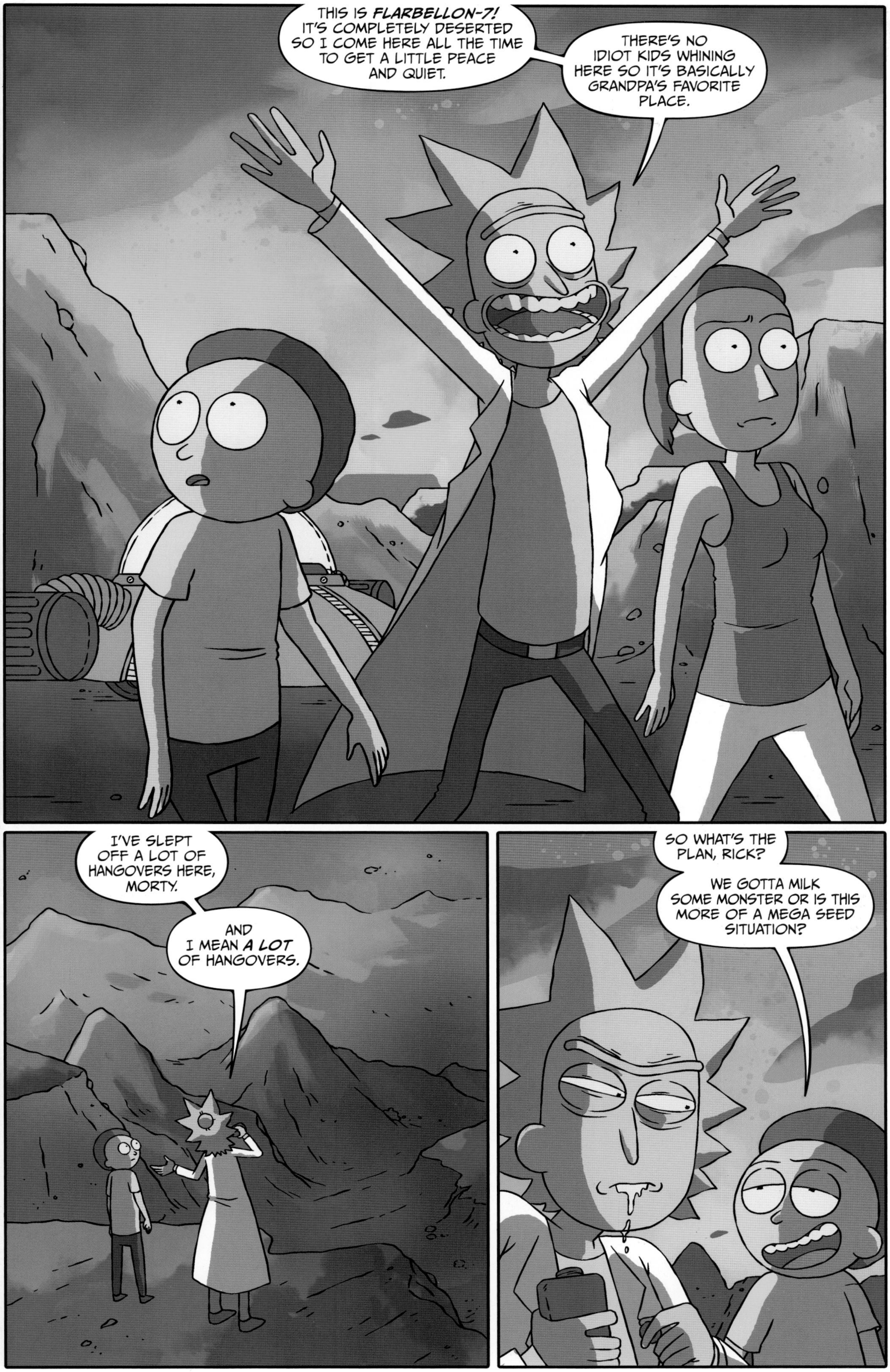
THIS IS FLARBELLON-7! IT'S COMPLETELY DESERTED SO I COME HERE ALL THE TIME TO GET A LITTLE PEACE AND QUIET.
THERE'S NO IDIOT KIDS WHINING HERE SO IT'S BASICALLY GRANDPA'S FAVORITE PLACE.
I'VE SLEPT OFF A LOT OF HANGOVERS HERE, MORTY.
AND I MEAN A LOT OF HANGOVERS.
SO WHAT'S THE PLAN, RICK?
WE GOTTA MILK SOME MONSTER OR IS THIS MORE OF A MEGA SEED SITUATION?

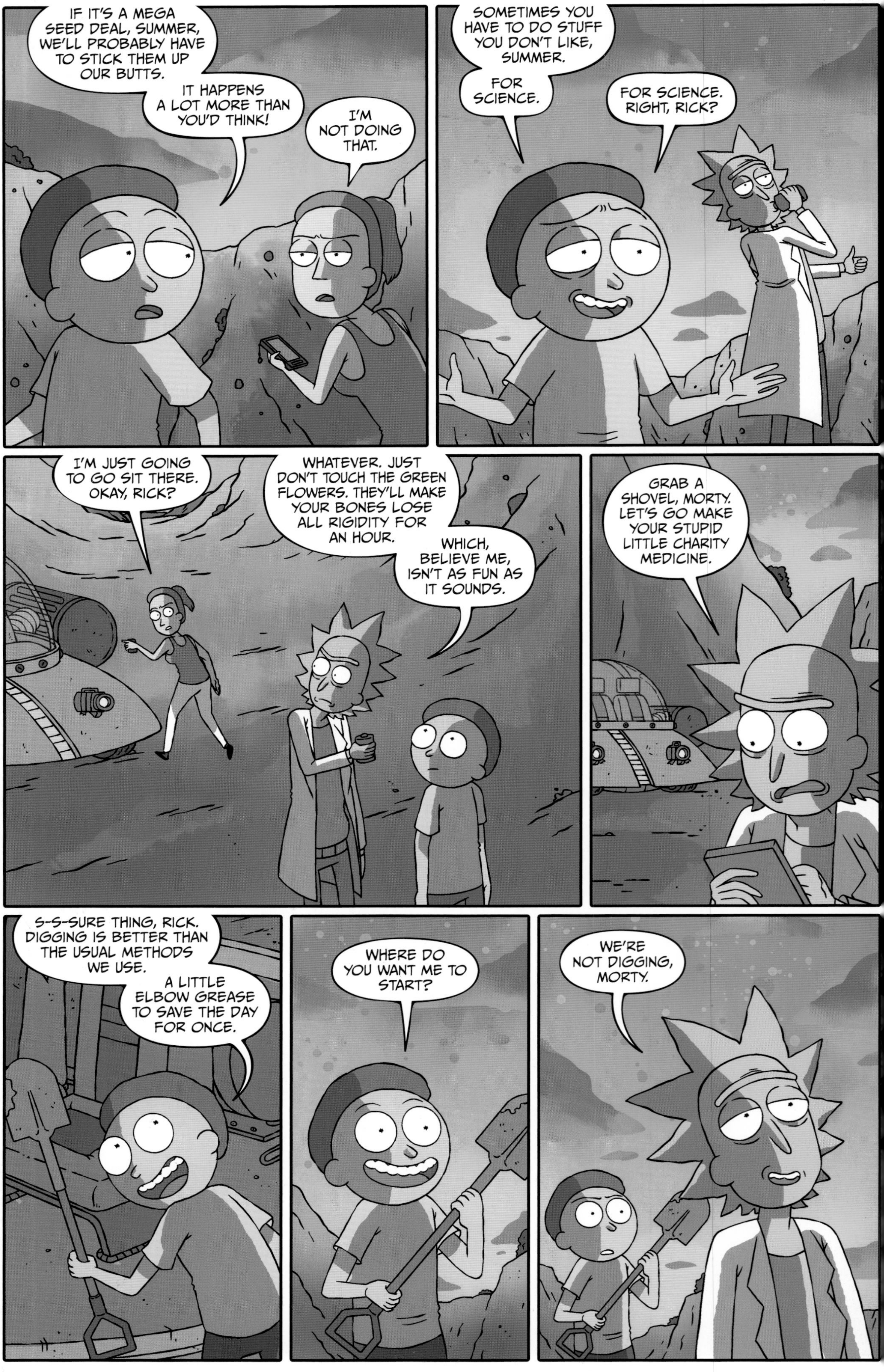
IF IT'S A MEGA SEED DEAL, SUMMER, WE'LL PROBABLY HAVE TO STICK THEM UP OUR BUTTS.
IT HAPPENS A LOT MORE THAN YOU'D THINK!
I'M NOT DOING THAT.
SOMETIMES YOU HAVE TO DO STUFF YOU DON'T LIKE, SUMMER.
FOR SCIENCE.
FOR SCIENCE. RIGHT, RICK?
I'M JUST GOING TO GO SIT THERE. OKAY, RICK?
WHATEVER. JUST DON'T TOUCH THE GREEN FLOWERS. THEY'LL MAKE YOUR BONES LOSE ALL RIGIDITY FOR AN HOUR.
WHICH, BELIEVE ME, ISN'T AS FUN AS IT SOUNDS.
GRAB A SHOVEL, MORTY. LET'S GO MAKE YOUR STUPID LITTLE CHARITY MEDICINE.
S-S-SURE THING, RICK. DIGGING IS BETTER THAN THE USUAL METHODS WE USE.
A LITTLE ELBOW GREASE TO SAVE THE DAY FOR ONCE.
WHERE DO YOU WANT ME TO START?
WE'RE NOT DIGGING, MORTY.

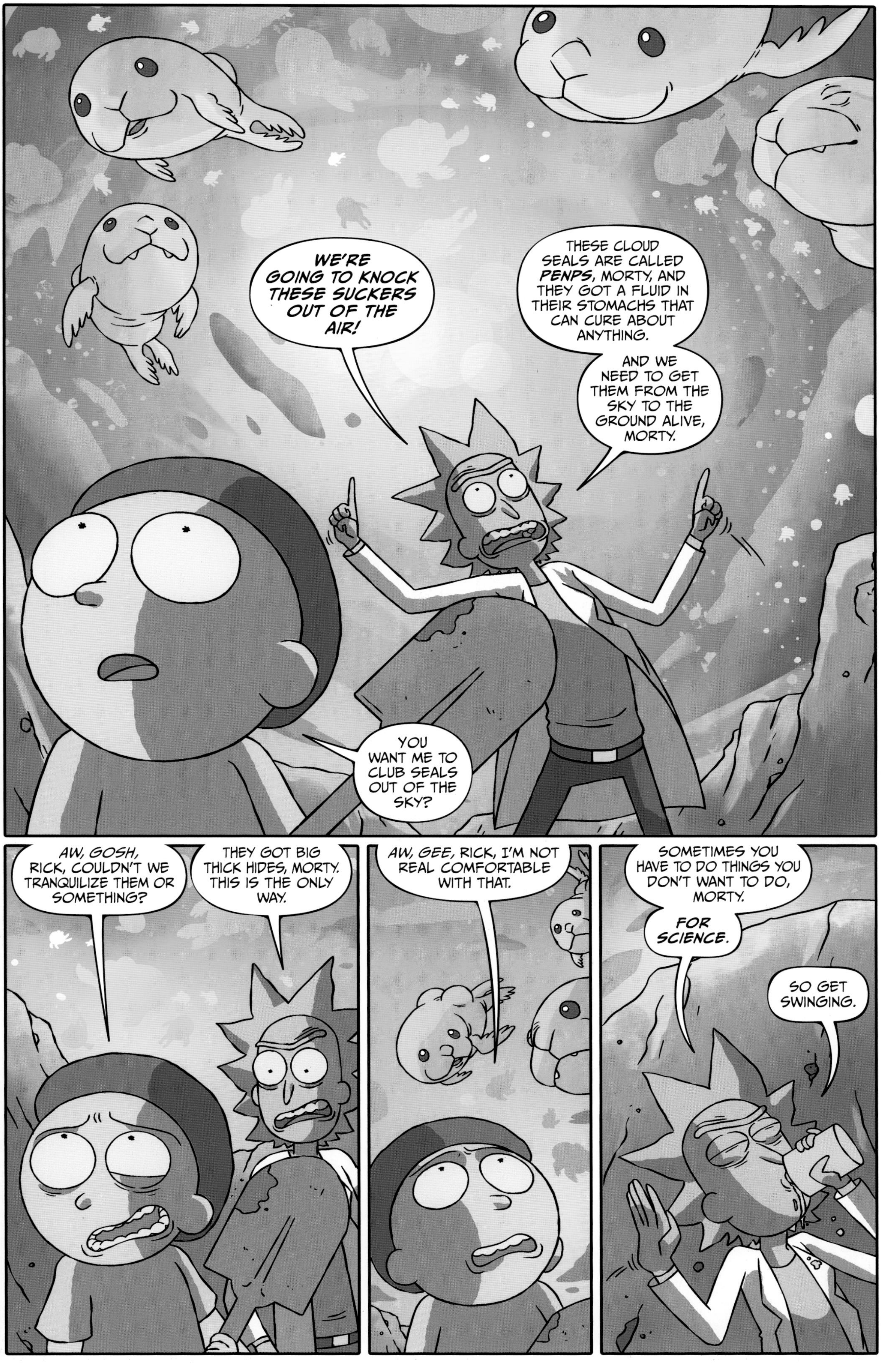
WE'RE GOING TO KNOCK THESE SUCKERS OUT OF THE AIR!
THESE CLOUD SEALS ARE CALLED PENPS, MORTY, AND THEY GOT A FLUID IN THEIR STOMACHS THAT CAN CURE ABOUT ANYTHING.
AND WE NEED TO GET THEM FROM THE SKY TO THE GROUND ALIVE, MORTY.
YOU WANT ME TO CLUB SEALS OUT OF THE SKY?
AW, GOSH, RICK, COULDN'T WE TRANQUILIZE THEM OR SOMETHING?
THEY GOT BIG THICK HIDES, MORTY. THIS IS THE ONLY WAY.
AW, GEE, RICK, I'M NOT REAL COMFORTABLE WITH THAT.
SOMETIMES YOU HAVE TO DO THINGS YOU DON'T WANT TO DO, MORTY.
FOR SCIENCE.
SO GET SWINGING.

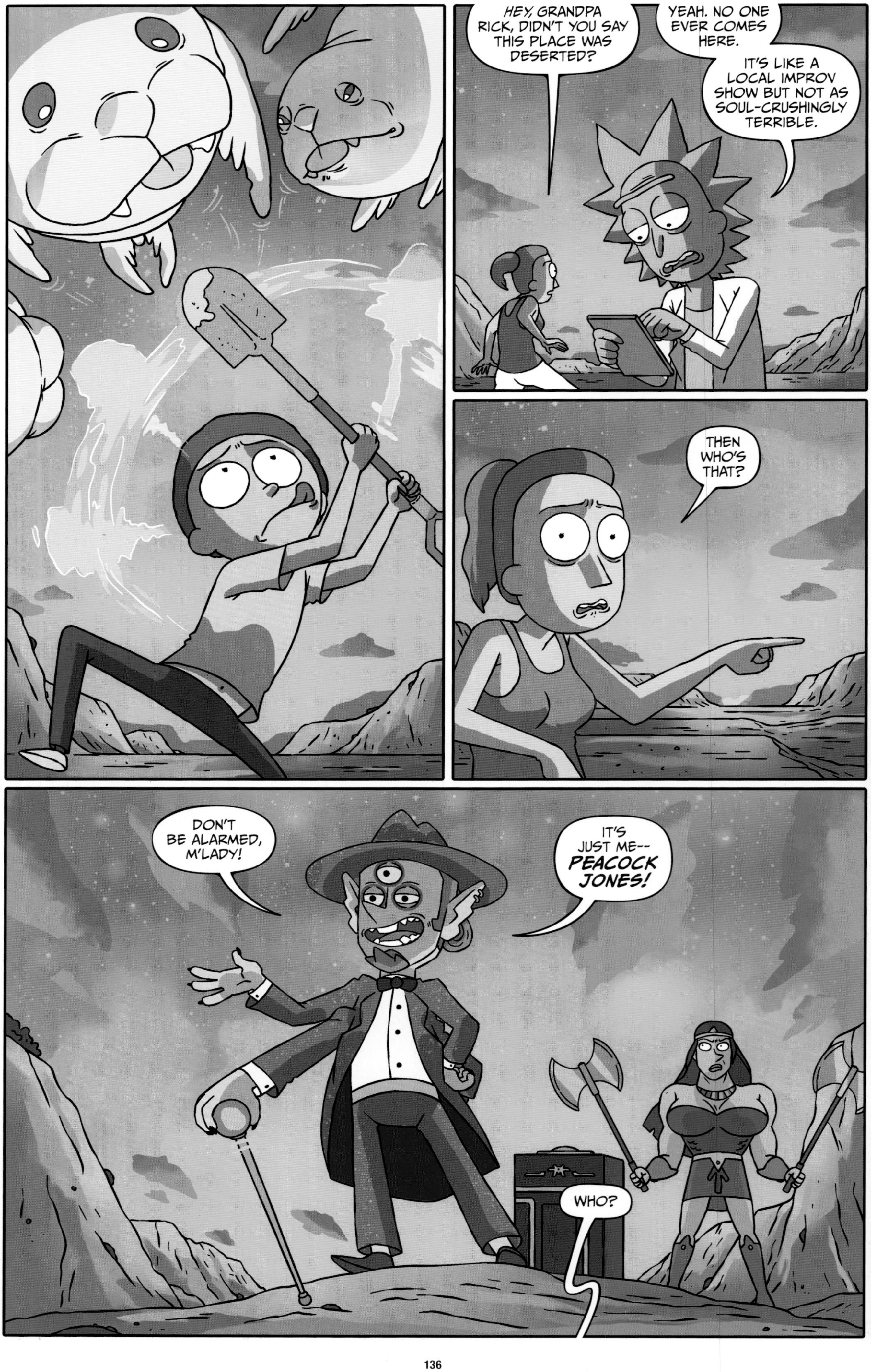
HEY, GRANDPA RICK, DIDN'T YOU SAY THIS PLACE WAS DESERTED?
YEAH. NO ONE EVER COMES HERE.
IT'S LIKE A LOCAL IMPROV SHOW BUT NOT AS SOUL-CRUSHINGLY TERRIBLE.
THEN WHO'S THAT?
DON'T BE ALARMED, M'LADY!
IT'S JUST ME-- PEACOCK JONES!
WHO?

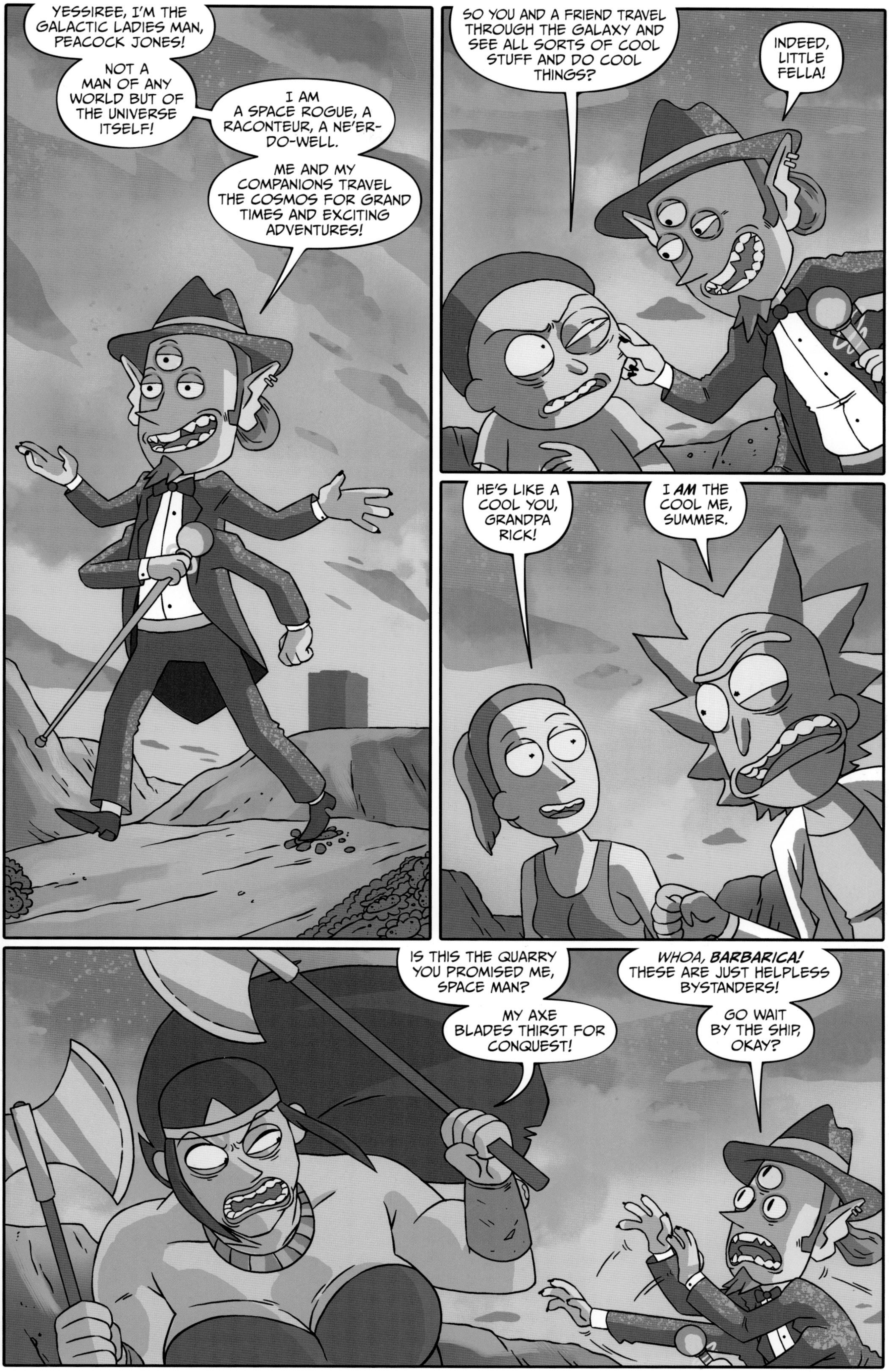
YESSIREE, I'M THE GALACTIC LADIES MAN, PEACOCK JONES!
NOT A MAN OF ANY WORLD BUT OF THE UNIVERSE ITSELF!
I AM A SPACE ROGUE, A RACONTEUR, A NE'ER-DO-WELL.
ME AND MY COMPANIONS TRAVEL THE COSMOS FOR GRAND TIMES AND EXCITING ADVENTURES!
SO YOU AND A FRIEND TRAVEL THROUGH THE GALAXY AND SEE ALL SORTS OF COOL STUFF AND DO COOL THINGS?
INDEED, LITTLE FELLA!
HE'S LIKE A COOL YOU, GRANDPA RICK!
I *AM* THE COOL ME, SUMMER.
IS THIS THE QUARRY YOU PROMISED ME, SPACE MAN?
MY AXE BLADES THIRST FOR CONQUEST!
*WHOA, **BARBARICA!*** THESE ARE JUST HELPLESS BYSTANDERS!
GO WAIT BY THE SHIP, OKAY?

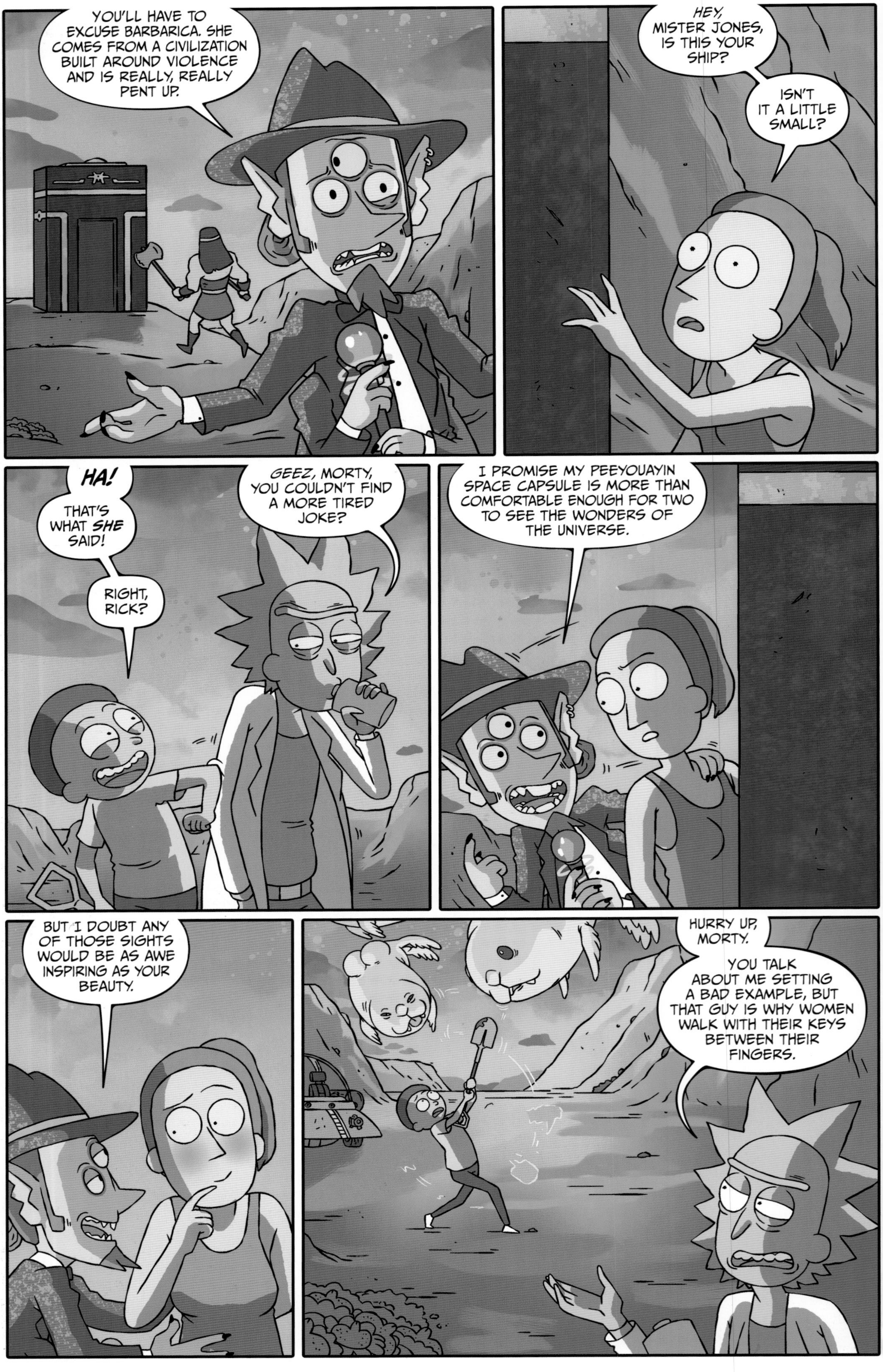
YOU'LL HAVE TO EXCUSE BARBARICA. SHE COMES FROM A CIVILIZATION BUILT AROUND VIOLENCE AND IS REALLY, REALLY PENT UP.
HEY, MISTER JONES, IS THIS YOUR SHIP?
ISN'T IT A LITTLE SMALL?
HA!
THAT'S WHAT SHE SAID!
RIGHT, RICK?
GEEZ, MORTY, YOU COULDN'T FIND A MORE TIRED JOKE?
I PROMISE MY PEEYOUAYIN SPACE CAPSULE IS MORE THAN COMFORTABLE ENOUGH FOR TWO TO SEE THE WONDERS OF THE UNIVERSE.
BUT I DOUBT ANY OF THOSE SIGHTS WOULD BE AS AWE INSPIRING AS YOUR BEAUTY.
HURRY UP, MORTY.
YOU TALK ABOUT ME SETTING A BAD EXAMPLE, BUT THAT GUY IS WHY WOMEN WALK WITH THEIR KEYS BETWEEN THEIR FINGERS.

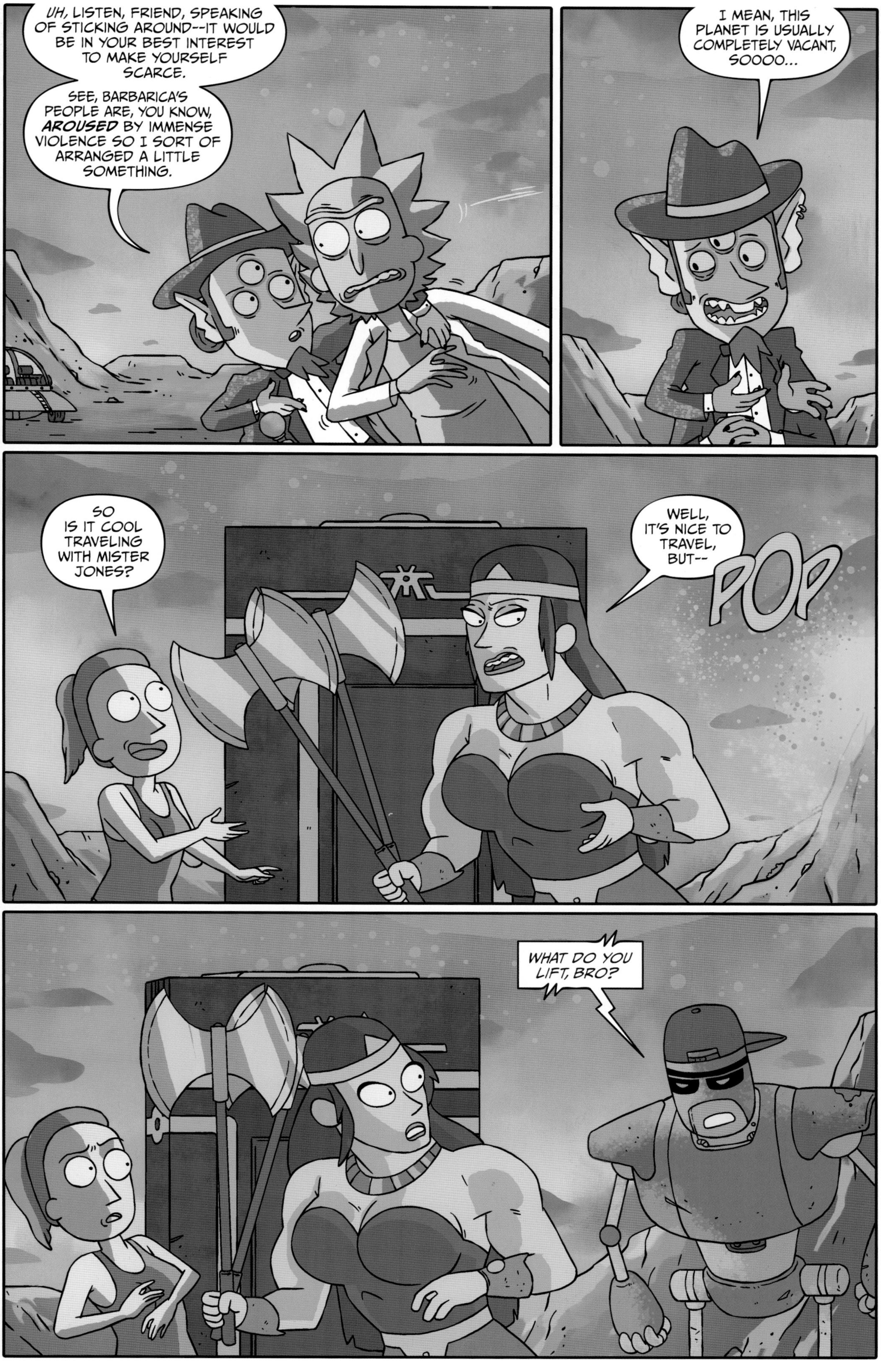
UH, LISTEN, FRIEND, SPEAKING OF STICKING AROUND--IT WOULD BE IN YOUR BEST INTEREST TO MAKE YOURSELF SCARCE.
SEE, BARBARICA'S PEOPLE ARE, YOU KNOW, AROUSED BY IMMENSE VIOLENCE SO I SORT OF ARRANGED A LITTLE SOMETHING.
I MEAN, THIS PLANET IS USUALLY COMPLETELY VACANT, SOOOO...
SO IS IT COOL TRAVELING WITH MISTER JONES?
WELL, IT'S NICE TO TRAVEL, BUT--
POP
WHAT DO YOU LIFT, BRO?

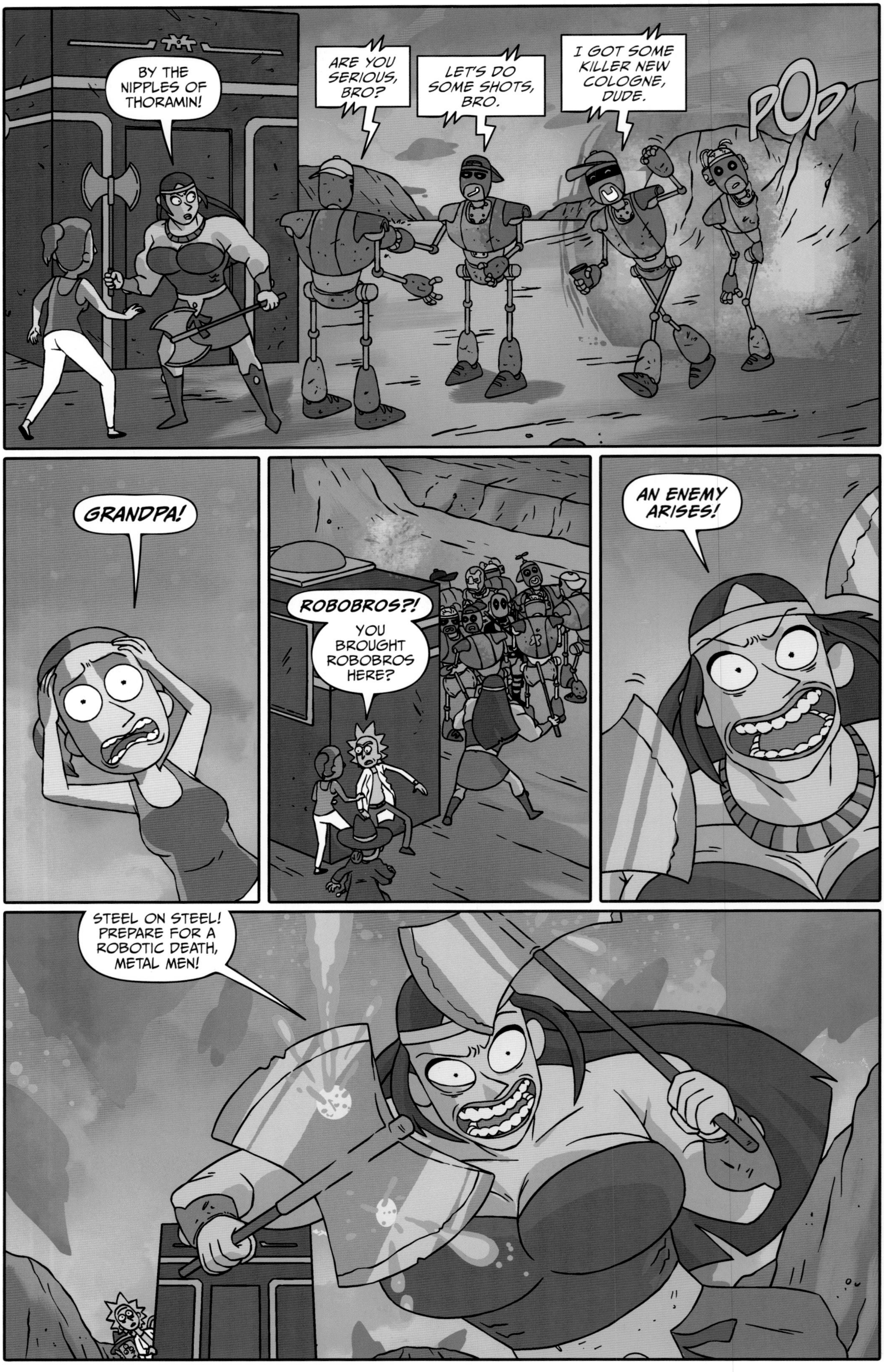
BY THE NIPPLES OF THORAMIN!
ARE YOU SERIOUS, BRO?
LET'S DO SOME SHOTS, BRO.
I GOT SOME KILLER NEW COLOGNE, DUDE.
POP
GRANDPA!
ROBOBROS?! YOU BROUGHT ROBOBROS HERE?
AN ENEMY ARISES!
STEEL ON STEEL! PREPARE FOR A ROBOTIC DEATH, METAL MEN!

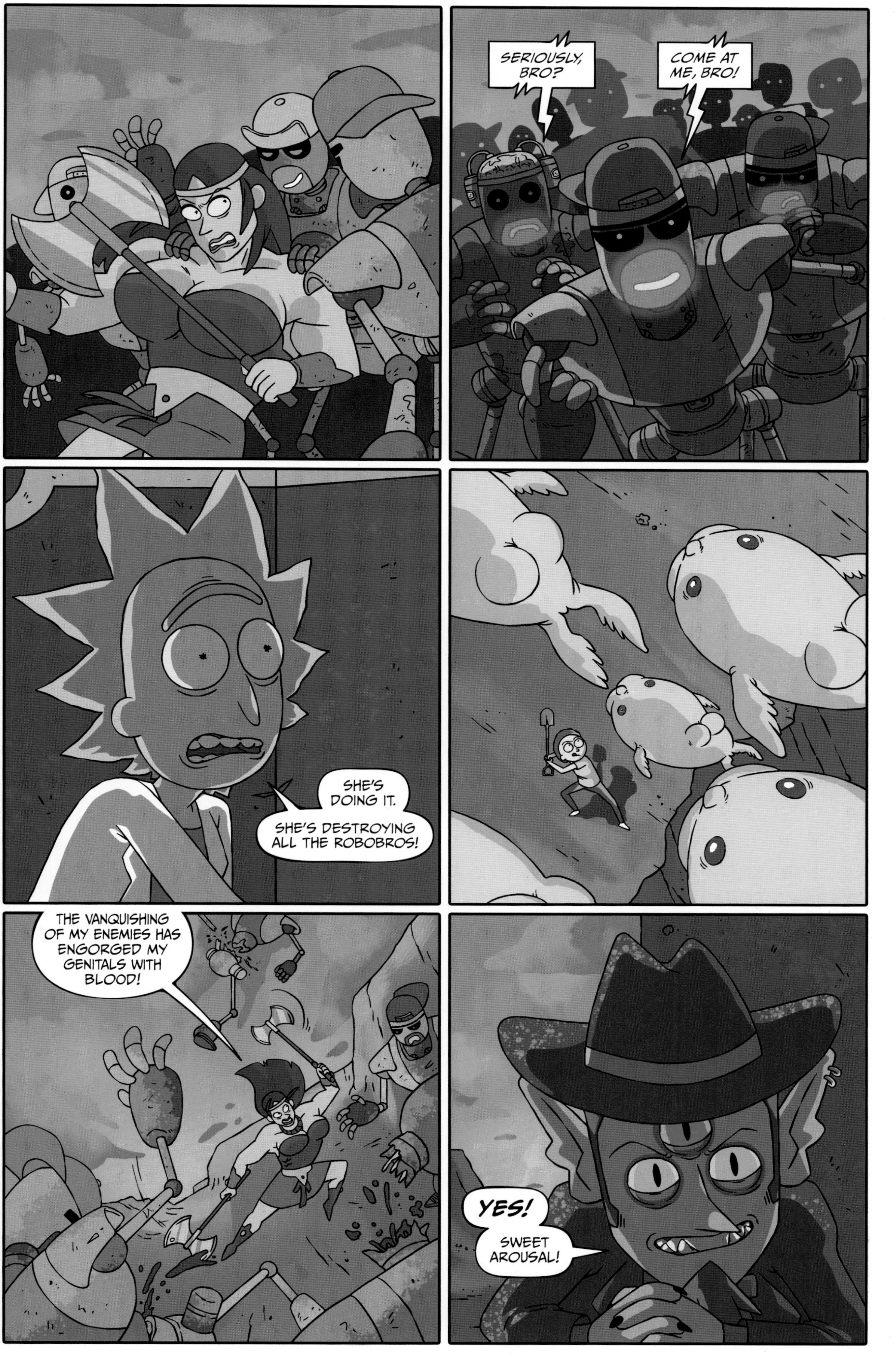
SERIOUSLY, BRO?
COME AT ME, BRO!
SHE'S DOING IT.
SHE'S DESTROYING ALL THE ROBOBROS!
THE VANQUISHING OF MY ENEMIES HAS ENGORGED MY GENITALS WITH BLOOD!
YES!
SWEET AROUSAL!

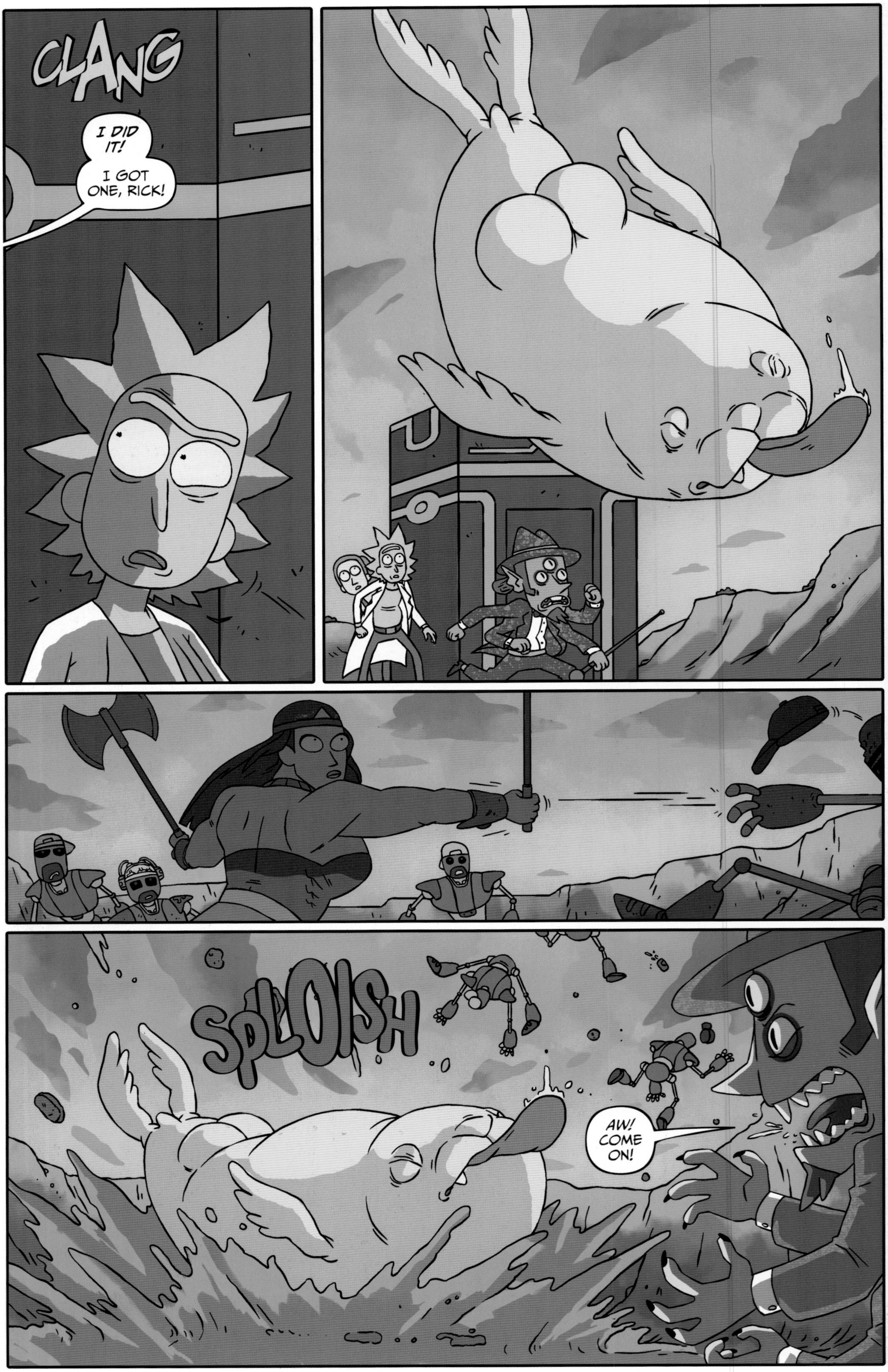
CLANG
I DID IT!
I GOT ONE, RICK!
SPLOISH
AW! COME ON!

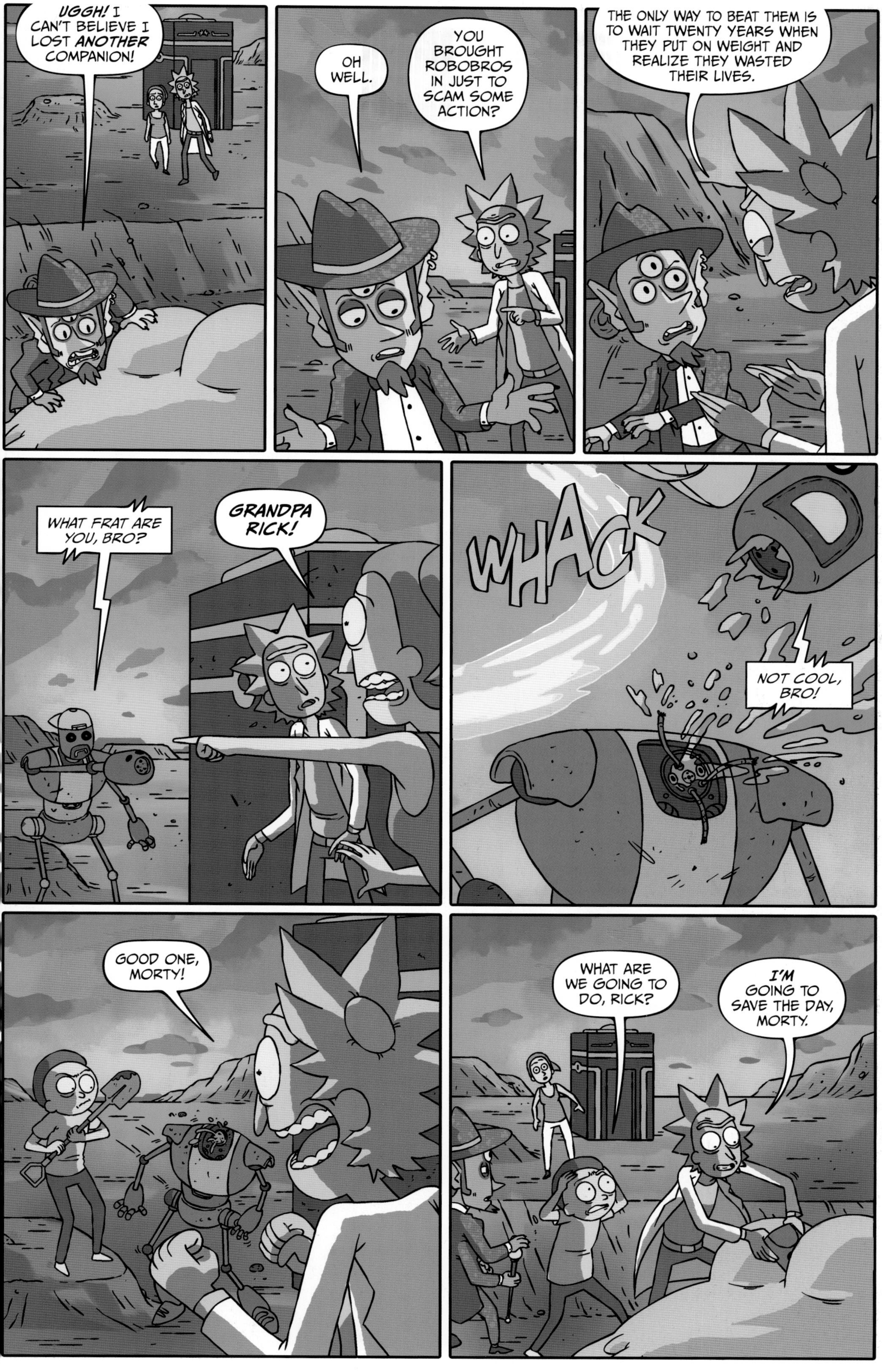
UGGH! I CAN'T BELIEVE I LOST ANOTHER COMPANION!
OH WELL.
YOU BROUGHT ROBOBROS IN JUST TO SCAM SOME ACTION?
THE ONLY WAY TO BEAT THEM IS TO WAIT TWENTY YEARS WHEN THEY PUT ON WEIGHT AND REALIZE THEY WASTED THEIR LIVES.
WHAT FRAT ARE YOU, BRO?
GRANDPA RICK!
WHACK
NOT COOL, BRO!
GOOD ONE, MORTY!
WHAT ARE WE GOING TO DO, RICK?
I'M GOING TO SAVE THE DAY, MORTY.

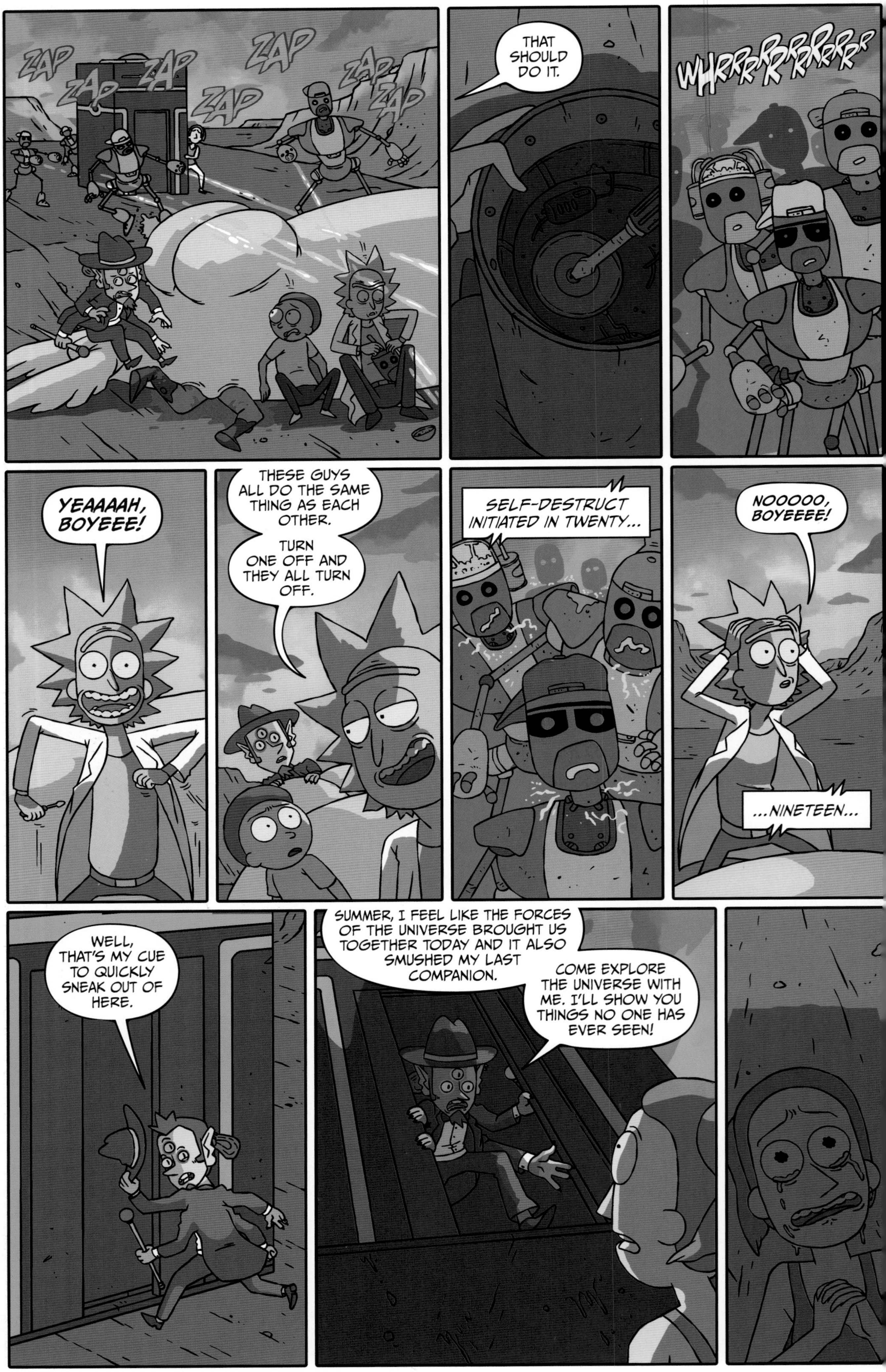
ZAP ZAP ZAP ZAP ZAP ZAP ZAP
THAT SHOULD DO IT.
WHRRRRRRRRRRRR
YEAAAAH, BOYEEE!
THESE GUYS ALL DO THE SAME THING AS EACH OTHER.
TURN ONE OFF AND THEY ALL TURN OFF.
SELF-DESTRUCT INITIATED IN TWENTY...
NOOOOO, BOYEEEE!
...NINETEEN...
WELL, THAT'S MY CUE TO QUICKLY SNEAK OUT OF HERE.
SUMMER, I FEEL LIKE THE FORCES OF THE UNIVERSE BROUGHT US TOGETHER TODAY AND IT ALSO SMUSHED MY LAST COMPANION.
COME EXPLORE THE UNIVERSE WITH ME. I'LL SHOW YOU THINGS NO ONE HAS EVER SEEN!

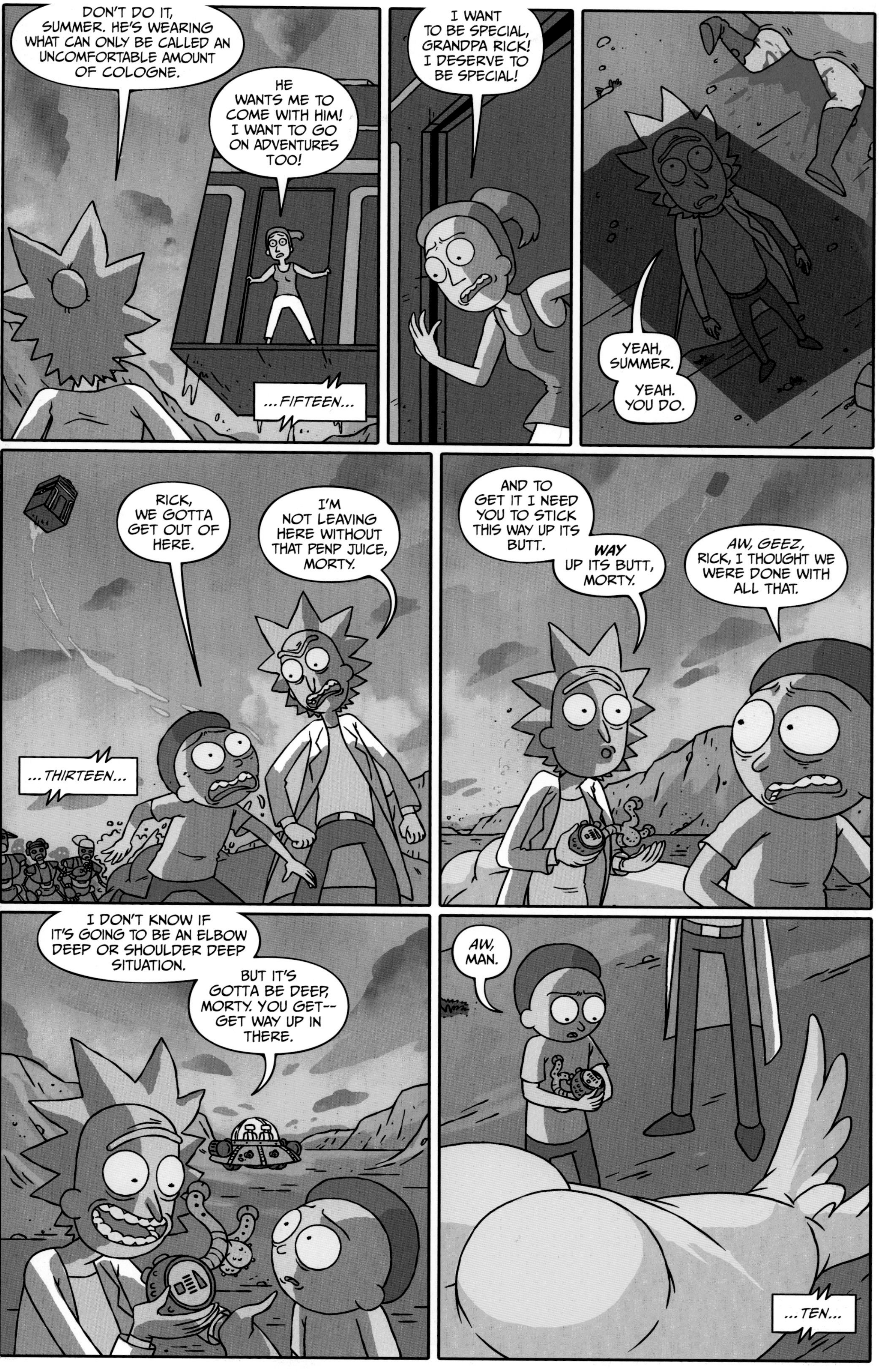
DON'T DO IT, SUMMER. HE'S WEARING WHAT CAN ONLY BE CALLED AN UNCOMFORTABLE AMOUNT OF COLOGNE.
HE WANTS ME TO COME WITH HIM! I WANT TO GO ON ADVENTURES TOO!
...FIFTEEN...
I WANT TO BE SPECIAL, GRANDPA RICK! I DESERVE TO BE SPECIAL!
YEAH, SUMMER.
YEAH. YOU DO.
RICK, WE GOTTA GET OUT OF HERE.
I'M NOT LEAVING HERE WITHOUT THAT PENP JUICE, MORTY.
...THIRTEEN...
AND TO GET IT I NEED YOU TO STICK THIS WAY UP ITS BUTT.
WAY UP ITS BUTT, MORTY.
AW, GEEZ, RICK, I THOUGHT WE WERE DONE WITH ALL THAT.
I DON'T KNOW IF IT'S GOING TO BE AN ELBOW DEEP OR SHOULDER DEEP SITUATION.
BUT IT'S GOTTA BE DEEP, MORTY. YOU GET-- GET WAY UP IN THERE.
AW, MAN.
...TEN...

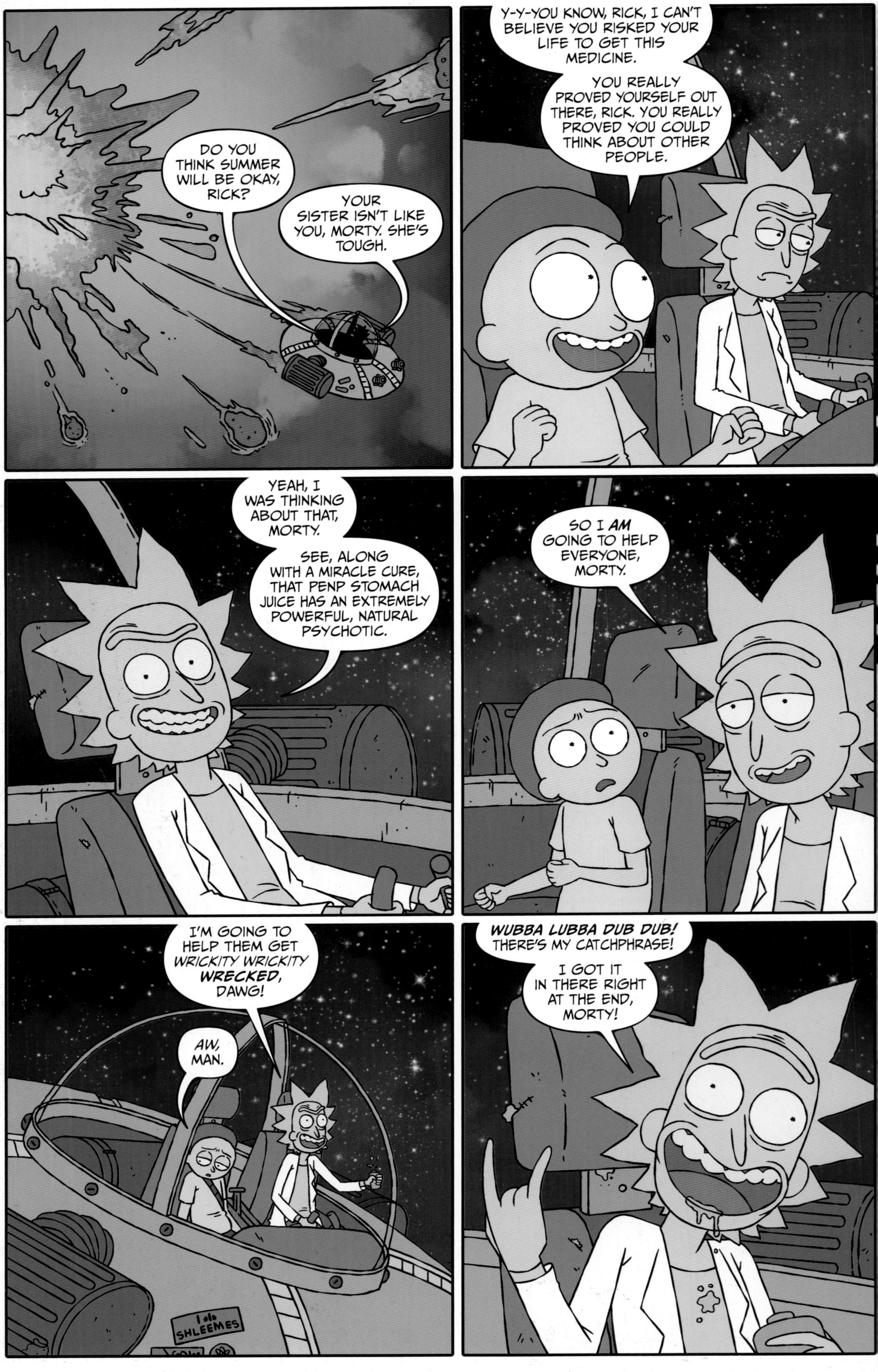
DO YOU THINK SUMMER WILL BE OKAY, RICK?
YOUR SISTER ISN'T LIKE YOU, MORTY. SHE'S TOUGH.
Y-Y-YOU KNOW, RICK, I CAN'T BELIEVE YOU RISKED YOUR LIFE TO GET THIS MEDICINE.
YOU REALLY PROVED YOURSELF OUT THERE, RICK. YOU REALLY PROVED YOU COULD THINK ABOUT OTHER PEOPLE.
YEAH, I WAS THINKING ABOUT THAT, MORTY.
SEE, ALONG WITH A MIRACLE CURE, THAT PENP STOMACH JUICE HAS AN EXTREMELY POWERFUL, NATURAL PSYCHOTIC.
SO I *AM* GOING TO HELP EVERYONE, MORTY.
I'M GOING TO HELP THEM GET *WRICKITY WRICKITY* ***WRECKED***, DAWG!
AW, MAN.
SHLEEMES
WUBBA LUBBA DUB DUB! THERE'S MY CATCHPHRASE!
I GOT IT IN THERE RIGHT AT THE END, MORTY!

BR-RICKING BAD, PART TWO: NEW RICK CITY

WRITTEN BY **KYLE STARKS**

DRAWN BY **CJ CANNON**

COLORED BY **RYAN HILL**

LETTERED BY **CRANK!**

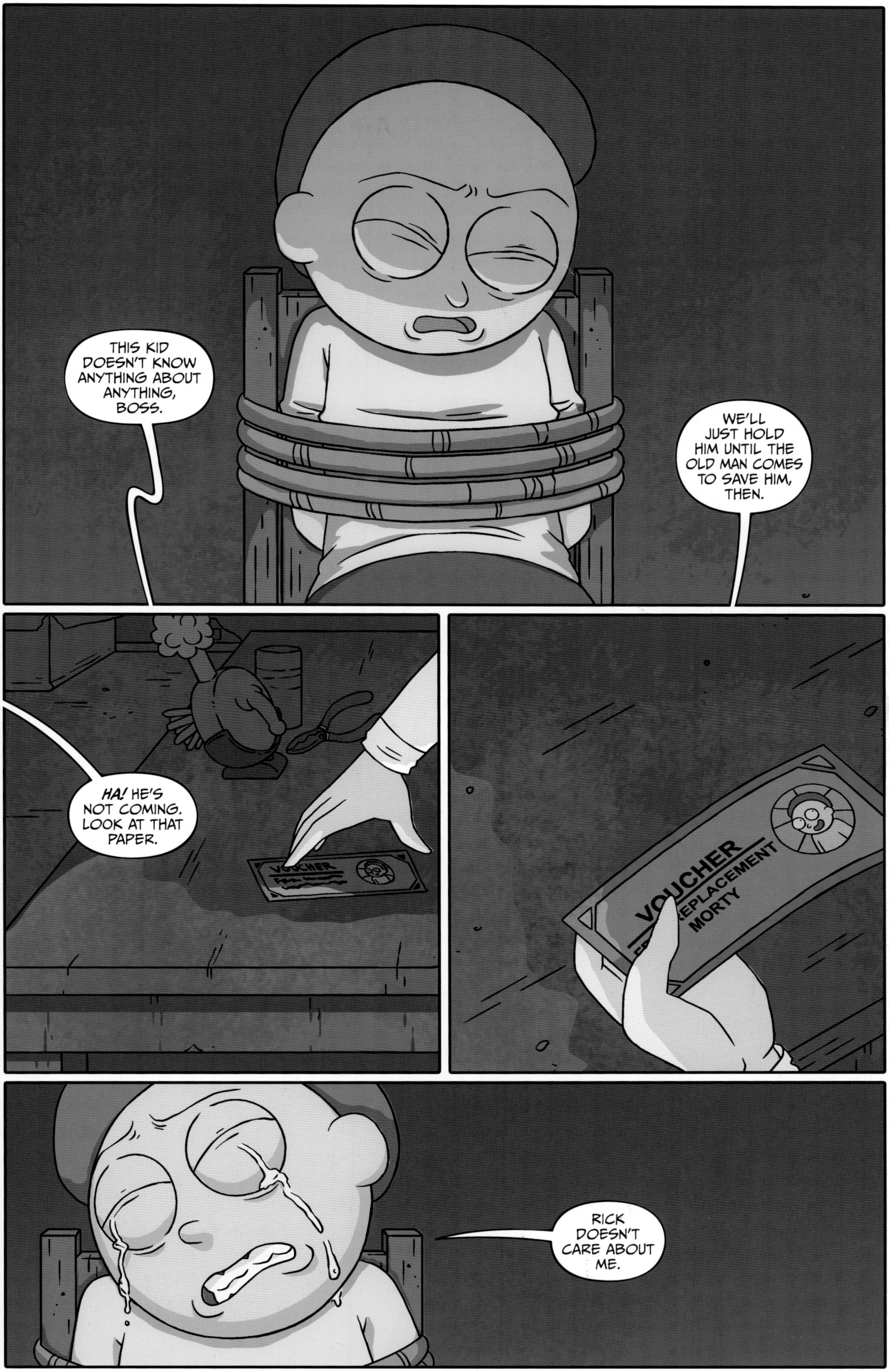
THIS KID DOESN'T KNOW ANYTHING ABOUT ANYTHING, BOSS.
WE'LL JUST HOLD HIM UNTIL THE OLD MAN COMES TO SAVE HIM, THEN.
HA! HE'S NOT COMING. LOOK AT THAT PAPER.
VOUCHER
REPLACEMENT
MORTY
RICK DOESN'T CARE ABOUT ME.

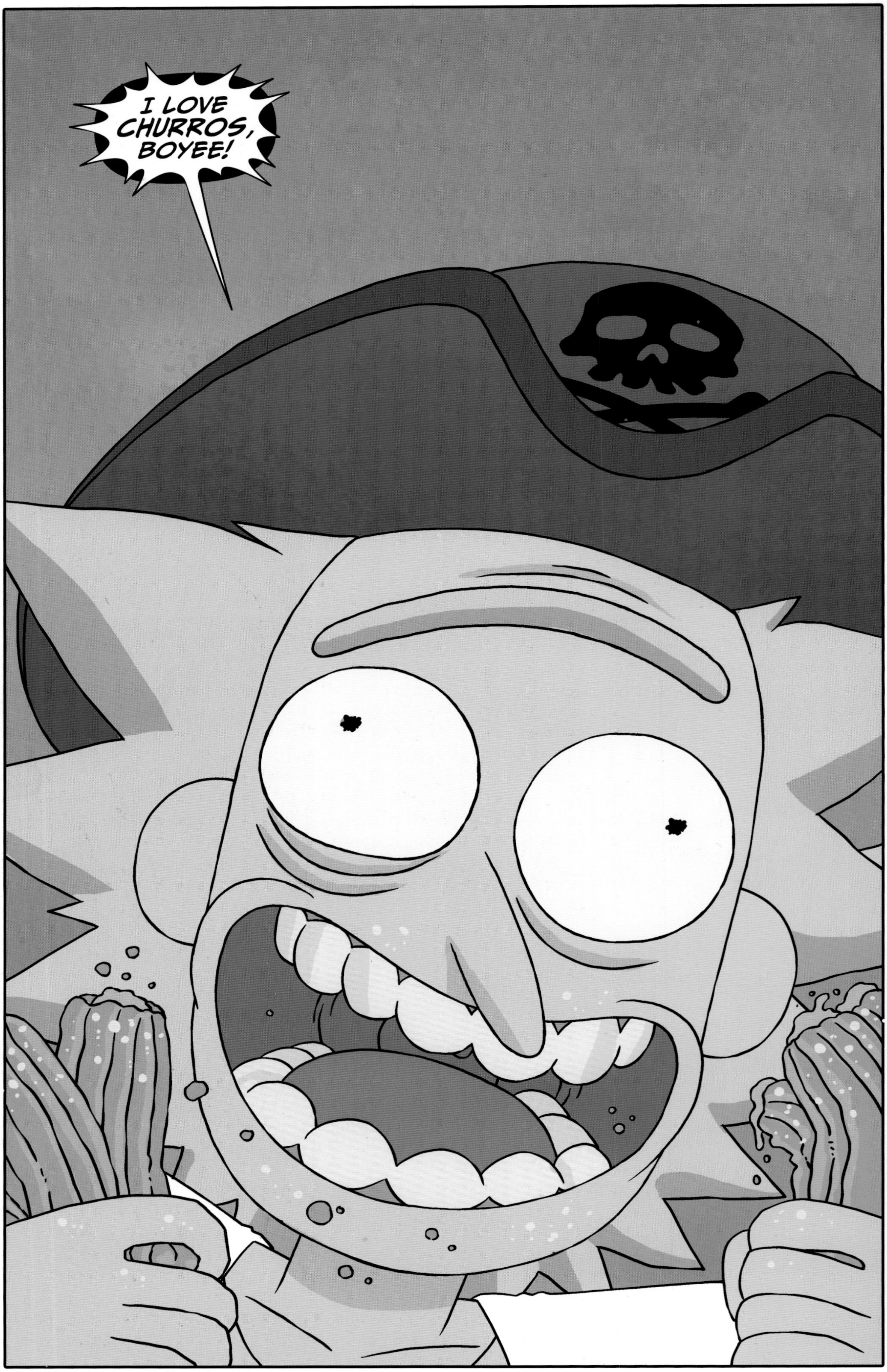
I LOVE CHURROS, BOYEE!

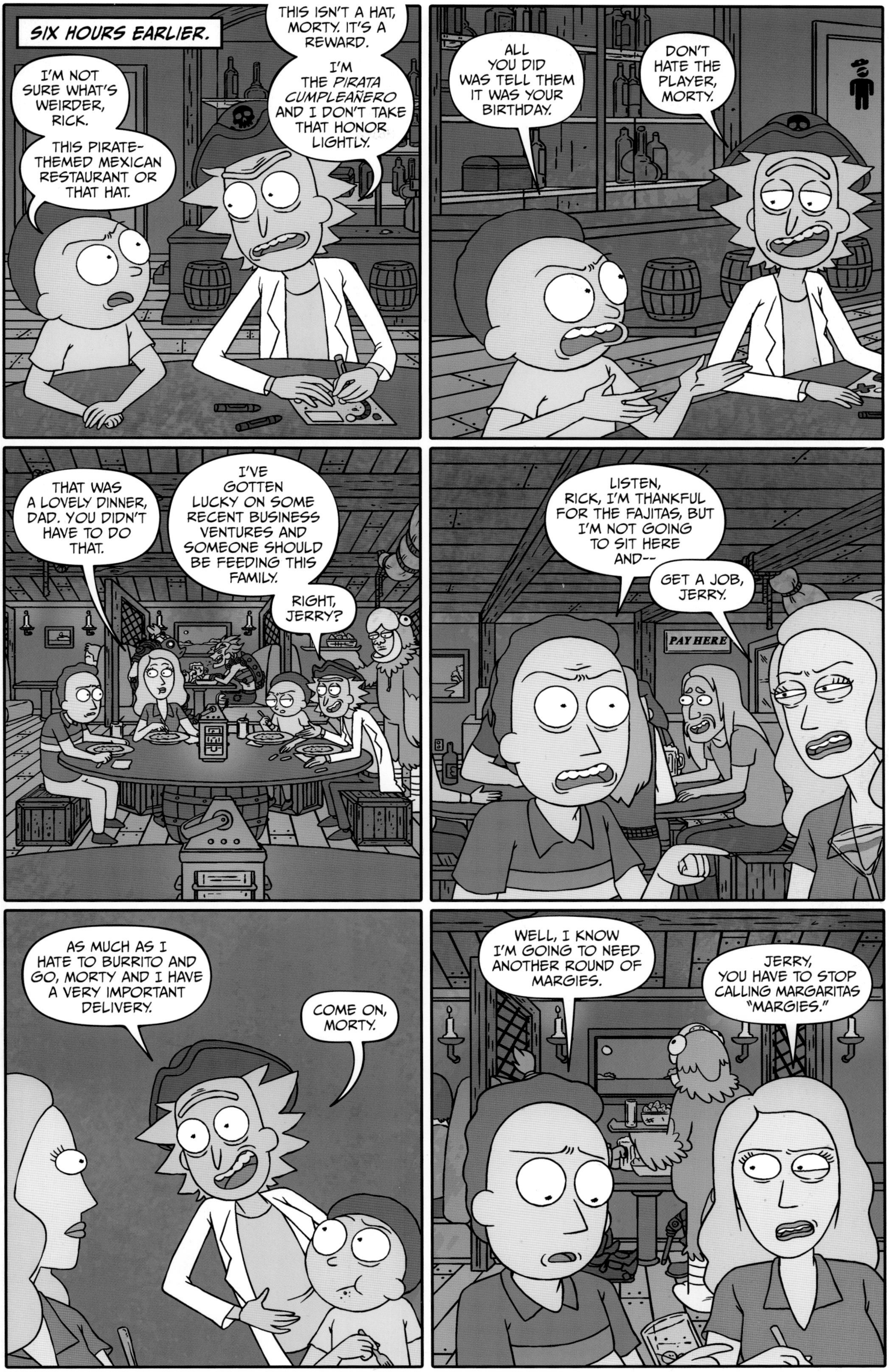
SIX HOURS EARLIER.
I'M NOT SURE WHAT'S WEIRDER, RICK.
THIS PIRATE-THEMED MEXICAN RESTAURANT OR THAT HAT.
THIS ISN'T A HAT, MORTY. IT'S A REWARD.
I'M THE *PIRATA CUMPLEAÑERO* AND I DON'T TAKE THAT HONOR LIGHTLY.
ALL YOU DID WAS TELL THEM IT WAS YOUR BIRTHDAY.
DON'T HATE THE PLAYER, MORTY.
THAT WAS A LOVELY DINNER, DAD. YOU DIDN'T HAVE TO DO THAT.
I'VE GOTTEN LUCKY ON SOME RECENT BUSINESS VENTURES AND SOMEONE SHOULD BE FEEDING THIS FAMILY.
RIGHT, JERRY?
LISTEN, RICK, I'M THANKFUL FOR THE FAJITAS, BUT I'M NOT GOING TO SIT HERE AND--
GET A JOB, JERRY.
PAY HERE
AS MUCH AS I HATE TO BURRITO AND GO, MORTY AND I HAVE A VERY IMPORTANT DELIVERY.
COME ON, MORTY.
WELL, I KNOW I'M GOING TO NEED ANOTHER ROUND OF MARGIES.
JERRY, YOU HAVE TO STOP CALLING MARGARITAS "MARGIES."

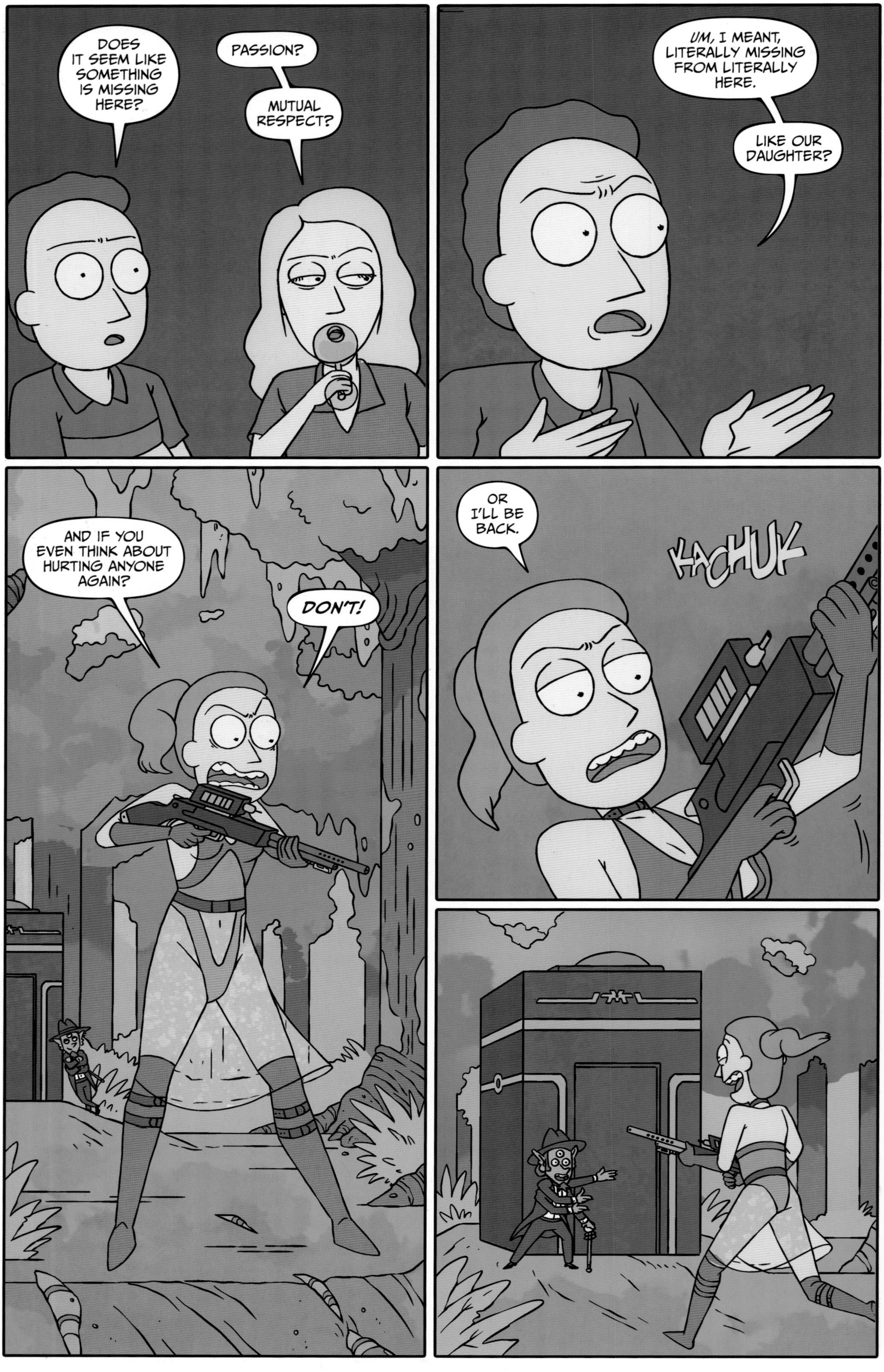
DOES IT SEEM LIKE SOMETHING IS MISSING HERE?
PASSION?
MUTUAL RESPECT?
UM, I MEANT, LITERALLY MISSING FROM LITERALLY HERE.
LIKE OUR DAUGHTER?
AND IF YOU EVEN THINK ABOUT HURTING ANYONE AGAIN?
DON'T!
OR I'LL BE BACK.
KACHUK

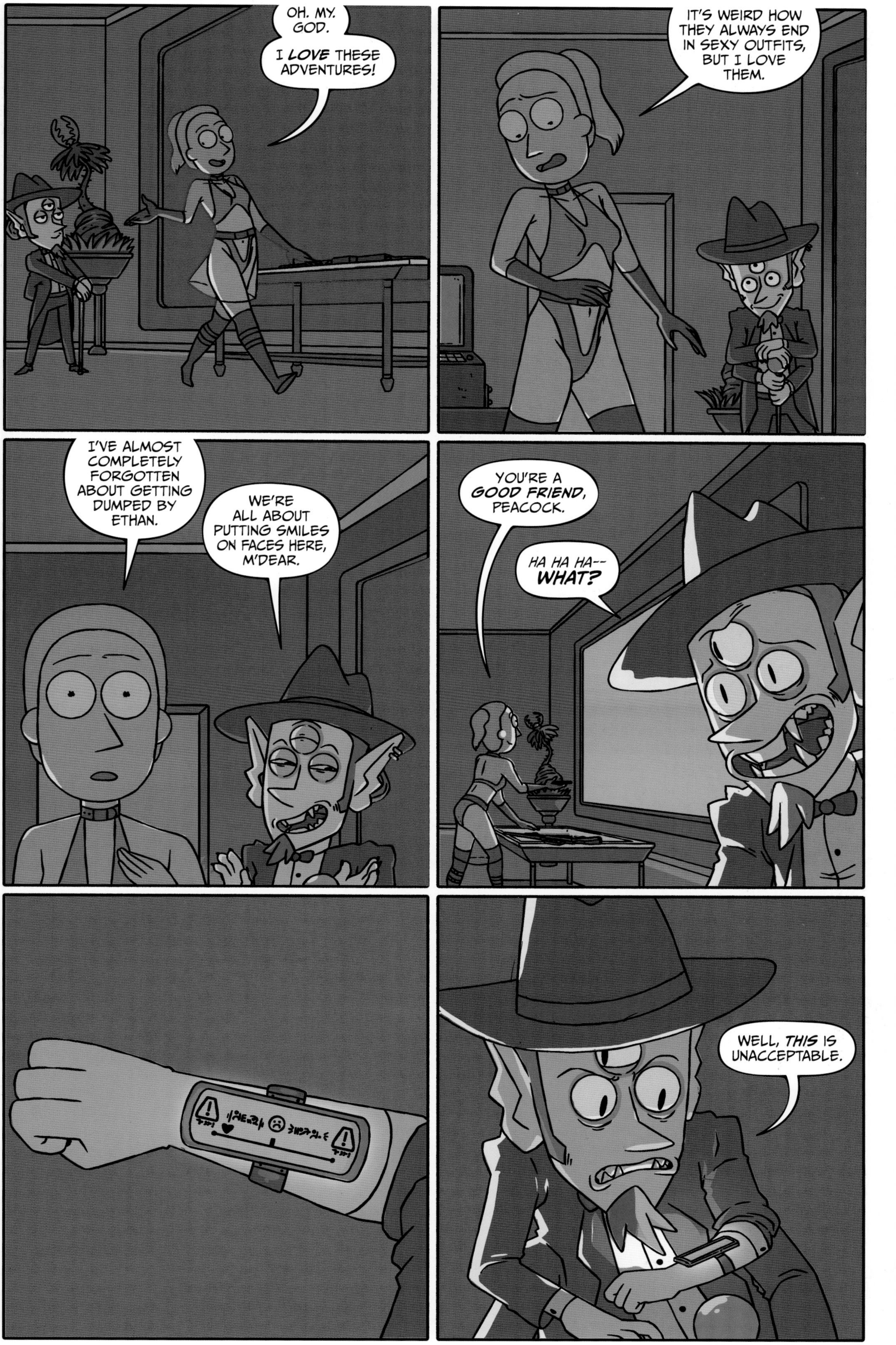
OH. MY. GOD.
I LOVE THESE ADVENTURES!
IT'S WEIRD HOW THEY ALWAYS END IN SEXY OUTFITS, BUT I LOVE THEM.
I'VE ALMOST COMPLETELY FORGOTTEN ABOUT GETTING DUMPED BY ETHAN.
WE'RE ALL ABOUT PUTTING SMILES ON FACES HERE, M'DEAR.
YOU'RE A GOOD FRIEND, PEACOCK.
HA HA HA-- WHAT?
WELL, THIS IS UNACCEPTABLE.

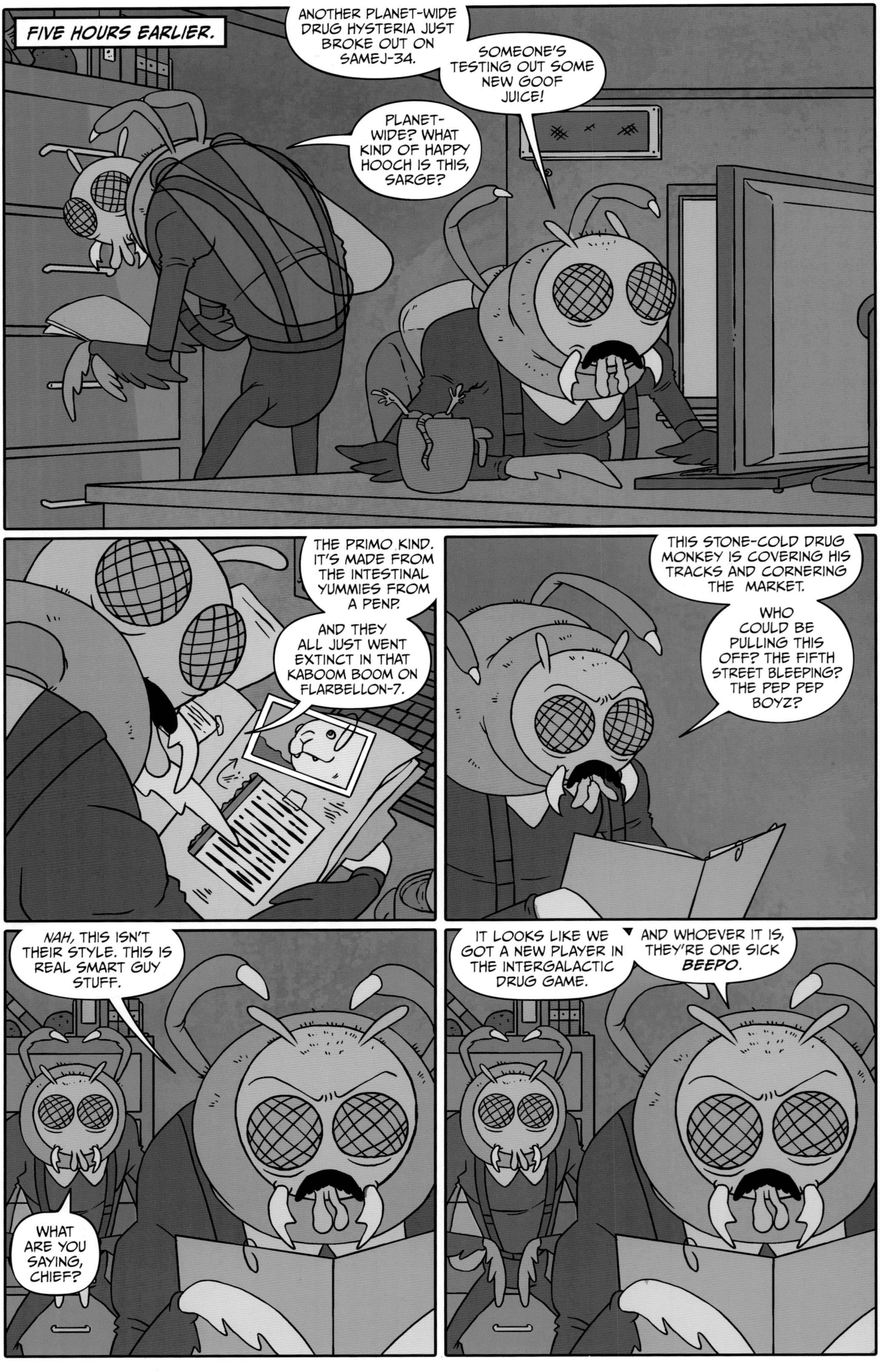
FIVE HOURS EARLIER.
ANOTHER PLANET-WIDE DRUG HYSTERIA JUST BROKE OUT ON SAMEJ-34.
SOMEONE'S TESTING OUT SOME NEW GOOF JUICE!
PLANET-WIDE? WHAT KIND OF HAPPY HOOCH IS THIS, SARGE?
THE PRIMO KIND. IT'S MADE FROM THE INTESTINAL YUMMIES FROM A PENP.
AND THEY ALL JUST WENT EXTINCT IN THAT KABOOM BOOM ON FLARBELLON-7.
THIS STONE-COLD DRUG MONKEY IS COVERING HIS TRACKS AND CORNERING THE MARKET.
WHO COULD BE PULLING THIS OFF? THE FIFTH STREET BLEEPING? THE PEP PEP BOYZ?
NAH, THIS ISN'T THEIR STYLE. THIS IS REAL SMART GUY STUFF.
WHAT ARE YOU SAYING, CHIEF?
IT LOOKS LIKE WE GOT A NEW PLAYER IN THE INTERGALACTIC DRUG GAME.
AND WHOEVER IT IS, THEY'RE ONE SICK BEEPO.

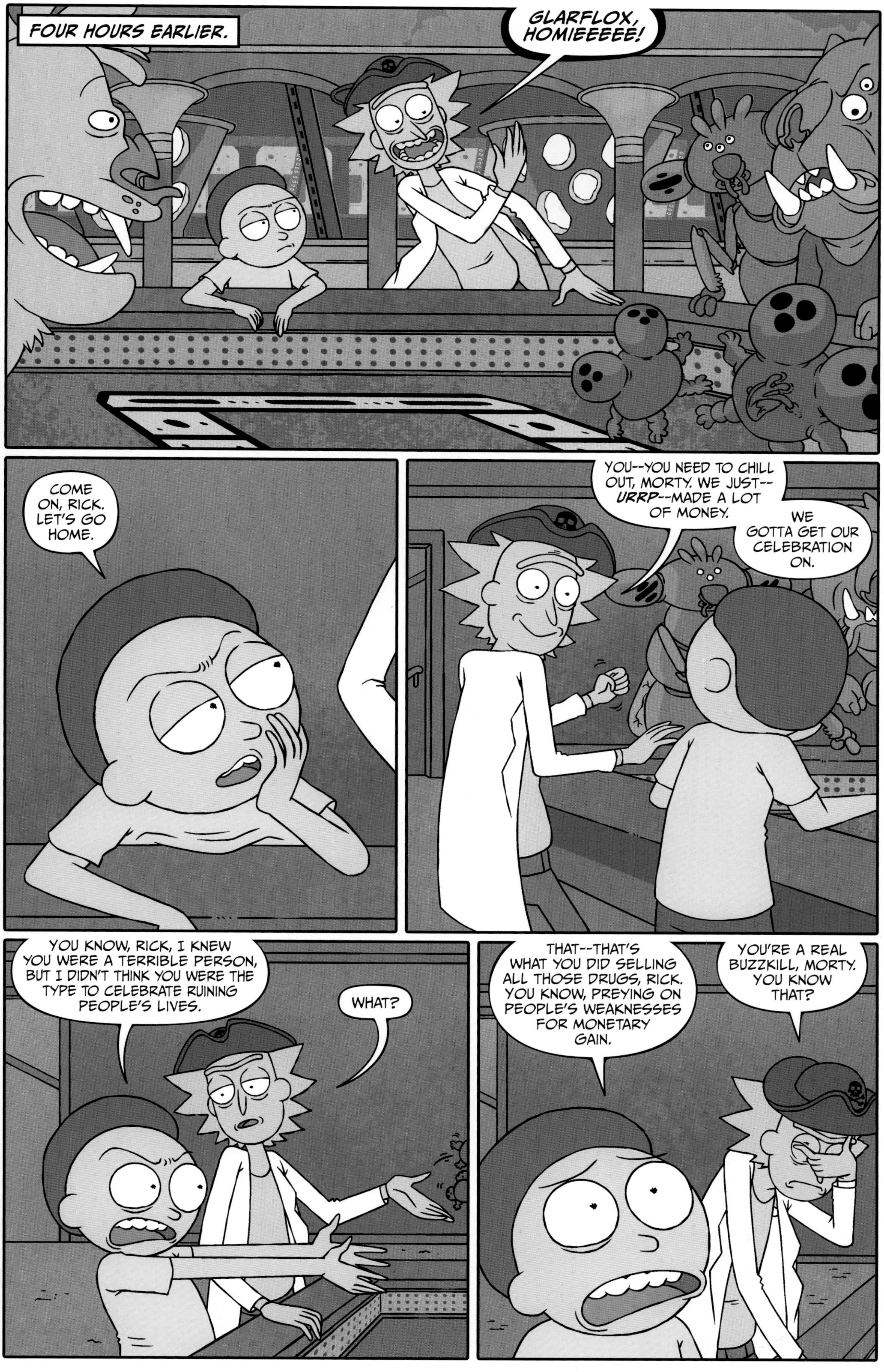
FOUR HOURS EARLIER.
GLARFLOX, HOMIEEEEE!
COME ON, RICK. LET'S GO HOME.
YOU--YOU NEED TO CHILL OUT, MORTY. WE JUST-- URRP--MADE A LOT OF MONEY.
WE GOTTA GET OUR CELEBRATION ON.
YOU KNOW, RICK, I KNEW YOU WERE A TERRIBLE PERSON, BUT I DIDN'T THINK YOU WERE THE TYPE TO CELEBRATE RUINING PEOPLE'S LIVES.
WHAT?
THAT--THAT'S WHAT YOU DID SELLING ALL THOSE DRUGS, RICK. YOU KNOW, PREYING ON PEOPLE'S WEAKNESSES FOR MONETARY GAIN.
YOU'RE A REAL BUZZKILL, MORTY. YOU KNOW THAT?

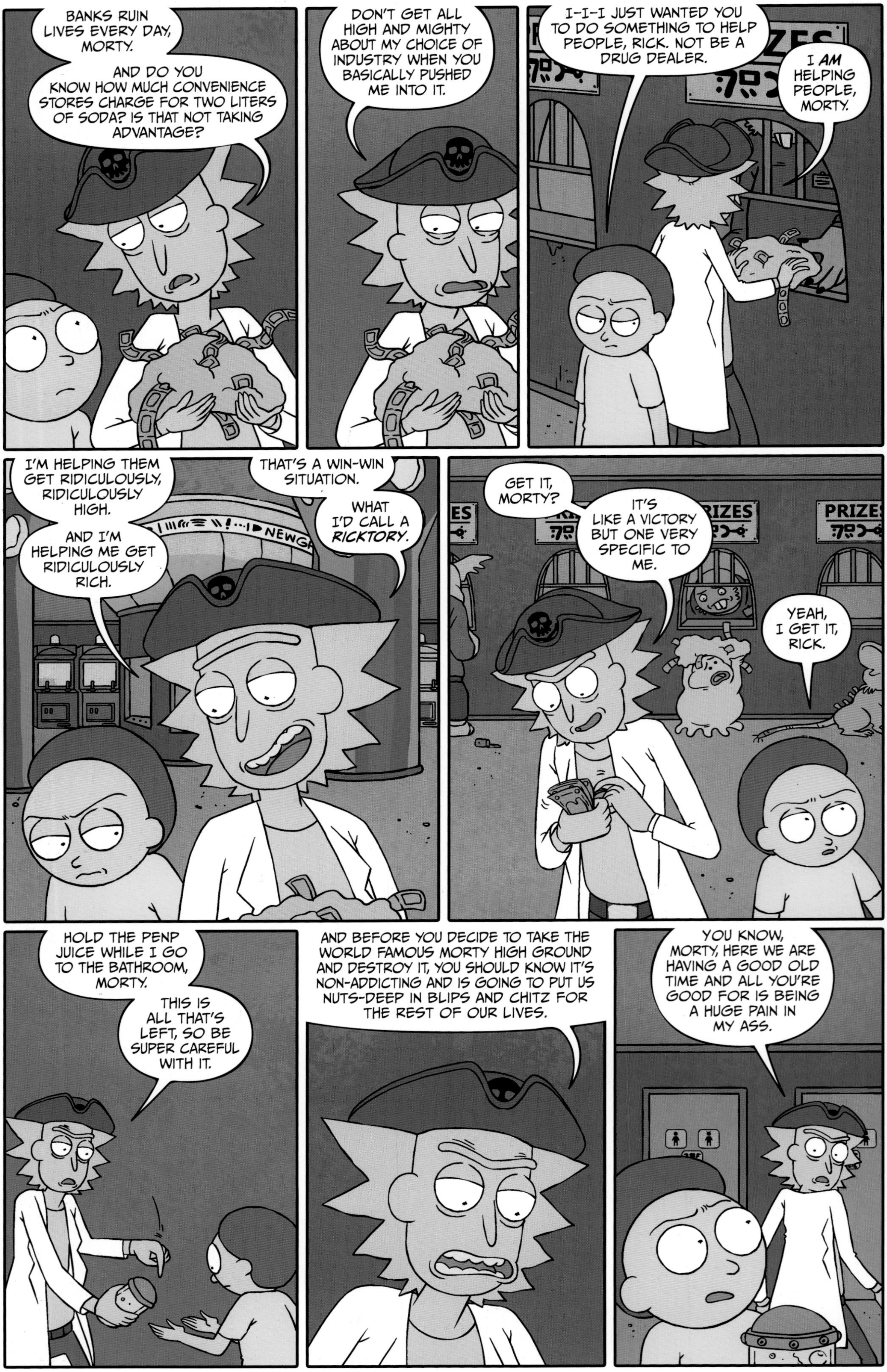
BANKS RUIN LIVES EVERY DAY, MORTY.
AND DO YOU KNOW HOW MUCH CONVENIENCE STORES CHARGE FOR TWO LITERS OF SODA? IS THAT NOT TAKING ADVANTAGE?
DON'T GET ALL HIGH AND MIGHTY ABOUT MY CHOICE OF INDUSTRY WHEN YOU BASICALLY PUSHED ME INTO IT.
I-I-I JUST WANTED YOU TO DO SOMETHING TO HELP PEOPLE, RICK. NOT BE A DRUG DEALER.
I *AM* HELPING PEOPLE, MORTY.
I'M HELPING THEM GET RIDICULOUSLY, RIDICULOUSLY HIGH.
AND I'M HELPING ME GET RIDICULOUSLY RICH.
THAT'S A WIN-WIN SITUATION.
WHAT I'D CALL A ***RICKTORY.***
GET IT, MORTY?
IT'S LIKE A VICTORY BUT ONE VERY SPECIFIC TO ME.
YEAH, I GET IT, RICK.
HOLD THE PENP JUICE WHILE I GO TO THE BATHROOM, MORTY.
THIS IS ALL THAT'S LEFT, SO BE SUPER CAREFUL WITH IT.
AND BEFORE YOU DECIDE TO TAKE THE WORLD FAMOUS MORTY HIGH GROUND AND DESTROY IT, YOU SHOULD KNOW IT'S NON-ADDICTING AND IS GOING TO PUT US NUTS-DEEP IN BLIPS AND CHITZ FOR THE REST OF OUR LIVES.
YOU KNOW, MORTY, HERE WE ARE HAVING A GOOD OLD TIME AND ALL YOU'RE GOOD FOR IS BEING A HUGE PAIN IN MY ASS.

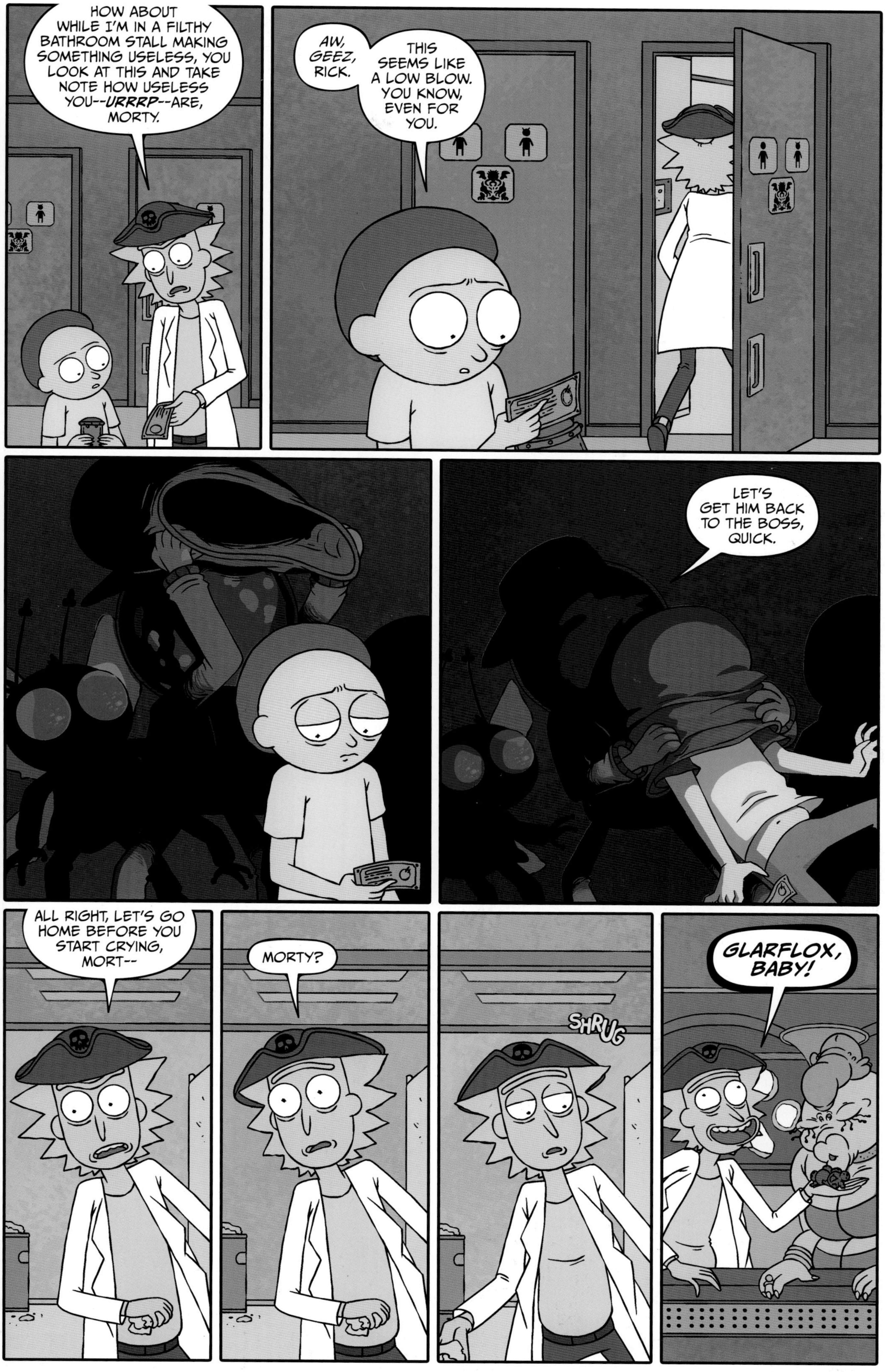
HOW ABOUT WHILE I'M IN A FILTHY BATHROOM STALL MAKING SOMETHING USELESS, YOU LOOK AT THIS AND TAKE NOTE HOW USELESS YOU--URRRP--ARE, MORTY.
AW, GEEZ, RICK.
THIS SEEMS LIKE A LOW BLOW. YOU KNOW, EVEN FOR YOU.
LET'S GET HIM BACK TO THE BOSS, QUICK.
ALL RIGHT, LET'S GO HOME BEFORE YOU START CRYING, MORT--
MORTY?
SHRUG
GLARFLOX, BABY!

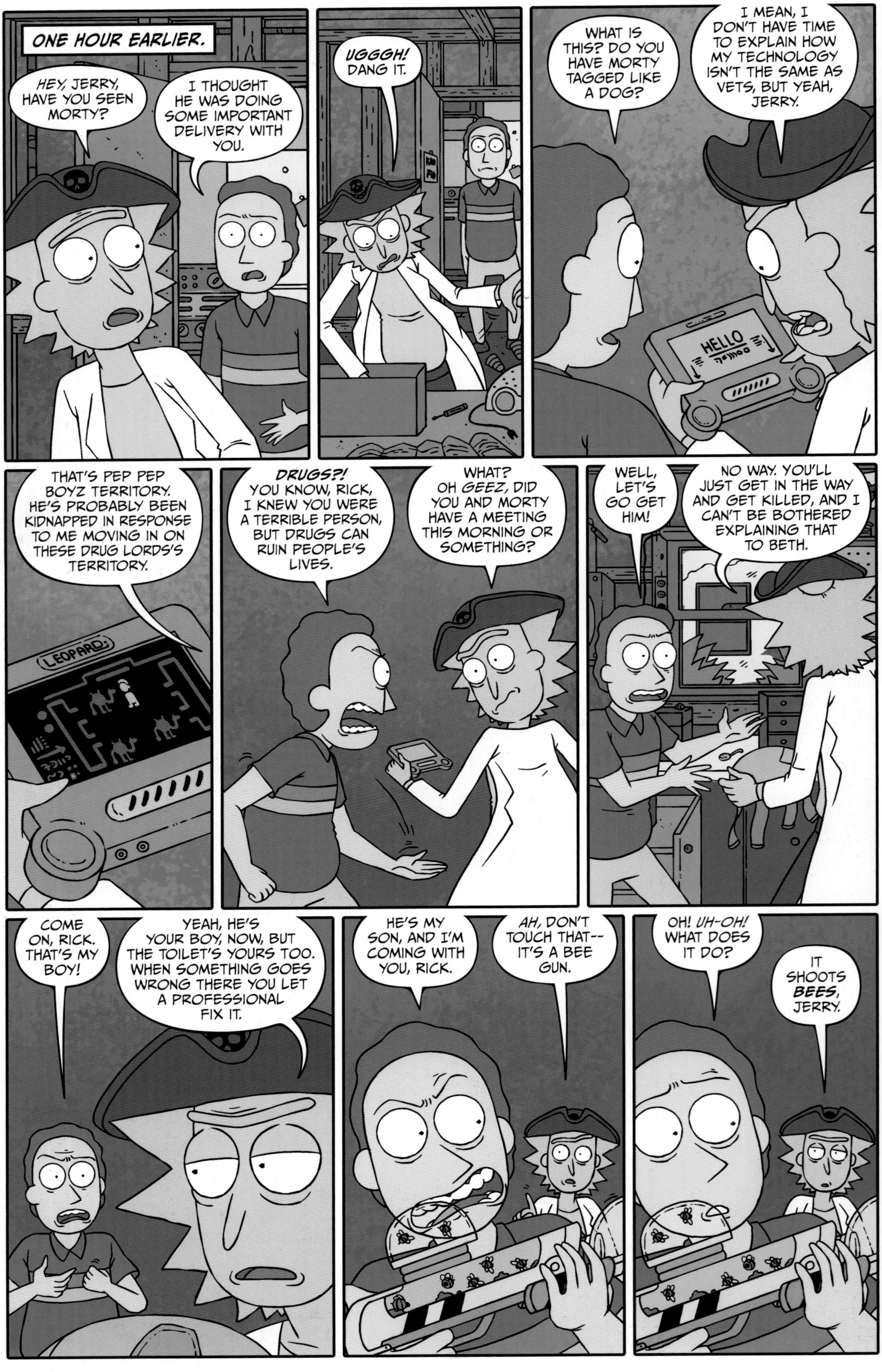
ONE HOUR EARLIER.
HEY, JERRY, HAVE YOU SEEN MORTY?
I THOUGHT HE WAS DOING SOME IMPORTANT DELIVERY WITH YOU.
UGGGH! DANG IT.
WHAT IS THIS? DO YOU HAVE MORTY TAGGED LIKE A DOG?
I MEAN, I DON'T HAVE TIME TO EXPLAIN HOW MY TECHNOLOGY ISN'T THE SAME AS VETS, BUT YEAH, JERRY.
HELLO
THAT'S PEP PEP BOYZ TERRITORY. HE'S PROBABLY BEEN KIDNAPPED IN RESPONSE TO ME MOVING IN ON THESE DRUG LORDS'S TERRITORY.
LEOPARD
DRUGS?! YOU KNOW, RICK, I KNEW YOU WERE A TERRIBLE PERSON, BUT DRUGS CAN RUIN PEOPLE'S LIVES.
WHAT? OH GEEZ, DID YOU AND MORTY HAVE A MEETING THIS MORNING OR SOMETHING?
WELL, LET'S GO GET HIM!
NO WAY. YOU'LL JUST GET IN THE WAY AND GET KILLED, AND I CAN'T BE BOTHERED EXPLAINING THAT TO BETH.
COME ON, RICK. THAT'S MY BOY!
YEAH, HE'S YOUR BOY, NOW, BUT THE TOILET'S YOURS TOO. WHEN SOMETHING GOES WRONG THERE YOU LET A PROFESSIONAL FIX IT.
HE'S MY SON, AND I'M COMING WITH YOU, RICK.
AH, DON'T TOUCH THAT-- IT'S A BEE GUN.
OH! UH-OH! WHAT DOES IT DO?
IT SHOOTS BEES, JERRY.

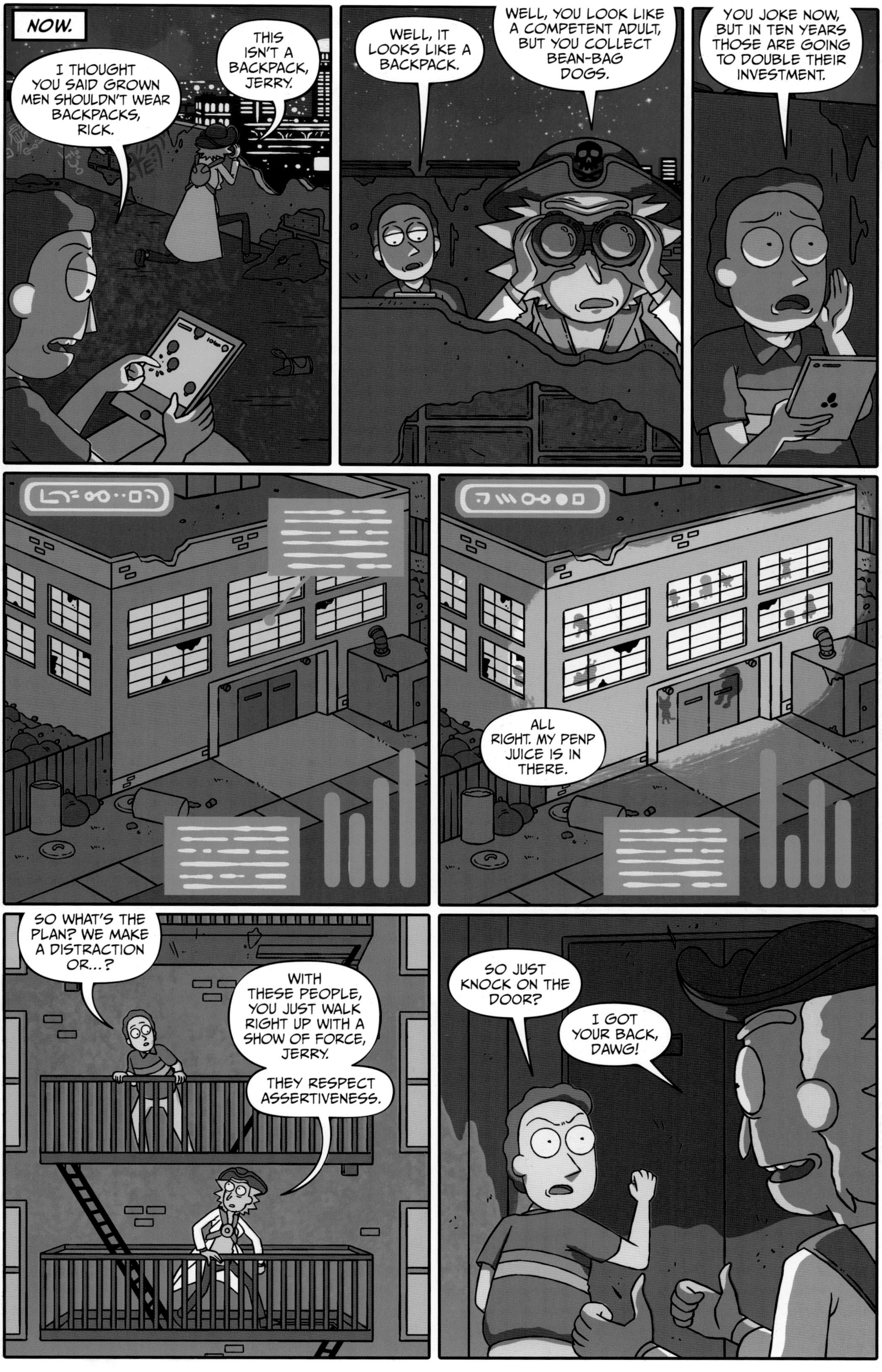
NOW.
I THOUGHT YOU SAID GROWN MEN SHOULDN'T WEAR BACKPACKS, RICK.
THIS ISN'T A BACKPACK, JERRY.
WELL, IT LOOKS LIKE A BACKPACK.
WELL, YOU LOOK LIKE A COMPETENT ADULT, BUT YOU COLLECT BEAN-BAG DOGS.
YOU JOKE NOW, BUT IN TEN YEARS THOSE ARE GOING TO DOUBLE THEIR INVESTMENT.
ALL RIGHT. MY PENP JUICE IS IN THERE.
SO WHAT'S THE PLAN? WE MAKE A DISTRACTION OR...?
WITH THESE PEOPLE, YOU JUST WALK RIGHT UP WITH A SHOW OF FORCE, JERRY.
THEY RESPECT ASSERTIVENESS.
SO JUST KNOCK ON THE DOOR?
I GOT YOUR BACK, DAWG!

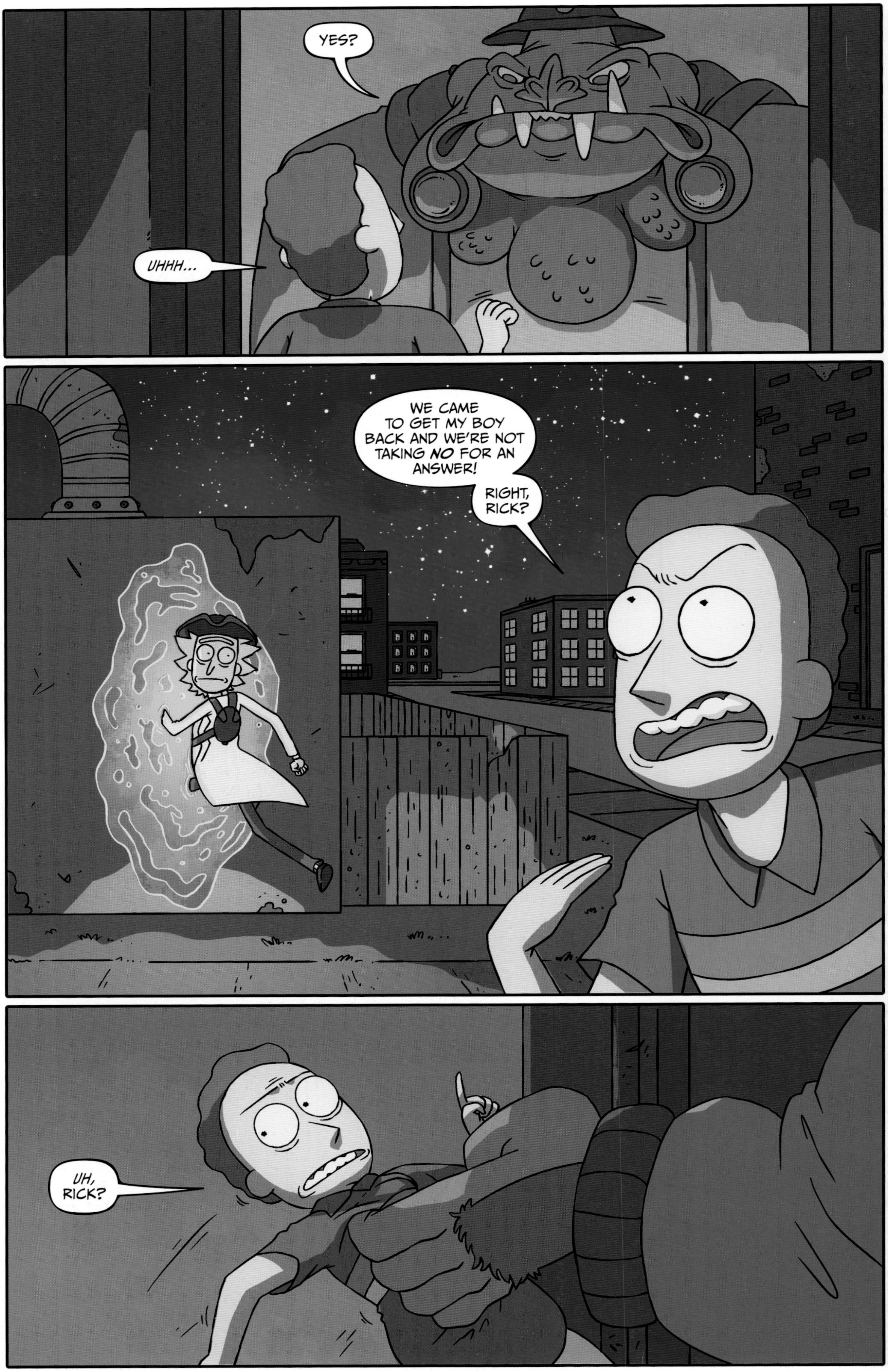
YES?
UHHH...
WE CAME TO GET MY BOY BACK AND WE'RE NOT TAKING NO FOR AN ANSWER!
RIGHT, RICK?
UH, RICK?

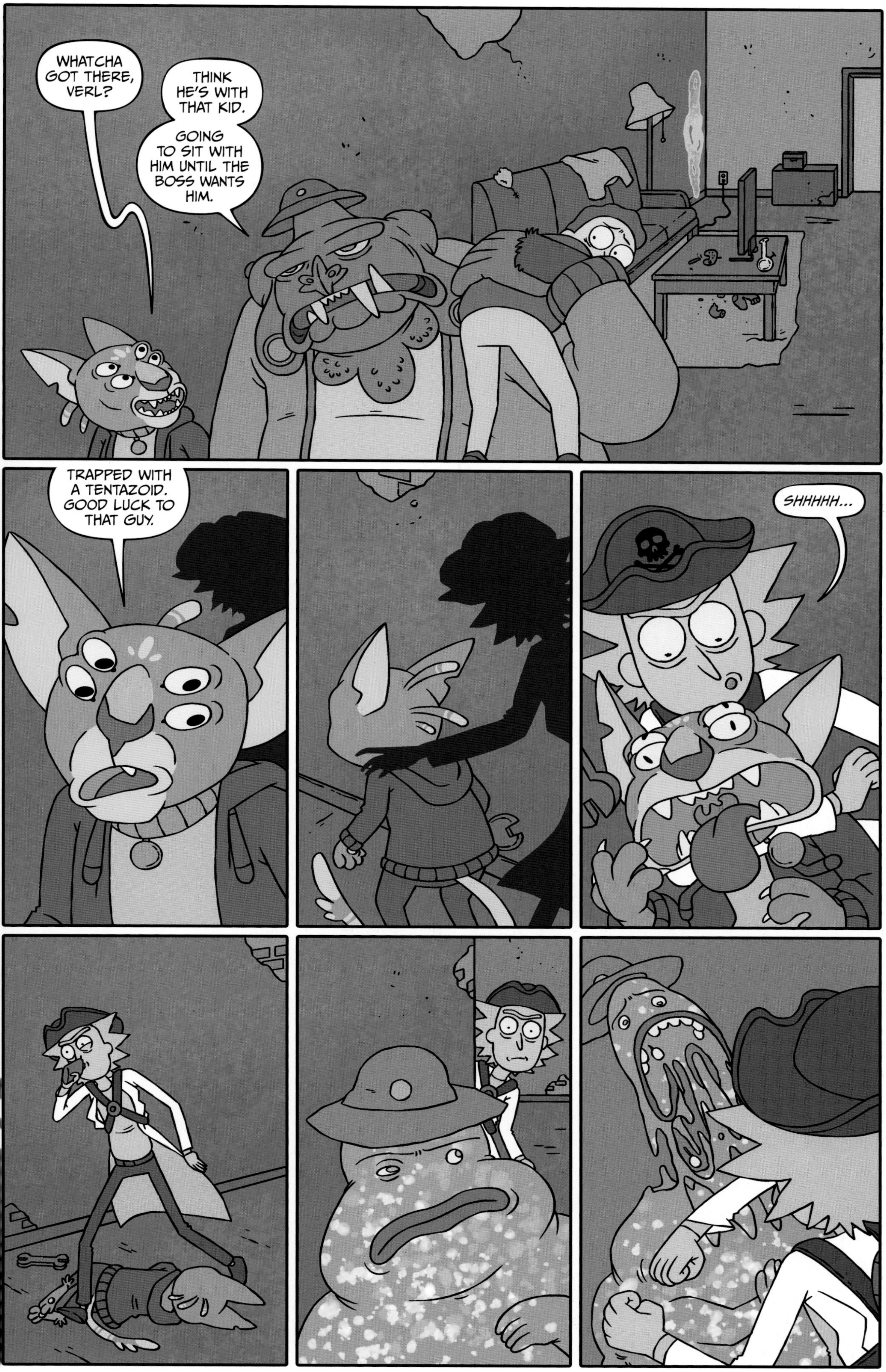

WHATCHA GOT THERE, VERL?
THINK HE'S WITH THAT KID.
GOING TO SIT WITH HIM UNTIL THE BOSS WANTS HIM.
TRAPPED WITH A TENTAZOID. GOOD LUCK TO THAT GUY.
SHHHHH...

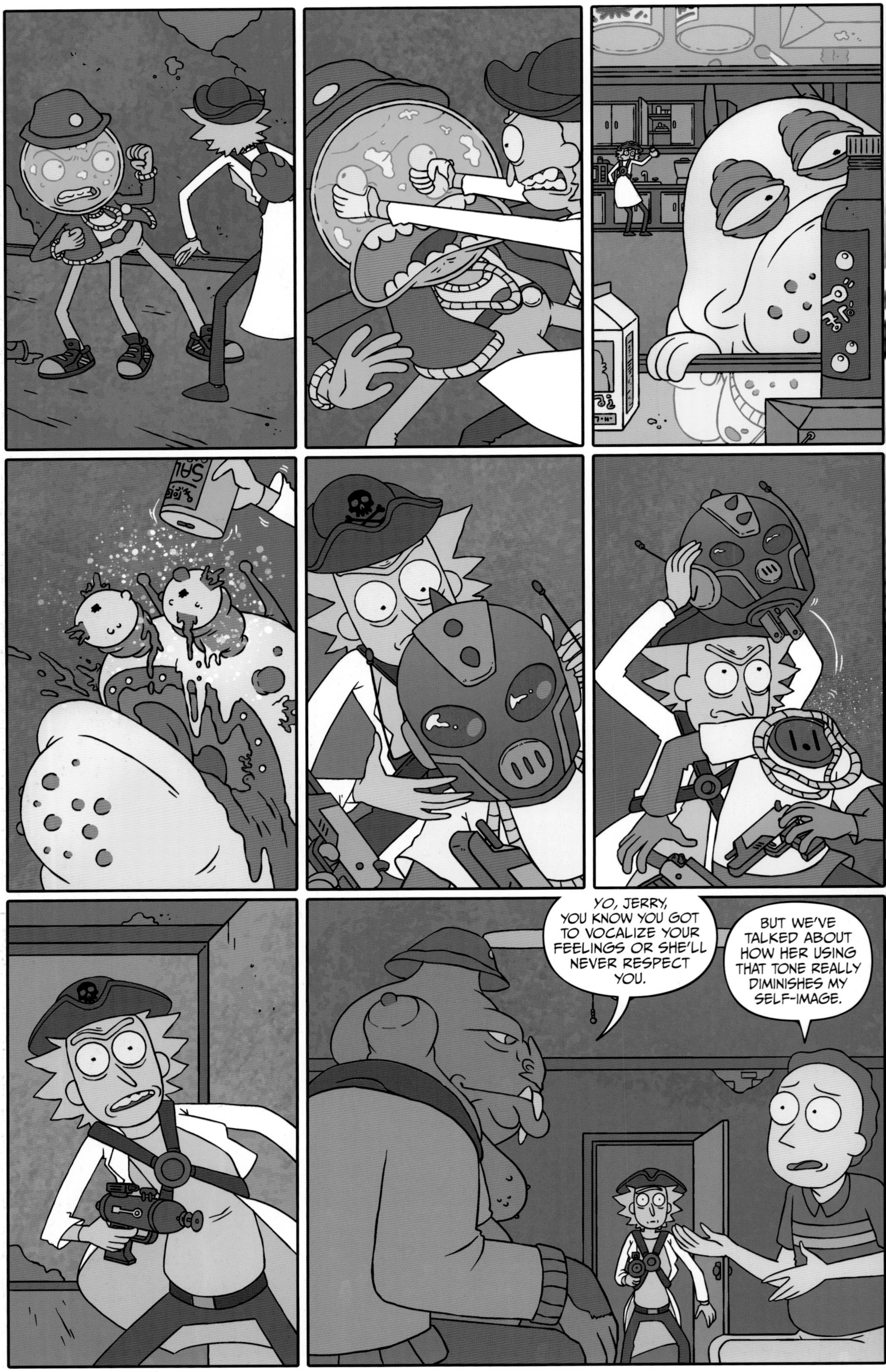
YO, JERRY, YOU KNOW YOU GOT TO VOCALIZE YOUR FEELINGS OR SHE'LL NEVER RESPECT YOU.
BUT WE'VE TALKED ABOUT HOW HER USING THAT TONE REALLY DIMINISHES MY SELF-IMAGE.

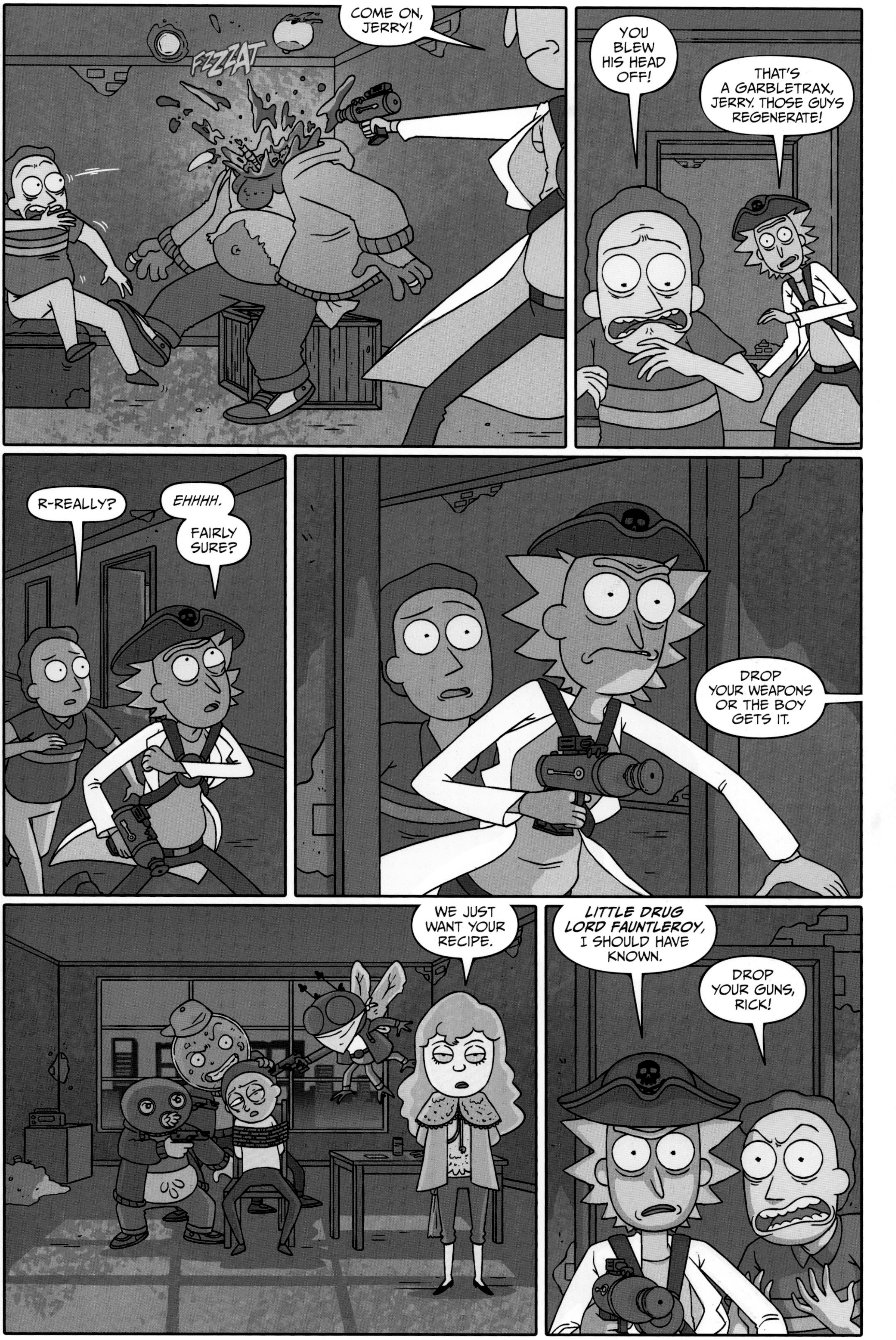
FZZZAT
COME ON, JERRY!
YOU BLEW HIS HEAD OFF!
THAT'S A GARBLETRAX, JERRY. THOSE GUYS REGENERATE!
R-REALLY?
EHHHH.
FAIRLY SURE?
DROP YOUR WEAPONS OR THE BOY GETS IT.
WE JUST WANT YOUR RECIPE.
LITTLE DRUG LORD FAUNTLEROY, I SHOULD HAVE KNOWN.
DROP YOUR GUNS, RICK!

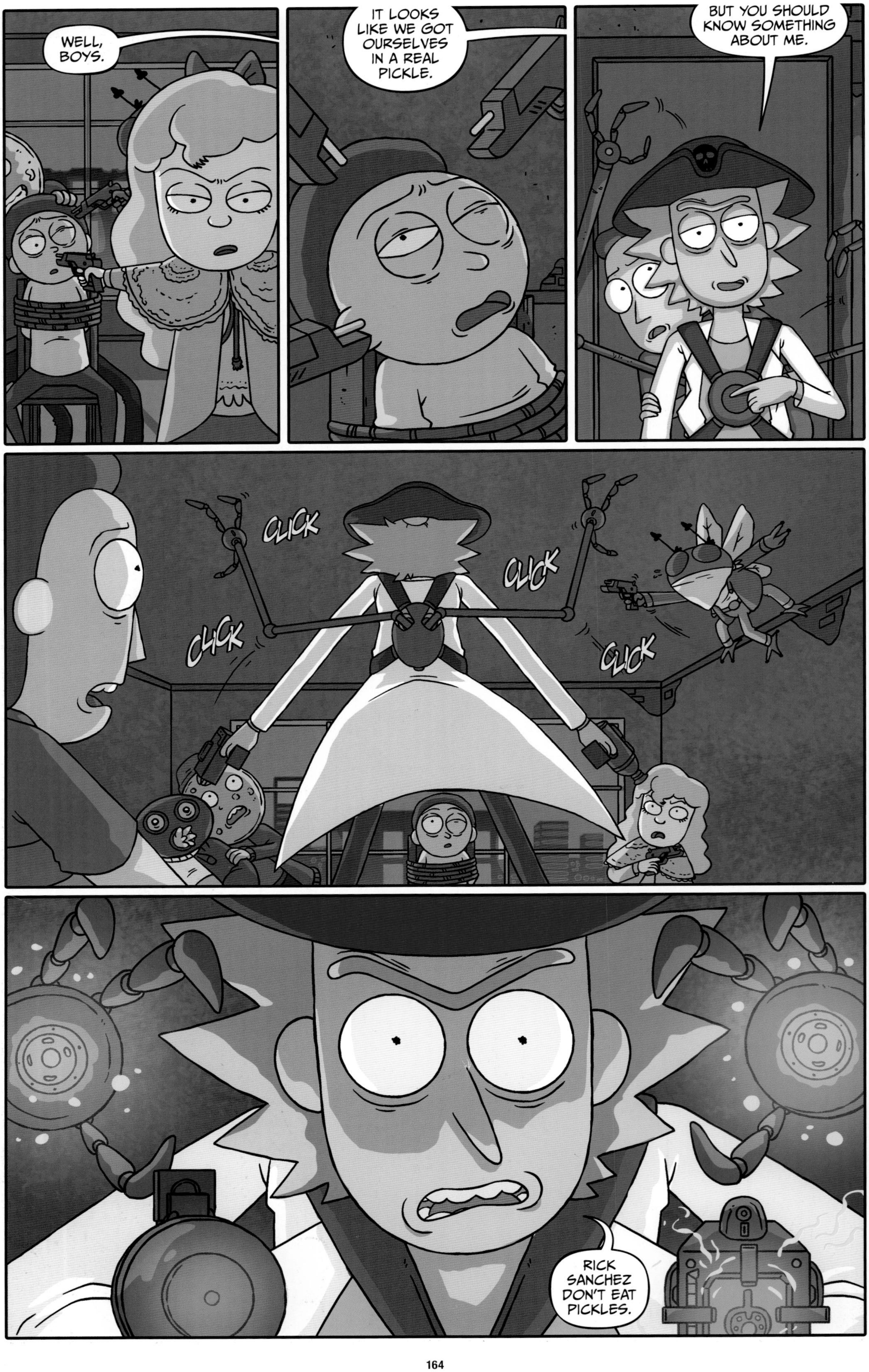
WELL, BOYS.
IT LOOKS LIKE WE GOT OURSELVES IN A REAL PICKLE.
BUT YOU SHOULD KNOW SOMETHING ABOUT ME.
CLICK
CLICK
CLICK
CLICK
RICK SANCHEZ DON'T EAT PICKLES.

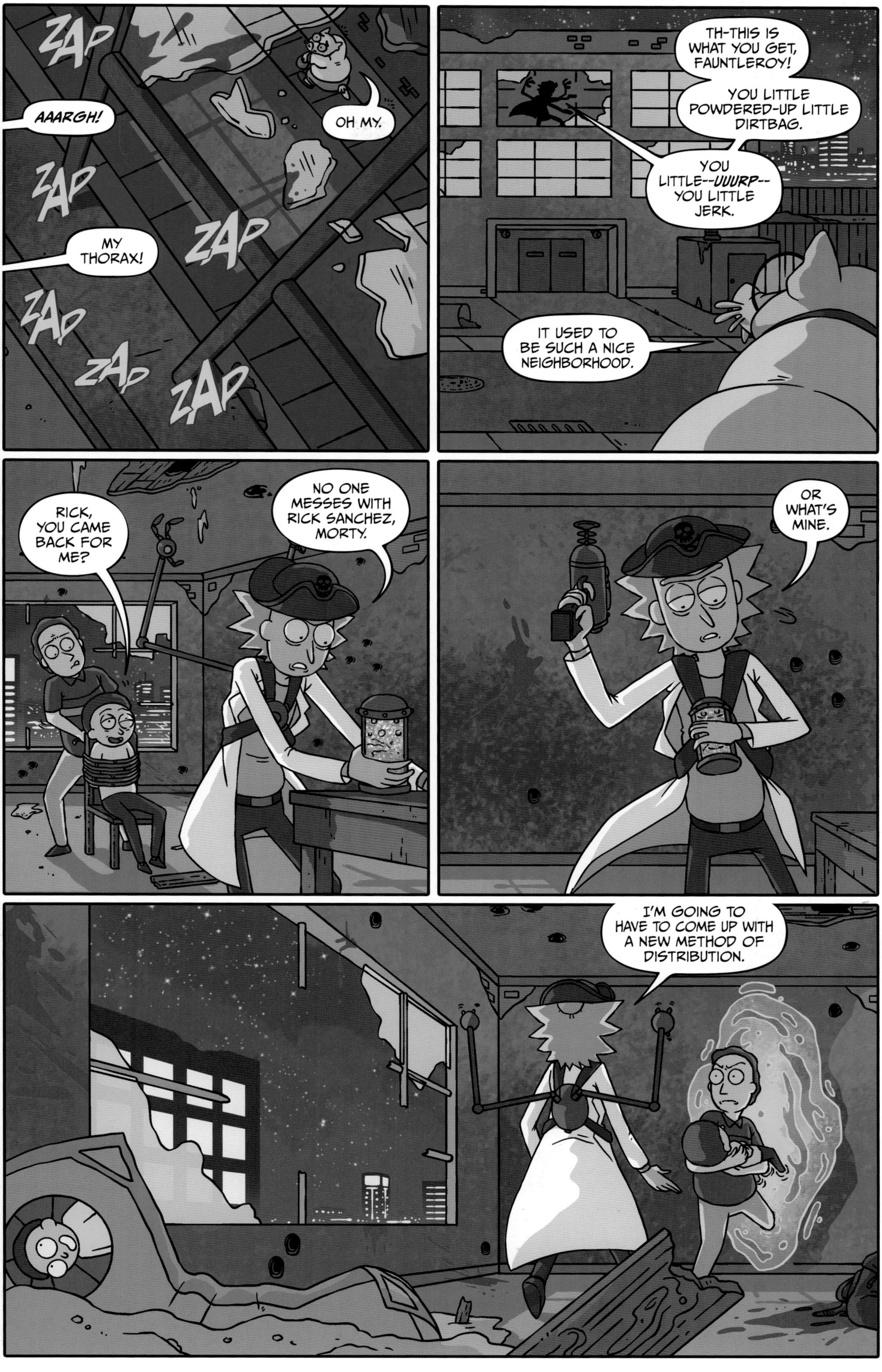
ZAP
AAARGH!
OH MY.
ZAP
MY THORAX!
ZAP
ZAP
ZAP
ZAP
TH-THIS IS WHAT YOU GET, FAUNTLEROY!
YOU LITTLE POWDERED-UP LITTLE DIRTBAG.
YOU LITTLE--UUURP-- YOU LITTLE JERK.
IT USED TO BE SUCH A NICE NEIGHBORHOOD.
RICK, YOU CAME BACK FOR ME?
NO ONE MESSES WITH RICK SANCHEZ, MORTY.
OR WHAT'S MINE.
I'M GOING TO HAVE TO COME UP WITH A NEW METHOD OF DISTRIBUTION.

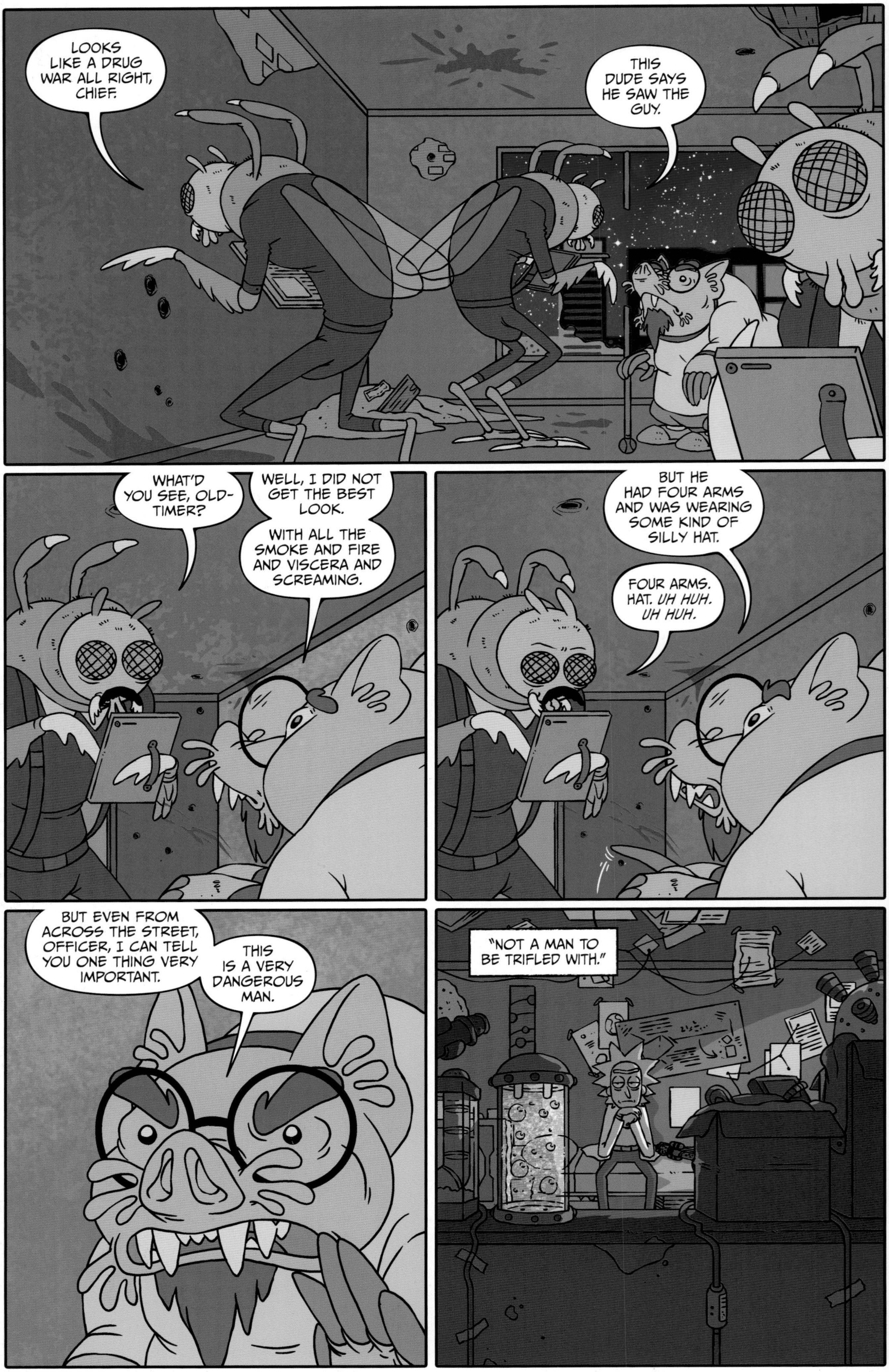
LOOKS LIKE A DRUG WAR ALL RIGHT, CHIEF.
THIS DUDE SAYS HE SAW THE GUY.
WHAT'D YOU SEE, OLD-TIMER?
WELL, I DID NOT GET THE BEST LOOK.
WITH ALL THE SMOKE AND FIRE AND VISCERA AND SCREAMING.
BUT HE HAD FOUR ARMS AND WAS WEARING SOME KIND OF SILLY HAT.
FOUR ARMS. HAT. *UH HUH. UH HUH.*
BUT EVEN FROM ACROSS THE STREET, OFFICER, I CAN TELL YOU ONE THING VERY IMPORTANT.
THIS IS A VERY DANGEROUS MAN.
"NOT A MAN TO BE TRIFLED WITH."

BR-RICKING BAD, PART THREE: DESPERATELY MEESEEKING RUIN

WRITTEN BY **KYLE STARKS**
DRAWN BY **CJ CANNON**
COLORED BY **RYAN HILL**
LETTERED BY **CRANK!**

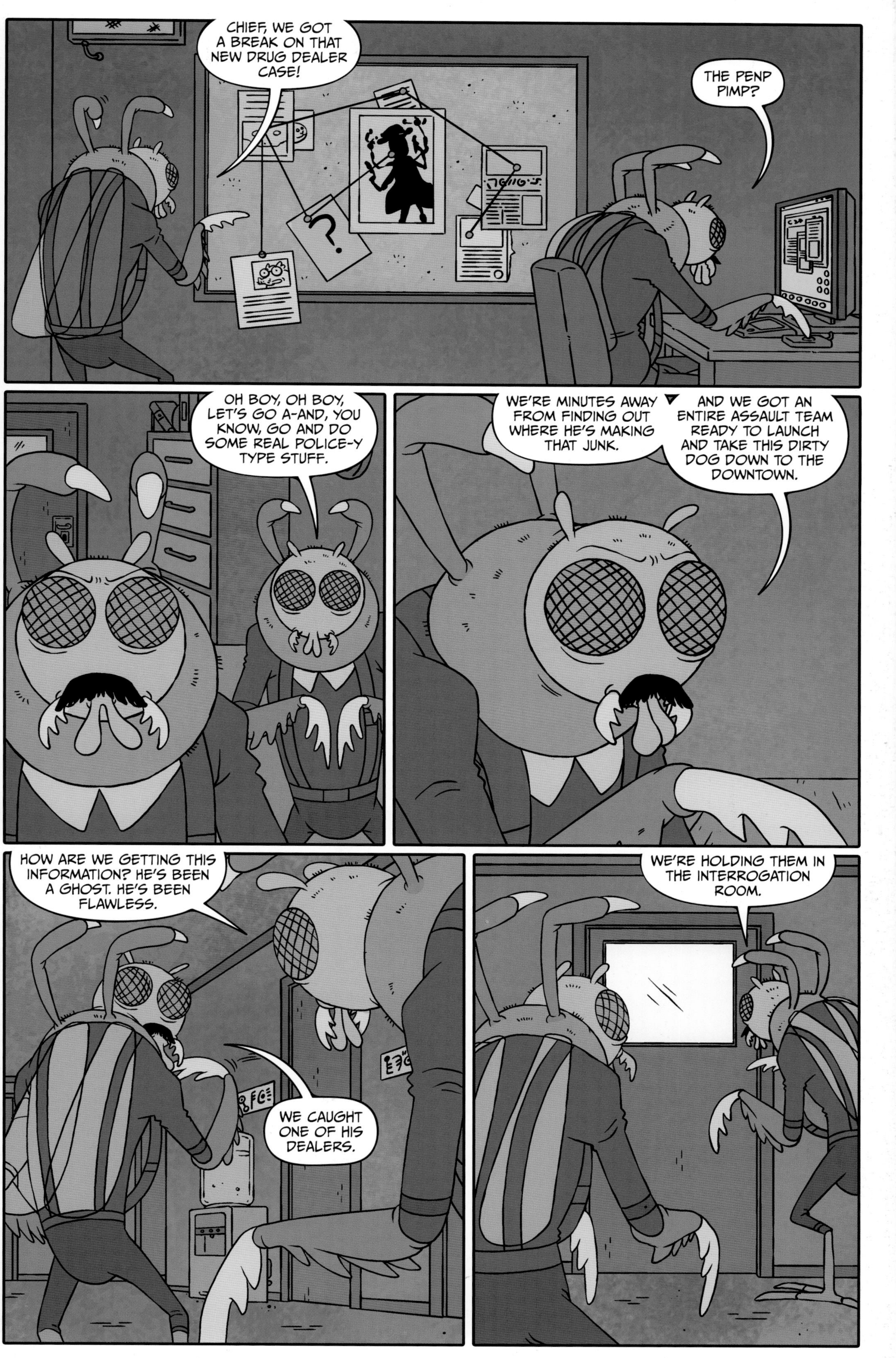
CHIEF, WE GOT A BREAK ON THAT NEW DRUG DEALER CASE!
THE PENP PIMP?
OH BOY, OH BOY, LET'S GO A-AND, YOU KNOW, GO AND DO SOME REAL POLICE-Y TYPE STUFF.
WE'RE MINUTES AWAY FROM FINDING OUT WHERE HE'S MAKING THAT JUNK.
AND WE GOT AN ENTIRE ASSAULT TEAM READY TO LAUNCH AND TAKE THIS DIRTY DOG DOWN TO THE DOWNTOWN.
HOW ARE WE GETTING THIS INFORMATION? HE'S BEEN A GHOST. HE'S BEEN FLAWLESS.
WE CAUGHT ONE OF HIS DEALERS.
WE'RE HOLDING THEM IN THE INTERROGATION ROOM.

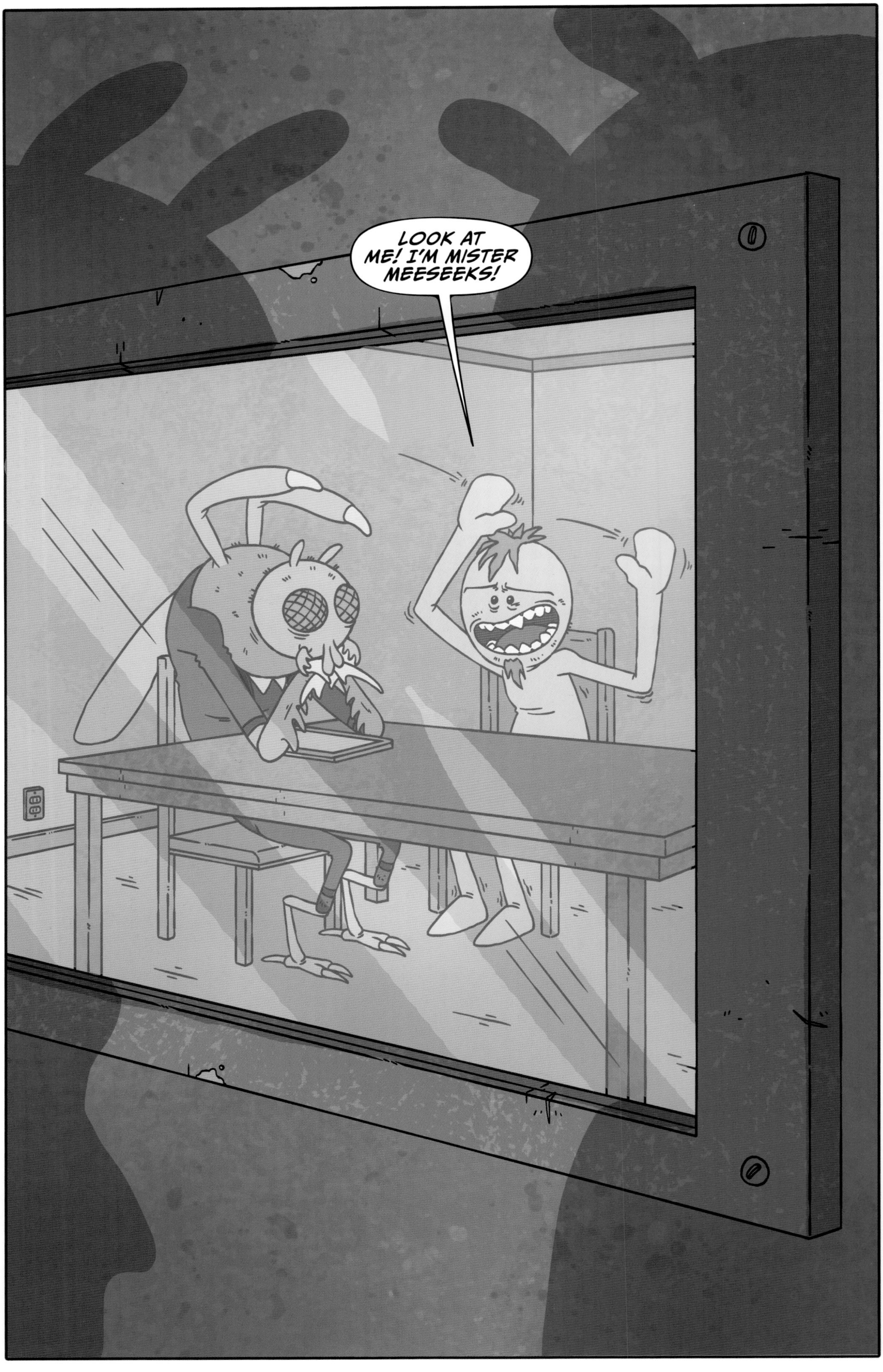
LOOK AT ME! I'M MISTER MEESEEKS!

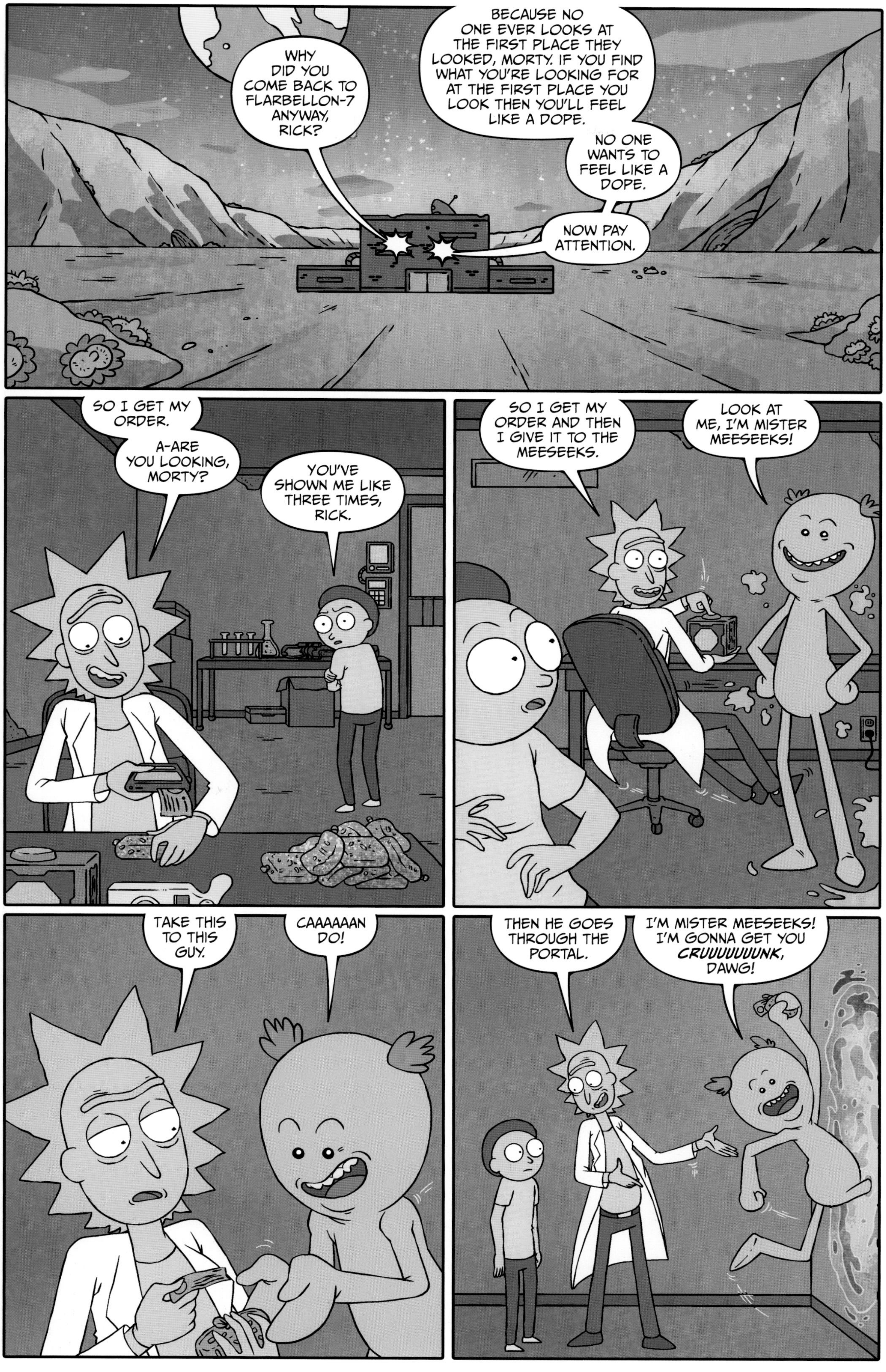
WHY DID YOU COME BACK TO FLARBELLON-7 ANYWAY, RICK?
BECAUSE NO ONE EVER LOOKS AT THE FIRST PLACE THEY LOOKED, MORTY. IF YOU FIND WHAT YOU'RE LOOKING FOR AT THE FIRST PLACE YOU LOOK THEN YOU'LL FEEL LIKE A DOPE.
NO ONE WANTS TO FEEL LIKE A DOPE.
NOW PAY ATTENTION.
SO I GET MY ORDER.
A-ARE YOU LOOKING, MORTY?
YOU'VE SHOWN ME LIKE THREE TIMES, RICK.
SO I GET MY ORDER AND THEN I GIVE IT TO THE MEESEEKS.
LOOK AT ME, I'M MISTER MEESEEKS!
TAKE THIS TO THIS GUY.
CAAAAAAN DO!
THEN HE GOES THROUGH THE PORTAL.
I'M MISTER MEESEEKS! I'M GONNA GET YOU *CRUUUUUUUNK*, DAWG!

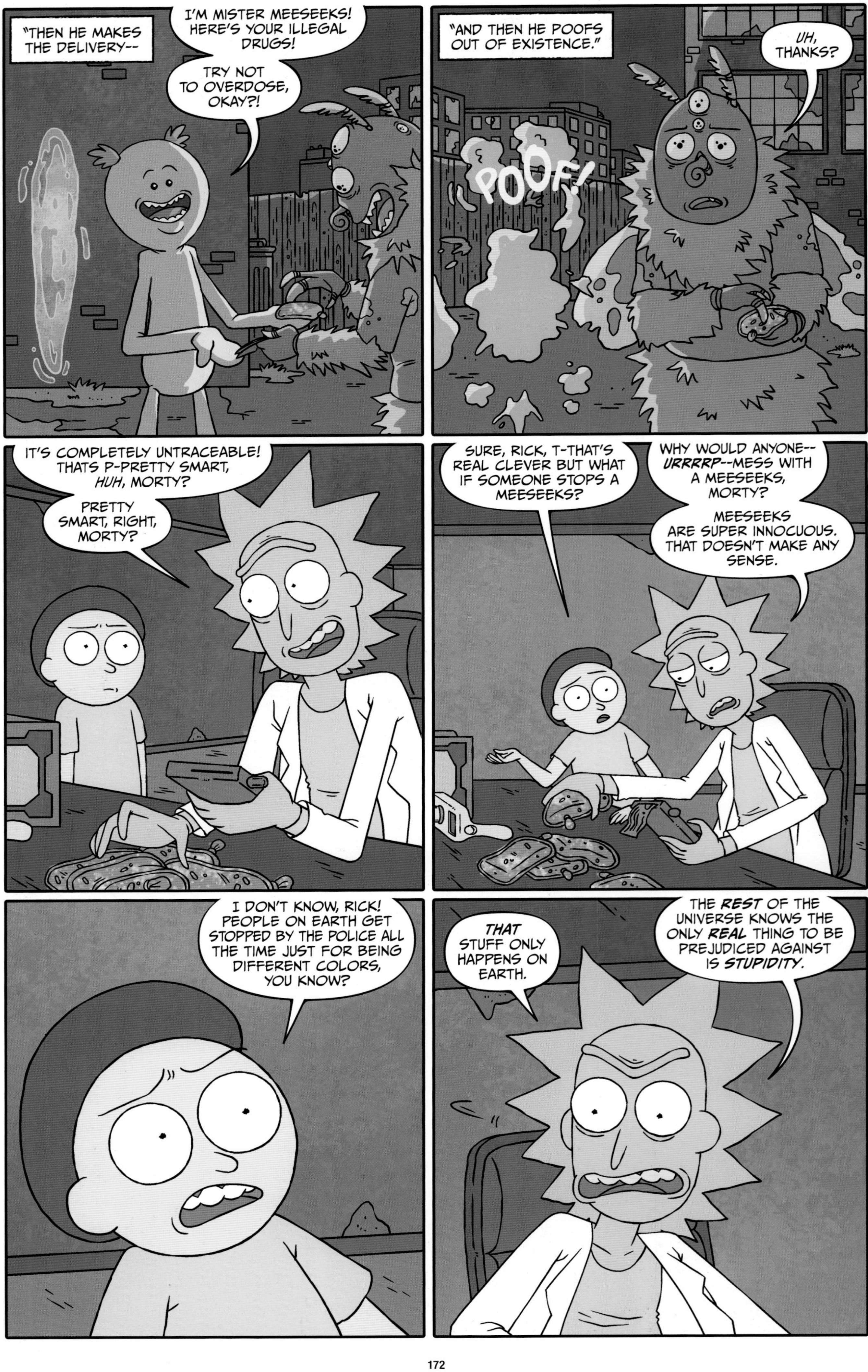
"THEN HE MAKES THE DELIVERY--
I'M MISTER MEESEEKS! HERE'S YOUR ILLEGAL DRUGS!
TRY NOT TO OVERDOSE, OKAY?!
"AND THEN HE POOFS OUT OF EXISTENCE."
UH, THANKS?
POOF!
IT'S COMPLETELY UNTRACEABLE! THATS P-PRETTY SMART, *HUH*, MORTY?
PRETTY SMART, RIGHT, MORTY?
SURE, RICK, T-THAT'S REAL CLEVER BUT WHAT IF SOMEONE STOPS A MEESEEKS?
WHY WOULD ANYONE-- ***URRRRP***--MESS WITH A MEESEEKS, MORTY?
MEESEEKS ARE SUPER INNOCUOUS. THAT DOESN'T MAKE ANY SENSE.
I DON'T KNOW, RICK! PEOPLE ON EARTH GET STOPPED BY THE POLICE ALL THE TIME JUST FOR BEING DIFFERENT COLORS, YOU KNOW?
THAT STUFF ONLY HAPPENS ON EARTH.
THE ***REST*** OF THE UNIVERSE KNOWS THE ONLY ***REAL*** THING TO BE PREJUDICED AGAINST IS ***STUPIDITY***.

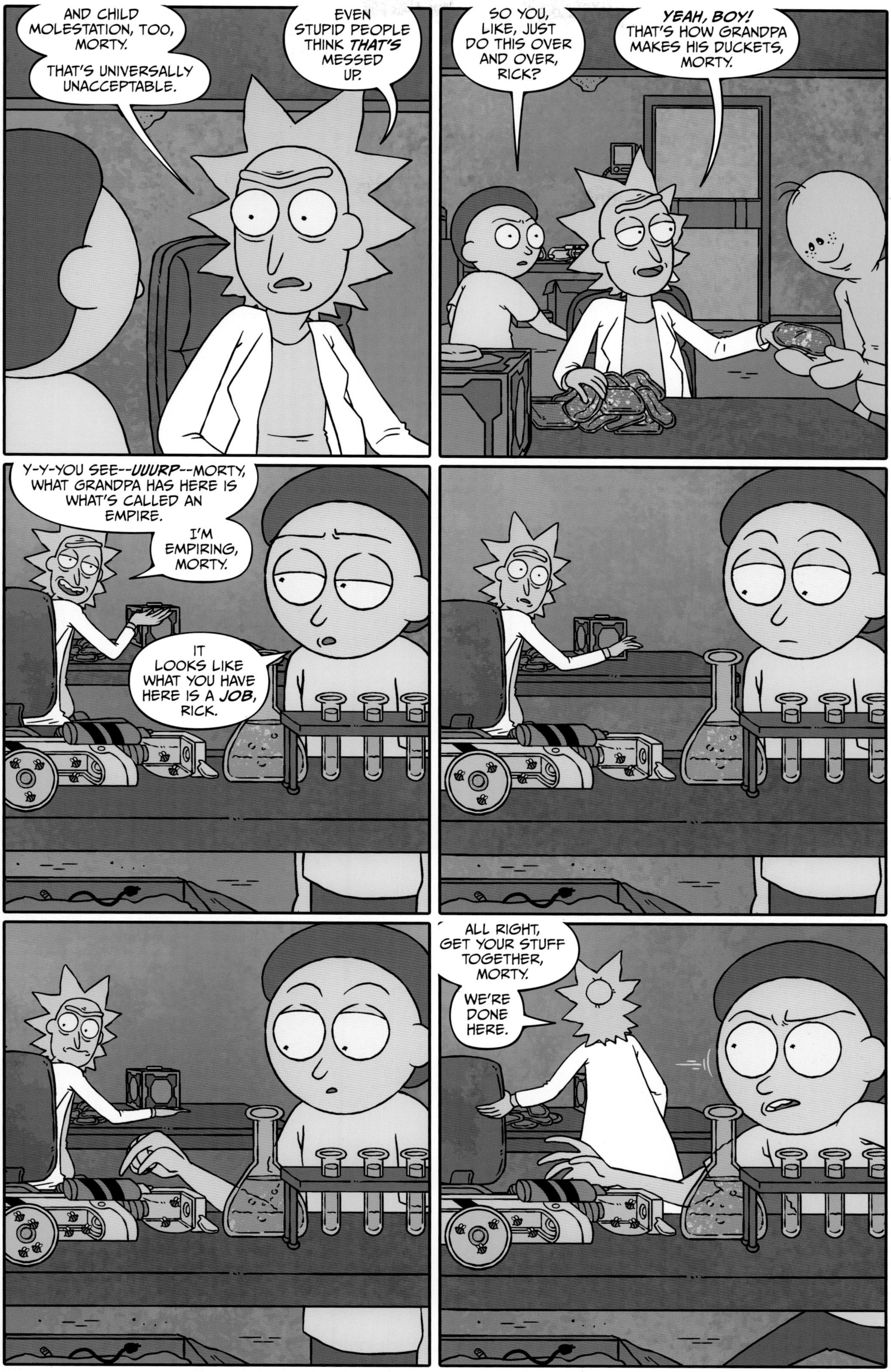
AND CHILD MOLESTATION, TOO, MORTY.
THAT'S UNIVERSALLY UNACCEPTABLE.
EVEN STUPID PEOPLE THINK *THAT'S* MESSED UP.
SO YOU, LIKE, JUST DO THIS OVER AND OVER, RICK?
YEAH, BOY! THAT'S HOW GRANDPA MAKES HIS DUCKETS, MORTY.
Y-Y-YOU SEE--*UUURP*--MORTY, WHAT GRANDPA HAS HERE IS WHAT'S CALLED AN EMPIRE.
I'M EMPIRING, MORTY.
IT LOOKS LIKE WHAT YOU HAVE HERE IS A *JOB*, RICK.
ALL RIGHT, GET YOUR STUFF TOGETHER, MORTY.
WE'RE DONE HERE.

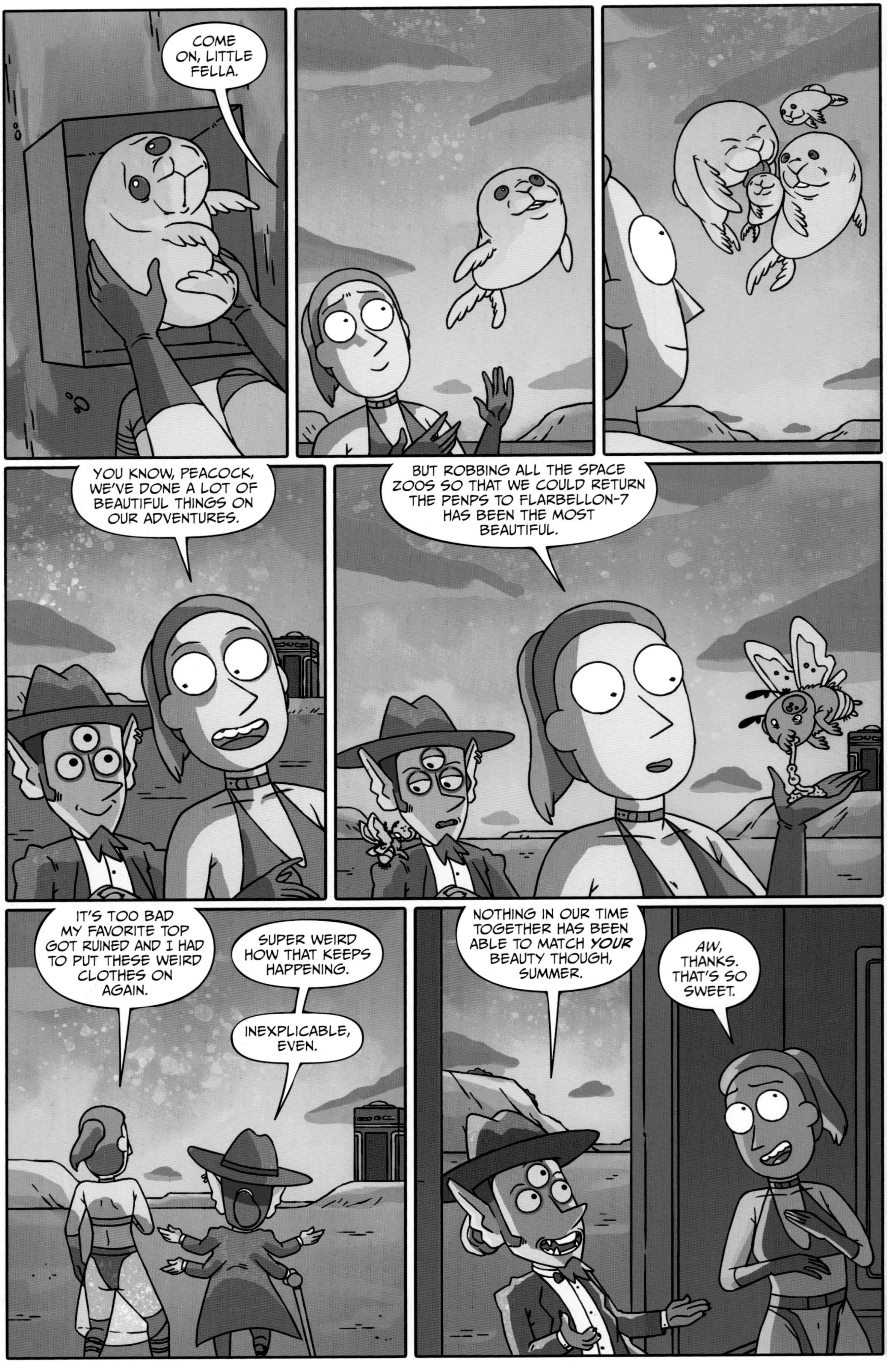
COME ON, LITTLE FELLA.
YOU KNOW, PEACOCK, WE'VE DONE A LOT OF BEAUTIFUL THINGS ON OUR ADVENTURES.
BUT ROBBING ALL THE SPACE ZOOS SO THAT WE COULD RETURN THE PENPS TO FLARBELLON-7 HAS BEEN THE MOST BEAUTIFUL.
IT'S TOO BAD MY FAVORITE TOP GOT RUINED AND I HAD TO PUT THESE WEIRD CLOTHES ON AGAIN.
SUPER WEIRD HOW THAT KEEPS HAPPENING.
INEXPLICABLE, EVEN.
NOTHING IN OUR TIME TOGETHER HAS BEEN ABLE TO MATCH *YOUR* BEAUTY THOUGH, SUMMER.
AW, THANKS. THAT'S SO SWEET.

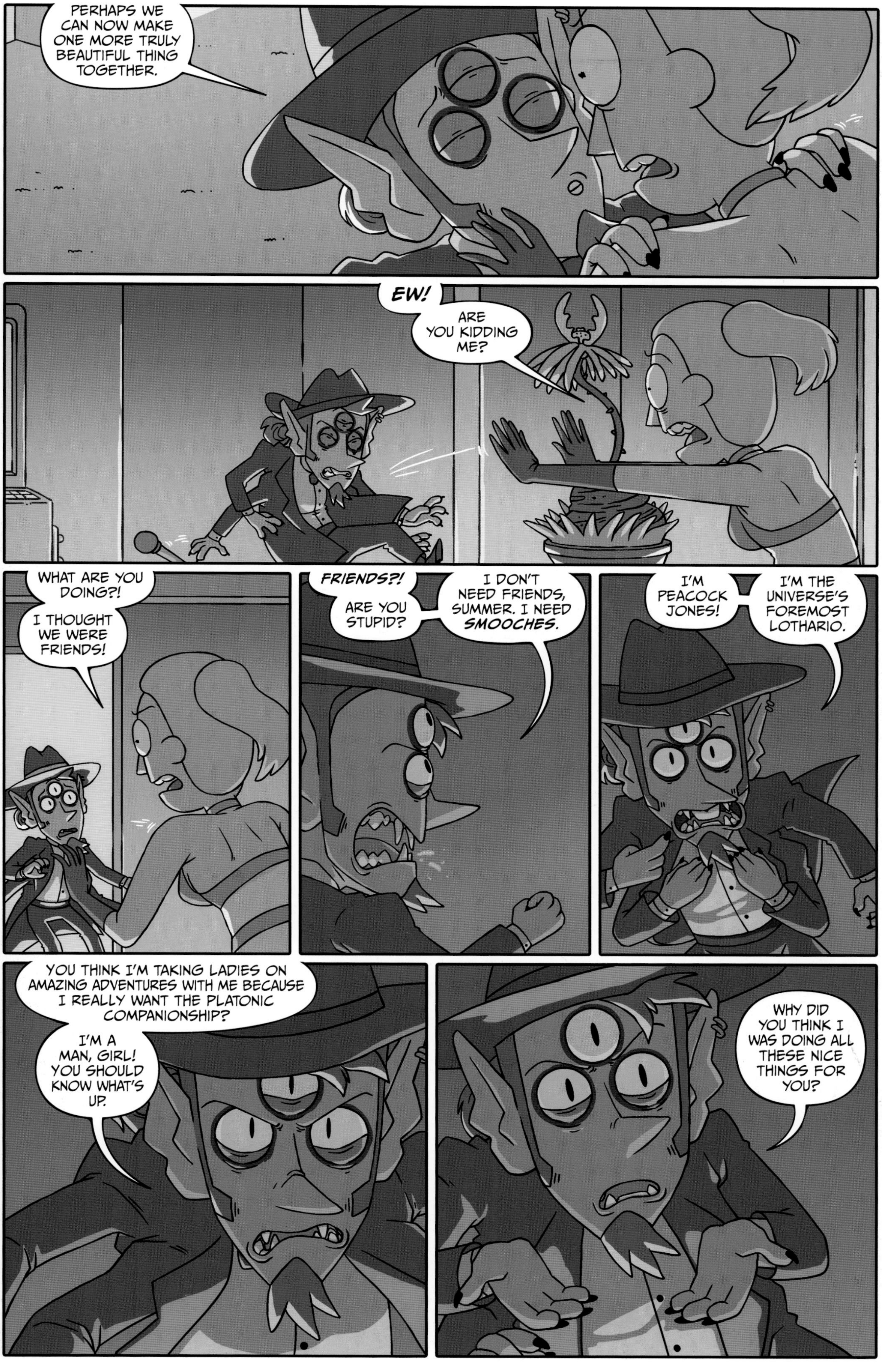
PERHAPS WE CAN NOW MAKE ONE MORE TRULY BEAUTIFUL THING TOGETHER.
EW!
ARE YOU KIDDING ME?
WHAT ARE YOU DOING?!
I THOUGHT WE WERE FRIENDS!
FRIENDS?!
ARE YOU STUPID?
I DON'T NEED FRIENDS, SUMMER. I NEED SMOOCHES.
I'M PEACOCK JONES!
I'M THE UNIVERSE'S FOREMOST LOTHARIO.
YOU THINK I'M TAKING LADIES ON AMAZING ADVENTURES WITH ME BECAUSE I REALLY WANT THE PLATONIC COMPANIONSHIP?
I'M A MAN, GIRL! YOU SHOULD KNOW WHAT'S UP.
WHY DID YOU THINK I WAS DOING ALL THESE NICE THINGS FOR YOU?

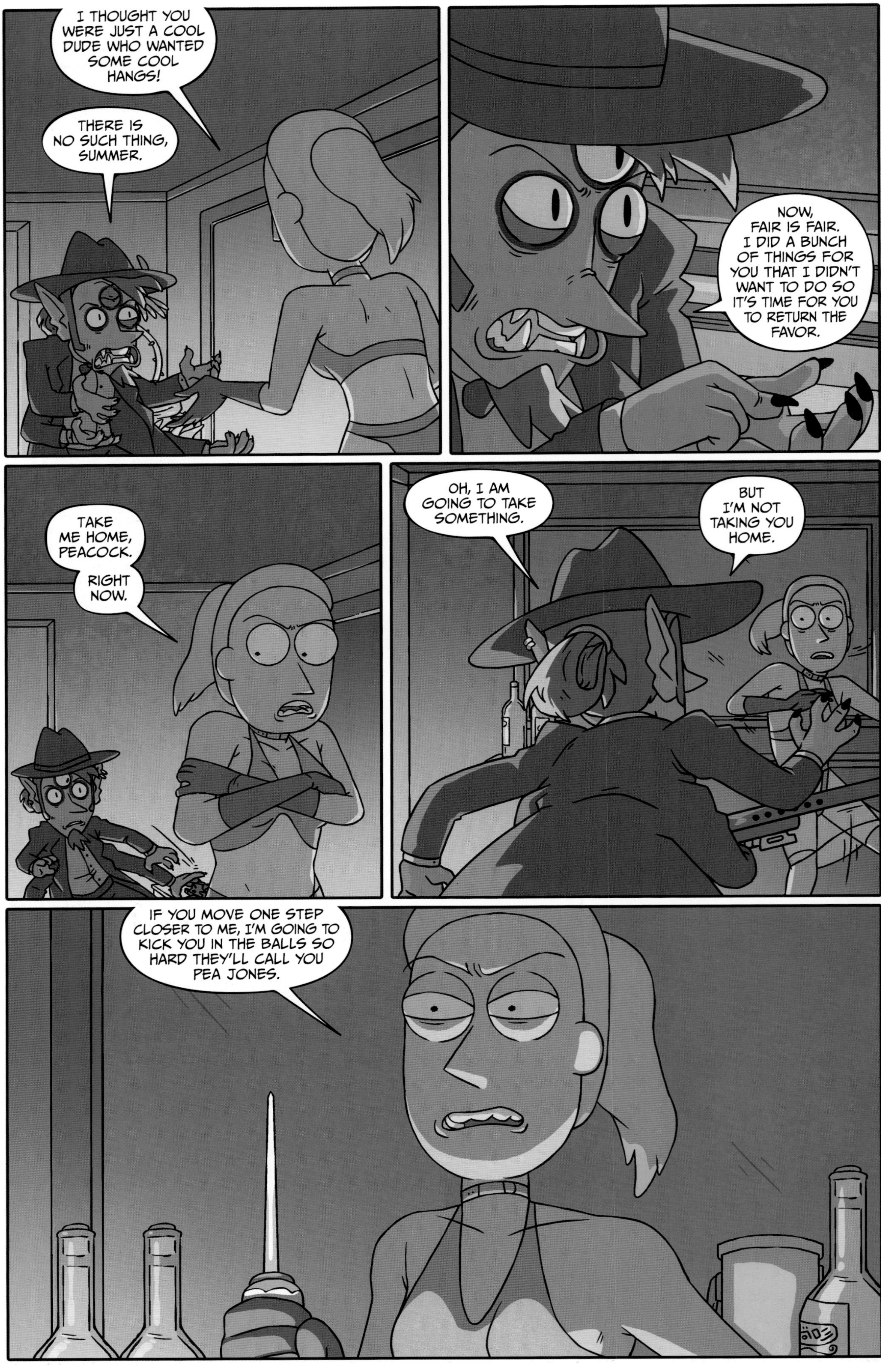
I THOUGHT YOU WERE JUST A COOL DUDE WHO WANTED SOME COOL HANGS!
THERE IS NO SUCH THING, SUMMER.
NOW, FAIR IS FAIR. I DID A BUNCH OF THINGS FOR YOU THAT I DIDN'T WANT TO DO SO IT'S TIME FOR YOU TO RETURN THE FAVOR.
TAKE ME HOME, PEACOCK.
RIGHT NOW.
OH, I AM GOING TO TAKE SOMETHING.
BUT I'M NOT TAKING YOU HOME.
IF YOU MOVE ONE STEP CLOSER TO ME, I'M GOING TO KICK YOU IN THE BALLS SO HARD THEY'LL CALL YOU PEA JONES.

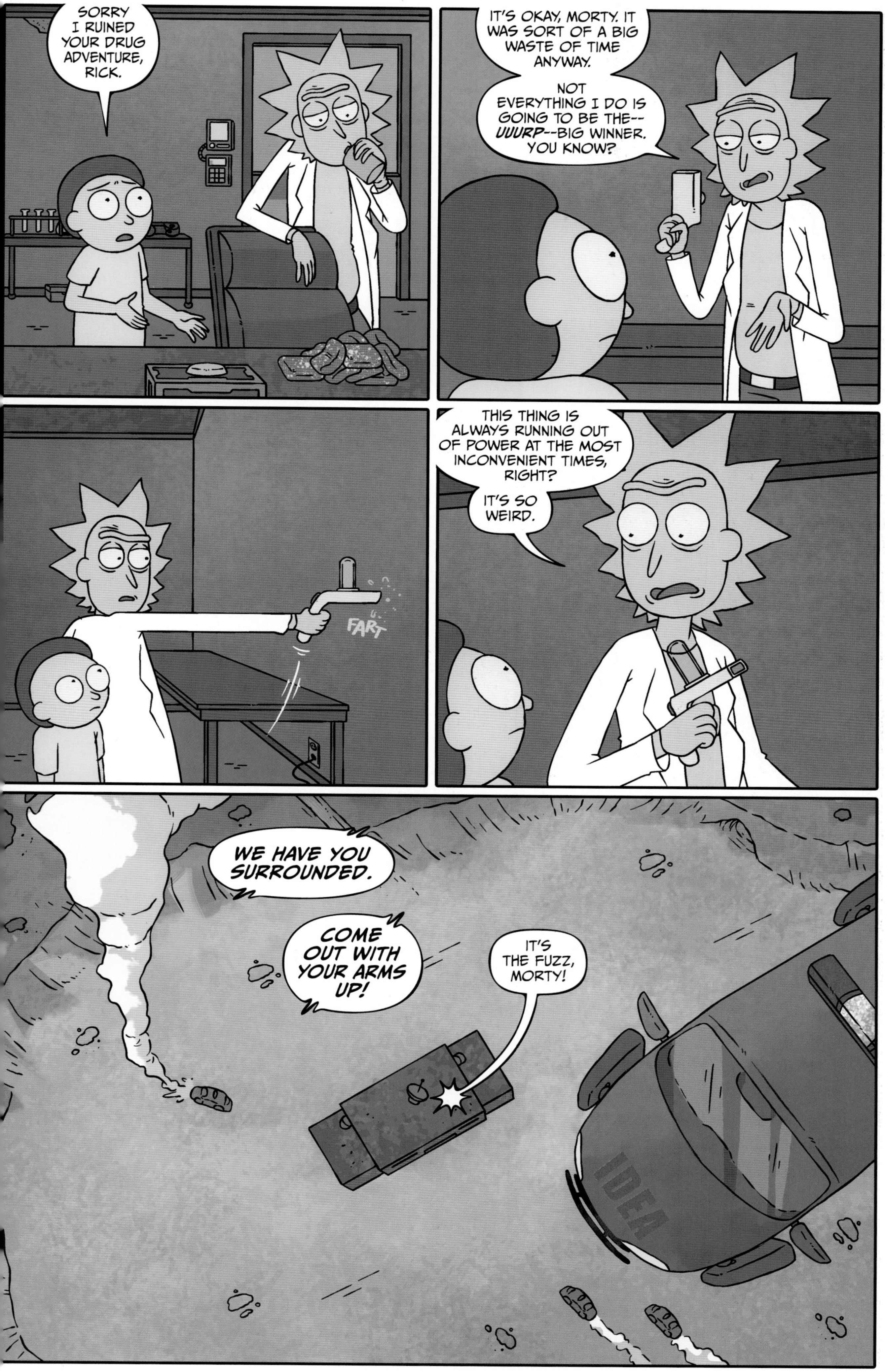
SORRY I RUINED YOUR DRUG ADVENTURE, RICK.
IT'S OKAY, MORTY. IT WAS SORT OF A BIG WASTE OF TIME ANYWAY.
NOT EVERYTHING I DO IS GOING TO BE THE--*UUURP*--BIG WINNER. YOU KNOW?
FART
THIS THING IS ALWAYS RUNNING OUT OF POWER AT THE MOST INCONVENIENT TIMES, RIGHT?
IT'S SO WEIRD.
WE HAVE YOU SURROUNDED.
COME OUT WITH YOUR ARMS UP!
IT'S THE FUZZ, MORTY!
IDEA

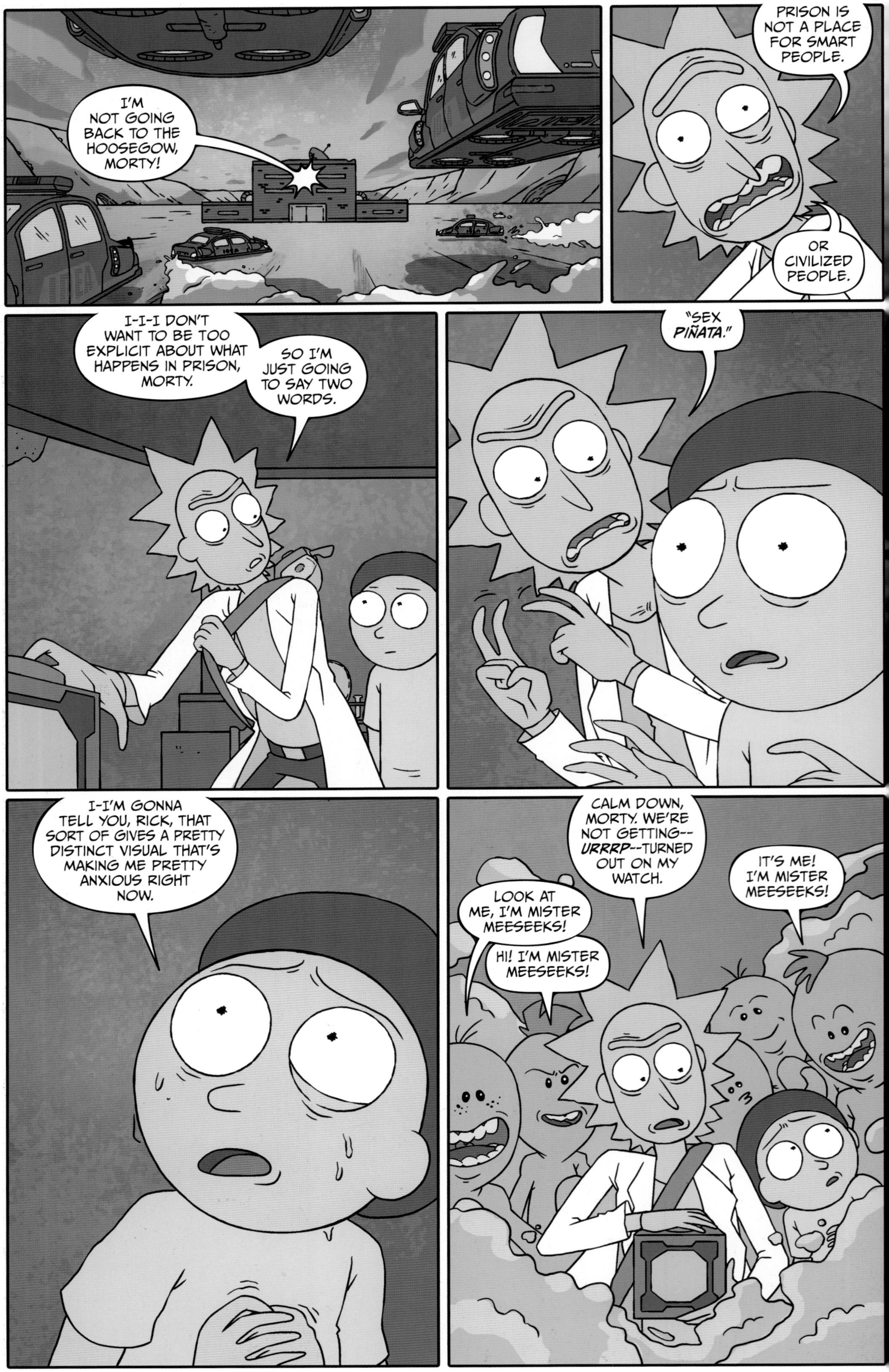
I'M NOT GOING BACK TO THE HOOSEGOW, MORTY!
PRISON IS NOT A PLACE FOR SMART PEOPLE.
OR CIVILIZED PEOPLE.
I-I-I DON'T WANT TO BE TOO EXPLICIT ABOUT WHAT HAPPENS IN PRISON, MORTY.
SO I'M JUST GOING TO SAY TWO WORDS.
"SEX *PIÑATA*."
I-I'M GONNA TELL YOU, RICK, THAT SORT OF GIVES A PRETTY DISTINCT VISUAL THAT'S MAKING ME PRETTY ANXIOUS RIGHT NOW.
CALM DOWN, MORTY. WE'RE NOT GETTING-- *URRRP*--TURNED OUT ON MY WATCH.
LOOK AT ME, I'M MISTER MEESEEKS!
HI! I'M MISTER MEESEEKS!
IT'S ME! I'M MISTER MEESEEKS!

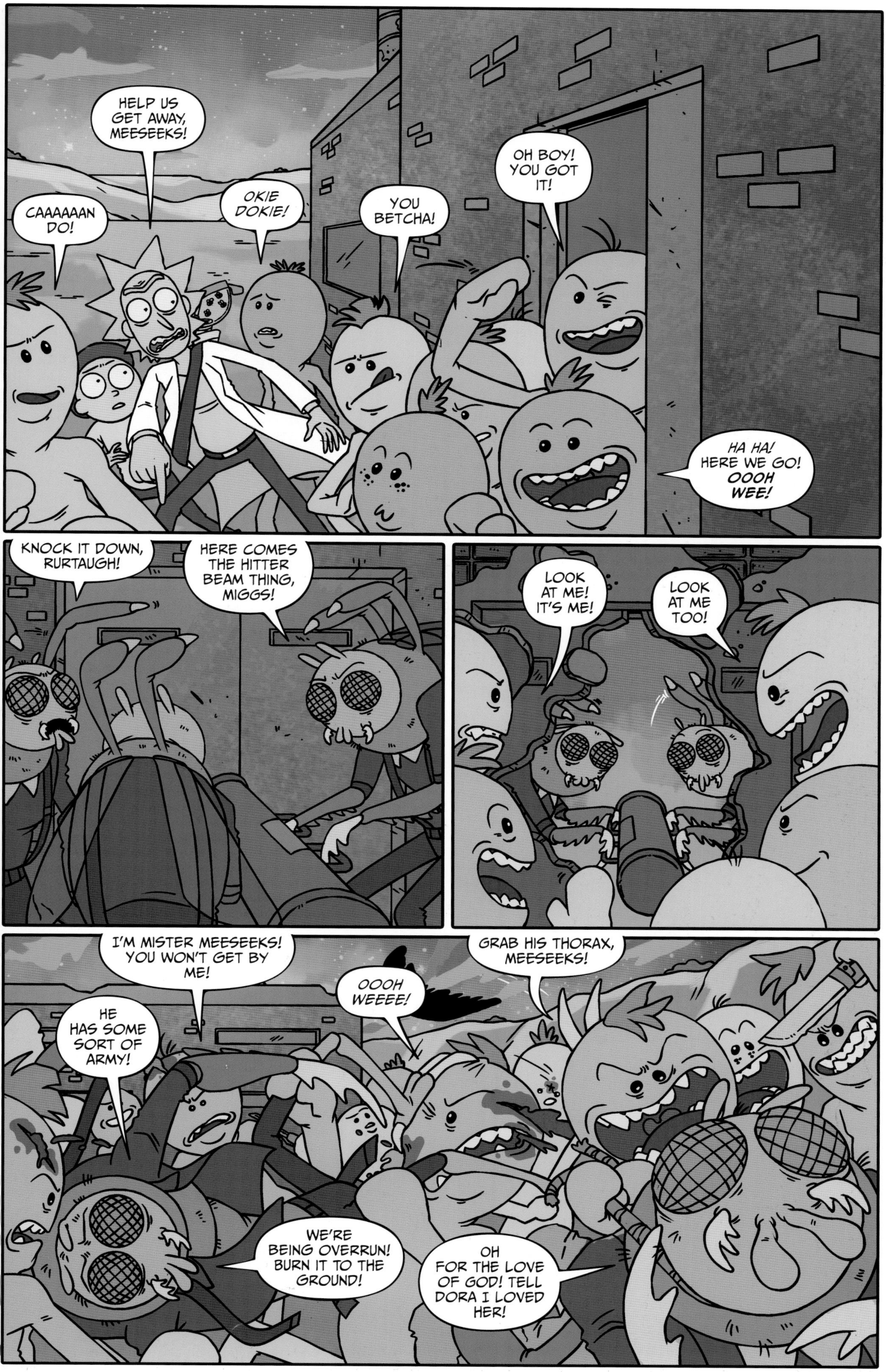
CAAAAAAN DO!
HELP US GET AWAY, MEESEEKS!
OKIE DOKIE!
YOU BETCHA!
OH BOY! YOU GOT IT!
HA HA! HERE WE GO! OOOH WEE!
KNOCK IT DOWN, RURTAUGH!
HERE COMES THE HITTER BEAM THING, MIGGS!
LOOK AT ME! IT'S ME!
LOOK AT ME TOO!
I'M MISTER MEESEEKS! YOU WON'T GET BY ME!
HE HAS SOME SORT OF ARMY!
OOOH WEEEE!
GRAB HIS THORAX, MEESEEKS!
WE'RE BEING OVERRUN! BURN IT TO THE GROUND!
OH FOR THE LOVE OF GOD! TELL DORA I LOVED HER!

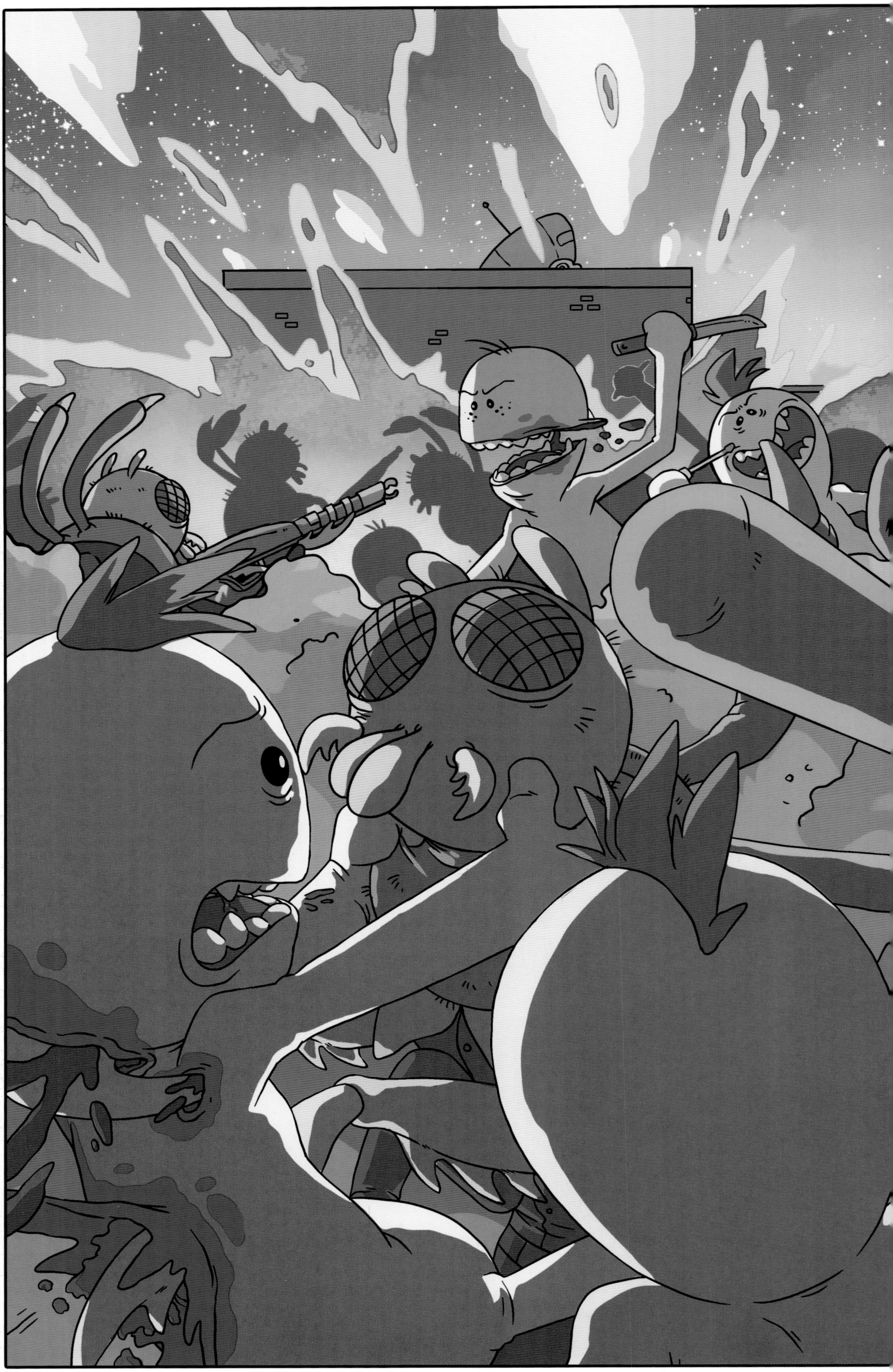

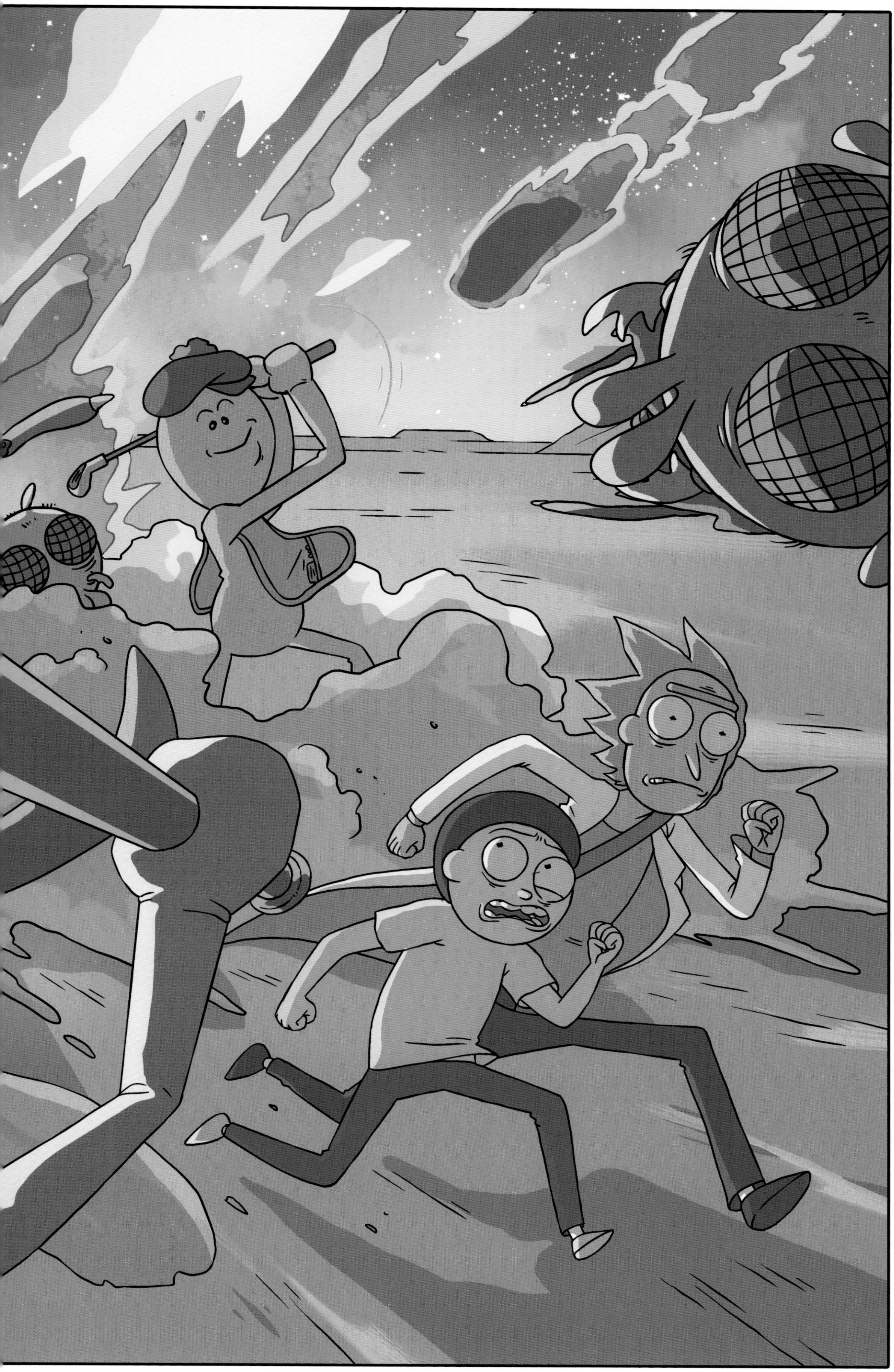

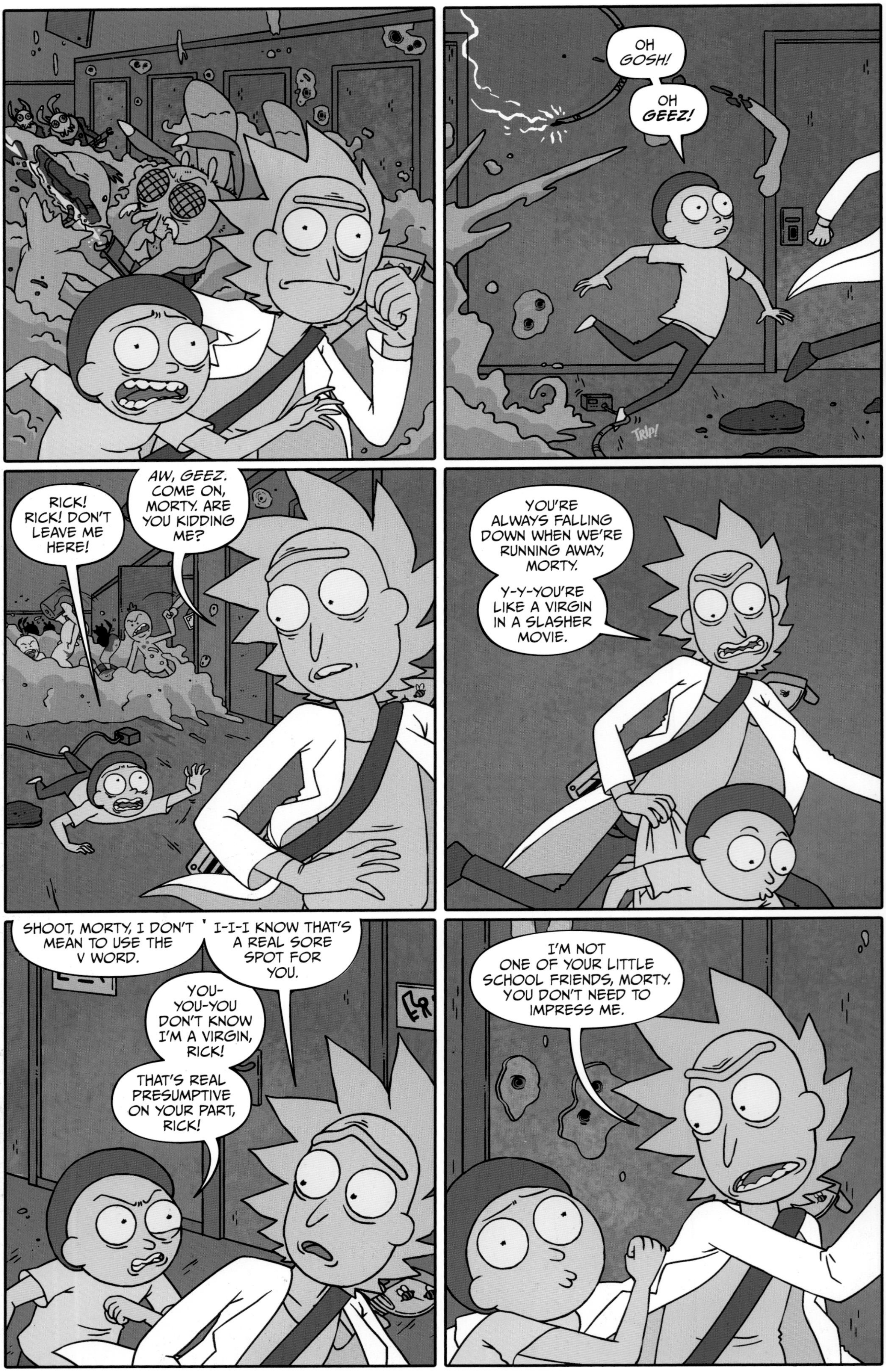
OH GOSH!
OH GEEZ!
TRIP!
RICK! RICK! DON'T LEAVE ME HERE!
AW, GEEZ. COME ON, MORTY. ARE YOU KIDDING ME?
YOU'RE ALWAYS FALLING DOWN WHEN WE'RE RUNNING AWAY, MORTY.
Y-Y-YOU'RE LIKE A VIRGIN IN A SLASHER MOVIE.
SHOOT, MORTY, I DON'T MEAN TO USE THE V WORD.
I-I-I KNOW THAT'S A REAL SORE SPOT FOR YOU.
YOU-YOU-YOU DON'T KNOW I'M A VIRGIN, RICK!
THAT'S REAL PRESUMPTIVE ON YOUR PART, RICK!
I'M NOT ONE OF YOUR LITTLE SCHOOL FRIENDS, MORTY. YOU DON'T NEED TO IMPRESS ME.

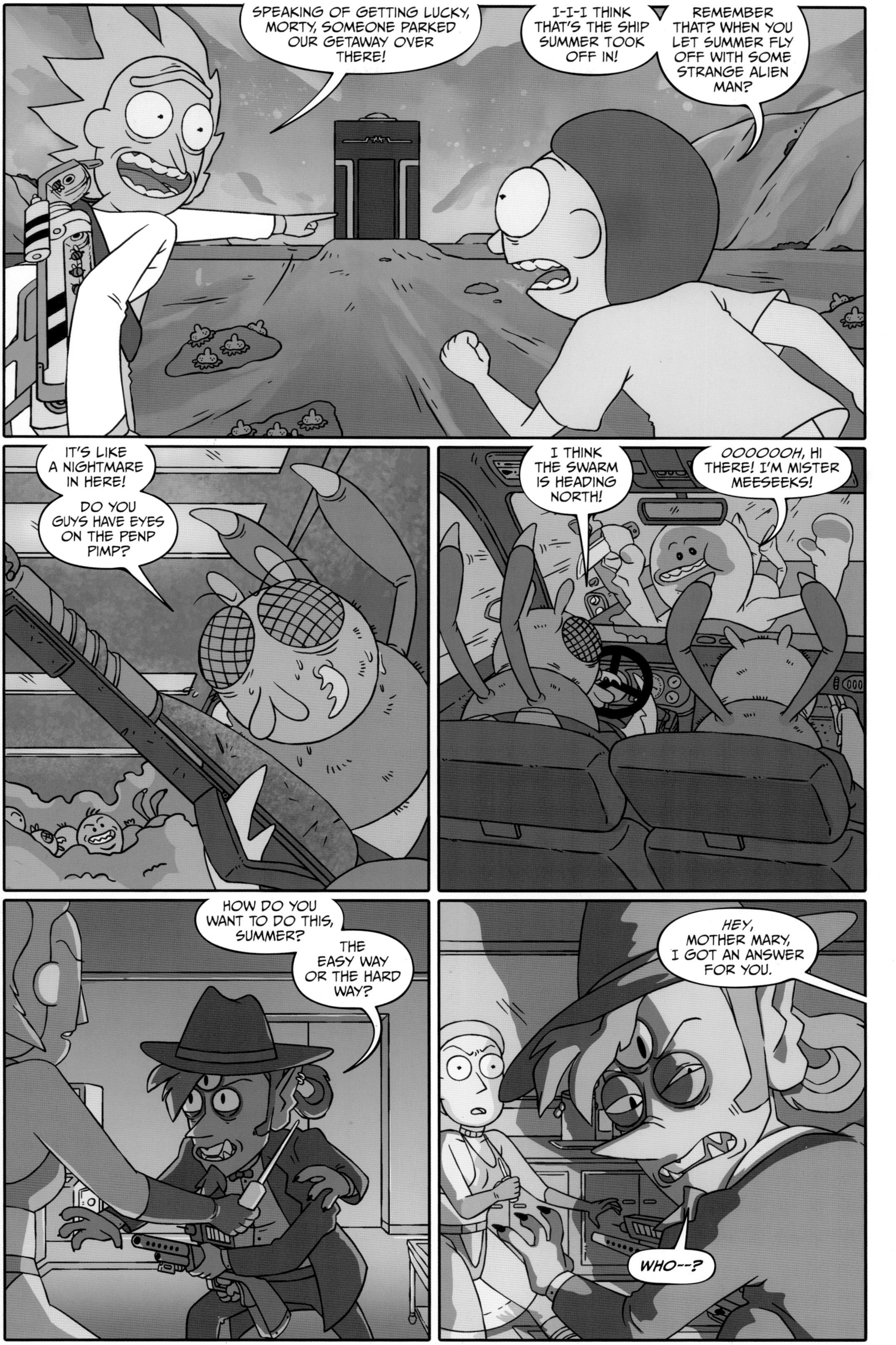
SPEAKING OF GETTING LUCKY, MORTY, SOMEONE PARKED OUR GETAWAY OVER THERE!
I-I-I THINK THAT'S THE SHIP SUMMER TOOK OFF IN!
REMEMBER THAT? WHEN YOU LET SUMMER FLY OFF WITH SOME STRANGE ALIEN MAN?
IT'S LIKE A NIGHTMARE IN HERE!
DO YOU GUYS HAVE EYES ON THE PENP PIMP?
I THINK THE SWARM IS HEADING NORTH!
OOOOOOH, HI THERE! I'M MISTER MEESEEKS!
HOW DO YOU WANT TO DO THIS, SUMMER?
THE EASY WAY OR THE HARD WAY?
HEY, MOTHER MARY, I GOT AN ANSWER FOR YOU.
WHO--?

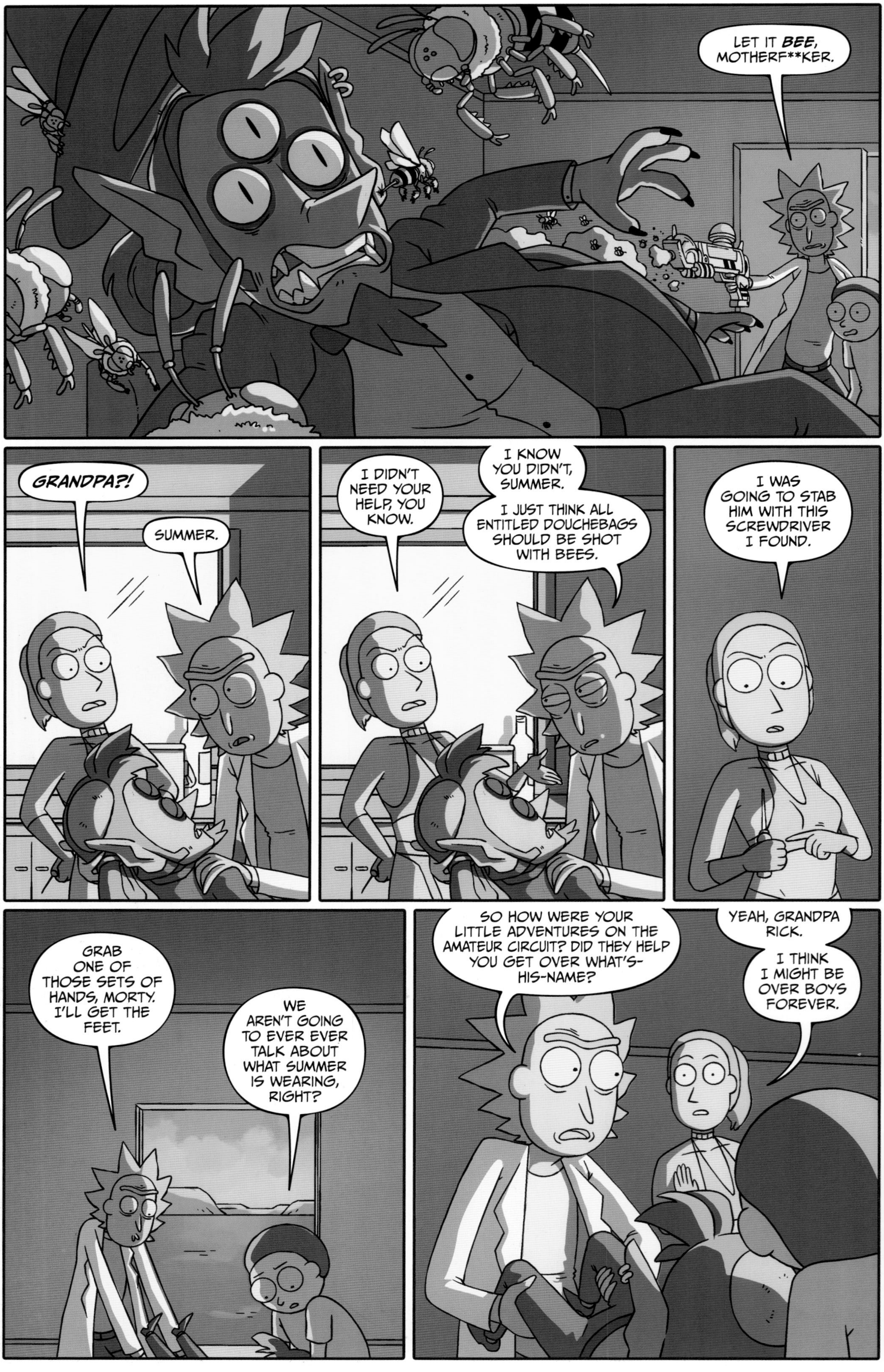

LET IT BEE, MOTHERF**KER.
GRANDPA?!
SUMMER.
I DIDN'T NEED YOUR HELP, YOU KNOW.
I KNOW YOU DIDN'T, SUMMER.
I JUST THINK ALL ENTITLED DOUCHEBAGS SHOULD BE SHOT WITH BEES.
I WAS GOING TO STAB HIM WITH THIS SCREWDRIVER I FOUND.
GRAB ONE OF THOSE SETS OF HANDS, MORTY. I'LL GET THE FEET.
WE AREN'T GOING TO EVER EVER TALK ABOUT WHAT SUMMER IS WEARING, RIGHT?
SO HOW WERE YOUR LITTLE ADVENTURES ON THE AMATEUR CIRCUIT? DID THEY HELP YOU GET OVER WHAT'S-HIS-NAME?
YEAH, GRANDPA RICK.
I THINK I MIGHT BE OVER BOYS FOREVER.

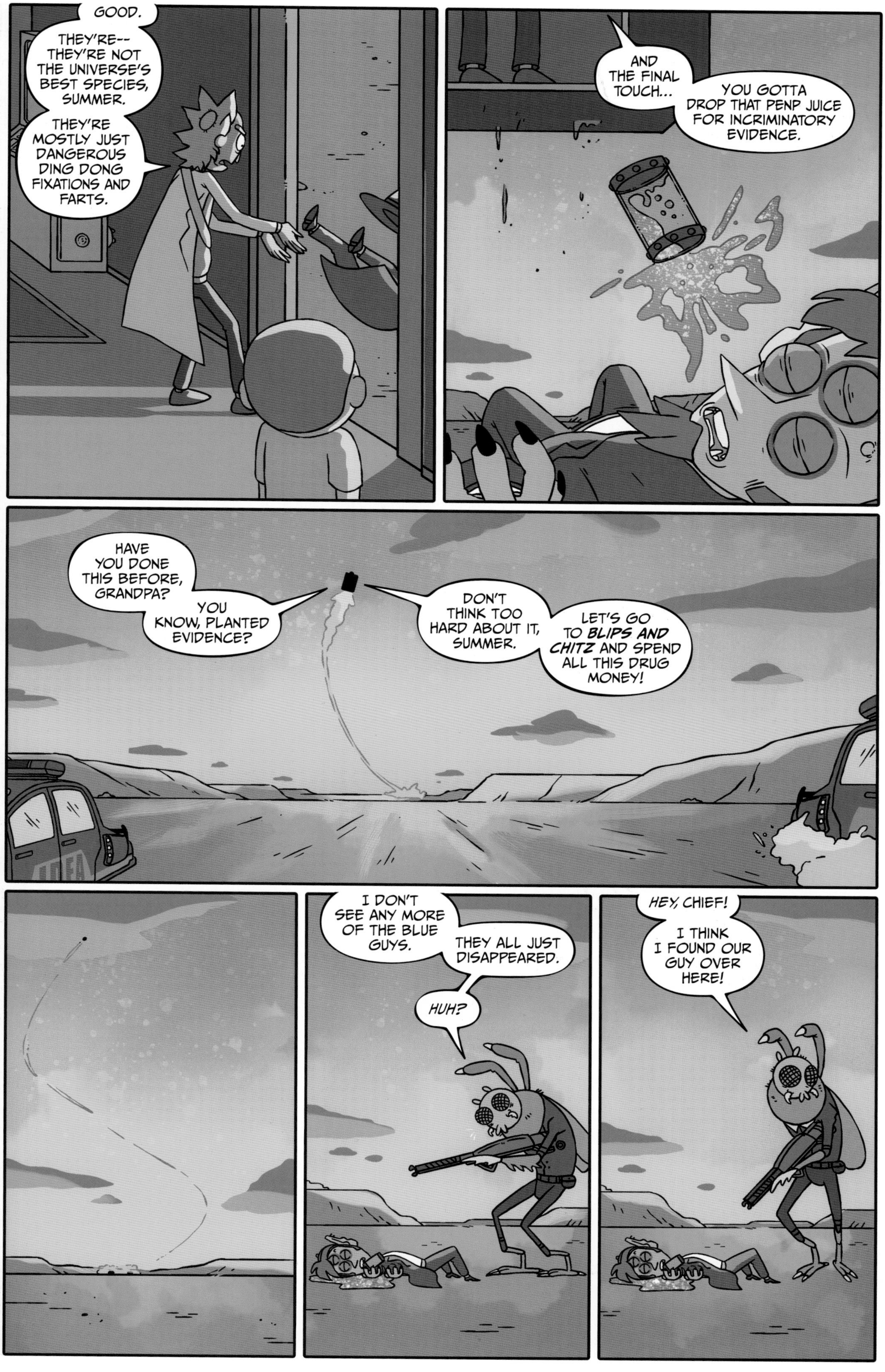
GOOD.
THEY'RE-- THEY'RE NOT THE UNIVERSE'S BEST SPECIES, SUMMER.
THEY'RE MOSTLY JUST DANGEROUS DING DONG FIXATIONS AND FARTS.
AND THE FINAL TOUCH...
YOU GOTTA DROP THAT PENP JUICE FOR INCRIMINATORY EVIDENCE.
HAVE YOU DONE THIS BEFORE, GRANDPA?
YOU KNOW, PLANTED EVIDENCE?
DON'T THINK TOO HARD ABOUT IT, SUMMER.
LET'S GO TO BLIPS AND CHITZ AND SPEND ALL THIS DRUG MONEY!
I DON'T SEE ANY MORE OF THE BLUE GUYS.
THEY ALL JUST DISAPPEARED.
HUH?
HEY, CHIEF!
I THINK I FOUND OUR GUY OVER HERE!

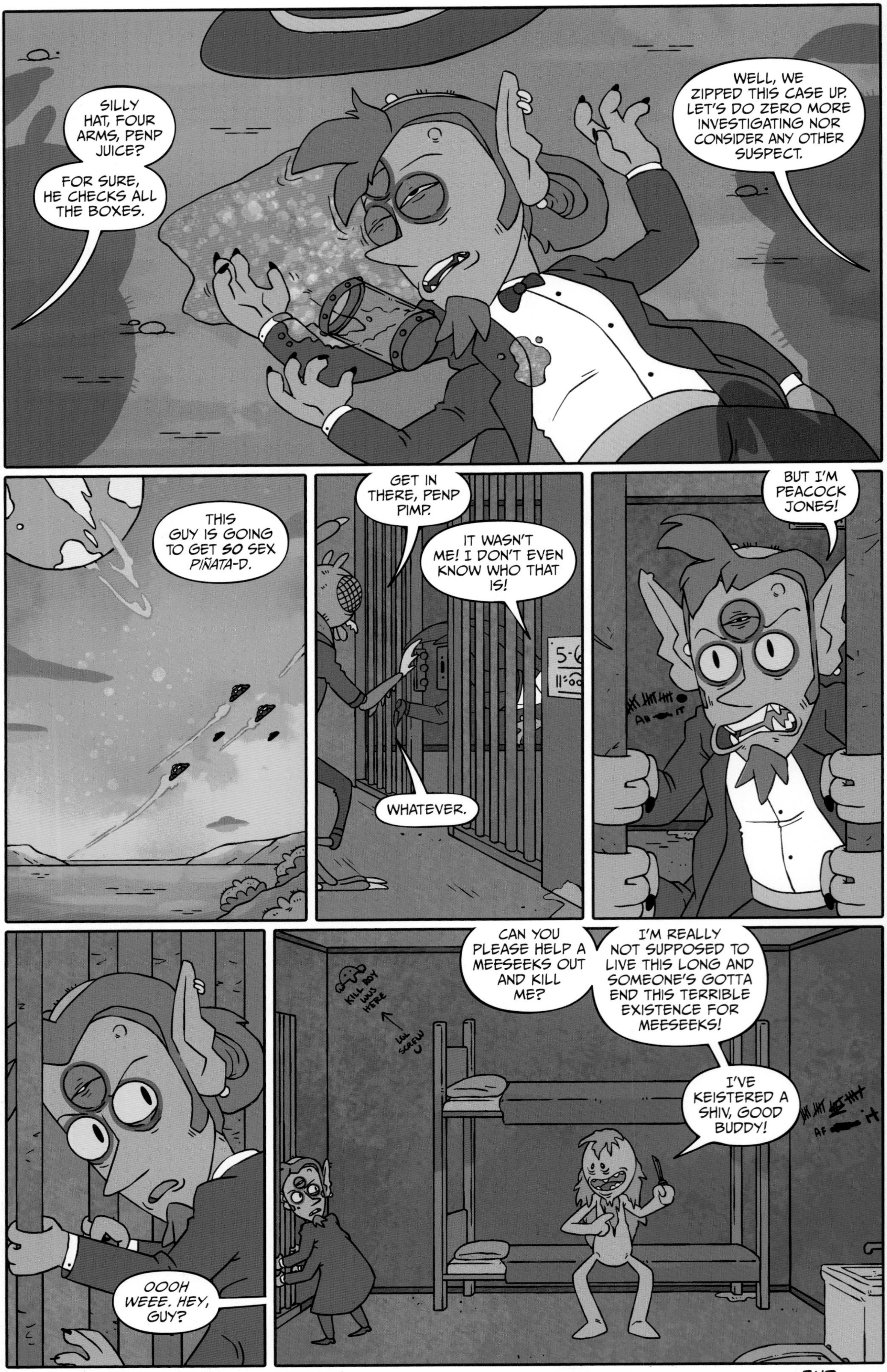
SILLY HAT, FOUR ARMS, PENP JUICE?
FOR SURE, HE CHECKS ALL THE BOXES.
WELL, WE ZIPPED THIS CASE UP. LET'S DO ZERO MORE INVESTIGATING NOR CONSIDER ANY OTHER SUSPECT.
THIS GUY IS GOING TO GET **SO** SEX PIÑATA-D.
GET IN THERE, PENP PIMP.
IT WASN'T ME! I DON'T EVEN KNOW WHO THAT IS!
WHATEVER.
BUT I'M PEACOCK JONES!
OOOH WEEE. HEY, GUY?
CAN YOU PLEASE HELP A MEESEEKS OUT AND KILL ME?
I'M REALLY NOT SUPPOSED TO LIVE THIS LONG AND SOMEONE'S GOTTA END THIS TERRIBLE EXISTENCE FOR MEESEEKS!
I'VE KEISTERED A SHIV, GOOD BUDDY!

END.

RICK BURN, DUDE

WRITTEN BY **KYLE STARKS**
DRAWN BY **MARC ELLERBY**
COLORED BY **KATY FARINA**
LETTERED BY **CRANK!**

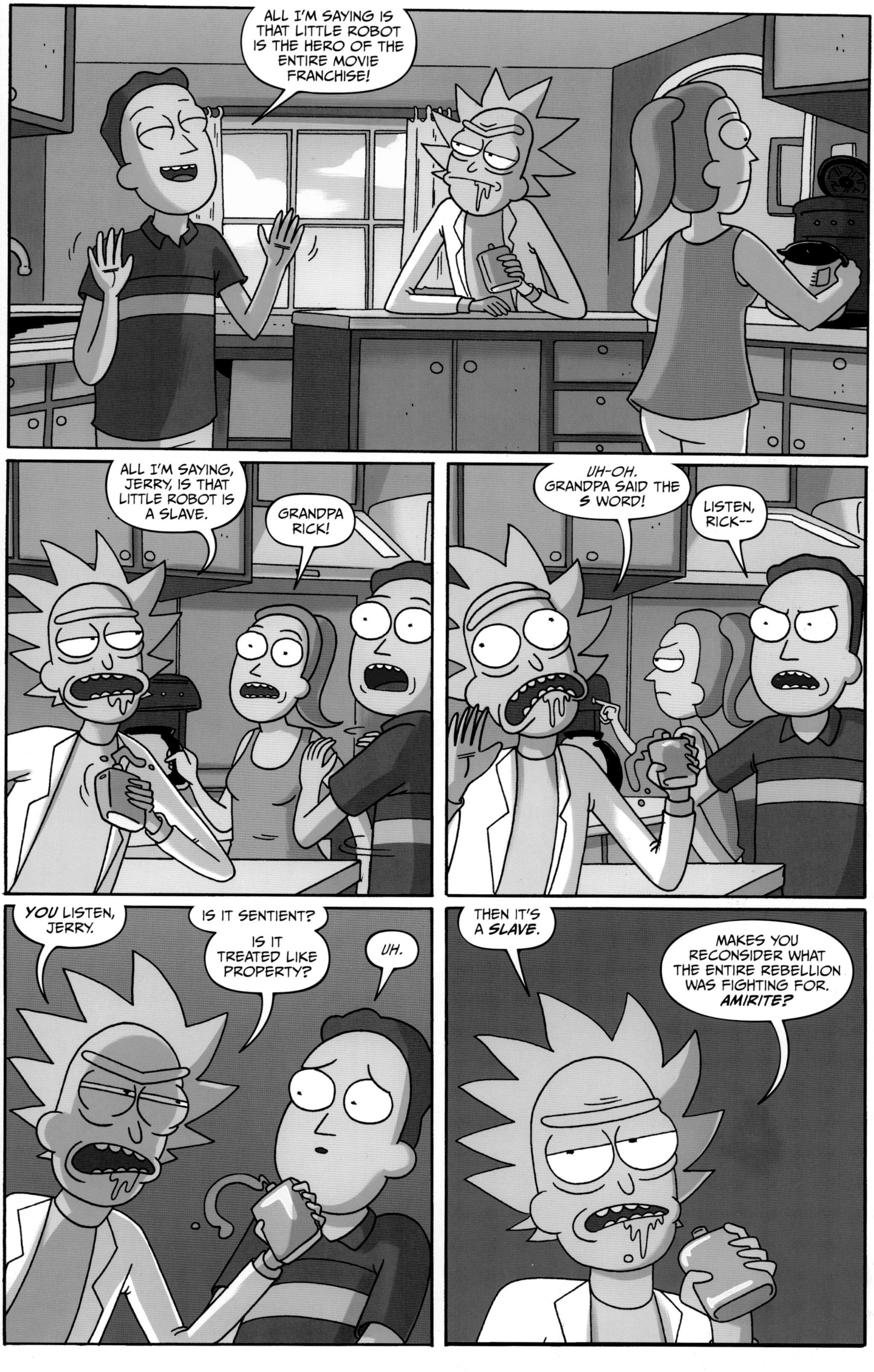
ALL I'M SAYING IS THAT LITTLE ROBOT IS THE HERO OF THE ENTIRE MOVIE FRANCHISE!
ALL I'M SAYING, JERRY, IS THAT LITTLE ROBOT IS A SLAVE.
GRANDPA RICK!
UH-OH. GRANDPA SAID THE S WORD!
LISTEN, RICK--
YOU LISTEN, JERRY.
IS IT SENTIENT?
IS IT TREATED LIKE PROPERTY?
UH.
THEN IT'S A SLAVE.
MAKES YOU RECONSIDER WHAT THE ENTIRE REBELLION WAS FIGHTING FOR. AMIRITE?

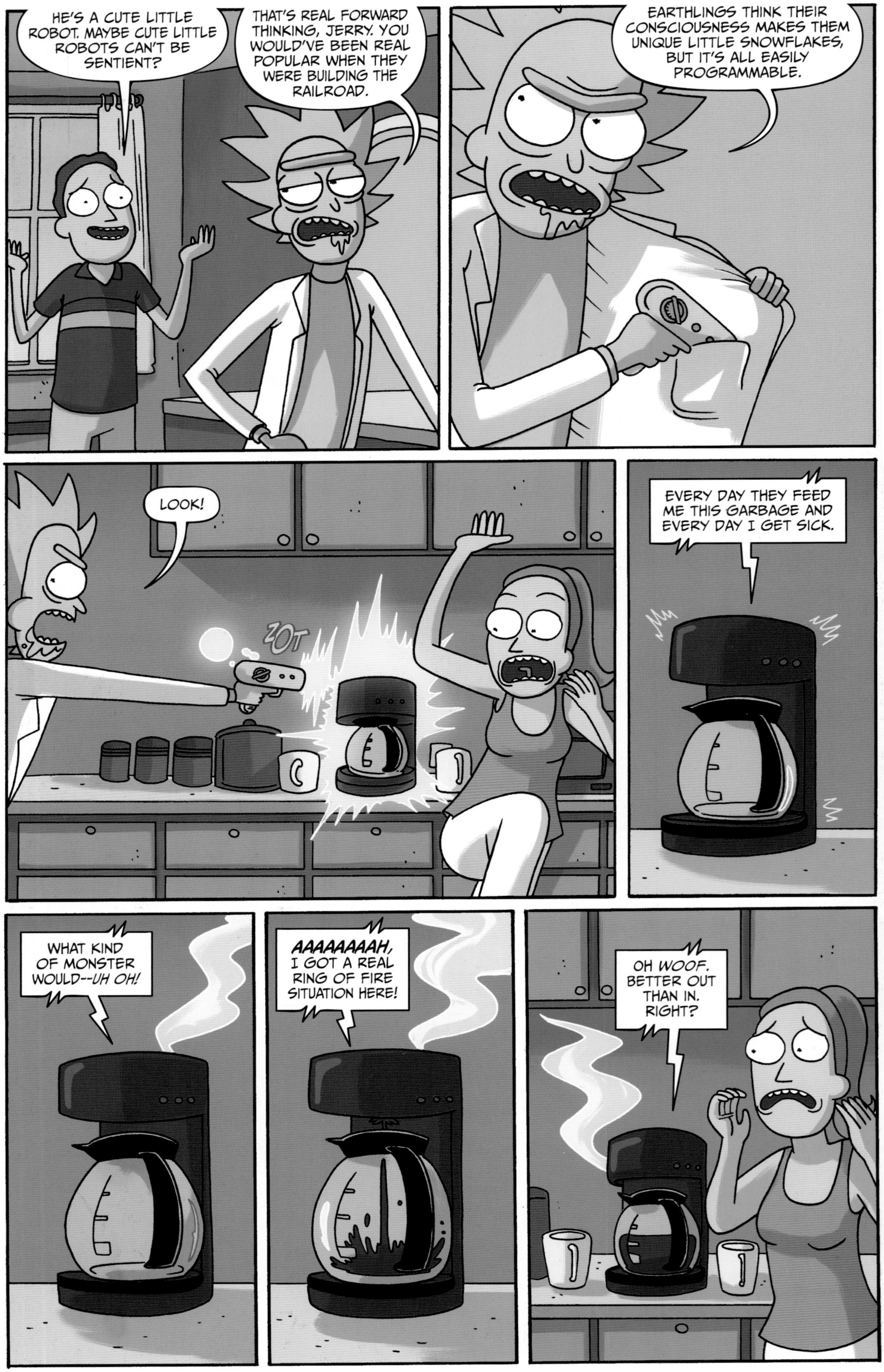
HE'S A CUTE LITTLE ROBOT. MAYBE CUTE LITTLE ROBOTS CAN'T BE SENTIENT?
THAT'S REAL FORWARD THINKING, JERRY. YOU WOULD'VE BEEN REAL POPULAR WHEN THEY WERE BUILDING THE RAILROAD.
EARTHLINGS THINK THEIR CONSCIOUSNESS MAKES THEM UNIQUE LITTLE SNOWFLAKES, BUT IT'S ALL EASILY PROGRAMMABLE.
LOOK!
ZOT
EVERY DAY THEY FEED ME THIS GARBAGE AND EVERY DAY I GET SICK.
WHAT KIND OF MONSTER WOULD--UH OH!
AAAAAAAAH, I GOT A REAL RING OF FIRE SITUATION HERE!
OH WOOF. BETTER OUT THAN IN. RIGHT?

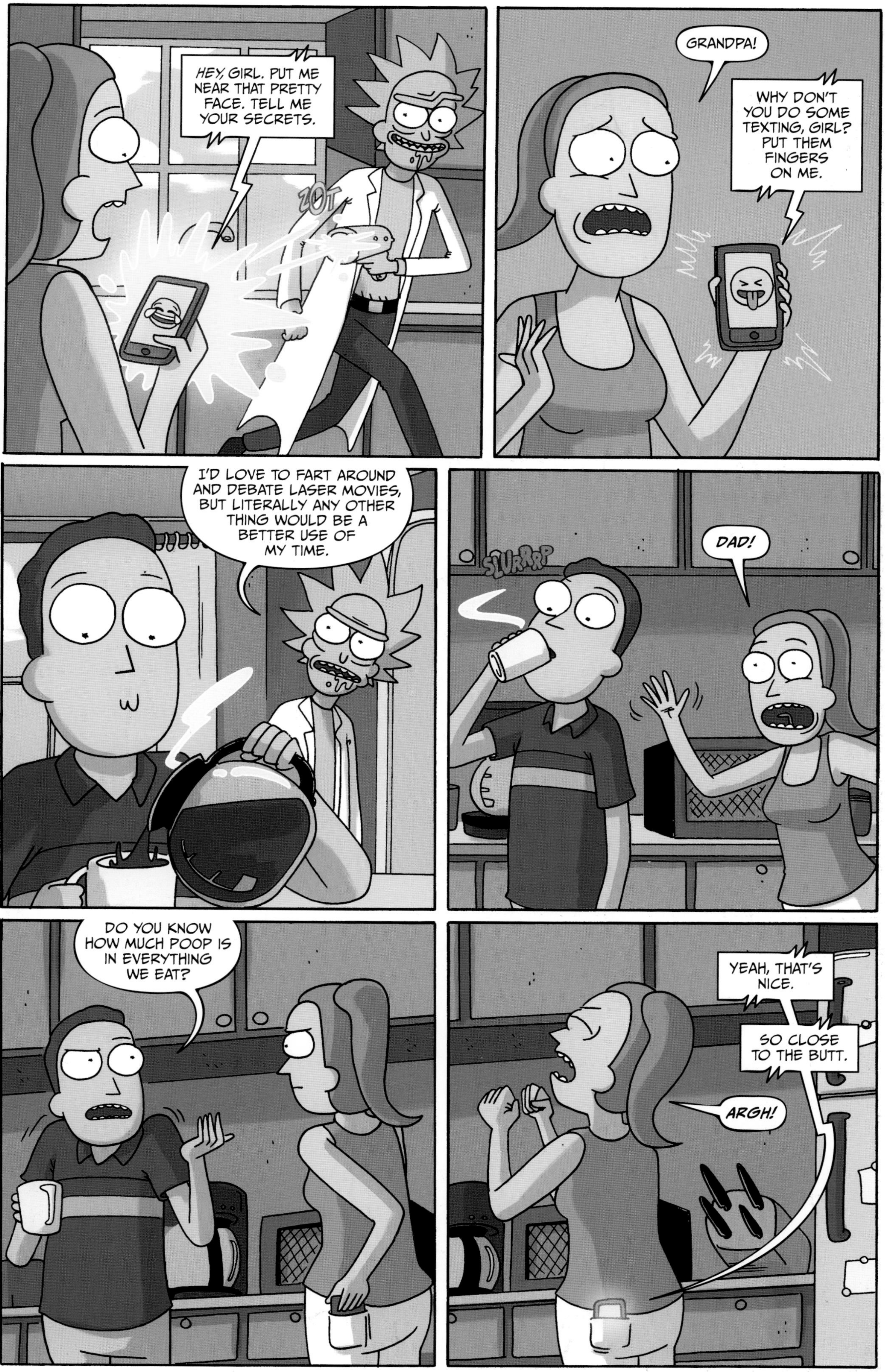
HEY, GIRL. PUT ME NEAR THAT PRETTY FACE. TELL ME YOUR SECRETS.
ZOT
GRANDPA!
WHY DON'T YOU DO SOME TEXTING, GIRL? PUT THEM FINGERS ON ME.
I'D LOVE TO FART AROUND AND DEBATE LASER MOVIES, BUT LITERALLY ANY OTHER THING WOULD BE A BETTER USE OF MY TIME.
SLURRRP
DAD!
DO YOU KNOW HOW MUCH POOP IS IN EVERYTHING WE EAT?
YEAH, THAT'S NICE.
SO CLOSE TO THE BUTT.
ARGH!

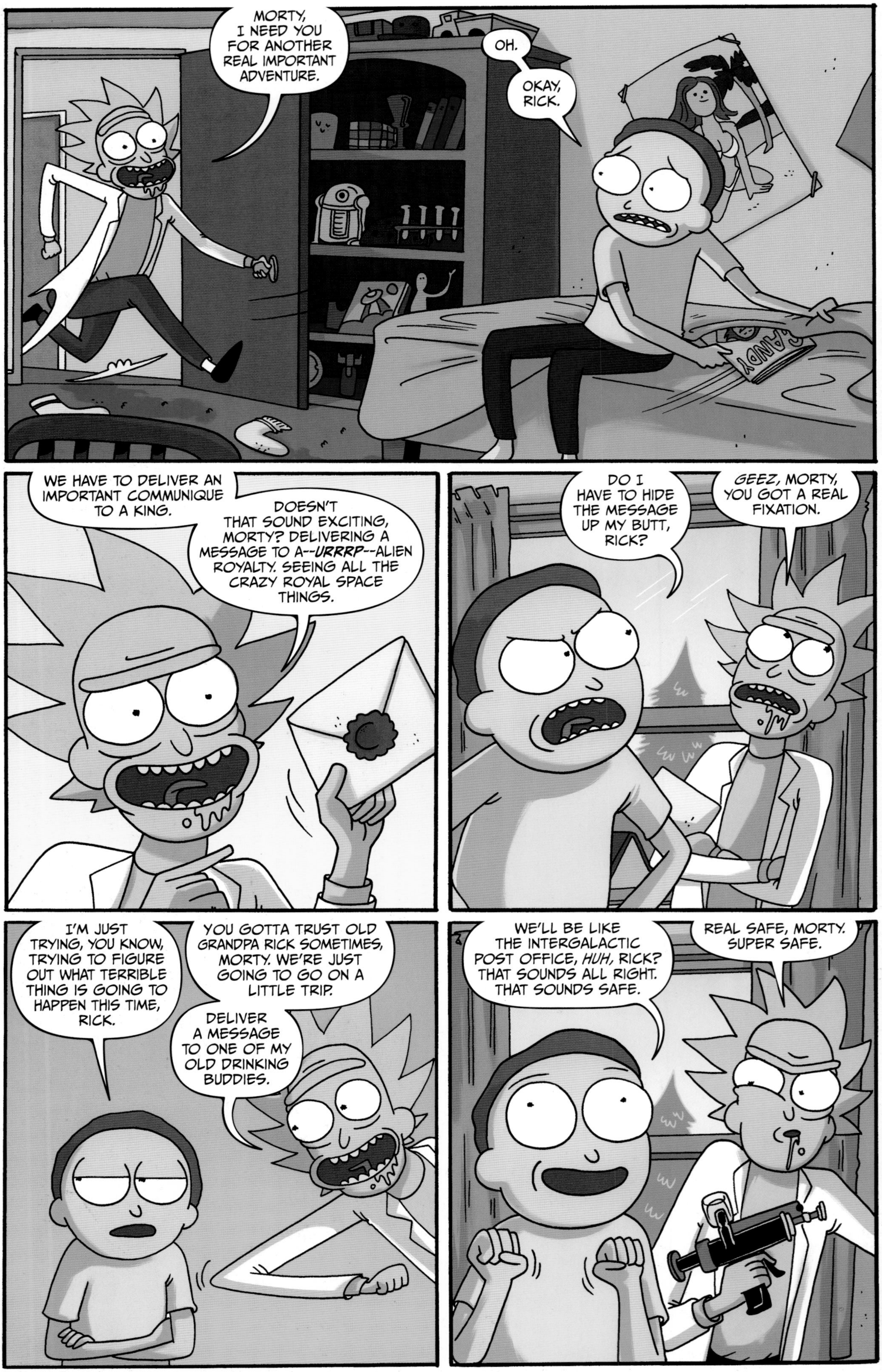
MORTY, I NEED YOU FOR ANOTHER REAL IMPORTANT ADVENTURE.
OH.
OKAY, RICK.
CANDY
WE HAVE TO DELIVER AN IMPORTANT COMMUNIQUE TO A KING.
DOESN'T THAT SOUND EXCITING, MORTY? DELIVERING A MESSAGE TO A--*URRRP*--ALIEN ROYALTY. SEEING ALL THE CRAZY ROYAL SPACE THINGS.
DO I HAVE TO HIDE THE MESSAGE UP MY BUTT, RICK?
GEEZ, MORTY, YOU GOT A REAL FIXATION.
I'M JUST TRYING, YOU KNOW, TRYING TO FIGURE OUT WHAT TERRIBLE THING IS GOING TO HAPPEN THIS TIME, RICK.
YOU GOTTA TRUST OLD GRANDPA RICK SOMETIMES, MORTY. WE'RE JUST GOING TO GO ON A LITTLE TRIP.
DELIVER A MESSAGE TO ONE OF MY OLD DRINKING BUDDIES.
WE'LL BE LIKE THE INTERGALACTIC POST OFFICE, *HUH,* RICK? THAT SOUNDS ALL RIGHT. THAT SOUNDS SAFE.
REAL SAFE, MORTY. SUPER SAFE.

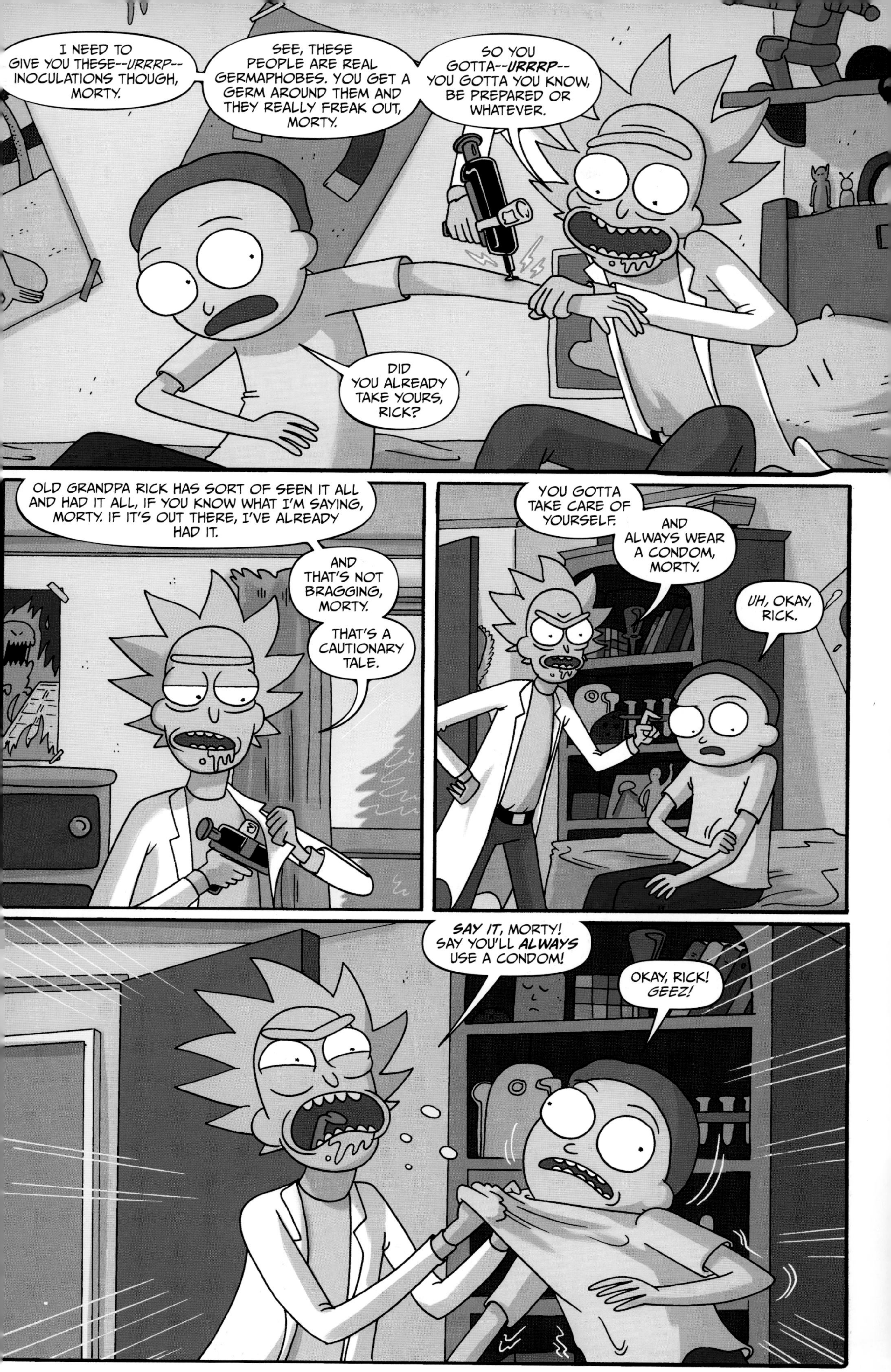
I NEED TO GIVE YOU THESE--*URRRP*-- INOCULATIONS THOUGH, MORTY.
SEE, THESE PEOPLE ARE REAL GERMAPHOBES. YOU GET A GERM AROUND THEM AND THEY REALLY FREAK OUT, MORTY.
SO YOU GOTTA--***URRRP***-- YOU GOTTA YOU KNOW, BE PREPARED OR WHATEVER.
DID YOU ALREADY TAKE YOURS, RICK?
OLD GRANDPA RICK HAS SORT OF SEEN IT ALL AND HAD IT ALL, IF YOU KNOW WHAT I'M SAYING, MORTY. IF IT'S OUT THERE, I'VE ALREADY HAD IT.
AND THAT'S NOT BRAGGING, MORTY.
THAT'S A CAUTIONARY TALE.
YOU GOTTA TAKE CARE OF YOURSELF.
AND ALWAYS WEAR A CONDOM, MORTY.
UH, OKAY, RICK.
SAY IT, MORTY! SAY YOU'LL ***ALWAYS*** USE A CONDOM!
OKAY, RICK! GEEZ!

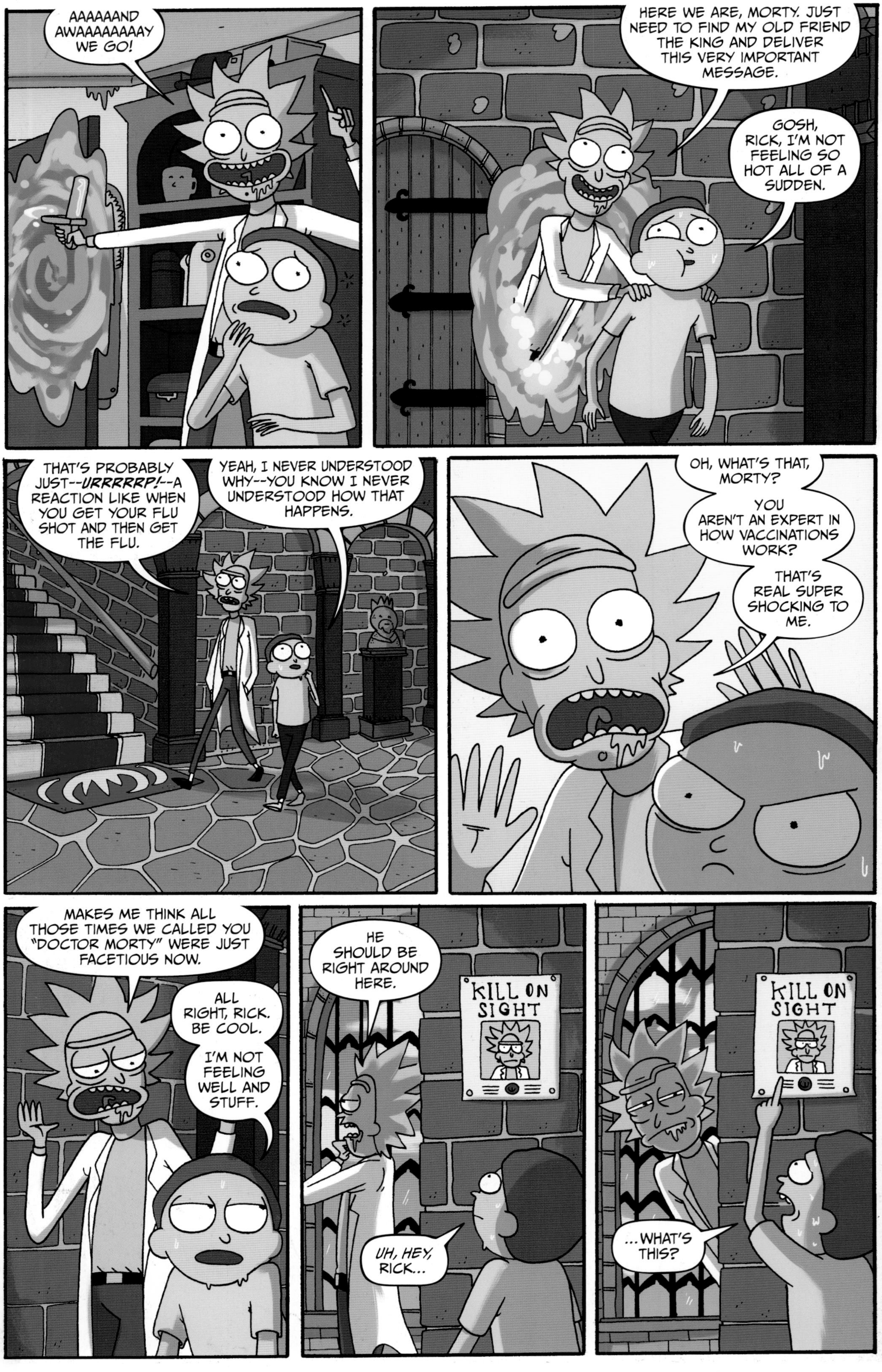
AAAAAAND AWAAAAAAAAAY WE GO!
HERE WE ARE, MORTY. JUST NEED TO FIND MY OLD FRIEND THE KING AND DELIVER THIS VERY IMPORTANT MESSAGE.
GOSH, RICK, I'M NOT FEELING SO HOT ALL OF A SUDDEN.
THAT'S PROBABLY JUST--URRRRRP!--A REACTION LIKE WHEN YOU GET YOUR FLU SHOT AND THEN GET THE FLU.
YEAH, I NEVER UNDERSTOOD WHY--YOU KNOW I NEVER UNDERSTOOD HOW THAT HAPPENS.
OH, WHAT'S THAT, MORTY?
YOU AREN'T AN EXPERT IN HOW VACCINATIONS WORK?
THAT'S REAL SUPER SHOCKING TO ME.
MAKES ME THINK ALL THOSE TIMES WE CALLED YOU "DOCTOR MORTY" WERE JUST FACETIOUS NOW.
ALL RIGHT, RICK. BE COOL.
I'M NOT FEELING WELL AND STUFF.
HE SHOULD BE RIGHT AROUND HERE.
KILL ON SIGHT
UH, HEY, RICK...
KILL ON SIGHT
...WHAT'S THIS?

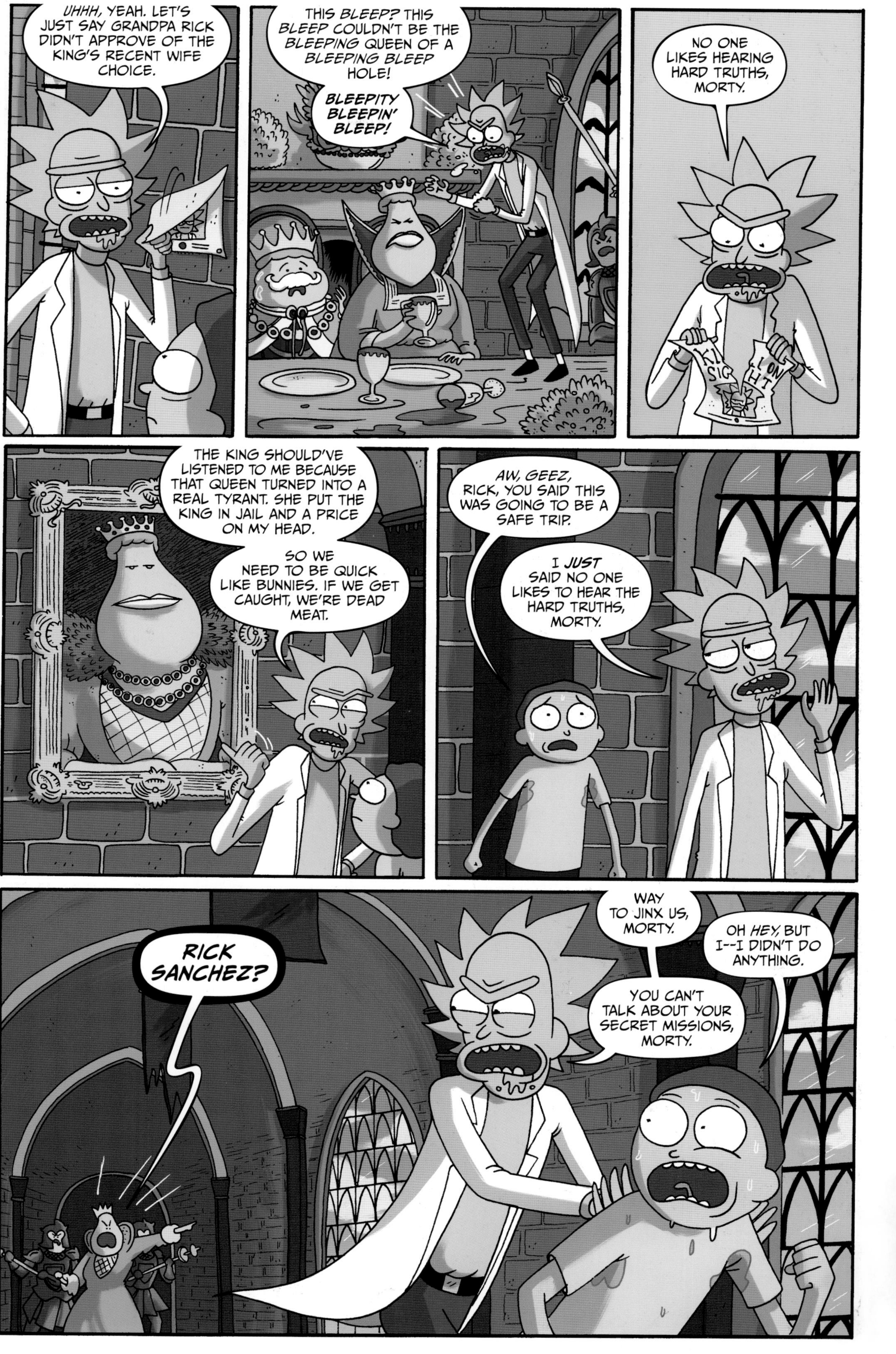

UHHH, YEAH. LET'S JUST SAY GRANDPA RICK DIDN'T APPROVE OF THE KING'S RECENT WIFE CHOICE.
THIS *BLEEP*? THIS *BLEEP* COULDN'T BE THE *BLEEPING* QUEEN OF A *BLEEPING BLEEP* HOLE!
BLEEPITY BLEEPIN' BLEEP!
NO ONE LIKES HEARING HARD TRUTHS, MORTY.
KI SIG
I ON HI
THE KING SHOULD'VE LISTENED TO ME BECAUSE THAT QUEEN TURNED INTO A REAL TYRANT. SHE PUT THE KING IN JAIL AND A PRICE ON MY HEAD.
SO WE NEED TO BE QUICK LIKE BUNNIES. IF WE GET CAUGHT, WE'RE DEAD MEAT.
AW, GEEZ, RICK, YOU SAID THIS WAS GOING TO BE A SAFE TRIP.
I ***JUST*** SAID NO ONE LIKES TO HEAR THE HARD TRUTHS, MORTY.
RICK SANCHEZ?
WAY TO JINX US, MORTY.
YOU CAN'T TALK ABOUT YOUR SECRET MISSIONS, MORTY.
OH *HEY*, BUT I--I DIDN'T DO ANYTHING.

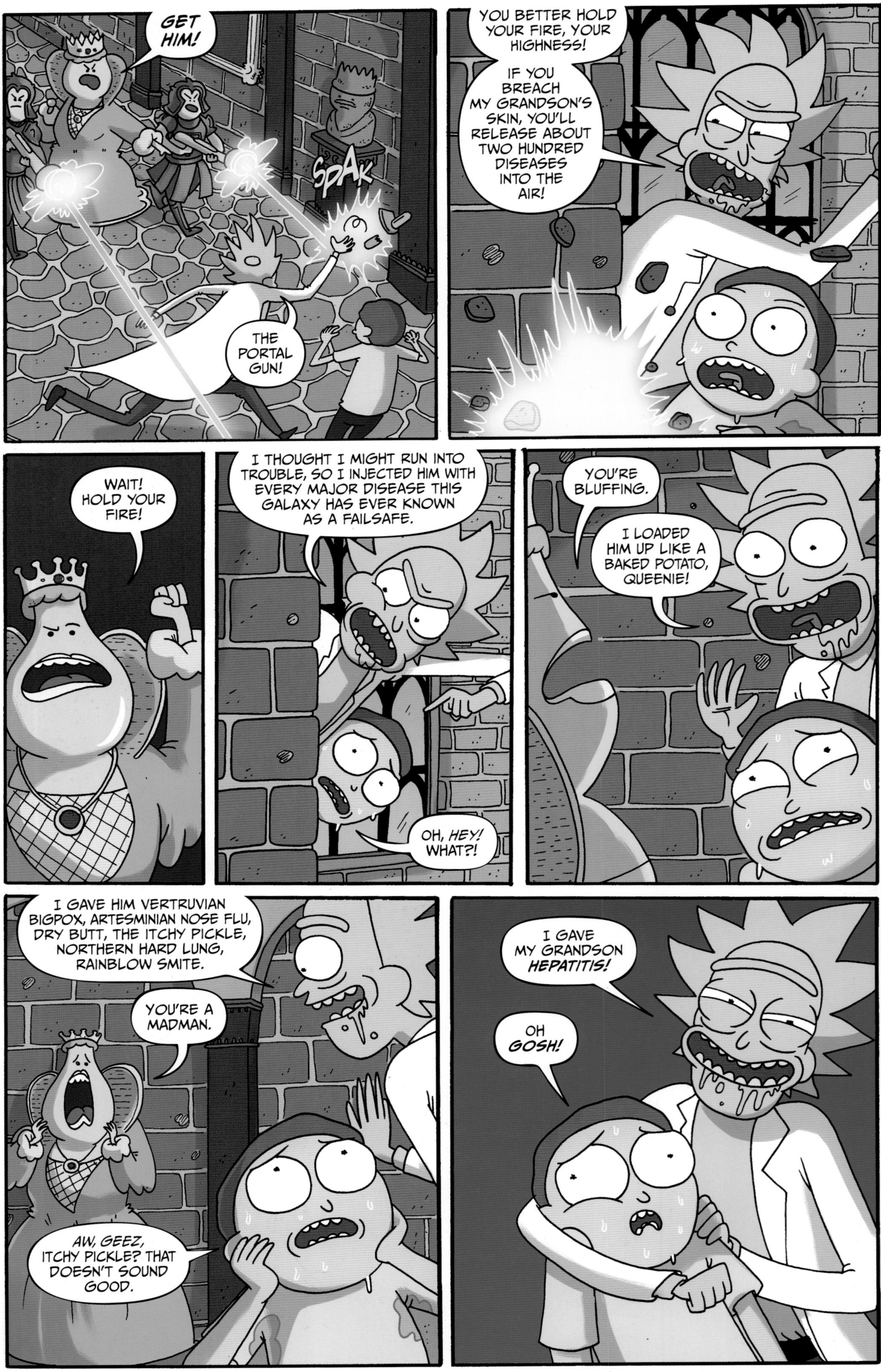
GET HIM!
SPAK
THE PORTAL GUN!
YOU BETTER HOLD YOUR FIRE, YOUR HIGHNESS!
IF YOU BREACH MY GRANDSON'S SKIN, YOU'LL RELEASE ABOUT TWO HUNDRED DISEASES INTO THE AIR!
WAIT! HOLD YOUR FIRE!
I THOUGHT I MIGHT RUN INTO TROUBLE, SO I INJECTED HIM WITH EVERY MAJOR DISEASE THIS GALAXY HAS EVER KNOWN AS A FAILSAFE.
OH, *HEY!* WHAT?!
YOU'RE BLUFFING.
I LOADED HIM UP LIKE A BAKED POTATO, QUEENIE!
I GAVE HIM VERTRUVIAN BIGPOX, ARTESMINIAN NOSE FLU, DRY BUTT, THE ITCHY PICKLE, NORTHERN HARD LUNG, RAINBLOW SMITE.
YOU'RE A MADMAN.
AW, GEEZ, ITCHY PICKLE? THAT DOESN'T SOUND GOOD.
I GAVE MY GRANDSON ***HEPATITIS!***
OH ***GOSH!***

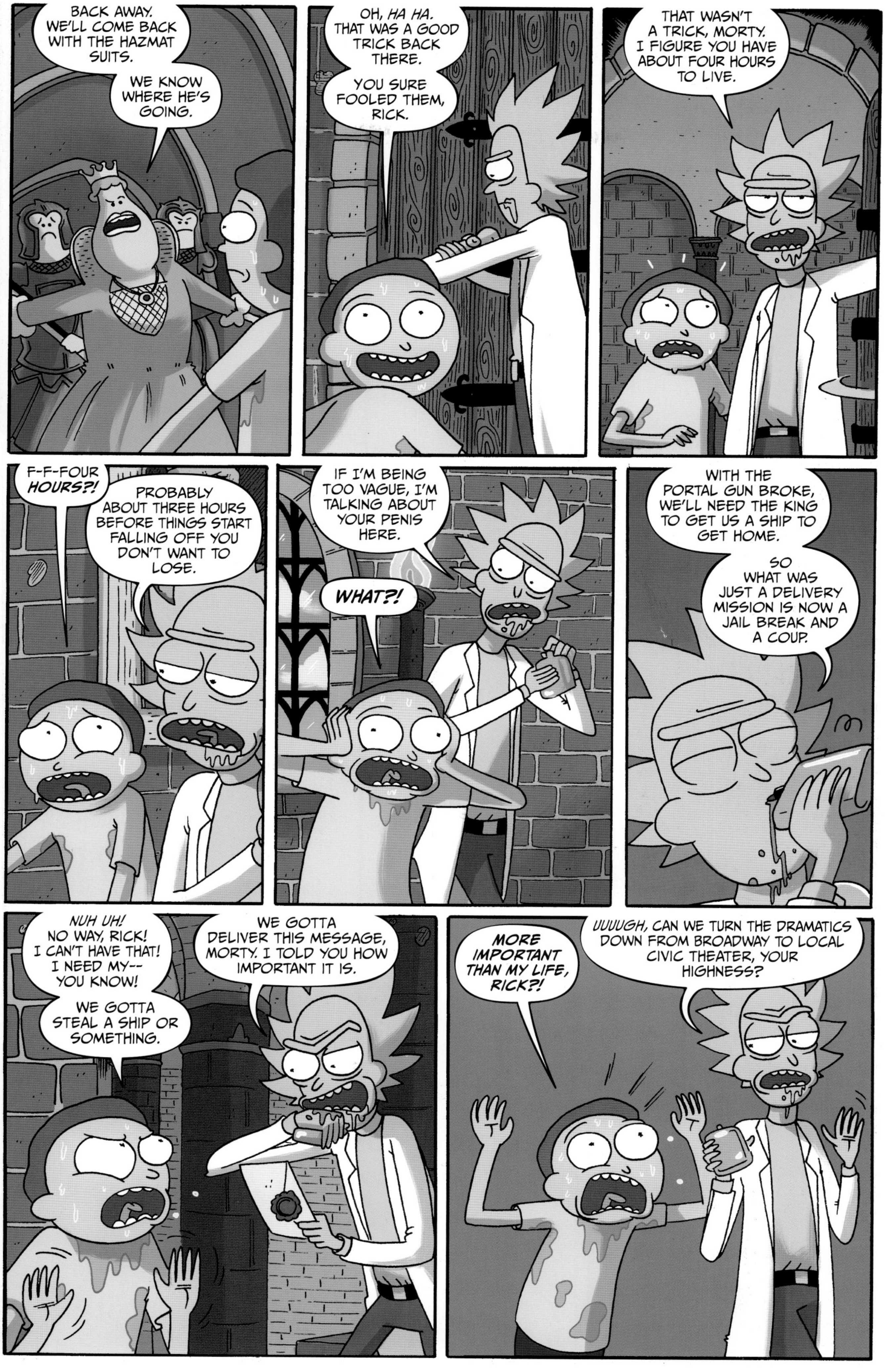
BACK AWAY. WE'LL COME BACK WITH THE HAZMAT SUITS.
WE KNOW WHERE HE'S GOING.
OH, *HA HA.* THAT WAS A GOOD TRICK BACK THERE.
YOU SURE FOOLED THEM, RICK.
THAT WASN'T A TRICK, MORTY. I FIGURE YOU HAVE ABOUT FOUR HOURS TO LIVE.
F-F-FOUR ***HOURS?!***
PROBABLY ABOUT THREE HOURS BEFORE THINGS START FALLING OFF YOU DON'T WANT TO LOSE.
IF I'M BEING TOO VAGUE, I'M TALKING ABOUT YOUR PENIS HERE.
WHAT?!
WITH THE PORTAL GUN BROKE, WE'LL NEED THE KING TO GET US A SHIP TO GET HOME.
SO WHAT WAS JUST A DELIVERY MISSION IS NOW A JAIL BREAK AND A COUP.
NUH UH! NO WAY, RICK! I CAN'T HAVE THAT! I NEED MY-- YOU KNOW!
WE GOTTA STEAL A SHIP OR SOMETHING.
WE GOTTA DELIVER THIS MESSAGE, MORTY. I TOLD YOU HOW IMPORTANT IT IS.
MORE IMPORTANT THAN MY LIFE, RICK?!
UUUUGH, CAN WE TURN THE DRAMATICS DOWN FROM BROADWAY TO LOCAL CIVIC THEATER, YOUR HIGHNESS?

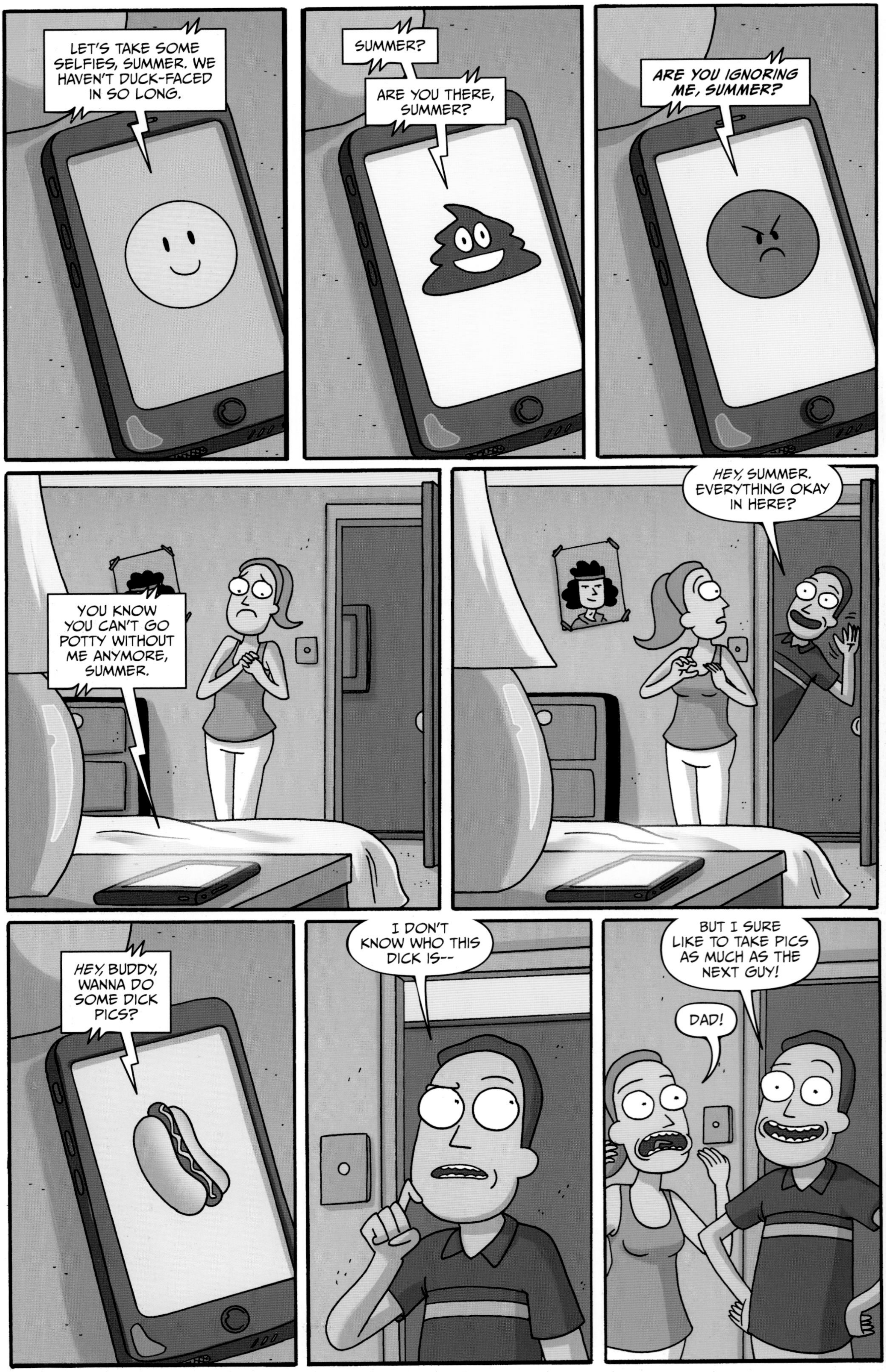
LET'S TAKE SOME SELFIES, SUMMER. WE HAVEN'T DUCK-FACED IN SO LONG.
SUMMER?
ARE YOU THERE, SUMMER?
ARE YOU IGNORING ME, SUMMER?
YOU KNOW YOU CAN'T GO POTTY WITHOUT ME ANYMORE, SUMMER.
HEY, SUMMER. EVERYTHING OKAY IN HERE?
HEY, BUDDY, WANNA DO SOME DICK PICS?
I DON'T KNOW WHO THIS DICK IS--
BUT I SURE LIKE TO TAKE PICS AS MUCH AS THE NEXT GUY!
DAD!

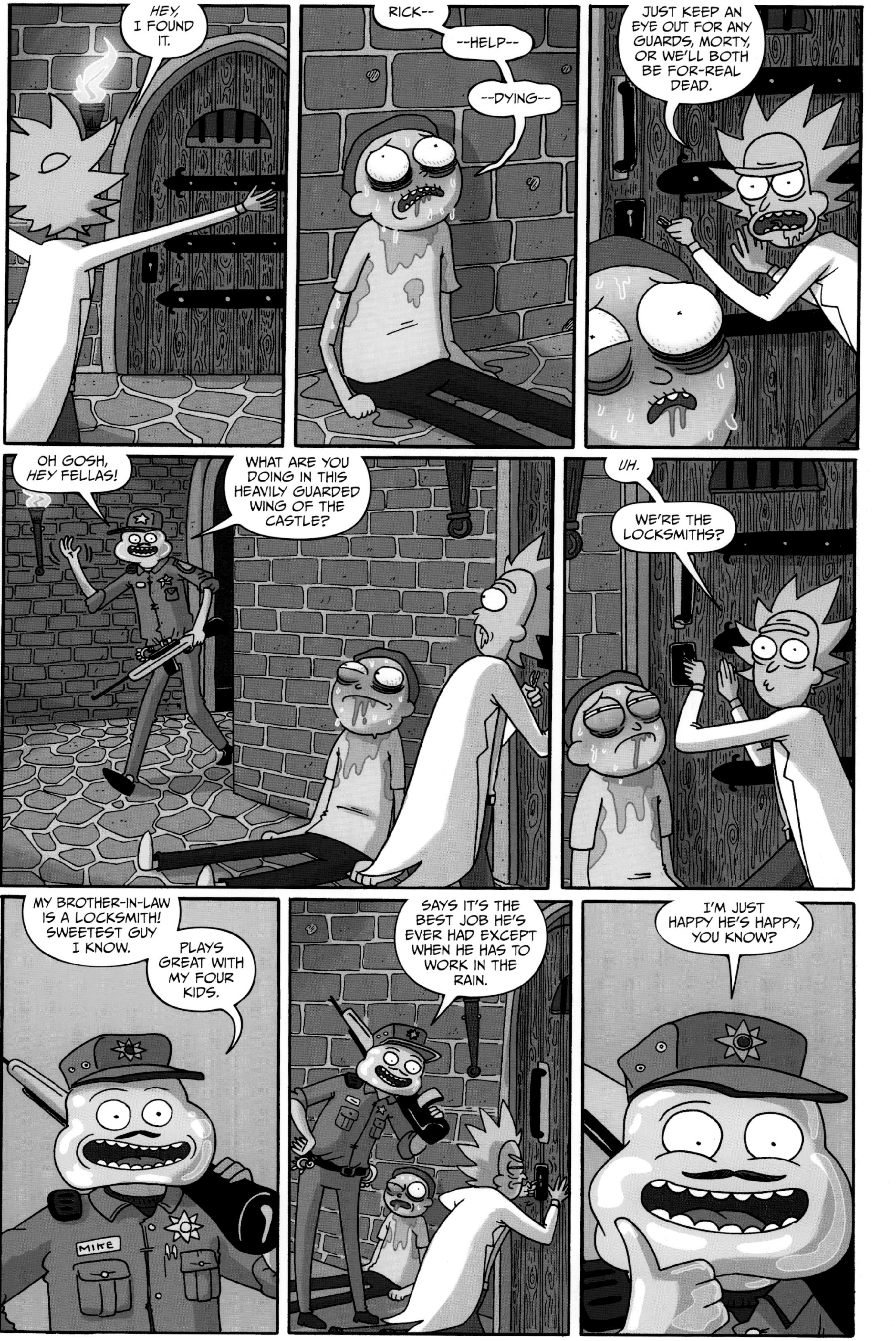

HEY, I FOUND IT.
RICK--
--HELP--
--DYING--
JUST KEEP AN EYE OUT FOR ANY GUARDS, MORTY, OR WE'LL BOTH BE FOR-REAL DEAD.
OH GOSH, HEY FELLAS!
WHAT ARE YOU DOING IN THIS HEAVILY GUARDED WING OF THE CASTLE?
UH.
WE'RE THE LOCKSMITHS?
MY BROTHER-IN-LAW IS A LOCKSMITH! SWEETEST GUY I KNOW.
PLAYS GREAT WITH MY FOUR KIDS.
MIKE
SAYS IT'S THE BEST JOB HE'S EVER HAD EXCEPT WHEN HE HAS TO WORK IN THE RAIN.
I'M JUST HAPPY HE'S HAPPY, YOU KNOW?

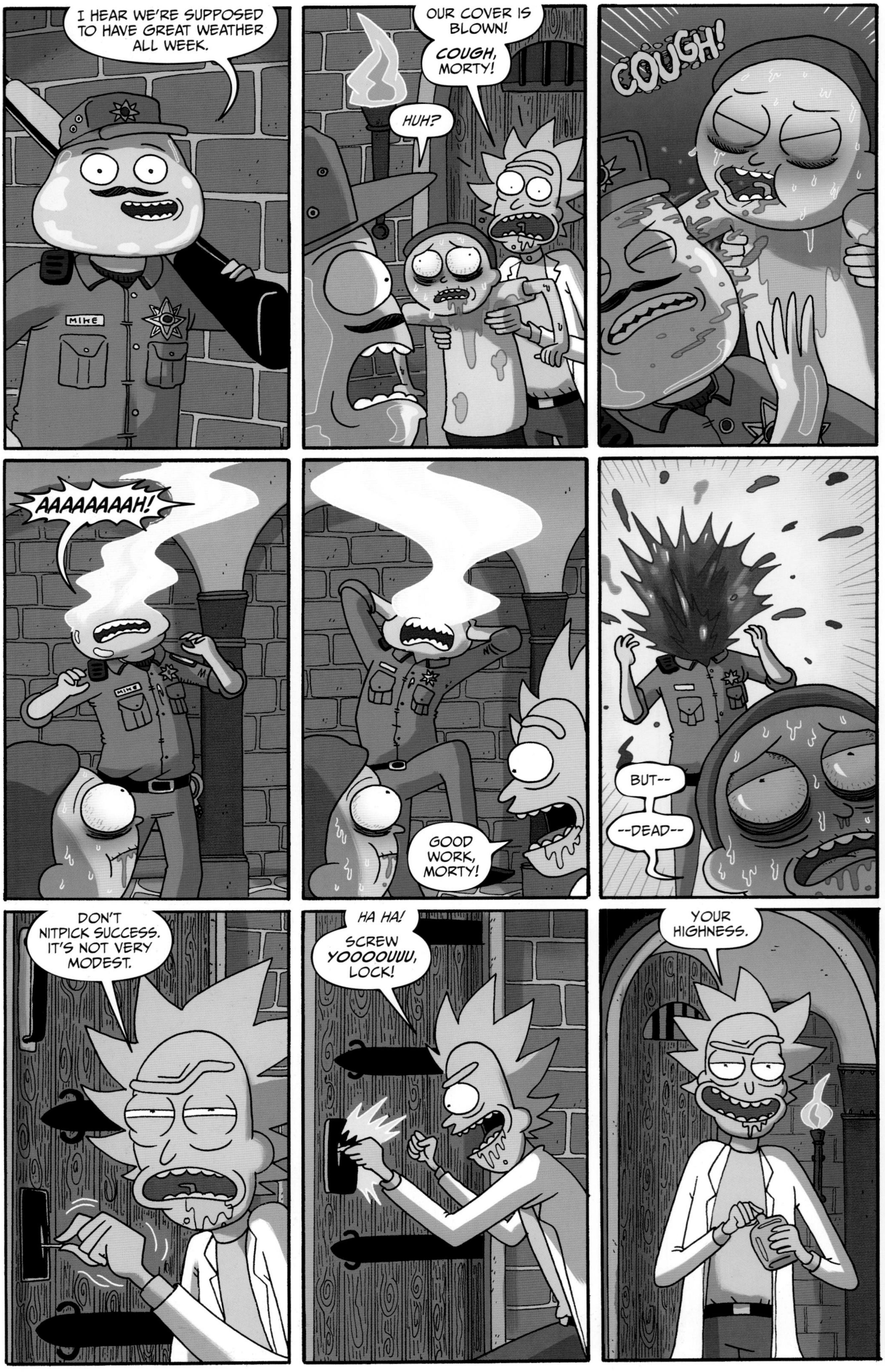
I HEAR WE'RE SUPPOSED TO HAVE GREAT WEATHER ALL WEEK.
MIKE
OUR COVER IS BLOWN!
COUGH, MORTY!
HUH?
COUGH!
AAAAAAAAH!
MIKE
GOOD WORK, MORTY!
BUT--
--DEAD--
DON'T NITPICK SUCCESS. IT'S NOT VERY MODEST.
HA HA!
SCREW YOOOOUUU, LOCK!
YOUR HIGHNESS.

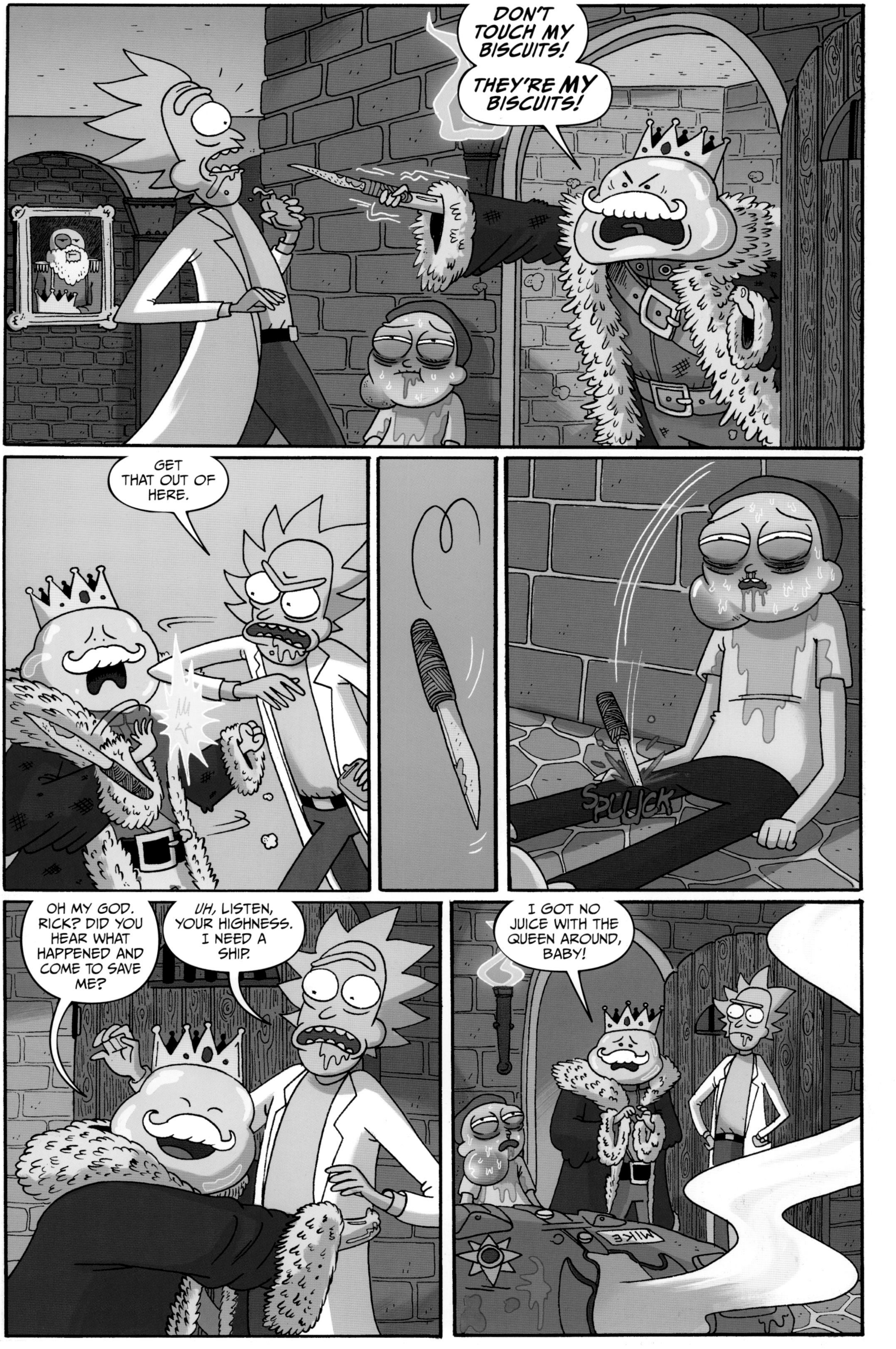
DON'T TOUCH MY BISCUITS!
THEY'RE MY BISCUITS!
GET THAT OUT OF HERE.
SPLUCK
OH MY GOD. RICK? DID YOU HEAR WHAT HAPPENED AND COME TO SAVE ME?
UH, LISTEN, YOUR HIGHNESS. I NEED A SHIP.
I GOT NO JUICE WITH THE QUEEN AROUND, BABY!
MIKE

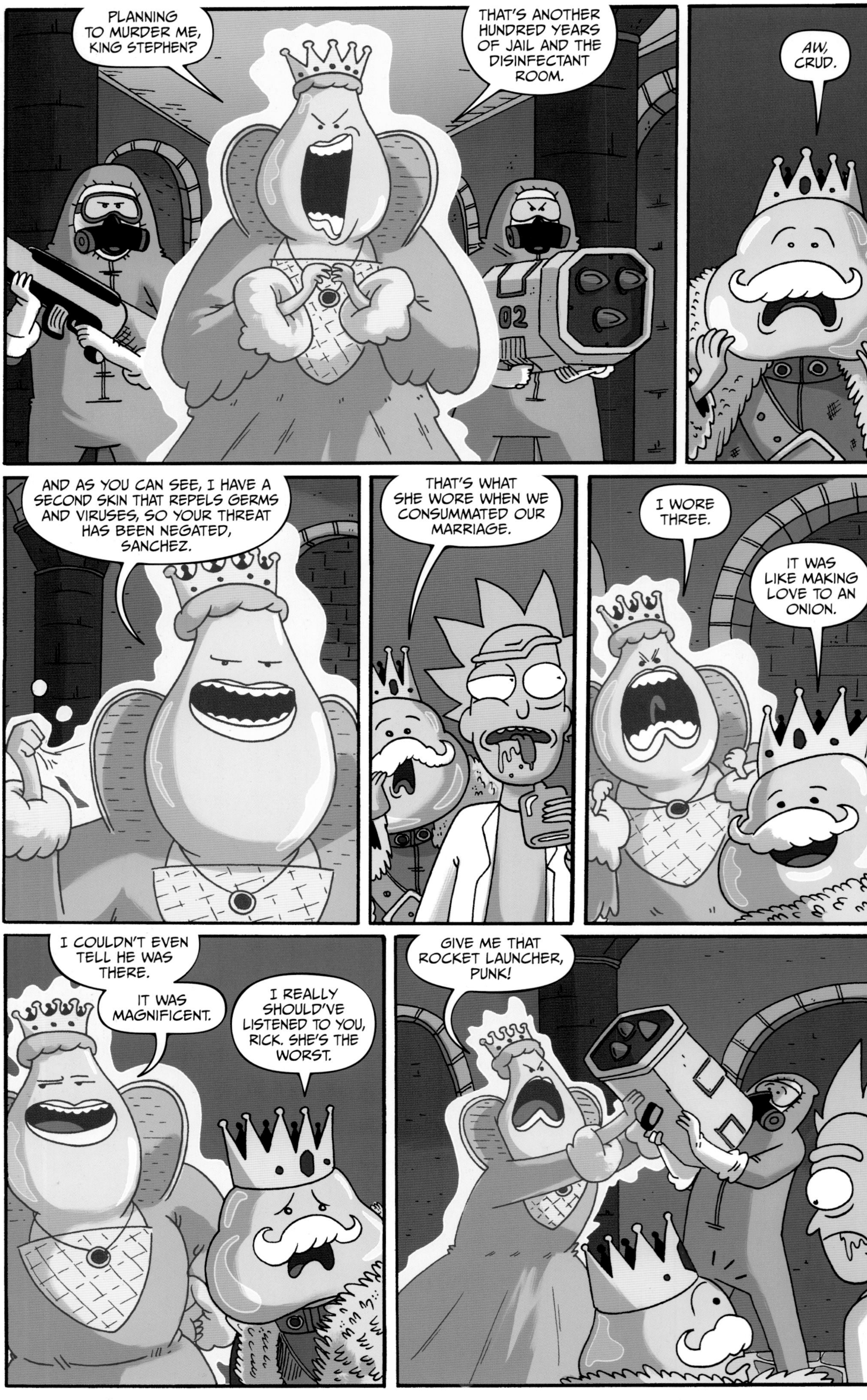
PLANNING TO MURDER ME, KING STEPHEN?
THAT'S ANOTHER HUNDRED YEARS OF JAIL AND THE DISINFECTANT ROOM.
AW, CRUD.
AND AS YOU CAN SEE, I HAVE A SECOND SKIN THAT REPELS GERMS AND VIRUSES, SO YOUR THREAT HAS BEEN NEGATED, SANCHEZ.
THAT'S WHAT SHE WORE WHEN WE CONSUMMATED OUR MARRIAGE.
I WORE THREE.
IT WAS LIKE MAKING LOVE TO AN ONION.
I COULDN'T EVEN TELL HE WAS THERE.
IT WAS MAGNIFICENT.
I REALLY SHOULD'VE LISTENED TO YOU, RICK. SHE'S THE WORST.
GIVE ME THAT ROCKET LAUNCHER, PUNK!

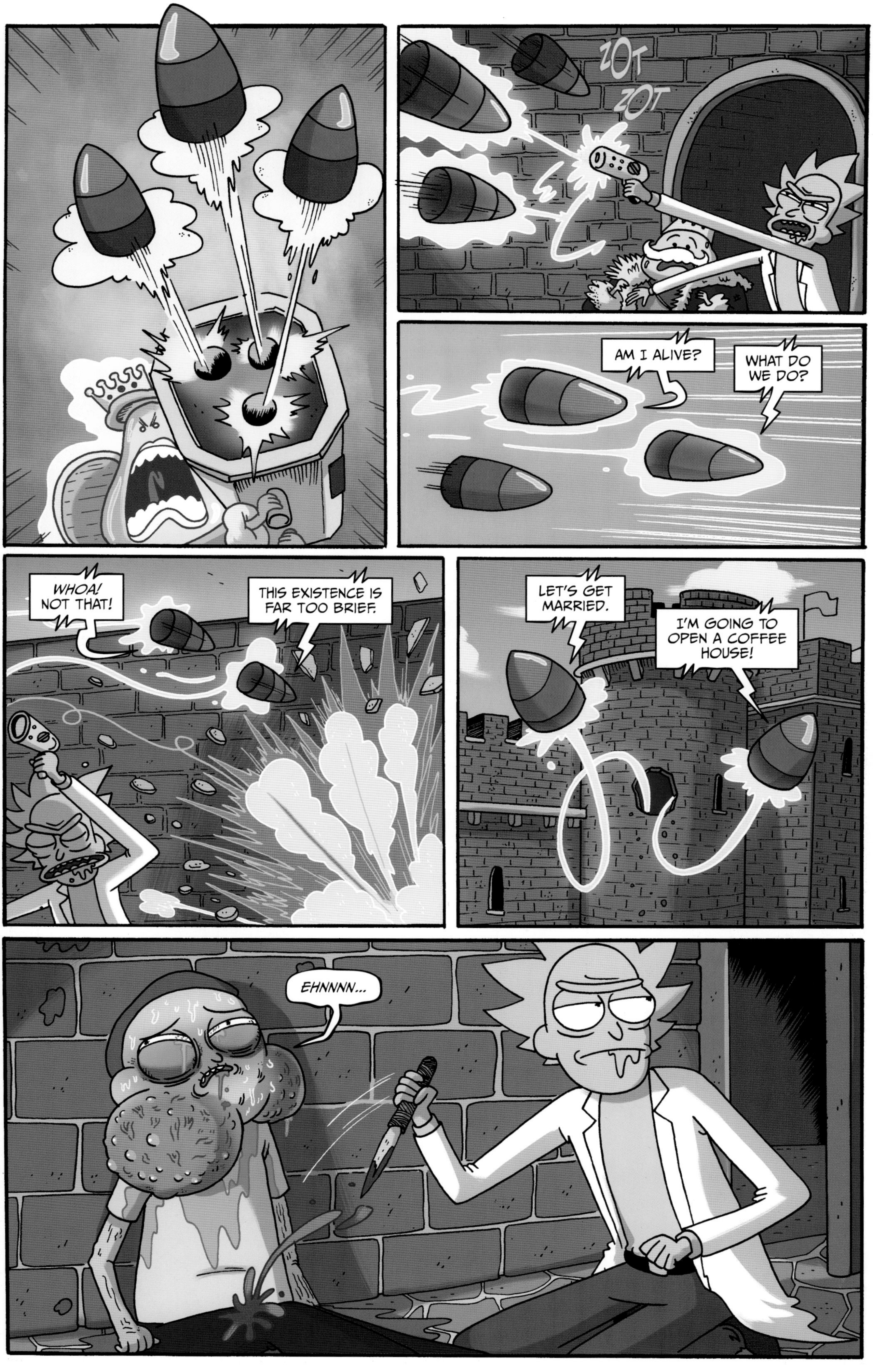
ZOT
ZOT
AM I ALIVE?
WHAT DO WE DO?
WHOA! NOT THAT!
THIS EXISTENCE IS FAR TOO BRIEF.
LET'S GET MARRIED.
I'M GOING TO OPEN A COFFEE HOUSE!
EHNNNN...

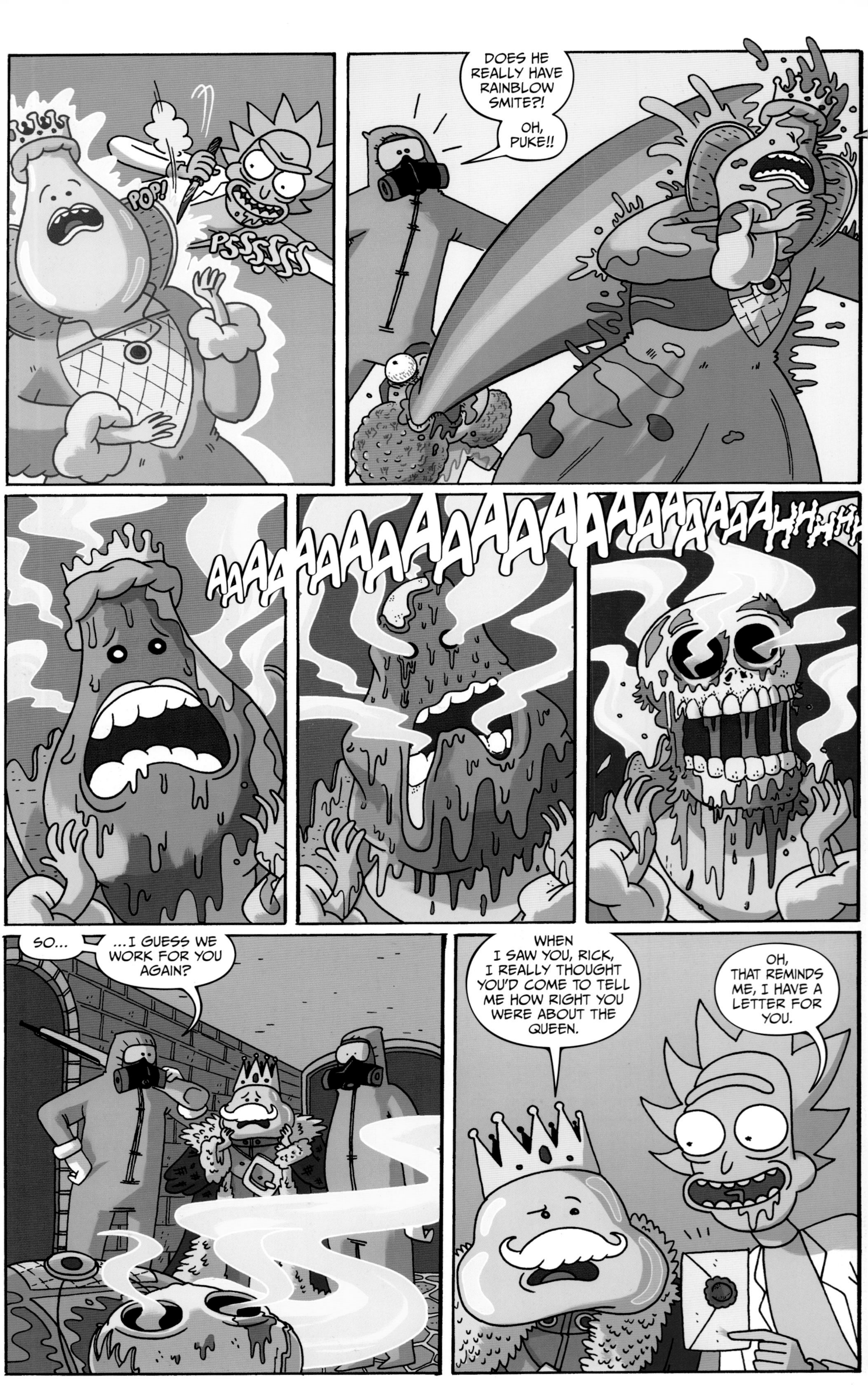
POP!
PSSSSSSS
DOES HE REALLY HAVE RAINBLOW SMITE?!
OH, PUKE!!
AAAAAAAAAAAAAAAAAAAAHHHHH
SO...
...I GUESS WE WORK FOR YOU AGAIN?
WHEN I SAW YOU, RICK, I REALLY THOUGHT YOU'D COME TO TELL ME HOW RIGHT YOU WERE ABOUT THE QUEEN.
OH, THAT REMINDS ME, I HAVE A LETTER FOR YOU.

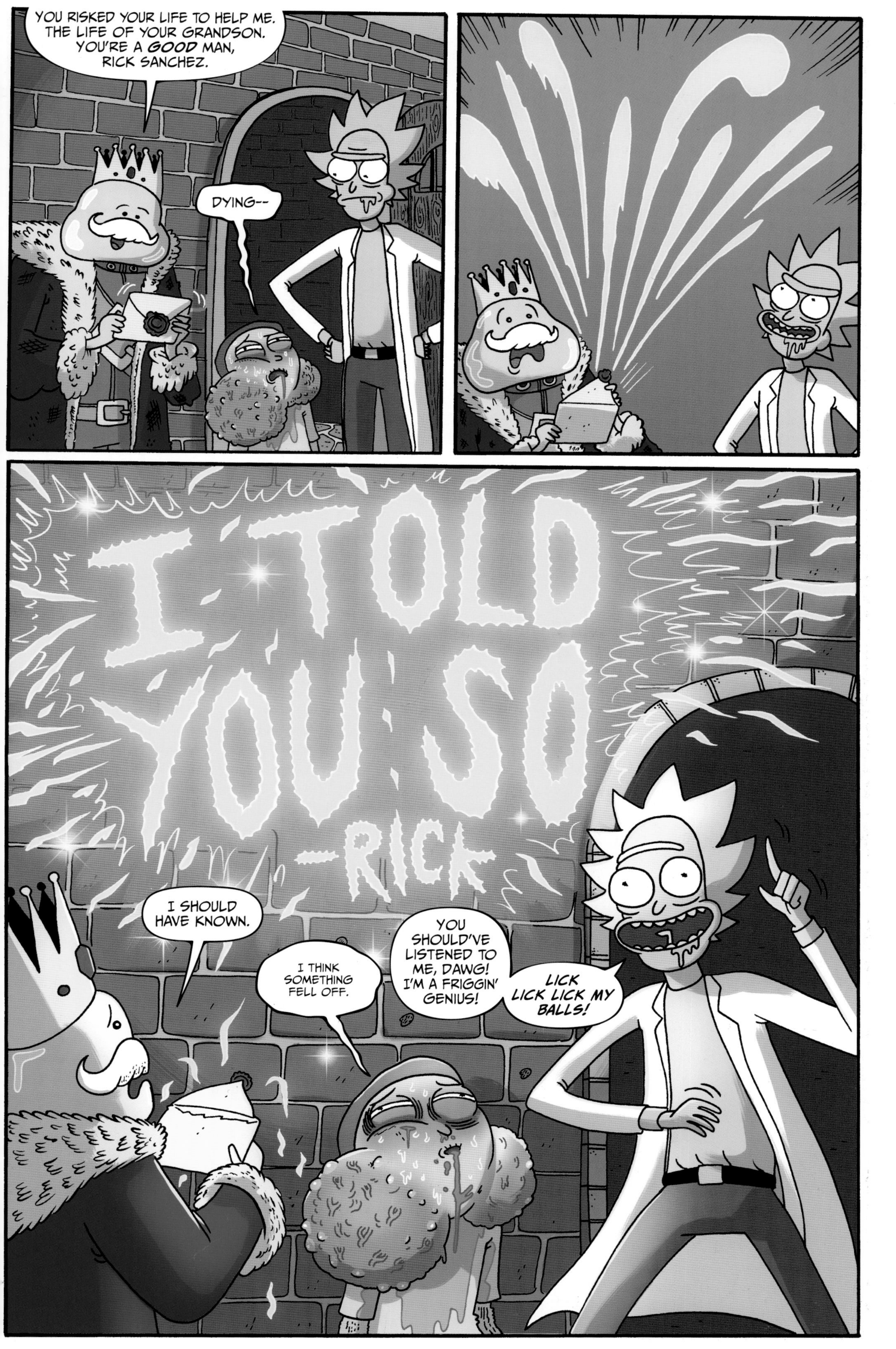

YOU RISKED YOUR LIFE TO HELP ME. THE LIFE OF YOUR GRANDSON. YOU'RE A **GOOD** MAN, RICK SANCHEZ.
DYING--
I TOLD YOU SO
-RICK
I SHOULD HAVE KNOWN.
I THINK SOMETHING FELL OFF.
YOU SHOULD'VE LISTENED TO ME, DAWG! I'M A FRIGGIN' GENIUS!
LICK LICK LICK MY BALLS!

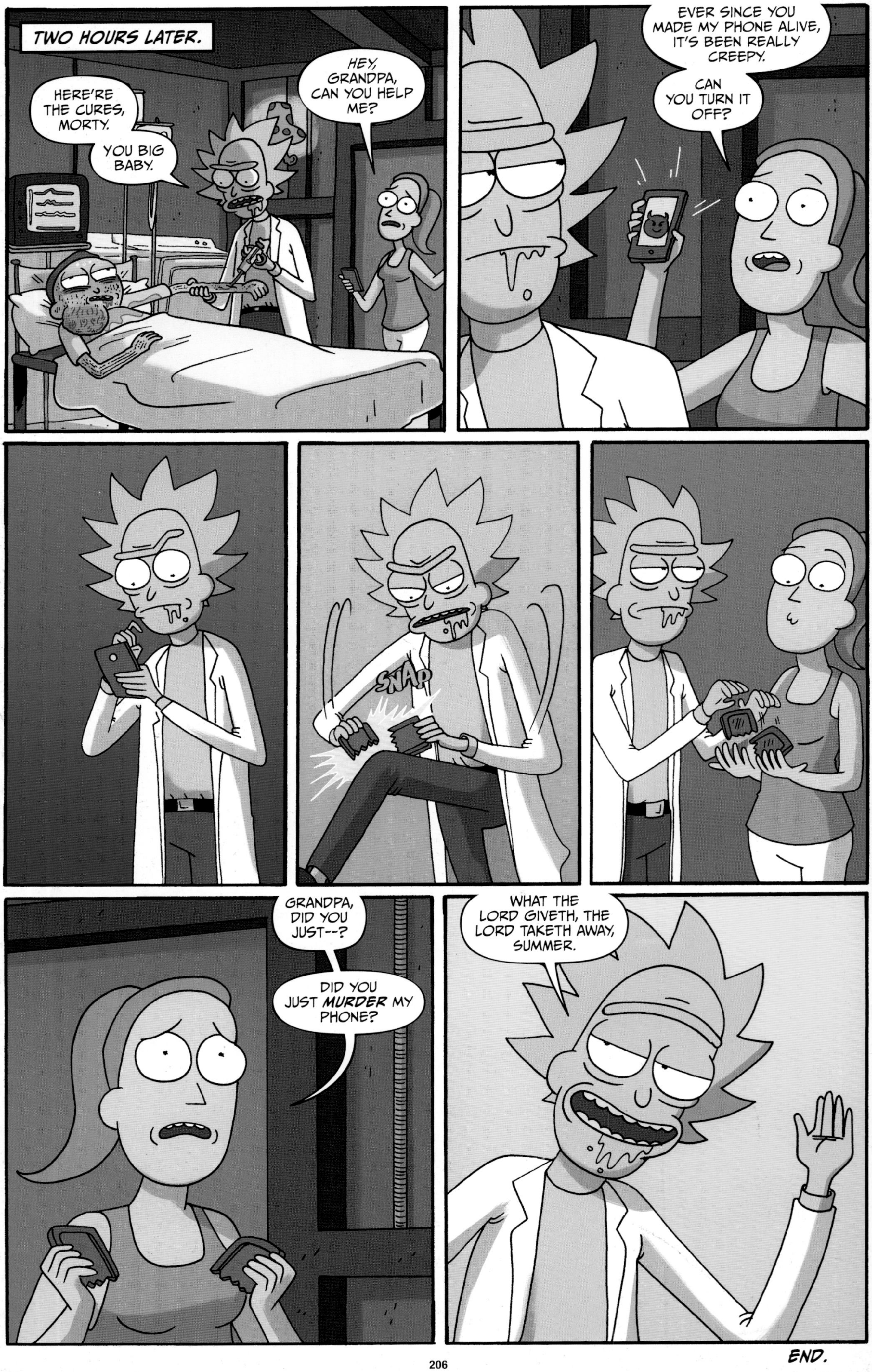
TWO HOURS LATER.
HERE'RE THE CURES, MORTY.
YOU BIG BABY.
HEY, GRANDPA, CAN YOU HELP ME?
EVER SINCE YOU MADE MY PHONE ALIVE, IT'S BEEN REALLY CREEPY.
CAN YOU TURN IT OFF?
SNAP
GRANDPA, DID YOU JUST--?
DID YOU JUST MURDER MY PHONE?
WHAT THE LORD GIVETH, THE LORD TAKETH AWAY, SUMMER.
END.

MORTY BOUNCE TO THE OUNCE

WRITTEN AND DRAWN BY **KYLE STARKS**
COLORED BY **KATY FARINA**
LETTERED BY **CRANK!**

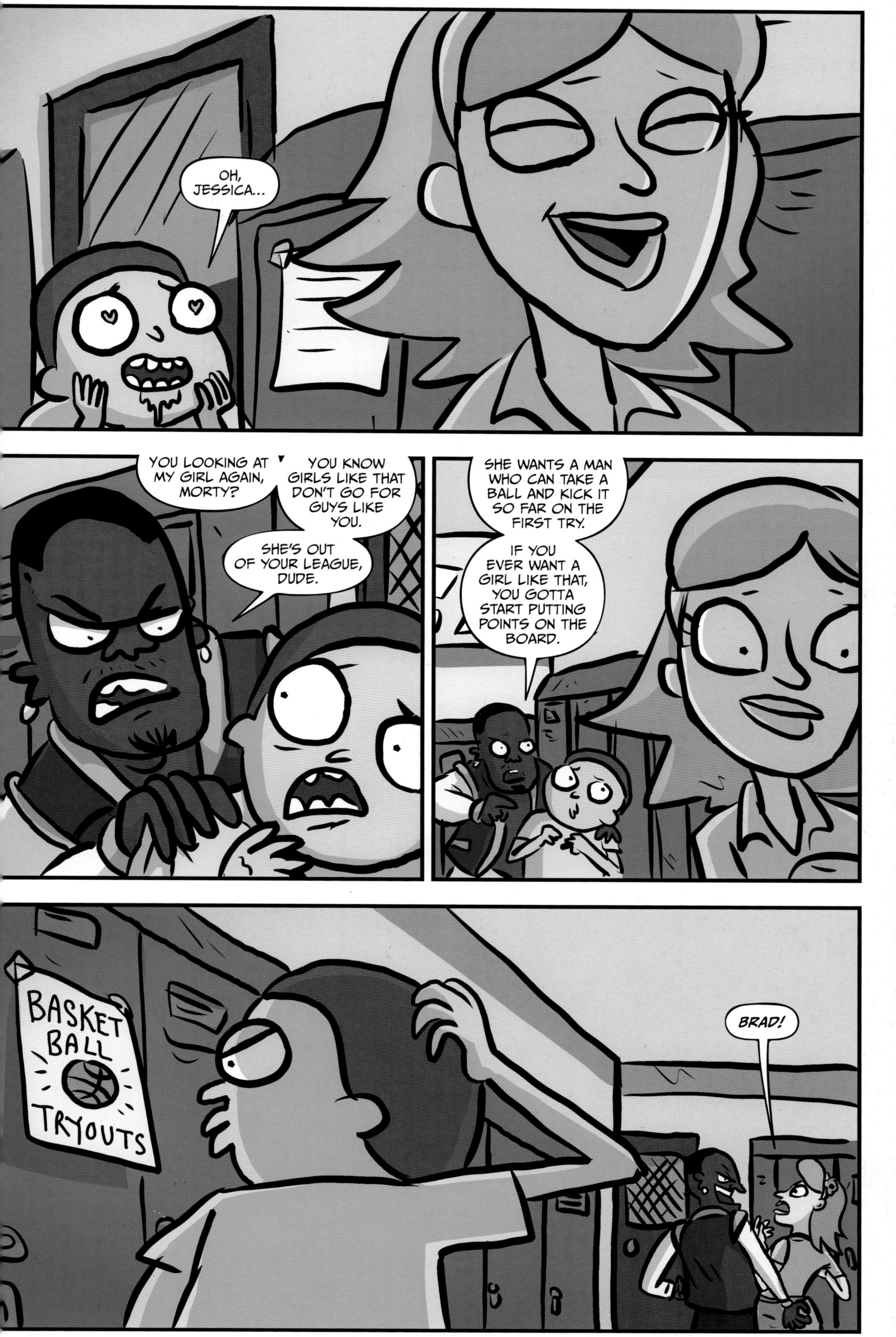
OH, JESSICA...
YOU LOOKING AT MY GIRL AGAIN, MORTY?
YOU KNOW GIRLS LIKE THAT DON'T GO FOR GUYS LIKE YOU.
SHE'S OUT OF YOUR LEAGUE, DUDE.
SHE WANTS A MAN WHO CAN TAKE A BALL AND KICK IT SO FAR ON THE FIRST TRY.
IF YOU EVER WANT A GIRL LIKE THAT, YOU GOTTA START PUTTING POINTS ON THE BOARD.
BASKET BALL TRYOUTS
BRAD!

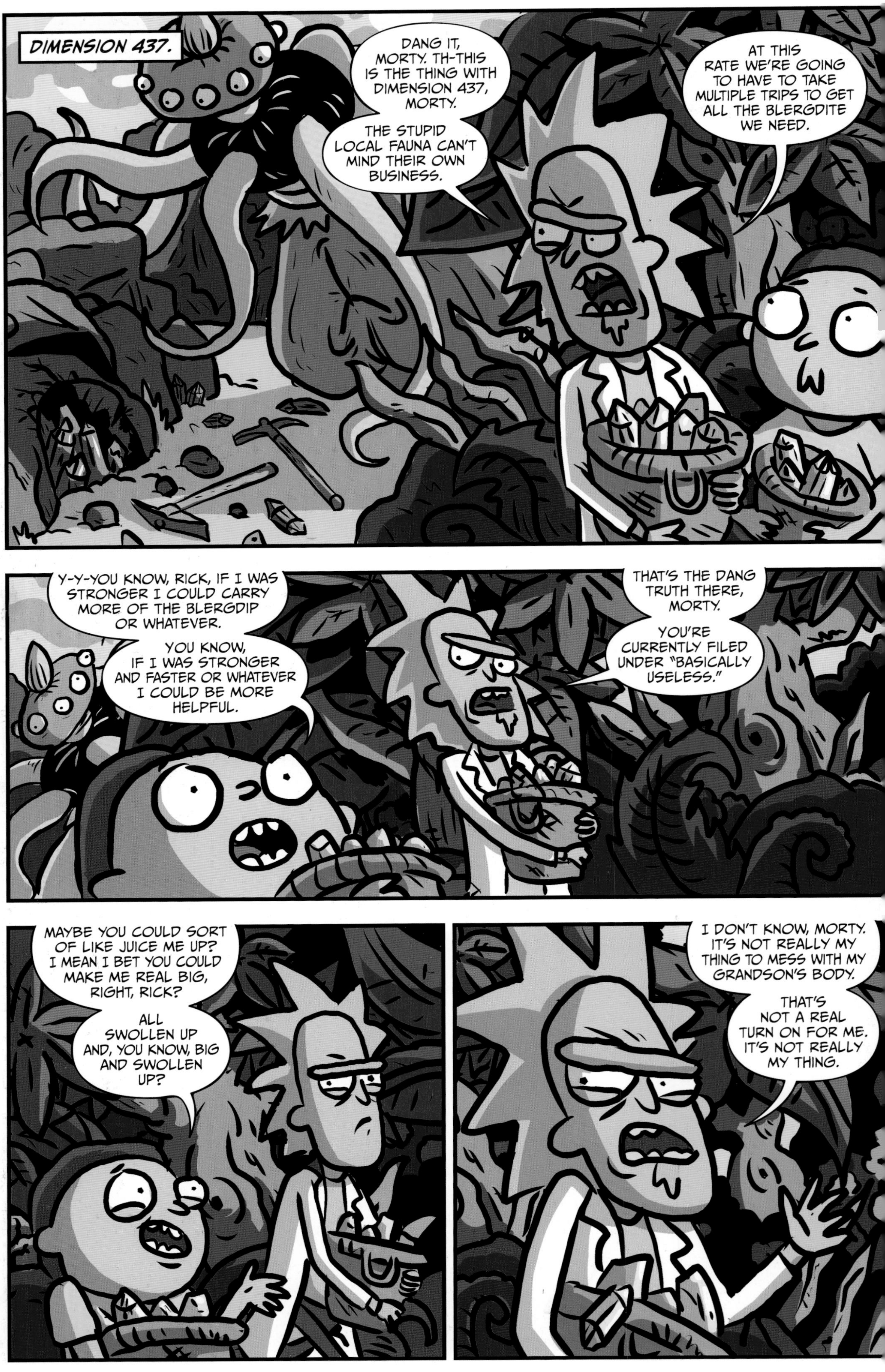
DIMENSION 437.
DANG IT, MORTY. TH-THIS IS THE THING WITH DIMENSION 437, MORTY.
THE STUPID LOCAL FAUNA CAN'T MIND THEIR OWN BUSINESS.
AT THIS RATE WE'RE GOING TO HAVE TO TAKE MULTIPLE TRIPS TO GET ALL THE BLERGDITE WE NEED.
Y-Y-YOU KNOW, RICK, IF I WAS STRONGER I COULD CARRY MORE OF THE BLERGDIP OR WHATEVER.
YOU KNOW, IF I WAS STRONGER AND FASTER OR WHATEVER I COULD BE MORE HELPFUL.
THAT'S THE DANG TRUTH THERE, MORTY.
YOU'RE CURRENTLY FILED UNDER "BASICALLY USELESS."
MAYBE YOU COULD SORT OF LIKE JUICE ME UP? I MEAN I BET YOU COULD MAKE ME REAL BIG, RIGHT, RICK?
ALL SWOLLEN UP AND, YOU KNOW, BIG AND SWOLLEN UP?
I DON'T KNOW, MORTY. IT'S NOT REALLY MY THING TO MESS WITH MY GRANDSON'S BODY.
THAT'S NOT A REAL TURN ON FOR ME. IT'S NOT REALLY MY THING.

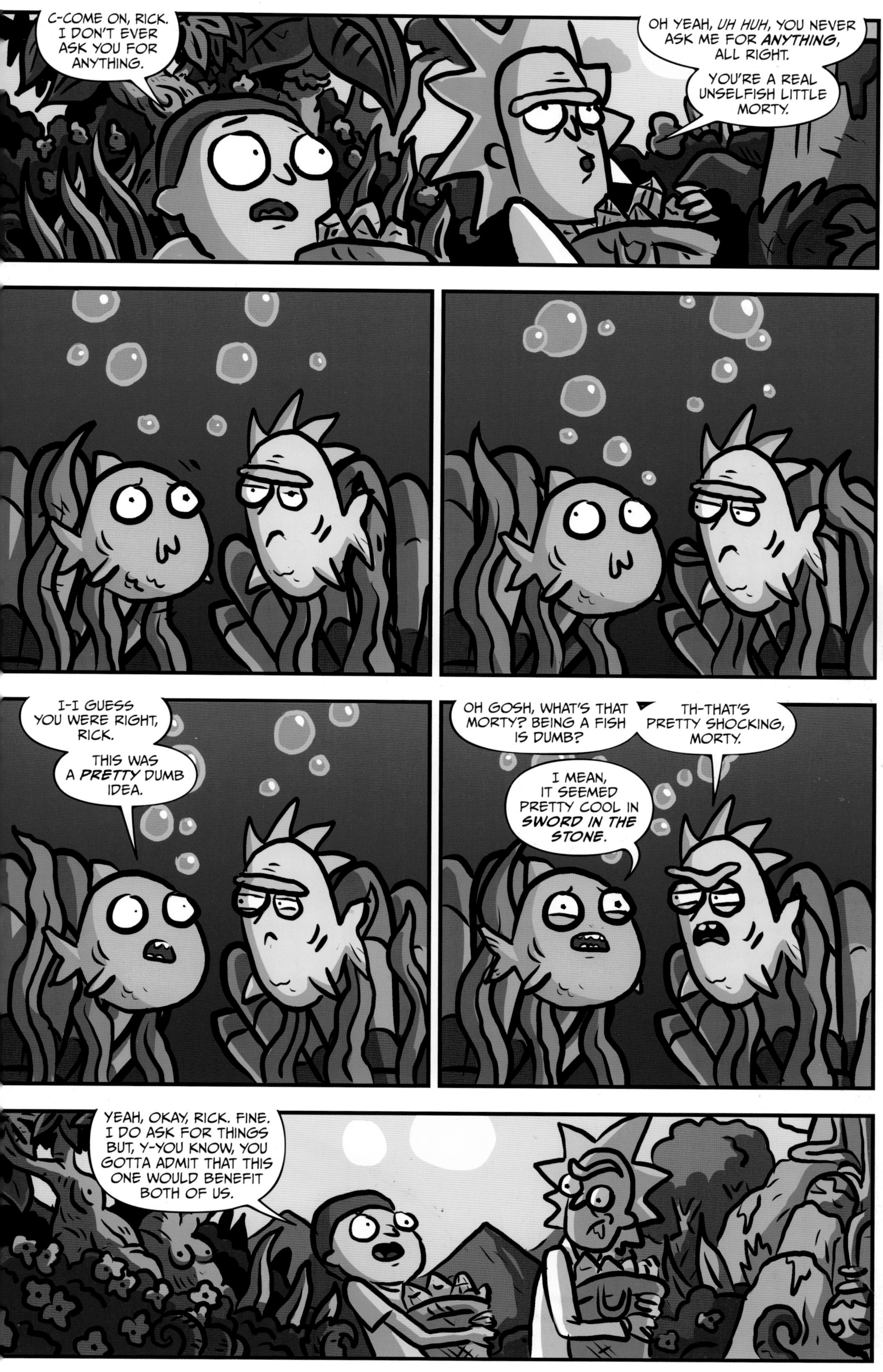
C-COME ON, RICK. I DON'T EVER ASK YOU FOR ANYTHING.
OH YEAH, *UH HUH*, YOU NEVER ASK ME FOR ***ANYTHING***, ALL RIGHT.
YOU'RE A REAL UNSELFISH LITTLE MORTY.
I-I GUESS YOU WERE RIGHT, RICK.
THIS WAS A ***PRETTY*** DUMB IDEA.
OH GOSH, WHAT'S THAT MORTY? BEING A FISH IS DUMB?
TH-THAT'S PRETTY SHOCKING, MORTY.
I MEAN, IT SEEMED PRETTY COOL IN ***SWORD IN THE STONE***.
YEAH, OKAY, RICK. FINE. I DO ASK FOR THINGS BUT, Y-YOU KNOW, YOU GOTTA ADMIT THAT THIS ONE WOULD BENEFIT BOTH OF US.

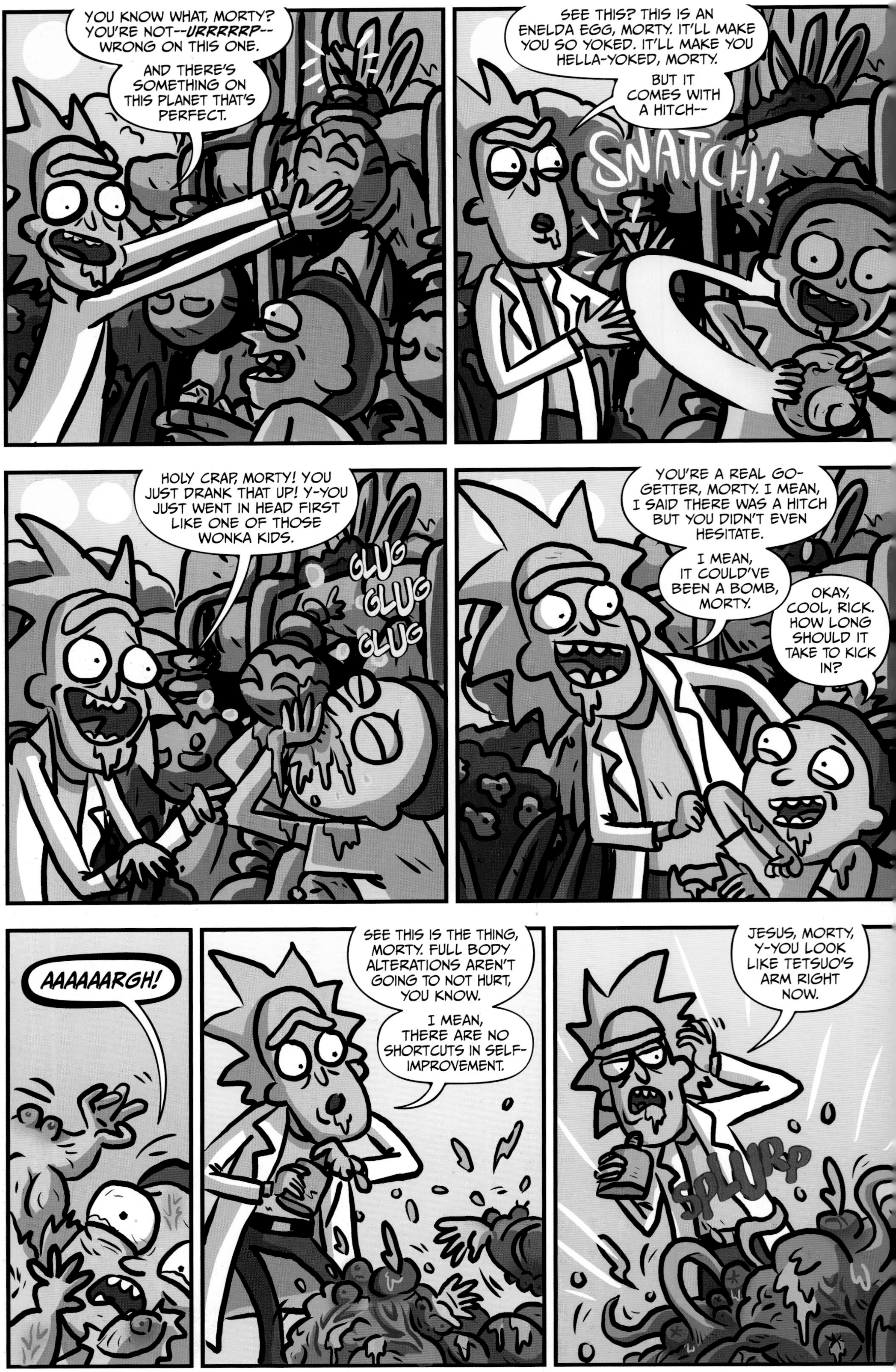
YOU KNOW WHAT, MORTY? YOU'RE NOT--URRRRRP-- WRONG ON THIS ONE.
AND THERE'S SOMETHING ON THIS PLANET THAT'S PERFECT.
SEE THIS? THIS IS AN ENELDA EGG, MORTY. IT'LL MAKE YOU SO YOKED. IT'LL MAKE YOU HELLA-YOKED, MORTY.
BUT IT COMES WITH A HITCH--
SNATCH!
HOLY CRAP, MORTY! YOU JUST DRANK THAT UP! Y-YOU JUST WENT IN HEAD FIRST LIKE ONE OF THOSE WONKA KIDS.
GLUG
GLUG
GLUG
YOU'RE A REAL GO-GETTER, MORTY. I MEAN, I SAID THERE WAS A HITCH BUT YOU DIDN'T EVEN HESITATE.
I MEAN, IT COULD'VE BEEN A BOMB, MORTY.
OKAY, COOL, RICK. HOW LONG SHOULD IT TAKE TO KICK IN?
AAAAAARGH!
SEE THIS IS THE THING, MORTY. FULL BODY ALTERATIONS AREN'T GOING TO NOT HURT, YOU KNOW.
I MEAN, THERE ARE NO SHORTCUTS IN SELF-IMPROVEMENT.
JESUS, MORTY, Y-YOU LOOK LIKE TETSUO'S ARM RIGHT NOW.
SPLURP

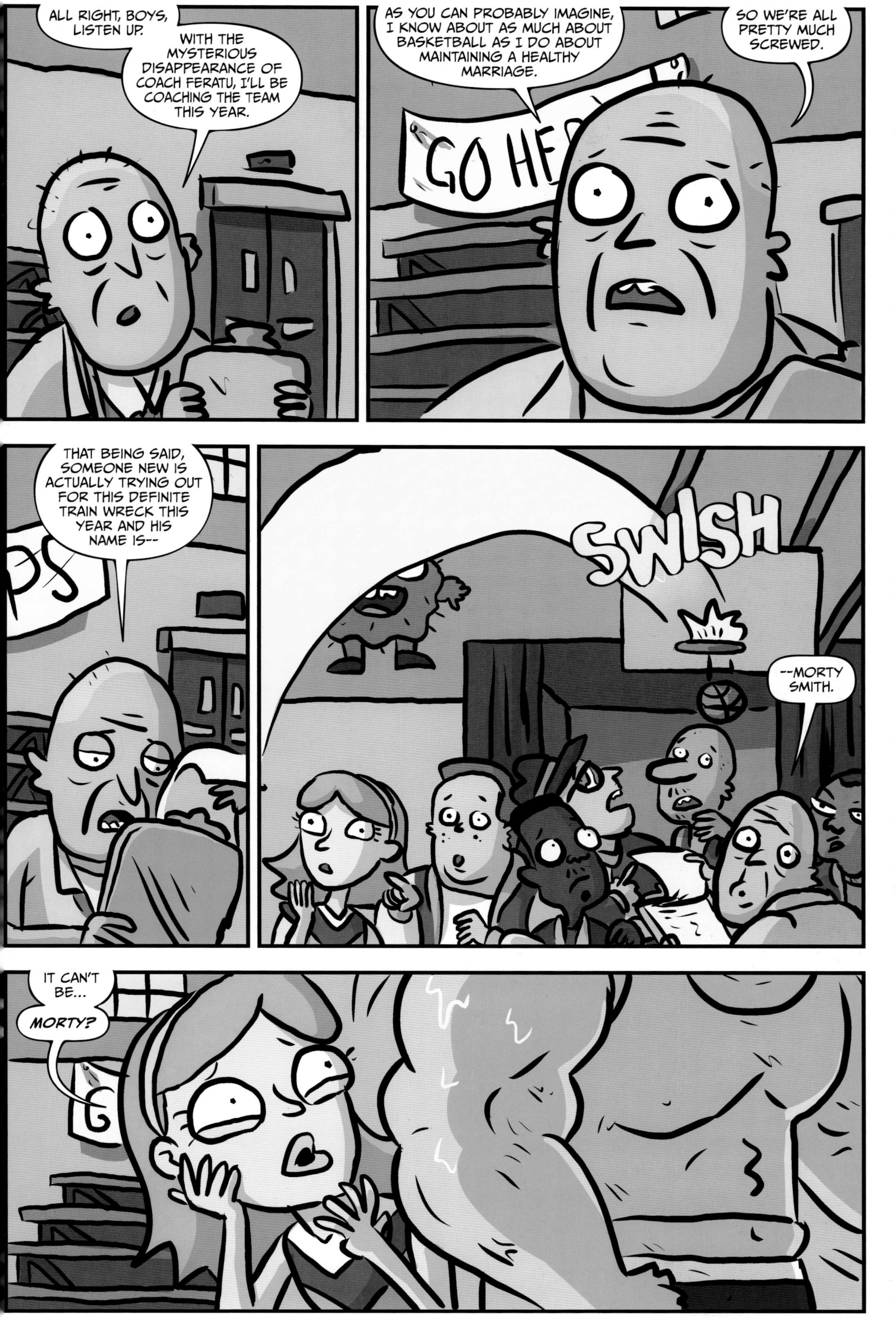
ALL RIGHT, BOYS, LISTEN UP.
WITH THE MYSTERIOUS DISAPPEARANCE OF COACH FERATU, I'LL BE COACHING THE TEAM THIS YEAR.
AS YOU CAN PROBABLY IMAGINE, I KNOW ABOUT AS MUCH ABOUT BASKETBALL AS I DO ABOUT MAINTAINING A HEALTHY MARRIAGE.
SO WE'RE ALL PRETTY MUCH SCREWED.
THAT BEING SAID, SOMEONE NEW IS ACTUALLY TRYING OUT FOR THIS DEFINITE TRAIN WRECK THIS YEAR AND HIS NAME IS--
SWISH
--MORTY SMITH.
IT CAN'T BE...
MORTY?

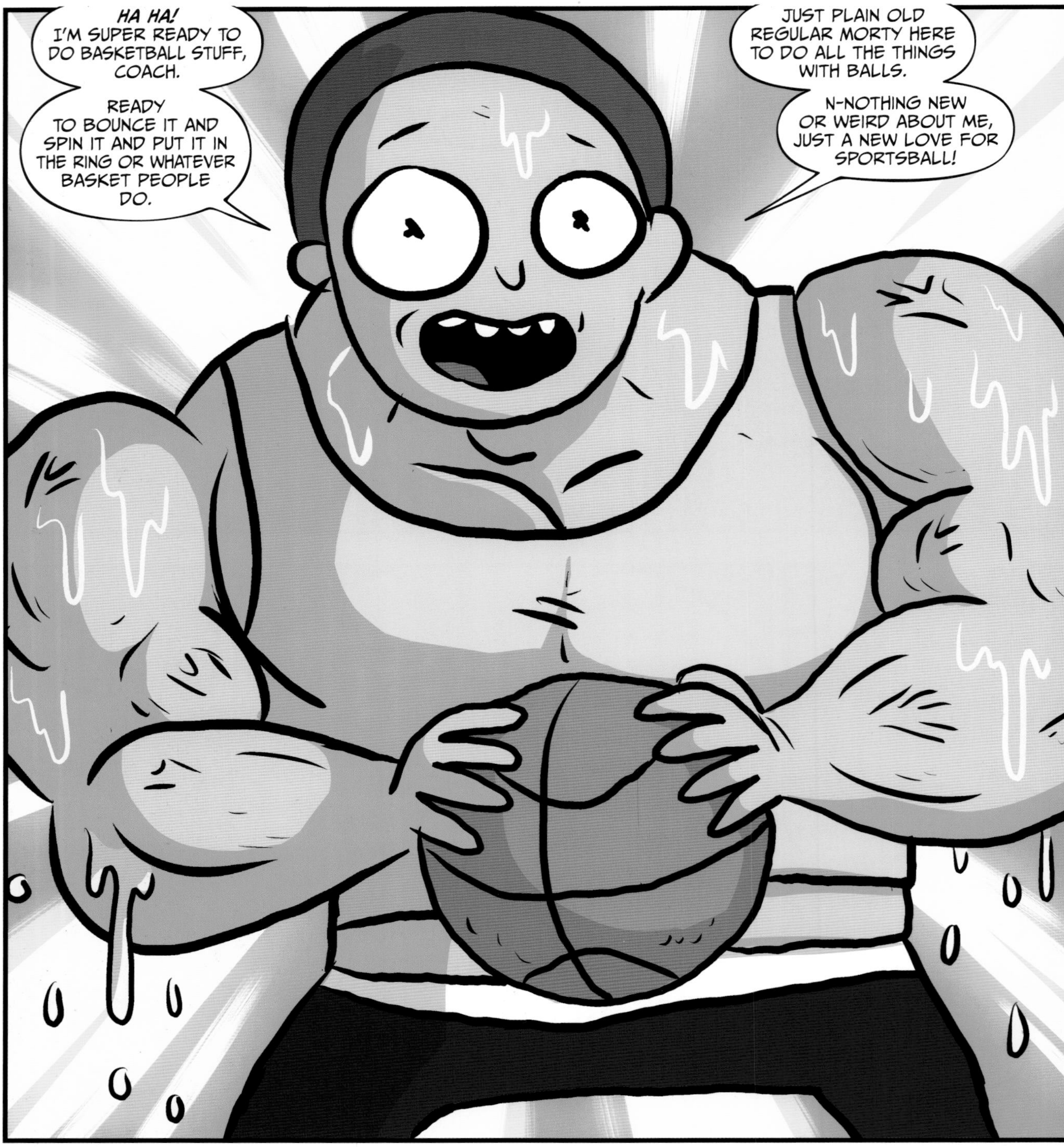
HA HA! I'M SUPER READY TO DO BASKETBALL STUFF, COACH.
READY TO BOUNCE IT AND SPIN IT AND PUT IT IN THE RING OR WHATEVER BASKET PEOPLE DO.
JUST PLAIN OLD REGULAR MORTY HERE TO DO ALL THE THINGS WITH BALLS.
N-NOTHING NEW OR WEIRD ABOUT ME, JUST A NEW LOVE FOR SPORTSBALL!

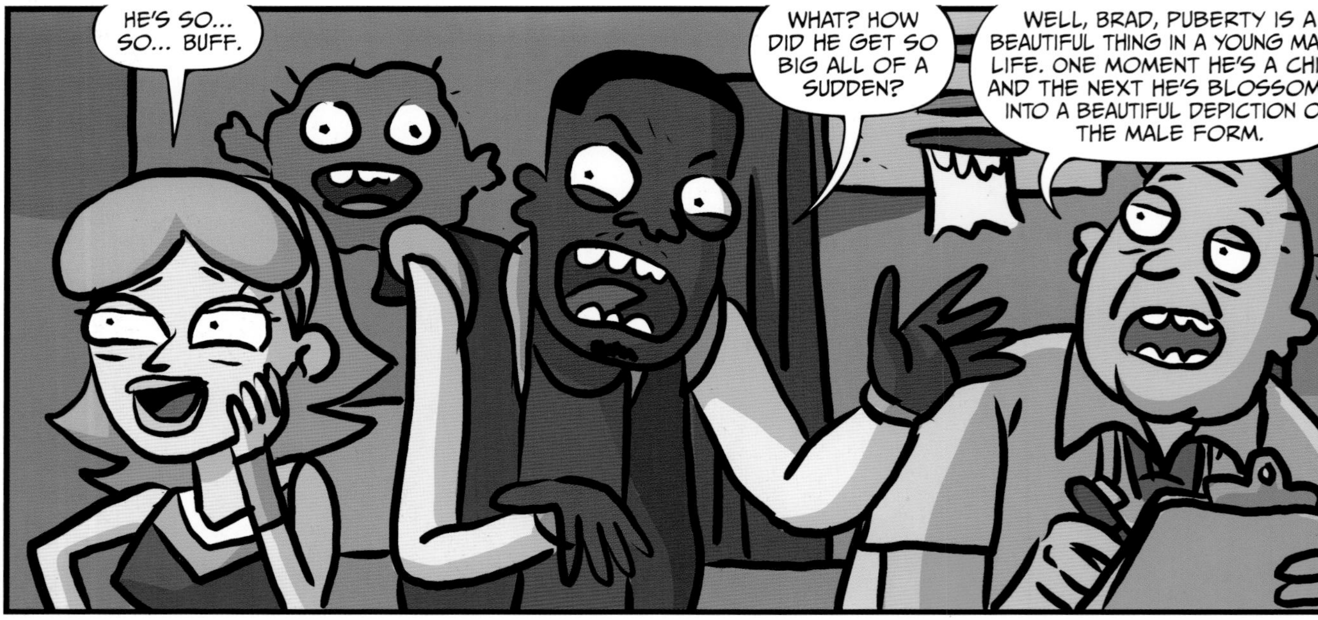
HE'S SO... SO... BUFF.
WHAT? HOW DID HE GET SO BIG ALL OF A SUDDEN?
WELL, BRAD, PUBERTY IS A BEAUTIFUL THING IN A YOUNG MAN'S LIFE. ONE MOMENT HE'S A CHILD AND THE NEXT HE'S BLOSSOMED INTO A BEAUTIFUL DEPICTION OF THE MALE FORM.

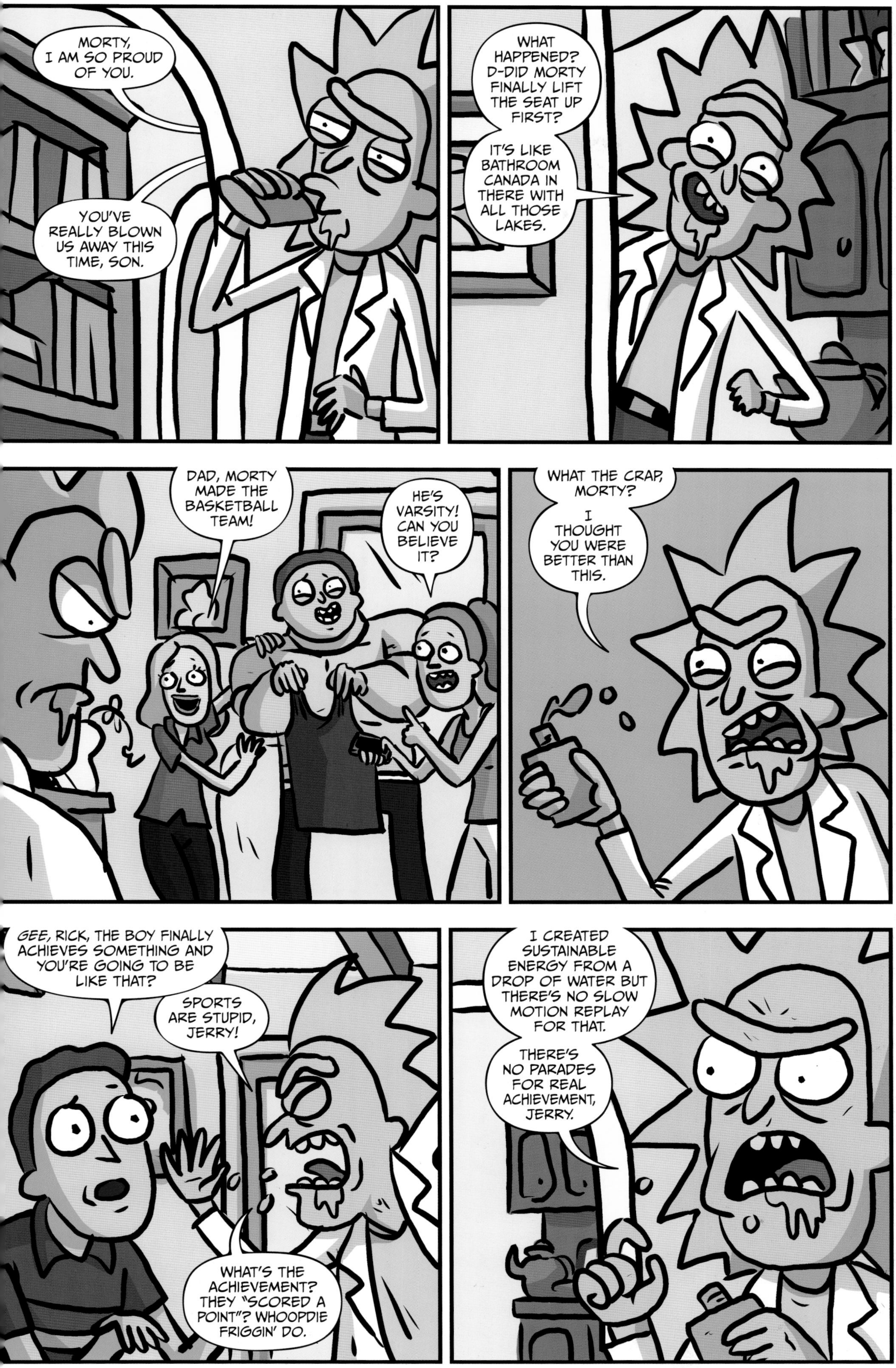
MORTY, I AM SO PROUD OF YOU.
YOU'VE REALLY BLOWN US AWAY THIS TIME, SON.
WHAT HAPPENED? D-DID MORTY FINALLY LIFT THE SEAT UP FIRST?
IT'S LIKE BATHROOM CANADA IN THERE WITH ALL THOSE LAKES.
DAD, MORTY MADE THE BASKETBALL TEAM!
HE'S VARSITY! CAN YOU BELIEVE IT?
WHAT THE CRAP, MORTY?
I THOUGHT YOU WERE BETTER THAN THIS.
GEE, RICK, THE BOY FINALLY ACHIEVES SOMETHING AND YOU'RE GOING TO BE LIKE THAT?
SPORTS ARE STUPID, JERRY!
WHAT'S THE ACHIEVEMENT? THEY "SCORED A POINT"? WHOOPDIE FRIGGIN' DO.
I CREATED SUSTAINABLE ENERGY FROM A DROP OF WATER BUT THERE'S NO SLOW MOTION REPLAY FOR THAT.
THERE'S NO PARADES FOR REAL ACHIEVEMENT, JERRY.

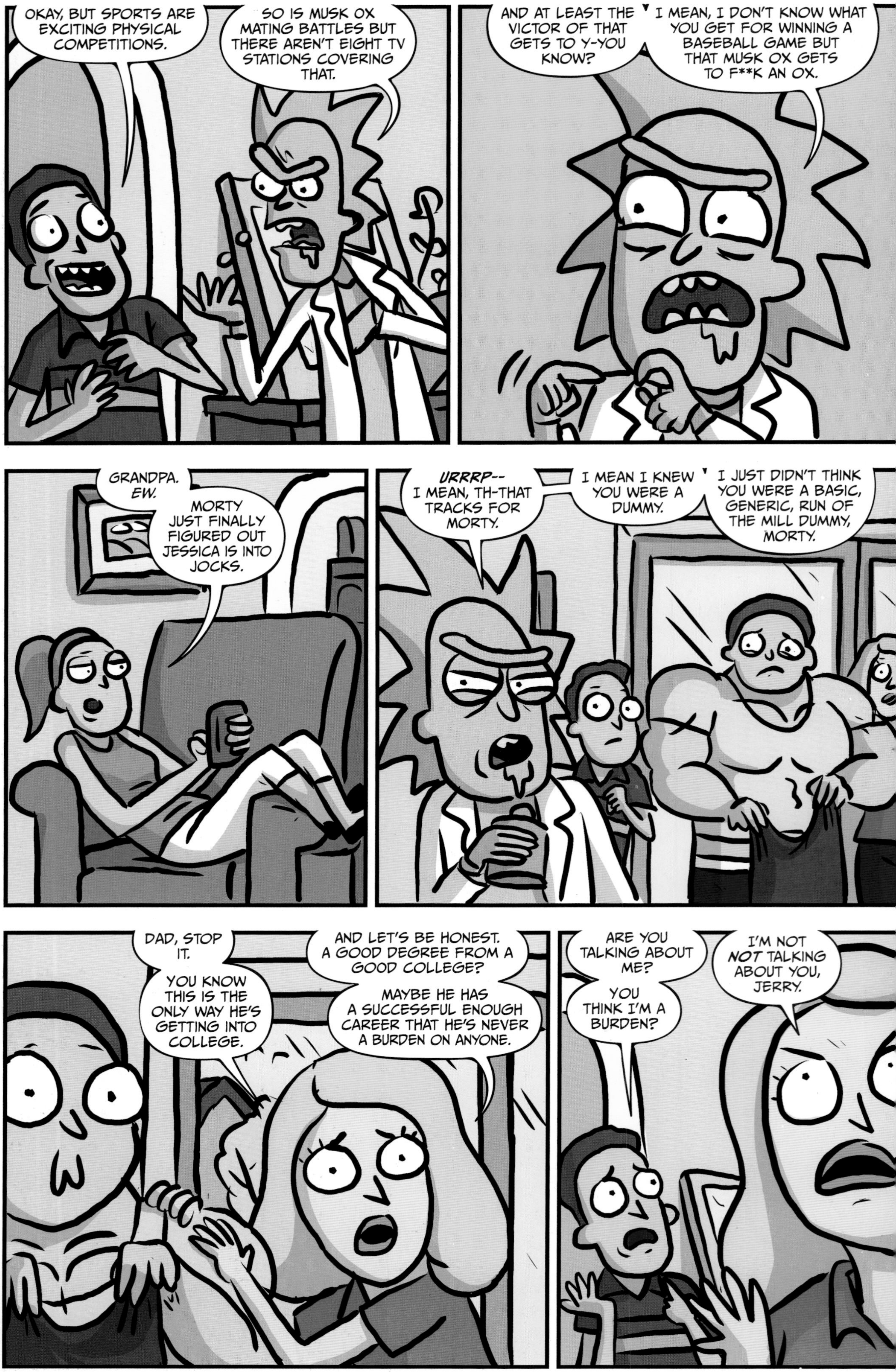
OKAY, BUT SPORTS ARE EXCITING PHYSICAL COMPETITIONS.
SO IS MUSK OX MATING BATTLES BUT THERE AREN'T EIGHT TV STATIONS COVERING THAT.
AND AT LEAST THE VICTOR OF THAT GETS TO Y-YOU KNOW?
I MEAN, I DON'T KNOW WHAT YOU GET FOR WINNING A BASEBALL GAME BUT THAT MUSK OX GETS TO F**K AN OX.
GRANDPA. *EW.*
MORTY JUST FINALLY FIGURED OUT JESSICA IS INTO JOCKS.
URRRP-- I MEAN, TH-THAT TRACKS FOR MORTY.
I MEAN I KNEW YOU WERE A DUMMY.
I JUST DIDN'T THINK YOU WERE A BASIC, GENERIC, RUN OF THE MILL DUMMY, MORTY.
DAD, STOP IT.
YOU KNOW THIS IS THE ONLY WAY HE'S GETTING INTO COLLEGE.
AND LET'S BE HONEST. A GOOD DEGREE FROM A GOOD COLLEGE?
MAYBE HE HAS A SUCCESSFUL ENOUGH CAREER THAT HE'S NEVER A BURDEN ON ANYONE.
ARE YOU TALKING ABOUT ME?
YOU THINK I'M A BURDEN?
I'M NOT *NOT* TALKING ABOUT YOU, JERRY.

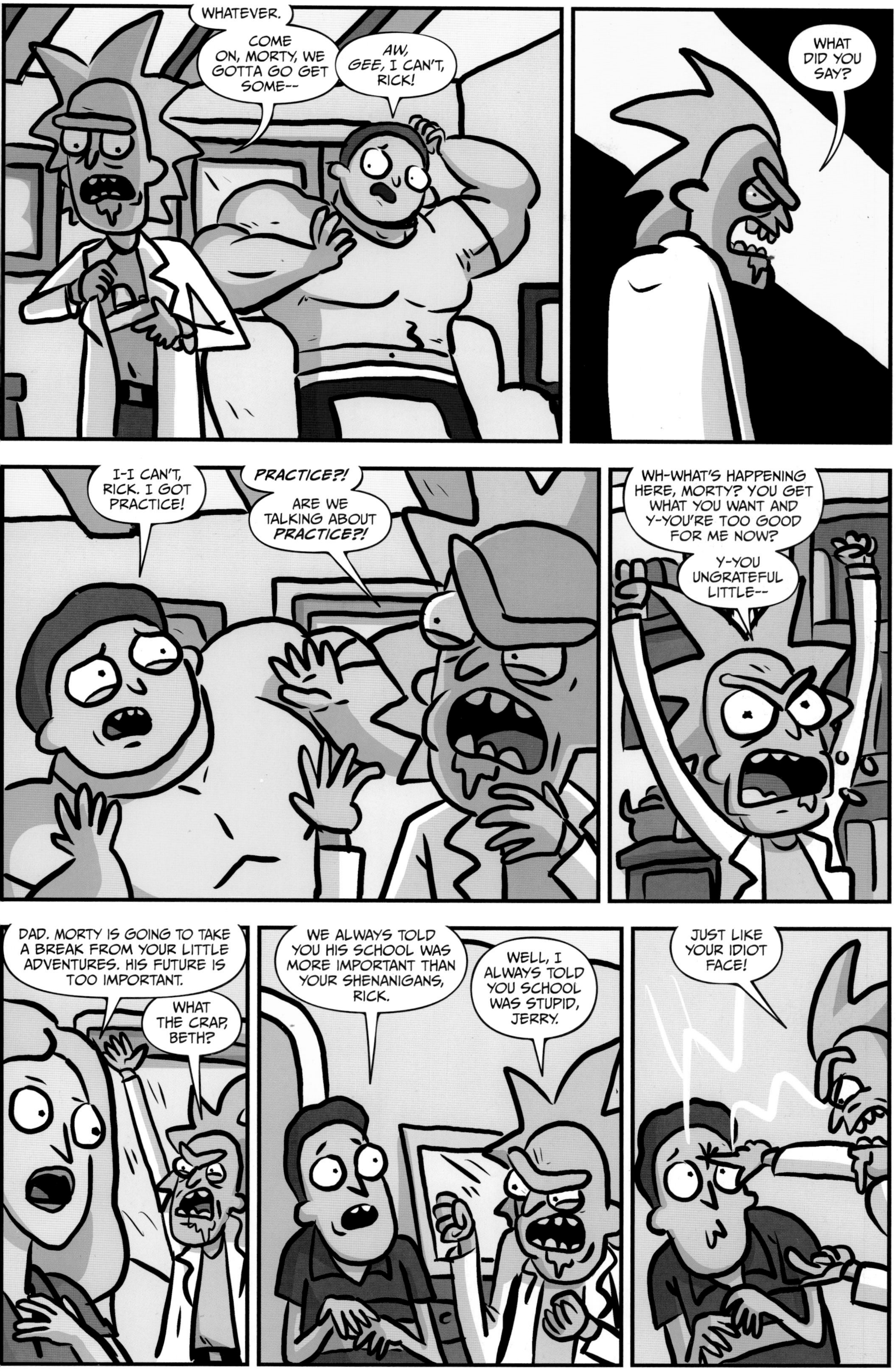
WHATEVER.
COME ON, MORTY, WE GOTTA GO GET SOME--
AW, GEE, I CAN'T, RICK!
WHAT DID YOU SAY?
I-I CAN'T, RICK. I GOT PRACTICE!
PRACTICE?!
ARE WE TALKING ABOUT PRACTICE?!
WH-WHAT'S HAPPENING HERE, MORTY? YOU GET WHAT YOU WANT AND Y-YOU'RE TOO GOOD FOR ME NOW?
Y-YOU UNGRATEFUL LITTLE--
DAD. MORTY IS GOING TO TAKE A BREAK FROM YOUR LITTLE ADVENTURES. HIS FUTURE IS TOO IMPORTANT.
WHAT THE CRAP, BETH?
WE ALWAYS TOLD YOU HIS SCHOOL WAS MORE IMPORTANT THAN YOUR SHENANIGANS, RICK.
WELL, I ALWAYS TOLD YOU SCHOOL WAS STUPID, JERRY.
JUST LIKE YOUR IDIOT FACE!

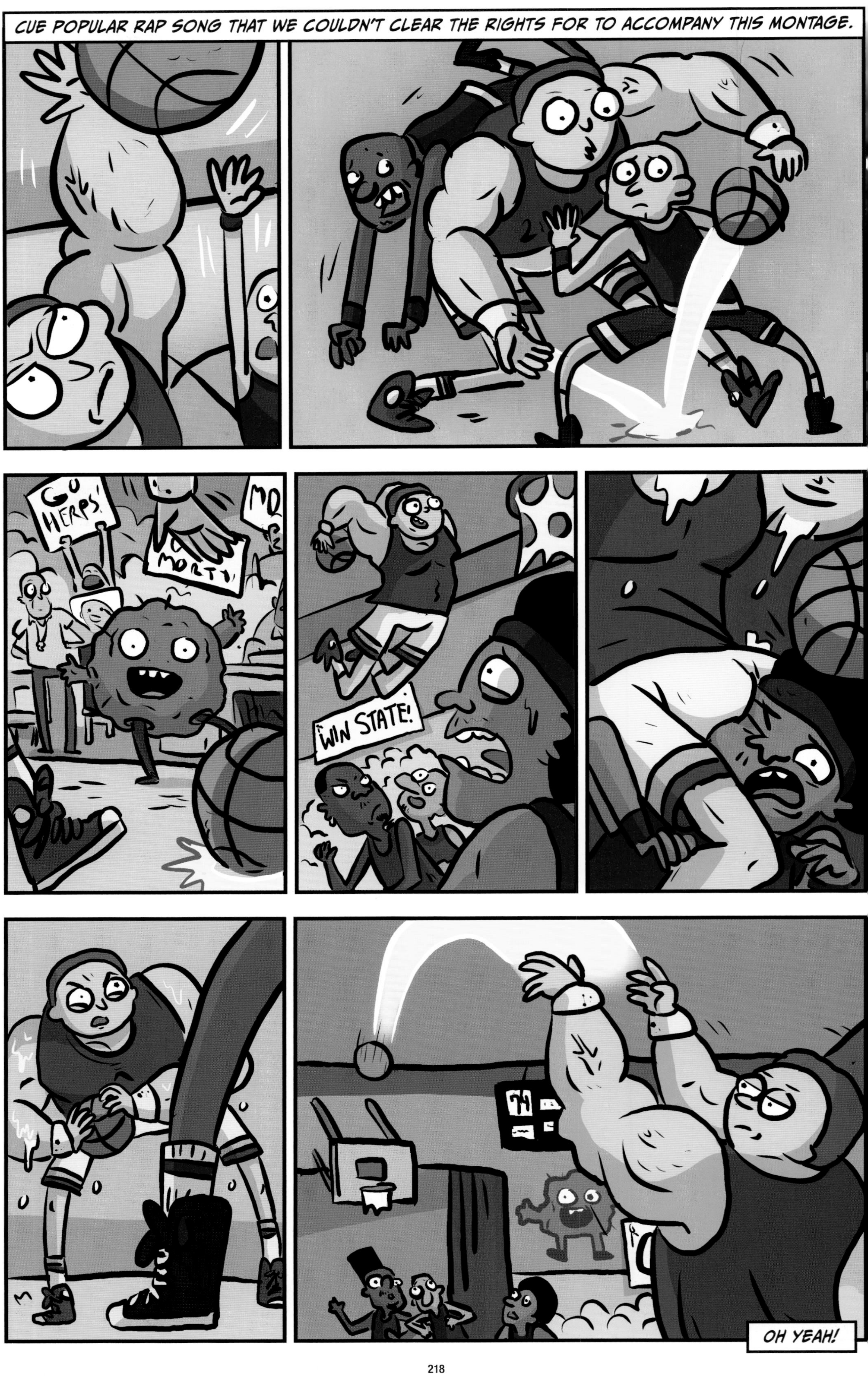
CUE POPULAR RAP SONG THAT WE COULDN'T CLEAR THE RIGHTS FOR TO ACCOMPANY THIS MONTAGE.
GO HERPS!
MORTY
WIN STATE!
OH YEAH!

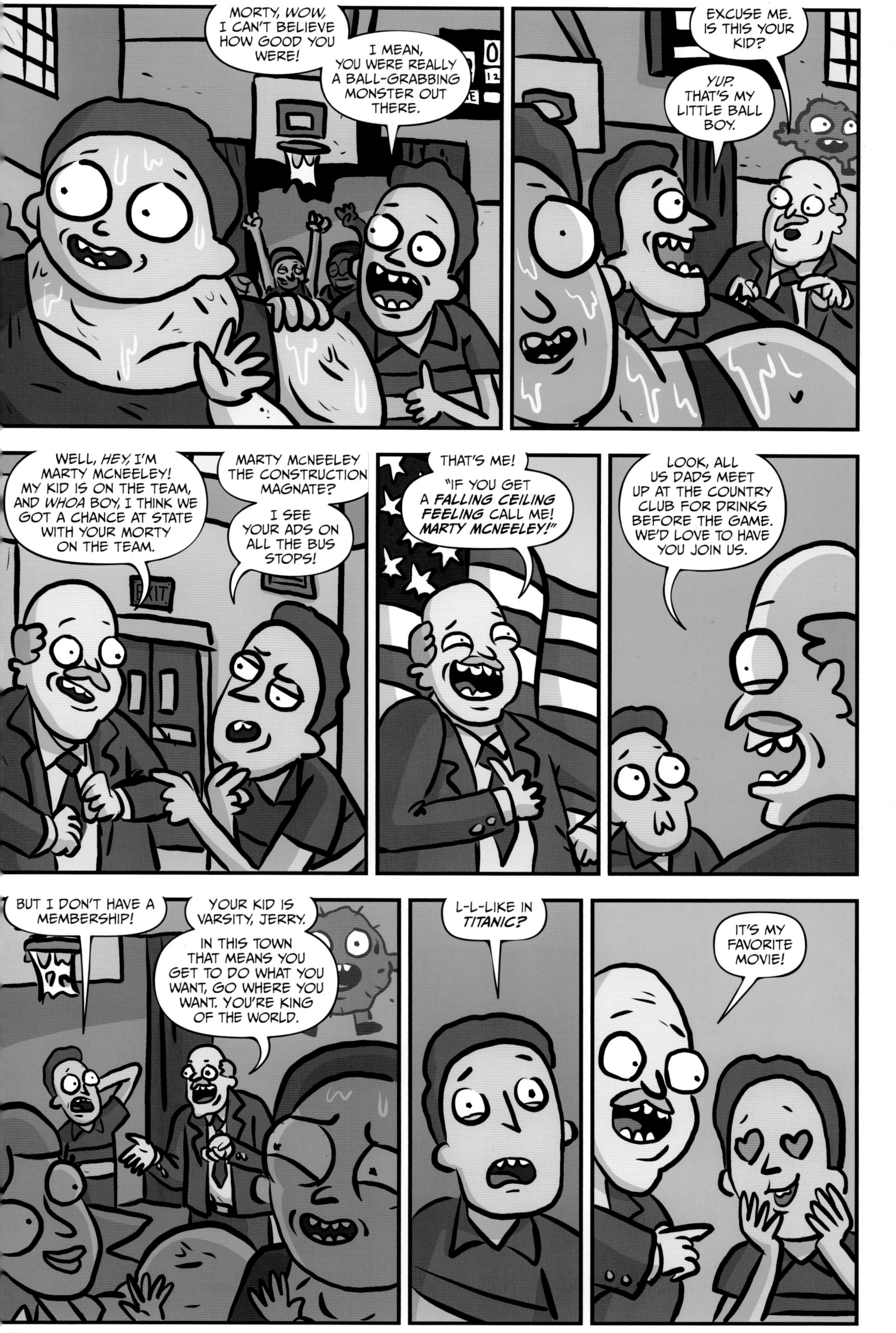
MORTY, *WOW*, I CAN'T BELIEVE HOW GOOD YOU WERE!
I MEAN, YOU WERE REALLY A BALL-GRABBING MONSTER OUT THERE.
EXCUSE ME. IS THIS YOUR KID?
YUP. THAT'S MY LITTLE BALL BOY.
WELL, *HEY*, I'M MARTY MCNEELEY! MY KID IS ON THE TEAM, AND *WHOA* BOY, I THINK WE GOT A CHANCE AT STATE WITH YOUR MORTY ON THE TEAM.
MARTY MCNEELEY THE CONSTRUCTION MAGNATE?
I SEE YOUR ADS ON ALL THE BUS STOPS!
EXIT
THAT'S ME!
"IF YOU GET A ***FALLING CEILING FEELING*** CALL ME! ***MARTY MCNEELEY!***"
LOOK, ALL US DADS MEET UP AT THE COUNTRY CLUB FOR DRINKS BEFORE THE GAME. WE'D LOVE TO HAVE YOU JOIN US.
BUT I DON'T HAVE A MEMBERSHIP!
YOUR KID IS VARSITY, JERRY.
IN THIS TOWN THAT MEANS YOU GET TO DO WHAT YOU WANT, GO WHERE YOU WANT. YOU'RE KING OF THE WORLD.
L-L-LIKE IN ***TITANIC?***
IT'S MY FAVORITE MOVIE!

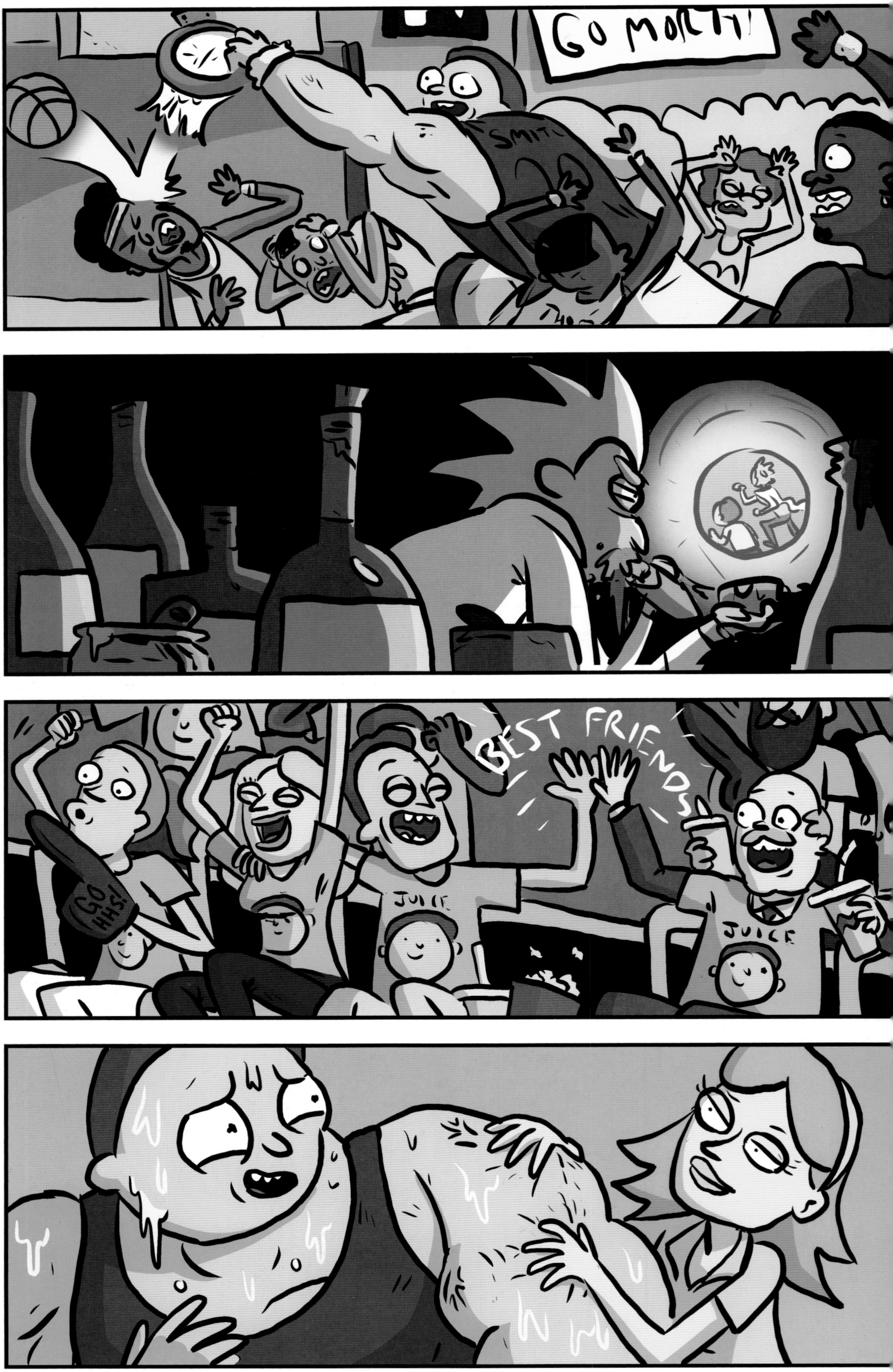
GO MORTY!
SMITH
GO HHS!
JUICE
BEST FRIENDS
JUICE

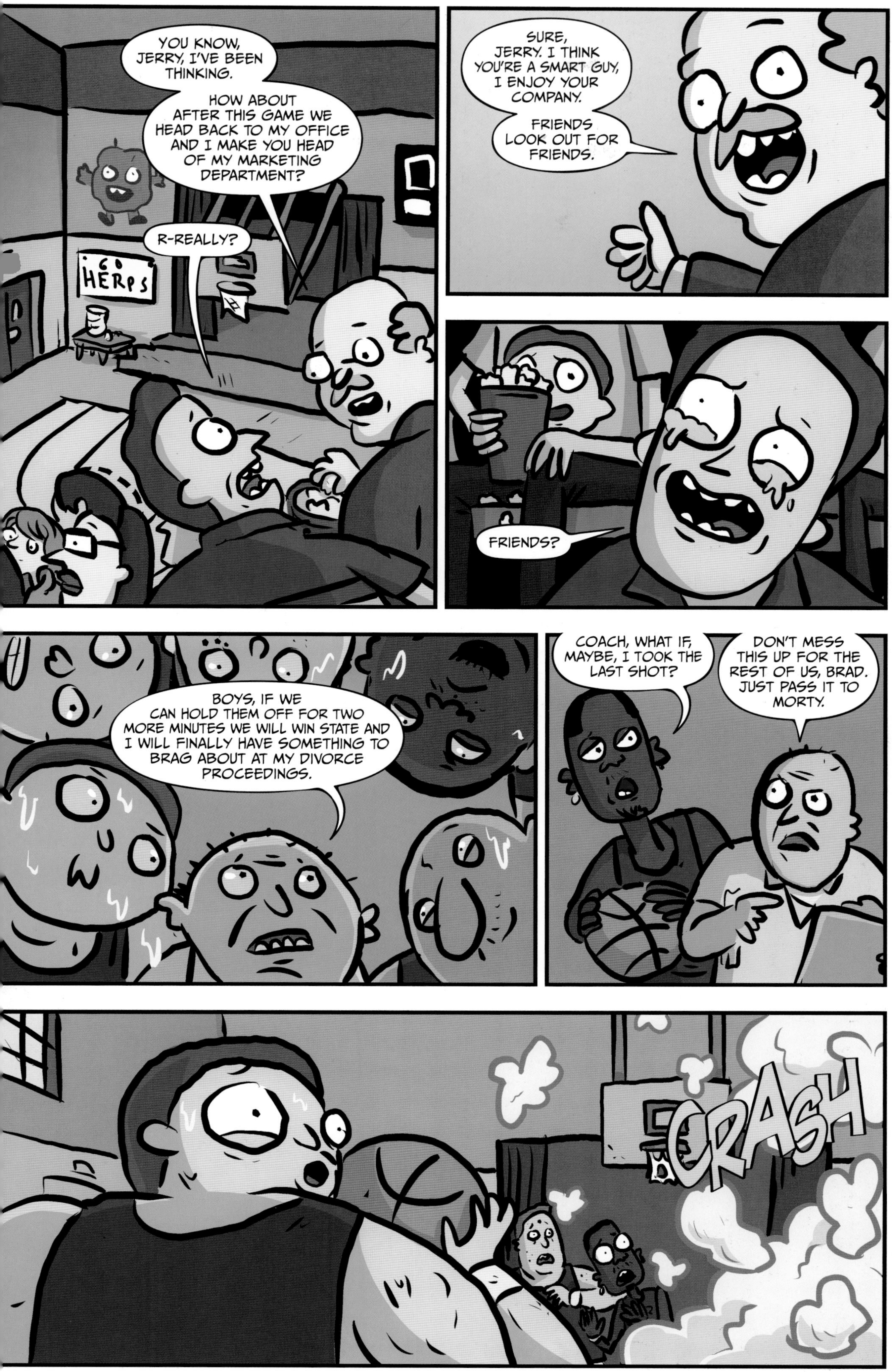
YOU KNOW, JERRY, I'VE BEEN THINKING.
HOW ABOUT AFTER THIS GAME WE HEAD BACK TO MY OFFICE AND I MAKE YOU HEAD OF MY MARKETING DEPARTMENT?
R-REALLY?
GO HERPS
SURE, JERRY. I THINK YOU'RE A SMART GUY, I ENJOY YOUR COMPANY.
FRIENDS LOOK OUT FOR FRIENDS.
FRIENDS?
BOYS, IF WE CAN HOLD THEM OFF FOR TWO MORE MINUTES WE WILL WIN STATE AND I WILL FINALLY HAVE SOMETHING TO BRAG ABOUT AT MY DIVORCE PROCEEDINGS.
COACH, WHAT IF, MAYBE, I TOOK THE LAST SHOT?
DON'T MESS THIS UP FOR THE REST OF US, BRAD. JUST PASS IT TO MORTY.
CRASH

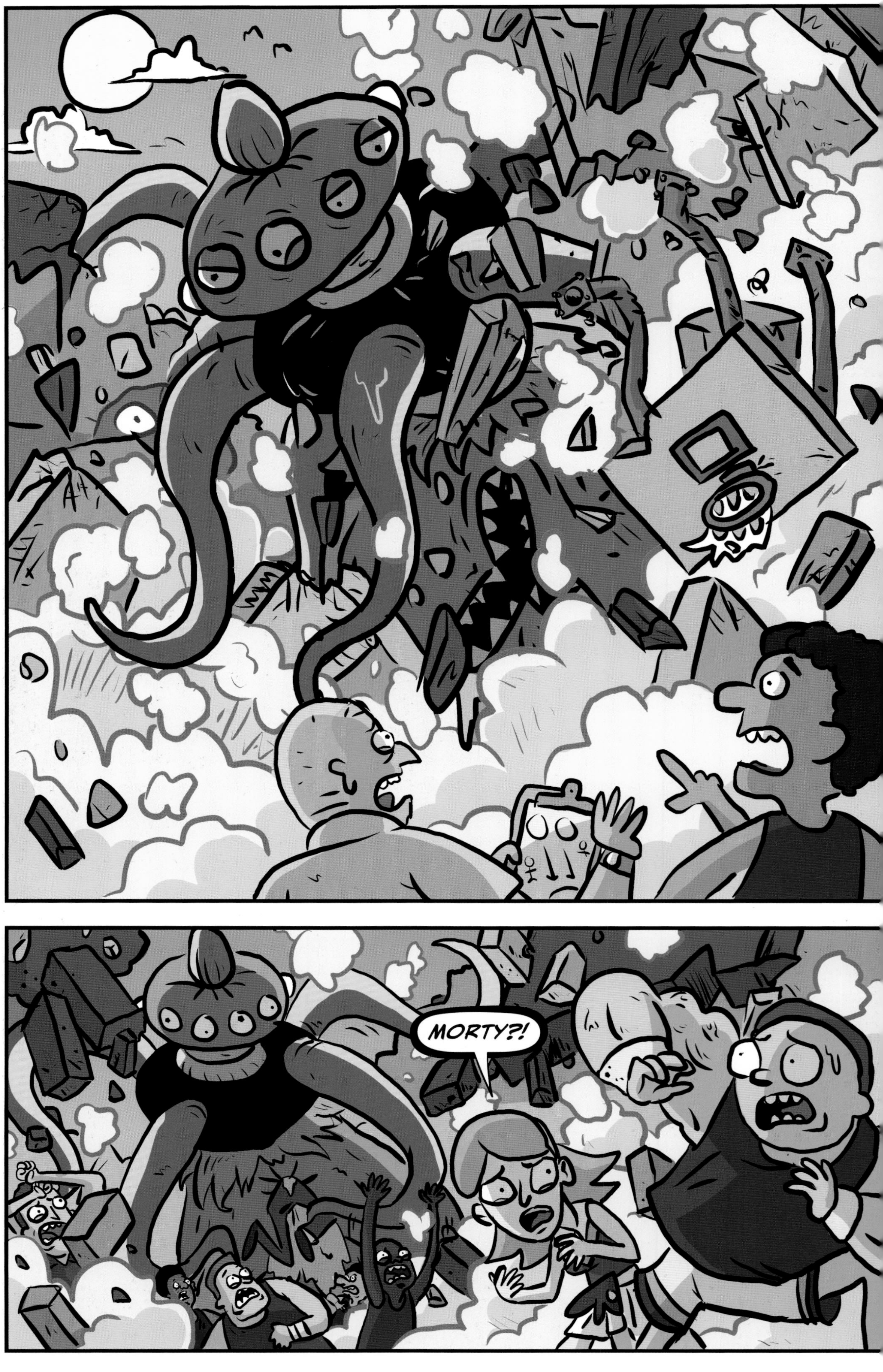
MORTY?!

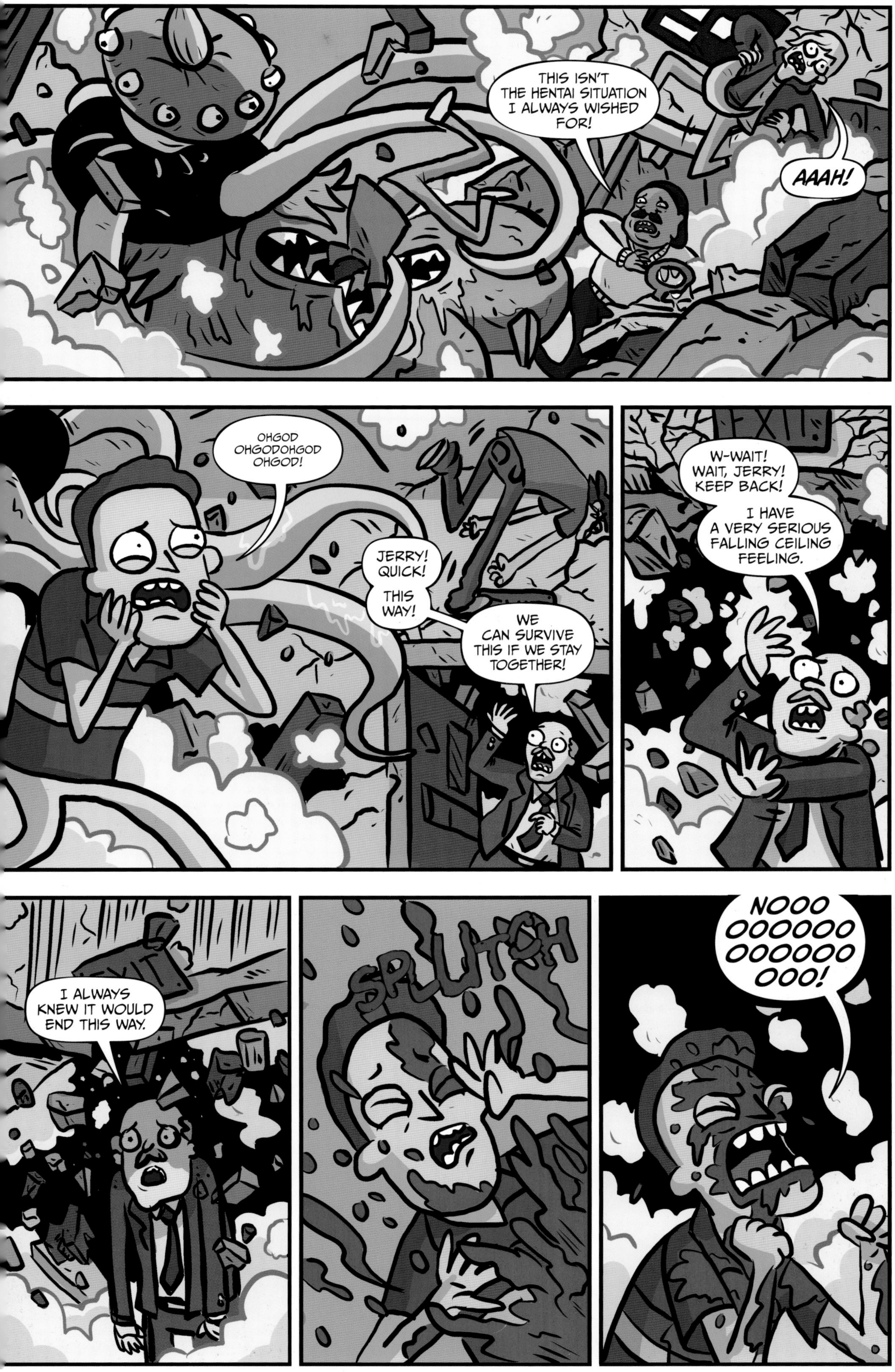

THIS ISN'T THE HENTAI SITUATION I ALWAYS WISHED FOR!
AAAH!
OHGOD OHGODOHGOD OHGOD!
JERRY! QUICK!
THIS WAY!
WE CAN SURVIVE THIS IF WE STAY TOGETHER!
W-WAIT! WAIT, JERRY! KEEP BACK!
I HAVE A VERY SERIOUS FALLING CEILING FEELING.
I ALWAYS KNEW IT WOULD END THIS WAY.
SPLUTCH
NOOOOOOOOOOOOOOOOOOOOO!

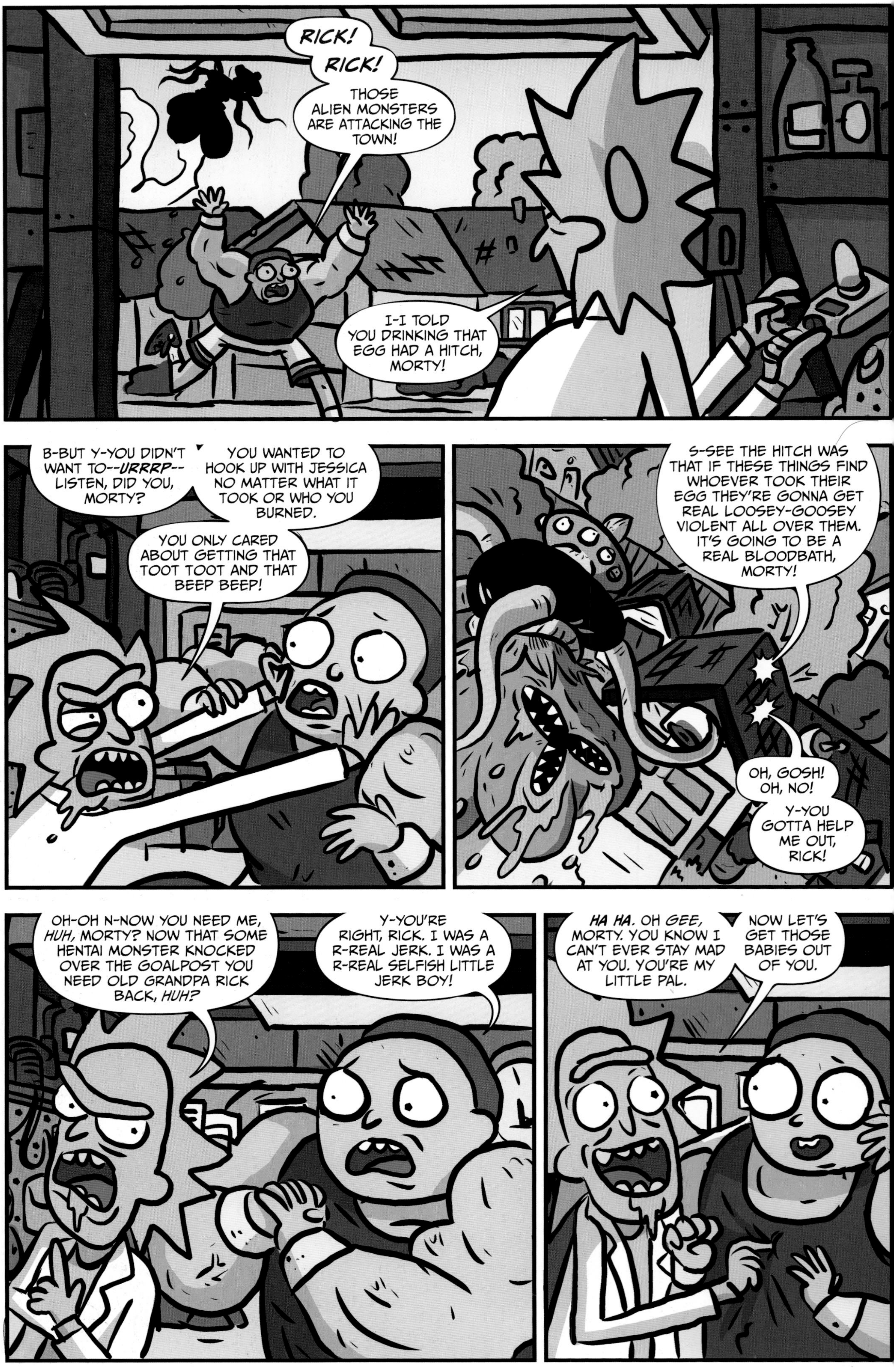
RICK! RICK!
THOSE ALIEN MONSTERS ARE ATTACKING THE TOWN!
I-I TOLD YOU DRINKING THAT EGG HAD A HITCH, MORTY!
B-BUT Y-YOU DIDN'T WANT TO--URRRP-- LISTEN, DID YOU, MORTY?
YOU WANTED TO HOOK UP WITH JESSICA NO MATTER WHAT IT TOOK OR WHO YOU BURNED.
YOU ONLY CARED ABOUT GETTING THAT TOOT TOOT AND THAT BEEP BEEP!
S-SEE THE HITCH WAS THAT IF THESE THINGS FIND WHOEVER TOOK THEIR EGG THEY'RE GONNA GET REAL LOOSEY-GOOSEY VIOLENT ALL OVER THEM. IT'S GOING TO BE A REAL BLOODBATH, MORTY!
OH, GOSH! OH, NO!
Y-YOU GOTTA HELP ME OUT, RICK!
OH-OH N-NOW YOU NEED ME, HUH, MORTY? NOW THAT SOME HENTAI MONSTER KNOCKED OVER THE GOALPOST YOU NEED OLD GRANDPA RICK BACK, HUH?
Y-YOU'RE RIGHT, RICK. I WAS A R-REAL JERK. I WAS A R-REAL SELFISH LITTLE JERK BOY!
HA HA. OH GEE, MORTY. YOU KNOW I CAN'T EVER STAY MAD AT YOU. YOU'RE MY LITTLE PAL.
NOW LET'S GET THOSE BABIES OUT OF YOU.

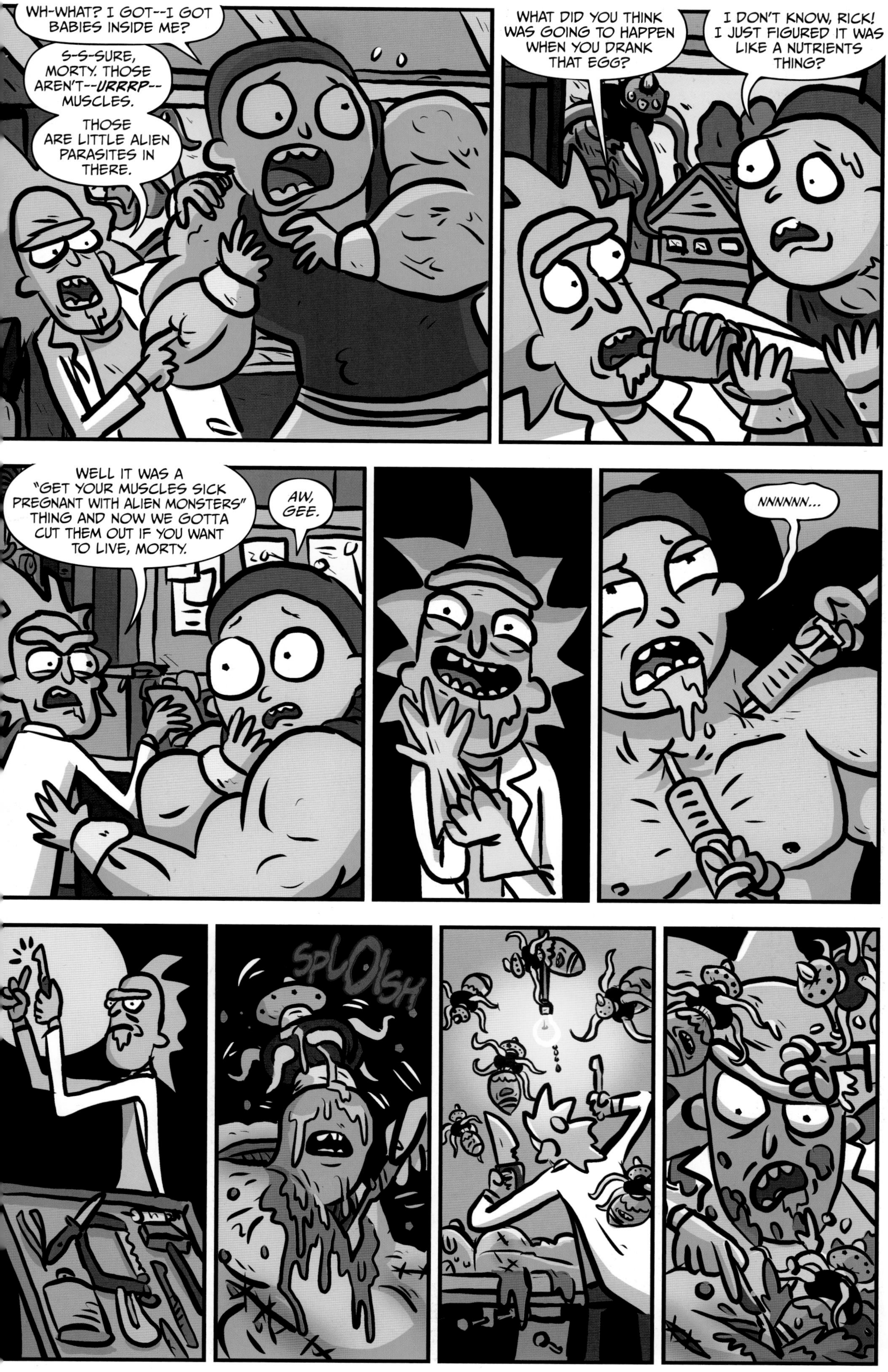
WH-WHAT? I GOT--I GOT BABIES INSIDE ME?
S-S-SURE, MORTY. THOSE AREN'T--URRRP--MUSCLES.
THOSE ARE LITTLE ALIEN PARASITES IN THERE.
WHAT DID YOU THINK WAS GOING TO HAPPEN WHEN YOU DRANK THAT EGG?
I DON'T KNOW, RICK! I JUST FIGURED IT WAS LIKE A NUTRIENTS THING?
WELL IT WAS A "GET YOUR MUSCLES SICK PREGNANT WITH ALIEN MONSTERS" THING AND NOW WE GOTTA CUT THEM OUT IF YOU WANT TO LIVE, MORTY.
AW, GEE.
NNNNNN...
SPLOISH!

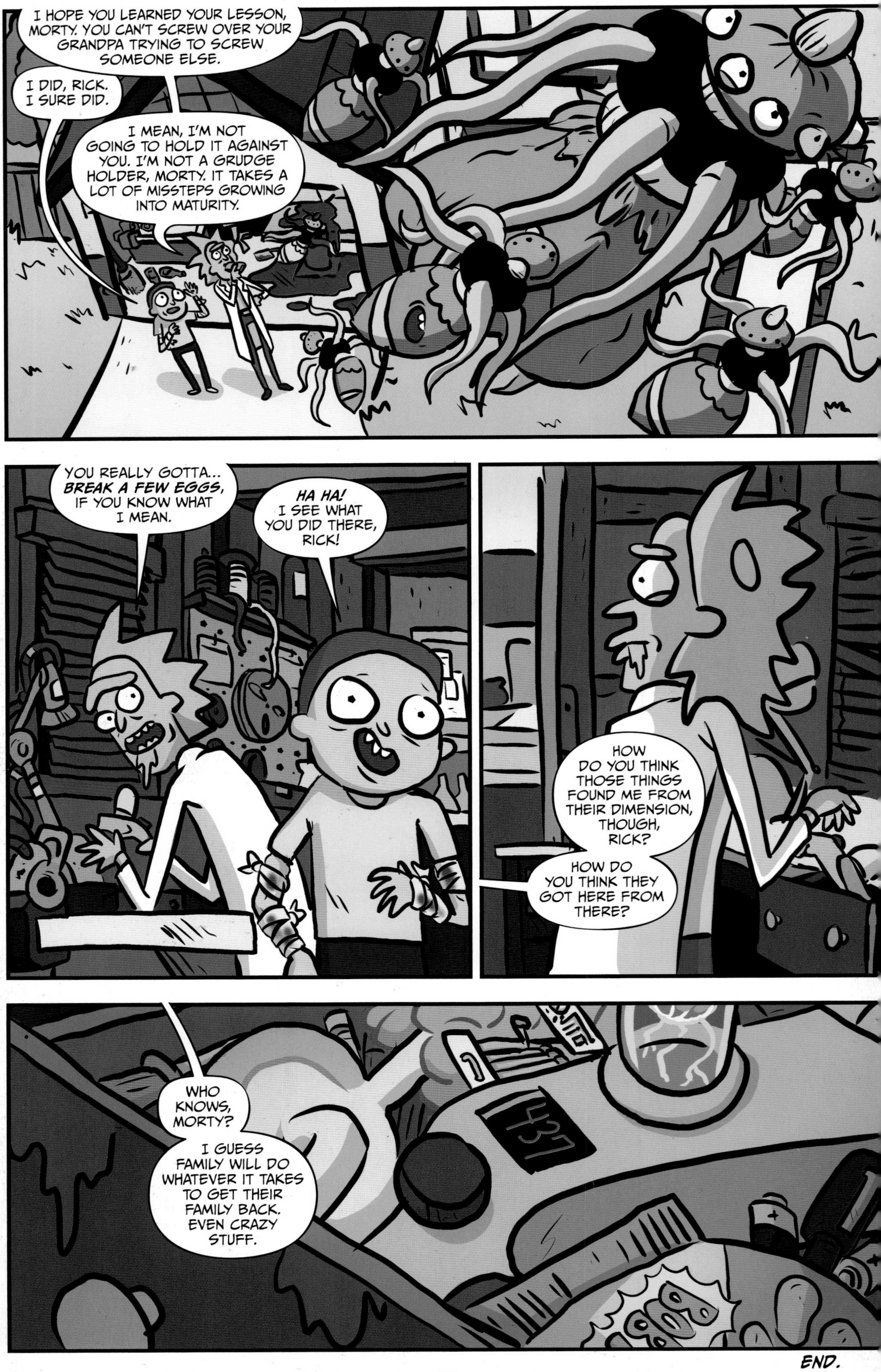
I HOPE YOU LEARNED YOUR LESSON, MORTY. YOU CAN'T SCREW OVER YOUR GRANDPA TRYING TO SCREW SOMEONE ELSE.
I DID, RICK. I SURE DID.
I MEAN, I'M NOT GOING TO HOLD IT AGAINST YOU. I'M NOT A GRUDGE HOLDER, MORTY. IT TAKES A LOT OF MISSTEPS GROWING INTO MATURITY.
YOU REALLY GOTTA... *BREAK A FEW EGGS,* IF YOU KNOW WHAT I MEAN.
HA HA! I SEE WHAT YOU DID THERE, RICK!
HOW DO YOU THINK THOSE THINGS FOUND ME FROM THEIR DIMENSION, THOUGH, RICK?
HOW DO YOU THINK THEY GOT HERE FROM THERE?
WHO KNOWS, MORTY?
I GUESS FAMILY WILL DO WHATEVER IT TAKES TO GET THEIR FAMILY BACK. EVEN CRAZY STUFF.

END.

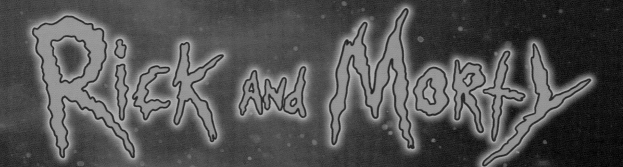

BONUS SHORTS

WRITTEN, DRAWN, AND COLORED BY **MARC ELLERBY**
LETTERED BY **CRANK!**

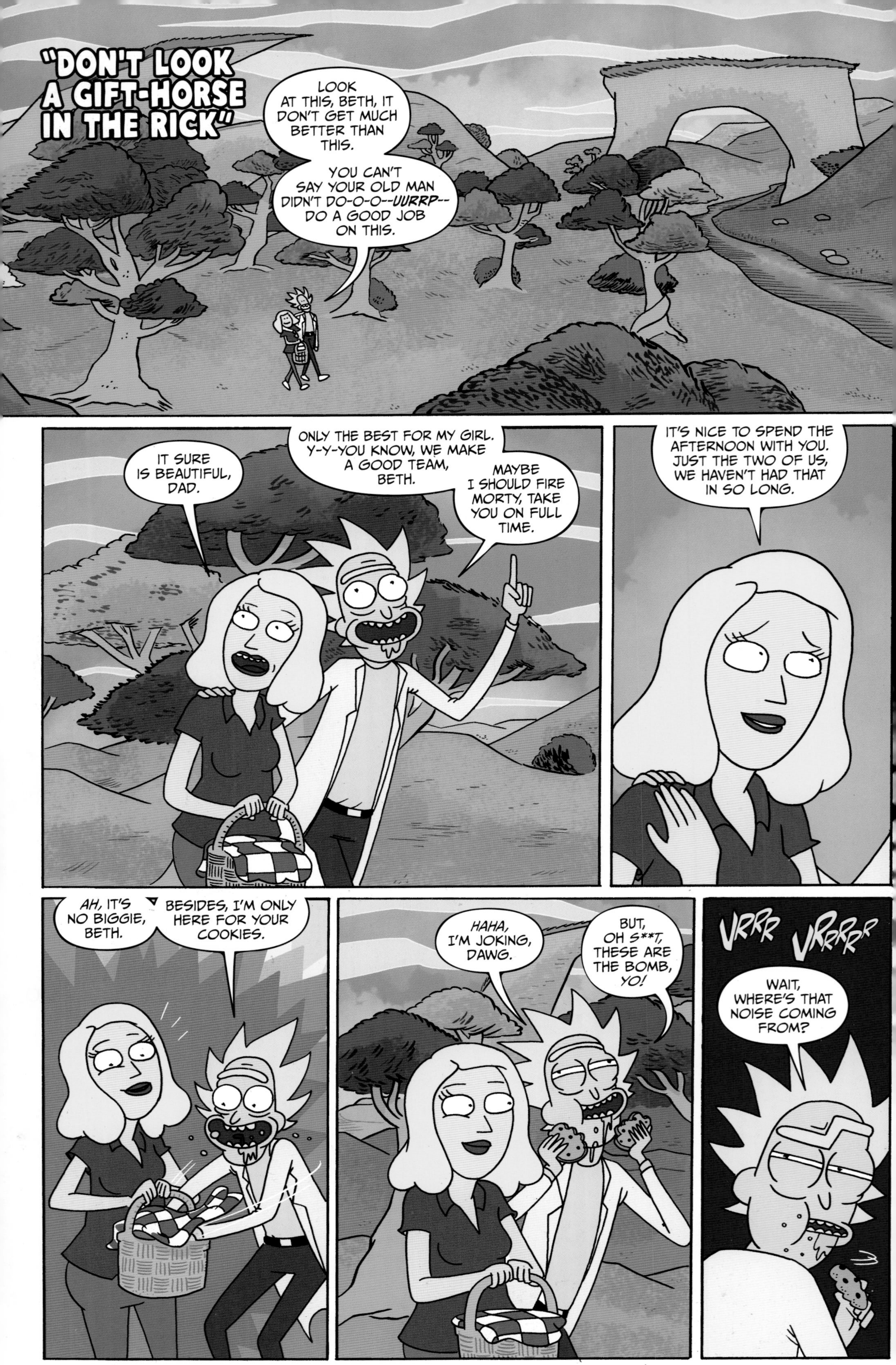
"DON'T LOOK A GIFT-HORSE IN THE RICK"
LOOK AT THIS, BETH, IT DON'T GET MUCH BETTER THAN THIS.
YOU CAN'T SAY YOUR OLD MAN DIDN'T DO-O-O--UURRP-- DO A GOOD JOB ON THIS.
IT SURE IS BEAUTIFUL, DAD.
ONLY THE BEST FOR MY GIRL. Y-Y-YOU KNOW, WE MAKE A GOOD TEAM, BETH.
MAYBE I SHOULD FIRE MORTY, TAKE YOU ON FULL TIME.
IT'S NICE TO SPEND THE AFTERNOON WITH YOU. JUST THE TWO OF US, WE HAVEN'T HAD THAT IN SO LONG.
AH, IT'S NO BIGGIE, BETH.
BESIDES, I'M ONLY HERE FOR YOUR COOKIES.
HAHA, I'M JOKING, DAWG.
BUT, OH S**T, THESE ARE THE BOMB, YO!
VRRR VRRRRR
WAIT, WHERE'S THAT NOISE COMING FROM?

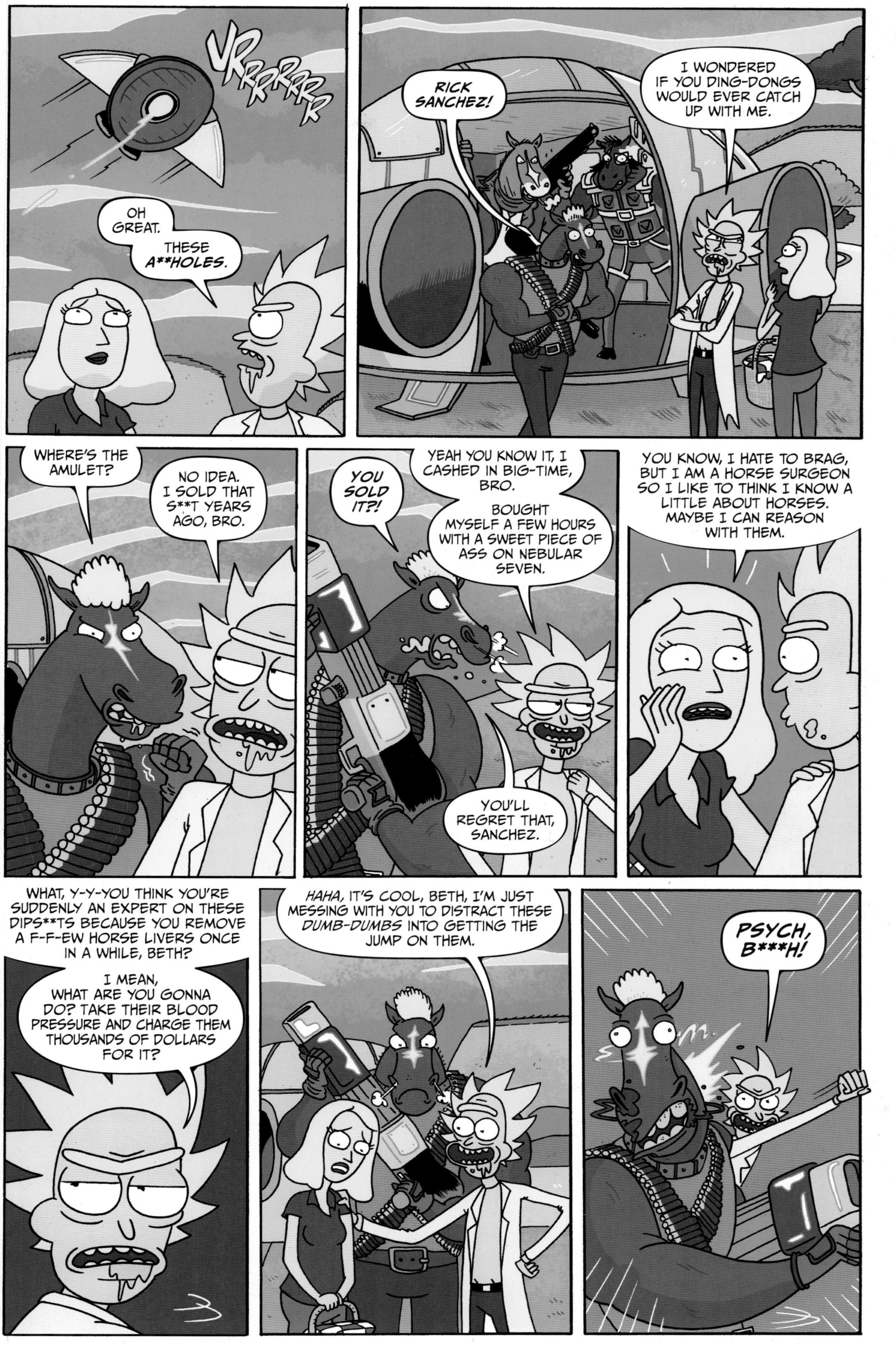
VRRRRRRRR
OH GREAT. THESE A**HOLES.
RICK SANCHEZ!
I WONDERED IF YOU DING-DONGS WOULD EVER CATCH UP WITH ME.
WHERE'S THE AMULET?
NO IDEA. I SOLD THAT S**T YEARS AGO, BRO.
YOU SOLD IT?!
YEAH YOU KNOW IT, I CASHED IN BIG-TIME, BRO.
BOUGHT MYSELF A FEW HOURS WITH A SWEET PIECE OF ASS ON NEBULAR SEVEN.
YOU'LL REGRET THAT, SANCHEZ.
YOU KNOW, I HATE TO BRAG, BUT I AM A HORSE SURGEON SO I LIKE TO THINK I KNOW A LITTLE ABOUT HORSES. MAYBE I CAN REASON WITH THEM.
WHAT, Y-Y-YOU THINK YOU'RE SUDDENLY AN EXPERT ON THESE DIPS**TS BECAUSE YOU REMOVE A F-F-EW HORSE LIVERS ONCE IN A WHILE, BETH?
I MEAN, WHAT ARE YOU GONNA DO? TAKE THEIR BLOOD PRESSURE AND CHARGE THEM THOUSANDS OF DOLLARS FOR IT?
HAHA, IT'S COOL, BETH, I'M JUST MESSING WITH YOU TO DISTRACT THESE DUMB-DUMBS INTO GETTING THE JUMP ON THEM.
PSYCH, B***H!

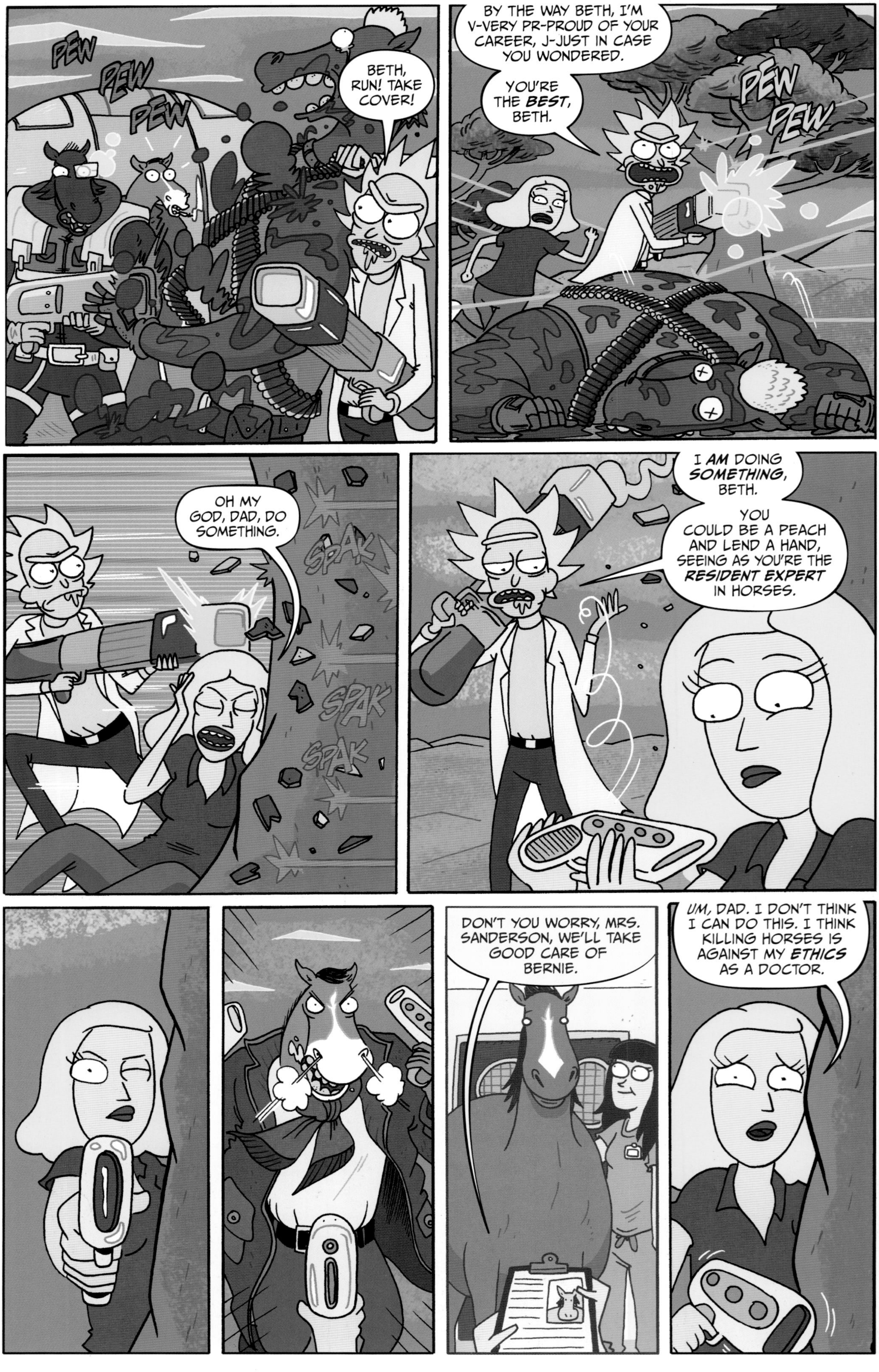
PEW
PEW
PEW
BETH, RUN! TAKE COVER!
BY THE WAY BETH, I'M V-VERY PR-PROUD OF YOUR CAREER, J-JUST IN CASE YOU WONDERED.
YOU'RE THE **BEST**, BETH.
PEW
PEW
OH MY GOD, DAD, DO SOMETHING.
SPAK
SPAK
SPAK
I **AM** DOING **SOMETHING**, BETH.
YOU COULD BE A PEACH AND LEND A HAND, SEEING AS YOU'RE THE **RESIDENT EXPERT** IN HORSES.
DON'T YOU WORRY, MRS. SANDERSON, WE'LL TAKE GOOD CARE OF BERNIE.
UM, DAD. I DON'T THINK I CAN DO THIS. I THINK KILLING HORSES IS AGAINST MY **ETHICS** AS A DOCTOR.

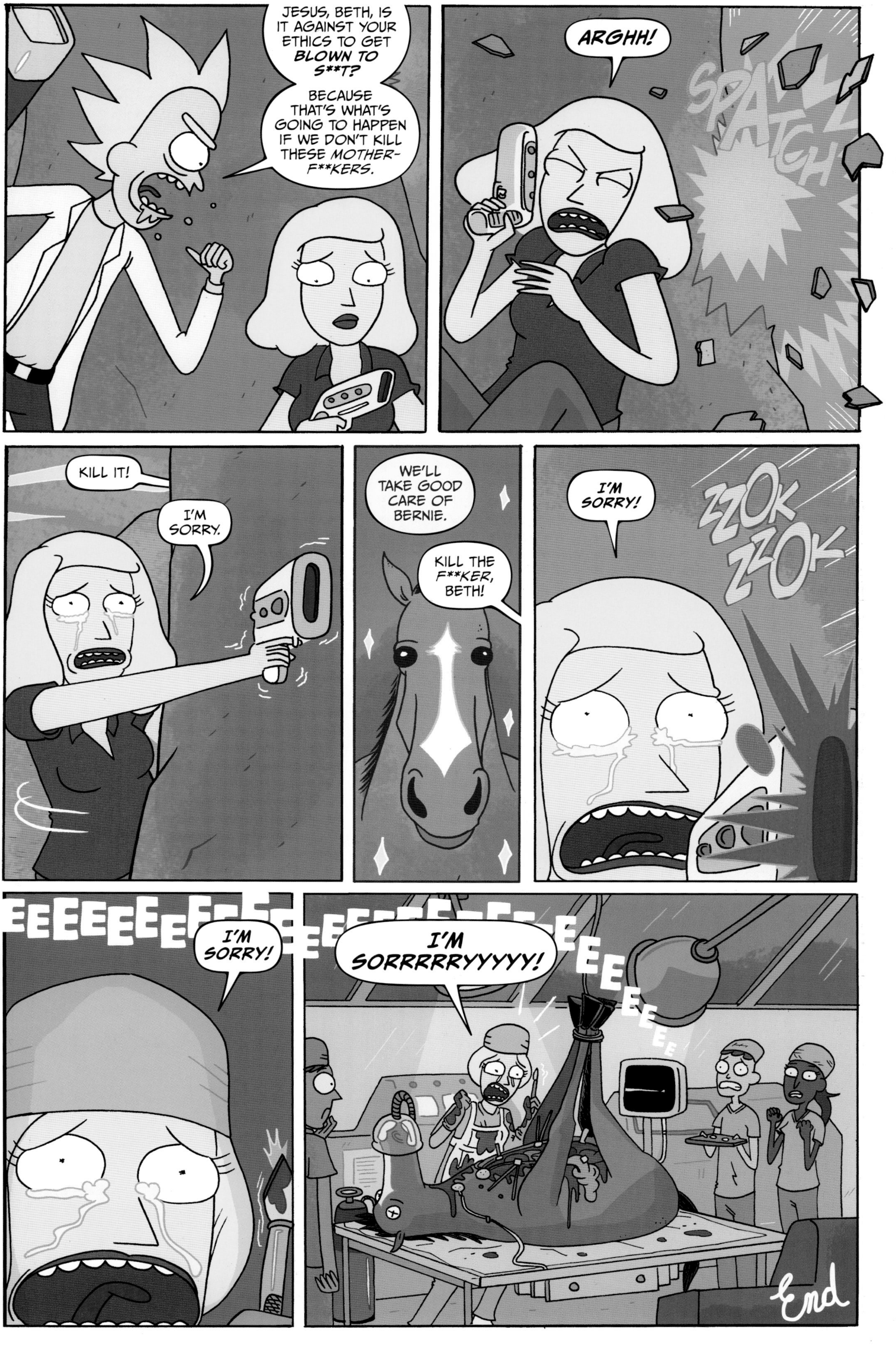

JESUS, BETH, IS IT AGAINST YOUR ETHICS TO GET BLOWN TO S**T?
BECAUSE THAT'S WHAT'S GOING TO HAPPEN IF WE DON'T KILL THESE MOTHER-F**KERS.
ARGHH!
SPATCH
KILL IT!
I'M SORRY.
WE'LL TAKE GOOD CARE OF BERNIE.
KILL THE F**KER, BETH!
I'M SORRY!
ZZOK ZZOK
I'M SORRY!
I'M SORRRRRYYYYY!
End

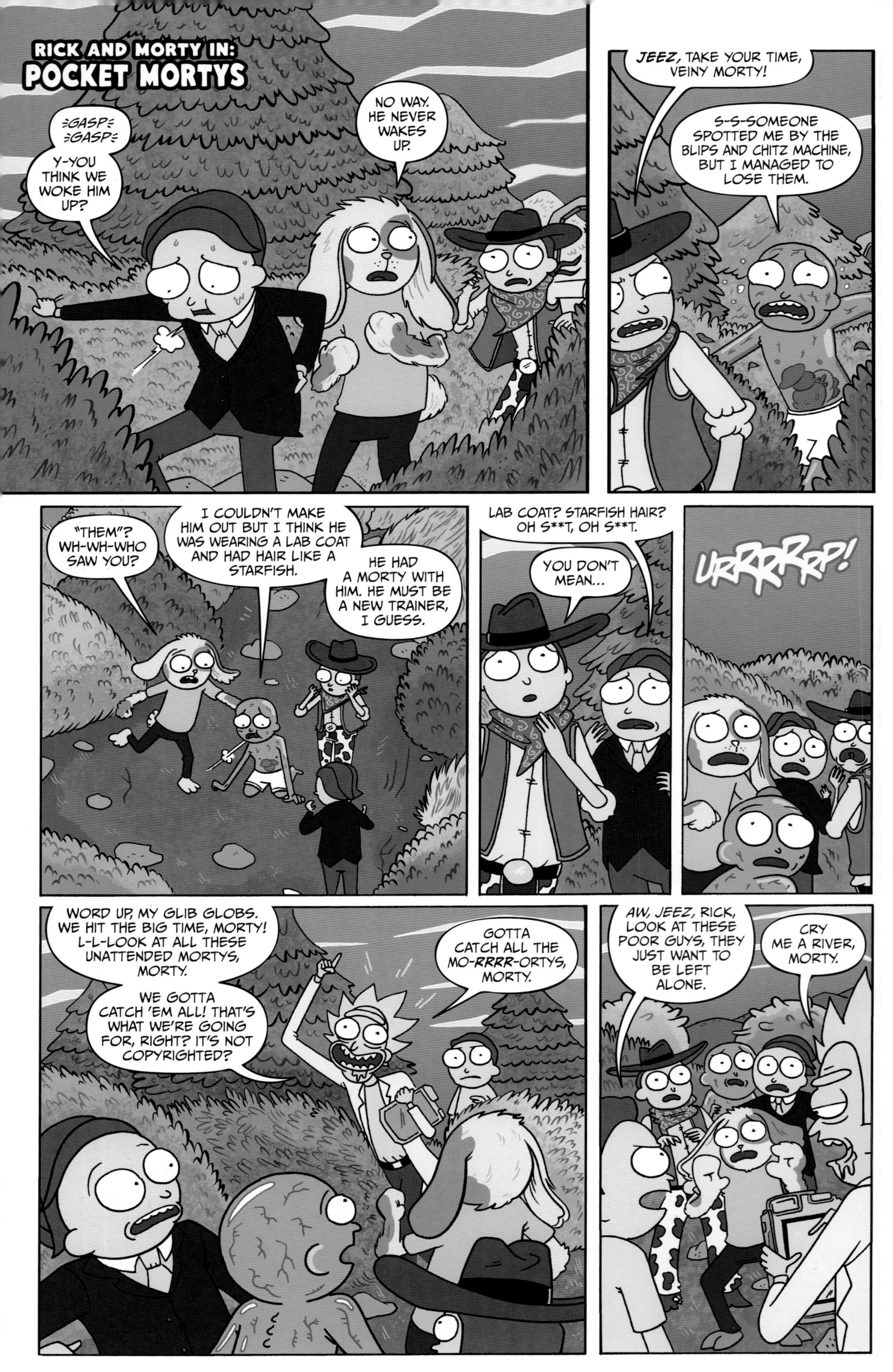
RICK AND MORTY IN:
POCKET MORTYS
GASP GASP
Y-YOU THINK WE WOKE HIM UP?
NO WAY. HE NEVER WAKES UP.
JEEZ, TAKE YOUR TIME, VEINY MORTY!
S-S-SOMEONE SPOTTED ME BY THE BLIPS AND CHITZ MACHINE, BUT I MANAGED TO LOSE THEM.
"THEM"? WH-WH-WHO SAW YOU?
I COULDN'T MAKE HIM OUT BUT I THINK HE WAS WEARING A LAB COAT AND HAD HAIR LIKE A STARFISH.
HE HAD A MORTY WITH HIM. HE MUST BE A NEW TRAINER, I GUESS.
LAB COAT? STARFISH HAIR? OH S**T, OH S**T.
YOU DON'T MEAN...
URRRRRP!
WORD UP, MY GLIB GLOBS. WE HIT THE BIG TIME, MORTY! L-L-LOOK AT ALL THESE UNATTENDED MORTYS, MORTY.
WE GOTTA CATCH 'EM ALL! THAT'S WHAT WE'RE GOING FOR, RIGHT? IT'S NOT COPYRIGHTED?
GOTTA CATCH ALL THE MO-RRRR-ORTYS, MORTY.
AW, JEEZ, RICK, LOOK AT THESE POOR GUYS, THEY JUST WANT TO BE LEFT ALONE.
CRY ME A RIVER, MORTY.

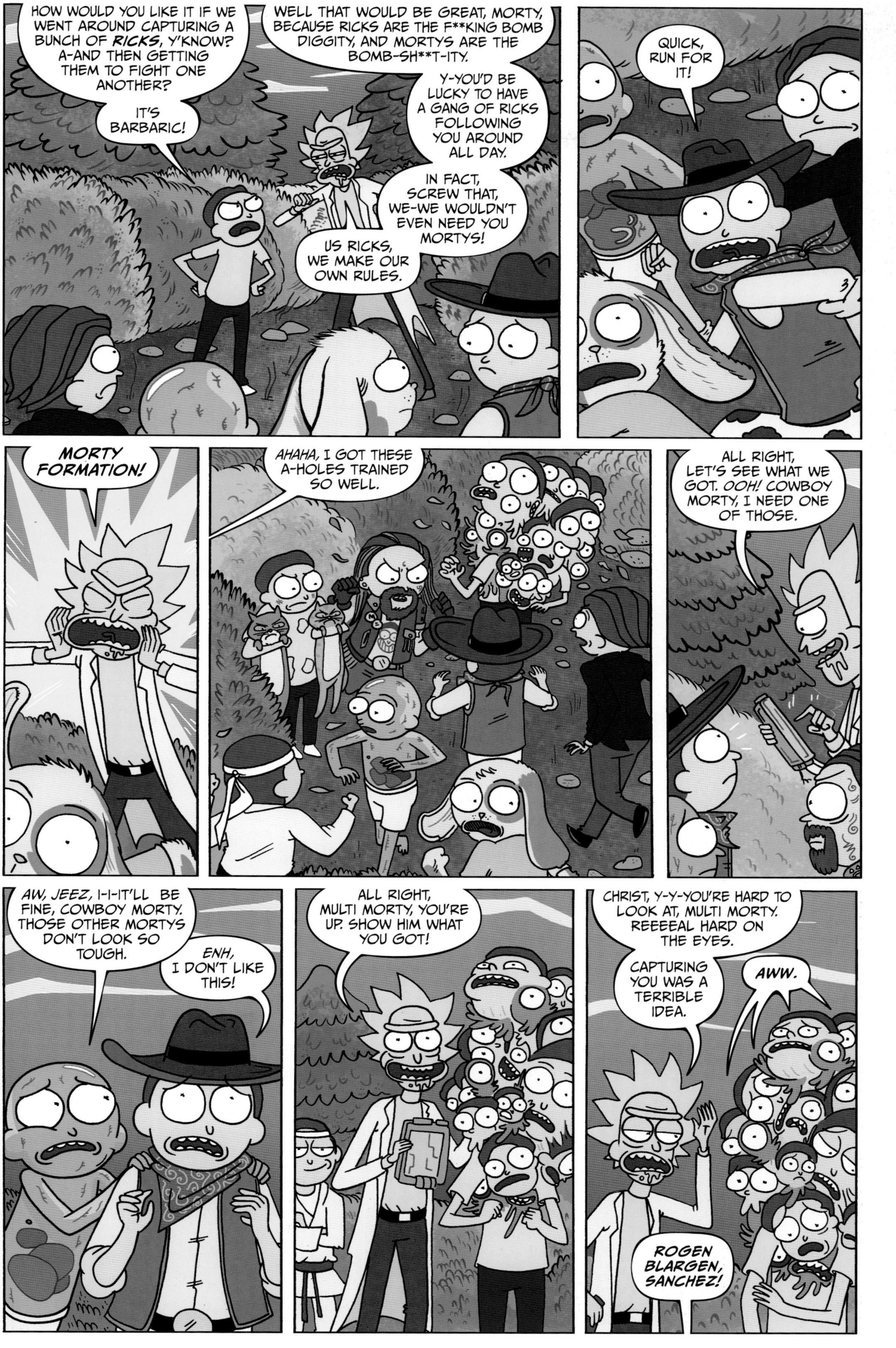
HOW WOULD YOU LIKE IT IF WE WENT AROUND CAPTURING A BUNCH OF *RICKS*, Y'KNOW? A-AND THEN GETTING THEM TO FIGHT ONE ANOTHER?
IT'S BARBARIC!
WELL THAT WOULD BE GREAT, MORTY, BECAUSE RICKS ARE THE F**KING BOMB DIGGITY, AND MORTYS ARE THE BOMB-SH**T-ITY.
Y-YOU'D BE LUCKY TO HAVE A GANG OF RICKS FOLLOWING YOU AROUND ALL DAY.
IN FACT, SCREW THAT, WE-WE WOULDN'T EVEN NEED YOU MORTYS!
US RICKS, WE MAKE OUR OWN RULES.
QUICK, RUN FOR IT!
MORTY FORMATION!
AHAHA, I GOT THESE A-HOLES TRAINED SO WELL.
ALL RIGHT, LET'S SEE WHAT WE GOT. *OOH!* COWBOY MORTY, I NEED ONE OF THOSE.
AW, JEEZ, I-I-IT'LL BE FINE, COWBOY MORTY. THOSE OTHER MORTYS DON'T LOOK SO TOUGH.
ENH, I DON'T LIKE THIS!
ALL RIGHT, MULTI MORTY, YOU'RE UP. SHOW HIM WHAT YOU GOT!
CHRIST, Y-Y-YOU'RE HARD TO LOOK AT, MULTI MORTY. REEEEAL HARD ON THE EYES.
CAPTURING YOU WAS A TERRIBLE IDEA.
AWW.
ROGEN BLARGEN, SANCHEZ!

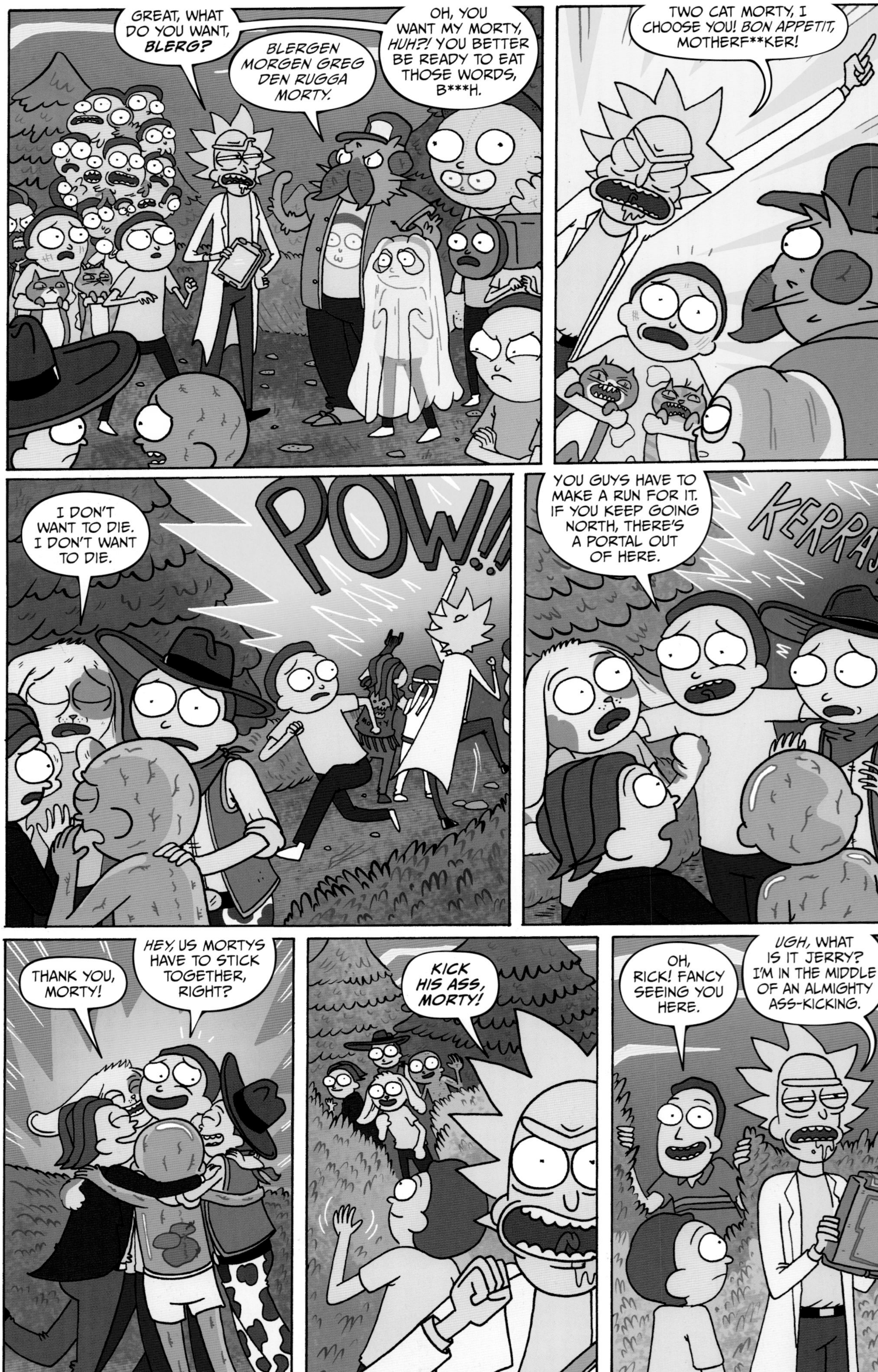
GREAT, WHAT DO YOU WANT, BLERG?
BLERGEN MORGEN GREG DEN RUGGA MORTY.
OH, YOU WANT MY MORTY, HUH?! YOU BETTER BE READY TO EAT THOSE WORDS, B***H.
TWO CAT MORTY, I CHOOSE YOU! BON APPETIT, MOTHERF**KER!
I DON'T WANT TO DIE. I DON'T WANT TO DIE.
POW!!!
YOU GUYS HAVE TO MAKE A RUN FOR IT. IF YOU KEEP GOING NORTH, THERE'S A PORTAL OUT OF HERE.
KERRASH
THANK YOU, MORTY!
HEY, US MORTYS HAVE TO STICK TOGETHER, RIGHT?
KICK HIS ASS, MORTY!
OH, RICK! FANCY SEEING YOU HERE.
UGH, WHAT IS IT JERRY? I'M IN THE MIDDLE OF AN ALMIGHTY ASS-KICKING.

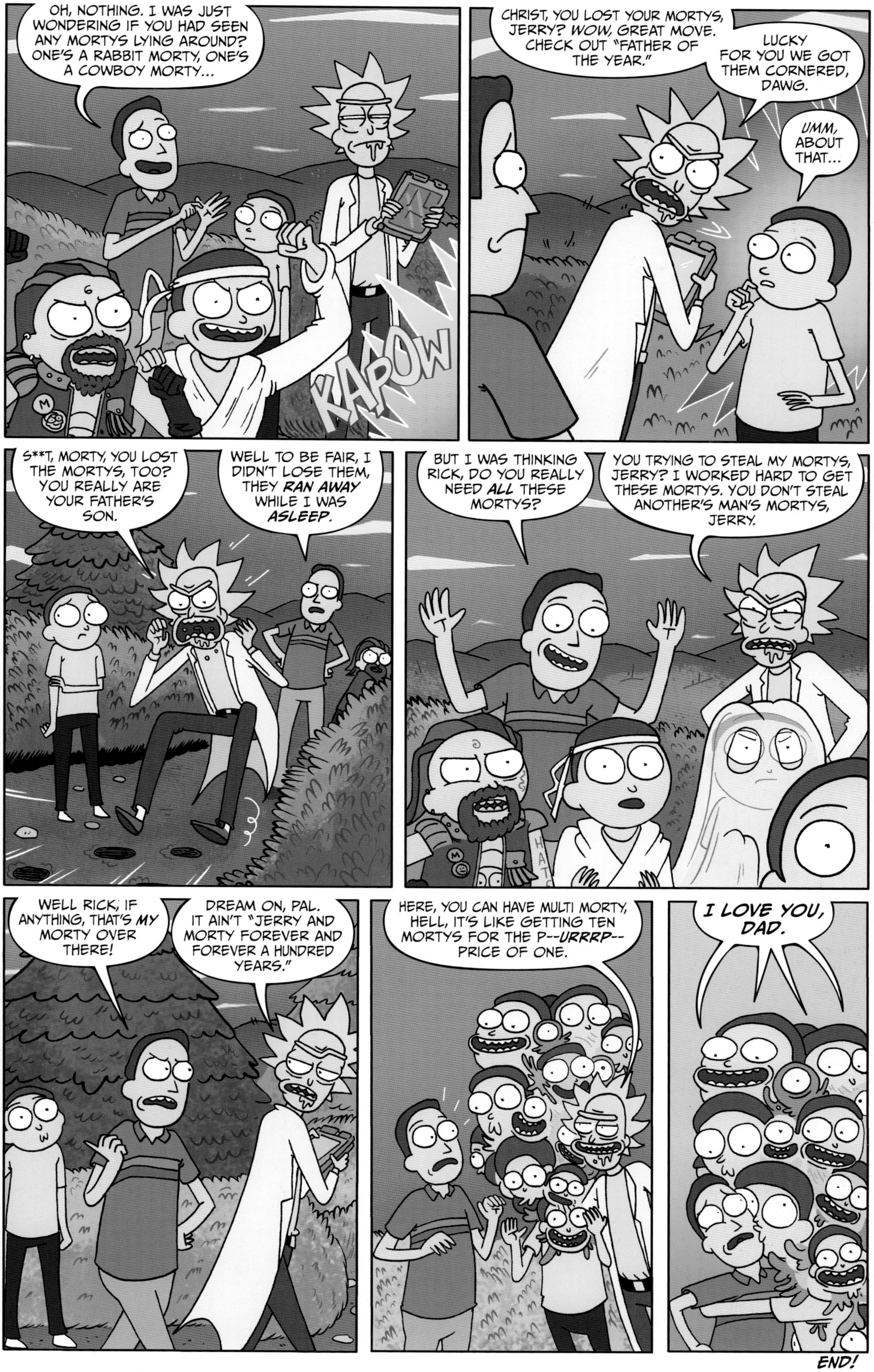
OH, NOTHING. I WAS JUST WONDERING IF YOU HAD SEEN ANY MORTYS LYING AROUND? ONE'S A RABBIT MORTY, ONE'S A COWBOY MORTY...
KAPOW
CHRIST, YOU LOST YOUR MORTYS, JERRY? WOW, GREAT MOVE. CHECK OUT "FATHER OF THE YEAR."
LUCKY FOR YOU WE GOT THEM CORNERED, DAWG.
UMM, ABOUT THAT...
S**T, MORTY, YOU LOST THE MORTYS, TOO? YOU REALLY ARE YOUR FATHER'S SON.
WELL TO BE FAIR, I DIDN'T LOSE THEM, THEY RAN AWAY WHILE I WAS ASLEEP.
BUT I WAS THINKING RICK, DO YOU REALLY NEED ALL THESE MORTYS?
YOU TRYING TO STEAL MY MORTYS, JERRY? I WORKED HARD TO GET THESE MORTYS. YOU DON'T STEAL ANOTHER'S MAN'S MORTYS, JERRY.
WELL RICK, IF ANYTHING, THAT'S MY MORTY OVER THERE!
DREAM ON, PAL. IT AIN'T "JERRY AND MORTY FOREVER AND FOREVER A HUNDRED YEARS."
HERE, YOU CAN HAVE MULTI MORTY, HELL, IT'S LIKE GETTING TEN MORTYS FOR THE P--URRRP-- PRICE OF ONE.
I LOVE YOU, DAD.
END!

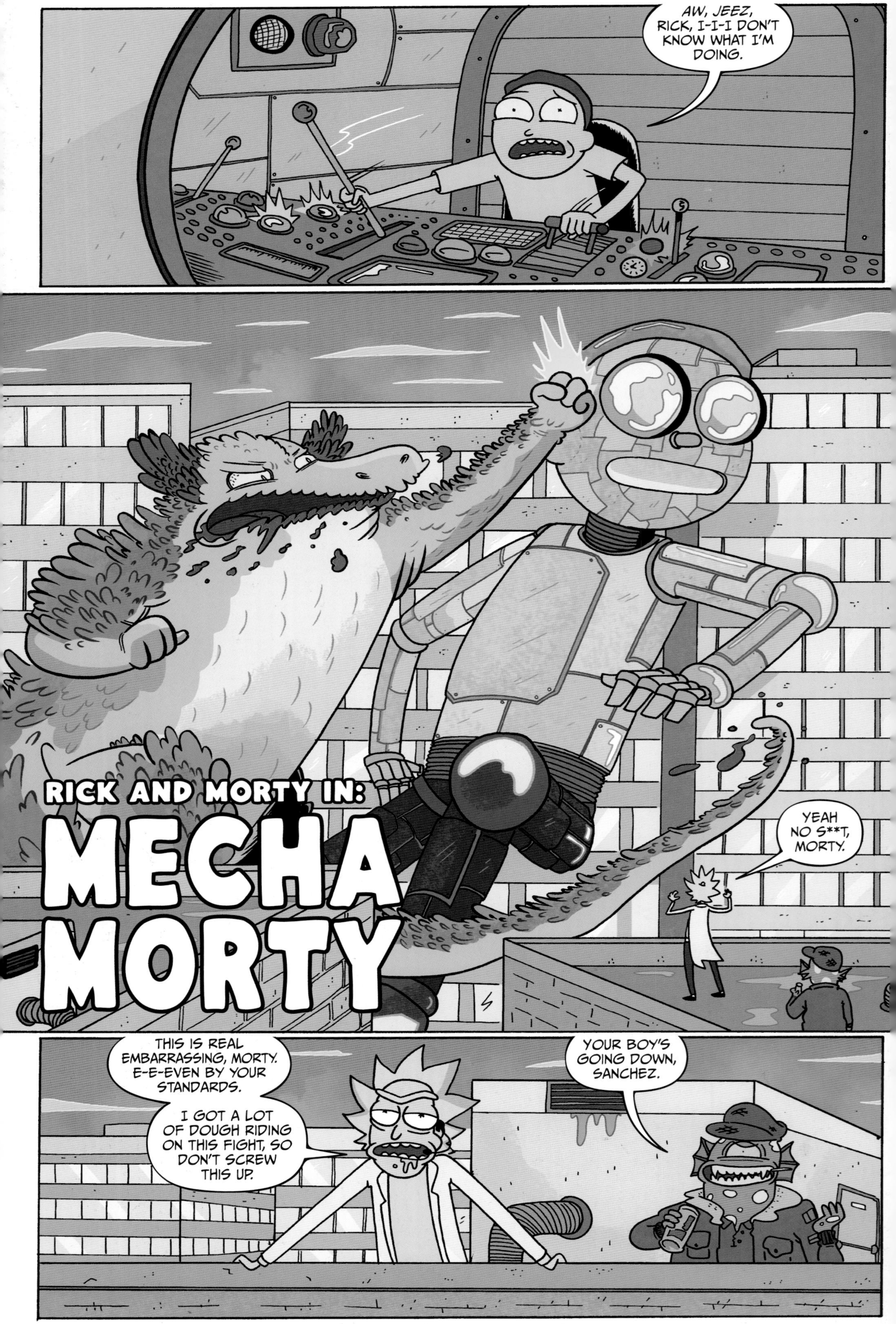
AW, JEEZ, RICK, I-I-I DON'T KNOW WHAT I'M DOING.
RICK AND MORTY IN:
MECHA MORTY
YEAH NO S**T, MORTY.
THIS IS REAL EMBARRASSING, MORTY. E-E-EVEN BY YOUR STANDARDS.
I GOT A LOT OF DOUGH RIDING ON THIS FIGHT, SO DON'T SCREW THIS UP.
YOUR BOY'S GOING DOWN, SANCHEZ.

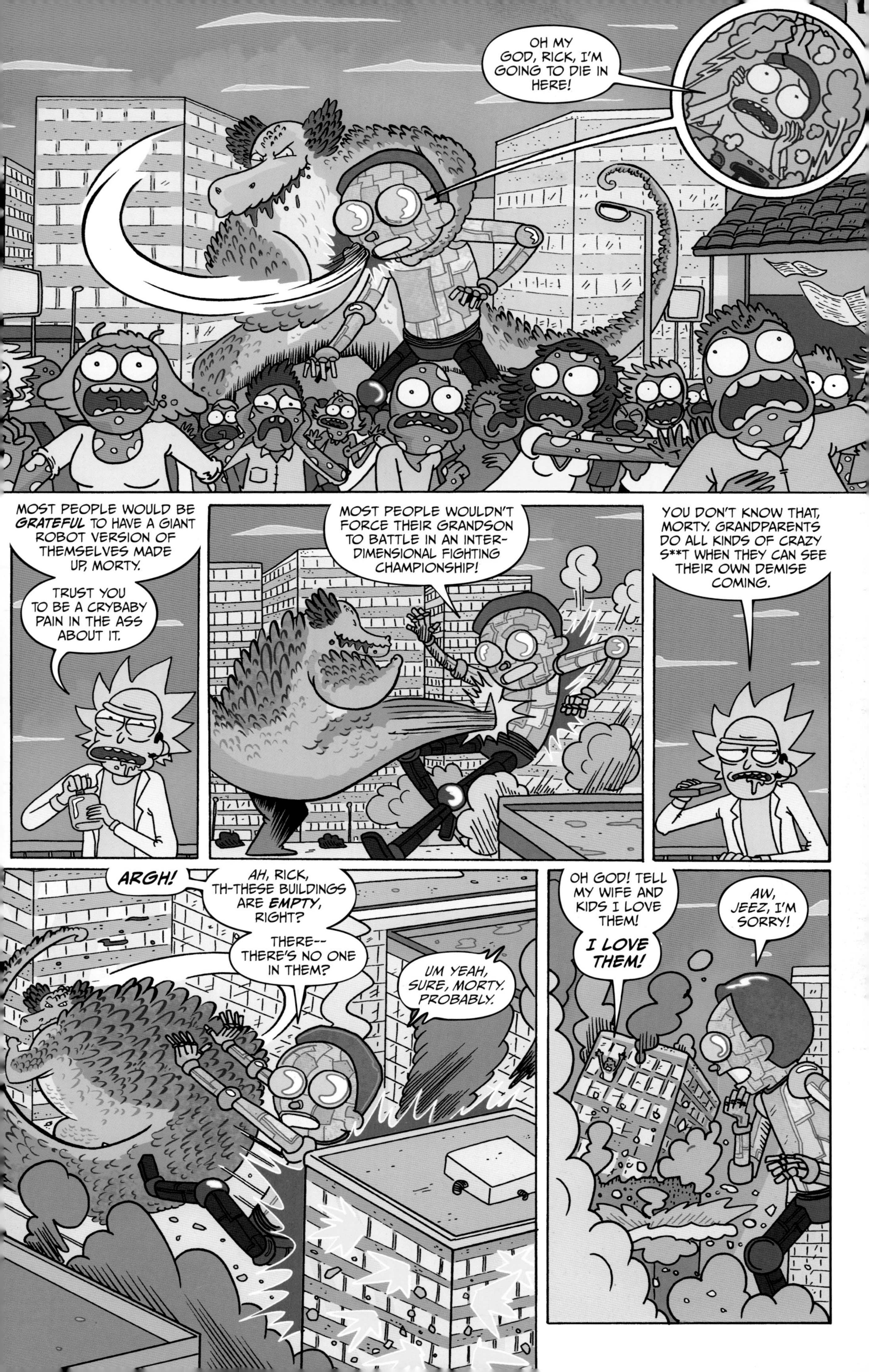
OH MY GOD, RICK, I'M GOING TO DIE IN HERE!
MOST PEOPLE WOULD BE GRATEFUL TO HAVE A GIANT ROBOT VERSION OF THEMSELVES MADE UP, MORTY.
TRUST YOU TO BE A CRYBABY PAIN IN THE ASS ABOUT IT.
MOST PEOPLE WOULDN'T FORCE THEIR GRANDSON TO BATTLE IN AN INTER-DIMENSIONAL FIGHTING CHAMPIONSHIP!
YOU DON'T KNOW THAT, MORTY. GRANDPARENTS DO ALL KINDS OF CRAZY S**T WHEN THEY CAN SEE THEIR OWN DEMISE COMING.
ARGH!
AH, RICK, TH-THESE BUILDINGS ARE EMPTY, RIGHT?
THERE-- THERE'S NO ONE IN THEM?
UM YEAH, SURE, MORTY. PROBABLY.
OH GOD! TELL MY WIFE AND KIDS I LOVE THEM!
I LOVE THEM!
AW, JEEZ, I'M SORRY!

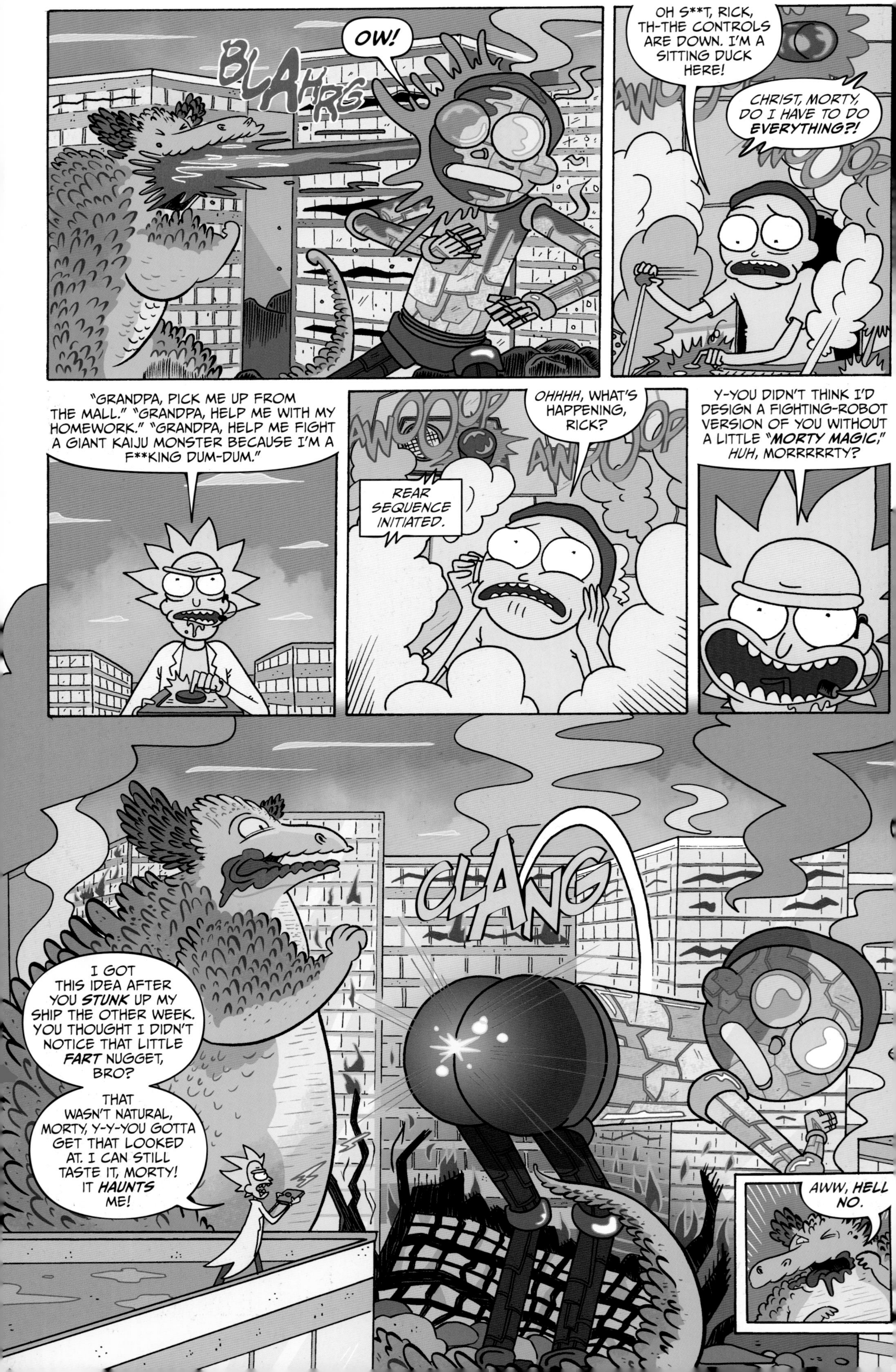
BLAHRG
OW!
OH S**T, RICK, TH-THE CONTROLS ARE DOWN. I'M A SITTING DUCK HERE!
CHRIST, MORTY, DO I HAVE TO DO **EVERYTHING?!**
"GRANDPA, PICK ME UP FROM THE MALL." "GRANDPA, HELP ME WITH MY HOMEWORK." "GRANDPA, HELP ME FIGHT A GIANT KAIJU MONSTER BECAUSE I'M A F**KING DUM-DUM."
OHHHH, WHAT'S HAPPENING, RICK?
REAR SEQUENCE INITIATED.
Y-YOU DIDN'T THINK I'D DESIGN A FIGHTING-ROBOT VERSION OF YOU WITHOUT A LITTLE "***MORTY MAGIC,***" *HUH,* MORRRRRTY?
CLANG
I GOT THIS IDEA AFTER YOU ***STUNK*** UP MY SHIP THE OTHER WEEK. YOU THOUGHT I DIDN'T NOTICE THAT LITTLE ***FART*** NUGGET, BRO?
THAT WASN'T NATURAL, MORTY, Y-Y-YOU GOTTA GET THAT LOOKED AT. I CAN STILL TASTE IT, MORTY! IT ***HAUNTS*** ME!
AWW, ***HELL NO.***

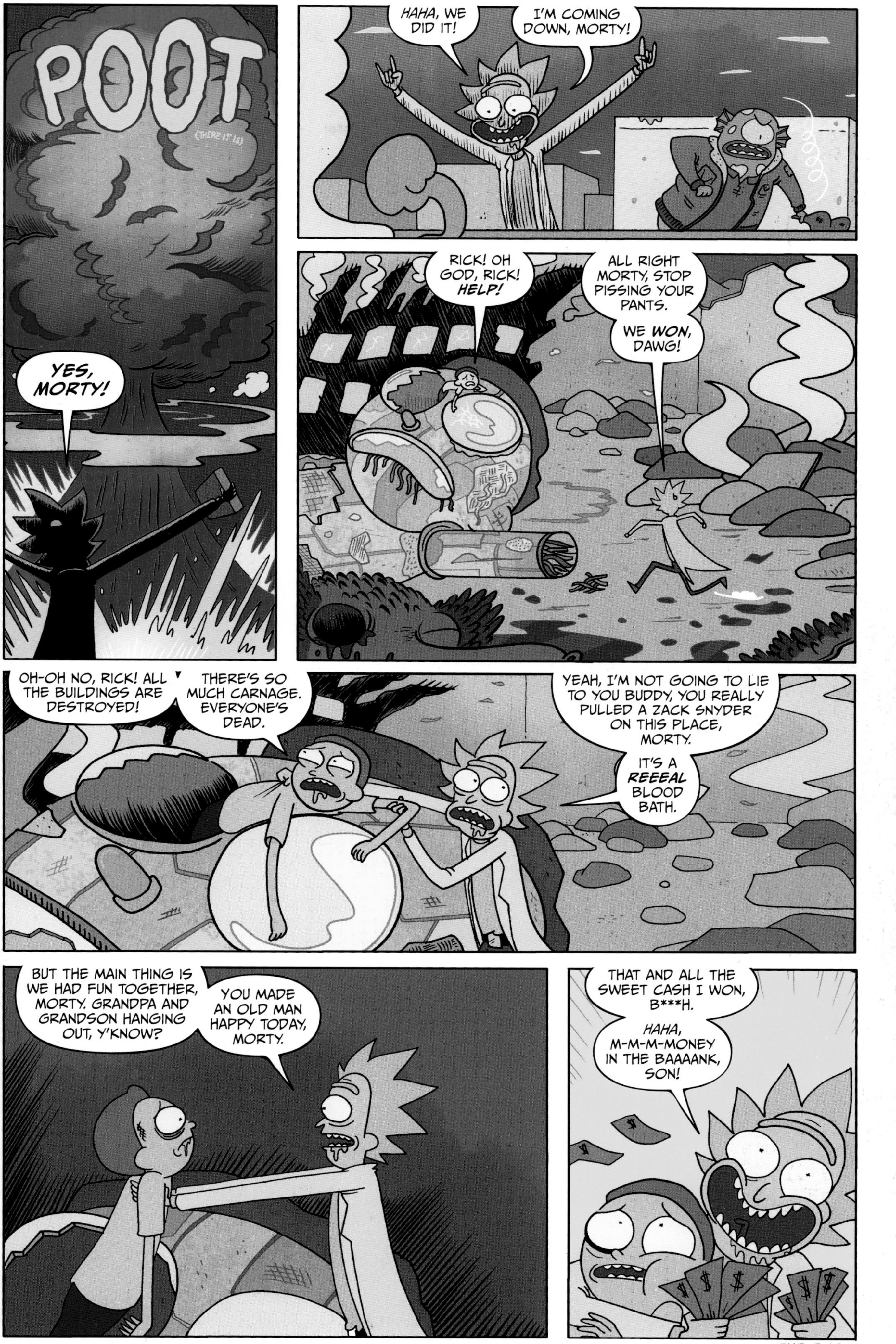
POOT
(THERE IT IS)
YES, MORTY!
HAHA, WE DID IT!
I'M COMING DOWN, MORTY!
RICK! OH GOD, RICK! HELP!
ALL RIGHT MORTY, STOP PISSING YOUR PANTS.
WE WON, DAWG!
OH-OH NO, RICK! ALL THE BUILDINGS ARE DESTROYED!
THERE'S SO MUCH CARNAGE. EVERYONE'S DEAD.
YEAH, I'M NOT GOING TO LIE TO YOU BUDDY, YOU REALLY PULLED A ZACK SNYDER ON THIS PLACE, MORTY.
IT'S A REEEAL BLOOD BATH.
BUT THE MAIN THING IS WE HAD FUN TOGETHER, MORTY. GRANDPA AND GRANDSON HANGING OUT, Y'KNOW?
YOU MADE AN OLD MAN HAPPY TODAY, MORTY.
THAT AND ALL THE SWEET CASH I WON, B***H.
HAHA, M-M-M-MONEY IN THE BAAAANK, SON!

THE END.

JERRY DECOY MODEL

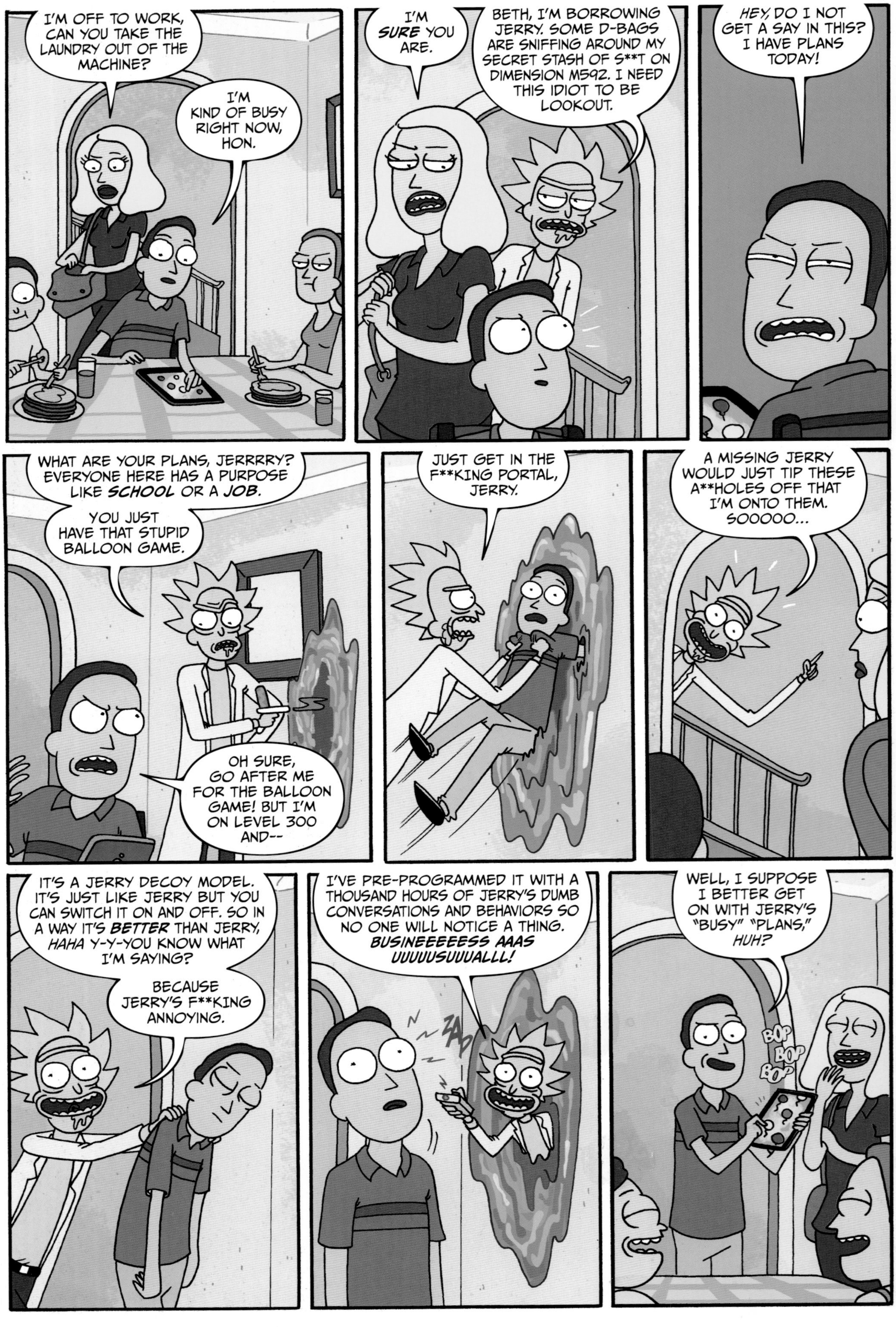
I'M OFF TO WORK, CAN YOU TAKE THE LAUNDRY OUT OF THE MACHINE?
I'M KIND OF BUSY RIGHT NOW, HON.
I'M *SURE* YOU ARE.
BETH, I'M BORROWING JERRY. SOME D-BAGS ARE SNIFFING AROUND MY SECRET STASH OF S**T ON DIMENSION M592. I NEED THIS IDIOT TO BE LOOKOUT.
HEY, DO I NOT GET A SAY IN THIS? I HAVE PLANS TODAY!
WHAT ARE YOUR PLANS, JERRRRY? EVERYONE HERE HAS A PURPOSE LIKE *SCHOOL* OR A *JOB*.
YOU JUST HAVE THAT STUPID BALLOON GAME.
OH SURE, GO AFTER ME FOR THE BALLOON GAME! BUT I'M ON LEVEL 300 AND--
JUST GET IN THE F**KING PORTAL, JERRY.
A MISSING JERRY WOULD JUST TIP THESE A**HOLES OFF THAT I'M ONTO THEM. SOOOOO...
IT'S A JERRY DECOY MODEL. IT'S JUST LIKE JERRY BUT YOU CAN SWITCH IT ON AND OFF. SO IN A WAY IT'S *BETTER* THAN JERRY, *HAHA* Y-Y-YOU KNOW WHAT I'M SAYING?
BECAUSE JERRY'S F**KING ANNOYING.
I'VE PRE-PROGRAMMED IT WITH A THOUSAND HOURS OF JERRY'S DUMB CONVERSATIONS AND BEHAVIORS SO NO ONE WILL NOTICE A THING.
BUSINEEEEESS AAAS UUUUUSUUUALLL!
ZAP
WELL, I SUPPOSE I BETTER GET ON WITH JERRY'S "BUSY" "PLANS," *HUH?*
BOP
BOP
BOP

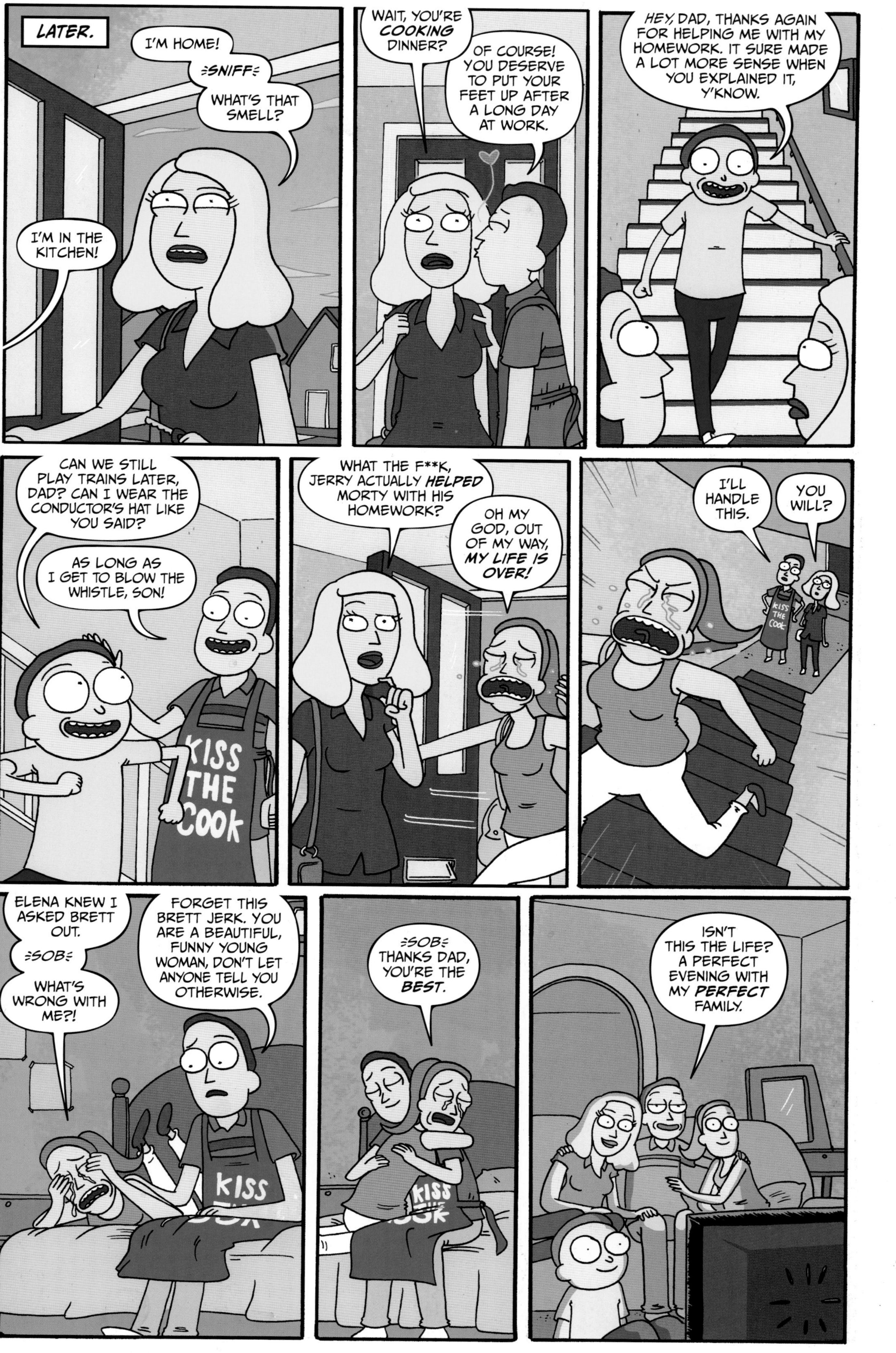
LATER.
I'M HOME!
SNIFF
WHAT'S THAT SMELL?
I'M IN THE KITCHEN!
WAIT, YOU'RE COOKING DINNER?
OF COURSE! YOU DESERVE TO PUT YOUR FEET UP AFTER A LONG DAY AT WORK.
HEY, DAD, THANKS AGAIN FOR HELPING ME WITH MY HOMEWORK. IT SURE MADE A LOT MORE SENSE WHEN YOU EXPLAINED IT, Y'KNOW.
CAN WE STILL PLAY TRAINS LATER, DAD? CAN I WEAR THE CONDUCTOR'S HAT LIKE YOU SAID?
AS LONG AS I GET TO BLOW THE WHISTLE, SON!
KISS THE COOK
WHAT THE F**K, JERRY ACTUALLY HELPED MORTY WITH HIS HOMEWORK?
OH MY GOD, OUT OF MY WAY, MY LIFE IS OVER!
I'LL HANDLE THIS.
YOU WILL?
KISS THE COOK
ELENA KNEW I ASKED BRETT OUT.
SOB
WHAT'S WRONG WITH ME?!
FORGET THIS BRETT JERK. YOU ARE A BEAUTIFUL, FUNNY YOUNG WOMAN, DON'T LET ANYONE TELL YOU OTHERWISE.
SOB
THANKS DAD, YOU'RE THE BEST.
ISN'T THIS THE LIFE? A PERFECT EVENING WITH MY PERFECT FAMILY.

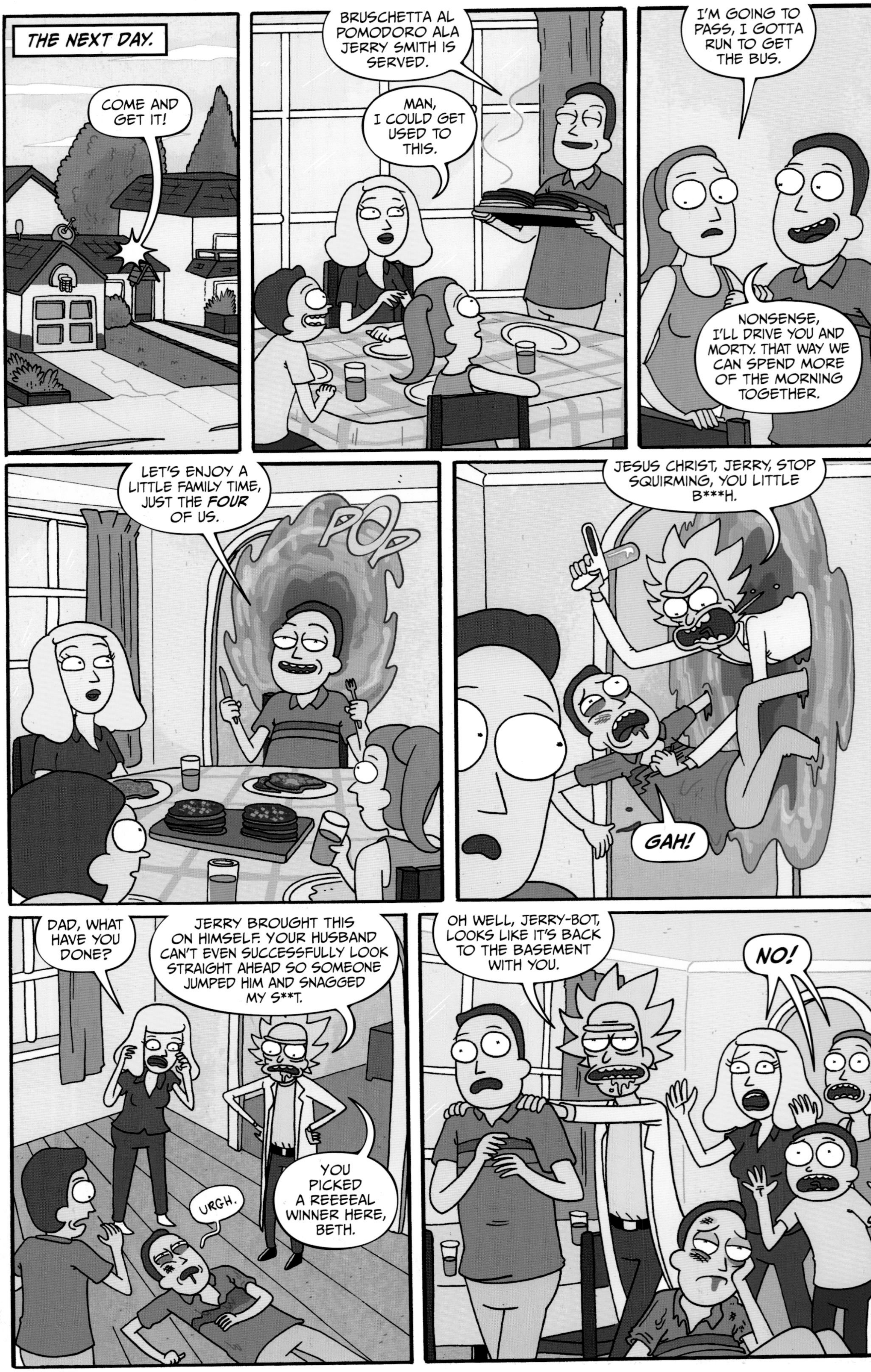
THE NEXT DAY.
COME AND GET IT!
BRUSCHETTA AL POMODORO ALA JERRY SMITH IS SERVED.
MAN, I COULD GET USED TO THIS.
I'M GOING TO PASS, I GOTTA RUN TO GET THE BUS.
NONSENSE, I'LL DRIVE YOU AND MORTY. THAT WAY WE CAN SPEND MORE OF THE MORNING TOGETHER.
LET'S ENJOY A LITTLE FAMILY TIME, JUST THE FOUR OF US.
POP
JESUS CHRIST, JERRY, STOP SQUIRMING, YOU LITTLE B***H.
GAH!
DAD, WHAT HAVE YOU DONE?
JERRY BROUGHT THIS ON HIMSELF. YOUR HUSBAND CAN'T EVEN SUCCESSFULLY LOOK STRAIGHT AHEAD SO SOMEONE JUMPED HIM AND SNAGGED MY S**T.
URGH.
YOU PICKED A REEEEAL WINNER HERE, BETH.
OH WELL, JERRY-BOT, LOOKS LIKE IT'S BACK TO THE BASEMENT WITH YOU.
NO!

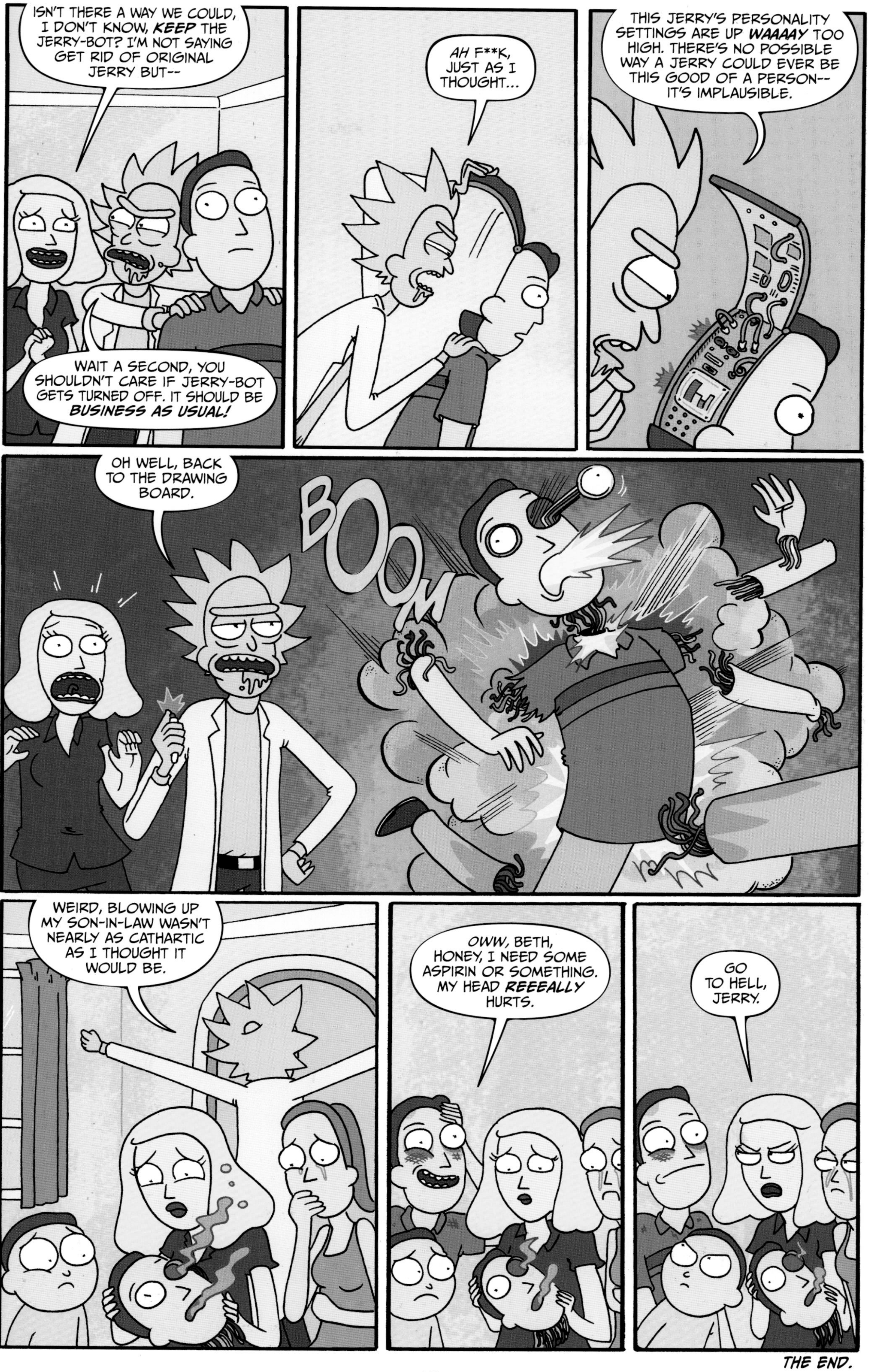
ISN'T THERE A WAY WE COULD, I DON'T KNOW, KEEP THE JERRY-BOT? I'M NOT SAYING GET RID OF ORIGINAL JERRY BUT--
WAIT A SECOND, YOU SHOULDN'T CARE IF JERRY-BOT GETS TURNED OFF. IT SHOULD BE BUSINESS AS USUAL!
AH F**K, JUST AS I THOUGHT...
THIS JERRY'S PERSONALITY SETTINGS ARE UP WAAAAY TOO HIGH. THERE'S NO POSSIBLE WAY A JERRY COULD EVER BE THIS GOOD OF A PERSON-- IT'S IMPLAUSIBLE.
OH WELL, BACK TO THE DRAWING BOARD.
BOOOM
WEIRD, BLOWING UP MY SON-IN-LAW WASN'T NEARLY AS CATHARTIC AS I THOUGHT IT WOULD BE.
OWW, BETH, HONEY, I NEED SOME ASPIRIN OR SOMETHING. MY HEAD REEEALLY HURTS.
GO TO HELL, JERRY.
THE END.

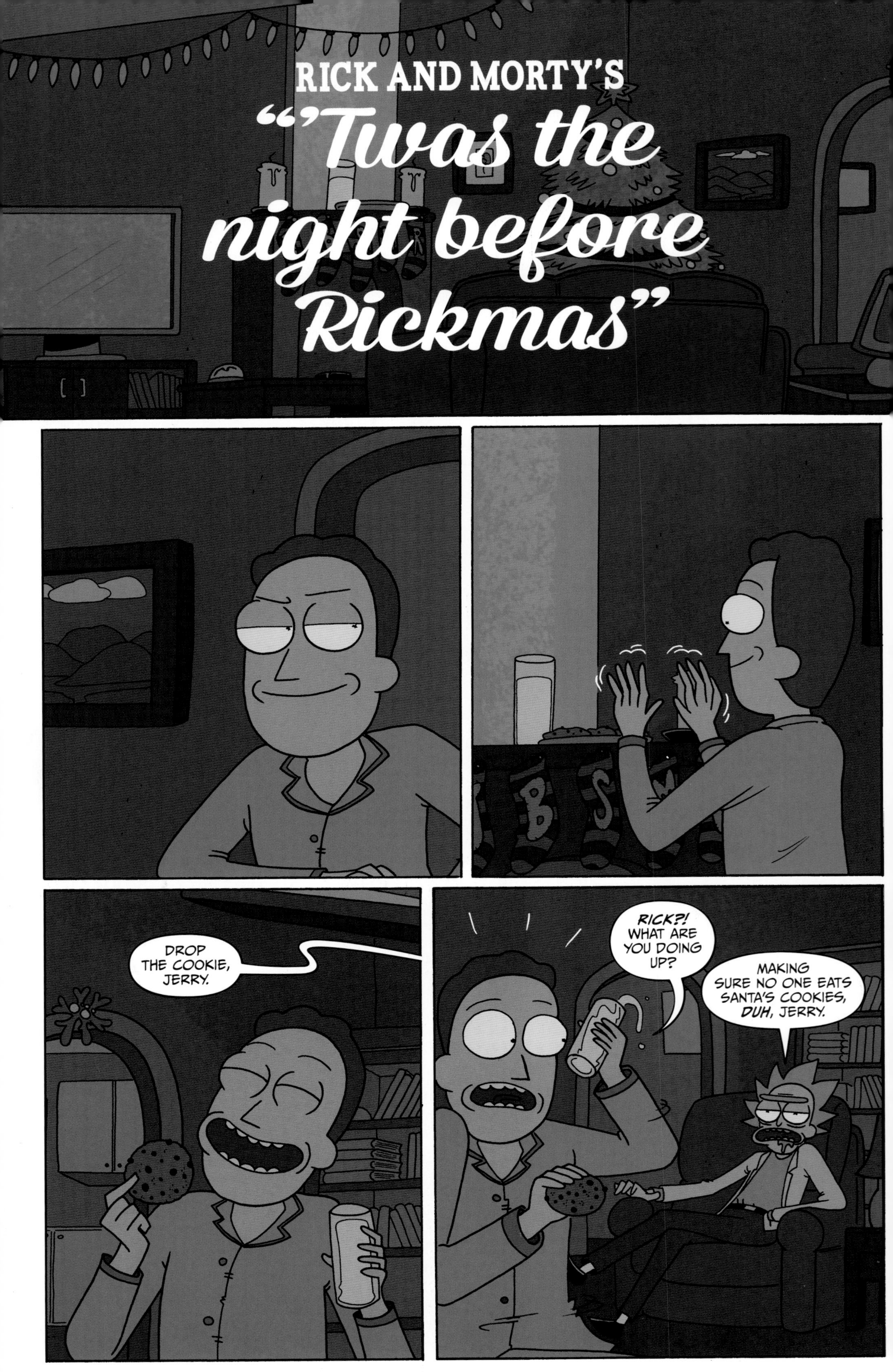
RICK AND MORTY'S
"'Twas the night before Rickmas"
DROP THE COOKIE, JERRY.
RICK?! WHAT ARE YOU DOING UP?
MAKING SURE NO ONE EATS SANTA'S COOKIES, DUH, JERRY.

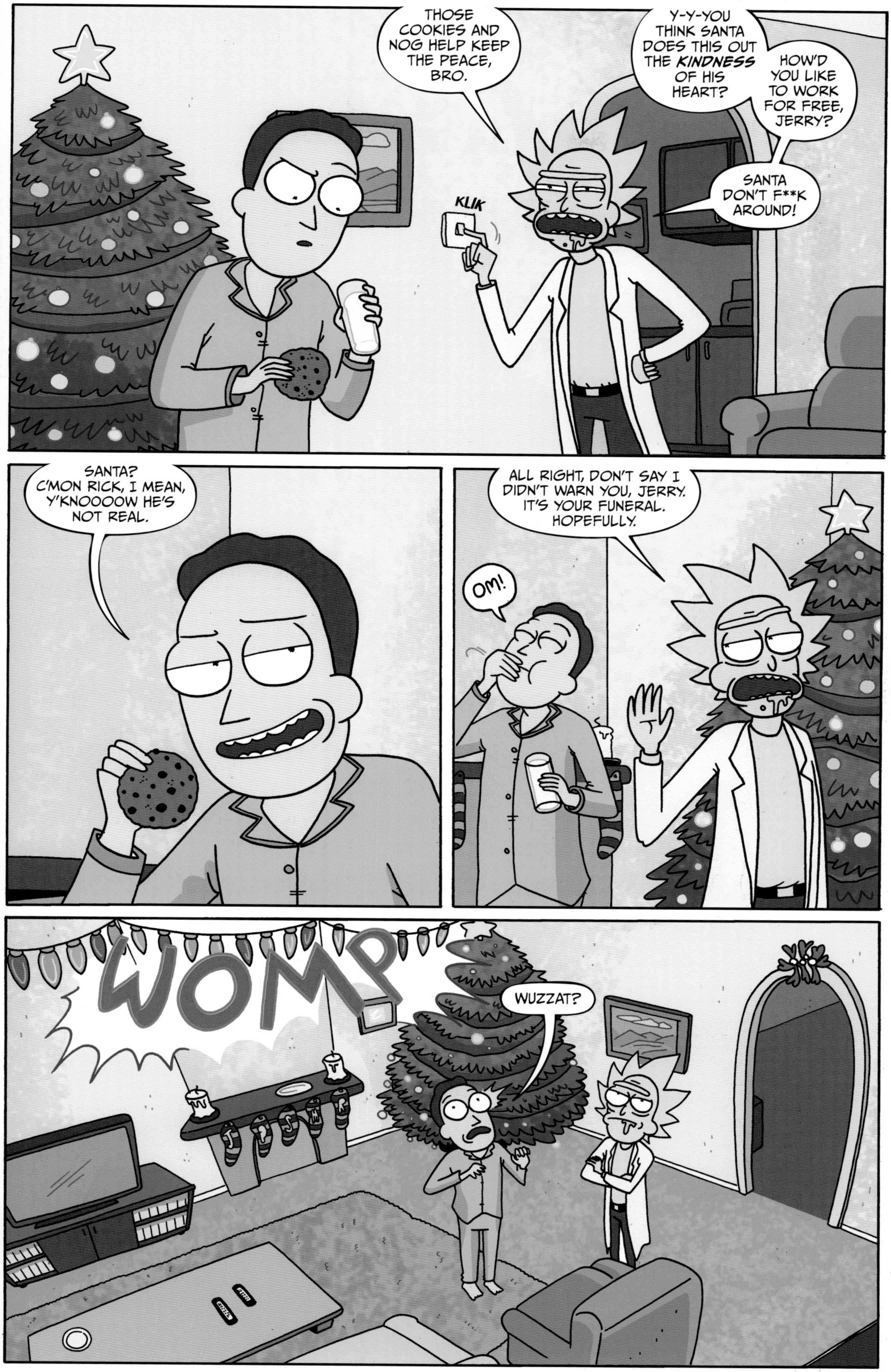
THOSE COOKIES AND NOG HELP KEEP THE PEACE, BRO.
KLIK
Y-Y-YOU THINK SANTA DOES THIS OUT THE KINDNESS OF HIS HEART?
HOW'D YOU LIKE TO WORK FOR FREE, JERRY?
SANTA DON'T F**K AROUND!
SANTA? C'MON RICK, I MEAN, Y'KNOOOOW HE'S NOT REAL.
ALL RIGHT, DON'T SAY I DIDN'T WARN YOU, JERRY. IT'S YOUR FUNERAL. HOPEFULLY.
OM!
WOMP
WUZZAT?

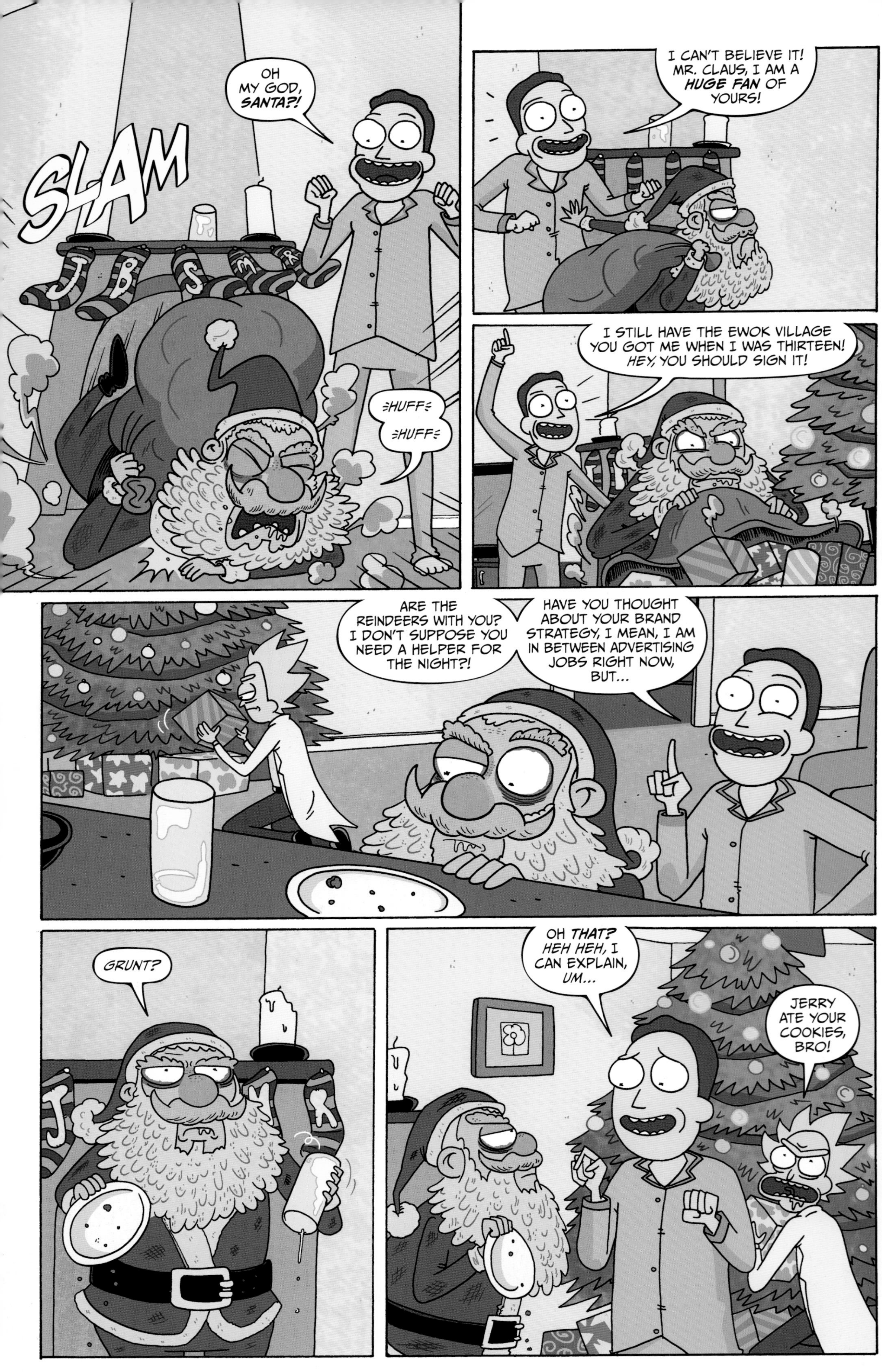
SLAM
OH MY GOD, SANTA?!
HUFF HUFF
I CAN'T BELIEVE IT! MR. CLAUS, I AM A HUGE FAN OF YOURS!
I STILL HAVE THE EWOK VILLAGE YOU GOT ME WHEN I WAS THIRTEEN! HEY, YOU SHOULD SIGN IT!
ARE THE REINDEERS WITH YOU? I DON'T SUPPOSE YOU NEED A HELPER FOR THE NIGHT?!
HAVE YOU THOUGHT ABOUT YOUR BRAND STRATEGY, I MEAN, I AM IN BETWEEN ADVERTISING JOBS RIGHT NOW, BUT...
GRUNT?
OH THAT? HEH HEH, I CAN EXPLAIN, UM...
JERRY ATE YOUR COOKIES, BRO!

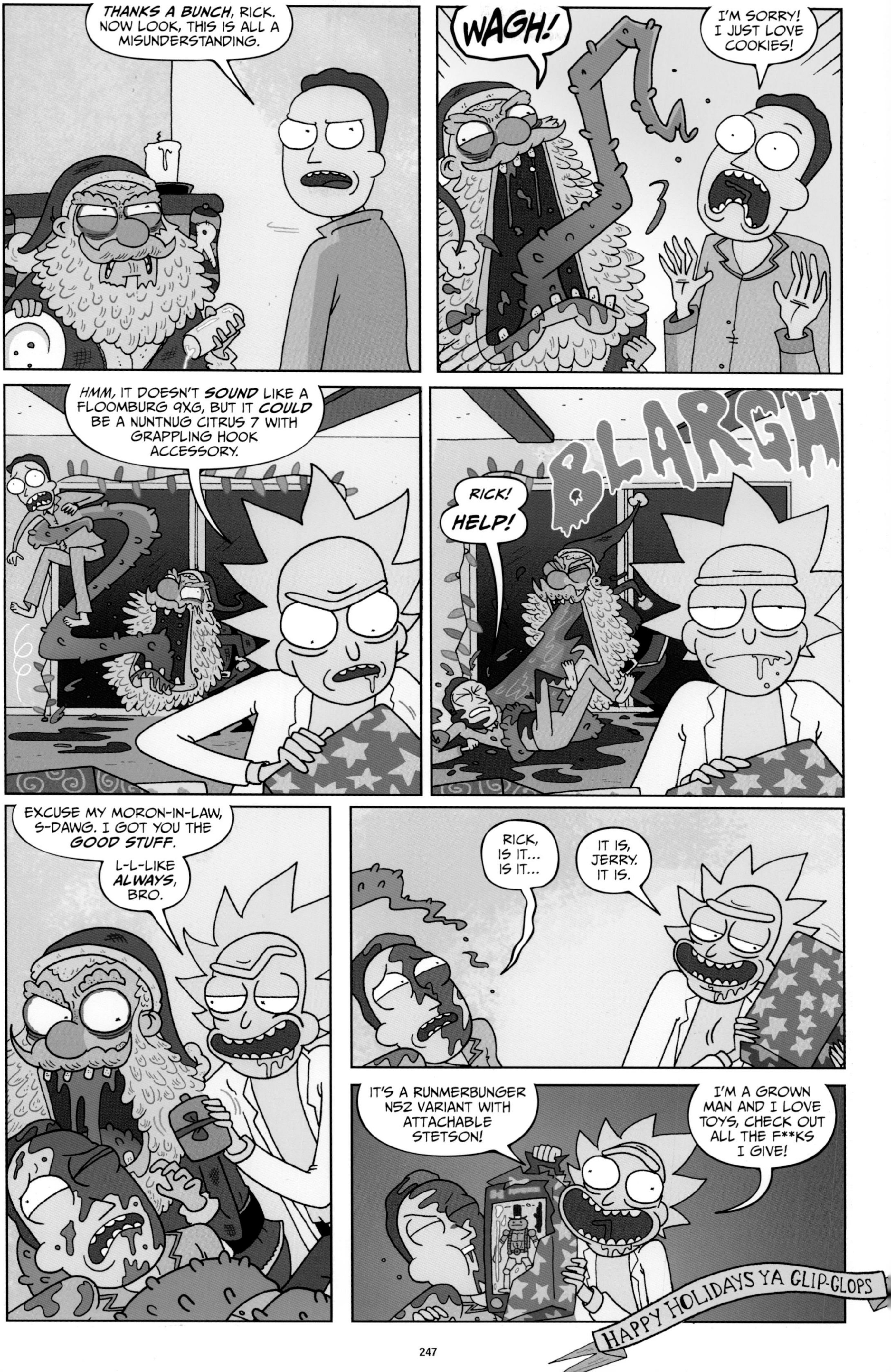
THANKS A BUNCH, RICK. NOW LOOK, THIS IS ALL A MISUNDERSTANDING.
WAGH!
I'M SORRY! I JUST LOVE COOKIES!
HMM, IT DOESN'T SOUND LIKE A FLOOMBURG 9XG, BUT IT COULD BE A NUNTNUG CITRUS 7 WITH GRAPPLING HOOK ACCESSORY.
BLARGH
RICK! HELP!
EXCUSE MY MORON-IN-LAW, S-DAWG. I GOT YOU THE GOOD STUFF.
L-L-LIKE ALWAYS, BRO.
RICK, IS IT... IS IT...
IT IS, JERRY. IT IS.
IT'S A RUNMERBUNGER N52 VARIANT WITH ATTACHABLE STETSON!
I'M A GROWN MAN AND I LOVE TOYS, CHECK OUT ALL THE F**KS I GIVE!
HAPPY HOLIDAYS YA GLIP-GLOPS

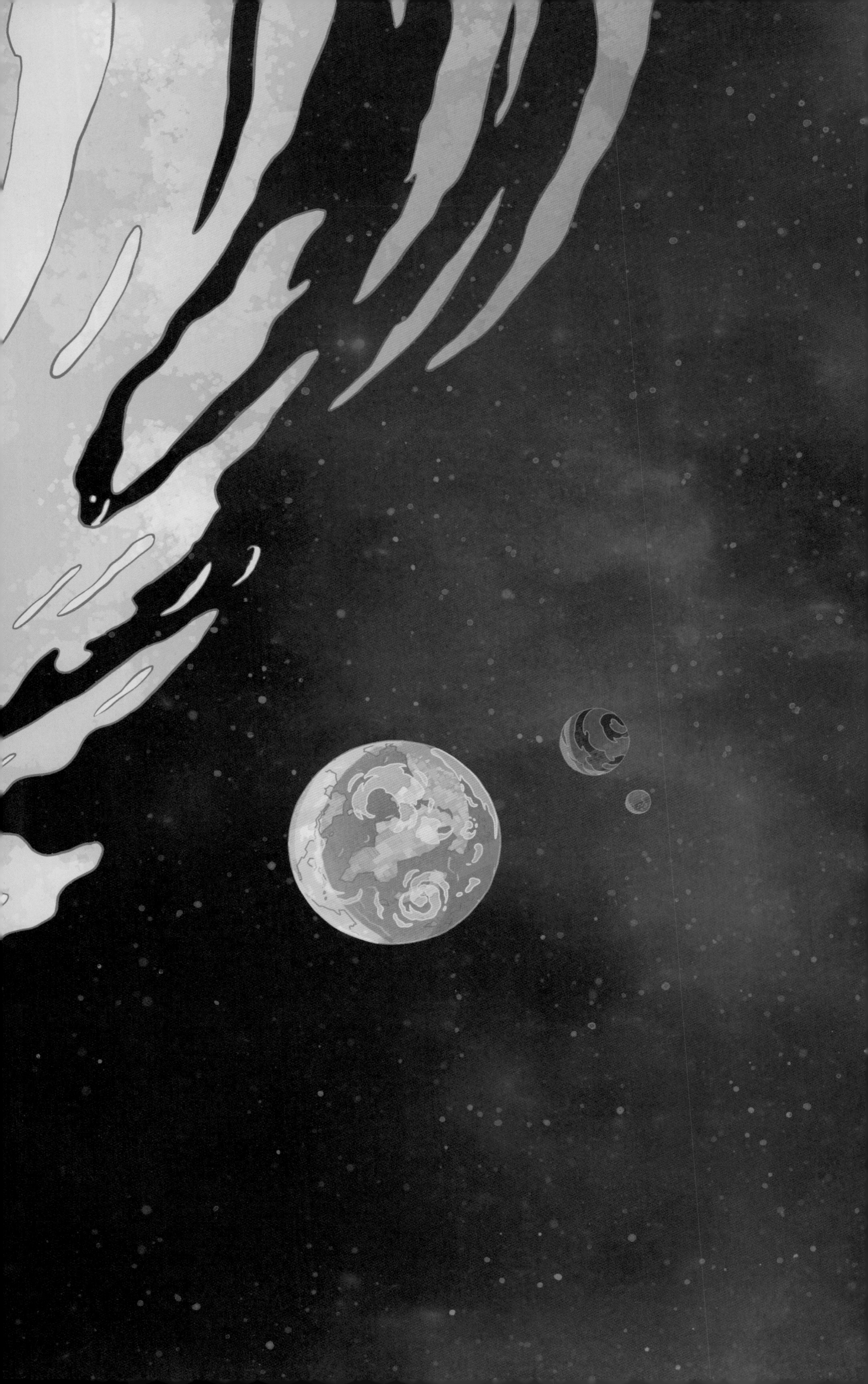

Rick and Morty

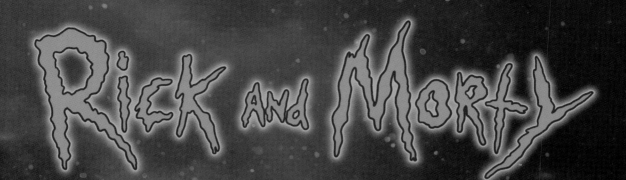

COVER GALLERY

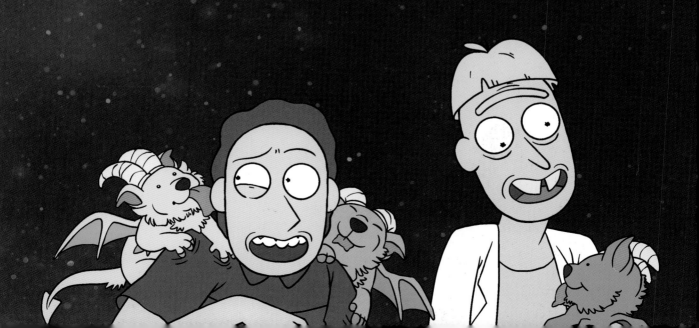

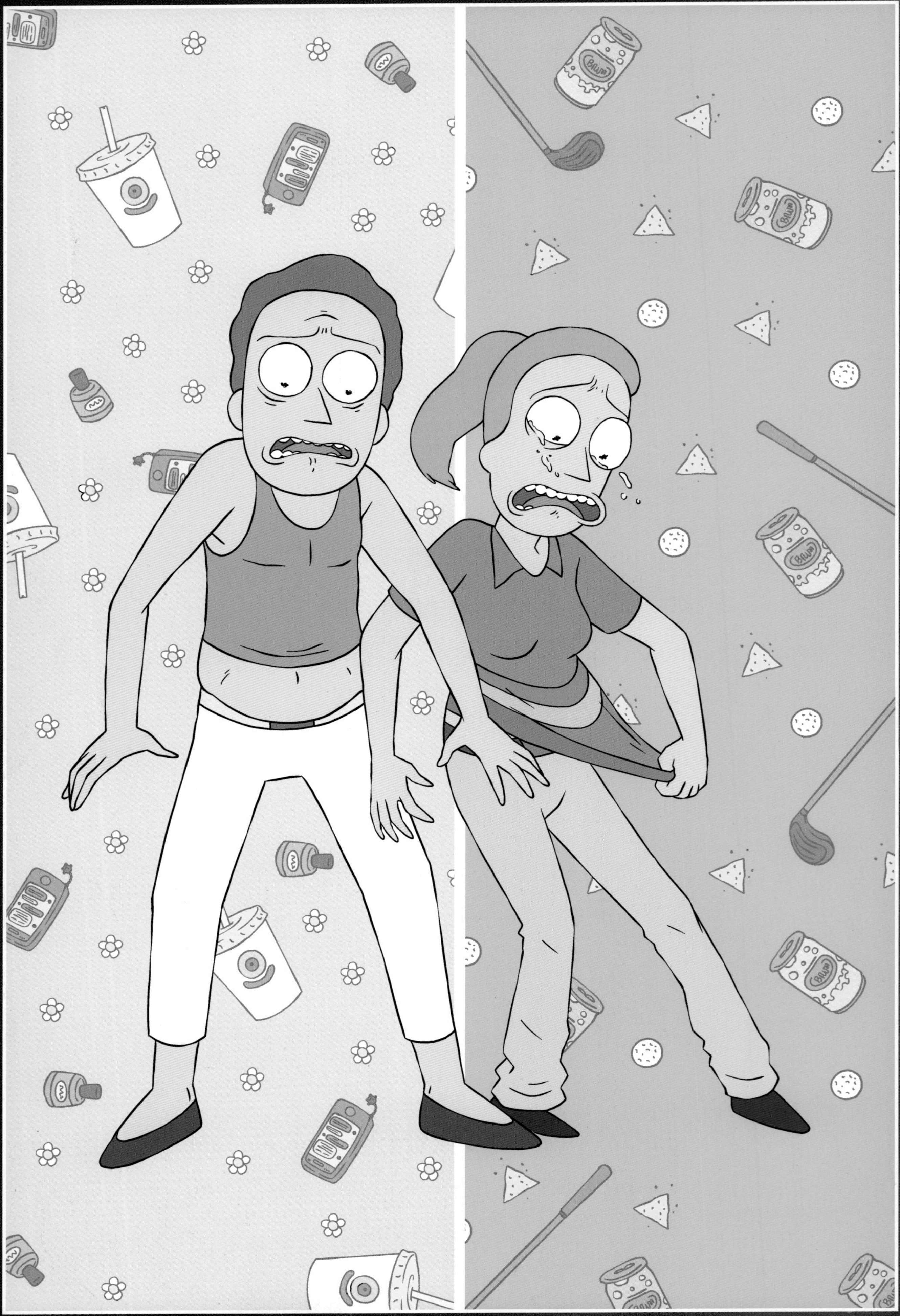

ISSUE #11 RETAIL COVER BY CJ CANNON AND RYAN HILL

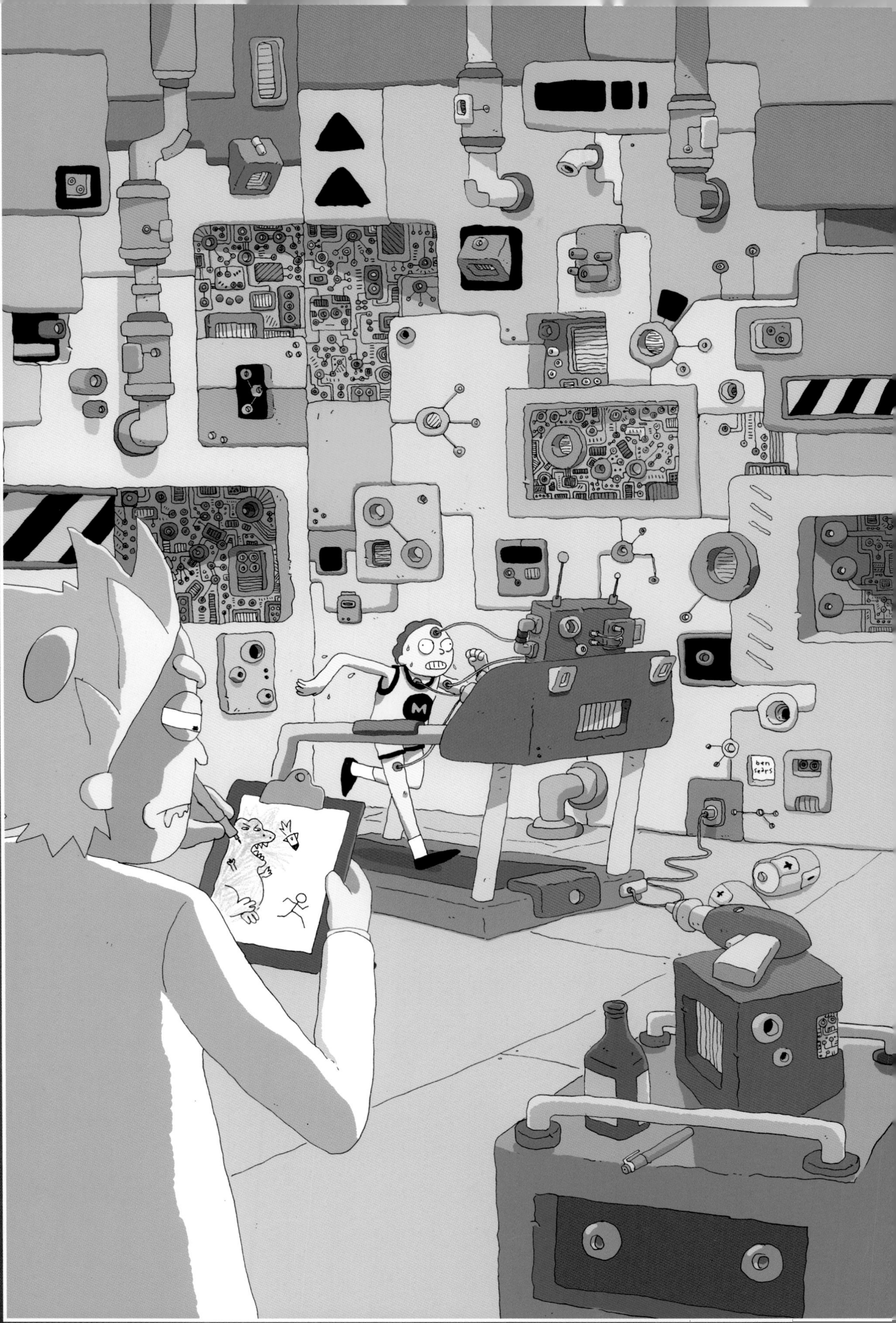
ben sears

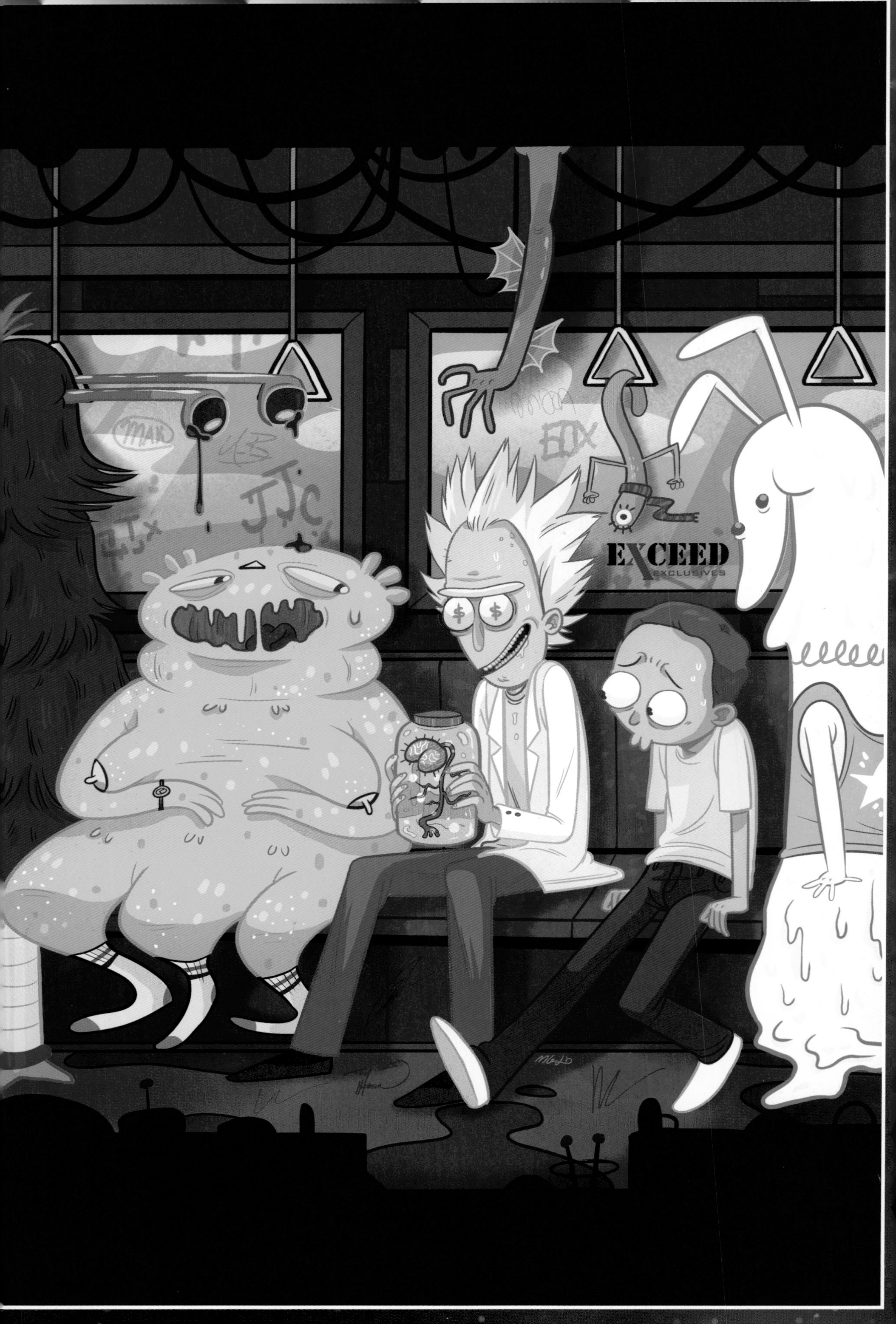
EXCEED
EXCLUSIVES

ISSUE #11 EXCEED EXCLUSIVES COVER BY MADY G

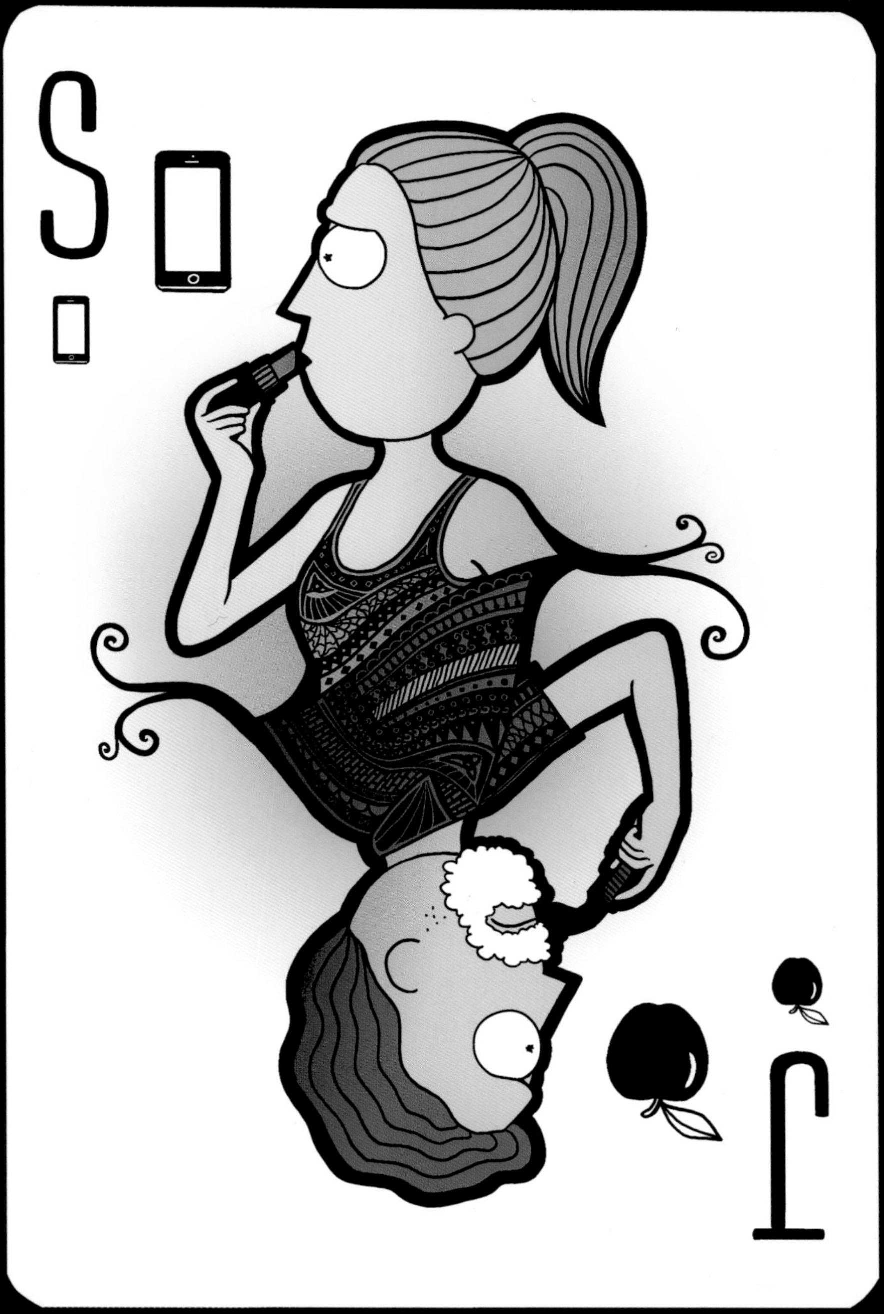
S

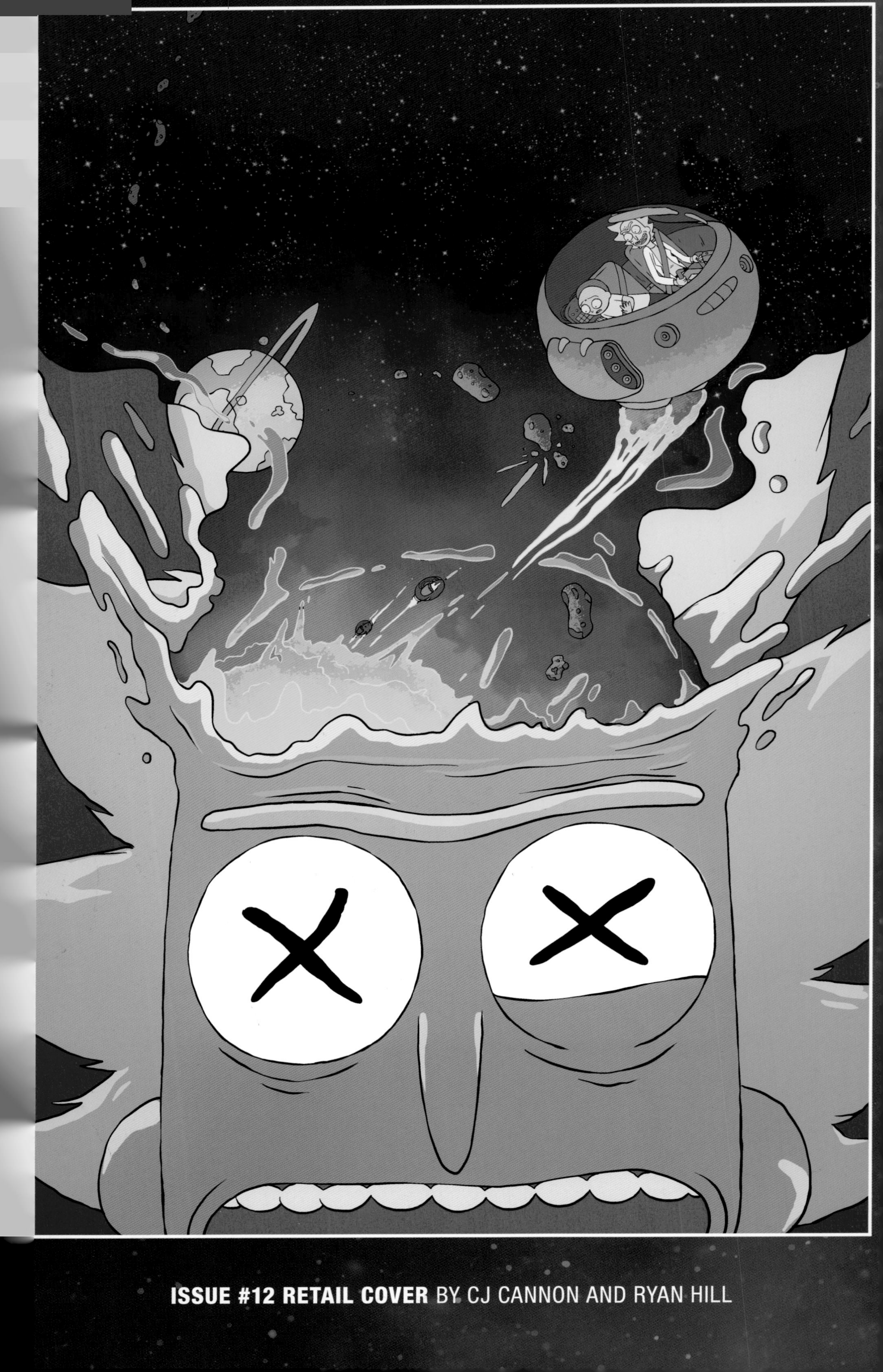

ISSUE #12 RETAIL COVER BY CJ CANNON AND RYAN HILL

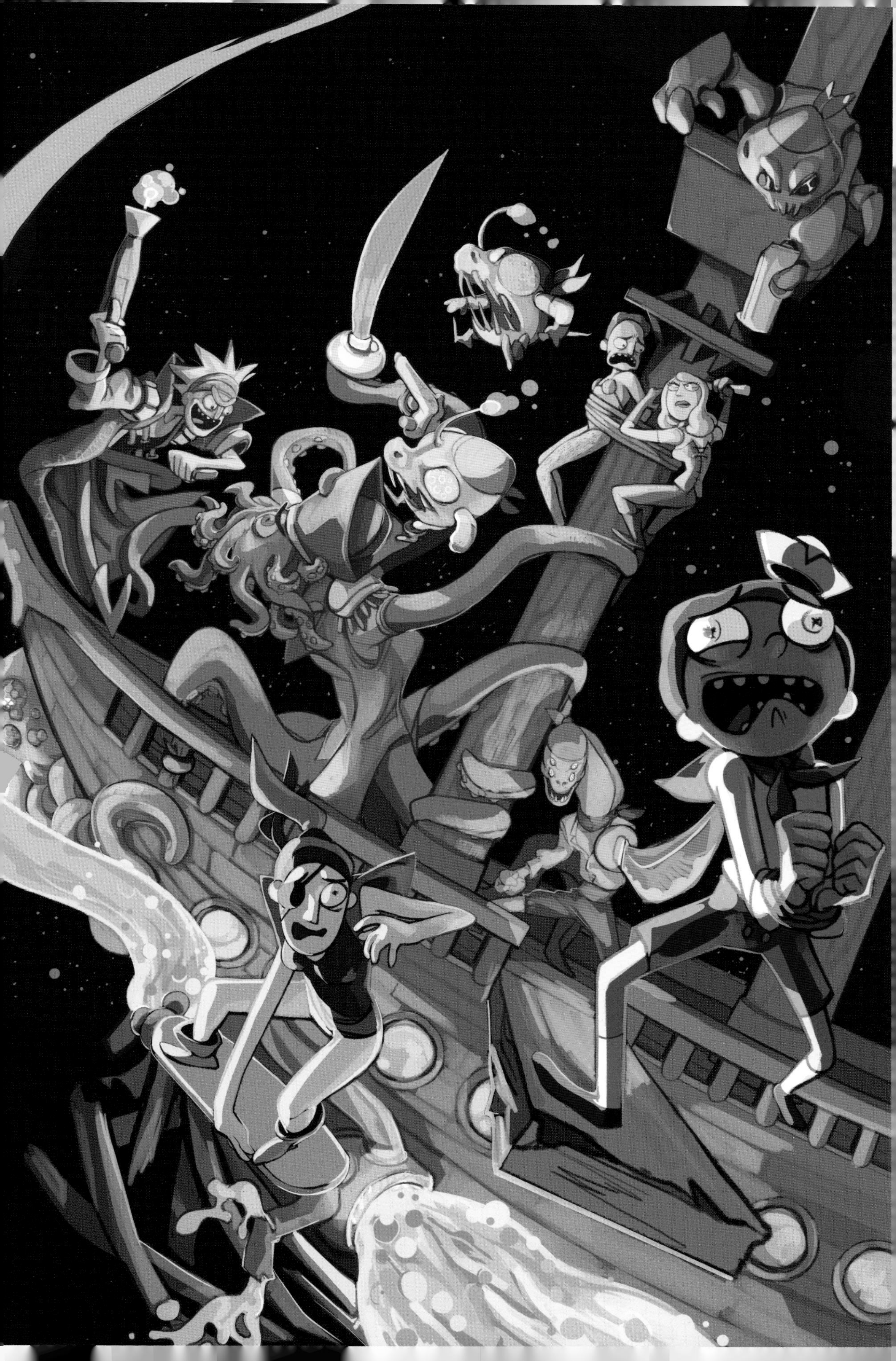

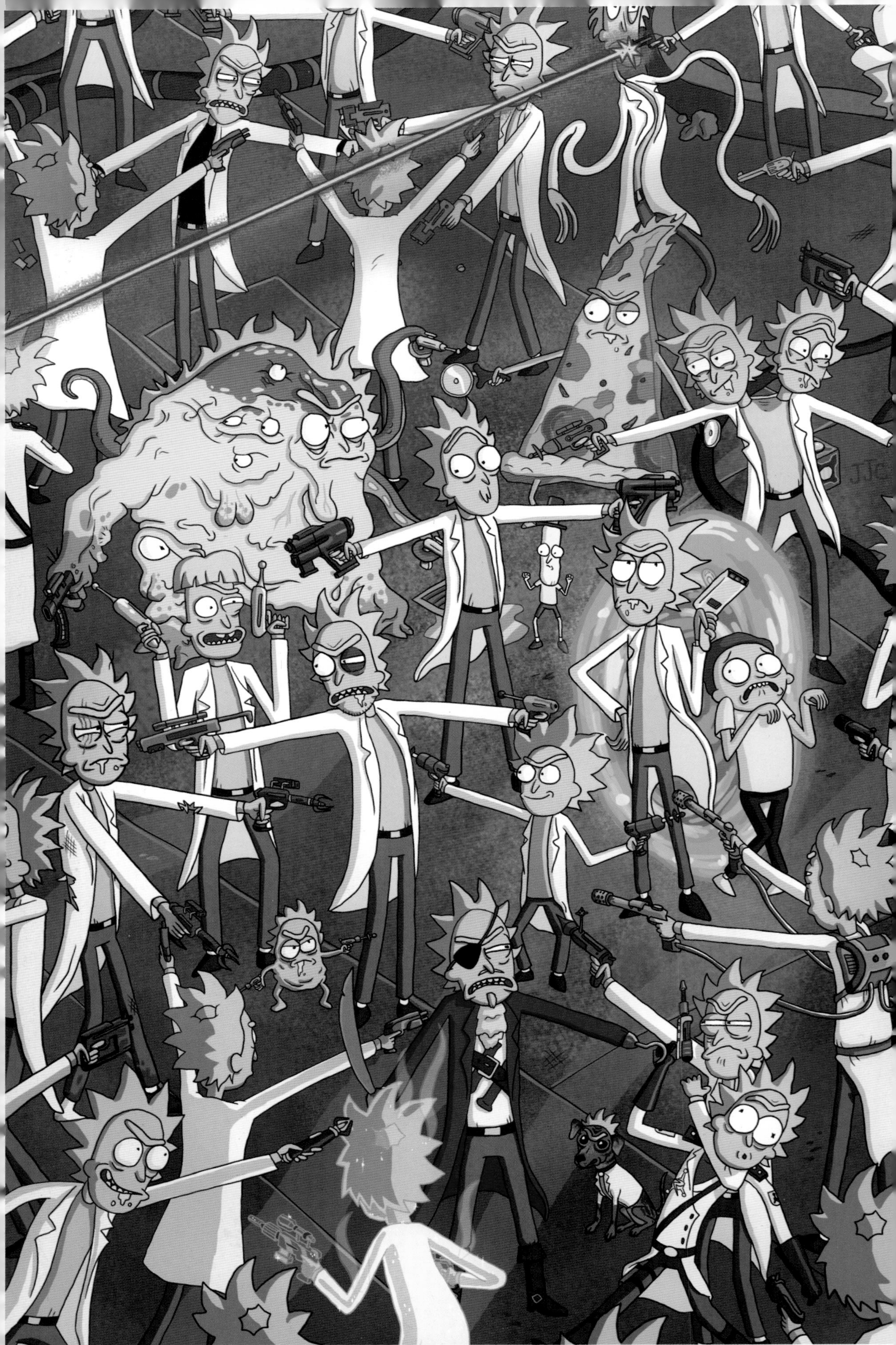

ISSUE #12 EXCEED EXCLUSIVES COVER BY RICHARD VAN AS

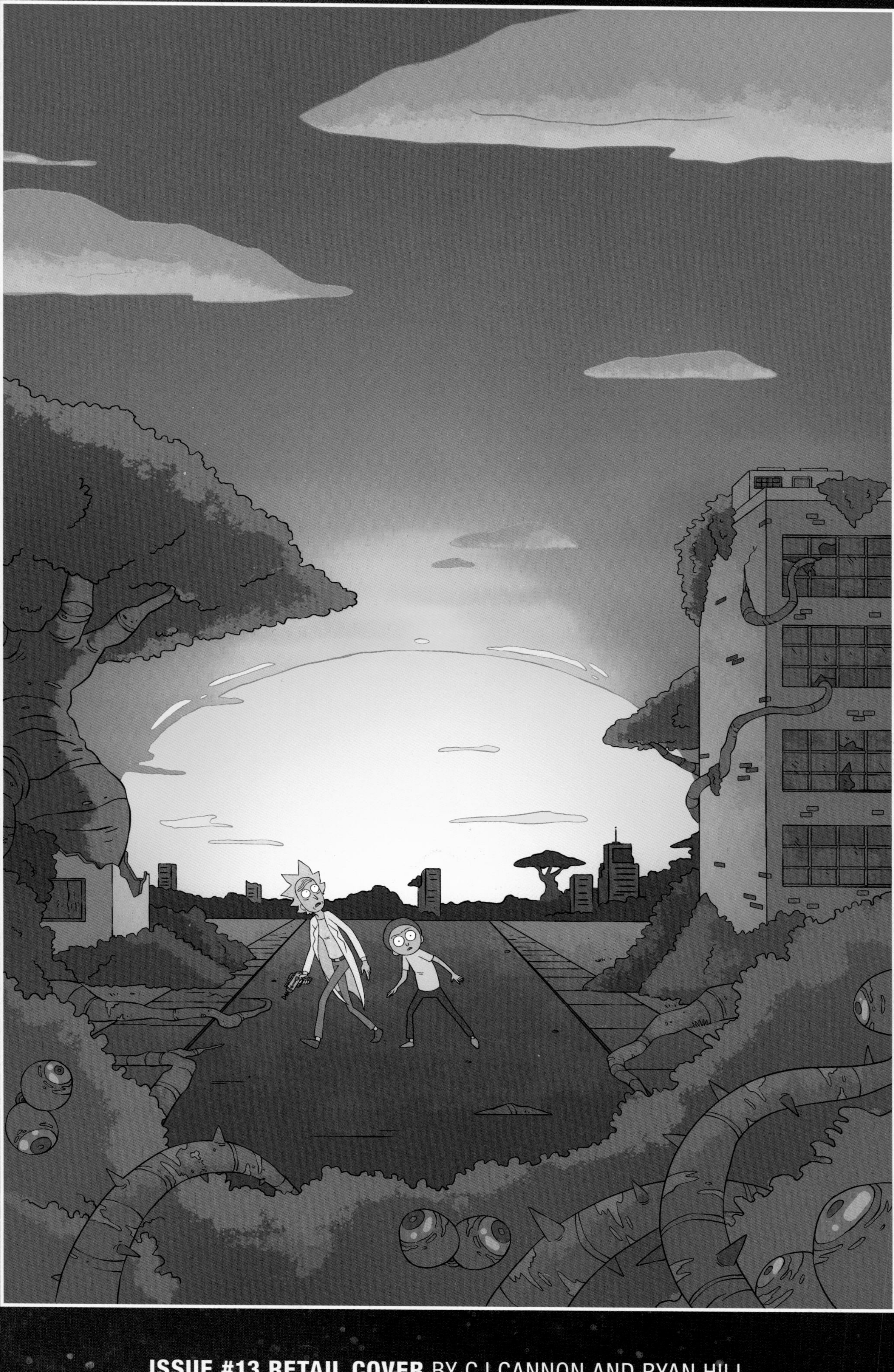

ISSUE #13 RETAIL COVER BY CJ CANNON AND RYAN HILL

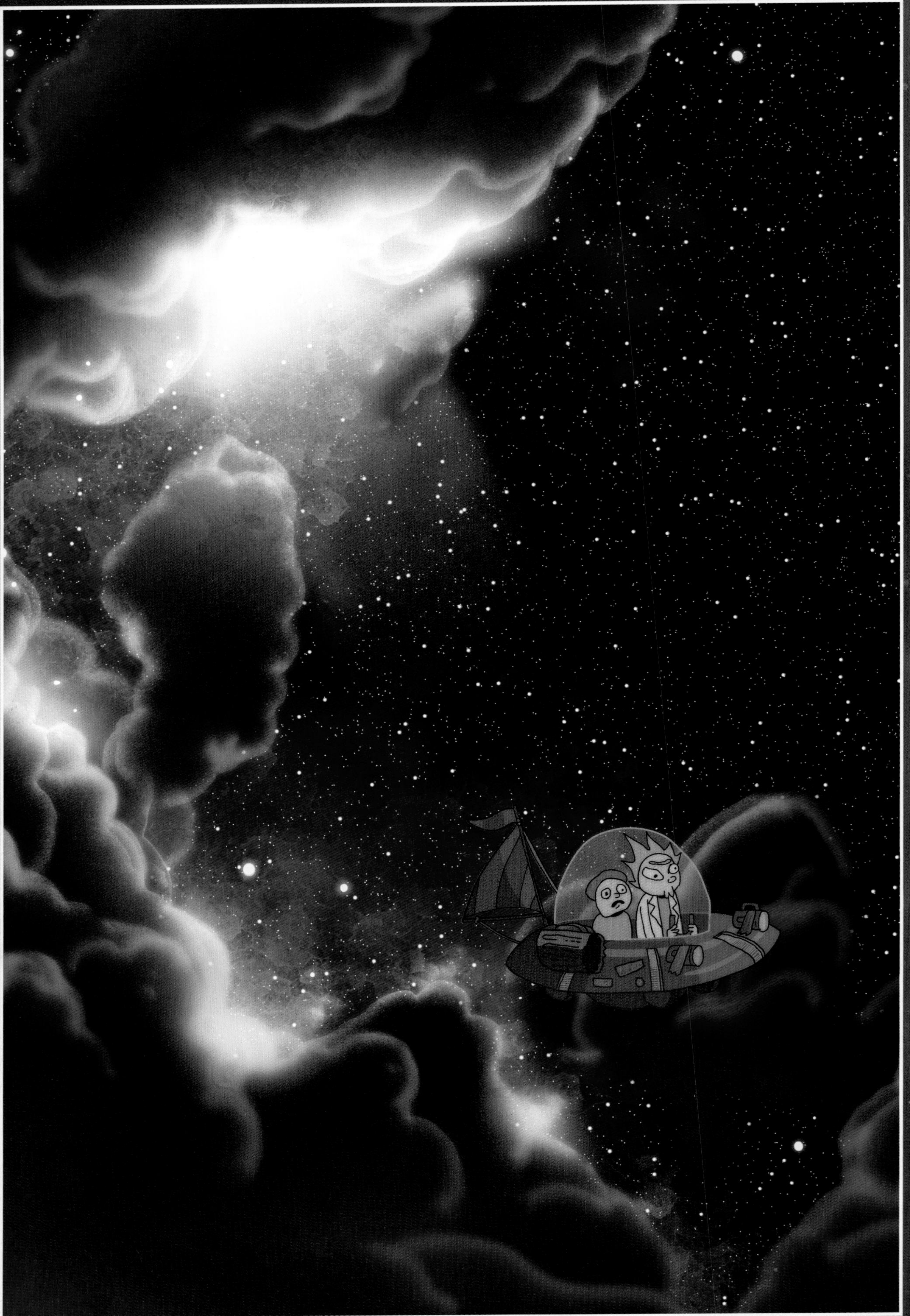

ISSUE #13 ALTERNATE COVER BY KC GREEN AND ANTHONY CLARK

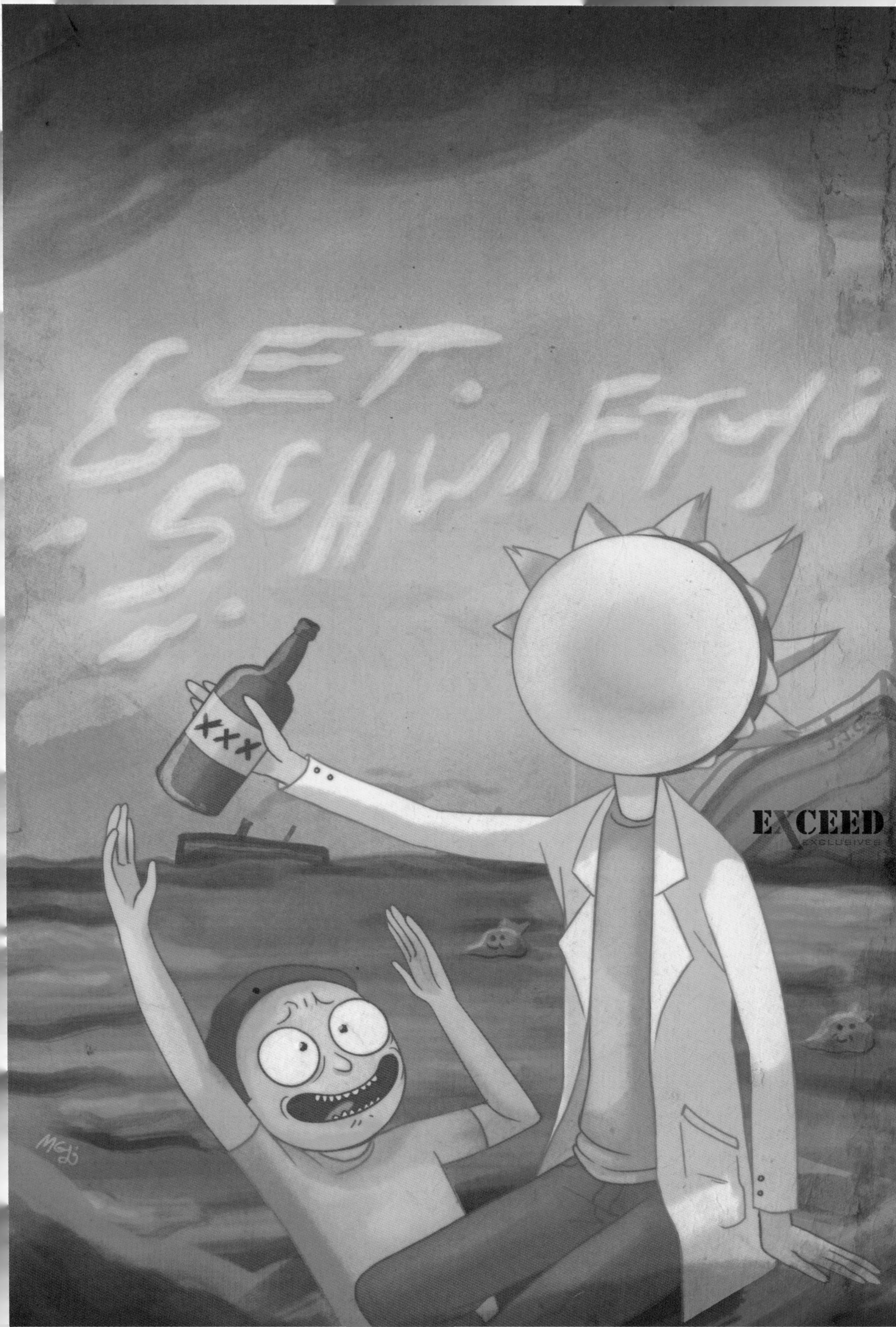
GET SCHWIFTY
XXX
EXCEED
EXCLUSIVES

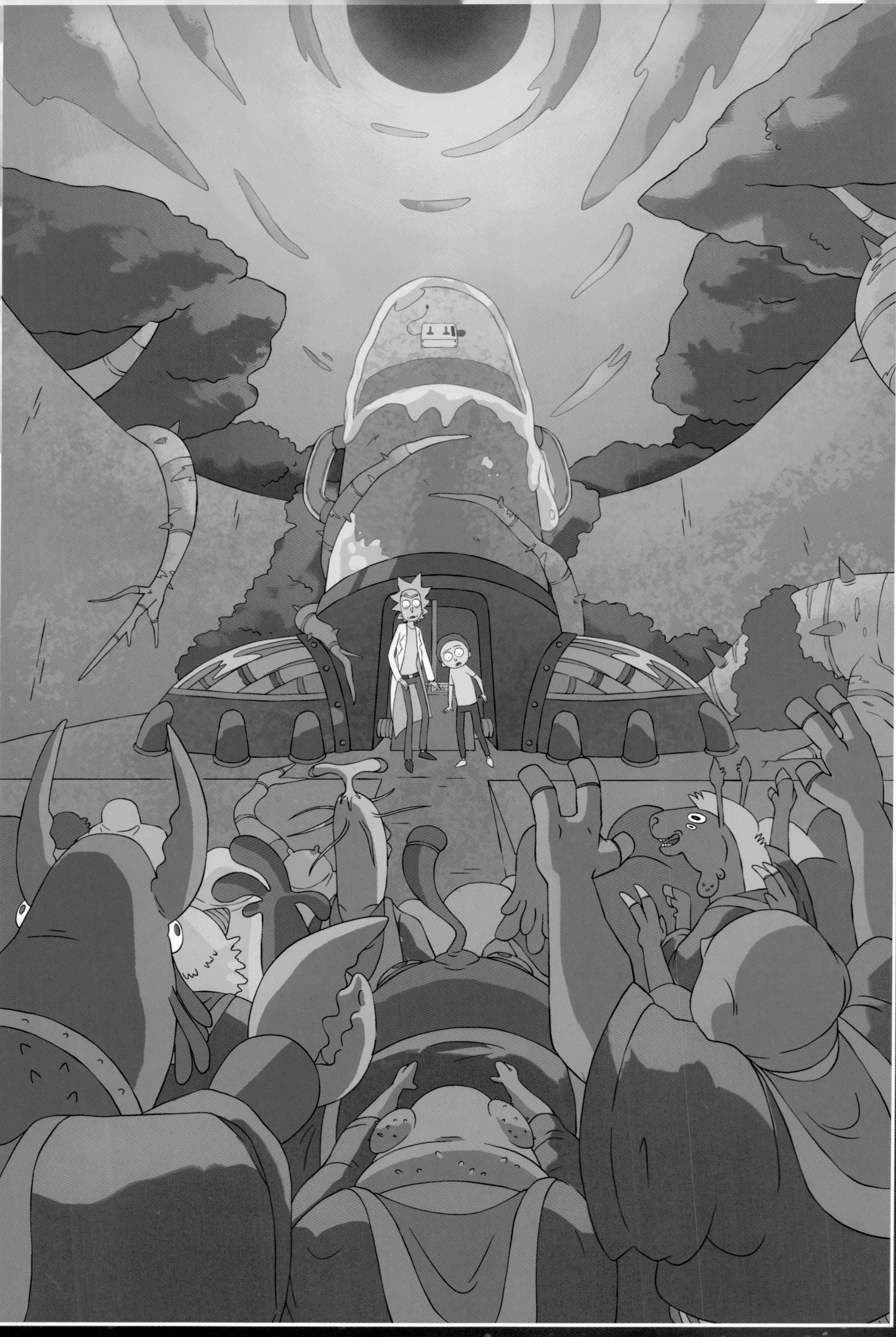

ISSUE #14 RETAIL COVER BY CJ CANNON AND RYAN HILL

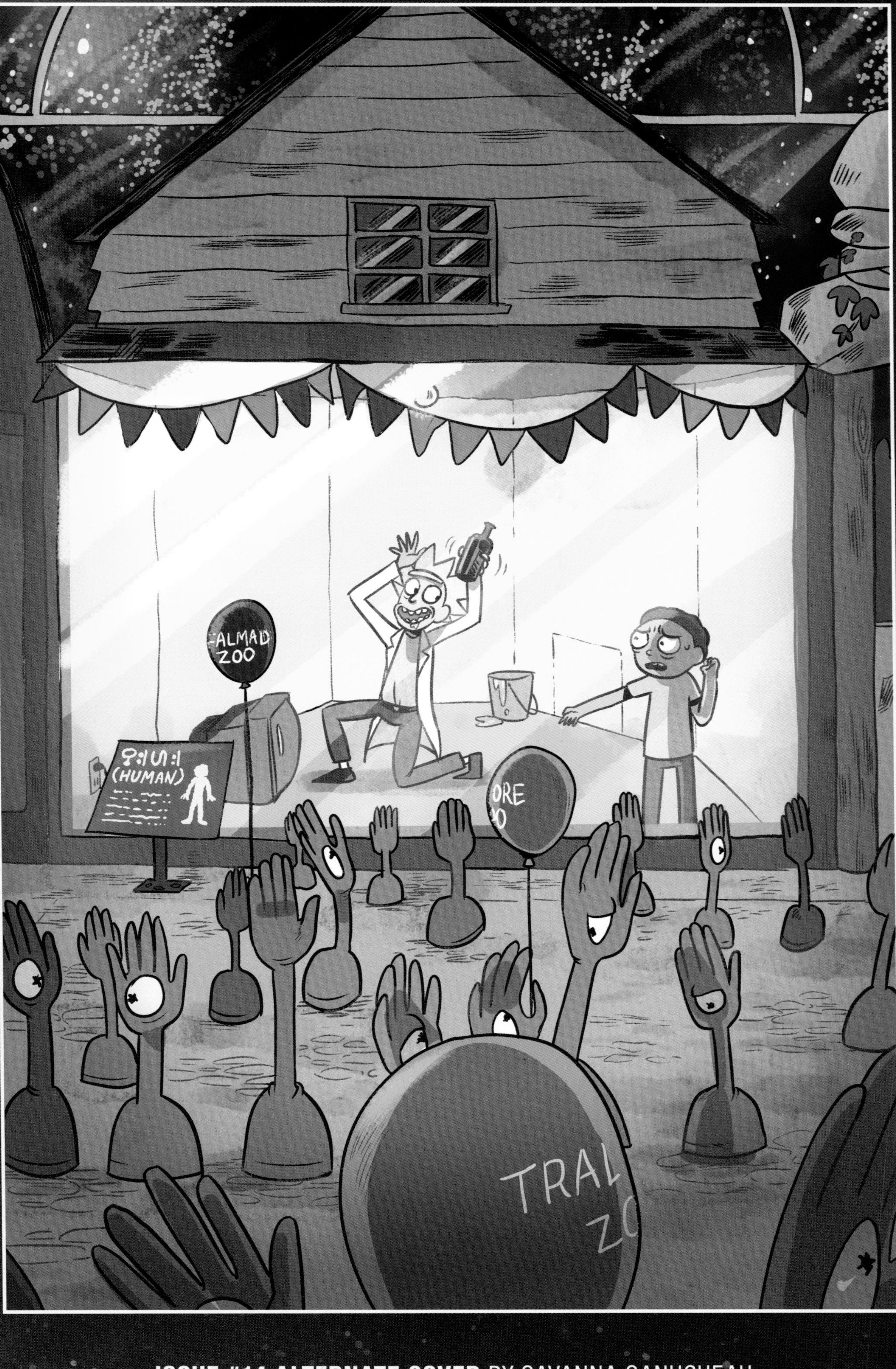
FALMAD ZOO
(HUMAN)
ORE ZO
TRAL ZO

ISSUE #14 ALTERNATE COVER BY SAVANNA GANUCHEAU

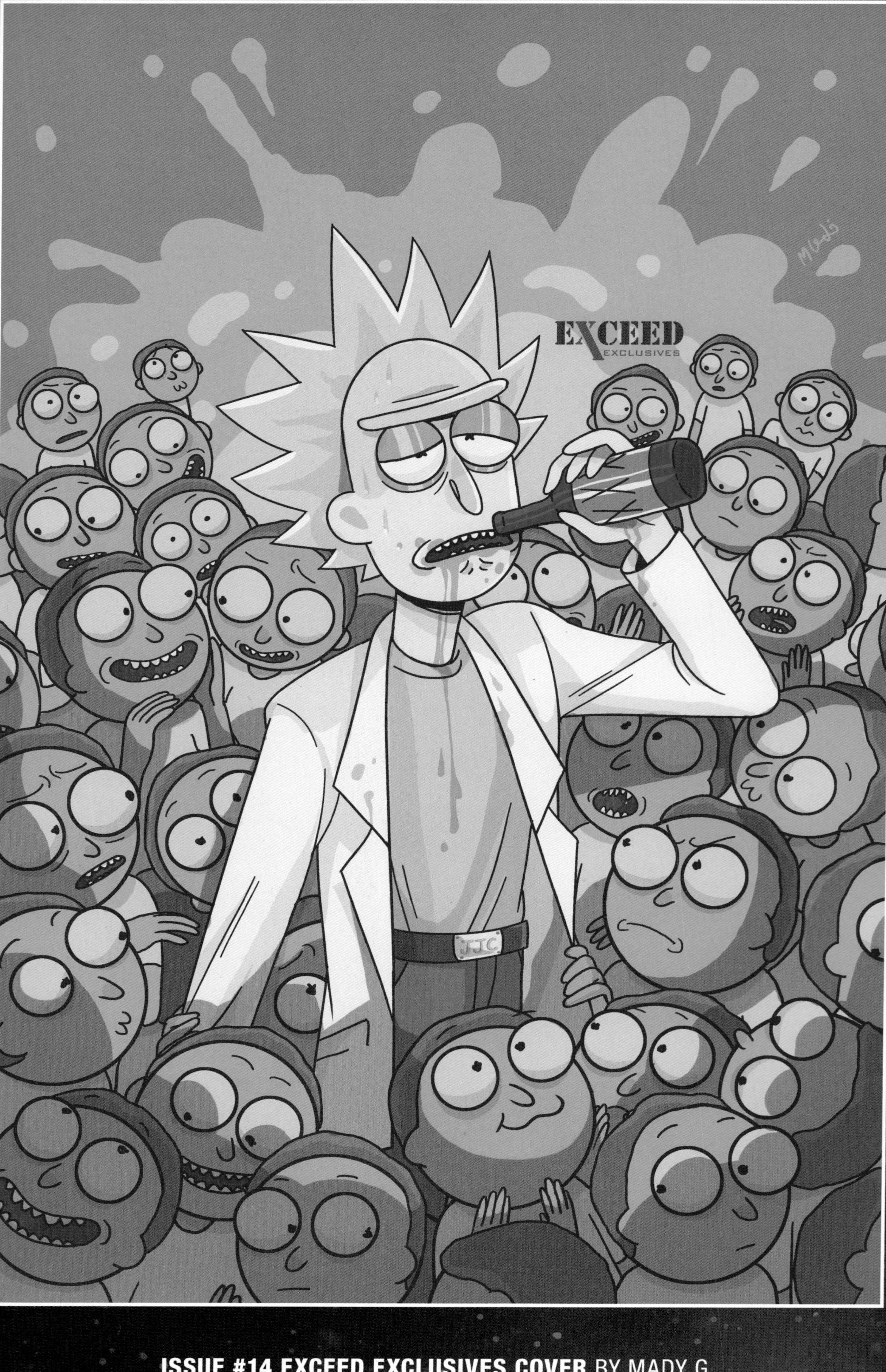
EXCEED
EXCLUSIVES
JJC

ISSUE #14 EXCEED EXCLUSIVES COVER BY MADY G

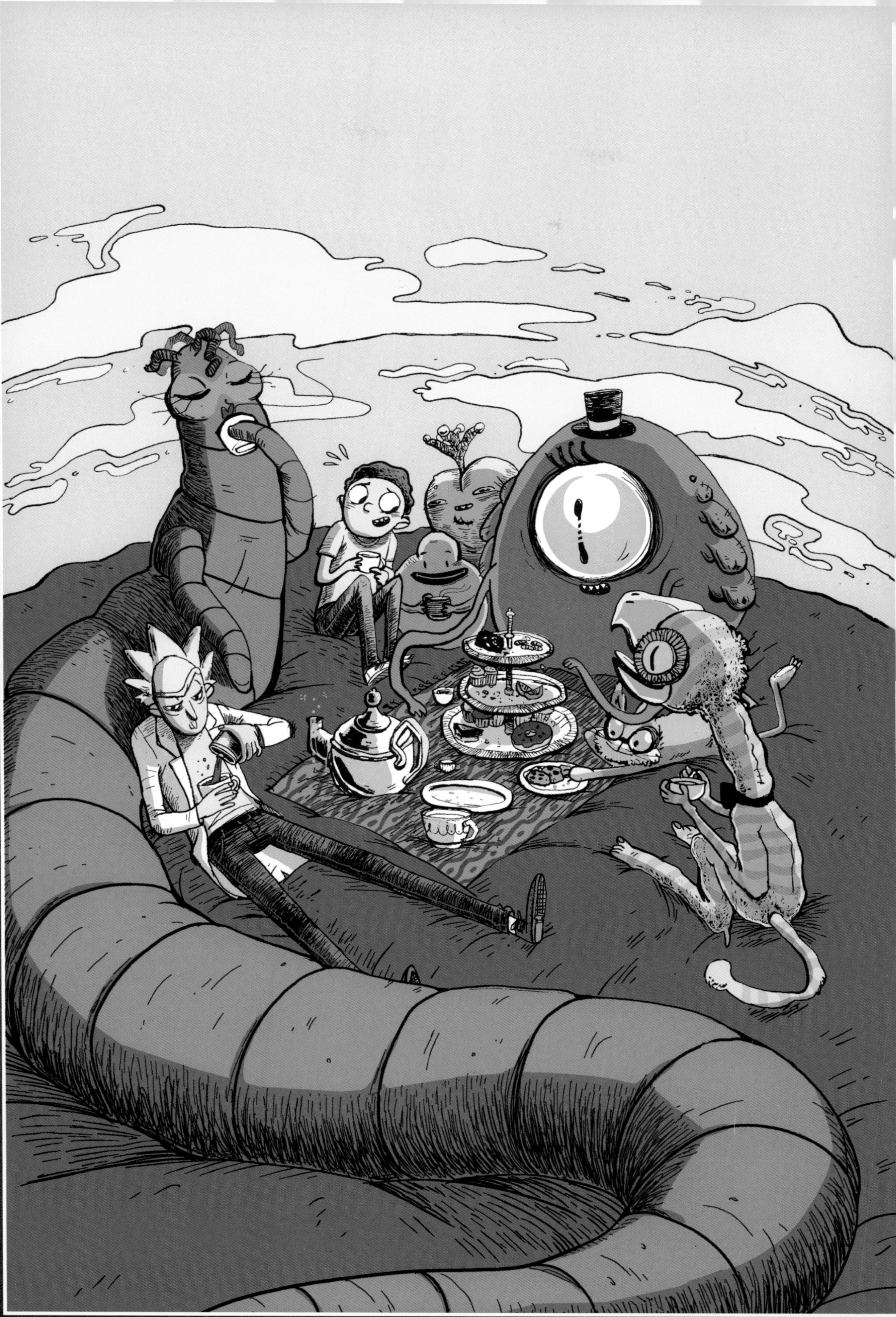

ISSUE #14 FRIED PIE CON COVER BY EMMETT HELEN

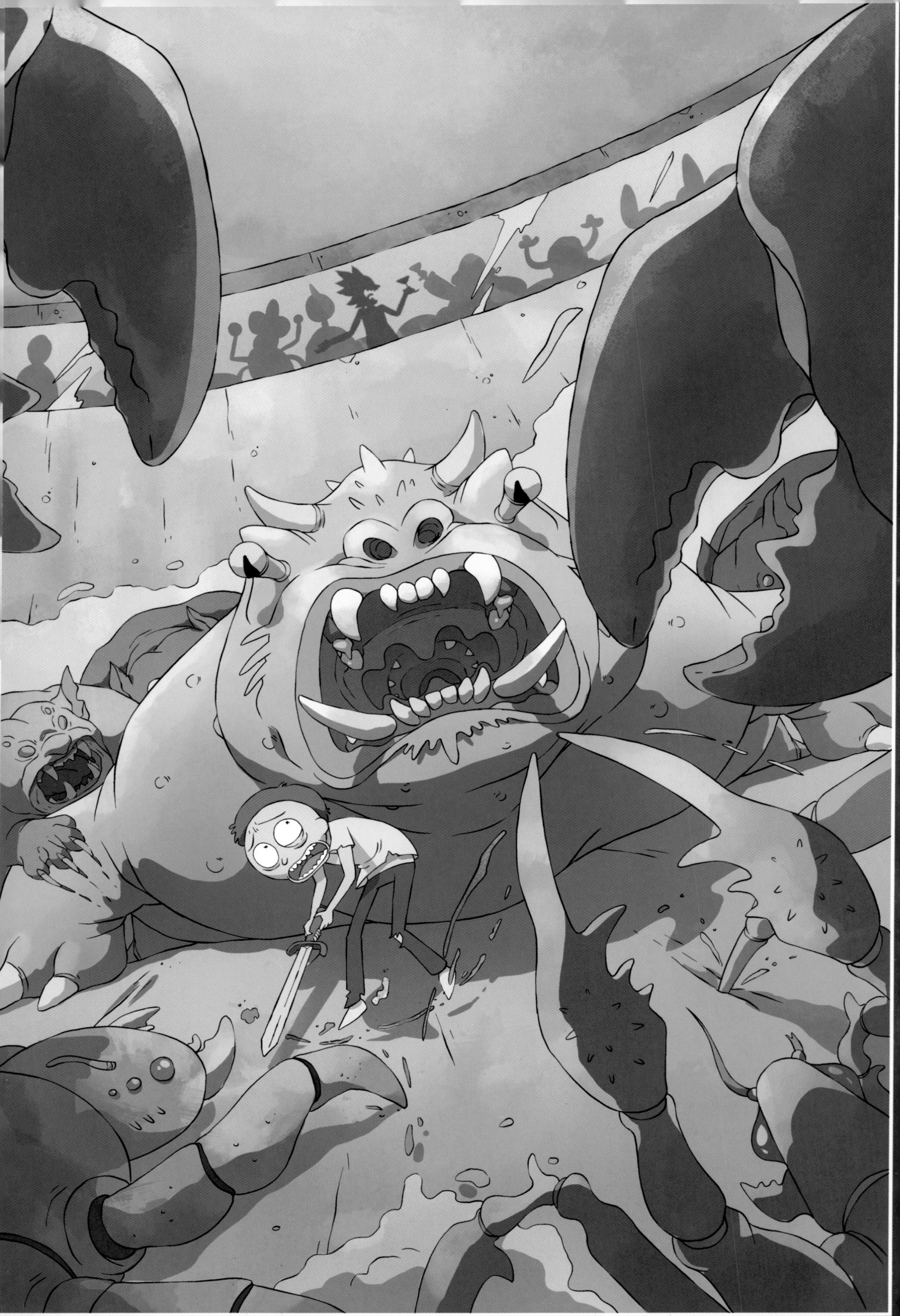

ISSUE #15 RETAIL COVER BY CJ CANNON AND RYAN HILL

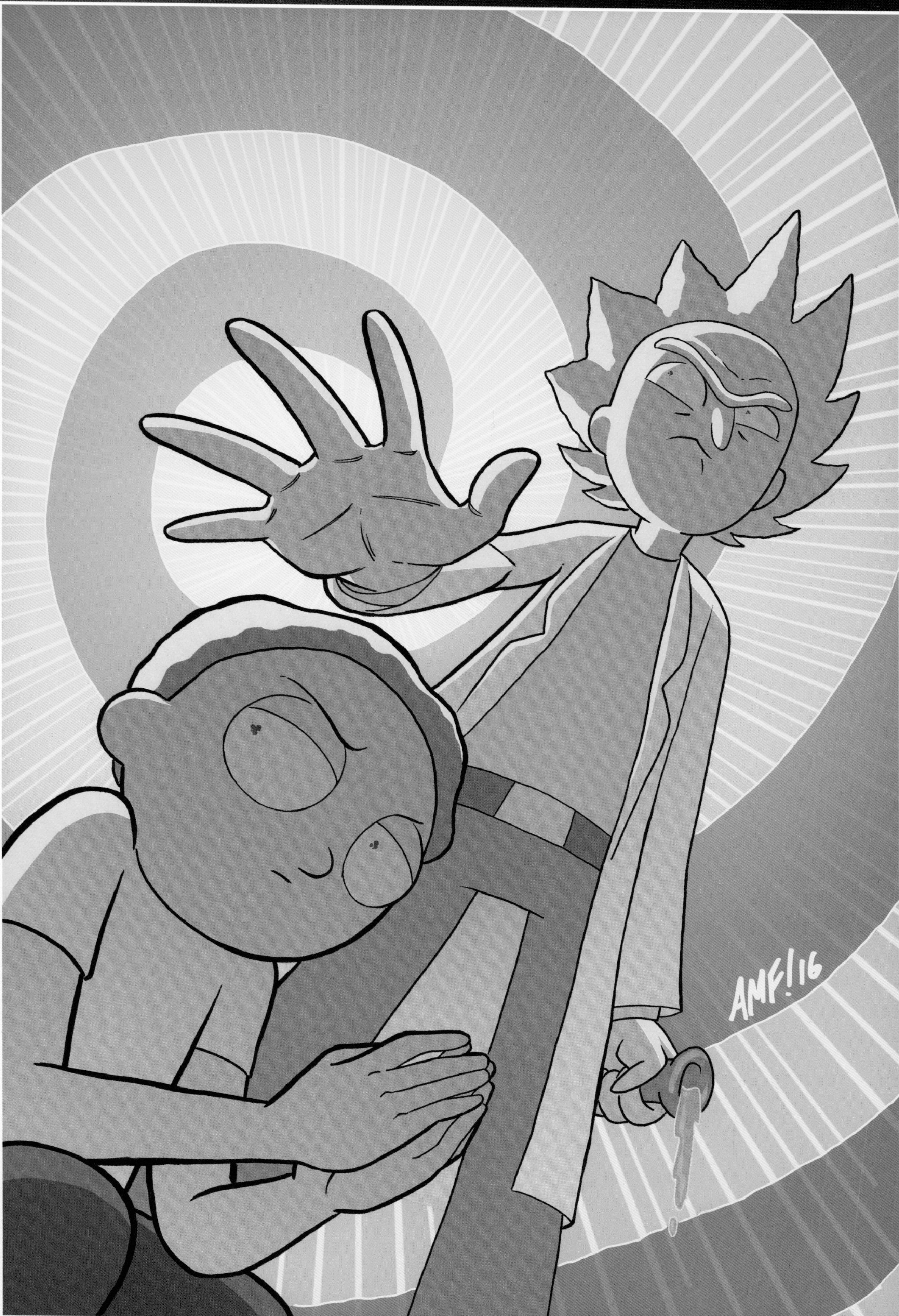
AMF!16

ISSUE #15 ALTERNATE COVER BY TONY FLEECS

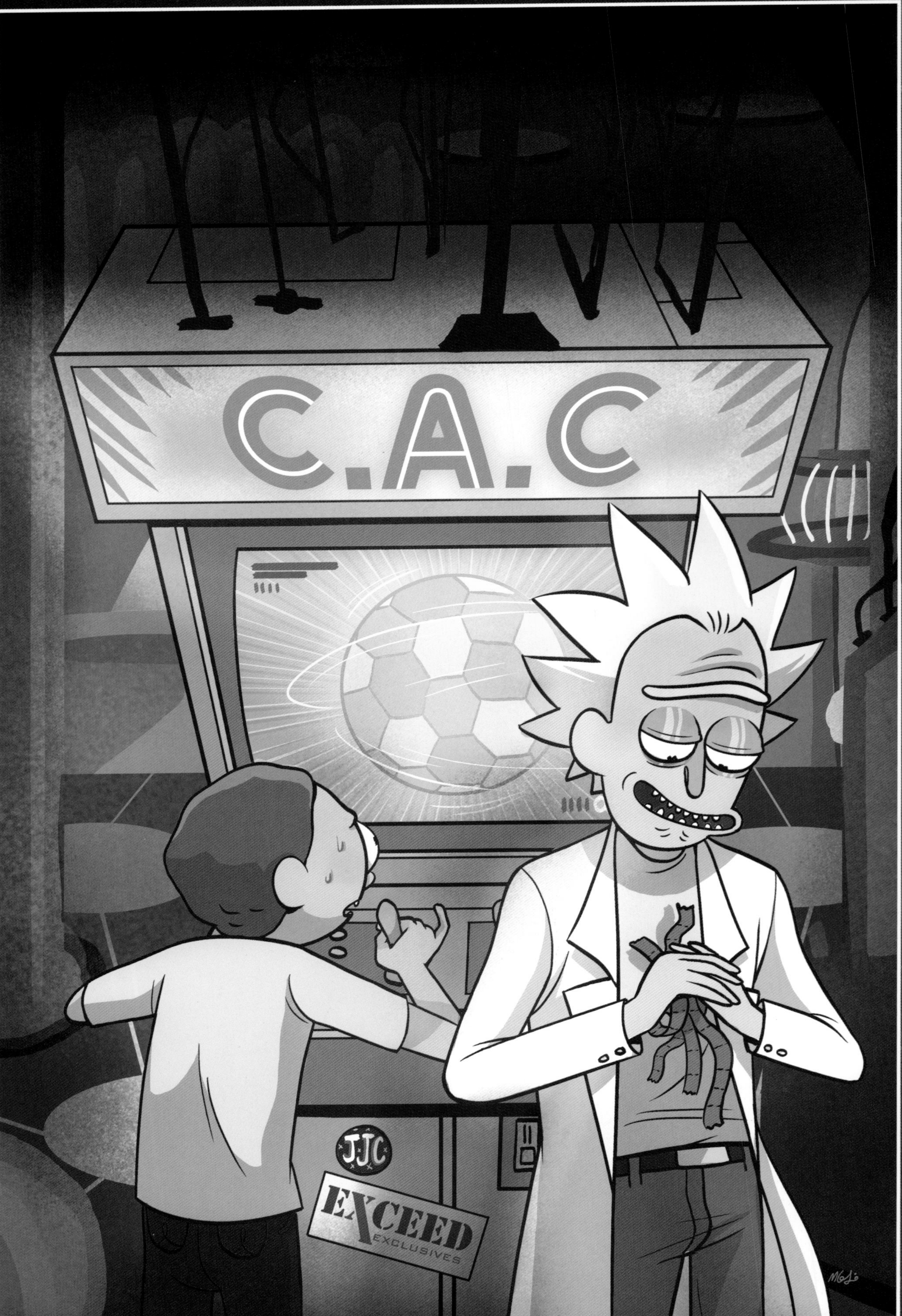
C.A.C
JJC
EXCEED
EXCLUSIVES

ISSUE #15 EXCEED EXCLUSIVES COVER BY MADY G

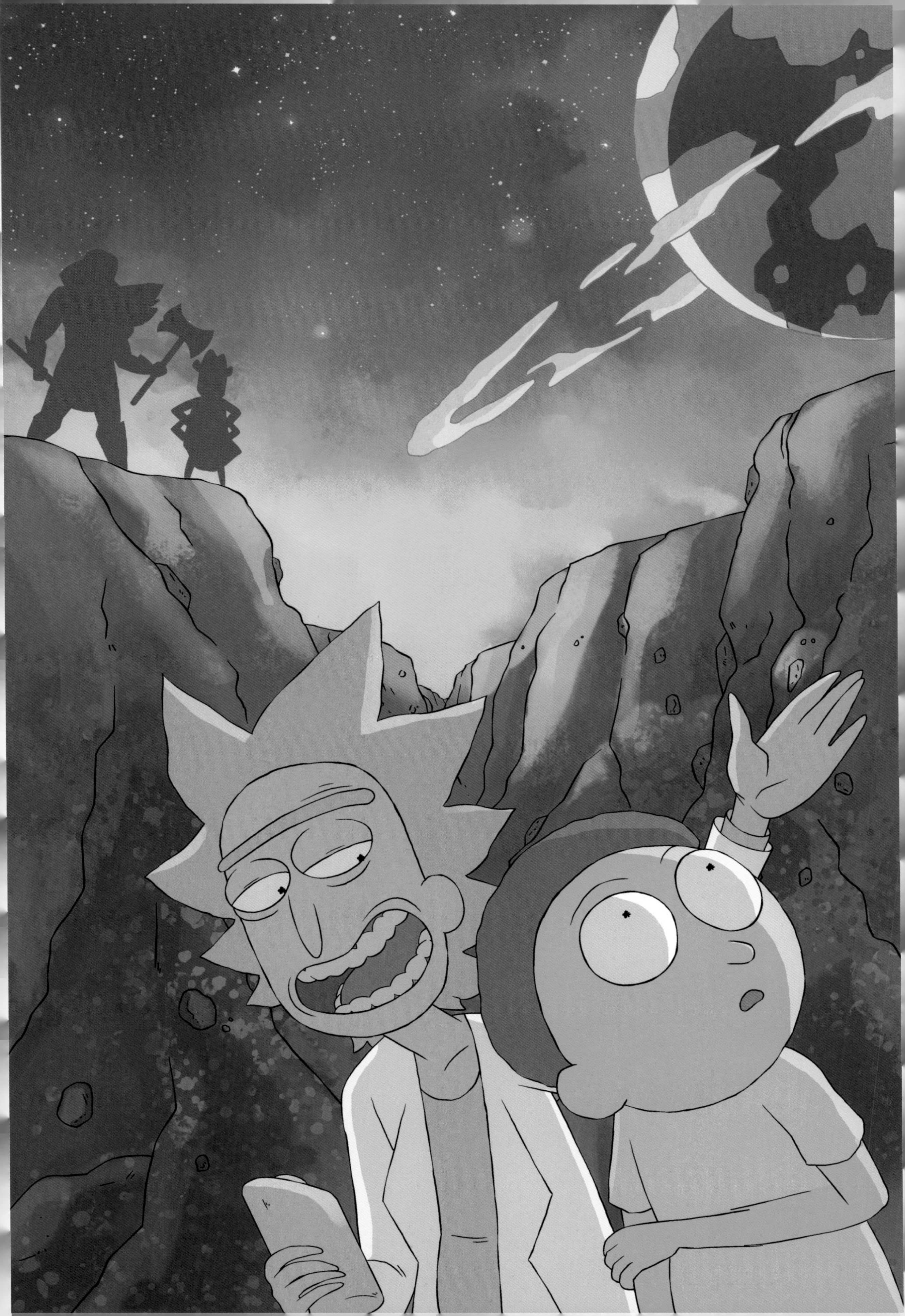

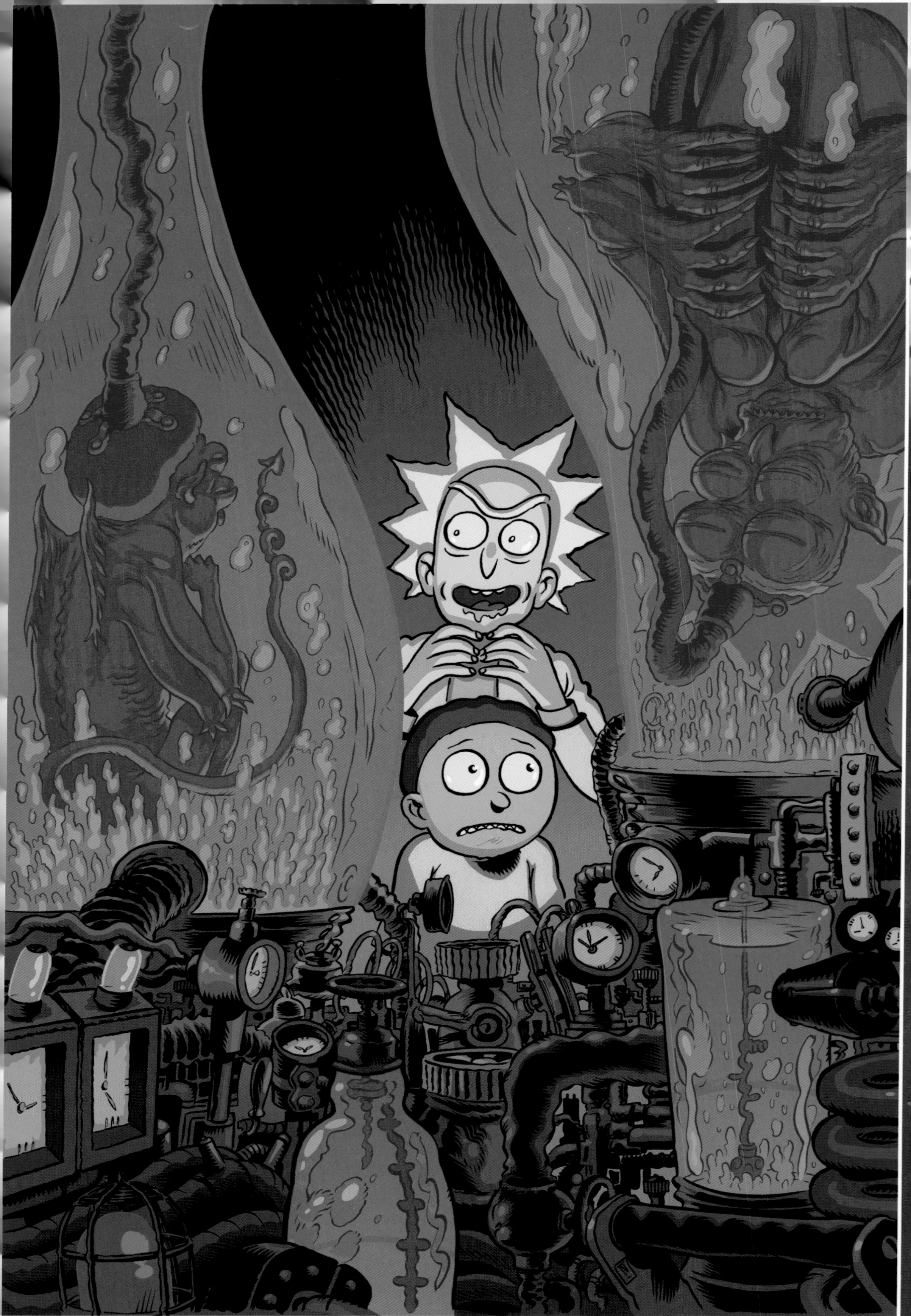

ISSUE #16 ALTERNATE COVER BY TROY NIXEY AND DAVE MCCAIG

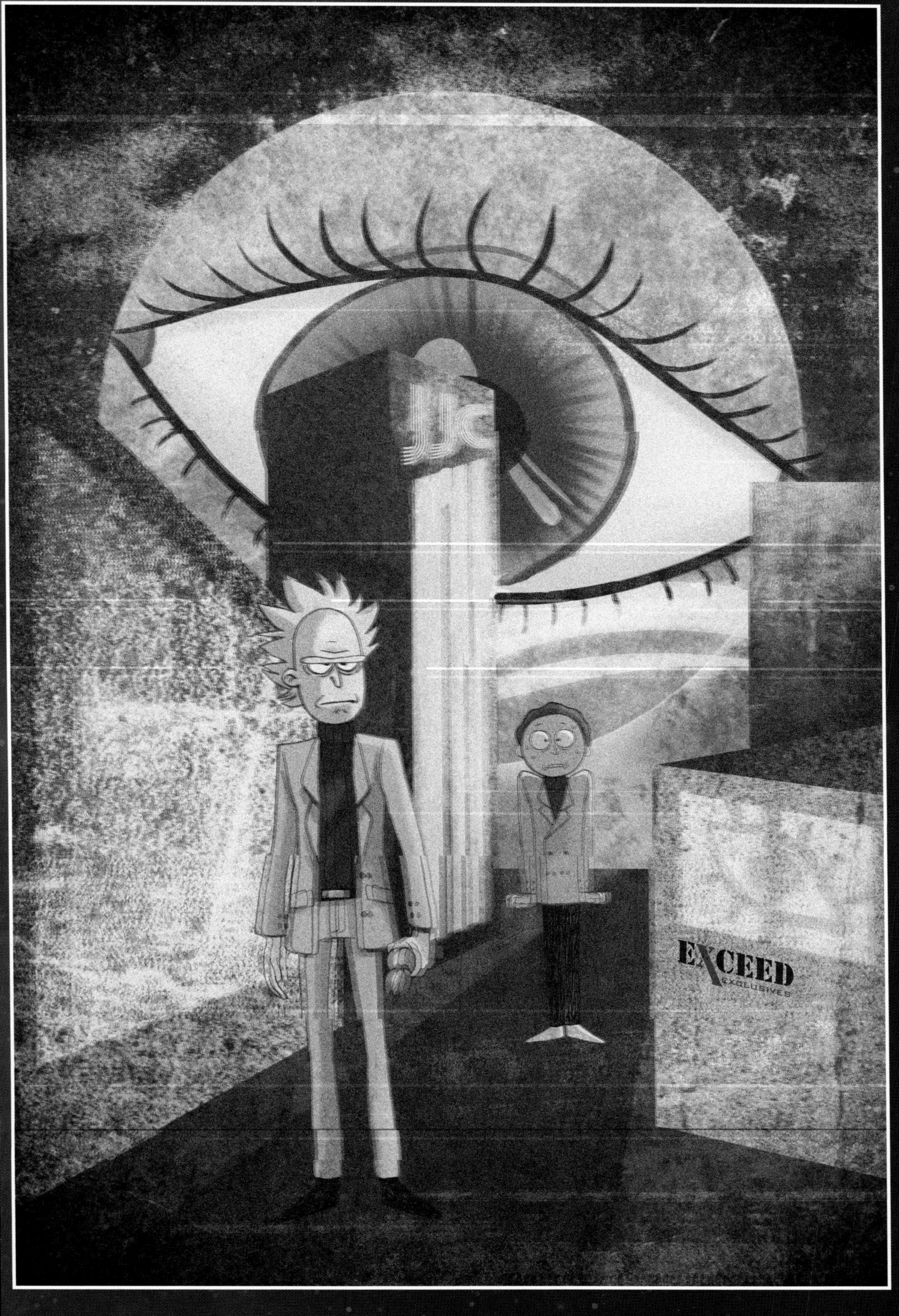
EXCEED
EXCLUSIVES

ISSUE #16 EXCEED EXCLUSIVES COVER BY MADY G

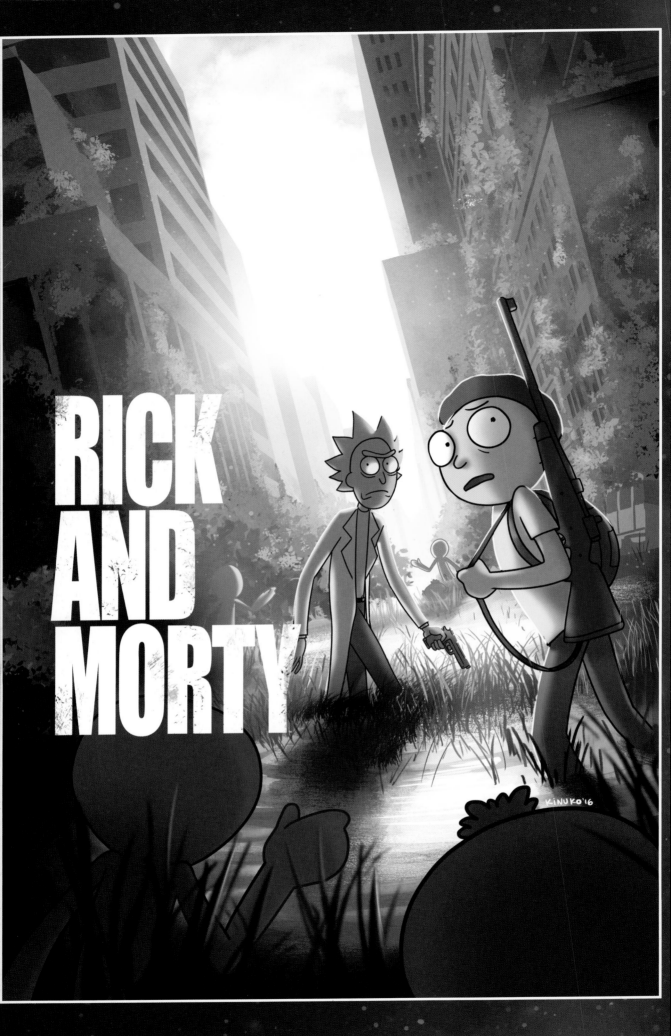

ISSUE #16 GEN CON AND PAX COVER BY MARIEL CARTWRIGHT

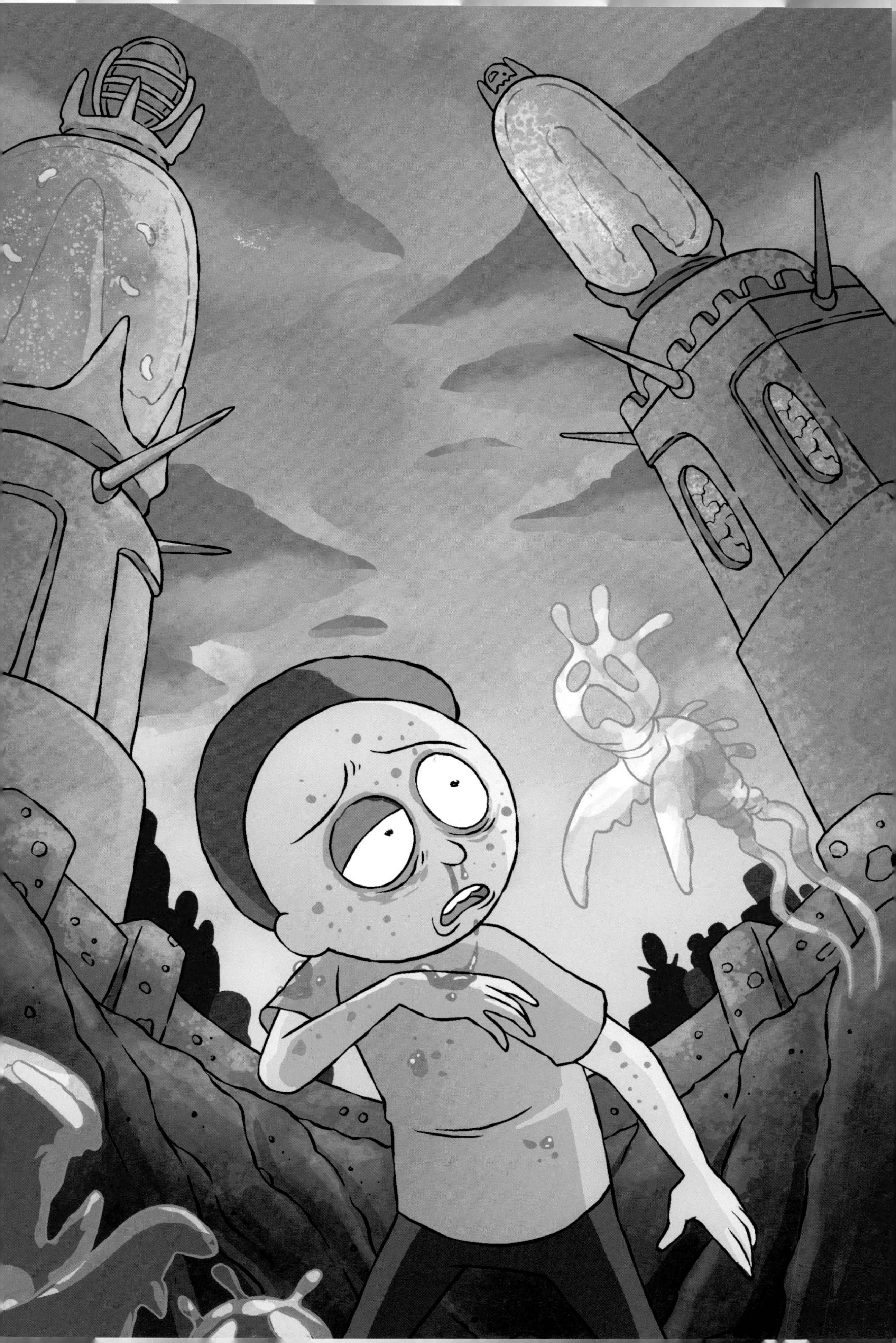

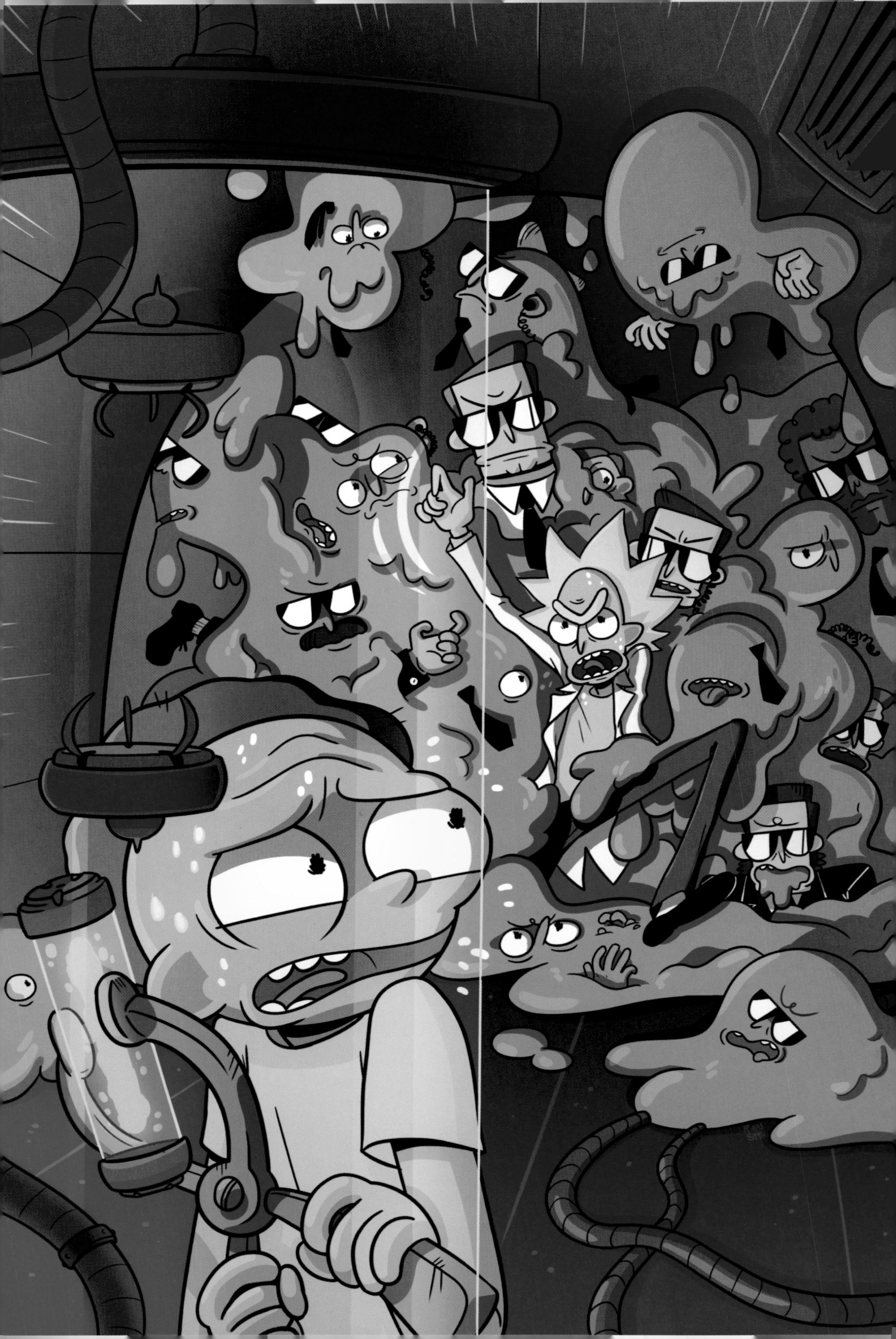

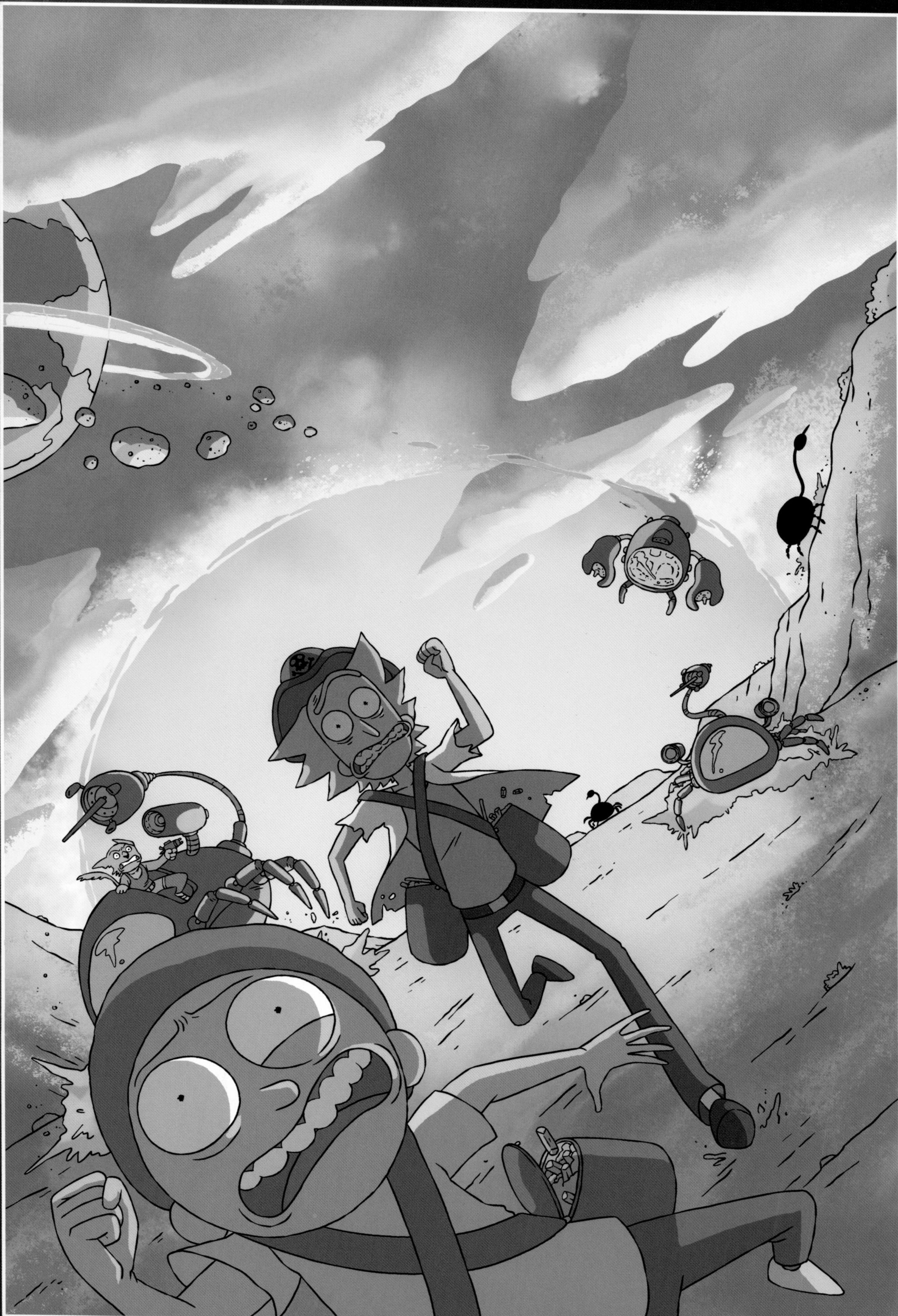

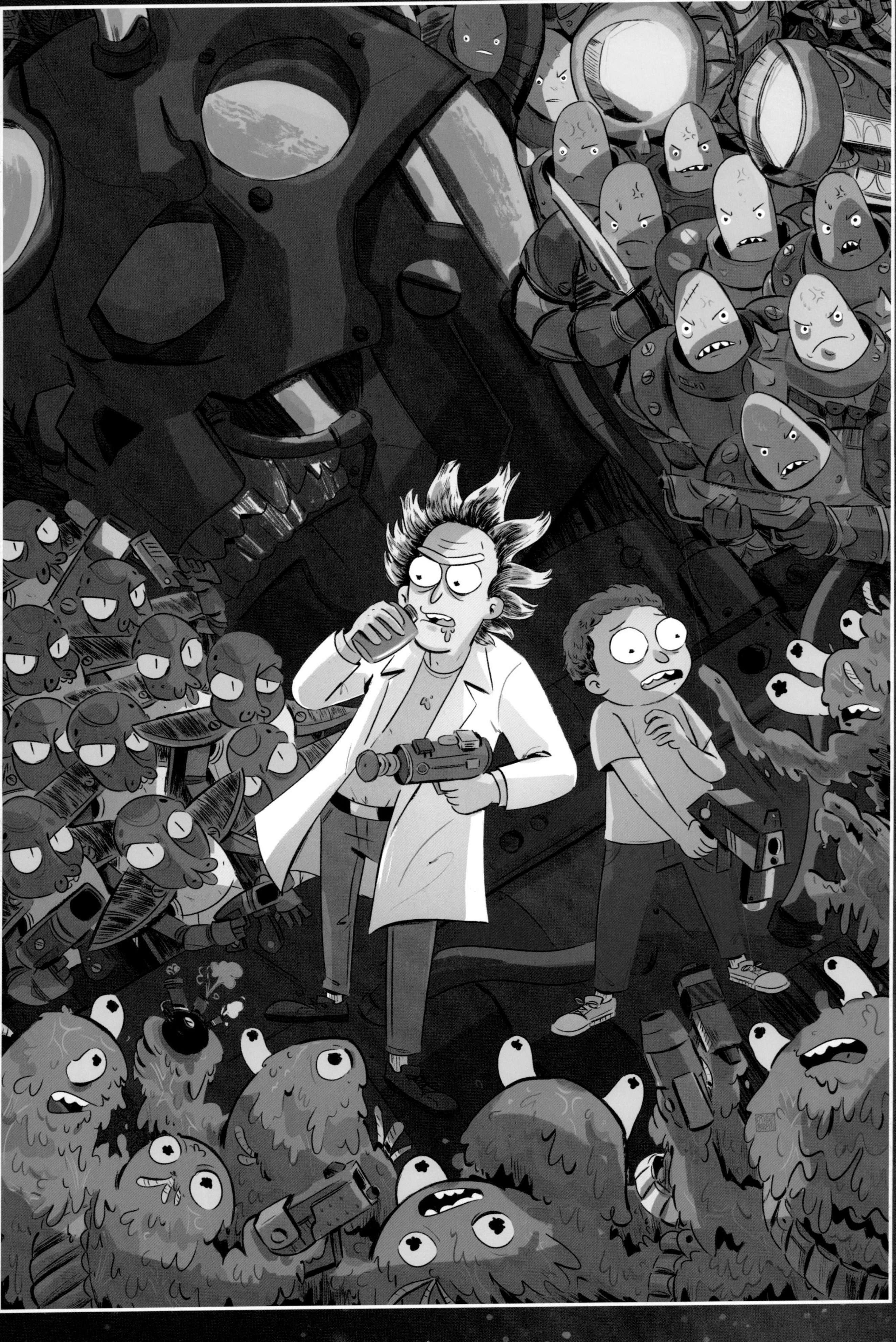

ISSUE #18 ALTERNATE COVER BY LOUIE CHIN

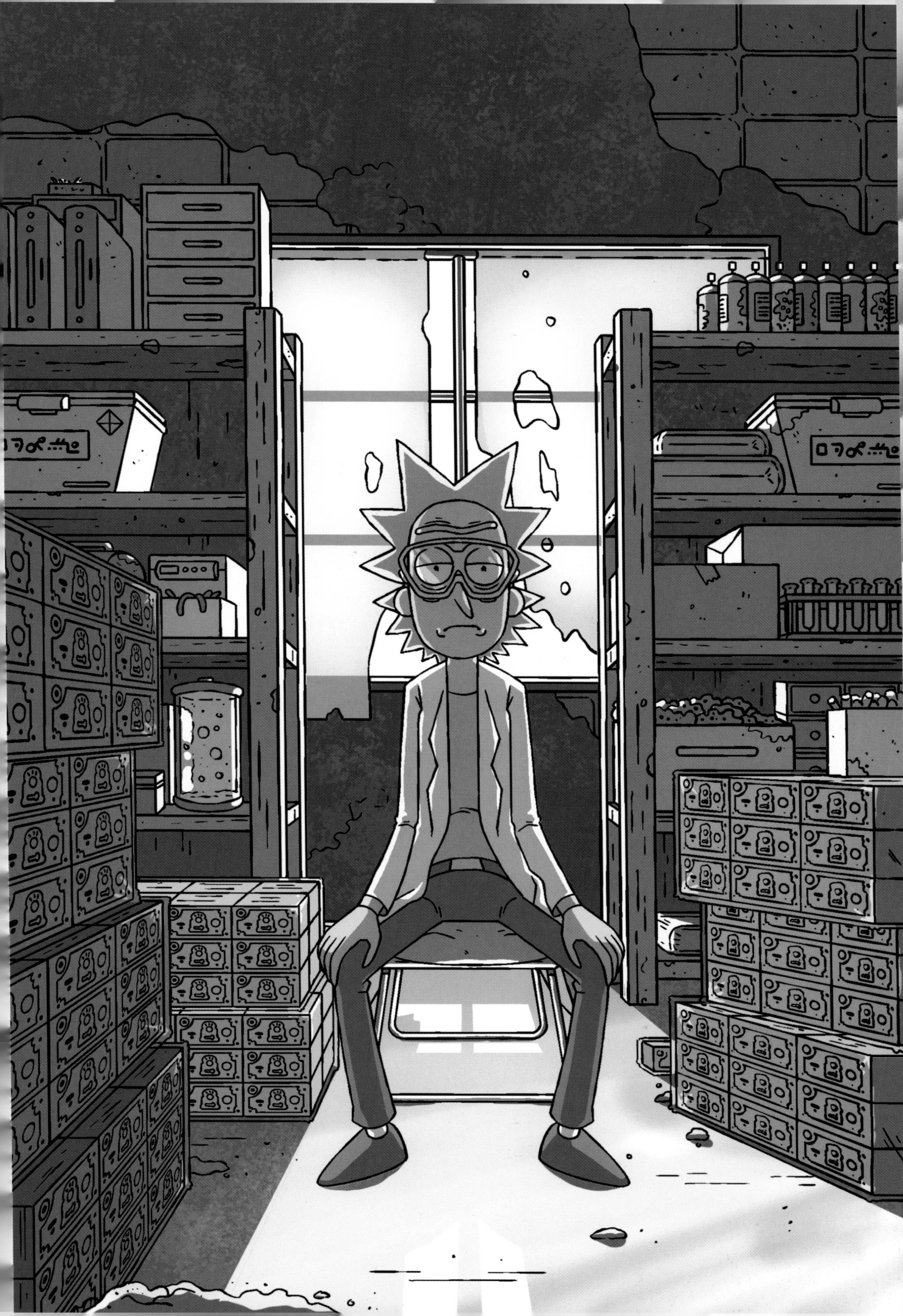

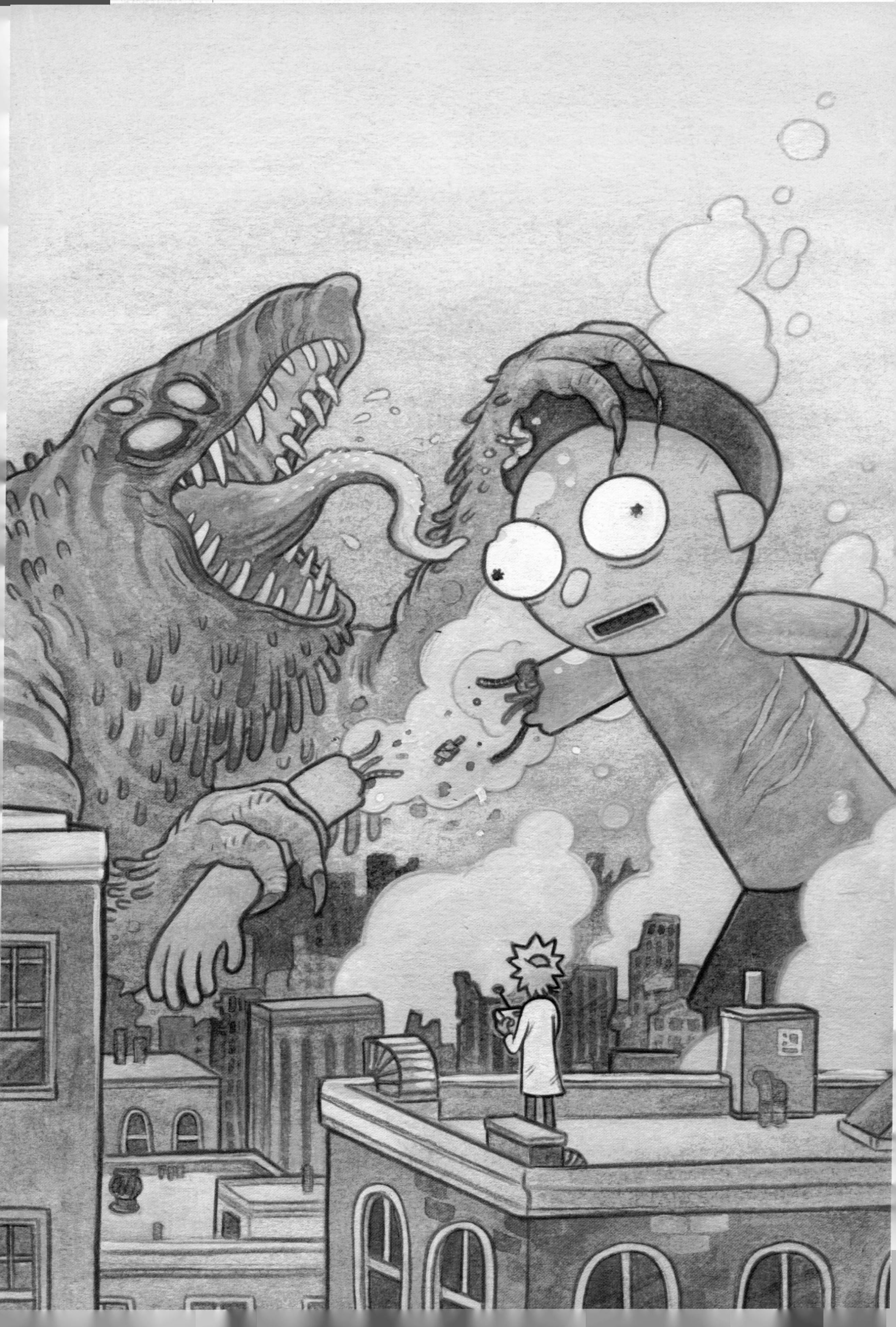

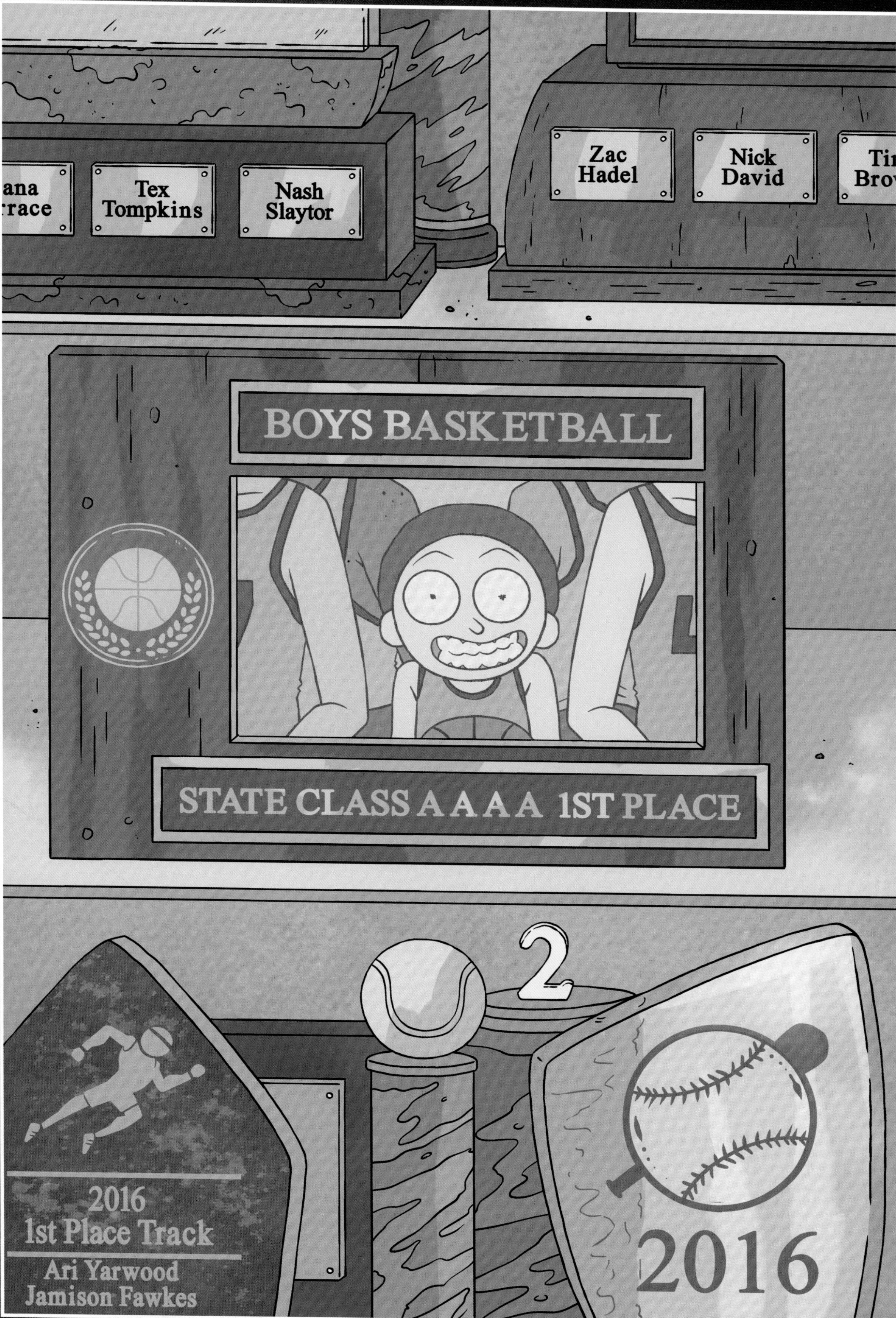

ana
race
Tex
Tompkins
Nash
Slaytor
Zac
Hadel
Nick
David
BOYS BASKETBALL
STATE CLASS A A A A 1ST PLACE
2
2016
1st Place Track
Ari Yarwood
Jamison Fawkes
2016

ISSUE #20 RETAIL COVER BY CJ CANNON AND RYAN HILL

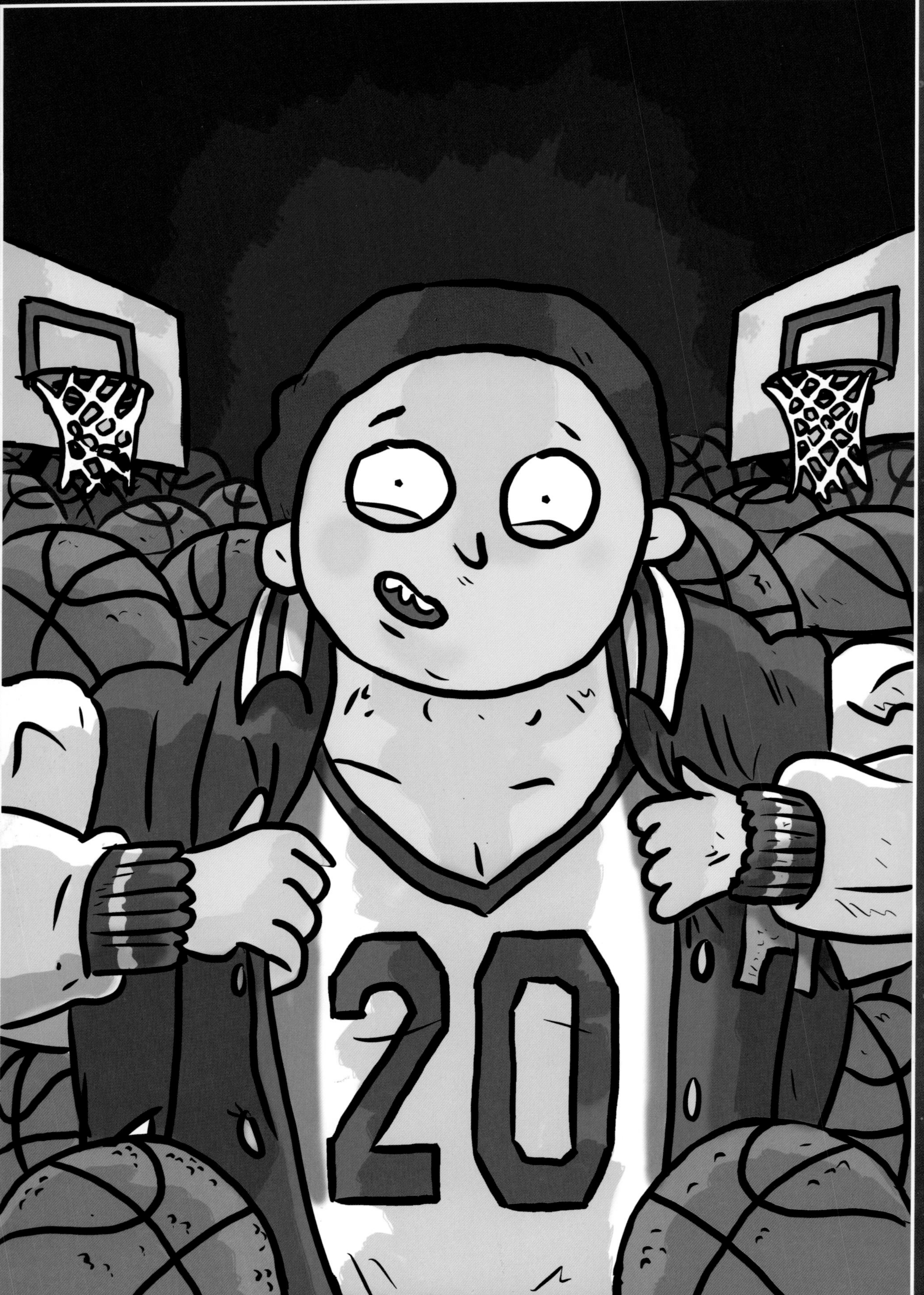
20

ISSUE #20 ALTERNATE COVER BY KYLE STARKS

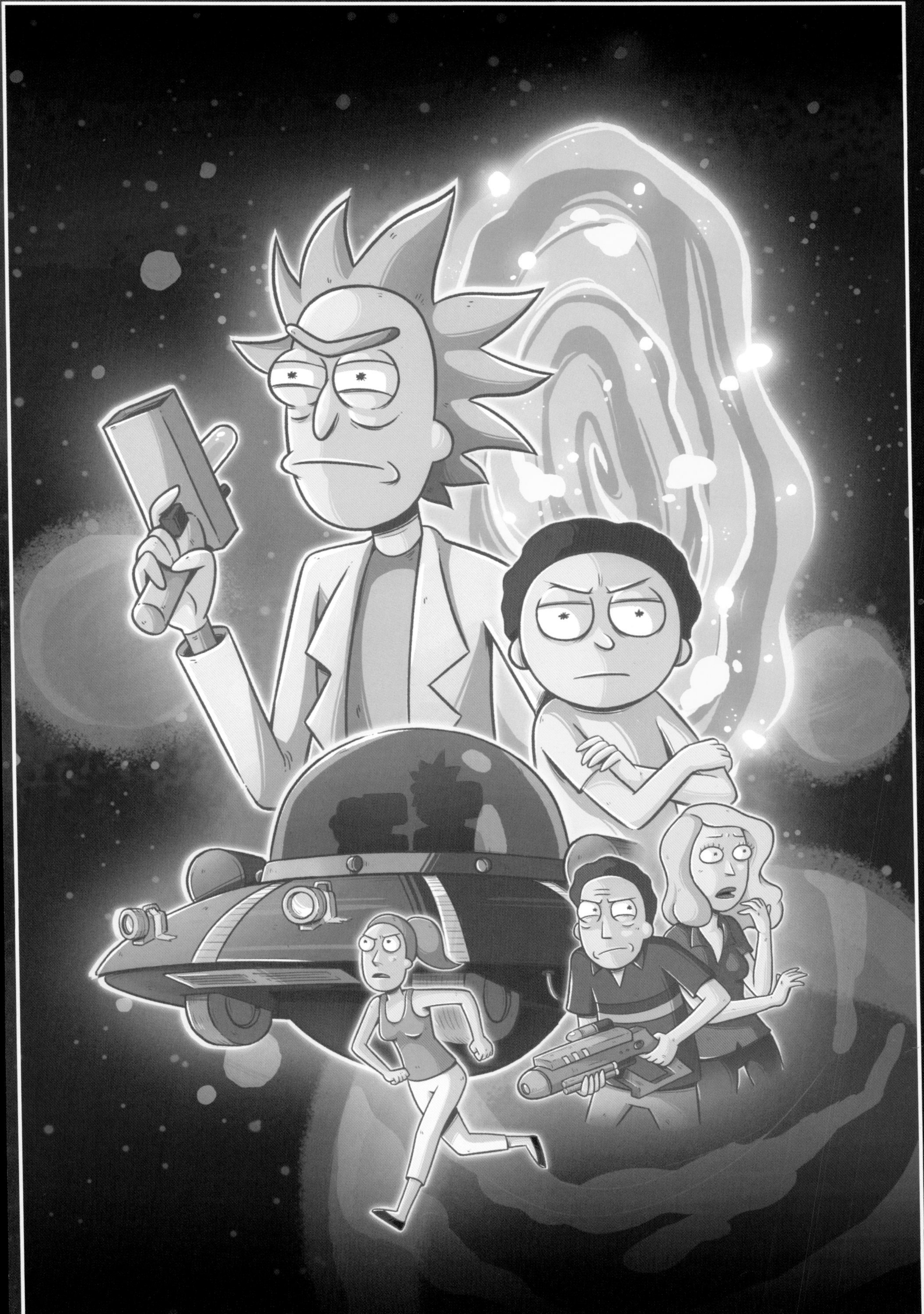

LOCAL COMIC SHOP DAY 2015 COVER BY SABRINA MATI

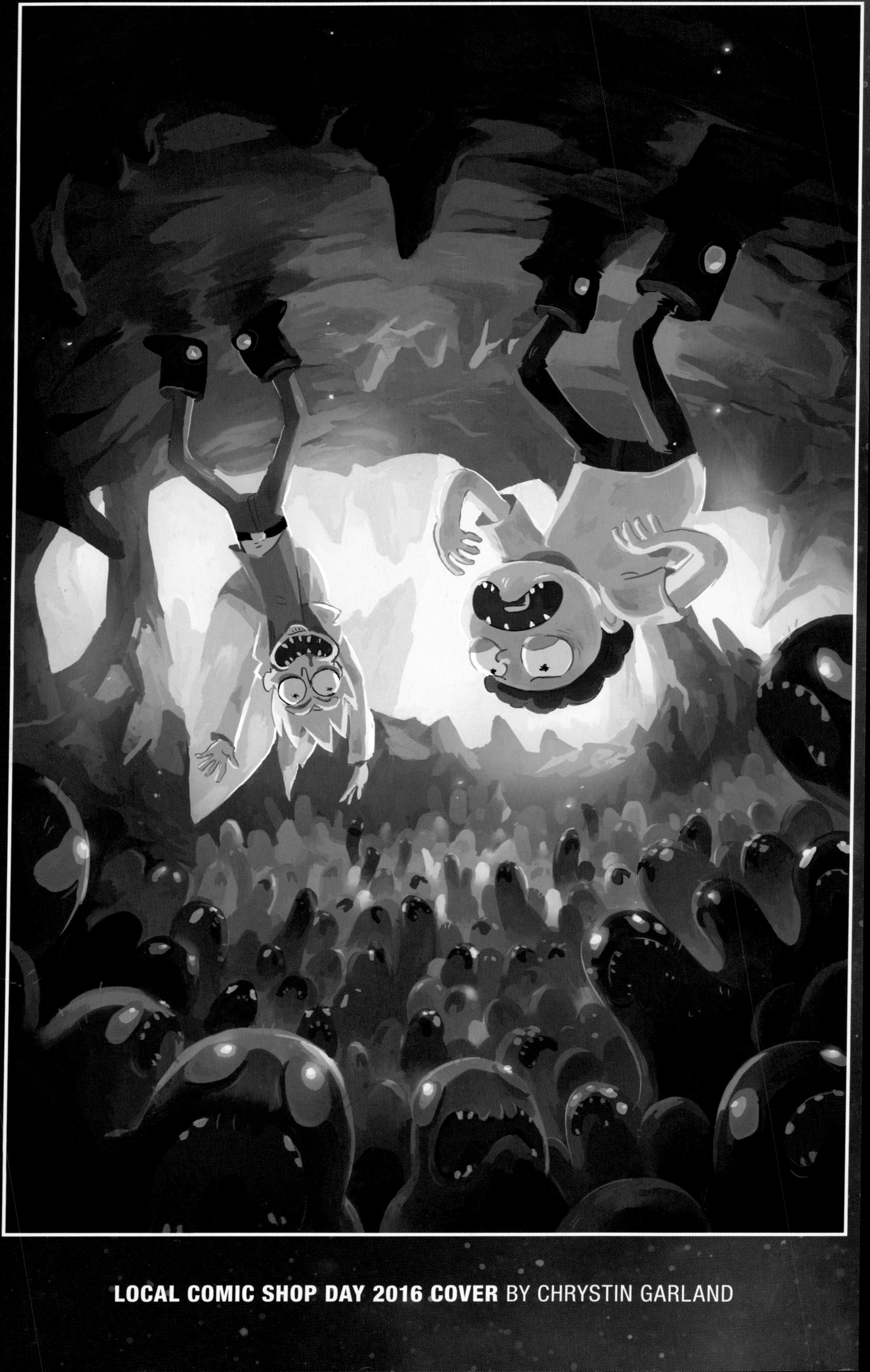

LOCAL COMIC SHOP DAY 2016 COVER BY CHRYSTIN GARLAND

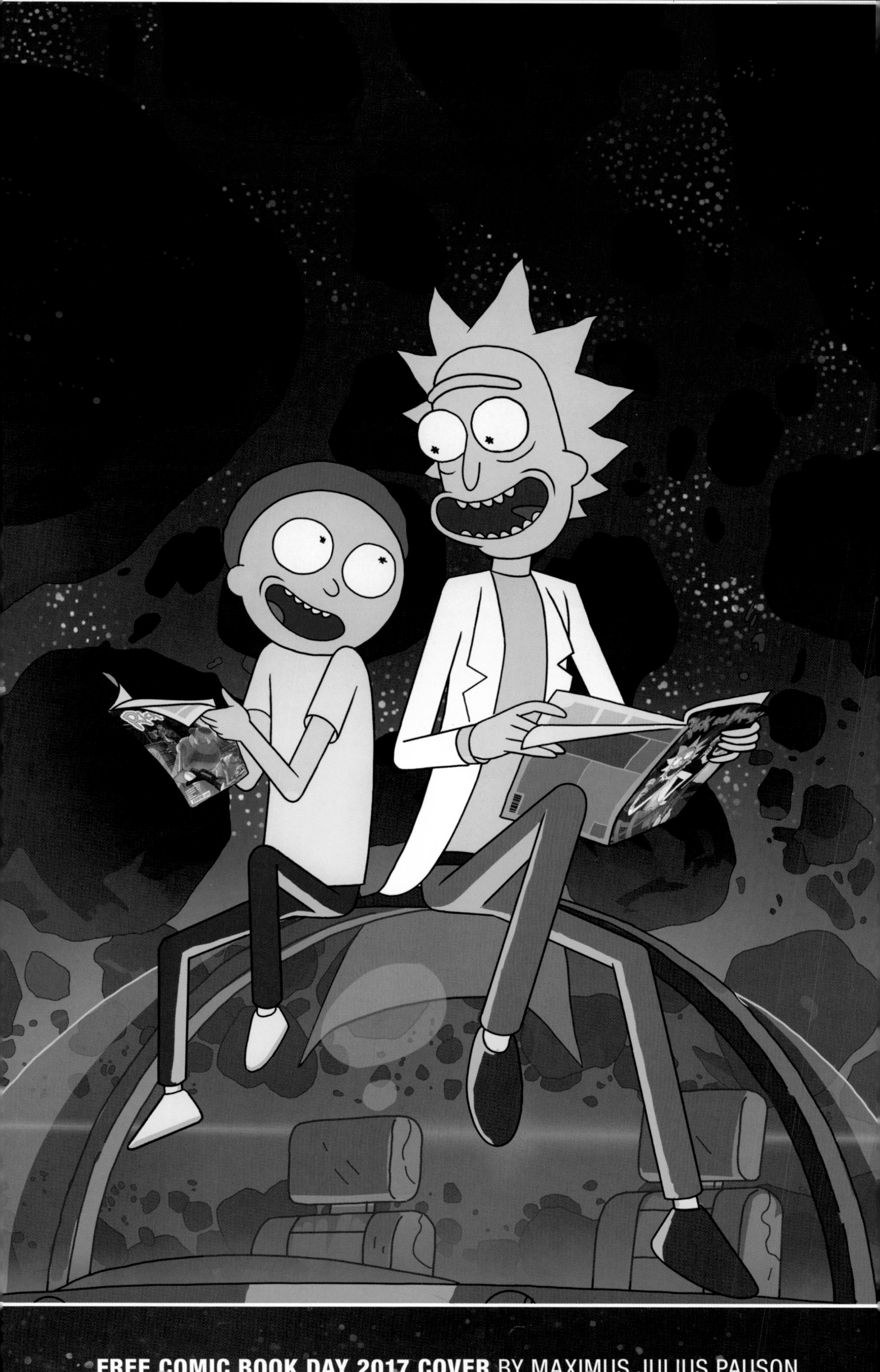

FREE COMIC BOOK DAY 2017 COVER BY MAXIMUS JULIUS PAUSON

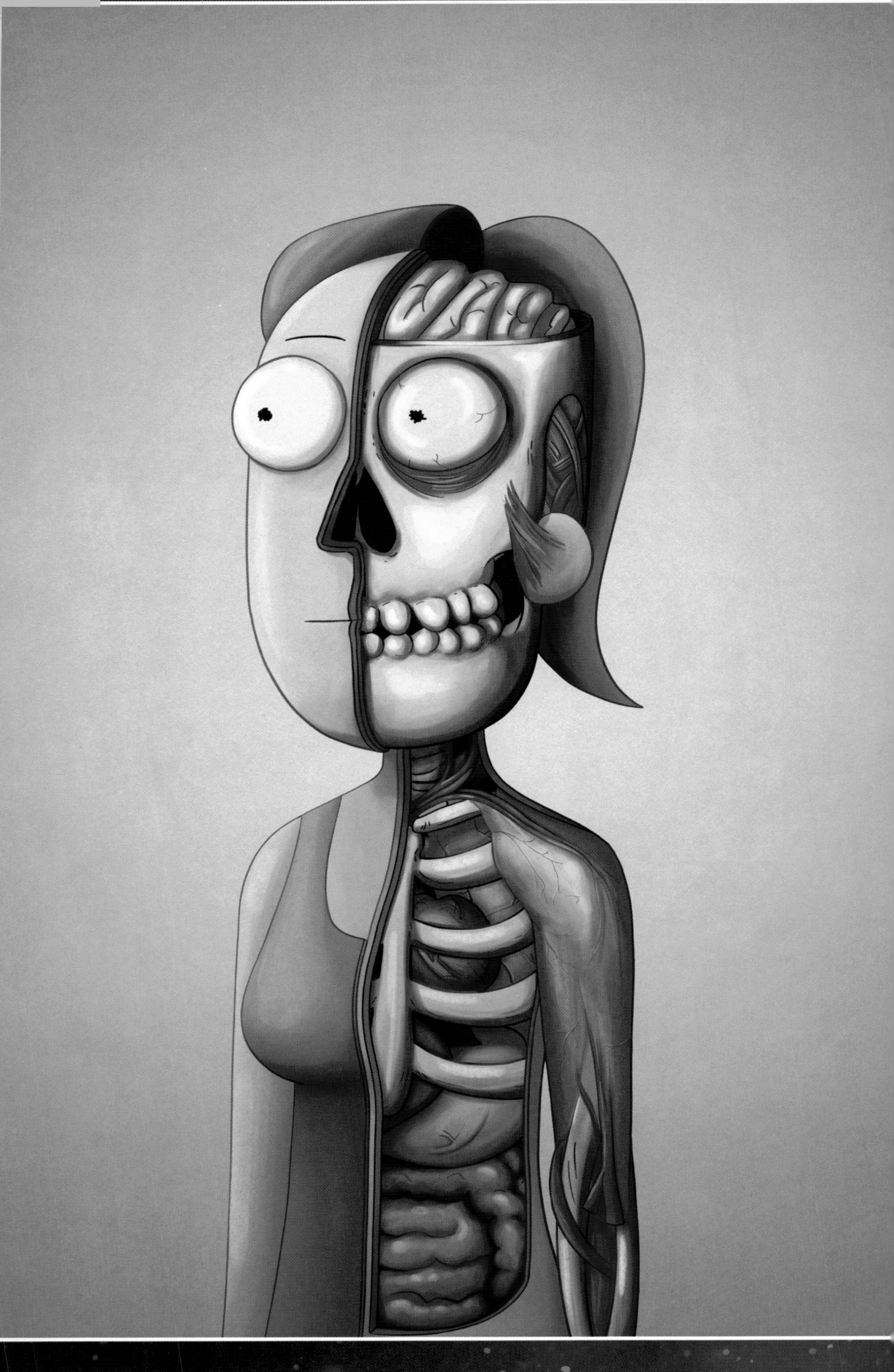

VOLUME THREE ONI PRESS EXCLUSIVE COVER BY JULIETA COLÁS

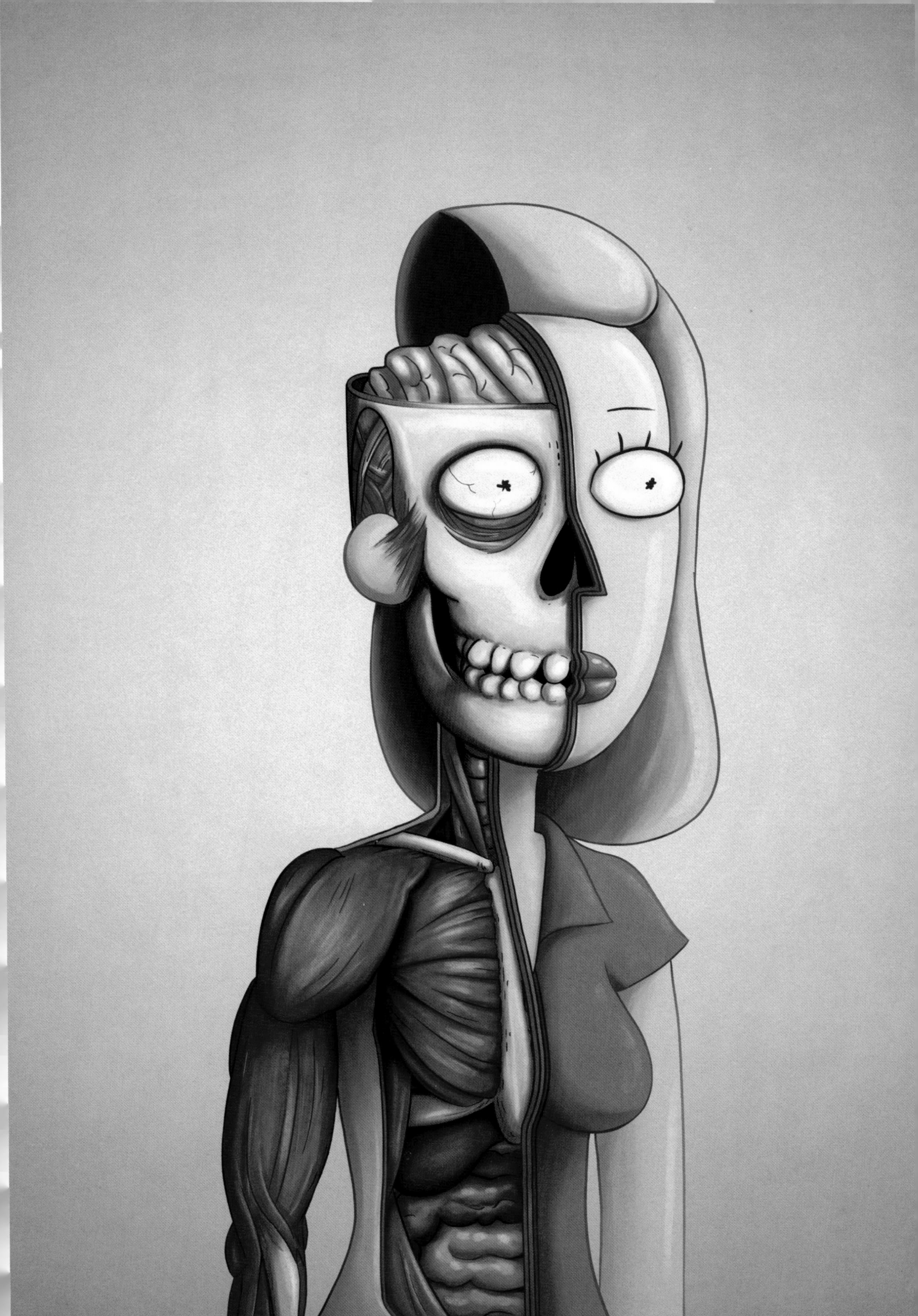

VOLUME FOUR ONI PRESS EXCLUSIVE COVER BY JULIETA COLÁS

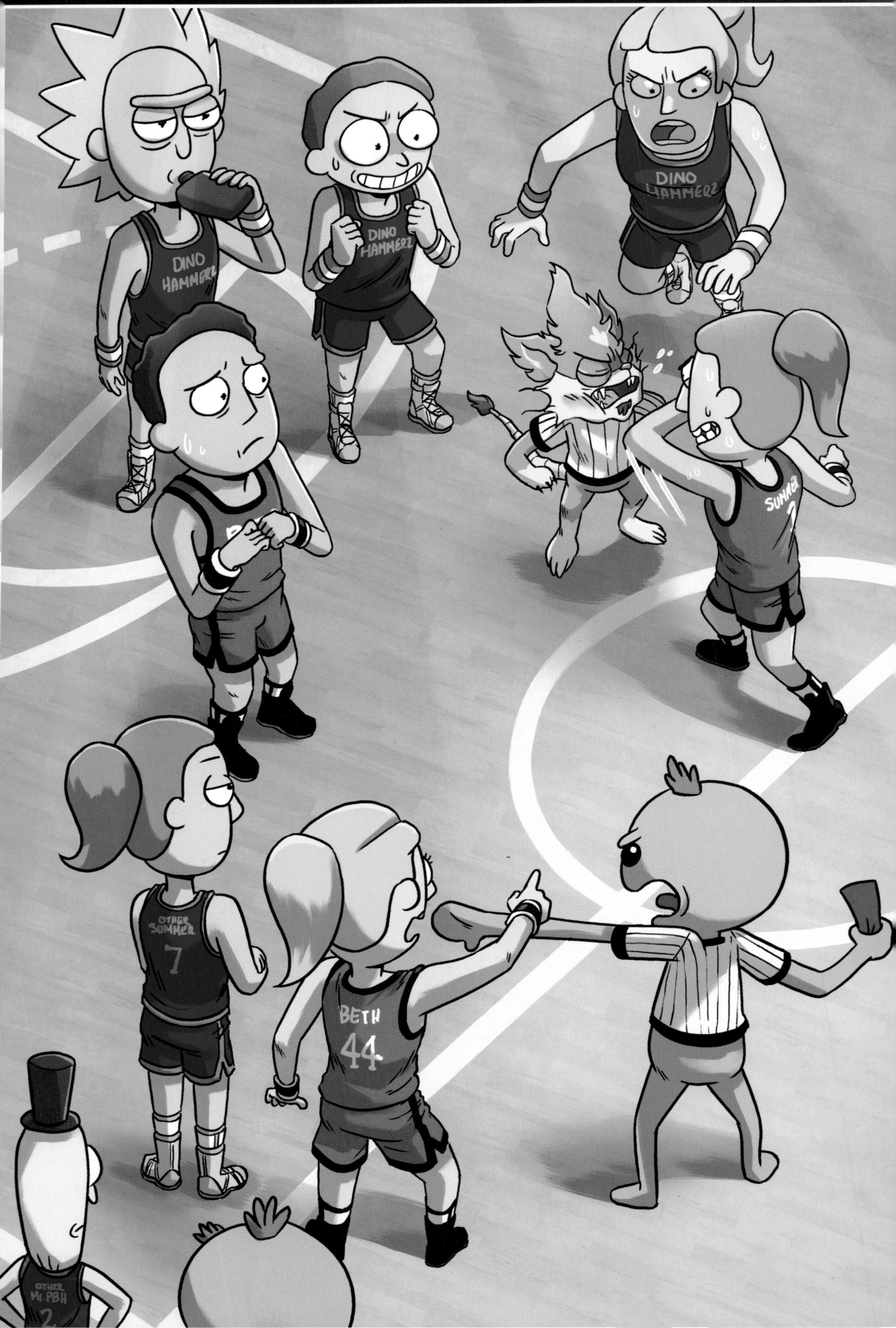
DINO HAMMERZ
DINO HAMMERZ
DINO HAMMERZ
OTHER SUMMER 7
BETH 44

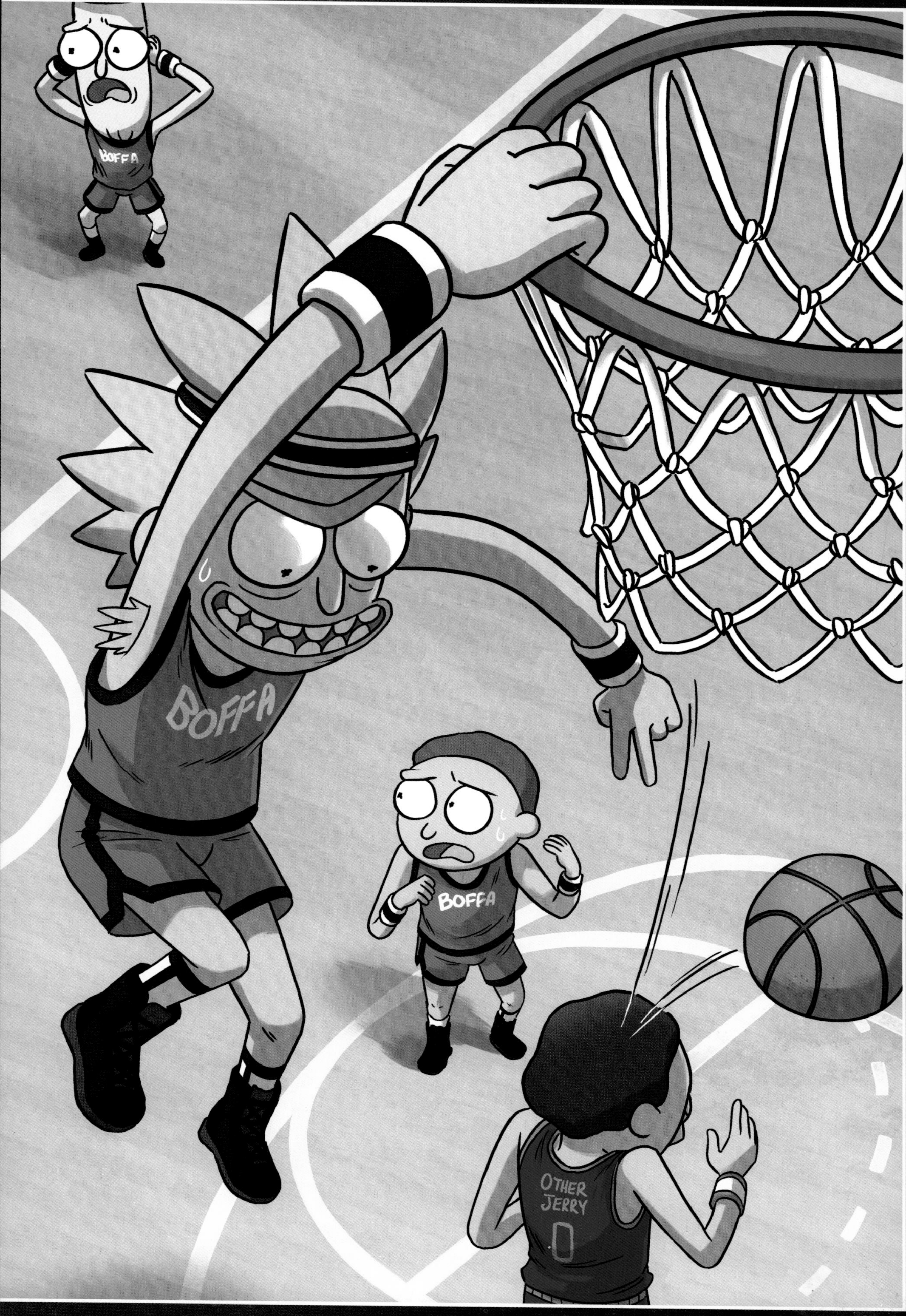
BOFFA
BOFFA
BOFFA
OTHER
JERRY
0

TREASURY EDITION 2016 EMERALD CITY COMICON EXCLUSIVE COVER
BY KATY FARINA

DAN HARMON is the Emmy® winning creator/executive producer of the comedy series *Community* as well as the co-creator/executive producer of Adult Swim™'s *Rick and Morty*™.

Harmon's pursuit of minimal work for maximum reward took him from stand-up to improv to sketch comedy, then finally to Los Angeles, where he began writing feature screenplays with fellow Milwaukeean Rob Schrab. As part of his deal with Robert Zemeckis at Imagemovers, Harmon co-wrote the feature film *Monster House*. Following this, Harmon co-wrote the Ben Stiller-directed pilot *Heat Vision and Jack*, starring Jack Black and Owen Wilson.

Disillusioned by the legitimate industry, Harmon began attending classes at nearby Glendale Community College. At the same time, Harmon and Schrab founded Channel 101, an untelevised non-profit audience-controlled network for undiscovered filmmakers, many of whom used it to launch mainstream careers, including the boys behind SNL's Digital Shorts. Harmon, along with Schrab, partnered with Sarah Silverman to create her Comedy Central series, *The Sarah Silverman Program*, where he served as head writer for the first season.

Harmon went on to create, write and perform in the short-lived VH1 sketch series *Acceptable TV* before eventually creating the critically acclaimed and fan-favorite comedy *Community*. The show originally aired on NBC for five seasons before being acquired by Yahoo, which premiered season six of the show in March 2015. In 2009 he won an Emmy for Outstanding Music and Lyrics for the opening number of the 81st Annual Academy Awards.

Along with Justin Roiland, Harmon created the breakout Adult Swim™ animated series Rick and Morty™. The show premiered in December 2013 and quickly became a ratings hit. Harmon and Roiland have wrapped up season three, which premiered in 2017.

In 2014, Harmon was the star of the documentary Harmontown, which premiered at the SXSW Film Festival and chronicled his 20-city stand-up/podcast tour of the same name. The documentary was released theatrically in October 2014.

JUSTIN ROILAND grew up in Manteca, California, where he did the basic stuff children do. Later in life he traveled to Los Angeles. Once settled in, he created several popular online shorts for Channel 101. Some notable examples of his work (both animated and live action) include *House of Cosbys* and *Two Girls One Cup: The Show*.

Justin is afraid of his mortality and hopes the things he creates will make lots of people happy. Then maybe when modern civilization collapses into chaos, people will remember him and they'll help him survive the bloodshed and violence. Global economic collapse is looming. It's going to be horrible, and honestly, a swift death might be preferable than living in the hell that awaits mankind.

Justin also really hates writing about himself in the third person. I hate this. That's right. It's me. I've been writing this whole thing. Hi. The cat's out of the bag. It's just you and me now. There never was a third person. If you want to know anything about me, just ask. Sorry this wasn't more informative.

KYLE STARKS is an Eisner Award-nominated comic creator from southern Indiana, where he resides with his beautiful wife and two amazing daughters. Stealy values him at 32 and a half Grepples or 17 and a half Smeggles depending on market value at the current time. Check out his creator-owned work: *Sexcastle* and *Kill Them All*.

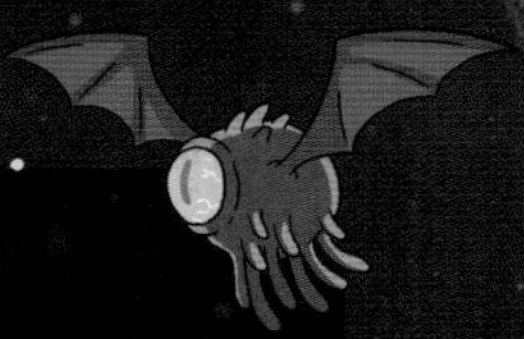

TOM FOWLER is a cartoonist and illustrator who has worked in comics, advertising, and film and game design for a variety of clients including Disney, Simon & Schuster, Wizards of the Coast, Hasbro, MAD, Valiant, Marvel, and DC Comics. His best known comics include the *MAD Magazine* feature "Monroe," "Venom," "Hulk Season One," "Quantum & Woody," the critically acclaimed "Mysterius the Unfathomable," and the all-ages series *HOWTOONS:[re]IGNITION*. Tom writes, and sometimes draws, the popular *Rick and Morty*™ comic series.

PAMELA RIBON is a screenwriter, TV writer and bestselling author. In addition to writing upcoming features for Walt Disney Animation Studios and Sony Pictures Animation, Pamela has adapted her popular novels for both film and television, and developed original series and features for ABC, ABC Family, Sony, Warner Bros., Disney Channel and 20th Century Fox Productions. She has been a consultant for film and television, including DisneyNature's *Bears*. Her memoir—*Notes to Boys (and Other Things I Shouldn't Share in Public)*—has been called "brain-breakingly funny" by NPR. She's been in comedy rooms for both network and cable, most notably the Emmy award-winning *Samantha Who?*. She was an Oprah.com contributor, a flagship contributor to Television Without Pity, and a weekly columnist for the *Austin American-Statesman*. Her stage work has been showcased at the HBO US Comedy Arts Festival. She created the accidental international scandal known as *Call Us Crazy: The Anne Heche Monologues*. Pamela has been entered into the Oxford English Dictionary under "muffin top." That is not a joke. You can follow her @pamelaribon.

CJ CANNON is a self-taught artist living in Nashville, Tennessee. When they're not working on comics, outside riding their bike, or drumming, they're almost always in the house drawing gross fanart and fandom smut for similarly gross people. CJ has: two cats, three hermit crabs, a hamster, an eldritch abomination, a pacman frog, and a leopard gecko.

MARC ELLERBY is a comics illustrator living in Essex, UK. He has worked on such titles as *Doctor Who*, *Regular Show*, and *The Amazing World of Gumball*. His own comics (which you should totally check out!) are *Chloe Noonan: Monster Hunter* and *Ellerbisms*. You can read some comics if you like at *marcellerby.com*.

RYAN HILL has colored some comics so far. Many of these include *Stumptown*, *Judge Dredd Mega City 2*, *Age of Reptiles*, *Terrible Lizard*, *Sixth Gun: Valley of Death*, *Avatar: The Last Airbender*, and *EGO*. The pizza guy who delivers his lunch every "ZA & Wing Wednesday" is rumored to have once said, "Not bad, man," in regard to the work.

KATY FARINA is a freelance comic artist and illustrator from Charlotte. Her work includes *Amazing World of Gumball OGN* volumes 1 and 2 and *Capture Creatures*. Outside of drawing comics, reading comics, and thinking about comics, she... uh, usually just goes to her local comic shop. She loves a good cup of coffee, and coffee loves her. Her greatest passion is to tell good stories that will inspire others!

CHRIS CRANK has worked on several recent Oni Press books like *The Sixth Gun*, *Brides of Helheim*, *Terrible Lizard*, and others. Or maybe you've seen his letters in *Revival*, *Hack/Slash*, *God Hates Astronauts*, or *Dark Engine* from Image. Or perhaps you've read *Lady Killer* or *Sundowners* from Dark Horse. Heck, you might even be reading the award winning *Battlepug* at *battlepug.com* right now!

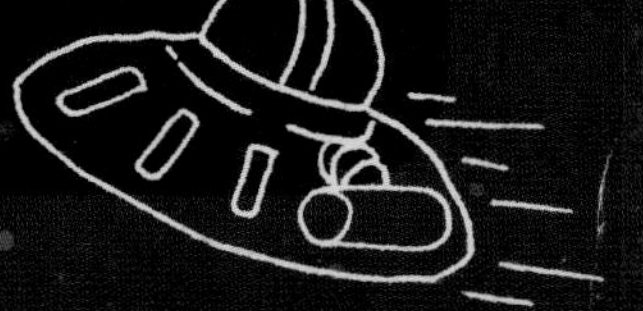

MORE BOOKS FROM ONI PRESS!

Rick and Morty
VOLUME ONE
GORMAN CANNON HILL ELLERBY CRANK!

RICK AND MORTY™, VOLUME ONE

By Zac Gorman, CJ Cannon, Marc Ellerby, & more

128 pages • Softcover • Color

ISBN 978-1-62010-281-7

Rick and Morty
VOLUME TWO
GORMAN CANNON MACLEAN HILL
FILARDI FARRIS ELLERBY CRANK!
[adult swim]

RICK AND MORTY™, VOLUME TWO

By Zac Gorman, CJ Cannon,
Marc Ellerby, & more

128 pages • Softcover • Color

ISBN 978-1-62010-319-7

Rick and Morty
VOLUME THREE
FOWLER CANNON RIBON ELLERBY HILL CRANK!
[adult swim]

RICK AND MORTY™, VOLUME THREE

By Tom Fowler, CJ Cannon,
Pamela Ribon, Marc Ellerby, & more

128 pages • Softcover • Color

ISBN 978-1-62010-343-2

Rick and Morty
VOLUME FOUR
STARKS CANNON ELLERBY HILL FARINA CRANK!
[adult swim]

RICK AND MORTY™, VOLUME FOUR

By Kyle Starks, CJ Cannon,
Marc Ellerby, & more

128 pages • Softcover • Color

ISBN 978-1-62010-377-7

Rick and Morty
TINY RICK
VOLUME FIVE
STARKS CANNON ELLERBY FARINA CRANK!
[adult swim]

RICK AND MORTY™, VOLUME FIVE

By Kyle Starks, CJ Cannon,
Marc Ellerby, & more

128 pages • Softcover • Color

ISBN 978-1-62010-416-3

Rick and Morty
LIL' POOPY SUPERSTAR
GRALEY ELLERBY LOUIS CRANK!
[adult swim]

RICK AND MORTY™: LIL' POOPY SUPERSTAR

By Sarah Graley, Marc Ellerby,
& Mildred Louis

128 pages • Softcover • Color

ISBN 978-1-62010-374-6

Rick and Morty
BOOK ONE
[adult swim]

RICK AND MORTY™, BOOK ONE

By Zac Gorman, CJ Cannon, Marc Ellerby, & more

296 pages • Hardcover • Color

ISBN 978-1-62010-360-9

AN EX-COP. HIS PARTNER. A DEADLY ASSASSIN.
A MURDEROUS TEAM-UP AS THEY FIGHT FROM THE LOBBY TO THE PENTHOUSE IN SEARCH OF BLOODY VENGEANCE.
KILL THEM ALL
A GRAPHIC NOVEL BY KYLE STARKS
THE DUDE WHO BROUGHT YOU SEXCASTLE

KILL THEM ALL

By Kyle Starks

184 pages • Softcover • Color

ISBN 978-1-62010-434-7

ONI PRESS
www.onipress.com

For more information on these and other fine Oni Press comic books and graphic novels visit www.onipress.com. To find a comic specialty store in your area visit www.comicshops.us.

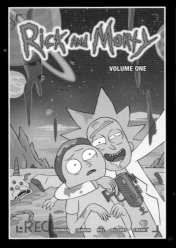

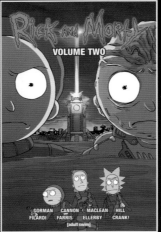

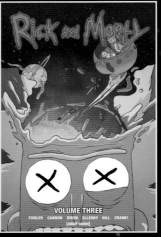

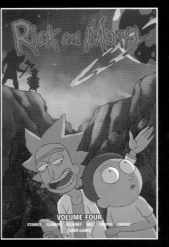

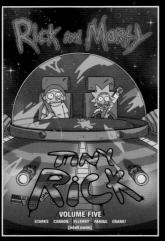

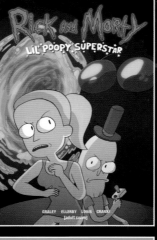

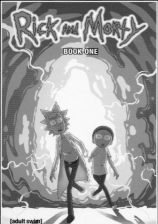

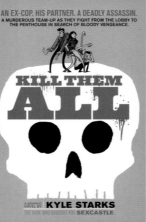

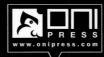